Toyota Corolla RWD Automotive Repair Manual

by Larry Warren, Robert Maddox and John H Haynes
Member of the Guild of Motoring Writers

Models covered:

All Toyota Corolla rear-wheel drive models
1980 through 1987

(1Z5 – 92032)

(961)

ABCDE
FGHIJ
KLM

2

Haynes Publishing Group
Sparkford Nr Yeovil
Somerset BA22 7JJ England

Haynes North America, Inc
861 Lawrence Drive
Newbury Park
California 91320 USA

Acknowledgements

We are grateful for the help and cooperation of Toyota Motor Corporation for their assistance with technical information.

A book in the **Haynes Automotive Repair Manual Series**

Printed in the USA

ISBN 1 85010 632 0

Library of Congress Catalog Card Number 90-81412

Contents

1985 Toyota Corolla GT-S Coupe

About this manual

Its purpose

The purpose of this manual is to help you get the best value from your vehicle. It can do so in several ways. It can help you decide what work must be done, even if you choose to have it done by a dealer service department or a repair shop; it provides information and procedures for routine maintenance and servicing; and it offers diagnostic and repair procedures to follow when trouble occurs.

We hope you use the manual to tackle the work yourself. For many simpler jobs, doing it yourself may be quicker than arranging an appointment to get the vehicle into a shop and making the trips to leave it and pick it up. More importantly, a lot of money can be saved by avoiding the expense the shop must pass on to you to cover its labor and overhead costs. An added benefit is the sense of satisfaction and accomplishment that you feel after doing the job yourself.

Using the manual

The manual is divided into Chapters. Each Chapter is divided into numbered Sections, which are headed in bold type between horizontal lines. Each Section consists of consecutively numbered paragraphs.

At the beginning of each numbered section you will be referred to any illustrations which apply to the procedures in that section. The reference numbers used in illustration captions pinpoint the pertinent Section and the Step within that section. That is, illustration 3.2 means the illustration refers to Section 3 and Step (or paragraph) 2 within that Section.

Procedures, once described in the text, are not normally repeated. When it's necessary to refer to another Chapter, the reference will be given as Chapter and Section number. Cross references given without use of the word "Chapter" apply to Sections and/or paragraphs in the same Chapter. For example, "see Section 8" means in the same Chapter.

References to the left or right side of the vehicle assume you are sitting in the driver's seat, facing forward.

Even though we have prepared this manual with extreme care, neither the publisher nor the author can accept responsibility for any errors in, or omissions from, the information given.

NOTE

A **Note** provides information necessary to properly complete a procedure or information which will make the procedure easier to understand.

CAUTION

A **Caution** provides a special procedure or special steps which must be taken while completing the procedure where the **Caution** is found. Not heeding a **Caution** can result in damage to the assembly being worked on.

WARNING

A **Warning** provides a special procedure or special steps which must be taken while completing the procedure where the **Warning** is found. Not heeding a **Warning** can result in personal injury.

Introduction to the rear-wheel drive Toyota Corolla

The Toyota Corolla is a conventional front engine/rear-wheel drive design.

The inline four-cylinder engines used in these vehicles are equipped with either a carburetor or port-type fuel injection. The engine drives the rear wheels through either a four or five-speed manual or an automatic transmission via a driveshaft and solid rear axle.

Front suspension is independent, featuring torsion bars, with power-assisted steering available on later models. Leaf springs are used in the rear.

Brakes are power assisted discs at the front and self-adjusting drums at the rear.

Vehicle identification numbers

Modifications are a continuing and unpublicized part of vehicle manufacturing. Since spare parts manuals and lists are compiled on a numerical basis, the individual vehicle numbers are essential to correctly identify the component required.

Vehicle Identification Number (VIN)

The VIN is very important because it's used for title and registration purposes. The VIN is stamped into a metal plate fastened to the dashboard close to the windshield on the driver's side of the vehicle. It's also fastened to the driver's door jamb and the firewall in the engine compartment **(see illustration)**. It contains valuable information such as where and when the vehicle was manufactured, the model year and the body style.

Engine identification number

The engine identification number is stamped on a pad on the left side of the block, near the rear **(see illustration)**.

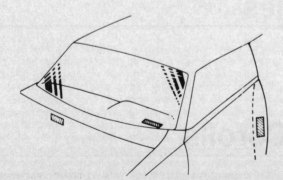

The VIN number can be found in three locations – on the firewall, the top of the dash on the driver's side (visible through the windshield) and on the driver's side door jamb

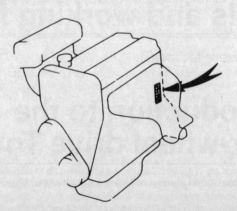

The engine identification number is stamped into the rear of the block on the driver's side

Buying parts

Replacement parts are available from many sources, which generally fall into one of two categories – authorized dealer parts departments and independent retail auto parts stores. Our advice concerning these parts is as follows:

Retail auto parts stores: Good auto parts stores will stock frequently needed components which wear out relatively fast, such as clutch components, exhaust systems, brake parts, tune-up parts, etc. These stores often supply new or reconditioned parts on an exchange basis, which can save a considerable amount of money. Discount auto parts stores are often very good places to buy materials and parts needed for general vehicle maintenance such as oil, grease, filters, spark plugs, belts, touch-up paint, bulbs, etc. They also usually sell tools and general accessories, have convenient hours, charge lower prices and can often be found not far from home.

Authorized dealer parts department: This is the best source for parts which are unique to the vehicle and not generally available elsewhere (such as major engine parts, transmission parts, trim pieces, etc.).

Warranty information: *If the vehicle is still covered under warranty, be sure that any replacement parts purchased – regardless of the source – do not invalidate the warranty!*

To be sure of obtaining the correct parts, have engine and chassis numbers available and, if possible, take the old parts along for positive identification.

Maintenance techniques, tools and working facilities

Maintenance techniques

There are a number of techniques involved in maintenance and repair that will be referred to throughout this manual. Application of these techniques will enable the home mechanic to be more efficient, better organized and capable of performing the various tasks properly, which will ensure that the repair job is thorough and complete.

Fasteners

Fasteners are nuts, bolts, studs and screws used to hold two or more parts together. There are a few things to keep in mind when working with fasteners. Almost all of them use a locking device of some type, either a lockwasher, locknut, locking tab or thread adhesive. All threaded fasteners should be clean and straight, with undamaged threads and undamaged corners on the hex head where the wrench fits. Develop the habit of replacing all damaged nuts and bolts with new ones. Special locknuts with nylon or fiber inserts can only be used once. If they are removed, they lose their locking ability and must be replaced with new ones.

Rusted nuts and bolts should be treated with a penetrating fluid to ease removal and prevent breakage. Some mechanics use turpentine in a spout-type oil can, which works quite well. After applying the rust penetrant, let it work for a few minutes before trying to loosen the nut or bolt. Badly rusted fasteners may have to be chiseled or sawed off or removed with a special nut breaker, available at tool stores.

If a bolt or stud breaks off in an assembly, it can be drilled and removed with a special tool commonly available for this purpose. Most automotive machine shops can perform this task, as well as other repair procedures, such as the repair of threaded holes that have been stripped out.

Flat washers and lockwashers, when removed from an assembly, should always be replaced exactly as removed. Replace any damaged washers with new ones. Never use a lockwasher on any soft metal surface (such as aluminum), thin sheet metal or plastic.

Fastener sizes

For a number of reasons, automobile manufacturers are making wider and wider use of metric fasteners. Therefore, it is important to be able to tell the difference between standard (sometimes called U.S. or SAE) and metric hardware, since they cannot be interchanged.

All bolts, whether standard or metric, are sized according to diameter, thread pitch and length. For example, a standard 1/2 – 13 x 1 bolt is 1/2 inch in diameter, has 13 threads per inch and is 1 inch long. An M12 – 1.75 x 25 metric bolt is 12 mm in diameter, has a thread pitch of 1.75 mm (the distance between threads) and is 25 mm long. The two bolts are nearly identical, and easily confused, but they are not interchangeable.

In addition to the differences in diameter, thread pitch and length, metric and standard bolts can also be distinguished by examining the bolt heads. To begin with, the distance across the flats on a standard bolt head is measured in inches, while the same dimension on a metric bolt is sized in millimeters (the same is true for nuts). As a result, a standard wrench should not be used on a metric bolt and a metric wrench should not be used on a standard bolt. Also, most standard bolts have slashes radiating out from the center of the head to denote the grade or strength of the bolt, which is an indication of the amount of torque that can be applied to it. The greater the number of slashes, the greater the strength of the bolt. Grades 0 through 5 are commonly used on automobiles. Metric bolts have a property class (grade) number, rather than a slash, molded into their heads to indicate bolt strength. In this case, the higher the number, the stronger the bolt. Property class numbers 8.8, 9.8 and 10.9 are commonly used on automobiles.

Strength markings can also be used to distinguish standard hex nuts from metric hex nuts. Many standard nuts have dots stamped into one side, while metric nuts are marked with a number. The greater the number of dots, or the higher the number, the greater the strength of the nut.

Metric studs are also marked on their ends according to property class (grade). Larger studs are numbered (the same as metric bolts), while smaller studs carry a geometric code to denote grade.

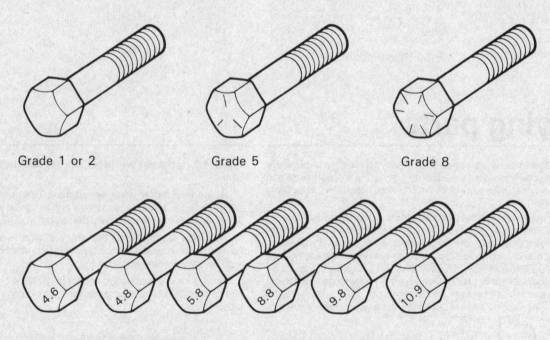

Grade 1 or 2   Grade 5   Grade 8

Bolt strength markings (top – standard/SAE/USS; bottom – metric)

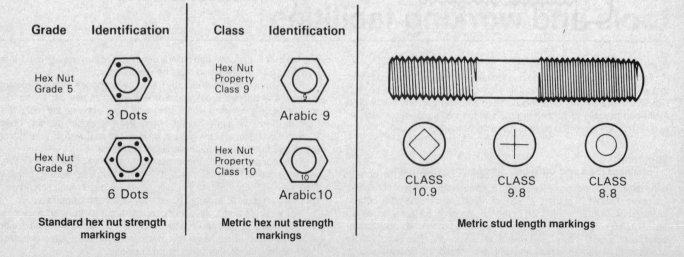

Grade	Identification	Class	Identification
Hex Nut Grade 5	3 Dots	Hex Nut Property Class 9	Arabic 9
Hex Nut Grade 8	6 Dots	Hex Nut Property Class 10	Arabic 10

Standard hex nut strength markings

Metric hex nut strength markings

CLASS 10.9   CLASS 9.8   CLASS 8.8

Metric stud length markings

It should be noted that many fasteners, especially Grades 0 through 2, have no distinguishing marks on them. When such is the case, the only way to determine whether it is standard or metric is to measure the thread pitch or compare it to a known fastener of the same size.

Standard fasteners are often referred to as SAE, as opposed to metric. However, it should be noted that SAE technically refers to a non-metric *fine thread* fastener only. Coarse thread non-metric fasteners are referred to as USS sizes.

Since fasteners of the same size (both standard and metric) may have different strength ratings, be sure to reinstall any bolts, studs or nuts removed from your vehicle in their original locations. Also, when replacing a fastener with a new one, make sure that the new one has a strength rating equal to or greater than the original.

Tightening sequences and procedures

Most threaded fasteners should be tightened to a specific torque value (torque is the twisting force applied to a threaded component such as a nut or bolt). Overtightening the fastener can weaken it and cause it to break, while undertightening can cause it to eventually come loose. Bolts, screws and studs, depending on the material they are made of and their thread diameters, have specific torque values, many of which are noted in the Specifications at the beginning of each Chapter. Be sure to follow the torque recommendations closely. For fasteners not assigned a specific torque, a general torque value chart is presented here as a guide. These torque values are for dry (unlubricated) fasteners threaded into steel or cast iron (not aluminum). As was previously mentioned, the size and grade of a fastener determine the amount of torque that can safely be

Metric thread sizes	Ft-lbs	Nm
M-6	6 to 9	9 to 12
M-8	14 to 21	19 to 28
M-10	28 to 40	38 to 54
M-12	50 to 71	68 to 96
M-14	80 to 140	109 to 154

Pipe thread sizes		
1/8	5 to 8	7 to 10
1/4	12 to 18	17 to 24
3/8	22 to 33	30 to 44
1/2	25 to 35	34 to 47

U.S. thread sizes		
1/4 – 20	6 to 9	9 to 12
5/16 – 18	12 to 18	17 to 24
5/16 – 24	14 to 20	19 to 27
3/8 – 16	22 to 32	30 to 43
3/8 – 24	27 to 38	37 to 51
7/16 – 14	40 to 55	55 to 74
7/16 – 20	40 to 60	55 to 81
1/2 – 13	55 to 80	75 to 108

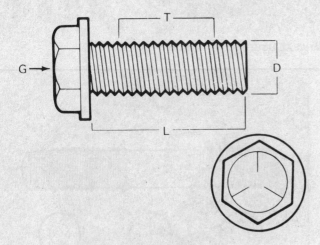

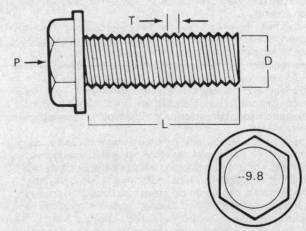

Standard (SAE and USS) bolt dimensions/grade marks

- G   Grade marks (bolt length)
- L   Length (in inches)
- T   Thread pitch (number of threads per inch)
- D   Nominal diameter (in inches)

Metric bolt dimensions/grade marks

- P   Property class (bolt strength)
- L   Length (in millimeters)
- T   Thread pitch (distance between threads in millimeters)
- D   Diameter

applied to it. The figures listed here are approximate for Grade 2 and Grade 3 fasteners. Higher grades can tolerate higher torque values.

Fasteners laid out in a pattern, such as cylinder head bolts, oil pan bolts, differential cover bolts, etc., must be loosened or tightened in sequence to avoid warping the component. This sequence will normally be shown in the appropriate Chapter. If a specific pattern is not given, the following procedures can be used to prevent warping.

Initially, the bolts or nuts should be assembled finger-tight only. Next, they should be tightened one full turn each, in a criss-cross or diagonal pattern. After each one has been tightened one full turn, return to the first one and tighten them all one-half turn, following the same pattern. Finally, tighten each of them one-quarter turn at a time until each fastener has been tightened to the proper torque. To loosen and remove the fasteners, the procedure would be reversed.

Component disassembly

Component disassembly should be done with care and purpose to help ensure that the parts go back together properly. Always keep track of the sequence in which parts are removed. Make note of special characteristics or marks on parts that can be installed more than one way, such as a grooved thrust washer on a shaft. It is a good idea to lay the disassembled parts out on a clean surface in the order that they were removed. It may also be helpful to make sketches or take instant photos of components before removal.

When removing fasteners from a component, keep track of their locations. Sometimes threading a bolt back in a part, or putting the washers and nut back on a stud, can prevent mix-ups later. If nuts and bolts cannot be returned to their original locations, they should be kept in a compartmented box or a series of small boxes. A cupcake or muffin tin is ideal for this purpose, since each cavity can hold the bolts and nuts from a particular area (i.e. oil pan bolts, valve cover bolts, engine mount bolts, etc.). A pan of this type is especially helpful when working on assemblies with very small parts, such as the carburetor, alternator, valve train or interior dash and trim pieces. The cavities can be marked with paint or tape to identify the contents.

Whenever wiring looms, harnesses or connectors are separated, it is a good idea to identify the two halves with numbered pieces of masking tape so they can be easily reconnected.

Gasket sealing surfaces

Throughout any vehicle, gaskets are used to seal the mating surfaces between two parts and keep lubricants, fluids, vacuum or pressure contained in an assembly.

Many times these gaskets are coated with a liquid or paste-type gasket sealing compound before assembly. Age, heat and pressure can sometimes cause the two parts to stick together so tightly that they are very difficult to separate. Often, the assembly can be loosened by striking it with a soft-face hammer near the mating surfaces. A regular hammer can be used if a block of wood is placed between the hammer and the part. Do not hammer on cast parts or parts that could be easily damaged. With any particularly stubborn part, always recheck to make sure that every fastener has been removed.

Avoid using a screwdriver or bar to pry apart an assembly, as they can easily mar the gasket sealing surfaces of the parts, which must remain smooth. If prying is absolutely necessary, use an old broom handle, but keep in mind that extra clean up will be necessary if the wood splinters.

After the parts are separated, the old gasket must be carefully scraped off and the gasket surfaces cleaned. Stubborn gasket material can be soaked with rust penetrant or treated with a special chemical to soften it so it can be easily scraped off. A scraper can be fashioned from a piece of copper tubing by flattening and sharpening one end. Copper is recommended because it is usually softer than the surfaces to be scraped, which reduces the chance of gouging the part. Some gaskets can be removed with a wire brush, but regardless of the method used, the mating surfaces must be left clean and smooth. If for some reason the gasket surface is gouged, then a gasket sealer thick enough to fill scratches will have to be used during reassembly of the components. For most applications, a non-drying (or semi-drying) gasket sealer should be used.

Hose removal tips

Warning: *If the vehicle is equipped with air conditioning, do not disconnect any of the A/C hoses without first having the system depressurized by a dealer service department or a service station.*

Hose removal precautions closely parallel gasket removal precautions. Avoid scratching or gouging the surface that the hose mates against or the connection may leak. This is especially true for radiator hoses. Because of various chemical reactions, the rubber in hoses can bond itself to the metal spigot that the hose fits over. To remove a hose, first loosen the hose clamps that secure it to the spigot. Then, with slip-joint pliers, grab the hose at the clamp and rotate it around the spigot. Work it back and forth until it is completely free, then pull it off. Silicone or other lubricants will ease removal if they can be applied between the hose and the outside of the spigot. Apply the same lubricant to the inside of the hose and the outside of the spigot to simplify installation.

As a last resort (and if the hose is to be replaced with a new one anyway), the rubber can be slit with a knife and the hose peeled from the spigot. If this must be done, be careful that the metal connection is not damaged.

If a hose clamp is broken or damaged, do not reuse it. Wire-type clamps usually weaken with age, so it is a good idea to replace them with screw-type clamps whenever a hose is removed.

Tools

A selection of good tools is a basic requirement for anyone who plans to maintain and repair his or her own vehicle. For the owner who has few tools, the initial investment might seem high, but when compared to the spiraling costs of professional auto maintenance and repair, it is a wise one.

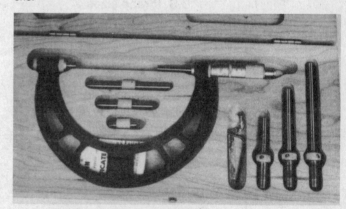

Micrometer set

Dial indicator set

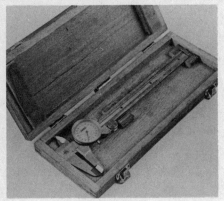

Dial caliper

Hand-operated vacuum pump

Timing light

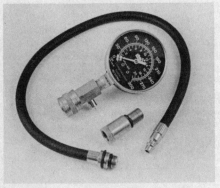

Compression gauge with spark plug hole adapter

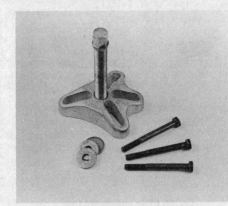

Damper/steering wheel puller

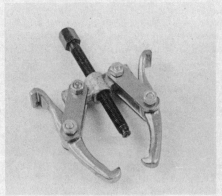

General purpose puller

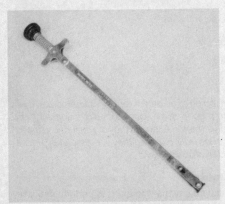

Hydraulic lifter removal tool

Valve spring compressor

Valve spring compressor

Ridge reamer

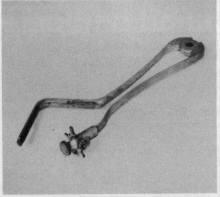

Piston ring groove cleaning tool

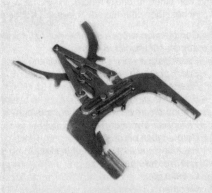

Ring removal/installation tool

Ring compressor

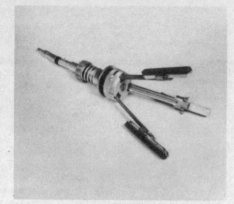

Cylinder hone

Brake hold-down spring tool

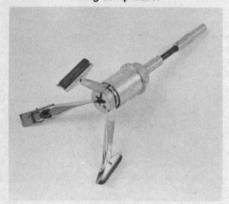

Brake cylinder hone

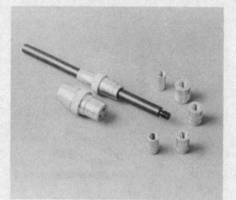

Clutch plate alignment tool

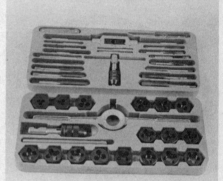

Tap and die set

To help the owner decide which tools are needed to perform the tasks detailed in this manual, the following tool lists are offered: *Maintenance and minor repair, Repair/overhaul* and *Special.*

The newcomer to practical mechanics should start off with the maintenance and minor repair tool kit, which is adequate for the simpler jobs performed on a vehicle. Then, as confidence and experience grow, the owner can tackle more difficult tasks, buying additional tools as they are needed. Eventually the basic kit will be expanded into the repair and overhaul tool set. Over a period of time, the experienced do-it-yourselfer will assemble a tool set complete enough for most repair and overhaul procedures and will add tools from the special category when it is felt that the expense is justified by the frequency of use.

Maintenance and minor repair tool kit

The tools in this list should be considered the minimum required for performance of routine maintenance, servicing and minor repair work. We recommend the purchase of combination wrenches (box-end and open-end combined in one wrench). While more expensive than open end wrenches, they offer the advantages of both types of wrench.

Combination wrench set (1/4-inch to 1 inch or 6 mm to 19 mm)
Adjustable wrench, 8 inch
Spark plug wrench with rubber insert
Spark plug gap adjusting tool
Feeler gauge set
Brake bleeder wrench
Standard screwdriver (5/16-inch x 6 inch)
Phillips screwdriver (No. 2 x 6 inch)
Combination pliers – 6 inch
Hacksaw and assortment of blades
Tire pressure gauge
Grease gun
Oil can
Fine emery cloth
Wire brush

Battery post and cable cleaning tool
Oil filter wrench
Funnel (medium size)
Safety goggles
Jackstands(2)
Drain pan

Note: *If basic tune-ups are going to be part of routine maintenance, it will be necessary to purchase a good quality stroboscopic timing light and combination tachometer/dwell meter. Although they are included in the list of special tools, it is mentioned here because they are absolutely necessary for tuning most vehicles properly.*

Repair and overhaul tool set

These tools are essential for anyone who plans to perform major repairs and are in addition to those in the maintenance and minor repair tool kit. Included is a comprehensive set of sockets which, though expensive, are invaluable because of their versatility, especially when various extensions and drives are available. We recommend the 1/2-inch drive over the 3/8-inch drive. Although the larger drive is bulky and more expensive, it has the capacity of accepting a very wide range of large sockets. Ideally, however, the mechanic should have a 3/8-inch drive set and a 1/2-inch drive set.

Socket set(s)
Reversible ratchet
Extension – 10 inch
Universal joint
Torque wrench (same size drive as sockets)
Ball peen hammer – 8 ounce
Soft-face hammer (plastic/rubber)
Standard screwdriver (1/4-inch x 6 inch)
Standard screwdriver (stubby – 5/16-inch)
Phillips screwdriver (No. 3 x 8 inch)
Phillips screwdriver (stubby – No. 2)

Pliers – vise grip
Pliers – lineman's
Pliers – needle nose
Pliers – snap-ring (internal and external)
Cold chisel – 1/2-inch
Scribe
Scraper (made from flattened copper tubing)
Centerpunch
Pin punches (1/16, 1/8, 3/16-inch)
Steel rule/straightedge – 12 inch
Allen wrench set (1/8 to 3/8-inch or 4 mm to 10 mm)
A selection of files
Wire brush (large)
Jackstands (second set)
Jack (scissor or hydraulic type)

Note: *Another tool which is often useful is an electric drill with a chuck capacity of 3/8-inch and a set of good quality drill bits.*

Special tools

The tools in this list include those which are not used regularly, are expensive to buy, or which need to be used in accordance with their manufacturer's instructions. Unless these tools will be used frequently, it is not very economical to purchase many of them. A consideration would be to split the cost and use between yourself and a friend or friends. In addition, most of these tools can be obtained from a tool rental shop on a temporary basis.

This list primarily contains only those tools and instruments widely available to the public, and not those special tools produced by the vehicle manufacturer for distribution to dealer service departments. Occasionally, references to the manufacturer's special tools are included in the text of this manual. Generally, an alternative method of doing the job without the special tool is offered. However, sometimes there is no alternative to their use. Where this is the case, and the tool cannot be purchased or borrowed, the work should be turned over to the dealer service department or an automotive repair shop.

Valve spring compressor
Piston ring groove cleaning tool
Piston ring compressor
Piston ring installation tool
Cylinder compression gauge
Cylinder ridge reamer
Cylinder surfacing hone
Cylinder bore gauge
Micrometers and/or dial calipers
Hydraulic lifter removal tool
Balljoint separator
Universal-type puller
Impact screwdriver
Dial indicator set
Stroboscopic timing light (inductive pick-up)
Hand operated vacuum/pressure pump
Tachometer/dwell meter
Universal electrical multimeter
Cable hoist
Brake spring removal and installation tools
Floor jack

Buying tools

For the do-it-yourselfer who is just starting to get involved in vehicle maintenance and repair, there are a number of options available when purchasing tools. If maintenance and minor repair is the extent of the work to be done, the purchase of individual tools is satisfactory. If, on the other hand, extensive work is planned, it would be a good idea to purchase a modest tool set from one of the large retail chain stores. A set can usually be bought at a substantial savings over the individual tool prices, and they often come with a tool box. As additional tools are needed, add–on sets, individual tools and a larger tool box can be purchased to expand the tool selection. Building a tool set gradually allows the cost of the tools to be spread over a longer period of time and gives the mechanic the freedom to choose only those tools that will actually be used.

Tool stores will often be the only source of some of the special tools that are needed, but regardless of where tools are bought, try to avoid cheap ones, especially when buying screwdrivers and sockets, because they won't last very long. The expense involved in replacing cheap tools will eventually be greater than the initial cost of quality tools.

Care and maintenance of tools

Good tools are expensive, so it makes sense to treat them with respect. Keep them clean and in usable condition and store them properly when not in use. Always wipe off any dirt, grease or metal chips before putting them away. Never leave tools lying around in the work area. Upon completion of a job, always check closely under the hood for tools that may have been left there so they won't get lost during a test drive.

Some tools, such as screwdrivers, pliers, wrenches and sockets, can be hung on a panel mounted on the garage or workshop wall, while others should be kept in a tool box or tray. Measuring instruments, gauges, meters, etc. must be carefully stored where they cannot be damaged by weather or impact from other tools.

When tools are used with care and stored properly, they will last a very long time. Even with the best of care, though, tools will wear out if used frequently. When a tool is damaged or worn out, replace it. Subsequent jobs will be safer and more enjoyable if you do.

Working facilities

Not to be overlooked when discussing tools is the workshop. If anything more than routine maintenance is to be carried out, some sort of suitable work area is essential.

It is understood, and appreciated, that many home mechanics do not have a good workshop or garage available, and end up removing an engine or doing major repairs outside. It is recommended, however, that the overhaul or repair be completed under the cover of a roof.

A clean, flat workbench or table of comfortable working height is an absolute necessity. The workbench should be equipped with a vise that has a jaw opening of at least four inches.

As mentioned previously, some clean, dry storage space is also required for tools, as well as the lubricants, fluids, cleaning solvents, etc. which soon become necessary.

Sometimes waste oil and fluids, drained from the engine or cooling system during normal maintenance or repairs, present a disposal problem. To avoid pouring them on the ground or into a sewage system, pour the used fluids into large containers, seal them with caps and take them to an authorized disposal site or recycling center. Plastic jugs, such as old antifreeze containers, are ideal for this purpose.

Always keep a supply of old newspapers and clean rags available. Old towels are excellent for mopping up spills. Many mechanics use rolls of paper towels for most work because they are readily available and disposable. To help keep the area under the vehicle clean, a large cardboard box can be cut open and flattened to protect the garage or shop floor.

Whenever working over a painted surface, such as when leaning over a fender to service something under the hood, always cover it with an old blanket or bedspread to protect the finish. Vinyl covered pads, made especially for this purpose, are available at auto parts stores.

Booster battery (jump) starting

Observe these precautions when using a booster battery to start a vehicle:

a) Before connecting the booster battery, make sure the ignition switch is in the Off position.
b) Turn off the lights, heater and other electrical loads.
c) Your eyes should be shielded. Safety goggles are a good idea.
d) Make sure the booster battery is the same voltage as the dead one in the vehicle.
e) The two vehicles MUST NOT TOUCH each other!
f) Make sure the transmission is in Neutral (manual) or Park (automatic).
g) If the booster battery is not a maintenance-free type, remove the vent caps and lay a cloth over the vent holes.

Connect the red jumper cable to the positive (+) terminals of each battery.

Connect one end of the black jumper cable to the negative (–) terminal of the booster battery. The other end of this cable should be connected to a good ground on the vehicle to be started, such as a bolt or bracket on the engine block **(see illustration)**. Make sure the cable will not come into contact with the fan, drivebelts or other moving parts of the engine.

Start the engine using the booster battery, then, with the engine running at idle speed, disconnect the jumper cables in the reverse order of connection.

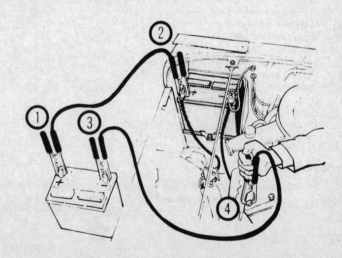

Make the booster battery cable connections in the numerical order shown (note that the negative cable of the booster battery is NOT attached to the negative terminal of the dead battery)

Jacking and towing

Jacking

Warning: *The jack supplied with the vehicle should only be used for raising the vehicle when changing a tire or placing jackstands under the frame. Never work under the vehicle or start the engine while the jack is being used as the only means of support.*

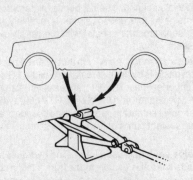

Jacking locations

The vehicle must be on a level surface with the wheels blocked and the transmission in Park (automatic) or Reverse (manual). Apply the parking brake if the front of the vehicle must be raised. Make sure no one is in the vehicle as it's being raised with the jack.

Remove the jack, lug nut wrench and spare tire (if needed) from the vehicle. If a tire is being replaced, use the lug wrench to remove the wheel cover. **Warning:** *Wheel covers may have sharp edges – be very careful not to cut yourself.* Loosen the lug nuts one-half turn, but leave them in place until the tire is raised off the ground.

Position the jack under the vehicle at the indicated jacking point. There's a front and rear jacking point on each side of the vehicle **(see illustration)**. It should be engaged with the seam in the rocker panel, between the two dimples.

Turn the jack handle clockwise until the tire clears the ground. Remove the lug nuts, pull the tire off and replace it with the spare. Replace the lug nuts with the beveled side facing in and tighten them snugly. Don't attempt to tighten them completely until the vehicle is lowered or it could slip off the jack.

Turn the jack handle counterclockwise to lower the vehicle. Remove the jack and tighten the lug nuts in a criss-cross pattern. If possible, tighten the nuts with a torque wrench (see Chapter 1 for the torque figures). If you don't have access to a torque wrench, have the nuts checked by a service station or repair shop as soon as possible.

Stow the tire, jack and wrench and unblock the wheels.

Towing

The vehicle can be towed with all four wheels on the ground, as long as speeds don't exceed 35 mph and the distance is less than 50 miles, otherwise transmission damage can result.

Towing equipment specifically designed for this purpose should be used and it must be attached to the main structural members of the vehicle, not the bumper or brackets.

Safety is a major consideration when towing and all applicable state and local laws must be obeyed. A safety chain must be used.

While towing, the parking brake should be released and the transmission should be in Neutral. The steering must be unlocked (ignition switch in the Off position). Remember that power steering and brakes won't work with the engine off.

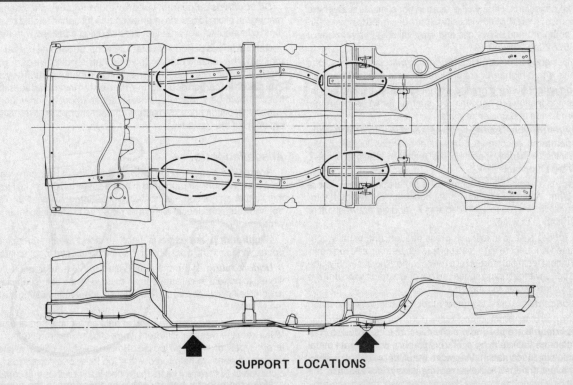

SUPPORT LOCATIONS

Support locations (for hoist pads or jackstands) on the under side of the body

Automotive chemicals and lubricants

A number of automotive chemicals and lubricants are available for use during vehicle maintenance and repair. They include a wide variety of products ranging from cleaning solvents and degreasers to lubricants and protective sprays for rubber, plastic and vinyl.

Cleaners

Carburetor cleaner and choke cleaner is a strong solvent for gum, varnish and carbon. Most carburetor cleaners leave a dry-type lubricant film which will not harden or gum up. Because of this film it is not recommended for use on electrical components.

Brake system cleaner is used to remove grease and brake fluid from the brake system, where clean surfaces are absolutely necessary. It leaves no residue and often eliminates brake squeal caused by contaminants.

Electrical cleaner removes oxidation, corrosion and carbon deposits from electrical contacts, restoring full current flow. It can also be used to clean spark plugs, carburetor jets, voltage regulators and other parts where an oil-free surface is desired.

Demoisturants remove water and moisture from electrical components such as alternators, voltage regulators, electrical connectors and fuse blocks. They are non-conductive, non-corrosive and non-flammable.

Degreasers are heavy-duty solvents used to remove grease from the outside of the engine and from chassis components. They can be sprayed or brushed on and, depending on the type, are rinsed off either with water or solvent.

Lubricants

Motor oil is the lubricant formulated for use in engines. It normally contains a wide variety of additives to prevent corrosion and reduce foaming and wear. Motor oil comes in various weights (viscosity ratings) from 5 to 80. The recommended weight of the oil depends on the season, temperature and the demands on the engine. Light oil is used in cold climates and under light load conditions. Heavy oil is used in hot climates and where high loads are encountered. Multi-viscosity oils are designed to have characteristics of both light and heavy oils and are available in a number of weights from 5W-20 to 20W-50.

Gear oil is designed to be used in differentials, manual transmissions and other areas where high-temperature lubrication is required.

Chassis and wheel bearing grease is a heavy grease used where increased loads and friction are encountered, such as for wheel bearings, balljoints, tie-rod ends and universal joints.

High-temperature wheel bearing grease is designed to withstand the extreme temperatures encountered by wheel bearings in disc brake equipped vehicles. It usually contains molybdenum disulfide (moly), which is a dry-type lubricant.

White grease is a heavy grease for metal-to-metal applications where water is a problem. White grease stays soft under both low and high temperatures (usually from −100 to +190-degrees F), and will not wash off or dilute in the presence of water.

Assembly lube is a special extreme pressure lubricant, usually containing moly, used to lubricate high-load parts (such as main and rod bearings and cam lobes) for initial start-up of a new engine. The assembly lube lubricates the parts without being squeezed out or washed away until the engine oiling system begins to function.

Silicone lubricants are used to protect rubber, plastic, vinyl and nylon parts.

Graphite lubricants are used where oils cannot be used due to contamination problems, such as in locks. The dry graphite will lubricate metal parts while remaining uncontaminated by dirt, water, oil or acids. It is electrically conductive and will not foul electrical contacts in locks such as the ignition switch.

Moly penetrants loosen and lubricate frozen, rusted and corroded fasteners and prevent future rusting or freezing.

Heat-sink grease is a special electrically non-conductive grease that is used for mounting electronic ignition modules where it is essential that heat is transferred away from the module.

Sealants

RTV sealant is one of the most widely used gasket compounds. Made from silicone, RTV is air curing, it seals, bonds, waterproofs, fills surface irregularities, remains flexible, doesn't shrink, is relatively easy to remove, and is used as a supplementary sealer with almost all low and medium temperature gaskets.

Anaerobic sealant is much like RTV in that it can be used either to seal gaskets or to form gaskets by itself. It remains flexible, is solvent resistant and fills surface imperfections. The difference between an anaerobic sealant and an RTV-type sealant is in the curing. RTV cures when exposed to air, while an anaerobic sealant cures only in the absence of air. This means that an anaerobic sealant cures only after the assembly of parts, sealing them together.

Thread and pipe sealant is used for sealing hydraulic and pneumatic fittings and vacuum lines. It is usually made from a teflon compound, and comes in a spray, a paint-on liquid and as a wrap-around tape.

Chemicals

Anti–seize compound prevents seizing, galling, cold welding, rust and corrosion in fasteners. High-temperature anti-seize, usually made with copper and graphite lubricants, is used for exhaust system and exhaust manifold bolts.

Anaerobic locking compounds are used to keep fasteners from vibrating or working loose and cure only after installation, in the absence of air. Medium strength locking compound is used for small nuts, bolts and screws that may be removed later. High-strength locking compound is for large nuts, bolts and studs which aren't removed on a regular basis.

Oil additives range from viscosity index improvers to chemical treatments that claim to reduce internal engine friction. It should be noted that most oil manufacturers caution against using additives with their oils.

Gas additives perform several functions, depending on their chemical makeup. They usually contain solvents that help dissolve gum and varnish that build up on carburetor, fuel injection and intake parts. They also serve to break down carbon deposits that form on the inside surfaces of the combustion chambers. Some additives contain upper cylinder lubricants for valves and piston rings, and others contain chemicals to remove condensation from the gas tank.

Miscellaneous

Brake fluid is specially formulated hydraulic fluid that can withstand the heat and pressure encountered in brake systems. Care must be taken so this fluid does not come in contact with painted surfaces or plastics. An opened container should always be resealed to prevent contamination by water or dirt.

Weatherstrip adhesive is used to bond weatherstripping around doors, windows and trunk lids. It is sometimes used to attach trim pieces.

Undercoating is a petroleum-based, tar-like substance that is designed to protect metal surfaces on the underside of the vehicle from corrosion. It also acts as a sound-deadening agent by insulating the bottom of the vehicle.

Waxes and polishes are used to help protect painted and plated surfaces from the weather. Different types of paint may require the use of different types of wax and polish. Some polishes utilize a chemical or abrasive cleaner to help remove the top layer of oxidized (dull) paint on older vehicles. In recent years many non-wax polishes that contain a wide variety of chemicals such as polymers and silicones have been introduced. These non-wax polishes are usually easier to apply and last longer than conventional waxes and polishes.

Safety first!

Regardless of how enthusiastic you may be about getting on with the job at hand, take the time to ensure that your safety is not jeopardized. A moment's lack of attention can result in an accident, as can failure to observe certain simple safety precautions. The possibility of an accident will always exist, and the following points should not be considered a comprehensive list of all dangers. Rather, they are intended to make you aware of the risks and to encourage a safety conscious approach to all work you carry out on your vehicle.

Essential DOs and DON'Ts

DON'T rely on a jack when working under the vehicle. Always use approved jackstands to support the weight of the vehicle and place them under the recommended lift or support points.

DON'T attempt to loosen extremely tight fasteners (i.e. wheel lug nuts) while the vehicle is on a jack – it may fall.

DON'T start the engine without first making sure that the transmission is in Neutral (or Park where applicable) and the parking brake is set.

DON'T remove the radiator cap from a hot cooling system – let it cool or cover it with a cloth and release the pressure gradually.

DON'T attempt to drain the engine oil until you are sure it has cooled to the point that it will not burn you.

DON'T touch any part of the engine or exhaust system until it has cooled sufficiently to avoid burns.

DON'T siphon toxic liquids such as gasoline, antifreeze and brake fluid by mouth, or allow them to remain on your skin.

DON'T inhale brake lining dust – it is potentially hazardous (see Asbestos below)

DON'T allow spilled oil or grease to remain on the floor – wipe it up before someone slips on it.

DON'T use loose fitting wrenches or other tools which may slip and cause injury.

DON'T push on wrenches when loosening or tightening nuts or bolts. Always try to pull the wrench toward you. If the situation calls for pushing the wrench away, push with an open hand to avoid scraped knuckles if the wrench should slip.

DON'T attempt to lift a heavy component alone – get someone to help you.

DON'T rush or take unsafe shortcuts to finish a job.

DON'T allow children or animals in or around the vehicle while you are working on it.

DO wear eye protection when using power tools such as a drill, sander, bench grinder, etc. and when working under a vehicle.

DO keep loose clothing and long hair well out of the way of moving parts.

DO make sure that any hoist used has a safe working load rating adequate for the job.

DO get someone to check on you periodically when working alone on a vehicle.

DO carry out work in a logical sequence and make sure that everything is correctly assembled and tightened.

DO keep chemicals and fluids tightly capped and out of the reach of children and pets.

DO remember that your vehicle's safety affects that of yourself and others. If in doubt on any point, get professional advice.

Asbestos

Certain friction, insulating, sealing, and other products – such as brake linings, brake bands, clutch linings, torque converters, gaskets, etc. – contain asbestos. *Extreme care must be taken to avoid inhalation of dust from such products since it is hazardous to health*. If in doubt, assume that they *do* contain asbestos.

Fire

Remember at all times that gasoline is highly flammable. Never smoke or have any kind of open flame around when working on a vehicle. But the risk does not end there. A spark caused by an electrical short circuit, by two metal surfaces contacting each other, or even by static electricity built up in your body under certain conditions, can ignite gasoline vapors, which in a confined space are highly explosive. Do not, under any circumstances, use gasoline for cleaning parts. Use an approved safety solvent.

Always disconnect the battery ground (–) cable *at the battery* before working on any part of the fuel system or electrical system. Never risk spilling fuel on a hot engine or exhaust component.

It is strongly recommended that a fire extinguisher suitable for use on fuel and electrical fires be kept handy in the garage or workshop at all times. Never try to extinguish a fuel or electrical fire with water.

Fumes

Certain fumes are highly toxic and can quickly cause unconsciousness and even death if inhaled to any extent. Gasoline vapor falls into this category, as do the vapors from some cleaning solvents. Any draining or pouring of such volatile fluids should be done in a well ventilated area.

When using cleaning fluids and solvents, read the instructions on the container carefully. Never use materials from unmarked containers.

Never run the engine in an enclosed space, such as a garage. Exhaust fumes contain carbon monoxide, which is extremely poisonous. If you need to run the engine, always do so in the open air, or at least have the rear of the vehicle outside the work area.

If you are fortunate enough to have the use of an inspection pit, never drain or pour gasoline and never run the engine while the vehicle is over the pit. The fumes, being heavier than air, will concentrate in the pit with possibly lethal results.

The battery

Never create a spark or allow a bare light bulb near a battery. They normally give off a certain amount of hydrogen gas, which is highly explosive.

Always disconnect the battery ground (–) cable *at the battery* before working on the fuel or electrical systems.

If possible, loosen the filler caps or cover when charging the battery from an external source (this does not apply to sealed or maintenancefree batteries). Do not charge at an excessive rate or the battery may burst.

Take care when adding water to a non maintenance–free battery and when carrying a battery. The electrolyte, even when diluted, is very corrosive and should not be allowed to contact clothing or skin.

Always wear eye protection when cleaning the battery to prevent the caustic deposits from entering your eyes.

Household current

When using an electric power tool, inspection light, etc., which operates on household current, always make sure that the tool is correctly connected to its plug and that, where necessary, it is properly grounded. Do not use such items in damp conditions and, again, do not create a spark or apply excessive heat in the vicinity of fuel or fuel vapor.

Secondary ignition system voltage

A severe electric shock can result from touching certain parts of the ignition system (such as the spark plug wires) when the engine is running or being cranked, particularly if components are damp or the insulation is defective. In the case of an electronic ignition system, the secondary system voltage is much higher and could prove fatal.

Conversion factors

Length (distance)

Inches (in)	X	25.4	=	Millimetres (mm)	X	0.0394	= Inches (in)
Feet (ft)	X	0.305	=	Metres (m)	X	3.281	= Feet (ft)
Miles	X	1.609	=	Kilometres (km)	X	0.621	= Miles

Volume (capacity)

Cubic inches (cu in; in³)	X	16.387	=	Cubic centimetres (cc; cm³)	X	0.061	= Cubic inches (cu in; in³)
Imperial pints (Imp pt)	X	0.568	=	Litres (l)	X	1.76	= Imperial pints (Imp pt)
Imperial quarts (Imp qt)	X	1.137	=	Litres (l)	X	0.88	= Imperial quarts (Imp qt)
Imperial quarts (Imp qt)	X	1.201	=	US quarts (US qt)	X	0.833	= Imperial quarts (Imp qt)
US quarts (US qt)	X	0.946	=	Litres (l)	X	1.057	= US quarts (US qt)
Imperial gallons (Imp gal)	X	4.546	=	Litres (l)	X	0.22	= Imperial gallons (Imp gal)
Imperial gallons (Imp gal)	X	1.201	=	US gallons (US gal)	X	0.833	= Imperial gallons (Imp gal)
US gallons (US gal)	X	3.785	=	Litres (l)	X	0.264	= US gallons (US gal)

Mass (weight)

Ounces (oz)	X	28.35	=	Grams (g)	X	0.035	= Ounces (oz)
Pounds (lb)	X	0.454	=	Kilograms (kg)	X	2.205	= Pounds (lb)

Force

Ounces-force (ozf; oz)	X	0.278	=	Newtons (N)	X	3.6	= Ounces-force (ozf; oz)
Pounds-force (lbf; lb)	X	4.448	=	Newtons (N)	X	0.225	= Pounds-force (lbf; lb)
Newtons (N)	X	0.1	=	Kilograms-force (kgf; kg)	X	9.81	= Newtons (N)

Pressure

Pounds-force per square inch (psi; lbf/in²; lb/in²)	X	0.070	=	Kilograms-force per square centimetre (kgf/cm²; kg/cm²)	X	14.223	= Pounds-force per square inch (psi; lbf/in²; lb/in²)
Pounds-force per square inch (psi; lbf/in²; lb/in²)	X	0.068	=	Atmospheres (atm)	X	14.696	= Pounds-force per square inch (psi; lbf/in²; lb/in²)
Pounds-force per square inch (psi; lbf/in²; lb/in²)	X	0.069	=	Bars	X	14.5	= Pounds-force per square inch (psi; lbf/in²; lb/in²)
Pounds-force per square inch (psi; lbf/in²; lb/in²)	X	6.895	=	Kilopascals (kPa)	X	0.145	= Pounds-force per square inch (psi; lbf/in²; lb/in²)
Kilopascals (kPa)	X	0.01	=	Kilograms-force per square centimetre (kgf/cm²; kg/cm²)	X	98.1	= Kilopascals (kPa)
Millibar (mbar)	X	100	=	Pascals (Pa)	X	0.01	= Millibar (mbar)
Millibar (mbar)	X	0.0145	=	Pounds-force per square inch (psi; lbf/in²; lb/in²)	X	68.947	= Millibar (mbar)
Millibar (mbar)	X	0.75	=	Millimetres of mercury (mmHg)	X	1.333	= Millibar (mbar)
Millibar (mbar)	X	0.401	=	Inches of water (inH₂O)	X	2.491	= Millibar (mbar)
Millimetres of mercury (mmHg)	X	0.535	=	Inches of water (inH₂O)	X	1.868	= Millimetres of mercury (mmHg)
Inches of water (inH₂O)	X	0.036	=	Pounds-force per square inch (psi; lbf/in²; lb/in²)	X	27.68	= Inches of water (inH₂O)

Torque (moment of force)

Pounds-force inches (lbf in; lb in)	X	1.152	=	Kilograms-force centimetre (kgf cm; kg cm)	X	0.868	= Pounds-force inches (lbf in; lb in)
Pounds-force inches (lbf in; lb in)	X	0.113	=	Newton metres (Nm)	X	8.85	= Pounds-force inches (lbf in; lb in)
Pounds-force inches (lbf in; lb in)	X	0.083	=	Pounds-force feet (lbf ft; lb ft)	X	12	= Pounds-force inches (lbf in; lb in)
Pounds-force feet (lbf ft; lb ft)	X	0.138	=	Kilograms-force metres (kgf m; kg m)	X	7.233	= Pounds-force feet (lbf ft; lb ft)
Pounds-force feet (lbf ft; lb ft)	X	1.356	=	Newton metres (Nm)	X	0.738	= Pounds-force feet (lbf ft; lb ft)
Newton metres (Nm)	X	0.102	=	Kilograms-force metres (kgf m; kg m)	X	9.804	= Newton metres (Nm)

Power

Horsepower (hp)	X	745.7	=	Watts (W)	X	0.0013	= Horsepower (hp)

Velocity (speed)

Miles per hour (miles/hr; mph)	X	1.609	=	Kilometres per hour (km/hr; kph)	X	0.621	= Miles per hour (miles/hr; mph)

Fuel consumption*

Miles per gallon, Imperial (mpg)	X	0.354	=	Kilometres per litre (km/l)	X	2.825	= Miles per gallon, Imperial (mpg)
Miles per gallon, US (mpg)	X	0.425	=	Kilometres per litre (km/l)	X	2.352	= Miles per gallon, US (mpg)

Temperature

Degrees Fahrenheit = (°C x 1.8) + 32

Degrees Celsius (Degrees Centigrade; °C) = (°F - 32) x 0.56

*It is common practice to convert from miles per gallon (mpg) to litres/100 kilometres (l/100km), where mpg (Imperial) x l/100 km = 282 and mpg (US) x l/100 km = 235

Troubleshooting

Contents

This section is an easy reference guide to the more common problems which may occur during the operation of your vehicle. The problems and their possible causes are grouped under headings denoting various components or systems, such as Engine, Cooling system, etc. They also refer you to the Chapter and/or Section which deals with the problem.

Remember, successful troubleshooting isn't a mysterious "black art" practiced only by professional mechanics. It's simply the result of the right knowledge combined with an intelligent, systematic approach to a problem. Always use the process of elimination, starting with the simplest solution and working through to the most complex – and never overlook the obvious. Anyone can run the gas tank dry or leave the lights on overnight, so don't assume that it can't happen to you.

Finally, always try to establish a clear idea why a problem has occurred and take steps to ensure it doesn't happen again. For example, if the electrical system fails because of a poor connection, check all other connections in the system to make sure they don't fail as well. If a particular fuse continues to blow, find out why – don't just replace one fuse after another. Remember, failure of a small component often indicates potential failure or malfunction of a more important component or system.

Engine and performance

1   Engine will not rotate when attempting to start

1   Battery terminal connections loose or corroded. Check the cable terminals at the battery; tighten cable clamp and/or clean off corrosion as necessary (see Chapter 1).
2   Battery discharged or faulty. If the cable ends are clean and tight on the battery posts, turn the key to the On position and switch on the headlights or windshield wipers. If they won't run, the battery is discharged.
3   Automatic transmission not engaged in park (P) or Neutral (N).
4   Broken, loose or disconnected wires in the starting circuit. Inspect all wires and connectors at the battery, starter solenoid and ignition switch (on steering column).
5   Starter motor pinion jammed in flywheel ring gear. If manual transmission, place transmission in gear and rock the vehicle to manually turn the engine. Remove starter (Chapter 5) and inspect pinion and flywheel (Chapter 2) at earliest convenience.
6   Starter solenoid faulty (Chapter 5).
7   Starter motor faulty (Chapter 5).
8   Ignition switch faulty (Chapter 13).
9   Engine seized. Try to turn the crankshaft with a large socket and breaker bar on the pulley bolt.

2   Engine rotates but will not start

1   Fuel tank empty.
2   Battery discharged (engine rotates slowly). Check the operation of electrical components as described in previous Section.
3   Battery terminal connections loose or corroded. See previous Section.
4   Fuel not reaching carburetor or fuel injector. Check for clogged fuel filter or lines and defective fuel pump. Also make sure the tank vent lines aren't clogged (Chapter 4).
5   Choke not operating properly (Chapter 1).
6   Faulty distributor components. Check the cap and rotor (Chapter 1).
7   Low cylinder compression. Check as described in Chapter 2.
8   Valve clearances not properly adjusted (Chapter 1).
9   Water in fuel. Drain tank and fill with new fuel.
10 Defective IC ignition unit (Chapter 5).
11 Dirty or clogged carburetor jets or fuel injector. Carburetor out of adjustment.
12 Wet or damaged ignition components (Chapters 1 and 5).
13 Worn, faulty or incorrectly gapped spark plugs (Chapter 1).

14 Broken, loose or disconnected wires in the starting circuit (see previous Section).
15 Loose distributor (changing ignition timing). Turn the distributor body as necessary to start the engine, then adjust the ignition timing as soon as possible (Chapter 1).
16 Broken, loose or disconnected wires at the ignition coil or faulty coil (Chapter 5).
17 Timing belt or chain failure or wear affecting valve timing (Chapter 2).

3   Starter motor operates without turning engine

1   Starter pinion sticking. Remove the starter (Chapter 5) and inspect.
2   Starter pinion or flywheel/driveplate teeth worn or broken. Remove the inspection cover on the left side of the engine and inspect.

4   Engine hard to start when cold

1   Battery discharged or low. Check as described in Chapter 1.
2   Fuel not reaching the carburetor or fuel injectors. Check the fuel filter and lines (Chapters 1 and 4).
3   Choke inoperative (Chapters 1 and 4).
4   Defective spark plugs (Chapter 1).

5   Engine hard to start when hot

1   Air filter dirty (Chapter 1).
2   Fuel not reaching carburetor or fuel injectors (see Section 4). Check for a vapor lock situation, brought about by clogged fuel tank vent lines.
3   Bad engine ground connection.
4   Choke sticking (Chapter 1).
5   Defective pick-up coil in distributor (Chapter 5).
6   Float level too high.

6   Starter motor noisy or engages roughly

1   Pinion or flywheel/driveplate teeth worn or broken. Remove the inspection cover on the left side of the engine and inspect.
2   Starter motor mounting bolts loose or missing.

7   Engine starts but stops immediately

1   Loose or damaged wire harness connections at distributor, coil or alternator.
2   Intake manifold vacuum leaks. Make sure all mounting bolts/nuts are tight and all vacuum hoses connected to the manifold are attached properly and in good condition.

8   Engine "lopes" while idling or idles erratically

1   Vacuum leaks. Check mounting bolts at the intake manifold for tightness. Make sure that all vacuum hoses are connected and in good condition. Use a stethoscope or a length of fuel hose held against your ear to listen for vacuum leaks while the engine is running. A hissing sound will be heard. A soapy water solution will also detect leaks. Check the intake manifold gasket surfaces.
2   Leaking EGR valve or plugged PCV valve (see Chapters 1 and 6).
3   Air filter clogged (Chapter 1).
4   Leaking head gasket. Perform a cylinder compression check (Chapter 2).
5   Timing chain or belt worn or (Chapter 2).
6   Camshaft lobes worn (Chapter 2).
7   Valve clearance out of adjustment (Chapter 1). Valves burned or otherwise leaking (Chapter 2).

8 Ignition timing out of adjustment (Chapter 1).
9 Ignition system not operating properly (Chapters 1 and 5).
10 Thermostatic air cleaner not operating properly (Chapter 1).
11 Choke not operating properly (Chapter 1).
12 Dirty or clogged injectors. Carburetor dirty, clogged or out of adjustment (Chapter 4).
13 Idle speed out of adjustment (Chapters 1 and 4).

9 Engine misses at idle speed

1 Spark plugs faulty or not gapped properly (Chapter 1).
2 Faulty spark plug wires (Chapter 1).
3 Wet or damaged distributor components (Chapter 1).
4 Short circuits in ignition, coil or spark plug wires.
5 Sticking or faulty emissions systems (see Chapter 6).
6 Clogged fuel filter and/or foreign matter in fuel. Remove the fuel filter (Chapter 1) and inspect.
7 Vacuum leaks at intake manifold or hose connections. Check as described in Section 8.
8 Incorrect idle speed (Chapter 1) or idle mixture.
9 Incorrect ignition timing (Chapter 1).
10 Low or uneven cylinder compression. Check as described in Chapter 2, Part C.
11 Choke not operating properly (Chapter 1).
12 Clogged or dirty fuel injectors (Chapter 4).

10 Excessively high idle speed

1 Sticking throttle linkage (Chapter 4).
2 Choke opened excessively at idle (Chapter 4).
3 Idle speed incorrectly adjusted (Chapter 1).
4 Valve clearances incorrectly adjusted (Chapter 1).
5 Dash pot out of adjustment (Chapter 6).

11 Battery will not hold a charge

1 Alternator drivebelt defective or not adjusted properly (Chapter 1).
2 Battery cables loose or corroded (Chapter 1).
3 Alternator not charging properly (Chapter 5).
4 Loose, broken or faulty wires in the charging circuit (Chapter 5).
5 Short circuit causing a continuous drain on the battery (Chapter 12).
6 Battery defective internally.
7 Faulty regulator (Chapter 5).

12 Alternator light stays on

1 Fault in alternator or charging circuit (Chapter 5).
2 Alternator drivebelt defective or not properly adjusted (Chapter 1).

13 Alternator light fails to come on when key is turned on

1 Faulty bulb (Chapter 12).
2 Defective alternator (Chapter 5).
3 Fault in the printed circuit, dash wiring or bulb holder (Chapter 12).

14 Engine misses throughout driving speed range

1 Fuel filter clogged and/or impurities in the fuel system. Check fuel filter (Chapter 1) or clean system (Chapter 4).
2 Faulty or incorrectly gapped spark plugs (Chapter 1).
3 Incorrect ignition timing (Chapter 1).

4 Cracked distributor cap, disconnected distributor wires or damaged distributor components (Chapter 1).
5 Defective spark plug wires (Chapter 1).
6 Emissions system components faulty (Chapter 6).
7 Low or uneven cylinder compression pressures. Check as described in Chapter 2.
8 Weak or faulty ignition coil (Chapter 5).
9 Weak or faulty ignition system (Chapter 5).
10 Vacuum leaks at intake manifold or vacuum hoses (Section 8).
11 Dirty or clogged carburetor or fuel injector (Chapter 4).
12 Leaky EGR valve (Chapter 6).
13 Carburetor out of adjustment (Chapter 4).
14 Idle speed out of adjustment (Chapter 1).

15 Hesitation or stumble during acceleration

1 Ignition timing incorrect (Chapter 1).
2 Ignition system not operating properly (Chapter 5).
3 Dirty or clogged carburetor or fuel injector (Chapter 4).
4 Low fuel pressure. Check for proper operation of the fuel pump and for restrictions in the fuel filter and lines (Chapter 4).
5 Carburetor out of adjustment (Chapter 4).

16 Engine stalls

1 Idle speed incorrect (Chapter 1).
2 Fuel filter clogged and/or water and impurities in the fuel system (Chapter 1).
3 Choke not operating properly (Chapter 1).
4 Damaged or wet distributor cap and wires.
5 Emissions system components faulty (Chapter 6).
6 Faulty or incorrectly gapped spark plugs (Chapter 1). Also check the spark plug wires (Chapter 1).
7 Vacuum leak at the carburetor, intake manifold or vacuum hoses. Check as described in Section 8.
8 Valve clearances incorrect (Chapter 1).

17 Engine lacks power

1 Incorrect ignition timing (Chapter 1).
2 Excessive play in distributor shaft. At the same time check for faulty distributor cap, wires, etc. (Chapter 1).
3 Faulty or incorrectly gapped spark plugs (Chapter 1).
4 Air filter dirty (Chapter 1).
5 Spark timing control system not operating properly (see Chapter 6).
6 Faulty ignition coil (Chapter 5).
7 Brakes binding (Chapters 1 and 9).
8 Automatic transmission fluid level incorrect, causing slippage (Chapter 1).
9 Clutch slipping (Chapter 8).
10 Fuel filter clogged and/or impurities in the fuel system (Chapters 1 and 4).
11 EGR system not functioning properly (Chapter 6).
12 Use of sub-standard fuel. Fill tank with proper octane fuel.
13 Low or uneven cylinder compression pressures. Check as described in Chapter 2.
14 Air leak at carburetor or intake manifold (check as described in Section 8).
15 Dirty or clogged carburetor jets or malfunctioning choke (Chapter 1).

18 Engine backfires

1 EGR system not functioning properly (Chapter 6).
2 Ignition timing incorrect (Chapter 1).

3　Thermostatic air cleaner system not operating properly (Chapter 6).
4　Vacuum leak (refer to Section 8).
5　Valve clearances incorrect (Chapter 1).
6　Damaged valve springs or sticking valves (Chapter 2).
7　Intake air leak (see Section 8).
8　Carburetor float level out of adjustment.

19　Engine surges while holding accelerator steady

1　Intake air leak (see Section 8).
2　Fuel pump not working properly.

20　Pinging or knocking engine sounds when engine is under load

1　Incorrect grade of fuel. Fill tank with fuel of the proper octane rating.
2　Ignition timing incorrect (Chapter 1).
3　Carbon build-up in combustion chambers. Remove cylinder head(s) and clean combustion chambers (Chapter 2).
4　Incorrect spark plugs (Chapter 1).

21　Engine diesels (continues to run) after being turned off

1　Idle speed too high (Chapter 1).
2　Ignition timing incorrect (Chapter 1).
3　Incorrect spark plug heat range (Chapter 1).
4　Intake air leak (see Section 8).
5　Carbon build-up in combustion chambers. Remove the cylinder head(s) and clean the combustion chambers (Chapter 2).
6　Valves sticking (Chapter 2).
7　BCDD or FICD system not operating properly (Chapter 6).
8　Valve clearance incorrect (Chapter 1).
9　EGR system not operating properly (Chapter 6).
10　Fuel shut-off system not operating properly (Chapter 6).
11　Check for causes of overheating (Section 27).

22　Low oil pressure

1　Improper grade of oil.
2　Oil pump regulator valve not operating properly (Chapter 2).
3　Oil pump worn or damaged (Chapter 2).
4　Engine overheating (refer to Section 27).
5　Clogged oil filter (Chapter 1).
6　Clogged oil strainer (Chapter 2).
7　Oil pressure gauge not working properly (Chapter 2).

23　Excessive oil consumption

1　Loose oil drain plug.
2　Loose bolts or damaged oil pan gasket (Chapter 2).
3　Loose bolts or damaged front cover gasket (Chapter 2).
4　Front or rear crankshaft oil seal leaking (Chapter 2).
5　Loose bolts or damaged rocker arm cover gasket (Chapter 2).
6　Loose oil filter (Chapter 1).
7　Loose or damaged oil pressure switch (Chapter 2).
8　Pistons and cylinders excessively worn (Chapter 2).
9　Piston rings not installed correctly on pistons (Chapter 2).
10　Worn or damaged piston rings (Chapter 2).
11　Intake and/or exhaust valve oil seals worn or damaged (see Chapter 2).
12　Worn valve stems.
13　Worn or damaged valves/guides (Chapter 2).

24　Excessive fuel consumption

1　Dirty or clogged air filter element (Chapter 1).
2　Incorrect ignition timing (Chapter 1).
3　Incorrect idle speed (Chapter 1).
4　Low tire pressure or incorrect tire size (Chapter 10).
5　Fuel leakage. Check all connections, lines and components in the fuel system (Chapter 4).
6　Choke not operating properly (Chapter 1).
7　Dirty or clogged carburetor jets or fuel injectors (see Chapter 4).

25　Fuel odor

1　Fuel leakage. Check all connections, lines and components in the fuel system (Chapter 4).
2　Fuel tank overfilled. Fill only to automatic shut-off.
3　Charcoal canister filter in Evaporative Emissions Control system clogged (Chapter 1).
4　Vapor leaks from Evaporative Emissions Control system lines (Chapter 6).

26　Miscellaneous engine noises

1　A strong dull noise that becomes more rapid as the engine accelerates indicates worn or damaged crankshaft bearings or an unevenly worn crankshaft. To pinpoint the trouble spot, remove the spark plug wire from one plug at a time and crank the engine over. If the noise stops, the cylinder with the removed plug wire indicates the problem area. Replace the bearing and/or service or replace the crankshaft (Chapter 2).
2　A similar (yet slightly higher pitched) noise to the crankshaft knocking described in the previous paragraph, that becomes more rapid as the engine accelerates, indicates worn or damaged connecting rod bearings (Chapter 2). The procedure for locating the problem cylinder is the same as described in Paragraph 1.
3　An overlapping metallic noise that increases in intensity as the engine speed increases, yet diminishes as the engine warms up indicates abnormal piston and cylinder wear (Chapter 2). To locate the problem cylinder, use the procedure described in Paragraph 1.
4　A rapid clicking noise that becomes faster as the engine accelerates indicates a worn piston pin or piston pin hole. This sound will happen each time the piston hits the highest and lowest points in the stroke (Chapter 2). The procedure for locating the problem piston is described in Paragraph 1.
5　A metallic clicking noise coming from the water pump indicates worn or damaged water pump bearings or pump. Replace the water pump with a new one (Chapter 3).
6　A rapid tapping sound or clicking sound that becomes faster as the engine speed increases indicates "valve tapping" or improperly adjusted valve clearances. This can be identified by holding one end of a section of hose to your ear and placing the other end at different spots along the rocker arm cover. The point where the sound is loudest indicates the problem valve. Adjust the valve clearance (Chapter 1).
7　A steady metallic rattling or rapping sound coming from the area of the timing chain cover indicates a worn, damaged or out-of-adjustment timing chain. Service or replace the chain and related components (Chapter 2).

Cooling system

27　Overheating

1　Insufficient coolant in system (Chapter 1).
2　Drivebelt defective or not adjusted properly (Chapter 1).
3　Radiator core blocked or radiator grille dirty and restricted (Chapter 3).
4　Thermostat faulty (Chapter 3).

5   Fan not functioning properly (Chapter 3).
6   Radiator cap not maintaining proper pressure. Have cap pressure tested by gas station or repair shop.
7   Ignition timing incorrect (Chapter 1).
8   Defective water pump (Chapter 3).
9   Improper grade of engine oil.
10 Inaccurate temperature gauge (Chapter 12).

28   Overcooling

1   Thermostat faulty (Chapter 3).
2   Inaccurate temperature gauge (Chapter 12).

29   External coolant leakage

1   Deteriorated or damaged hoses. Loose clamps at hose connections (Chapter 1).
2   Water pump seals defective. If this is the case, water will drip from the weep hole in the water pump body (Chapter 3).
3   Leakage from radiator core or header tank. This will require the radiator to be professionally repaired (see Chapter 3 for removal procedures).
4   Engine drain plugs or water jacket freeze plugs leaking (see Chapters 1 and 2).
5   Leak from coolant temperature switch (Chapter 3).
6   Leak from damaged gaskets or small cracks (Chapter 2).
7   Damaged head gasket. This can be verified by checking the condition of the engine oil as noted in Section 30.

30   Internal coolant leakage

Note: *Internal coolant leaks can usually be detected by examining the oil. Check the dipstick and inside the rocker arm/camshaft cover for water deposits and an oil consistency resembling a milkshake.*
1   Leaking cylinder head gasket. Have the system pressure tested or remove the cylinder head (Chapter 2) and inspect.
2   Cracked cylinder bore or cylinder head. Dismantle engine and inspect (Chapter 2).
3   Loose cylinder head bolts (tighten as described in Chapter 2).

31   Abnormal coolant loss

1   Overfilling system (Chapter 1).
2   Coolant boiling away due to overheating (see causes in Section 27).
3   Internal or external leakage (see Sections 29 and 30).
4   Faulty radiator cap. Have the cap pressure tested.
5   Cooling system being pressurized by engine compression. This could be due to a cracked head or block or leaking head gasket(s).

32   Poor coolant circulation

1   Inoperative water pump. A quick test is to pinch the top radiator hose closed with your hand while the engine is idling, then release it. You should feel a surge of coolant if the pump is working properly (Chapter 3).
2   Restriction in cooling system. Drain, flush and refill the system (Chapter 1). If necessary, remove the radiator (Chapter 3) and have it reverse flushed or professionally cleaned.
3   Loose water pump drivebelt (Chapter 1).
4   Thermostat sticking (Chapter 3).
5   Insufficient coolant (Chapter 1).

33   Corrosion

1   Excessive impurities in the water. Soft, clean water is recommended. Distilled or rainwater is satisfactory.
2   Insufficient antifreeze solution (refer to Chapter 1 for the proper ratio of water to antifreeze).
3   Infrequent flushing and draining of system. Regular flushing of the cooling system should be carried out at the specified intervals as described in Chapter 1.

Clutch

Note: *All clutch related service information is in Chapter 8, unless otherwise indicated.*

34   Fails to release (pedal pressed to the floor – shift lever does not move freely in and out of Rverse)

1   Clutch contaminated with oil. Remove clutch plate and inspect.
2   Clutch plate warped, distorted or otherwise damaged.
3   Diaphragm spring fatigued. Remove clutch cover/pressure plate assembly and inspect.
4   Leakage of fluid from clutch hydraulic system. Inspect master cylinder, operating cylinder and connecting lines.
5   Air in clutch hydraulic system. Bleed the system.
6   Insufficient pedal stroke. Check and adjust as necessary.
7   Piston seal in operating cylinder deformed or damaged.
8   Lack of grease on pilot bushing.
9   Damaged transmission input shaft splines.

35   Clutch slips (engine speed increases with no increase in vehicle speed)

1   Worn or oil soaked clutch plate.
2   Clutch plate not broken in. It may take 30 or 40 normal starts for a new clutch to seat.
3   Diaphragm spring weak or damaged. Remove clutch cover/pressure plate assembly and inspect.
4   Flywheel warped or scored (Chapter 2).
5   Debris in master cylinder preventing the piston from returning to its normal position.
6   Clutch hydraulic line damaged.

36   Grabbing (chattering) as clutch is engaged

1   Oil on clutch plate. Remove and inspect. Repair any leaks.
2   Worn or loose engine or transmission mounts. They may move slightly when clutch is released. Inspect mounts and bolts.
3   Worn splines on transmission input shaft. Remove clutch components and inspect.
4   Warped pressure plate or flywheel. Remove clutch components and inspect.
5   Diaphragm spring fatigued. Remove clutch cover/pressure plate assembly and inspect.
6   Clutch linings hardened or warped.
7   Clutch lining rivets loose.
8   Engine and transmission not in alignment. Check for foreign object between bellhousing and engine block. Check for loose bellhousing bolts.

37   Squeal or rumble with clutch engaged (pedal released)

1   Improper pedal adjustment. Adjust pedal free play.
2   Release bearing binding on transmission shaft. Remove clutch components and check bearing. Remove any burrs or nicks, clean and relubricate before reinstallation.
3   Clutch rivets loose.
4   Clutch plate cracked.
5   Fatigued clutch plate torsion springs. Replace clutch plate.

38   Squeal or rumble with clutch disengaged (pedal depressed)

1   Worn or damaged release bearing.
2   Worn or broken pressure plate diaphragm fingers.
3   Worn or damaged pilot bearing.

39   Clutch pedal stays on floor when disengaged

1   Binding linkage or release bearing. Inspect linkage or remove clutch components as necessary.
2   Linkage springs being over extended. Adjust linkage for proper free play. Make sure proper pedal stop (bumper) is installed.

Manual transmission

Note: *All manual transmission service information is in Chapter 7, unless otherwise indicated.*

40   Noisy in Neutral with engine running

1   Input shaft bearing worn.
2   Damaged main drive gear bearing.
3   Insufficient transmission oil (Chapter 1).
4   Transmission oil in poor condition. Drain and fill with proper grade oil. Check old oil for water and debris (Chapter 1).
5   Noise can be caused by variations in engine torque. Change the idle speed and see if noise disappears.

41   Noisy in all gears

1   Any of the above causes, and/or:
2   Worn or damaged output gear bearings or shaft.

42   Noisy in one particular gear

1   Worn, damaged or chipped gear teeth.
2   Worn or damaged synchronizer.

43   Slips out of gear

1   Transmission loose on clutch housing.
2   Stiff shift lever seal.
3   Shift linkage binding.
4   Broken or loose input gear bearing retainer.
5   Dirt between clutch lever and engine housing.
6   Worn linkage.
7   Damaged or worn check balls, fork rod ball grooves or check springs.

8   Worn mainshaft or countershaft bearings.
9   Loose engine mounts (Chapter 2).
10   Excessive gear end play.
11   Worn synchronizers.

44   Oil leaks

1   Excessive amount of lubricant in transmission (see Chapter 1 for correct checking procedures). Drain lubricant as required.
2   Side cover loose or gasket damaged.
3   Rear oil seal or speedometer oil seal damaged.
4   To pinpoint a leak, first remove all built-up dirt and grime from the transmission. Degreasing agents and/or steam cleaning will achieve this. With the underside clean, drive the vehicle at low speeds so the air flow will not blow the leak far from its source. Raise the vehicle and determine where the leak is located.

45   Difficulty engaging gears

1   Clutch not releasing completely.
2   Loose or damaged shift linkage. Make a thorough inspection, replacing parts as necessary.
3   Insufficient transmission oil (Chapter 1).
4   Transmission oil in poor condition. Drain and fill with proper grade oil. Check oil for water and debris (Chapter 1).
5   Worn or damaged striking rod.
6   Sticking or jamming gears.

46   Noise occurs while shifting gears

1   Check for proper operation of the clutch (Chapter 8).
2   Faulty synchronizer assemblies. Measure baulk ring-to-gear clearance. Also, check for wear or damage to baulk rings or any parts of the synchromesh assemblies.

Automatic transmission

Note: *Due to the complexity of the automatic transmission, it's difficult for the home mechanic to properly diagnose and service. For problems other than the following, the vehicle should be taken to a reputable mechanic.*

47   Fluid leakage

1   Automatic transmission fluid is a deep red color, and fluid leaks should not be confused with engine oil which can easily be blown by air flow to the transmission.
2   To pinpoint a leak, first remove all built-up dirt and grime from the transmission. Degreasing agents and/or steam cleaning will achieve this. With the underside clean, drive the vehicle at low speeds so the air flow will not blow the leak far from its source. Raise the vehicle and determine where the leak is located. Common areas of leakage are:
   a) Fluid pan: tighten mounting bolts and/or replace pan gasket as necessary (Chapter 1).
   b) Rear extension: tighten bolts and/or replace oil seal as necessary.
   c) Filler pipe: replace the rubber oil seal where pipe enters transmission case.
   d) Transmission oil lines: tighten fittings where lines enter transmission case and/or replace lines.
   e) Vent pipe: transmission overfilled and/or water in fluid (see checking procedures, Chapter 1).
   f) Speedometer connector: replace the O-ring where speedometer cable enters transmission case.

48 General shift mechanism problems

Chapter 7 deals with checking and adjusting the shift linkage on automatic transmissions. Common problems which may be caused by out of adjustment linkage are:
  a) Engine starting in gears other than P (park) or N (Neutral).
  b) Indicator pointing to a gear other than the one actually engaged.
  c) Vehicle moves with transmission in P (Park) position.

49 Transmission will not downshift with the accelerator pedal pressed to the floor

Chapter 7 deals with adjusting the kickdown switch to enable the transmission to downshift properly.

50 Engine will start in gears other than Park or Neutral

Chapter 7 deals with adjusting the Neutral start switch installed on automatic transmissions.

51 Transmission slips, shifts rough, is noisy or has no drive in forward or Reverse gears

1   There are many probable causes for the above problems, but the home mechanic should concern himself only with one possibility; fluid level.
2   Before taking the vehicle to a shop, check the fluid level and condition as described in Chapter 1. Add fluid, if necessary, or change the fluid and filter if needed. If problems persist, have a professional diagnose the transmission.

Driveshaft

52 Leaks at front of driveshaft

Defective transmission rear seal. See Chapter 7 for replacement procedure. As this is done, check the splined yoke for burrs or roughness that could damage the new seal. Remove burrs with a fine file or whetstone.

53 Knock or clunk when transmission is under initial load (just after transmission is put into gear)

1   Loose or disconnected rear suspension components. Check all mounting bolts and bushings (Chapters 1 and 11).
2   Loose driveshaft bolts. Inspect all bolts and nuts and tighten them securely.
3   Worn or damaged universal joint bearings. Replace driveshaft (Chapter 8).
4   Worn sleeve yoke and mainshaft spline.
5   Defective center bearing or insulator.

54 Metallic grating sound consistent with vehicle speed

Pronounced wear in the universal joint bearings. Replace U-joints or driveshafts, as necessary.

55 Vibration

Note: *Before blaming the driveshaft, make sure the tires are perfectly balanced and perform the following test.*

1   Install a tachometer inside the vehicle to monitor engine speed as the vehicle is driven. Drive the vehicle and note the engine speed at which the vibration (roughness) is most pronounced. Now shift the transmission to a different gear and bring the engine speed to the same point.
2   If the vibration occurs at the same engine speed (rpm) regardless of which gear the transmission is in, the driveshaft is NOT at fault since the driveshaft speed varies.
3   If the vibration decreases or is eliminated when the transmission is in a different gear at the same engine speed, refer to the following probable causes.
4   Bent or dented driveshaft. Inspect and replace as necessary.
5   Undercoating or built-up dirt, etc. on the driveshaft. Clean the shaft thoroughly.
6   Worn universal joint bearings. Replace the U-joints or driveshaft as necessary.
7   Driveshaft and/or companion flange out-of-balance. Check for missing weights on the shaft. Remove driveshaft and reinstall 177-degrees from original position, then recheck. Have the driveshaft balanced if problem persists.
8   Loose driveshaft mounting bolts/nuts.
9   Defective center bearing, if so equipped.
10 Worn transmission rear bushing (Chapter 7).

56 Scraping noise

Make sure the dust cover on the sleeve yoke isn't rubbing on the transmission extension housing.

57 Whining or whistling noise

Defective center bearing, if so equipped.

Rear axle and differential

Note: *For differential servicing information, refer to Chapter 8, unless otherwise indicated.*

58 Noise – same when in drive as when vehicle is coasting

1   Road noise. No corrective action available.
2   Tire noise. Inspect tires and check tire pressures (see Chapter 1).
3   Front wheel bearings loose, worn or damaged (Chapter 1).
4   Insufficient differential oil (Chapter 1).
5   Defective differential.

59 Knocking sound when starting or shifting gears

Defective or incorrectly adjusted differential.

60 Noise when turning

Defective differential.

61   Vibration

See probable causes under Driveshaft. Proceed under the guidelines listed for the driveshaft. If the problem persists, check the rear wheel bearings by raising the rear of the vehicle and spinning the wheels by hand. Listen for evidence of rough (noisy) bearings. Remove and inspect (Chapter 8).

62   Oil leaks

1   Pinion oil seal damaged (Chapter 8).
2   Axleshaft oil seals damaged (Chapter 8).
3   Differential cover leaking. Tighten mounting bolts or replace the gasket as required.
4   Loose filler or drain plug on differential (Chapter 1).
5   Clogged or damaged breather on differential.

Brakes

Note: *Before assuming a brake problem exists, make sure the tires are in good condition and inflated properly, the front end alignment is correct and the vehicle isn't loaded with weight in an unequal manner. All service procedures for the brakes are included in Chapter 9, unless otherwise indicated.*

63   Vehicle pulls to one side during braking

1   Defective, damaged or oil contaminated brake pad on one side. Inspect as described in Chapter 1. Refer to Chapter 9 if replacement is required.
2   Excessive wear of brake pad material or disc on one side. Inspect and repair as necessary.
3   Loose or disconnected front suspension components. Inspect and tighten all bolts securely (Chapters 1 and 11).
4   Defective caliper assembly. Remove caliper and inspect for stuck piston or damage.
5   Brake pad to disc adjustment needed. Inspect automatic adjusting mechanism for proper operation.
6   Scored or out-of-round disc.
7   Loose caliper mounting bolts.
8   Incorrect wheel bearing adjustment.

64   Noise (high-pitched squeal)

1   Front brake pads worn out. This noise comes from the wear sensor rubbing against the disc. Replace pads with new ones immediately!
2   Glazed or contaminated pads.
3   Dirty or scored disc.
4   Bent support plate.

65   Excessive brake pedal travel

1   Partial brake system failure. Inspect entire system (Chapter 1) and correct as required.
2   Insufficient fluid in master cylinder. Check (Chapter 1) and add fluid – bleed system if necessary.
3   Air in system. Bleed system.
4   Excessive lateral disc play.
5   Brakes out of adjustment. Check the operation of the automatic adjusters.
6   Defective check valve. Replace valve and bleed system.

66   Brake pedal feels spongy when depressed

1   Air in brake lines. Bleed the brake system.
2   Deteriorated rubber brake hoses. Inspect all system hoses and lines. Replace parts as necessary.
3   Master cylinder mounting nuts loose. Inspect master cylinder bolts (nuts) and tighten them securely.
4   Master cylinder faulty.
5   Incorrect shoe or pad clearance.
6   Defective check valve. Replace valve and bleed system.
7   Clogged reservoir cap vent hole.
8   Deformed rubber brake lines.
9   Soft or swollen caliper seals.
10   Poor quality brake fluid. Bleed entire system and fill with new approved fluid.

67   Excessive effort required to stop vehicle

1   Power brake booster not operating properly.
2   Excessively worn linings or pads. Check and replace if necessary.
3   One or more caliper pistons seized or sticking. Inspect and rebuild as required.
4   Brake pads or linings contaminated with oil or grease. Inspect and replace as required.
5   New pads or linings installed and not yet seated. It'll take a while for the new material to seat against the disc or drum.
6   Worn or damaged master cylinder or caliper assemblies. Check particularly for frozen pistons.
7   Also see causes listed under Section 66.

68   Pedal travels to the floor with little resistance

Little or no fluid in the master cylinder reservoir caused by leaking caliper piston(s) or loose, damaged or disconnected brake lines. Inspect entire system and repair as necessary.

69   Brake pedal pulsates during brake application

1   Wheel bearings damaged, worn or out of adjustment (Chapter 1).
2   Caliper not sliding properly due to improper installation or obstructions. Remove and inspect.
3   Disc not within specifications. Remove the disc and check for excessive lateral runout and parallelism. Have the discs resurfaced or replace them with new ones. Also make sure that all discs are the same thickness.
4   Out-of-round rear brake drums. Remove the drums and have them turned or replace them with new ones.

70   Brakes drag (indicated by sluggish engine performance or wheels being very hot after driving)

1   Output rod adjustment incorrect at the brake pedal.
2   Obstructed master cylinder compensator. Disassemble master cylinder and clean.
3   Master cylinder piston seized in bore. Overhaul master cylinder.
4   Caliper assembly in need of overhaul.
5   Brake pads or shoes worn out.
6   Piston cups in master cylinder or caliper assembly deformed. Overhaul master cylinder.
7   Disc not within specifications (Section 69).
8   Parking brake assembly will not release.
9   Clogged brake lines.

10 Wheel bearings out of adjustment (Chapter 1).
11 Brake pedal height improperly adjusted.
12 Wheel cylinder needs overhaul.
13 Improper shoe to drum clearance. Adjust as necessary.

71 Rear brakes lock up under light brake application

1 Tire pressures too high.
2 Tires excessively worn (Chapter 1).
3 Defective LSPB valve.

72 Rear brakes lock up under heavy brake application

1 Tire pressures too high.
2 Tires excessively worn (Chapter 1).
3 Front brake pads contaminated with oil, mud or water. Clean or replace the pads.
4 Front brake pads excessively worn.
5 Defective master cylinder or caliper assembly.

Suspension and steering

Note: *All service procedures for the suspension and steering systems are included in Chapter 10, unless otherwise indicated.*

73 Vehicle pulls to one side

1 Tire pressures uneven (Chapter 1).
2 Defective tire (Chapter 1).
3 Excessive wear in suspension or steering components (see Chapter 1).
4 Front end alignment incorrect.
5 Front brakes dragging. Inspect as described in Section 70.
6 Wheel bearings improperly adjusted (Chapter 1).
7 Wheel lug nuts loose.
8 Worn upper or lower link or tension rod bushings.

74 Shimmy, shake or vibration

1 Tire or wheel out-of-balance or out-of-round. Have them balanced on the vehicle.
2 Loose, worn or out of adjustment wheel bearings (Chapter 1).
3 Shock absorbers and/or suspension components worn or damaged. Check for worn bushings in the upper and lower links.
4 Wheel lug nuts loose.
5 Incorrect tire pressures.
6 Excessively worn or damaged tire.
7 Loosely mounted steering gear housing.
8 Steering gear improperly adjusted.
9 Loose, worn or damaged steering components.
10 Damaged idler arm.
11 Worn balljoint.

75 Excessive pitching and/or rolling around corners or during braking

1 Defective shock absorbers. Replace as a set.
2 Broken or weak springs and/or suspension components.
3 Worn or damaged stabilizer bar or bushings.
4 Worn or damaged upper or lower links or bushings.

76 Wandering or general instability

1 Improper tire pressures.
2 Worn or damaged upper and lower link or strut bar bushings.
3 Incorrect front end alignment.
4 Worn or damaged steering linkage or upper or lower link.
5 Improperly adjusted steering gear.
6 out-of-balance wheels.
7 Loose wheel lug nuts.
8 Worn rear shock absorbers.
9 Fatigued or damaged rear leaf springs.

77 Excessively stiff steering

1 Lack of lubricant in power steering fluid reservoir, where appropriate (Chapter 1).
2 Incorrect tire pressures (Chapter 1).
3 Lack of lubrication at balljoints (Chapter 1).
4 Front end out of alignment.
5 Steering gear out of adjustment or lacking lubrication.
6 Improperly adjusted wheel bearings.
7 Worn or damaged steering gear.
8 Interference of steering column with turn signal switch.
9 Low tire pressures.
10 Worn or damaged balljoints.
11 Worn or damaged steering linkage.
12 See also Section 76.

78 Excessive play in steering

1 Loose wheel bearings (Chapter 1).
2 Excessive wear in upper or lower link or strut bar bushings (Chapter 1).
3 Steering gear improperly adjusted.
4 Incorrect front end alignment.
5 Steering gear mounting bolts loose.
6 Worn steering linkage.

79 Lack of power assistance

1 Steering pump drivebelt faulty or not adjusted properly (Chapter 1).
2 Fluid level low (Chapter 1).
3 Hoses or pipes restricting the flow. Inspect and replace parts as necessary.
4 Air in power steering system. Bleed system.
5 Defective power steering pump.

80 Steering wheel fails to return to straight-ahead position

1 Incorrect front end alignment.
2 Tire pressures low.
3 Steering gears improperly engaged.
4 Steering column out of alignment.
5 Worn or damaged balljoint.
6 Worn or damaged steering linkage.
7 Improperly lubricated idler arm.
8 Insufficient oil in steering gear.
9 Lack of fluid in power steering pump.

81   Steering effort not the same in both directions (power system)

1   Leaks in steering gear.
2   Clogged fluid passage in steering gear.

82   Noisy power steering pump

1   Insufficient oil in pump.
2   Clogged hoses or oil filter in pump.
3   Loose pulley.
4   Improperly adjusted drivebelt (Chapter 1).
5   Defective pump.

83   Miscellaneous noises

1   Improper tire pressures.
2   Insufficiently lubricated balljoint or steering linkage.
3   Loose or worn steering gear, steering linkage or suspension components.
4   Defective shock absorber.
5   Defective wheel bearing.
6   Worn or damaged upper or lower link or strut bar bushing.
7   Damaged spring.
8   Loose wheel lug nuts.
9   Worn or damaged rear axleshaft spline.
10 Worn or damaged rear shock absorber mounting bushing.

11 Incorrect rear axle end play.
12 See also causes of noises at the rear axle and driveshaft.

84   Excessive tire wear (not specific to one area)

1   Incorrect tire pressures.
2   Tires out-of-balance. Have them balanced on the vehicle.
3   Wheels damaged. Inspect and replace as necessary.
4   Suspension or steering components worn (Chapter 1).

85   Excessive tire wear on outside edge

1   Incorrect tire pressure
2   Excessive speed in turns.
3   Front end alignment incorrect (excessive toe-in and/or camber).

86   Excessive tire wear on inside edge

1   Incorrect tire pressure.
2   Front end alignment incorrect (toe-out and/or negative camber).
3   Loose or damaged steering components (Chapter 1).

87   Tire tread worn in one place

1   Tires out-of-balance. Have them balanced on the vehicle.
2   Damaged or buckled wheel. Inspect and replace if necessary.
3   Defective tire.

Chapter 1 Tune-up and routine maintenance

Contents

Specifications

Recommended lubricants and fluids

Engine oil
  Type .... API grade SF or SF/CC
  Viscosity .... See accompanying chart
  Capacity (drain and refill, including filter change)
    3T-C engine .... 4.0 qts
    4A-C engine .... 3.5 qts
    4A-GE engine .... 4.0 qts

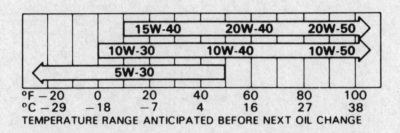

Engine oil
viscosity chart

Coolant
  Type .... Ethylene glycol based antifreeze and water
  Capacity .... 5.9 qts
Brake fluid .... DOT 3
Clutch fluid .... DOT 3 brake fluid
Automatic transmission fluid
  Type
    3-speed .... DEXRON II ATF
    4-speed .... Type F ATF
  Capacity
    3-speed
      Dry fill .... 6.7 qts
      Drain and refill .... 2.5 qts
    4-speed
      Dry fill .... 6.0 qts
      Drain and refill .... 2.5 qts
Power steering fluid .... DEXRON II ATF
Suspension balljoint grease .... Lithium base, NLGI no. 1 or 2 with moly
Steering gearbox lubricant (recirculating ball) ... API GL-4 (90 weight)
Wheel bearing grease .... Lithium base, multi-purpose, NLGI no. 2
Manual transmission lubricant
  Type .... API GL-4, SAE 75W90 or 80W90 gear oil
  Capacity .... 1.8 qts
Differential lubricant
  Type .... API GL-5, SAE 80W90 hypoid gear oil
  Capacity .... 1.5 qts

Brakes

Pedal
  Height
    1980 through 1982 .... 6-3/4 to 7-1/4 in
    1983-on .... 6-1/4 to 6-3/4 in
  Freeplay .... 1/8 to 1/4 in
  Reserve distance (at 110 lbs) .... 3 to 3-1/8 in
Disc brake pad lining thickness (minimum) .... 1/8 in
Drum brake shoe lining thickness (minimum) .... 1/16 in

Drivebelt tension
New belt .... 125 ± 25 lbs
Used belt .... 80 ± 20 lbs

Engine
Idle speed .... Refer to the *Emission Control Information* label in the engine compartment
Valve clearances
  OHV engine (hot)
    Intake .... 0.008 in (0.20 mm)
    Exhaust .... 0.013 in (0.33 mm)
  SOHC engine (hot)
    Intake .... 0.008 in (0.20 mm)
    Exhaust .... 0.012 in (0.30 mm)
  DOHC engine (cold)
    Intake .... 0.006 to 0.010 in (0.15 to 0.25 mm)
    Exhaust .... 0.008 to 0.012 in (0.20 to 0.30 mm)
Spark plug type and gap*
  3T-C and 4A-C engines .... ND W16EXR-U11 or equivalent @ 0.044 in
  4A-GE engines .... ND PQ16R or equivalent @ 0.044 in
Spark plug wire resistance .... Less than 25000 ohms
Ignition timing
  3T-C engines .... 7 degrees BTDC
  4A-C engines .... 5 degrees BTDC
  4A-GE engines .... 10 degrees BTDC
Throttle Positioner (TP) setting speed .... 1400 rpm
Firing order 1-3-4-2
Cylinder numbers (front-to-rear) 1–2–3–4

* If it differs from that shown here, use the information on the Emmission Control Information label in the engine compartment.

Clutch
Pedal freeplay .... 1/2 to 7/8 in
Pedal height
  1980 through 1982 .... 6-3/4 to 7-1/4 in
  1983-on .... 6-1/2 to 6-3/4 in

Suspension
Steering wheel freeplay .... 1 to 1-1/4 in
Balljoint vertical play limit .... 7/64 in
Front wheel bearing preload (Section 39)
  1980 through 1983 .... 0.7 to 1.5 ft-lbs
  1984-on (plus oil seal friction drag) .... 0 to 2.3 ft-lbs

Cylinder location and distributor rotation

Torque specifications
Ft-lbs (unless otherwise indicated)
Front wheel bearing adjusting nut* 21
Spark plugs .... 13 to 15
Automatic transmission pan bolts .... 24 to 36 in-lbs
Automatic transmission filter/strainer bolts ...... 48 in-lbs
Wheel lug nuts .... 65 to 87

** **Note:** Initial torque only – see text (Section 39) for complete tightening procedure.*

1 Introduction

This Chapter is designed to help the home mechanic maintain the Toyota Corolla with the goals of maximum performance, economy, safety and reliability in mind.

Included is a master maintenance schedule (page 32), followed by procedures dealing specifically with each item on the schedule. Visual checks, adjustments, component replacement and other helpful items are included. Refer to the accompanying illustrations of the engine compartment for the locations of various components.

Servicing your vehicle in accordance with the planned mileage/time maintenance schedule and the step-by-step procedures should result in maximum reliability and extend the life of your vehicle. Keep in mind that it's a comprehensive plan – maintaining some items but not others at the specified intervals will not produce the same results.

As you perform routine maintenance procedures, you'll find that many can, and should, be grouped together because of the nature of the procedures or because of the proximity of two otherwise unrelated components or systems.

For example, if the vehicle is raised for chassis lubrication, you should inspect the exhaust, suspension, steering and fuel systems while you're under the vehicle. When you're rotating the tires, it makes good sense to check the brakes since the wheels are already removed. Finally, let's suppose you have to borrow or rent a torque wrench. Even if you only need it to tighten the spark plugs, you might as well check the torque of as many critical fasteners as time allows.

The first step in this maintenance program is to prepare yourself before the actual work begins. Read through all the procedures you're planning to do, then gather up all the parts and tools needed. If it looks like you might run into problems during a particular job, seek advice from a mechanic or experienced do-it-yourselfer.

2 Toyota Corolla Maintenance schedule

The following maintenance intervals are based on the assumption that the vehicle owner will be doing the maintenance or service work, as opposed to having a dealer service department do the work. Although the time/mileage intervals are based on factory recommendations, most have been shortened to ensure, for example, that such items as lubricants and fluids are checked/changed at intervals that promote maximum engine/driveline service life. Also, subject to the preference of the individual owner interested in keeping the vehicle in peak condition at all times and with the vehicle's ultimate resale in mind, many of the maintenance procedures may be performed more often than recommended in the following schedule. We encourage such owner initiative.

Every 250 miles/weekly, whichever comes first

Check the engine oil level (Section 4)
Check the coolant level (Section 4)
Check the windshield washer fluid level (Section 4)
Check the brake and clutch fluid levels (Section 4)
Check the battery electrolyte level (Section 4)
Check the automatic transmission fluid level (Section 5)
Check the power steering fluid level (Section 6)
Check the tires and tire pressures (Section 7)

Every 3000 miles/3 months, whichever comes first

Change the engine oil and filter (Section 8)

Every 7500 miles/12 months, whichever comes first

Inspect/replace the windshield wiper blades (Section 9)
Check/adjust the brake pedal (Section 10)
Check and service the battery (Section 11)
Check the cooling system (Section 12)
Inspect/replace all underhood hoses (Section 13)
Inspect the exhaust system (Section 14)

Every 15,000/12 months, whichever comes first

Check/adjust the engine drivebelts (Section 15)
Check/adjust the engine idle speed (Section 16)

Check/adjust the idle mixture (1980 and 1981 Canadian models only) (Section 17)
Check the Throttle Positioner (TP) (carburetor-equipped models only) (Section 18)
Check/adjust the valve clearances (1980 through 1985 OHV and SOHC engines only) (Section 19)
Inspect the suspension and steering components (Section 20)
Check the fuel system (Section 21)
Rotate the tires (Section 22)
Check the brakes (Section 23)
Check the manual transmission lubricant level (Section 24)
Check the differential lubricant level (Section 25)
Lubricate the chassis components (Section 26)
Check the chassis and body bolt torques (Section 27)

Every 30,000 miles/24 months, whichever comes first

Check/adjust the engine idle speed (1987 models) (Section 16)
Check/adjust the valve clearances (1986 and 1987 SOHC engines only) (Section 19)
Check the clutch pedal freeplay (Section 28)
Replace the air filter (Section 29)
Check the PCV valve (Section 30)
Check the EVAP system (Section 31)
Replace the spark plugs (Section 32)
Check/replace the spark plug wires, distributor cap and rotor (Section 33)
Service the cooling system (drain, flush and refill) (Section 34)
Check the thermostatic air cleaner (carburetor-equipped models) (Section 35)
Check the carburetor choke operation (Section 36)
Check/adjust the ignition timing (Section 37)
Replace the fuel filter (Section 38)
Check and repack the front wheel bearings (Section 39)
Change the manual transmission lubricant (Section 40)
Change the automatic transmission fluid and filter (Section 41)
Change the differential lubricant (Section 42)

Every 60,000 miles/24 months, whichever comes first

Check/adjust the valve clearances (1985 through 1987 DOHC engines only) (Section 19)
Replace the fuel tank cap gasket (Section 43)
Replace the timing belt (1983 and later models) (Chapter 2)

Severe operating conditions

Severe operating conditions are defined as follows:

A   Pulling a trailer
B   Repeated short trips
C   Driving on rough or muddy roads
D   Driving on dusty roads
E   Operating in extremely cold weather and/or driving in areas using road salt
F   Repeated short trips in extremely cold weather

If your vehicle is operated under severe conditions, the maintenance schedule must be amended as follows . . .

Every 1500 miles/2 months, whichever comes first:

Change the engine oil and filter if condition(s) A, D or F exist (Section 8)
Check the steering linkage, gearbox oil and steering wheel freeplay if condition C exists (Section 20)
Check the balljoints and boots if condition(s) C, D or E exist (Section 20)
Lubricate the chassis if condition C exists (Section 26)
Check the air filter if condition D exists (Section 29)

Every 7500 miles/6 months, whichever comes first:

Check the exhaust pipes and brackets if conditions(s) A, B, C or E exist (Section 14)
Check the brake linings and drums if condition(s) A, B, C or D exist (Section 23)

Every 15,000 miles/12 months, whichever comes first:

Replace the air filter if condition D exists (Section 29)
Check the spark plug wires if condition E exists (Section 33) (**Note:** *In areas where road salt is used, inspection of the distributor cap should be done annually, just after the snow season ends.*)
Change the manual transmission lubricant if condition(s) A or C exist (Section 40)
Change the automatic transmission fluid if condition(s) A or C exist (Section 41)
Change the differential oil if condition(s) A or C exist (Section 42)

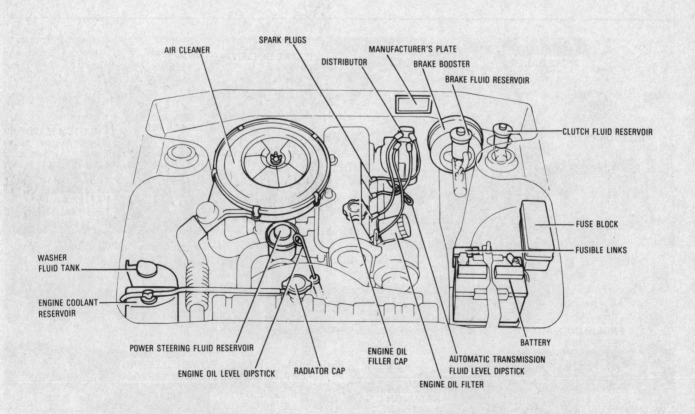

Engine compartment components – 1980 through 1983 OHV engine (typical)

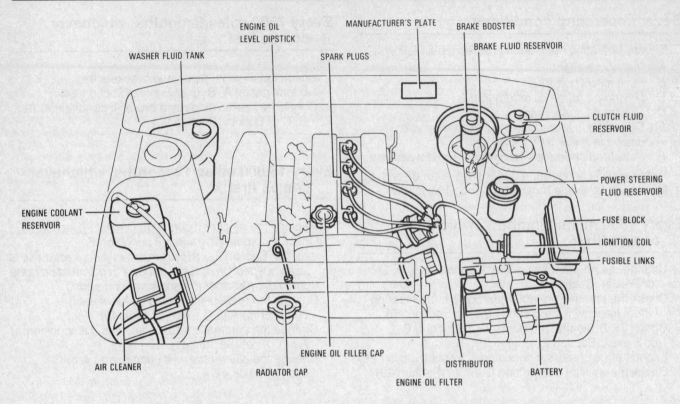

Engine compartment components – DOHC (16-valve) engine (typical)

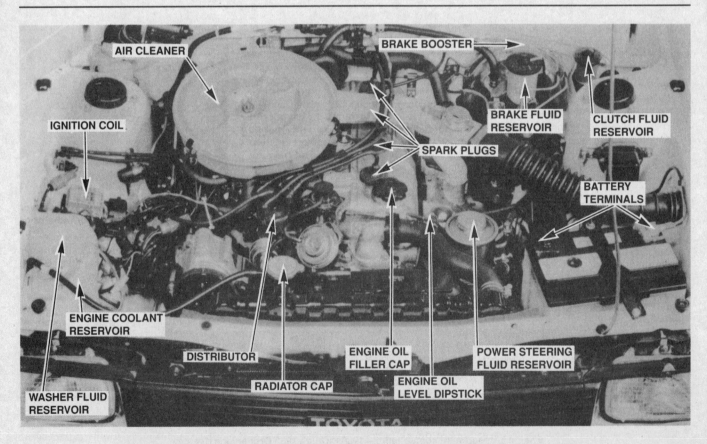

Engine compartment components – SOHC engine

3   Tune-up general information

The term tune-up is used in this manual to represent a combination of individual operations rather than one specific procedure.

If, from the time the vehicle is new, the routine maintenance schedule is followed closely and frequent checks are made of fluid levels and high wear items, as suggested throughout this manual, the engine will be kept in relatively good running condition and the need for additional work will be minimized.

More likely than not, however, there will be times when the engine is running poorly due to lack of regular maintenance. This is even more likely if a used vehicle, which has not received regular and frequent maintenance checks, is purchased. In such cases, an engine tune-up will be needed outside of the regular routine maintenance intervals.

The first step in any tune-up or diagnostic procedure to help correct a poor running engine is a cylinder compression check. A compression check (see Chapter 2 Part C) will help determine the condition of internal engine components and should be used as a guide for tune-up and repair procedures. If, for instance, a compression check indicates serious internal engine wear, a conventional tune-up will not improve the performance of the engine and would be a waste of time and money. Because of its importance, the compression check should be done by someone with the right equipment and the knowledge to use it properly.

The following procedures are those most often needed to bring a generally poor running engine back into a proper state of tune.

Minor tune-up

Check all engine related fluids (Section 4)
Clean and check the battery (Section 11)
Check all underhood hoses (Section 13)
Check the PCV valve (Section 30)
Check and adjust the drivebelts (Section 15)
Check and adjust the idle speed (Section 16)
Replace the air filter (Section 29)
Adjust the valve clearances (Section 19)
Check the cylinder compression (Chapter 2)
Replace the spark plugs (Section 32)
Inspect the distributor cap and rotor (Section 33)
Inspect the spark plug and coil wires (Section 33)
Check and adjust the ignition timing (Section 37)
Replace the fuel filter (Section 38)
Check and service the cooling system (Sections 12 and 34)

Major tune-up

All items listed under Minor tune-up, plus . . .
Check the charging system (Chapter 5)
Check the ignition system (Chapter 5)
Check the EGR system (Chapter 6)
Check the fuel system (Section 21 and Chapter 4)
Replace the spark plug wires, distributor cap and rotor (Section 33)

4   Fluid level checks

Note: *The following are fluid level checks to be done on a 250 mile or weekly basis. Additional fluid level checks can be found in specific maintenance procedures which follow. Regardless of how often the fluid levels are checked, watch for puddles under the vehicle – if leaks are noted, make repairs immediately.*

1   Fluids are an essential part of the lubrication, cooling, brake, clutch and windshield washer systems. Because the fluids gradually become depleted and/or contaminated during normal operation of the vehicle, they must be periodically replenished. See Recommended lubricants and fluids at the beginning of this Chapter before adding fluid to any of the following components. **Note:** *The vehicle must be on level ground when fluid levels are checked.*

Engine oil

Refer to illustrations 4.4 and 4.6

2   The engine oil level is checked with a dipstick that extends through a tube and into the oil pan at the bottom of the engine.

3   The oil level should be checked before the vehicle has been driven, or about 15 minutes after the engine has been shut off. If the oil is checked immediately after driving the vehicle, some of the oil will remain in the upper engine components, resulting in an inaccurate reading on the dipstick.

4   Pull the dipstick out of the tube (see the underhood component illustrations at the front of this Chapter) and wipe all the oil off the end with a clean rag or paper towel. Insert the clean dipstick all the way back into the tube, then pull it out again. Note the oil at the end of the dipstick. Add oil as necessary to keep the level between the L (low) and F (full) marks on the dipstick **(see illustration)**.

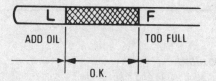

4.4   The engine oil level MUST be kept between the Low and Full marks on the dipstick or serious and costly engine damage could occur!

4.6   Oil can be added to the engine after unscrewing the filler cap on the rocker arm cover or camshaft cover – use a funnel to prevent spills

5   Don't overfill the engine by adding too much oil since this may result in oil fouled spark plugs, oil leaks or oil seal failures.

6   Oil is added to the engine after removing a threaded cap from the rocker arm cover/camshaft cover **(see illustration)**. A funnel will help reduce spills.

7   Checking the oil level is an important preventive maintenance step. A consistently low oil level indicates oil leakage through damaged seals, defective gaskets or past worn rings or valve guides. If the oil looks milky in color or has water droplets in it, the cylinder head gasket may be blown or the head or block may be cracked. The engine should be checked immediately. The condition of the oil should also be checked. Whenever you check the oil level, slide your thumb and index finger up the dipstick before wiping off the oil. If you see small dirt or metal particles clinging to the dipstick, the oil should be changed (Section 8).

4.9a   If the coolant level in the reservoir isn't between the two marks, . . .

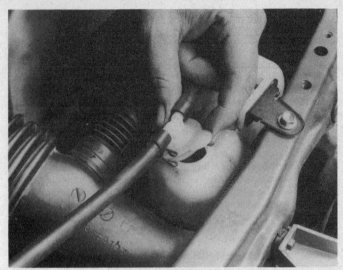

4.9b   . . . pry up on the cap to remove it and add more coolant to the reservoir – DO NOT overfill it!

Engine coolant

Refer to illustrations 4.9a and 4.9b

Warning: *Don't allow antifreeze to come in contact with your skin or painted surfaces of the vehicle. Flush contaminated areas immediately with plenty of water. Don't store new coolant or leave old coolant lying around where it's accessible to children or pets – they're attracted by its sweet smell. Ingestion of even a small amount of coolant can be fatal! Wipe up garage floor and drip pan coolant spills immediately. Keep antifreeze containers covered and repair leaks in your cooling system as soon as they're noticed.*

8   All vehicles covered by this manual are equipped with a pressurized coolant recovery system. A white plastic coolant reservoir located in the engine compartment is connected by a hose to the radiator filler neck. If the engine overheats, coolant escapes through a valve in the radiator cap and travels through the hose into the reservoir. As the engine cools, the coolant is automatically drawn back into the system to maintain the correct level.

9   The coolant level in the reservoir should be checked regularly. **Warning:** *Do not remove the radiator cap to check the coolant level when the engine is warm.* The level in the reservoir varies with the temperature of the engine. When the engine is cold, the coolant level should be at or slightly above the Low mark on the reservoir. Once the engine has warmed up, the level should be at or near the Full mark **(see illustration)**. If it isn't, allow the engine to cool, then remove the cap from the reservoir and add a 50/50 mixture of ethylene glycolbased antifreeze and water **(see illustration)**.

10   Drive the vehicle and recheck the coolant level. If only a small amount of coolant is required to bring the system up to the proper level, water can be used. However, repeated additions of water will dilute the antifreeze and water solution. In order to maintain the proper ratio of antifreeze and water, always top up the coolant level with the correct mixture. An empty plastic milk jug or bleach bottle makes an excellent container for mixing coolant. Do not use rust inhibitors or additives.

11   If the coolant level drops consistently, there may be a leak in the system. Inspect the radiator, hoses, filler cap, drain plugs and water pump (see Section 12). If no leaks are noted, have the radiator cap pressure tested by a service station.

12   If you have to remove the radiator cap, wait until the engine has cooled, then wrap a thick cloth around the cap and turn it to the first stop. If coolant or steam escapes, let the engine cool down longer, then remove the cap.

4.14   The windshield washer fluid level should be kept near the top of the reservoir – don't confuse the windshield washer and engine coolant reservoirs

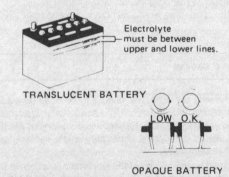

4.17   On original equipment batteries, the electrolyte level can be checked without removing the cell caps – it must be maintained between the lines on the case

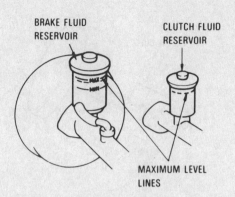

4.19 The brake and clutch fluid levels should be kept near the upper (MAX) mark on the reservoir – it's translucent so the cover doesn't have to be removed for the check

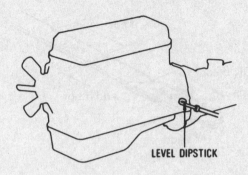

5.3 The automatic transmission fluid dipstick is located near the rear of the engine, on the driver's side

13 Check the condition of the coolant as well. It should be relatively clear. If it's brown or rust colored, the system should be drained, flushed and refilled. Even if the coolant appears to be normal, the corrosion inhibitors wear out, so it must be replaced at the specified intervals.

Windshield washer fluid

Refer to illustration 4.14

14 Fluid for the windshield washer system is stored in a plastic reservoir located near the battery (see illustration). If necessary, refer to the underhood component illustration(s) at the beginning of this Chapter to locate the reservoir.

15 In milder climates, plain water can be used in the reservoir, but it should be kept no more than 2/3 full to allow for expansion if the water freezes. In colder climates, use windshield washer system antifreeze, available at any auto parts store, to lower the freezing point of the fluid. Mix the antifreeze with water in accordance with the manufacturer's directions on the container. **Caution:** *Don't use cooling system antifreeze – it will damage the vehicle's paint.*

16 To help prevent icing in cold weather, warm the windshield with the defroster before using the washer.

Battery electrolyte

Refer to illustration 4.17

17 To check the electrolyte level in the battery, remove all of the cell caps. If the level is low, add distilled water until it's above the plates. Original equipment batteries are usually translucent so the electrolyte level can be checked by looking at the side of the case (see illustration). Most aftermarket replacement batteries have a split-ring indicator in each cell to help you judge when enough water has been added – don't overfill the cells!

Brake and clutch fluid

Refer to illustration 4.19

18 The brake master cylinder is mounted on the front of the power booster unit in the engine compartment. The clutch cylinder used on manual transmissions is mounted adjacent to it on the firewall.

19 The fluid inside is readily visible. The level should be between the MIN and MAX marks on the reservoirs (see illustration). If a low level is indicated, be sure to wipe the top of the reservoir cover with a clean rag to prevent contamination of the brake and/or clutch system before removing the cover.

20 When adding fluid, pour it carefully into the reservoir to avoid spilling it onto surrounding painted surfaces. Be sure the specified fluid is used,

since mixing different types of brake fluid can cause damage to the system. See Recommended lubricants and fluids at the front of this Chapter or your owner's manual. **Warning:** *Brake fluid can harm your eyes and damage painted surfaces, so be very careful when handling or pouring it. Don't use brake fluid that's been standing open or is more than one year old. Brake fluid absorbs moisture from the air. Excess moisture can cause a dangerous loss of brake efficiency.*

21 At this time the fluid and master cylinder can be inspected for contamination. The system should be drained and refilled if deposits, dirt particles or water droplets are seen in the fluid.

22 After filling the reservoir to the proper level, make sure the cover is on tight to prevent fluid leakage.

23 The brake fluid level in the master cylinder will drop slightly as the pads and the brake shoes at each wheel wear down during normal operation. If the master cylinder requires repeated additions to keep it at the proper level, it's an indication of leakage in the brake system, which should be corrected immediately. Check all brake lines and connections (see Section 24 for more information).

24 If, upon checking the master cylinder fluid level, you discover one or both reservoirs empty or nearly empty, the brake system should be bled (Chapter 9).

5 Automatic transmission fluid level check

Refer to illustrations 5.3 and 5.6

1 The automatic transmission fluid level should be carefully maintained. Low fluid level can lead to slipping or loss of drive, while overfilling can cause foaming and loss of fluid.

2 With the parking brake set, start the engine, then move the shift lever through all the gears, ending in Park. The fluid level must be checked with the vehicle level and the engine running at idle. **Note:** *Incorrect fluid level readings will result if the vehicle has just been driven at high speeds for an extended period, in hot weather in city traffic, or while pulling a trailer. If any of these conditions apply, wait until the fluid has cooled down (about 30 minutes).*

3 With the transmission at normal operating temperature, remove the dipstick from the filler tube. The dipstick is located at the rear of the engine compartment, usually on the driver's side (see illustration).

4 Carefully touch the fluid at the end of the dipstick to determine if it's cool (86 to 122-degrees F) or hot (123 to 176-degrees F). Wipe the fluid off the dipstick with a clean rag and push it back into the filler tube until the cap seats.

5 Pull the dipstick out again and note the fluid level.

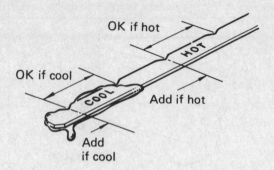

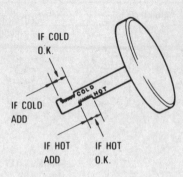

5.6　The fluid level on the dipstick will change, depending on the temperature of the transmission and fluid

6.6a　The power steering fluid dipstick has marks for checking the fluid level hot or cold (typical earlier model shown)

6　If the fluid felt cool, the level should be in the COLD range (between the cutouts) **(see illustration)**. If the fluid was hot, the level should be in the HOT range.

7　If additional fluid is required, add it directly into the tube using a funnel. It takes about one pint to raise the level from the lower mark to the upper mark in a hot transmission, so add the fluid a little at a time and keep checking the level until it's correct.

8　The condition of the fluid should also be checked along with the level. If the fluid at the end of the dipstick is a dark reddish-brown color, or if it smells burned, it should be changed. If you're in doubt about the condition of the fluid, purchase some new fluid and compare the two for color and smell.

6　Power steering fluid level check

Refer to illustrations 6.6a and 6.6b

1　Unlike manual steering, the power steering system relies on fluid which may, over a period of time, require replenishing.

2　The fluid reservoir for the power steering pump is located on the pump body at the front of the engine.

3　For the check, the front wheels should be pointed straight ahead and the engine should be off. The level can be checked with the fluid hot (normal engine operating temperature) or cold. The fluid can be considered

cold if the engine hasn't been run for at least five hours.

4　Use a clean rag to wipe off the reservoir cap and the area around it. This will help prevent any foreign matter from entering the reservoir during the check.

5　Twist off the cap – it has a dipstick attached to it.

6　Wipe off the fluid with a clean rag, reinsert the dipstick, then withdraw it and note the fluid level. The level should be within the range marked on the dipstick **(see illustrations)**. Never allow the fluid level to drop below the lower range mark.

7　If additional fluid is required, pour the specified type directly into the reservoir, using a funnel to prevent spills.

8　If the reservoir requires frequent fluid additions, all power steering hoses, hose connections and the power steering pump should be carefully checked for leaks.

7　Tire and tire pressure checks

Refer to illustrations 7.2, 7.3, 7.4a, 7.4b and 7.8

1　Periodic inspection of the tires may spare you the inconvenience of being stranded with a flat tire. It can also provide you with vital information regarding possible problems in the steering and suspension systems before major damage occurs.

2　The original tires on this vehicle are equipped with wear indicator bars

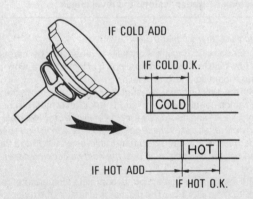

6.6b　Late model DOHC engine power steering dipstick marks

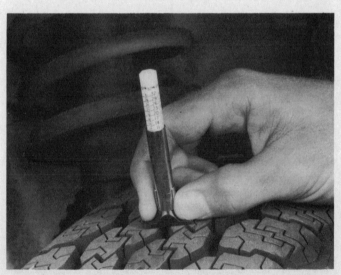

7.2　A tire tread depth indicator should be used to monitor tire wear – they're available at auto parts stores and service stations and cost very little

Condition	Probable cause	Corrective action	Condition	Probable cause	Corrective action
Shoulder wear	• Underinflation (both sides wear) • Incorrect wheel camber (one side wear) • Hard cornering • Lack of rotation	• Measure and adjust pressure. • Repair or replace axle and suspension parts. • Reduce speed. • Rotate tires.	Feathered edge **Toe wear**	• Incorrect toe	• Adjust toe-in.
Center wear	• Overinflation • Lack of rotation	• Measure and adjust pressure. • Rotate tires.	**Uneven wear**	• Incorrect camber or caster • Malfunctioning suspension • Unbalanced wheel • Out-of-round brake drum • Lack of rotation	• Repair or replace axle and suspension parts. • Repair or replace suspension parts. • Balance or replace. • Turn or replace. • Rotate tires.

7.3   This chart will help you determine the condition of the tires, the probable cause(s) of abnormal wear and the corrective action necessary

that will appear when tread depth reaches a predetermined limit, usually 1/16-inch, but they don't appear until the tires are worn out. Tread wear can be monitored with a simple, inexpensive device known as a tread depth indicator **(see illustration)**.

3   Note any abnormal tread wear **(see illustration)**. Tread pattern irregularities such as cupping, flat spots and more wear on one side than the other are indications of front end alignment and/or balance problems. If any of these conditions are noted, take the vehicle to a tire shop or service station to correct the problem.

4   Look closely for cuts, punctures and embedded nails or tacks. Sometimes a tire will hold air pressure for a short time or leak down very slowly

after a nail has embedded itself in the tread. If a slow leak persists, check the valve stem core to make sure it's tight **(see illustration)**. Examine the tread for an object that may have embedded itself in the tire or for a "plug" that may have begun to leak (radial tire punctures are repaired with a plug that's installed in a puncture). If a puncture is suspected, it can be easily verified by spraying a solution of soapy water onto the tread area **(see illustration)**. The soapy solution will bubble if there's a leak. Unless the puncture is unusually large, a tire shop or service station can usually repair the tire.

5   Carefully inspect the inner sidewall of each tire for evidence of brake fluid leakage. If you see any, inspect the brakes immediately.

7.4a   If a tire loses air on a steady basis, check the valve core first to make sure it's snug (special inexpensive wrenches are commonly available at auto parts stores)

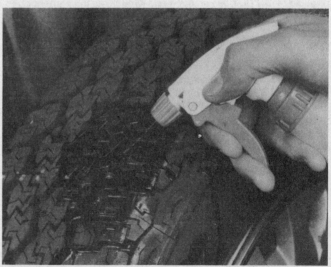

7.4b   If the valve core is tight, raise the corner of the vehicle with the low tire and spray a soapy water solution onto the tread as the tire is turned – slow leaks will cause small bubbles to appear

7.8   To extend the life of the tires, check the air pressure at least once a week with an accurate gauge (don't forget the spare!)

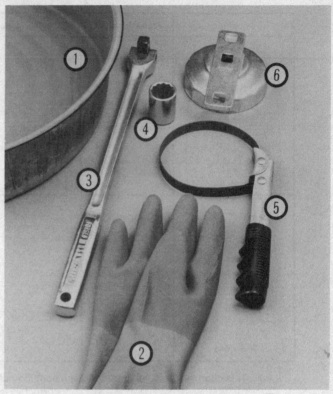

8.3   These tools are required when changing the engine oil and filter

1   *Drain pan – It should be fairly shallow in depth, but wide to prevent spills*
2   *Rubber gloves – When removing the drain plug and filter, you will get oil on your hands (the gloves will prevent burns)*
3   *Breaker bar – Sometimes the oil drain plug is tight and a long breaker bar is needed to loosen it*
4   *Socket – To be used with the breaker bar or a ratchet (must be the correct size to fit the drain plug – 6-point preferred)*
5   *Filter wrench – This is a metal band-type wrench, which requires clearance around the filter to be effective*
6   *Filter wrench – This type fits on the bottom of the filter and can be turned with a ratchet or breaker bar (different size wrenches are available for different types of filters)*

8.9   The engine oil drain plug is located at the bottom of the pan and should be removed with a box-end wrench or six-point socket – DO NOT use an open-end wrench, as the corners on the bolt hex are easily rounded off

6   Correct air pressure adds miles to the lifespan of the tires, improves mileage and enhances overall ride quality. Tire pressure cannot be accurately estimated by looking at a tire, especially if it's a radial. A tire pressure gauge is essential. Keep an accurate gauge in the vehicle. The pressure gauges attached to the nozzles of air hoses at gas stations are often inaccurate.

7   Always check tire pressure when the tires are cold. Cold, in this case, means the vehicle has not been driven over a mile in the three hours preceding a tire pressure check. A pressure rise of four to eight pounds is not uncommon once the tires are warm.

8   Unscrew the valve cap protruding from the wheel or hubcap and push the gauge firmly onto the valve stem **(see illustration)**. Note the reading on the gauge and compare the figure to the recommended tire pressure shown on the placard on the glove compartment door. Be sure to reinstall the valve cap to keep dirt and moisture out of the valve stem mechanism. Check all four tires and, if necessary, add enough air to bring them up to the recommended pressure.

9   Don't forget to keep the spare tire inflated to the specified pressure (refer to your owner's manual or the tire sidewall).

8   Engine oil and filter change

Refer to illustrations 8.3, 8.9, 8.14 and 8.18

1   Frequent oil changes are the most important preventive maintenance procedures that can be done by the home mechanic. As engine oil ages, it becomes diluted and contaminated, which leads to premature engine wear.

2   Although some sources recommend oil filter changes every other oil change, the minimal cost of an oil filter and the fact that it's easy to install dictate that a new filter be used every time the oil is changed.

3   Gather all necessary tools and materials before beginning this procedure **(see illustration)**.

4   You should have plenty of clean rags and newspapers handy to mop up any spills. Access to the underside of the vehicle is greatly improved if the vehicle can be lifted on a hoist, driven onto ramps or supported by jackstands. **Warning:** *Do not work under a vehicle which is supported only by a bumper, hydraulic or scissors-type jack!*

5   If this is your first oil change, get under the vehicle and familiarize yourself with the locations of the oil drain plug and the oil filter. The engine

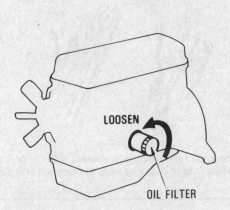

8.14   The oil filter is located on the left side of the block

8.18   Lubricate the gasket with clean oil before installing the filter on the engine

1

and exhaust components will be warm during the actual work, so note how they're situated to avoid touching them when working under the vehicle.

6   Warm the engine to normal operating temperature. If the new oil or any tools are needed, use the warm-up time to obtain everything necessary for the job. The correct oil for your application can be found in Recommended lubricants and fluids at the beginning of this Chapter.

7   With the engine oil warm (warm engine oil will drain better and more built-up sludge will be removed with it), raise and support the vehicle. Make sure it's safely supported!

8   Move all necessary tools, rags and newspapers under the vehicle. Set the drain pan under the drain plug. Keep in mind that the oil will initially flow from the pan with some force; position the pan accordingly.

9   Being careful not to touch any of the hot exhaust components, use a wrench to remove the drain plug near the bottom of the oil pan **(see illustration)**. Depending on how hot the oil is, you may want to wear gloves while unscrewing the plug the final few turns.

10   Allow the old oil to drain into the pan. It may be necessary to move the pan as the oil flow slows to a trickle.

11   After all the oil has drained, wipe off the drain plug with a clean rag. Small metal particles may cling to the plug and would immediately contaminate the new oil.

12   Clean the area around the drain plug opening and reinstall the plug. Tighten the plug securely with the wrench. If a torque wrench is available, use it to tighten the plug.

13   Move the drain pan into position under the oil filter.

14   Use the filter wrench to loosen the oil filter **(see illustration)**. Chain or metal band filter wrenches may distort the filter canister, but it doesn't matter since the filter will be discarded anyway.

15   Completely unscrew the old filter. Be careful; it's full of oil. Empty the oil inside the filter into the drain pan.

16   Compare the old filter with the new one to make sure they're the same type.

17   Use a clean rag to remove all oil, dirt and sludge from the area where the oil filter mounts to the engine. Check the old filter to make sure the rubber gasket isn't stuck to the engine. If the gasket is stuck to the engine, remove it.

18   Apply a light coat of clean oil to the rubber gasket on the new oil filter **(see illustration)**.

19   Attach the new filter to the engine, following the tightening directions printed on the filter canister or packing box. Most filter manufacturers recommend against using a filter wrench due to the possibility of overtighten-

ing and damage to the seal.

20   Remove all tools, rags, etc. from under the vehicle, being careful not to spill the oil in the drain pan, then lower the vehicle.

21   Move to the engine compartment and locate the oil filler cap.

22   Pour the fresh oil through the filler cap opening. A funnel may be needed to avoid spills.

23   Pour three or four quarts of fresh oil into the engine. Wait a few minutes to allow the oil to drain into the pan, then check the level on the oil dipstick (see Section 4 if necessary). If the oil level is above the L mark, start the engine and allow the new oil to circulate.

24   Run the engine for only about a minute and then shut it off. Immediately look under the vehicle and check for leaks at the oil pan drain plug and around the oil filter. If either one is leaking, tighten it a little more.

25   With the new oil circulated and the filter now completely full, recheck the level on the dipstick and add more oil as necessary.

26   During the first few trips after an oil change, make it a point to check frequently for leaks and correct oil level.

27   The old oil drained from the engine cannot be reused in its present state and should be disposed of. Oil reclamation centers, auto repair shops and gas stations will normally accept the oil, which can be refined and used again. After the oil has cooled it can be poured into a container (capped plastic jugs or bottles, milk cartons, etc.) for transport to a disposal site.

---

9   Wiper blade check and replacement

Refer to illustrations 9.5, 9.6, 9.7 and 9.8

1   The windshield and rear wiper (if equipped) and blade assembly should be inspected periodically for damage, loose components and cracked or worn blade elements.

2   Road film can build up on the wiper blades and affect their efficiency, so they should be washed regularly with a mild detergent and water solution.

3   The action of the wiping mechanism can loosen the fasteners, so they should be checked and tightened, as necessary, at the same time the wiper blades are checked.

4   If the wiper blade elements (sometimes called inserts) are cracked, worn or warped, they should be replaced with new ones.

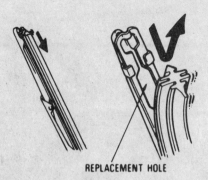

9.5   Pull the wiper blade element out of the end slot, then through the replacement hole

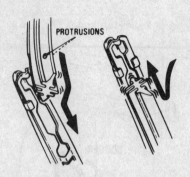

9.6   Insert the end of the new blade element with the protrusions into the replacement hole and slide the element into place

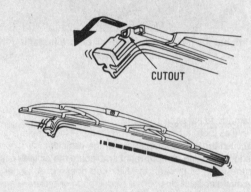

9.7   Pull the rear wiper blade free of the cutout, then slide it out of the frame

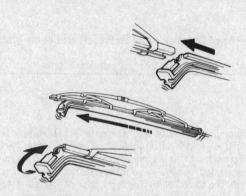

9.8   Work the new blade into the frame and secure it by stretching the tip over the end

Windshield wiper

5   Pull the top of the rubber element in until it's free of the end slot, revealing the replacement hole **(see illustration)**. Pull the rubber blade element out of the hole.
6   To install the new one, insert the end of the element with the small protrusions into the replacement hole and work the rubber along the slot into the frame **(see illustration)**. Once the entire blade is in the frame slot, allow it to expand and fill in the end.

Rear wiper

7   Pull the tip of the element out of the frame until the cutout is visible, disengage the tip from the cutout and slide the assembly down the frame in the opposite direction to remove it **(see illustration)**.
8   To install the new one, work it into the frame as far as it will go, then engage it by stretching the tip of the blade over the frame end **(see illustration)**.

---

10   Brake pedal check and adjustment

Pedal height

Refer to illustration 10.1

1   Make sure the pedal height is correct by measuring the distance from the floor board to the top of the pedal **(see illustration)**. See the Specifications at the front of this Chapter. If incorrect, adjust the pedal height.
2   Loosen the brake light switch.
3   Adjust the pedal height by turning the pushrod until the specified height is attained.

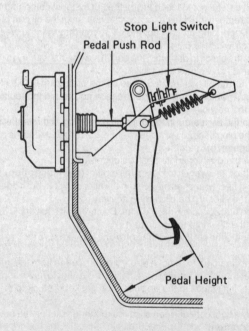

10.1   Brake pedal height adjustment details

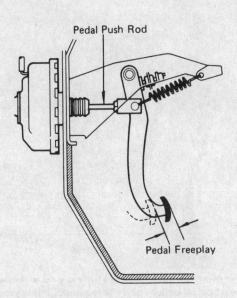

Pedal Push Rod

Pedal Freeplay

10.8 Brake pedal freeplay adjustment details

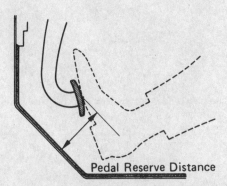

Pedal Reserve Distance

10.12 Brake pedal reserve distance must be as specified

4 Tighten the brake light switch until the switch body lightly contacts the pedal stop.

5 After adjusting the pedal height, check and adjust the pedal freeplay.

Pedal freeplay

Refer to illustration 10.8

6 With the engine off, depress the brake pedal several times until there is no more vacuum left in the booster.

7 Depress the pedal by hand until resistance is felt.

8 Measure the distance the pedal travels before resistance is felt **(see illustration)**. Compare the results to the Specifications.

9 If incorrect, adjust the pedal freeplay by turning the pushrod.

10 Start the engine and confirm that the pedal freeplay is correct.

11 After adjusting the pedal freeplay, recheck the pedal height.

Pedal reserve

Refer to illustration 10.12

12 With the brake pedal fully depressed, measure the distance from the floor board to a line parallel with the floor board at the center of the brake pedal **(see illustration)**. Confirm that this measurement is within the specified limits.

11.1 Tools and materials required for battery maintenance

1 *Face shield/safety goggles* – *When removing corrosion with a brush, the acidic particles can easily fly up into your eyes*

2 *Baking soda* – *A solution of baking soda and water can be used to neutralize corrosion*

3 *Petroleum jelly* – *A layer of this on the battery posts will help prevent corrosion*

4 *Battery post/cable cleaner* – *This wire brush cleaning tool will remove all traces of corrosion from the battery posts and cable clamps*

5 *Treated felt washers* – *Placing one of these on each post, directly under the cable clamps, will help prevent corrosion*

6 *Puller* – *Sometimes the cable clamps are very difficult to pull off the posts, even after the nut/bolt has been completely loosened. This tool pulls the clamp straight up and off the post without damage*

7 *Battery post/cable cleaner* – *Here is another cleaning tool which is a slightly different version of number 4 above, but it does the same thing*

8 *Rubber gloves* – *Another safety item to consider when servicing the battery; remember that's acid inside the battery!*

11 Battery check and maintenance

Refer to illustrations 11.1, 11.5a, 11.5b, 11.5c and 11.5d

Warning: *Several precautions must be followed when checking and servicing the battery. Hydrogen gas, which is highly flammable, is always present in the battery cells, so keep lighted tobacco and all other open flames and sparks away from the battery. The electrolyte in the cells is actually dilute sulfuric acid, which will cause injury if splashed on your skin or in your eyes. It'll also ruin clothes and painted surfaces. When removing the battery cables, always detach the negative cable first and hook it up last!*

Check

1 Battery maintenance is an important procedure which will help ensure that you aren't stranded because of a dead battery. Several tools are required for this procedure **(see illustration)**.

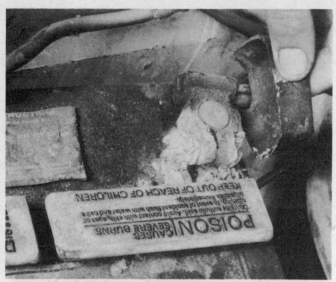

11.5a   Battery terminal corrosion usually appears as light, fluffy powder

11.5b   Removing the cable from the battery post with a wrench – sometimes a special battery pliers is required for this procedure if corrosion has caused deterioration of the nut hex (always remove the ground cable first and hook it up last!)

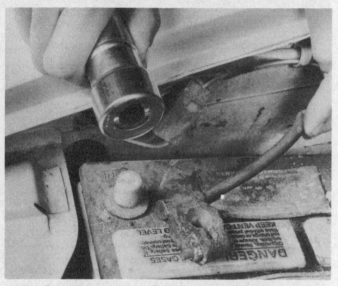

11.5c   Regardless of the type of tool used on the battery posts, a clean, shiny surface should be the result

11.5d   When cleaning the cable clamps, all corrosion must be removed (the inside of the clamp is tapered to match the taper of the post, so don't remove too much material)

2   The electrolyte level should be checked every week (see Section 4).

3   Periodically clean the top and sides of the battery. Remove all dirt and moisture. This will help prevent corrosion and ensure that the battery doesn't become partially discharged by leakage through moisture and dirt. Check the case for cracks and distortion.

4   Check the tightness of the battery cable bolts to ensure good electrical connections. Inspect the entire length of each cable, looking for cracked or abraded insulation and frayed conductors. Battery cable removal and installation is covered in Chapter 5.

5   If corrosion, which usually appears as white, fluffy deposits, is evident, remove the cables from the terminals, clean them with a battery brush and reinstall them (see illustrations). Corrosion can be kept to a minimum by applying a layer of petroleum jelly to the terminals after the cables are in place.

6   Make sure the battery carrier is in good condition and the holddown clamp is tight. If the battery is removed, make sure that nothing is in the bottom of the carrier when it's reinstalled and don't overtighten the clamp nuts.

7   The freezing point of electrolyte depends on its specific gravity. Since freezing can ruin a battery, it should be kept in a fully charged state to protect against freezing.

8   If you frequently have to add water to the battery and the case has been inspected for cracks that could cause leakage, but none are found, the battery is being overcharged; the charging system should be checked as described in Chapter 5.

9   If any doubt exists about the battery state of charge, a hydrometer should be used to test it by withdrawing a little electrolyte from each cell, one at a time.

10   The specific gravity of the electrolyte at 80-degrees F will be approximately 1.270 for a fully charged battery. For every 10-degrees F that the electrolyte temperature is above 80-degrees F, add 0.04 to the specific gravity. Subtract 0.04 if the temperature is below 80-degrees F.

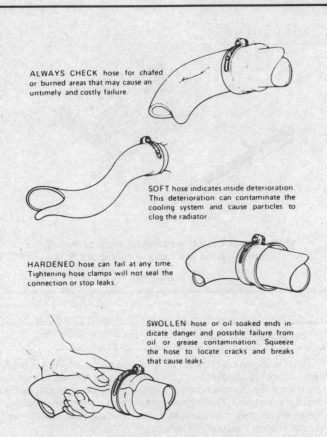

ALWAYS CHECK hose for chafed or burned areas that may cause an untimely and costly failure.

SOFT hose indicates inside deterioration. This deterioration can contaminate the cooling system and cause particles to clog the radiator.

HARDENED hose can fail at any time. Tightening hose clamps will not seal the connection or stop leaks.

SWOLLEN hose or oil soaked ends indicate danger and possible failure from oil or grease contamination. Squeeze the hose to locate cracks and breaks that cause leaks.

12.4   Hoses, like drivebelts, have a habit of failing at the worst possible time – to prevent the inconvenience of a blown radiator or heater hose, inspect them carefully as shown here

11   A specific gravity reading of 1.240 with an electrolyte temperature of 80-degrees F indicates a half-charged battery.

12   Some of the common causes of battery failure are:
  a) Accessories, especially headlights, left on overnight or for several hours.
  b) Slow average driving speeds for short intervals.
  c) The electrical load of the vehicle being more than the alternator output. This is very common when several high draw accessories are being used simultaneously (such as radio/stereo, air conditioning, window defoggers, lights, etc.).
  d) Charging system problems such as short circuits, slipping drivebelt, defective alternator or faulty voltage regulator.
  e) Battery neglect, such as loose or corroded terminals or loose battery hold-down clamp.

Battery charging

13   In winter when heavy demand is placed upon the battery, it's a good idea to occasionally have it charged from an external source.

14   When charging the battery, the negative cable should be disconnected. The charger leads should be connected to the battery before the charger is plugged in or turned on. If the leads are connected to the battery terminals after the charger is on, a spark could occur and the hydrogen gas given off by the battery could explode!

15   The battery should be charged at a low rate of about 4 to 6 amps, and should be left on for at least three or four hours. A trickle charger charging at the rate of 1.5 amps can be safely used overnight.

16   Special rapid boost charges which are claimed to restore the power of the battery in a short time can cause serious damage to the battery plates and should only be used in an emergency situation.

17   The battery should be left on the charger only until the specific gravity is brought up to a normal level. Don't overcharge the battery! **Note:** *Some battery chargers will automatically shut off after the battery is fully charged, making it unnecessary to keep a close watch on the state of charge.*

18   When disconnecting the charger, unplug it before disconnecting the charger leads from the battery.

12   Cooling system check

Refer to illustration 12.4

1   Many major engine failures can be attributed to a faulty cooling system. If the vehicle is equipped with an automatic transmission, the cooling system also cools the transmission fluid, prolonging transmission life.

2   The cooling system should be checked with the engine cold. Do this before the vehicle is driven for the day or after it has been shut off for at least three hours.

3   Remove the radiator cap by turning it counterclockwise until it reaches a stop. If you hear a hissing sound (indicating there's still pressure in the system), wait until it stops. Now press down on the cap with the palm of your hand and continue turning until it can be removed. Thoroughly clean the cap, inside and out, with clean water. Also clean the filler neck on the radiator. All traces of corrosion should be removed. The coolant inside the radiator should be relatively transparent. If it's rust colored, the system should be drained and refilled (Section 36). If the coolant level is not up to the top, add additional antifreeze/coolant mixture (see Section 4).

4   Carefully check the large upper and lower radiator hoses along with the smaller diameter heater hoses which run from the engine to the firewall. Inspect each hose along its entire length, replacing any hose that's cracked, swollen or deteriorated. Cracks may become more apparent if the hose is squeezed **(see illustration)**. Regardless of condition, it's a good idea to replace hoses with new ones every two years.

5   Make sure all hose connections are tight. A leak in the cooling system will usually show up as white or rust colored deposits on the areas adjoining the leak. If wire-type clamps are used at the ends of the hoses, it may be a good idea to replace them with more secure screw-type clamps.

6   Use compressed air or a soft brush to remove bugs, leaves, etc. from the front of the radiator or air conditioning condenser. Be careful not to damage the delicate cooling fins or cut yourself on them.

7   Every other inspection, or at the first indication of cooling system problems, have the cap and system pressure tested. If you don't have a pressure tester, most gas stations and repair shops will do this for a minimal charge.

13   Underhood hose check and replacement

General

1   **Caution:** *Replacement of air conditioning hoses must be left to a dealer service department or service station with the equipment to depressurize the system safely. Never remove air conditioning components or hoses until the system has been depressurized.*

2   High temperatures in the engine compartment can cause the deterioration of the rubber and plastic hoses used for engine, accessory and emission systems operation. Periodic inspection should be made for cracks, loose clamps, material hardening and leaks. Information specific to the cooling system hoses can be found in Section 12.

3   Some, but not all, hoses are secured to the fittings with clamps. Where clamps are used, check to be sure they haven't lost their tension, allowing the hose to leak. If clamps aren't used, make sure the hose hasn't expanded and/or hardened where it slips over the fitting, allowing it to leak.

Vacuum hoses

4   It's quite common for vacuum hoses, especially those in the emissions system, to be color coded or identified by colored stripes molded into them. Various systems require hoses with different wall thicknesses, collapse resistance and temperature resistance. When replacing hoses, be sure the new ones are made of the same material.

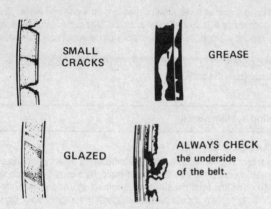

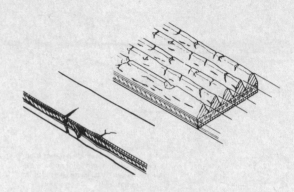

15.3a   Here are some of the more common problems associated with drivebelts (check the belts very carefully to prevent an untimely breakdown)

15.3b   Check the V-ribbed belt for signs of wear like these – if the belt looks worn, replace it

5   Often the only effective way to check a hose is to remove it completely from the vehicle. If more than one hose is removed, be sure to label the hoses and fittings to ensure correct installation.

6   When checking vacuum hoses, be sure to include any plastic T-fittings in the check. Inspect the fittings for cracks and the hose where it fits over the fitting for distortion, which could cause leakage.

7   A small piece of vacuum hose (1/4-inch inside diameter) can be used as a stethoscope to detect vacuum leaks. Hold one end of the hose to your ear and probe around vacuum hoses and fittings, listening for the "hissing" sound characteristic of a vacuum leak. **Warning:** *When probing with the vacuum hose stethoscope, be very careful not to come into contact with moving engine components such as the drivebelts and fan.*

Fuel hose

Warning: *There are certain precautions which must be taken when inspecting or servicing fuel system components. Work in a well ventilated area and don't allow open flames (cigarettes, appliance pilot lights, etc.) or bare light bulbs near the work area. Mop up any spills immediately and don't store fuel soaked rags where they could ignite. On vehicles equipped with fuel injection, the fuel system is under pressure, so if any fuel lines must be disconnected, the pressure in the system must be relieved first (see Chapter 4 for more information).*

8   Check all rubber fuel lines for deterioration and chafing. Check carefully for cracks in areas where the hoses bend and attach to fittings.

9   High quality fuel line, usually identified by the word Fluroelastomer printed on the hose, should be used for fuel line replacement. **Warning:** *Never, under any circumstances, use unreinforced vacuum line, clear plastic or vinyl tubing for fuel lines!*

10   Spring-type clamps are commonly used on fuel lines. They often lose their tension over a period of time, and can be "sprung" during removal. Replace all spring-type clamps with screw clamps when a hose is replaced.

Metal lines

11   Sections of steel tubing are often used for fuel line between the fuel pump and carburetor or fuel injection unit. Check carefully to be sure the line isn't bent or crimped and look for cracks.

12   If a section of metal fuel line must be replaced, only seamless steel tubing should be used, since copper and aluminum tubing don't have the strength necessary to withstand normal engine vibration.

13   Check the metal brake lines where they enter the master cylinder and brake proportioning unit (if used) for cracks and loose fittings. Any sign of brake fluid leakage means an immediate thorough inspection of the brake system should be done.

14   Exhaust system check

1   With the engine cold (at least three hours after the vehicle has been driven), check the complete exhaust system from the manifold to the end of the tailpipe. Be careful around the catalytic converter, which may be hot even after three hours. The inspection should be done with the vehicle on a hoist to permit unrestricted access. If a hoist isn't available, raise the vehicle and support it securely on jackstands.

2   Check the exhaust pipes and connections for signs of leakage and/or corrosion indicating a potential failure. Make sure that all brackets and hangers are in good condition and tight.

3   Inspect the underside of the body for holes, corrosion, open seams, etc. which may allow exhaust gases to enter the passenger compartment. Seal all body openings with silicone sealant or body putty.

4   Rattles and other noises can often be traced to the exhaust system, especially the hangers, mounts and heat shields. Try to move the pipes, mufflers and catalytic converter. If the components can come in contact with the body or suspension parts, secure the exhaust system with new brackets and hangers.

15   Drivebelt check, adjustment and replacement

Refer to illustrations 15.3a, 15.3b, 15.4, 15.5 and 15.9

1   The drivebelts, or V-belts as they are often called, are located at the front of the engine and play an important role in the overall operation of the engine and accessories. Due to their function and material makeup, the belts are prone to failure after a period of time and should be inspected and adjusted periodically to prevent major engine damage.

2   The number of belts used on a particular vehicle depends on the accessories installed. Drivebelts are used to turn the alternator, smog pump, power steering pump, water pump and air conditioning compressor. Depending on the pulley arrangement, more than one of the components may be driven by a single belt.

3   With the engine off, locate the drivebelts at the front of the engine. Using your fingers (and a flashlight, if necessary), move along the belts checking for cracks and separation of the belt plies. Also check for fraying and glazing, which gives the belt a shiny appearance **(see illustrations)**. Both sides of each belt should be inspected, which means you'll have to twist each belt to check the underside. Check the pulleys for nicks, cracks, distortion and corrosion.

4   To check the tension of each belt in accordance with factory recommendations, install a drivebelt tension gauge **(see illustration)**. Measure the tension in accordance with the tension gauge instructions and compare your measurement to the specified drivebelt tension for either a used

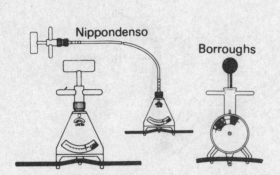

15.4 If you can borrow either a Nippondenso or Burroughs belt tension gauge, this is how it's installed on the belt – compare the reading on the scale with the specified drivebelt tension

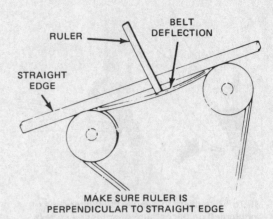

MAKE SURE RULER IS
PERPENDICULAR TO STRAIGHT EDGE

15.5 Measuring drivebelt deflection with a straightedge and ruler

or new belt. **Note:** *A "new" belt is defined as any belt which has not been run; a "used" belt is one that has been run for more than ten minutes.*

5   The special gauge is the most accurate way to check belt tension. However, if you don't have a gauge, and cannot borrow one, the following "rule-of-thumb" method is recommended as an alternative. Lay a straightedge across the longest free span (the distance between two pulleys) of the belt. Push down firmly on the belt at a point half way between the pulleys and see how much the belt moves (deflects). Measure the deflection with a ruler **(see illustration)**. The belt should deflect 1/8 to 1/4-inch if the distance from pulley center-to-pulley center is less than 12-inches; it should deflect from 1/8 to 3/8-inch if the distance from pulley center-to-pulley center is over 12-inches.

6   If adjustment is needed, either to make the belt tighter or looser, it's done by moving the belt-driven accessory on the bracket. Each component usually has an adjusting bolt and a pivot bolt. Both bolts must be loosened slightly to enable you to move the component.

7   After the two bolts have been loosened, move the component away from the engine to tighten the belt or toward the engine to loosen the belt. Hold the accessory in position and check the belt tension. If it's correct, tighten the two bolts until just snug, then recheck the tension. If the tension is correct, tighten the bolts.

8   You may have to use some sort of pry bar to move the accessory while the belt is adjusted. If this must be done to gain the proper leverage, be very careful not to damage the component being moved or the part being pried against (especially the smog pump).

9   To replace a belt, follow the above procedures for drivebelt adjustment but slip the belt off the pulleys and remove it. Since belts tend to wear out more or less at the same time, it's a good idea to replace all of them at the same time. Mark each belt and the corresponding pulley grooves so the replacement belts can be installed properly **(see illustration)**.

10   Take the old belts with you when purchasing new ones in order to

make a direct comparison for length, width and design.

11   Adjust the belts as described earlier in this Section.

16   Idle speed check and adjustment

1   Engine idle speed is the speed at which the engine operates when no accelerator pedal pressure is applied. The idle speed is critical to the performance of the engine itself, as well as many accessories. On carbureted engines, the fast idle speed must also be checked and adjusted.

2   To get an accurate reading, a hand-held tachometer must be used when adjusting idle speed. The exact hook-up for these meters depends on the manufacturer, so follow the directions included with the tachometer.

3   Apply the parking brake and block the wheels. Be sure the transmission is in Neutral (manual transmission) or Park (automatic transmission).

4   Turn off the air conditioner (if equipped), the headlights and all other accessories.

5   Start the engine and allow it to reach normal operating temperature.

Carburetor-equipped vehicles

Idle

Refer to illustrations 16.7a and 16.7b

6   Check the engine idle speed with the tachometer and compare it to the VECI label under the hood.

7   If the idle speed is incorrect, turn the idle speed adjusting screw to change it **(see illustrations)**.

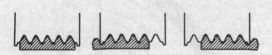

CORRECT   WRONG   WRONG

15.9 Make sure the V-ribbed belt is secure in the pulley grooves

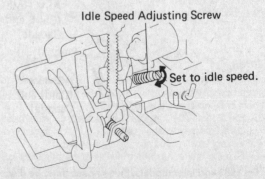

Idle Speed Adjusting Screw

Set to idle speed.

16.7a Carburetor idle speed adjusting screw location

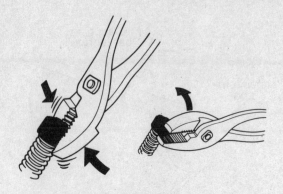

16.7b   Use pliers to remove the limiter caps (if equipped) on the carburetor adjusting screws

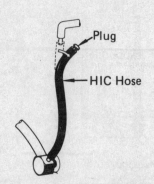

16.9   Disconnect and plug the Hot Idle Compensator (HIC) hose (1980 through 1982 models)

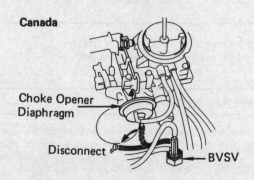

16.10a   Disconnect the hose between the BVSV and choke opener diaphragm (1980 through 1982 Canadian models)

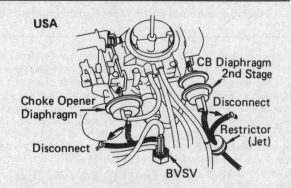

16.10b   On 1980 through 1982 US models, disconnect and plug the indicated hoses

Fast idle

Refer to illustrations 16.9, 16.10a, 16.10b, 16.11, 16.12, 16.13 and 16.15

8   Stop the engine and remove the air cleaner.

1980 through 1982

9   Disconnect and plug the Hot Idle Compensation (HIC) system hose **(see illustration)**.
10   Disconnect and plug the hose between the choke breaker second stage and the restricter jet **(see illustration)**. On Canadian models, disconnect and plug the hose between the choke opener diaphragm and BVSV at the diaphragm **(see illustration)**.

1983-on

11   Disconnect and plug the HIC, AS and ASC hoses **(see illustration)**.
12   Disconnect the hose from the TVSV M port and plug the port so the EGR system and choke opener will be deactivated during the fast idle adjustment procedure **(see illustration)**.

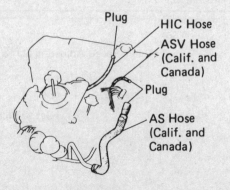

16.11   On 1983 and later models, these hoses must be disconnected and plugged before the fast idle speed can be checked

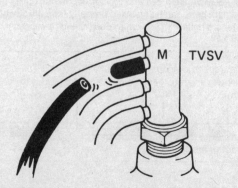

16.12   Plug the TVSV M port so the EGR system and choke opener won't affect the fast idle check

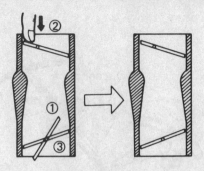

16.13   Hold the throttle valve (1) open slightly, push the choke valve (2) closed, then release the throttle valve so the valves appear as shown on the right

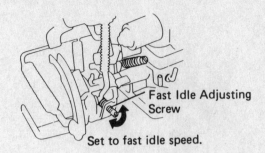

16.15   Turn the carburetor fast idle adjusting screw

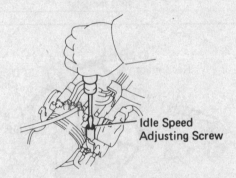

16.19   EFI idle speed adjusting screw location

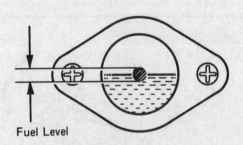

17.1   Always check the carburetor sight glass to verify the fuel level before checking or adjusting anything

All models

13   While holding the throttle valve slightly open, push the choke valve closed and hold it closed as you release the throttle valve **(see illustration)**.

14   Start the engine, but do not touch the accelerator pedal.

15   Check that the engine is operating at the correct fast idle speed. If not, turn the fast idle adjustment screw until the specified rpm is obtained **(see illustration)**.

16   Disconnect the tachometer, reconnect any hoses and install the air cleaner. When the hoses are reconnected, it is normal for the engine speed to drop noticeably. If it does not, check the choke opener diaphragm and fast idle linkage.

Fuel injected vehicles

Refer to illustration 16.19

17   Run the engine at 2500 rpm for about two minutes, then allow it to return to idle.

18   Check the engine idle speed with the tachometer and compare it to the VECI label under the hood.

19   If the idle speed is incorrect, remove the rubber plug (if equipped) from the throttle body and turn the idle speed adjusting screw to change it **(see illustration)**.

17   Idle mixture check and adjustment (1980 and 1981 Canadian models only)

Refer to illustrations 17.1, 17.3 and 17.4

1   The following conditions should be met before beginning this adjustment:
   a)   Air cleaner installed.
   b)   Choke valve fully open.

c)   Accessories switched off.
d)   All vacuum lines connected.
e)   Ignition timing set correctly (Section 37).
f)   Transmission in Neutral (manual transmission) or Park (automatic transmission) (parking brake set and wheels blocked to prevent movement).
g)   Engine idling at normal operating temperature.
h)   A hand-held tachometer attached according to the manufacturer's instructions.
i)   Cooling fan is off.
j)   Fuel level correct in sight glass **(see illustration)**.

2   If limiter caps are installed on the idle mixture and speed adjusting screws, break them off with pliers **(see illustration 16.7b)**.

3   Turn the idle mixture screw until the maximum engine rpm is obtained **(see illustration)**.

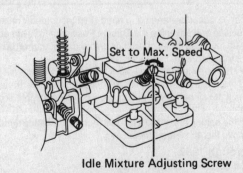

17.3   Turn the idle mixture screw until maximum engine speed is attained

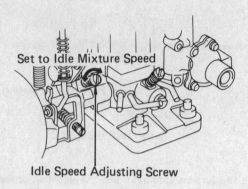

17.4 Turn the idle speed screw to obtain the specified idle speed

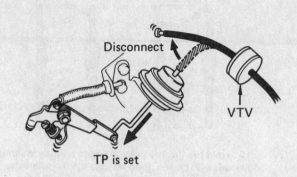

18.6 Disconnect and plug the Throttle Positioner (TP) vacuum hose – the engine rpm should increase (1980 through 1982 models)

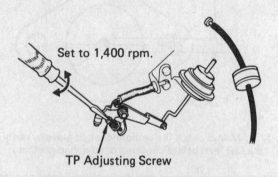

18.7 Turn the adjusting screw to obtain an engine speed of 1400 rpm (1980 through 1982 models)

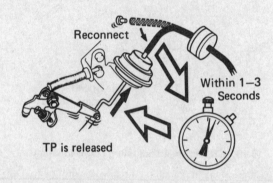

18.8 Reconnect the hose and make sure the idle takes from 1 to 3 seconds to return to normal

4   Turn the idle speed adjusting screw until the specified idle speed is obtained (see illustration).
5   Repeat the two Steps above until the engine rpm cannot be increased by turning the idle mixture screw.
6   Turn the idle speed adjusting screw until the idle speed listed in this Chapter's Specifications is obtained.
7   If originally so equipped, install new limiter caps on the idle mixture and idle speed screws.

18 Throttle Positioner (TP) check and adjustment (carburetor-equipped models only)

1   To get an accurate reading, a hand-held tachometer must be used when checking and adjusting the Throttle Positioner (TP) speed. The exact hook-up for these meters depends on the manufacturer, so follow the directions included with the tachometer.
2   Apply the parking brake and block the wheels. Be sure the transmission is in Neutral (manual transmission) or Park (automatic transmission).
3   Turn off the air conditioner (if equipped), the headlights and all other accessories.
4   Start the engine and allow it to reach normal operating temperature.
5   Remove the air cleaner for access.

1980 through 1982
Refer to illustrations 18.6, 18.7 and 18.8
6   Disconnect and plug the TP vacuum hose and verify that the rpm increases (see illustration).
7   If necessary, turn the adjusting screw in the TP linkage to obtain a

1400 rpm reading on the tachometer (see illustration).
8   Reconnect the hose and make sure the idle speed returns to normal idle speed within 1 to 3 seconds (see illustration). If it does not, check the VTV, TP diaphragm or the linkage itself. Disconnect the tachometer and install the air cleaner.

1983-on
Refer to illustrations 18.10, 18.11 and 18.12
9   Disconnect the vacuum hose from the M port of the TVSV and plug it so the EGR system and choke opener will be deactivated during this procedure (see illustration 16.12).
10   Disconnect and plug the TP vacuum hose and make sure the rpm goes up (see illustration).

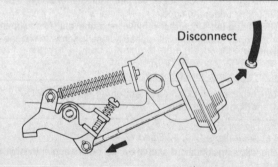

18.10 Disconnect and plug the TP vacuum hose (1983-on)

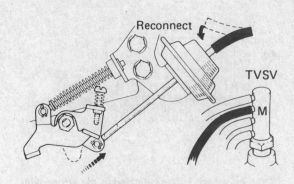

18.11   Adjust the engine speed by turning the TP adjusting screw (1983-on)

18.12   The idle rpm should return to normal when the hoses are reconnected (1983-on)

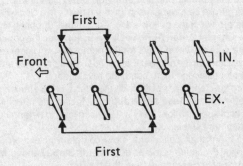

19.5   Adjust the valves indicated by the arrows with the number one piston at TDC on the compression stroke (OHV engine)

19.7   The valve clearance can be changed by turning the adjusting screw with a screwdriver – once the clearance is set, tighten the locknut with a wrench and withdraw the feeler gauge

11   Adjust the engine speed to 1400 rpm if necessary, by turning the adjusting screw **(see illustration)**.
12   Reconnect the TP hose and the TVSV M port hose and verify that the engine returns to normal idle speed **(see illustration)**. Disconnect the tachometer and install the air cleaner.

19   Valve clearance check and adjustment

OHV engine (1980 through 1982)

Refer to illustrations 19.5, 19.7 and 19.10

1   Start the engine and allow it to reach normal operating temperature, then shut it off.
2   Remove the air cleaner (Chapter 4) and the rocker arm cover (Chapter 2).
3   Position the number one piston at TDC on the compression stroke (see Chapter 2).
4   Make sure the rocker arms for the number one cylinder valves are loose and number four are tight. If they aren't, the number one piston is not at TDC on the compression stroke.
5   Check/adjust only the valves indicated by the arrows **(see illustration)**. The valve clearances can be found in the Specifications at the beginning of this Chapter.
6   The clearance is measured by inserting the specified size feeler gauge between the end of the valve stem and the adjusting screw. You should feel a slight amount of drag when the feeler gauge is moved back-and-forth.
7   If the gap is too large or too small, loosen the locknut and turn the adjusting screw to obtain the correct gap **(see illustration)**.

8   Once the gap has been set, hold the screw in position with a screwdriver and retighten the locknut. Recheck the valve clearance – sometimes it'll change slightly when the locknut is tightened. If so, readjust it until it's correct.
9   Repeat the procedure for the remaining valves **(see illustration 19.5),** then turn the crankshaft one complete revolution (360-degrees) and realign the notch in the pulley with the zero on the engine.
10   Adjust the valves indicated by the arrows **(see illustration)**.
11   Reinstall the rocker arm cover and the air cleaner assembly.

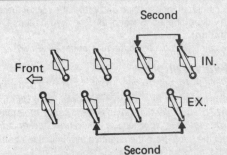

19.10   Turn the crankshaft one complete revolution (360-degrees), then adjust the valves marked with an arrow (OHV engine)

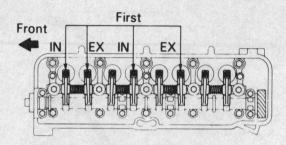

19.16   Adjust the valves indicated by the arrows with the number one piston at TDC on the compression stroke (SOHC engine)

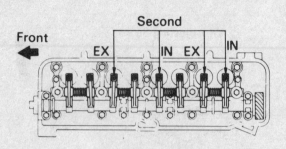

19.22   Turn the crankshaft one complete revolution (360-degrees), then adjust the valves marked with an arrow (SOHC engine)

SOHC engine (1983 through 1987 carburetor-equipped vehicles)

Refer to illustrations 19.16 and 19.22

12   The valve clearances are checked and adjusted with the engine at normal operating temperature.

13   Remove the air cleaner assembly (see Chapter 4).

14   Remove the camshaft cover (see Chapter 2, Part B).

15   Place the number one piston at Top Dead Center (TDC) on the compression stroke (see Chapter 2, Part B). The number one cylinder rocker arms (closest to the timing belt end of the engine) should be loose (able to move up-and-down slightly) and the camshaft lobes should be facing down, away from the rocker arms.

16   With the crankshaft in this position the valves labeled "First" can be checked and adjusted **(see illustration)**.

17   Check and adjust the intake valves. Insert the appropriate size feeler gauge between the intake valve stem and the adjusting screw. If adjustment is required, loosen the locknut and turn the adjusting screw until you can feel a slight drag on the feeler gauge as you withdraw it from between the stem and adjusting screw.

18   Hold the adjusting screw with a screwdriver (to keep it from turning) and tighten the locknut. Recheck the clearance to make sure it hasn't changed.

19   Next adjust both exhaust valves. Loosen the locknut on the exhaust valve adjusting screw. Turn the adjusting screw counterclockwise and insert the appropriate size feeler gauge between the valve stem and the adjusting screw. Carefully tighten the adjusting screw until you can feel a slight drag on the feeler gauge as you withdraw it from between the stem and adjusting screw.

20   Hold the adjusting screw with a screwdriver (to keep it from turning) and tighten the locknut **(see illustration 19.7)**. Recheck the clearance to make sure it hasn't changed.

21   Rotate the crankshaft one full revolution (360-degrees) until the number four piston is at TDC on the compression stroke. The number four cylinder rocker arms (closest to the transmission end of the engine) should be loose with the camshaft lobes facing away from the rocker arms.

22   Adjust the valves labelled "Second" as described in Steps 17 through 20 **(see illustration)**.

23   Install the camshaft cover and the air cleaner assembly.

DOHC (16-valve) engine

Refer to illustrations 19.28a, 19.28b, 19.29, 19.31a, 19.31b and 19.32

Note: *The following procedure requires a special valve lifter tool set (J 09248-A 070012 or equivalent). It's impossible to perform this task without one. The engine must be cold when the valves are checked/adjusted.*

24   Disconnect the cable from the negative terminal of the battery.

25   Remove the camshaft covers (see Chapter 2, Part A).

26   Blow out the recessed area between the camshafts with compressed air, if available, to remove any debris that might fall into the cylinders, then remove the spark plugs (see Section 32). **Warning:** *Wear eye protection when using compressed air.*

27   Position the number one piston at Top Dead Center (TDC) on the compression stroke by turning the crankshaft pulley in a clockwise direction until the groove in the pulley is aligned with the "0" on the stationary pointer (see Chapter 2, Part A). To verify the piston is on the compression stroke, make sure the valve lifters for the number one cylinder are loose and the valve lifters for the number four cylinder are tight. If they aren't, turn the crankshaft pulley one more complete revolution.

28   Measure the clearances of the indicated valves with a feeler gauge of the specified thickness **(see illustrations)**. Record the measurements which are out of specification. They will be used later to determine the required replacement shims.

29   Turn the crankshaft pulley one more complete revolution (360-degrees) and align the timing marks as described in Step 27 above. Measure the remaining valve clearances **(see illustration)**.

30   After all the valve clearances have been measured, turn the crankshaft pulley clockwise until the camshaft lobe above the first valve which you intend to adjust is pointing up, away from the shim.

31   Position the notch in the valve lifter toward the spark plug. Then press down the valve lifter with the special valve lifter tool **(see illustration)**. Place the special valve lifter tool in position as shown, with the longer jaw of the tool gripping the lower edge of the cast lifter boss and the upper, shorter jaw gripping the upper edge of the lifter. Press down the valve lifter by squeezing the handles of the valve lifter tool and remove the adjusting shim with a small screwdriver or a pair of tweezers **(see illustration)**. Note that the wire hook on the end of one valve lifter tool handle can be used to clamp both handles together to keep the lifter depressed while the shim is removed.

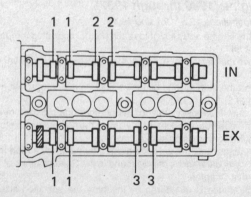

19.28a   When the number one piston is at TDC on the compression stroke, the valve clearances for the number one and number three exhaust valves and the number one and number two intake valves can be checked (DOHC engine)

19.28b Measure the clearance for each valve with a feeler gauge of the specified thickness – if the clearance is correct, you'll feel a slight drag on the gauge as it's pulled out (DOHC engine)

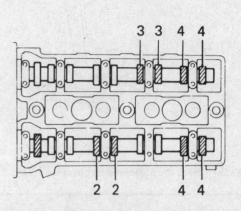

19.29 When the number four piston is at TDC on the compression stroke, the valve clearances for the number two and number four exhaust valves and the number three and number four intake valves can be checked (DOHC engine)

1

19.31a Install the valve lifter tool as shown and squeeze the handles together to lower the valve lifter so the shim can be removed (DOHC engine)

19.31b Remove the shim with a small screwdriver, a pair of tweezers or a magnet (DOHC engine)

32 Measure the thickness of the shim with a micrometer (see illustration). To calculate the correct thickness of a replacement shim that will place the valve clearance within the specified value, use the following formula:

Intake side: N = T + (A – 0.008 in)
Exhaust side: N = T + (A – 0.010 in)
T = thickness of the shim used
A = valve clearance measured
N = the thickness of the new shim

33 Select a shim with a thickness as close as possible to the valve clearance calculated. Shims, which are available in 17 sizes in increments of 0.0020-inch (0.050 mm), range in size from 0.984-inch (2.500 mm) to 0.1299-inch (3.300 mm). **Note:** *Through careful analysis of the shim sizes needed to bring all the out of specification valve clearances within specification, it's often possible to simply move a shim to another valve lifter requiring a shim of that particular size, thereby reducing the number of new shims that must be purchased.*

34 Depress the lifter and install the new shim. Measure the clearance with a feeler gauge to make sure that your calculations are correct.

35 Repeat this procedure until all the valve clearances are correct.

36 Installation of the remaining components is the reverse of removal.

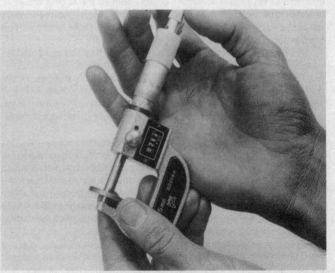

19.32 Measure the shim thickness with a micrometer (DOHC engine)

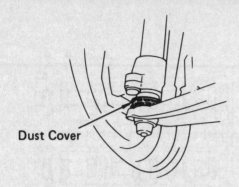

20.6a Check the balljoint dust cover for cracks

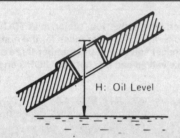

20.9 Unscrew the plug and check the steering box oil – it should be about 1-inch from the top of the hole (1980 through 1982 models)

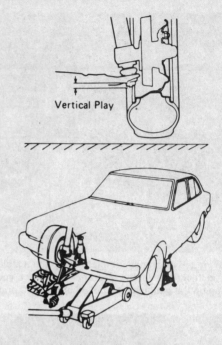

20.6b Check the suspension balljoints for vertical movement by prying up on the control arm as shown here – note that the chassis must be supported by a jack and jackstand and the tire must be resting on blocks with half the suspension weight on it

20 Suspension and steering check

Refer to illustrations 20.6a, 20.6b, 20.9 and 20.10

1   Whenever the front of the vehicle is raised for any reason, it's a good idea to visually check the suspension and steering components for wear.
2   Indications of steering or suspension problems include excessive play in the steering wheel before the front wheels react, excessive swaying around corners or body movement over rough roads and binding at some point as the steering wheel is turned.
3   Before the vehicle is raised for inspection, test the shock absorbers by pushing down aggressively at each corner. If the vehicle doesn't come back to a level position within one or two bounces, the shocks are worn and should be replaced. As this is done listen for squeaks and other noises from the suspension components. Information on shock absorber and suspension components can be found in Chapter 10.
4   Raise the front end of the vehicle and support it on jackstands. Make sure it's safely supported!
5   Crawl under the vehicle and check for loose bolts, broken or disconnected parts and deteriorated rubber bushings on all suspension and steering components. Look for grease or fluid leaking from around the steering gear assembly and shock absorbers. If equipped, check the power steering hoses and connections for leaks.
6   The balljoint seals or dust covers should be checked at this time. This includes not only the lower suspension balljoints, but those connecting the steering linkage parts as well. After cleaning around the balljoints, inspect the seals or covers for cracks and damage **(see illustration)**. Check the balljoints for wear by raising the front of the vehicle, supporting one wheel with a 7 to 8-inch high wood block and then lowering about half the vehicle weight onto the tire. Pry the control arm up-and-down to check the vertical play of the balljoint **(see illustration)**.
7   Grip the top and bottom of each wheel and try to move it in-and-out. It won't take a lot of effort to be able to feel any play in the wheel bearings. If the play is noticeable it would be a good idea to adjust it right away or it could confuse further inspections.
8   Grip each side of the wheel and try rocking it laterally. Steady pressure will, of course, turn the steering, but back-and-forth pressure will reveal a loose steering joint. If some play is felt it would be easier to get assistance from someone so while one person rocks the wheel from side-to-side, the other can look at the joints, bushings and connections in the steering linkage.
9   Inspect the universal joint or flexible coupling between the steering shaft and the steering gear housing. Check the steering gearbox or rack and pinion assembly for grease leakage or oozing. Make sure the bolts holding the steering gear to the frame are tight and the dust seals and boots are not damaged. While an assistant turns the wheel from side-to-side, look for loose bolts, broken or disconnected parts and binding. steering box while the other turns the steering wheel a little from side-to-side. The amount of lost motion between the steering wheel and the steering arm indicates the degree of wear in the steering box. On recirculating ball-type steering (used on 1980 through 1982 models) check the gearbox oil level as well. It should be about 1-inch from the top **(see illustration)**. Refer to the Recommended lubricants and fluids section in the Specifications if oil is needed.
10   Moving to the vehicle interior, check the play in the steering wheel by turning it slowly in both directions until the wheels can just be felt turning. The steering wheel free play should be as specified **(see illustration)**. Excessive play is another indication of wear in the steering gear or linkage.

20.10 Check the steering wheel freeplay – it's the distance the wheel will turn with no resistance

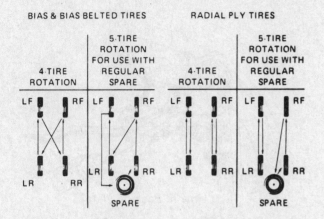

BIAS & BIAS BELTED TIRES   RADIAL PLY TIRES

4-TIRE ROTATION | 5-TIRE ROTATION FOR USE WITH REGULAR SPARE | 4-TIRE ROTATION | 5-TIRE ROTATION FOR USE WITH REGULAR SPARE

22.2   Tire rotation diagram

11   Following the inspection of the front, a similar inspection should be made of the rear suspension components, again checking for loose bolts, damaged and disconnected parts and deteriorated rubber bushings.

21   Fuel system check

Warning: *There are certain precautions to take when inspecting or servicing the fuel system components. Work in a well ventilated area and don't allow open flames (cigarettes, appliance pilot lights, etc.) in the work area. Mop up spills immediately and don't store fuel soaked rags where they could ignite. On fuel injection equipped models, the fuel system is under pressure. No components should be disconnected until the pressure has been relieved (see Chapter 4).*

1   On most models the main fuel tank is located at the rear of the vehicle.
2   The fuel system should be checked with the vehicle raised on a hoist so the components underneath the vehicle are readily visible and accessible.
3   If the smell of gasoline is noticed while driving or after the vehicle has been in the sun, the system should be thoroughly inspected immediately.
4   Remove the gas tank cap and check for damage, corrosion and an unbroken sealing imprint on the gasket. Replace the cap or gasket with a new one if necessary (Section 43).
5   With the vehicle raised, check the gas tank and filler neck for punctures, cracks and other damage. The connection between the filler neck and the tank is especially critical. Sometimes a rubber filler neck will leak due to loose clamps or deteriorated rubber, problems a home mechanic can usually rectify. **Warning:** *Do not, under any circumstances, try to repair a fuel tank yourself (except rubber components). A welding torch or any open flame can easily cause the fuel vapors to explode if the proper precautions are not taken!*
6   Carefully check all rubber hoses and metal lines leading away from the fuel tank. Look for loose connections, deteriorated hoses, crimped lines and other damage. Follow the lines to the front of the vehicle, carefully inspecting them all the way. Repair or replace damaged sections as necessary.
7   If a fuel odor is still evident after the inspection, check the EVAP system.

22   Tire rotation

Refer to illustration 22.2

1   The tires should be rotated at the specified intervals and whenever uneven wear is noticed. Since the vehicle will be raised and the tires removed, it would be a good time to check the brakes and repack the wheel bearings as well.

2   Refer to the accompanying illustration for the preferred tire rotation pattern.
3   Refer to the information in Jacking and towing at the front of this manual for the proper procedures to follow when raising the vehicle and changing a tire. If the brakes are to be checked, don't apply the parking brake as stated. Make sure the tires are blocked to prevent the vehicle from rolling as it's raised.
4   Preferably, the entire vehicle should be raised at the same time. This can be done on a hoist or by jacking up each corner and then lowering the vehicle onto jackstands placed under the frame rails. Always use four jackstands and make sure the vehicle is safely supported!
5   After rotation, check and adjust the tire pressures as necessary and be sure to check the lug nut tightness.
6   For additional information on the wheels and tires, refer to Chapter 10.

23   Brake check

Refer to illustrations 23.6a, 23.6b, 23.11 and 23.13
Note: *For detailed photographs of the brake system, refer to Chapter 9.*
Warning: *Brake system dust contains asbestos, which is hazardous to your health. DO NOT blow it out with compressed air and DO NOT inhale it. DO NOT use gasoline or solvents to remove the dust. Use brake system cleaner or denatured alcohol only!*

1   In addition to the specified intervals, the brakes should be inspected every time the wheels are removed.
2   To check the brakes, the vehicle must be raised and supported securely on jackstands.

Disc brakes

3   Disc brakes are used on the front (and on some later models, rear) wheels. Extensive rotor damage can occur if the pads are allowed to wear beyond the specified limit. Later models are equipped with a wear sensor. This is a small, bent piece of metal which rubs against the disc and makes a screeching sound, warning that the pads are worn to the limit.
4   Raise the vehicle and support it securely on jackstands, then remove all four wheels (see Jacking and Towing at the front of the manual if necessary).
5   The disc brake calipers, which contain the pads, are visible with the wheels removed. There's an outer pad and an inner pad in each caliper. All four pads should be inspected.
6   Each caliper has an opening, which will allow you to inspect the pads **(see illustrations)**. If the pad material has worn to about 1/8-inch or less, the pads should be replaced.

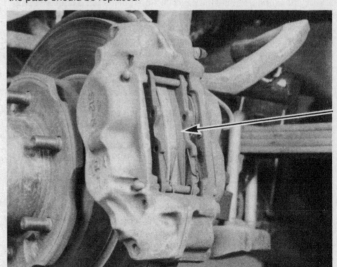

23.6a   To check the brake pads on early models, remove the inspection cover and note the thickness of the lining material (arrow) on both pads in each caliper

23.6b   Later model calipers don't have an inspection cover – the pad lining material (arrows) is visible through the large opening in the caliper

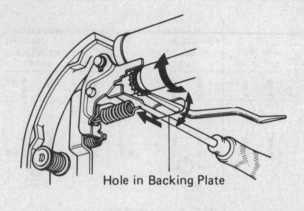

23.11   Hold the locking lever out of the way with a hooked tool and turn the star wheel with a screwdriver to move the brake shoes away from the drum

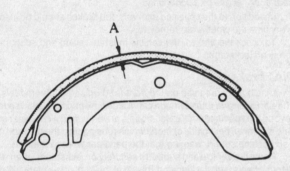

23.13   The rear brake shoe lining thickness (A) is measured from the outer surface of the lining to the metal shoe

24.3   Use a squeeze bottle or pump to add lubricant to the transmission through the filler hole

7   If you're unsure about the exact thickness of the remaining lining material, remove the pads for further inspection or replacement (refer to Chapter 9).

8   Before installing the wheels, check for leakage and/or damage (cracks, splitting, etc.) around the brake hose connections. Replace the hose or fittings as necessary, referring to Chapter 9.

9   Check the rotor. Look for score marks, deep scratches and burned spots. If these conditions exist, the hub/rotor assembly should be removed for servicing.

Drum brakes

10   Remove the drum by pulling it off the axle and brake assembly. If it's stuck, make sure the parking brake is released, then squirt penetrating oil into the joint between the hub and drum. Allow the oil to soak in and try to pull the drum off again.

11   If the drum still can't be pulled off, the brake shoes will have to be retracted. This is done by first removing the dust cover from the backing plate. With the cover removed, use a small screwdriver to turn the star wheel, which will move the brake shoes away from the drum (see illustration).

12   With the drum removed, be careful not to touch any brake dust (see the Warning at the beginning of this Section).

13   Note the thickness of the lining material on both the front and rear brake shoes. If the material has worn away to within 1/16-inch of the recessed rivets or metal backing, the shoes should be replaced (see illus-

tration). The shoes should also be replaced if they're cracked, glazed (shiny surface) or contaminated with brake fluid.

14   Make sure that all the brake assembly springs are connected and in good condition.

15   Check the brake components for signs of fluid leakage. Carefully pry back the rubber cups on the wheel cylinders located at the top of the brake shoes with your finger. Any leakage is an indication that the wheel cylinders should be overhauled immediately (Chapter 9). Also check the brake hoses and connections for leakage.

16   Wipe the inside of the drum with a clean rag and brake cleaner or denatured alcohol. Again, be careful not to breath the asbestos dust.

17   Check the inside of the drum for cracks, score marks, deep scratches and hard spots, which will appear as small discolorations. If imperfections cannot be removed with fine emery cloth, the drum must be taken to a machine shop equipped to turn the drums.

18   If all parts are in good working condition, reinstall the brake drum.

19   Install the wheels and lower the vehicle.

Parking brake

20   The parking brake operates from a hand lever and locks the rear brakes. The easiest, and perhaps most obvious method of periodically checking the operation of the parking brake assembly is to park the vehicle on a steep hill with the parking brake set and the transmission in Neutral. If the parking brake cannot prevent the vehicle from rolling, it's in need of adjustment (see Chapter 9).

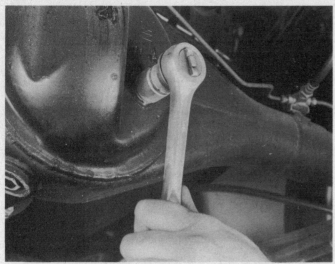

25.2 Remove the check/fill plug to check the differential lubricant level

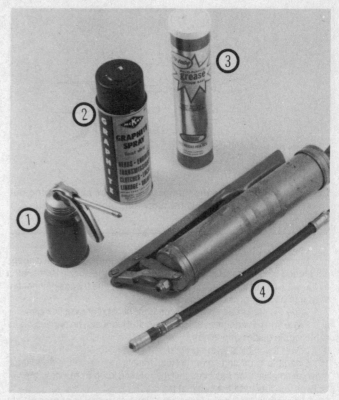

26.1 Materials required for chassis and body lubrication

24 Manual transmission lubricant level check

Refer to illustration 24.3

1 The manual transmission doesn't have a dipstick. The lubricant level is checked by removing a plug from the side of the transmission case. Locate the plug and use a rag to clean the plug and the area around it. If the vehicle is raised to gain access to the plug, be sure to support it safely on jackstands – DO NOT crawl under the vehicle when it's supported only by a jack!

2 With the engine and transmission cold, remove the plug. If lubricant immediately starts leaking out, thread the plug back into the transmission – the level is correct. If it doesn't, completely remove the plug and reach inside the hole with your little finger. The level should be even with the bottom of the plug hole.

3 If the transmission needs more lubricant, use a squeeze bottle or small pump to add it through the plug hole **(see illustration)**.

4 Thread the plug back into the transmission and tighten it securely. Drive the vehicle, then check for leaks around the plug.

25 Differential lubricant level check

Refer to illustration 25.2

1 The differential has a check/fill plug which must be removed to check the oil level. If the vehicle is raised to gain access to the plug, be sure to support it safely on jackstands – DO NOT crawl under the vehicle when it's supported only by a jack!

2 Remove the oil check/fill plug from the differential **(see illustration)**.

3 The oil level should be at the bottom of the plug opening. If not, use a syringe to add the recommended lubricant until it just starts to run out of the opening.

4 Install the plug and tighten it securely. Check for leaks after the first few miles of driving.

26 Chassis lubrication

Refer to illustrations 26.1, 26.5 and 26.6

1 A grease gun and cartridge filled with the recommended grease are the only items required for chassis lubrication other than some clean rags and equipment needed to raise and support the vehicle safely **(see illustration)**.

1 **Engine oil** – Light engine oil in a can like this can be used for door and hood hinges

2 **Graphite spray** – Used to lubricate lock cylinders

3 **Grease** – Grease, in a variety of types and weights, is available for use in a grease gun. Check the Specifications for your requirements.

4 **Grease gun** – A common grease gun, shown here with a detachable hose and nozzle, is needed for chassis lubrication. After use, clean it thoroughly!

2 For easier access under the vehicle, raise it with a jack and place jackstands under the frame. Make sure the vehicle is safely supported by the stands!

3 Locate the grease fittings on the balljoints.

4 Force a little of the grease out of the nozzle to remove any dirt from the end of the gun, then wipe it off with a rag.

5 To lubricate the suspension balljoints, remove the threaded plug and install a grease fitting in each hole **(see illustration)**

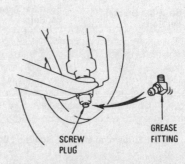

26.5 Remove the balljoint plug and install a grease fitting (1980 through 1982 models)

SCREW PLUG

GREASE FITTING

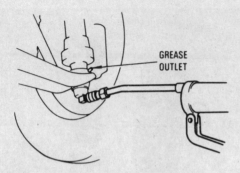

26.6   Pump grease into the fitting until it can be seen coming out the outlet (1980 through 1982 models)

6   Pump grease into the balljoints **(see illustration)**. If the grease seeps out around the gun nozzle, the fitting is clogged or the nozzle isn't seated all the way. Resecure the gun nozzle to the fitting and try again. If necessary, use another grease fitting.
7   Wipe excess grease from the components and grease fittings.
8   While you're under the vehicle, clean and lubricate the parking brake cable, cable guides and levers.
9   Lower the vehicle to the ground.
10   Open the hood and smear a little chassis grease on the hood latch mechanism. Have an assistant pull the release knob from inside the vehicle as you lubricate the cable at the latch.
11   Lubricate all the hinges (door, hood, tailgate) with a few drops of light engine oil.
12   The key lock cylinders can be lubricated with spray-on graphite, which is available at auto parts stores.

27   Chassis and body fastener check

Refer to illustration 27.1
    Tighten the following parts securely: front seat mounting bolts, front

suspension mounting bolts and the strut bar bracket bolts **(see illustration)**.

28   Clutch pedal height and freeplay check and adjustment

Refer to illustration 28.2
1   On vehicles equipped with a manual transmission, the clutch pedal height and freeplay must be correctly adjusted.
2   Clutch pedal height is the distance the pedal sits off the floor (measured from the center of the rubber pad). The distance should be as specified. If the pedal height is not within the specified range, loosen the locknut on the pedal stop and turn the stop in-or-out until the pedal height is correct **(see illustration)**. Retighten the locknut.
3   The freeplay is the pedal slack, or the distance the pedal can be depressed before it begins to have any effect on the clutch. The distance should be as specified. If it isn't, loosen the locknut on the clutch master cylinder pushrod, turn the pushrod until the freeplay is correct, then retighten the locknut.

29   Air filter replacement

1   At the specified intervals, the air filter should be replaced with a new one. A thorough program of preventive maintenance would also call for the filter to be inspected periodically between changes, especially if the vehicle is often driven in dusty conditions.

Carburetor-equipped vehicles
Refer to illustrations 29.3 and 29.4
2   The air filter is located inside the air cleaner housing, which is mounted on top of the carburetor.
3   Remove the wing nut that holds the top plate to the air cleaner body, release the clips and lift it off **(see illustration)**.
4   Lift the air filter out of the housing **(see illustration)**. If it's covered with dirt, it should be replaced.
5   Wipe out the inside of the air cleaner housing with a rag.
6   Place the old filter (if it's still in good condition) or the new filter (if replacement is necessary) into the air cleaner housing.

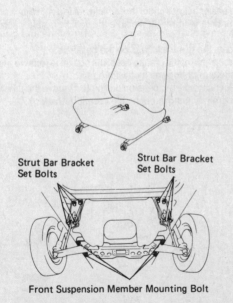

27.1   The mounting bolts for the front seats and front suspension must be periodically checked and tightened

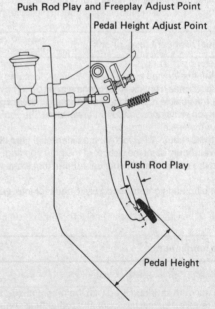

28.2   Clutch pedal height and freeplay details

29.3 Release the spring clips and remove the wing nut (arrow) to detach the air cleaner top plate, . . .

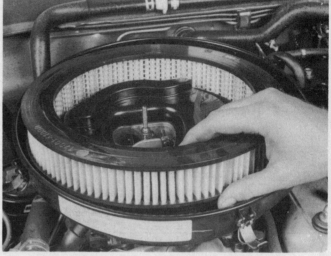

29.4 . . . then lift out the filter element

7   Reinstall the top plate on the air cleaner and make sure the arrow is aligned with the arrow on the housing. Tighten the wing nut, then snap the clips into place.

Fuel injected vehicles

Refer to illustration 29.8

8   The air filter housing is located in the front corner of the engine compartment. Release the spring clips and carefully lift up on the cover to expose the filter element **(see illustration)**.
9   Remove the filter and clean the seat area, then install the new filter. Make sure it's properly seated.
10   Reposition the cover and fasten the clips to hold it in place.

---

30   PCV valve check and replacement

Refer to illustration 30.2

1   The PCV valve is usually located in the rocker arm cover.
2   With the engine idling at normal operating temperature, pull the valve (with hose attached) out of the rubber grommet in the cover **(see illustration)**.
3   Place your finger over the valve opening. If there's no vacuum at the valve, check for a plugged hose, manifold port or valve. Replace any plugged or deteriorated hoses.
4   Turn off the engine and shake the PCV valve, listening for a rattle. If the valve doesn't rattle, replace it with a new one.
5   To replace the valve, release the clamp and pull it out of the end of the hose. Note which end is positioned in the hose.
6   When purchasing a replacement PCV valve, make sure it's for your particular vehicle and engine type. Compare the old valve with the new one to make sure they're the same.
7   Push the valve into the end of the hose until it's seated, then reposition the clamp.
8   Inspect the rubber grommet for damage and replace it with a new one if necessary.
9   Push the PCV valve and hose into the grommet until the valve is seated.

---

31   Fuel Evaporative Control (EVAP) system check

Refer to illustrations 31.3a, 31.3b, 31.3c, 31.3d and 31.3e
Note: *Refer to Chapter 6 for illustrations showing the EVAP system canister location(s).*

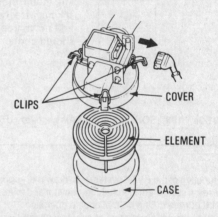

29.8 On EFI equipped vehicles, the air filter element can be removed after releasing the spring clips and pulling the housing cover up

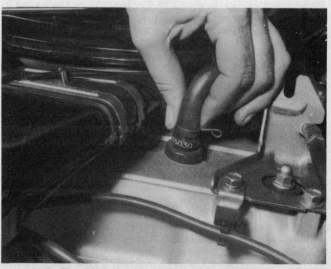

30.2 The PCV valve is located in the rocker arm cover

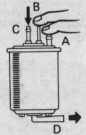

Air should flow through freely and no
charcoal should come out.

31.3a   1981 through 1985 model EVAP canister

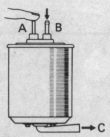

Air should flow through freely and
no charcoal should come out.

31.3b   1986 SOHC engine EVAP canister

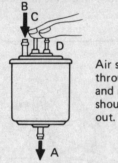

Air should flow
through freely
and no charcoal
should come
out.

31.3c   1987 SOHC engine EVAP canister (US models)

Air should flow
through freely
and no charcoal
should come
out.

31.3d   1987 SOHC engine EVAP canister (Canadian models)

1   The function of the EVAP system is to draw fuel vapors from the tank
and carburetor, store them in a charcoal canister and route them to the cylinders to be burned during normal engine operation.
2   The most common symptom of a faulty evaporative emissions system is a strong fuel odor is in the engine compartment. If a fuel odor is detected detected, inspect the canister, located in the engine compartment.
3   To perform a simple check of system operation, label and disconnect
the hoses. Inspect the canister for cracks or damage before beginning the
following tests. Check for a clogged filter and/or stuck check valve by
blowing air into the indicated pipe with no more than 43 psi and making
sure the air flows out of the tank pipe at the bottom of the canister **(see
illustrations)**.
4   The EVAP system is explained in more detail in Chapter 6.

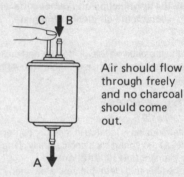

Air should flow through freely and no
charcoal should come out.

31.3e DOHC engine EVAP canister

32   Spark plug replacement

Refer to illustrations 32.2, 32.5a, 32.5b, 32.6, 32.8 and 32.10

1   Replace the spark plugs with new ones at the intervals recommended
in the Routine maintenance schedule.
2   In most cases, the tools necessary for spark plug replacement include
a spark plug socket which fits onto a ratchet (spark plug sockets are
padded inside to prevent damage to the porcelain insulators on the new
plugs), various extensions and a gap gauge to check and adjust the gaps
on the new plugs **(see illustration)**. A special plug wire removal tool is
available for separating the wire boots from the spark plugs, but it isn't absolutely necessary. A torque wrench should be used to tighten the new
plugs.

3   The best approach when replacing the spark plugs is to purchase the
new ones in advance, adjust them to the proper gap and replace them one
at a time. When buying the new spark plugs, be sure to obtain the correct
plug type for your particular engine. This information can be found on the
Emission Control Information label located under the hood and in the factory owner's manual. If differences exist between the plug specified on the
emissions label and in the owner's manual, assume the emissions label is
correct.
4   Allow the engine to cool completely before attempting to remove any
of the plugs. While you're waiting for the engine to cool, check the new
plugs for defects and adjust the gaps.

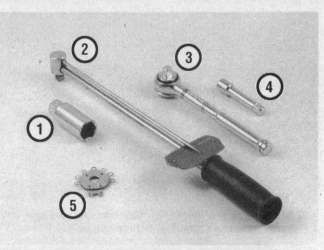

32.2 Tools required for changing spark plugs

1 **Spark plug socket** – *This will have special padding inside to protect the spark plug's porcelain insulator*
2 **Torque wrench** – *Although not mandatory, using this tool is the best way to ensure the plugs are tightened properly*
3 **Ratchet** – *Standard hand tool to fit the spark plug socket*
4 **Extension** – *Depending on model and accessories, you may need special extensions and universal joints to reach one or more of the plugs*
5 **Spark plug gap gauge** – *This gauge for checking the gap comes in a variety of styles. Make sure the gap for your engine is included.*

32.5a Spark plug manufacturers recommend using a wire-type gauge when checking the gap – if the wire doesn't slide between the electrodes with a slight drag, adjustment is required

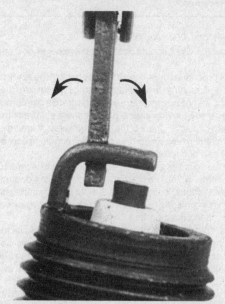

5 The gap is checked by inserting the proper thickness gauge between the electrodes at the tip of the plug **(see illustration)**. The gap between the electrodes should be the same as the one specified on the Emissions Control Information label. The wire should just slide between the electrodes with a slight amount of drag. If the gap is incorrect, use the adjuster on the gauge body to bend the curved side electrode slightly until the proper gap is obtained **(see illustration)**. If the side electrode is not exactly over the center electrode, bend it with the adjuster until it is. Check for cracks in the porcelain insulator (if any are found, the plug shouldn't be used).
6 With the engine cool, remove the spark plug wire from one spark plug. Pull only on the boot at the end of the wire – don't pull on the wire **(see illustration)**.
7 If compressed air is available, use it to blow any dirt or foreign material away from the spark plug hole. A common bicycle pump will also work. The idea here is to eliminate the possibility of debris falling into the cylinder as the spark plug is removed.
8 Place the spark plug socket over the plug and remove it from the engine by turning it in a counterclockwise direction **(see illustration)**.
9 Compare the spark plug to those shown in the photos on page 65 to get an indication of the general running condition of the engine.
10 Thread one of the new plugs into the hole until you can no longer turn it with your fingers, then tighten it with a torque wrench (if available) or the ratchet. It might be a good idea to slip a short length of rubber hose over the end of the plug to use as a tool to thread it into place **(see illustration)**. The hose will grip the plug well enough to turn it, but will start to slip if the plug begins to cross-thread in the hole – this will prevent damaged threads and the accompanying repair costs.
11 Before pushing the spark plug wire onto the end of the plug, inspect it following the procedures outlined in Section 33.
12 Attach the plug wire to the new spark plug, again using a twisting motion on the boot until it's seated on the spark plug.
13 Repeat the procedure for the remaining spark plugs, replacing them one at a time to prevent mixing up the spark plug wires.

32.5b To change the gap, bend the side electrode only, as indicated by the arrows, and be very careful not to crack or chip the porcelain insulator surrounding the center electrode

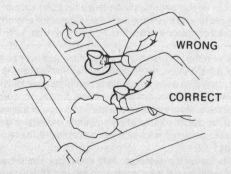

32.6 When removing the spark plug wires, grip the boot only and use a twisting/pulling motion (OHV engine shown)

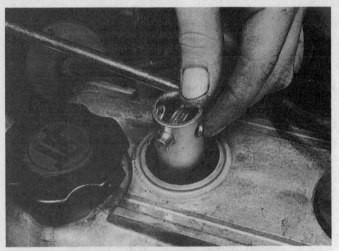

32.8   A deep socket is required when removing the spark plugs
from OHV and DOHC engines

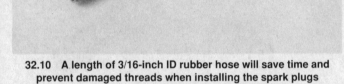

32.10   A length of 3/16-inch ID rubber hose will save time and
prevent damaged threads when installing the spark plugs

33   Spark plug wire, distributor cap and rotor check and replacement

Refer to illustrations 33.11 and 33.12

1   The spark plug wires should be checked whenever new spark plugs are installed.

2   Begin this procedure by making a visual check of the spark plug wires while the engine is running. In a darkened garage (make sure there is ventilation) start the engine and inspect each plug wire. Be careful not to come into contact with any moving engine parts. If there's a break in the wire, you'll see arcing or a small spark at the damaged area. If arcing is noticed, make a note to obtain new wires, then allow the engine to cool and check the distributor cap and rotor.

3   The spark plug wires should be inspected one at a time to prevent mixing up the order, which is essential for proper engine operation. Each original plug wire should be numbered to help identify its location. If the number is illegible, a piece of tape can be marked with the correct number and wrapped around the plug wire.

4   Disconnect the plug wire from the spark plug. A removal tool can be used or you can grasp the rubber boot with your hand, twist it back-and-forth and pull it off the plug. Don't pull on the wire **(see illustration 32.6).**

5   Check inside the boot for corrosion, which will look like a white crusty powder.

6   Push the wire and boot back onto the end of the spark plug. It should fit securely. If it doesn't, remove the wire and use pliers to carefully crimp the metal connector inside the boot until the fit is snug.

7   Using a clean rag, wipe the entire length of the wire to remove built-up dirt and grease. Once it's clean, check for burns, cracks and other damage. Do not bend the wire sharply, because the conductor might break.

8   Disconnect the wire from the distributor. Again, pull only on the rubber boot. Check for corrosion and a tight fit. Press the wire back into the distributor.

9   Check the remaining spark plug wires. Make sure each one is securely fastened at the distributor and spark plug when the check is complete.

10   If new spark plug wires are required, purchase a set for your specific engine model. Pre-cut wire sets with the boots already installed are available. Install the wires one at a time to avoid mix-ups in the firing order.

11   Detach the distributor cap by prying off the two retaining clips. Look inside it for cracks, carbon tracks and worn, burned or loose terminals **(see illustration).**

12   Pull the rotor off the distributor shaft and check it for cracks and carbon tracks **(see illustration).** On some models you'll have to remove a set screw before the rotor can be pulled off. Replace the cap and rotor if damage or defects are noted.

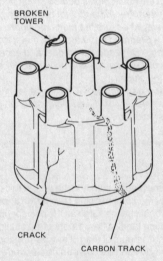

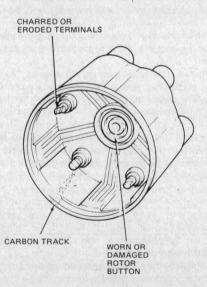

33.11   Shown here are some of the common defects to look for
when inspecting the distributor cap (if in doubt about its
condition, buy a new one)

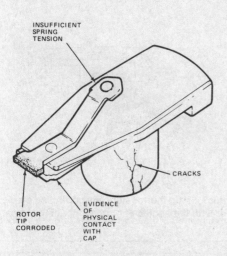

33.12   The ignition rotor should be checked for wear and corrosion as indicated here (if in doubt about its condition, buy a new one)

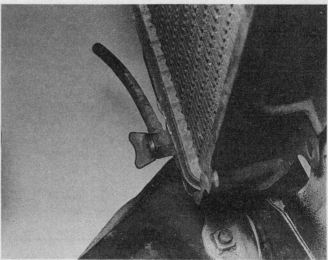

34.4   The drain fitting is located at the bottom of the radiator – before opening the valve, push a short section of 3/8-inch ID hose onto the fitting to prevent the coolant from splashing as it drains

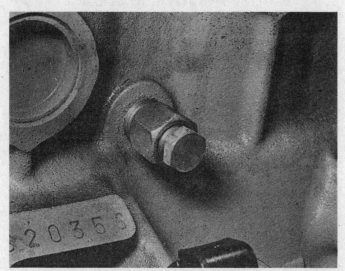

34.5   The engine block coolant drain plug is located on the left side, near the oil filter

13   It's common practice to install a new cap and rotor whenever new spark plug wires are installed, but if you reinstall the old cap, clean the terminals first.

14   When installing a new cap, remove the wires from the old cap one at a time and attach them to the new cap in the exact same location – do not remove all the wires from the old cap at the same time or firing order mixups may occur.

34   Cooling system servicing (draining, flushing and refilling)

Refer to illustrations 34.4 and 34.5

Warning: Antifreeze is a corrosive and poisonous solution, so be careful not to spill any of the coolant mixture on the vehicle's paint or your skin. If you do, rinse it off immediately with plenty of clean water. NEVER leave antifreeze lying around in an open container or in a puddle in the driveway or on the garage floor. Children and pets are attracted by it's sweet smell. Antifreeze is fatal if ingested. Consult local authorities regarding proper disposal of antifreeze before draining the cooling system. In many areas, reclamation centers have been established to collect used oil and coolant mixtures.

1   The cooling system should periodically be drained, flushed and re-filled to replenish the antifreeze mixture and prevent formation of rust and corrosion, which can impair the performance of the cooling system and cause engine damage. When the cooling system is serviced, all hoses and the radiator cap should be checked and replaced if necessary.

2   Apply the parking brake and block the wheels. If the vehicle has just been driven, wait several hours to allow the engine to cool down before beginning this procedure.

3   Once the engine is completely cool, remove the radiator cap. Place the heater temperature control in the maximum heat position.

4   Move a large container under the radiator drain to catch the coolant, then unscrew the drain plug (a pair of pliers may be required to turn it) **(see illustration)**.

5   After the coolant stops flowing out of the radiator, move the container under the engine block drain plug **(see illustration)**. Remove the plug and allow the coolant in the block to drain.

6   While the coolant is draining, check the condition of the radiator hoses, heater hoses and clamps (refer to Section 12 if necessary).

7   Replace any damaged clamps or hoses.

8   Once the system is completely drained, flush the radiator with fresh water from a garden hose until it runs clear at the drain. The flushing action of the water will remove sediments from the radiator but will not remove rust and scale from the engine and cooling tube surfaces.

9   These deposits can be removed with a chemical cleaner. Follow the procedure outlined in the manufacturer's instructions. If the radiator is severely corroded, damaged or leaking, it should be removed (Chapter 3) and taken to a radiator repair shop.

10   Remove the overflow hose from the coolant recovery reservoir. Drain the reservoir and flush it with clean water, then reconnect the hose.

11   Reinstall and tighten the radiator drain plug. Install and tighten the block drain plug(s).

12   Slowly add new coolant (a 50/50 mixture of water and antifreeze) to the radiator until it's full. Add coolant to the reservoir up to the lower mark.

13   Leave the radiator cap off and run the engine in a well-ventilated area until the thermostat opens (coolant will begin flowing through the radiator and the upper radiator hose will become hot).

14   Turn the engine off and let it cool. Add more coolant mixture to bring the level back up to the lip on the radiator filler neck.

15   Squeeze the upper radiator hose to expel air, then add more coolant mixture if necessary. Replace the radiator cap.

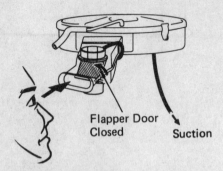

35.5   Position of the thermostatically controlled air cleaner flapper door with the engine cold

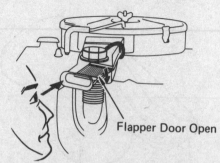

35.6   Position of the thermostatically controlled air cleaner flapper door with the engine at normal operating temperature

16   Start the engine, allow it to reach normal operating temperature and check for leaks.

35   Thermostatic air cleaner check

Refer to illustrations 35.5 and 35.6

1   All models are equipped with a thermostatically controlled air cleaner, which draws air to the carburetor from different locations depending on engine temperature.
2   This is a simple visual check. However, if access is tight, a small mirror may have to be used.
3   Open the hood and find the air control valve (flapper door) in the air cleaner assembly. It's located inside the long snorkel portion of the air cleaner housing.
4   If there's a flexible air duct attached to the end of the snorkel, disconnect it so you can look through the end of the snorkel and see the flapper door inside. A mirror may be needed if you can't safely look directly into the end of the snorkel.
5   The check should be done when the engine and outside air are cold. Start the engine and watch the flapper door, which should move up and close off the snorkel air passage **(see illustration)**. With the door closed, air can't enter through the end of the snorkel, but instead enters the air cleaner through the hot air duct attached to the exhaust manifold.
6   As the engine warms up to operating temperature, the door should open to allow air through the snorkel end **(see illustration)**. Depending on outside air temperature, this may take 10 to 15 minutes. To speed up the check you can reconnect the snorkel air duct, drive the vehicle and then check the position of the flapper door.
7   If the thermostatic air cleaner isn't operating properly, see Chapter 6 for more information.

36   Carburetor choke check

Refer to illustration 36.3

1   The choke only operates when the engine is cold, so this check should be done before the engine has been started for the day.
2   Open the hood and remove the top plate from the air cleaner assembly. It's held in place by a wing nut at the center and several spring clips around the edge. If any vacuum hoses must be disconnected, tag them to ensure reinstallation in their original locations.
3   Look at the center of the air cleaner housing. You'll notice a flat plate at the carburetor opening **(see illustration)**.
4   Have an assistant press the accelerator to the floor. The plate should close completely. Start the engine while watching the plate at the carbure-

tor. Don't position your face near the carburetor, as the engine could back-fire, causing serious burns! When the engine starts, the choke plate should open slightly.
5   Allow the engine to continue running at an idle speed. As the engine warms up to operating temperature, the plate should slowly open, allowing more air to enter through the top of the carburetor.
6   After a few minutes, the choke plate should be completely open to the vertical position. Blip the throttle to make sure the fast idle cam disengages.
7   You'll notice that engine speed corresponds to the plate opening. With the plate closed, the engine should run at fast idle. As the plate opens and the throttle is moved to disengage the fast idle cam, the engine speed will decrease.
8   With the engine off and the throttle held half-way open, open and close the choke several times. Check the linkage to see if it's hooked up correctly and make sure it doesn't bind.
9   If the choke or linkage binds, sticks or works sluggishly, clean it with choke cleaner (an aerosol spray available at auto parts stores). If the condition persists after cleaning, replace the troublesome parts.
10   Visually inspect all vacuum hoses to be sure they're securely connected and look for cracks and deterioration. Replace hoses as necessary.
11   If the choke fails to operate normally, but no mechanical causes can be found, refer to Chapter 4.

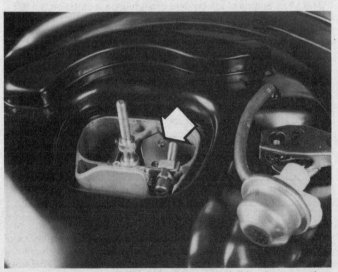

36.3   The carburetor choke plate (arrow) is visible after removing the air cleaner top plate

Common spark plug conditions

NORMAL

Symptoms: Brown to grayish-tan color and slight electrode wear. Correct heat range for engine and operating conditions.
Recommendation: When new spark plugs are installed, replace with plugs of the same heat range.

WORN

Symptoms: Rounded electrodes with a small amount of deposits on the firing end. Normal color. Causes hard starting in damp or cold weather and poor fuel economy.
Recommendation: Plugs have been left in the engine too long. Replace with new plugs of the same heat range. Follow the recommended maintenance schedule.

CARBON DEPOSITS

Symptoms: Dry sooty deposits indicate a rich mixture or weak ignition. Causes misfiring, hard starting and hesitation.
Recommendation: Make sure the plug has the correct heat range. Check for a clogged air filter or problem in the fuel system or engine management system. Also check for ignition system problems.

ASH DEPOSITS

Symptoms: Light brown deposits encrusted on the side or center electrodes or both. Derived from oil and/or fuel additives. Excessive amounts may mask the spark, causing misfiring and hesitation during acceleration.
Recommendation: If excessive deposits accumulate over a short time or low mileage, install new valve guide seals to prevent seepage of oil into the combustion chambers. Also try changing gasoline brands.

OIL DEPOSITS

Symptoms: Oily coating caused by poor oil control. Oil is leaking past worn valve guides or piston rings into the combustion chamber. Causes hard starting, misfiring and hesitation.
Recommendation: Correct the mechanical condition with necessary repairs and install new plugs.

GAP BRIDGING

Symptoms: Combustion deposits lodge between the electrodes. Heavy deposits accumulate and bridge the electrode gap. The plug ceases to fire, resulting in a dead cylinder.
Recommendation: Locate the faulty plug and remove the deposits from between the electrodes.

TOO HOT

Symptoms: Blistered, white insulator, eroded electrode and absence of deposits. Results in shortened plug life.
Recommendation: Check for the correct plug heat range, over-advanced ignition timing, lean fuel mixture, intake manifold vacuum leaks, sticking valves and insufficient engine cooling.

PREIGNITION

Symptoms: Melted electrodes. Insulators are white, but may be dirty due to misfiring or flying debris in the combustion chamber. Can lead to engine damage.
Recommendation: Check for the correct plug heat range, over-advanced ignition timing, lean fuel mixture, insufficient engine cooling and lack of lubrication.

HIGH SPEED GLAZING

Symptoms: Insulator has yellowish, glazed appearance. Indicates that combustion chamber temperatures have risen suddenly during hard acceleration. Normal deposits melt to form a conductive coating. Causes misfiring at high speeds.
Recommendation: Install new plugs. Consider using a colder plug if driving habits warrant.

DETONATION

Symptoms: Insulators may be cracked or chipped. Improper gap setting techniques can also result in a fractured insulator tip. Can lead to piston damage.
Recommendation: Make sure the fuel anti-knock values meet engine requirements. Use care when setting the gaps on new plugs. Avoid lugging the engine.

MECHANICAL DAMAGE

Symptoms: May be caused by a foreign object in the combustion chamber or the piston striking an incorrect reach (too long) plug. Causes a dead cylinder and could result in piston damage.
Recommendation: Repair the mechanical damage. Remove the foreign object from the engine and/or install the correct reach plug.

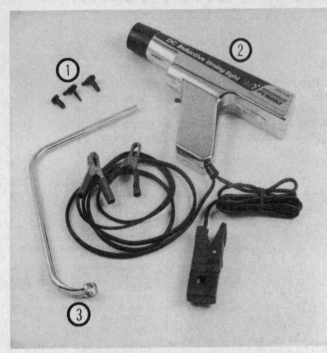

37.2   The timing plate and pulley notch (arrow) are located low on the front of the engine – be careful of moving engine parts when checking the timing!

37.1   Tools needed to check and adjust the ignition timing

1   *Vacuum plugs – Vacuum hoses will, in most cases, have to be disconnected and plugged. Molded plugs in various shapes and sizes are available for this.*
2   *Inductive pick-up timing light – Flashes a bright concentrated beam of light when the number one spark plug fires. Connect the leads according to the instructions supplied with the light.*
3   *Distributor wrench – On some models, the hold-down bolt for the distributor is difficult to reach and turn with conventional wrenches or sockets. A special wrench like this must be used.*

37   Ignition timing check and adjustment

Refer to illustrations 37.1, 37.2 and 37.9

1   The proper ignition timing setting for your vehicle is printed on the VECI label located on the under side of the hood. Some special tools will be required for this procedure **(see illustration)**.

2   Locate the timing plate on the front of the engine, near the crankshaft pulley **(see illustration)**. The 0 mark is Top Dead Center (TDC). To locate which mark the notch in the pulley must line up with for the timing to be correct, count back from the 0 mark the number of degrees BTDC (Before Top Dead Center) noted on the VECI label.
3   Locate the timing notch in the pulley and mark it with a dab of paint or chalk so it'll be visible under the strobe light. To locate the notch it may be necessary to have an assistant temporarily turn the ignition off and on in short bursts to turn the crankshaft. **Warning:** *Stay clear of all moving engine components if the engine is turned in this manner!*
4   Connect a tachometer according to the manufacturer's instructions and make sure the idle speed is correct. Adjust it if necessary as described in Section 16.
5   Allow the engine to reach normal operating temperature. Be sure the air conditioner, if equipped, is off. On some models, as noted on the VECI label, you must disconnect the distributor vacuum advance hose and plug it.
6   With the ignition switch off, connect the pick-up lead of the timing light to the number one spark plug wire – it's the front one. Use either a jumper lead between the wire and plug or an inductive-type pick up. Don't pierce the wire or attempt to insert a wire between the boot and plug wire. Connect the timing light power leads according to the manufacturer's instructions.

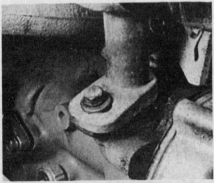

37.9   Loosen the bolt and rotate the distributor to adjust the ignition timing

38.3   Carburetor-equipped vehicle fuel filter details

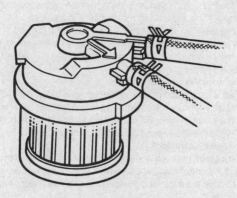

38.5   The arrow on the fuel filter indicates the outlet side (carburetor-equipped vehicles)

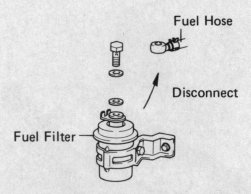

38.6   EFI fuel filter mounting details – always replace the sealing washers and tighten the banjo bolts by hand before using a wrench

1

7   Make sure the wiring for the timing light is clear of all moving engine components, then start the engine. Race the engine two or three times, then allow it to idle for a minute.

8   Point the flashing timing light at the timing marks, again being careful not to come in contact with moving parts. The marks you highlighted should appear stationary. If the marks are in alignment, the timing is correct. If the marks aren't aligned, turn off the engine.

9   Loosen the distributor bolt until the distributor can be rotated **(see illustration)**.

10   Start the engine and slowly rotate the distributor until the timing marks are aligned.

11   Shut off the engine and tighten the distributor bolt, being careful not to move the distributor.

12   Restart the engine and recheck the timing to make sure the marks are still in alignment.

13   Disconnect the timing light.

14   Race the engine two or three times, then allow it to run at idle. Recheck the idle speed with the tachometer. If it has changed from the correct setting readjust it.

15   Drive the vehicle and listen for "pinging" noises. They'll be noticeable when the engine is hot and under load (climbing a hill, accelerating from a stop). If you hear engine pinging, the ignition timing is too far advanced (Before Top Dead Center). Reconnect the timing light and turn the distributor to move the mark 1 or 2 degrees in the retard direction (counterclockwise). Road test the vehicle again to check for proper operation.

16   To keep "pinging" at a minimum, yet still allow you to operate the vehicle at the specified timing setting, use gasoline of the same octane at all times. Switching fuel brands and octane levels can decrease performance and economy, and possibly damage the engine.

38   Fuel filter replacement

Warning: *Gasoline is extremely flammable, so take extra precautions when working on any part of the fuel system. Don't smoke or allow open flames or bare light bulbs in or near the work area and don't work in a garage where a natural gas-type appliance (such as a water heater or clothes dryer) with a pilot light is present. If you spill gasoline on your skin, rinse it off immediately with soap and water. Have a fire extinguisher suitable for use on flammable liquid fires and know how to use it!*

1   This job should be done with the engine cold (after sitting at least three hours). Place a metal container, rags or newspapers under the filter to catch spilled fuel.

Carburetor-equipped vehicles
Refer to illustrations 38.3 and 38.5

2   The fuel filter is located in the engine compartment on the right (passenger) side.

3   To replace the filter, release the clamps and slide them down the hoses, past the fittings on the filter **(see illustration)**.

4   Carefully twist and pull on the hoses to separate them from the filter. If the hoses are in bad shape, now would be a good time to replace them with new ones. Slide off the old clamps and install new ones.

5   Pull the filter out of the clip and install the new one, then hook up the hoses and reposition the clamps. Note that the arrow on the filter must point in the direction of fuel flow (toward the carburetor) **(see illustration)**. Start the engine and check carefully for leaks at the filter hose connections.

Fuel injected vehicles
Refer to illustration 38.6

Warning: *Refer to Chapter 4 and depressurize the fuel system before removing the filter!*

6   Loosen the banjo bolts on both ends of the fuel filter **(see illustration)** with a box-end wrench. Disconnect both lines.

7   Remove both bracket bolts and detach the filter and the filter support bracket.

8   Remove the filter clamp bolt and separate the filter from the bracket. Note that the inlet and outlet lines are clearly labelled and the flanged end of the filter faces down.

9   Install the new filter and bracket assembly and tighten the bracket bolts securely.

10   Using the new sealing washers – two per banjo fitting – provided by the filter manufacturer, install the inlet and outlet banjo bolts and tighten them to the specified torque.

11   The remainder of installation is the reverse of the removal procedure.

39   Front wheel bearing check, repack and adjustment

Refer to illustrations 39.1, 39.6, 39.11, 39.15, 39.17, 39.19, and 39.23

1   In most cases the front wheel bearings will not need servicing until the brake pads are changed. However, the bearings should be checked whenever the front of the vehicle is raised for any reason. Several items, includ-

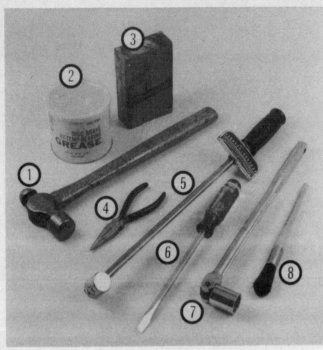

39.1   Tools and materials needed for front wheel bearing maintenance

1 **Hammer** – *A common hammer will do just fine*
2 **Grease** – *High-temperature grease which is formulated specially for front wheel bearings should be used*
3 **Wood block** – *If you have a scrap piece of 2x4, it can be used to drive the new seal into the hub*
4 **Needle-nose pliers** – *Used to straighten and remove the cotter pin in the spindle*
5 **Torque wrench** – *This is very important in this procedure; if the bearing is too tight, the wheel won't turn freely – if it's too loose, the wheel will "wobble" on the spindle. Either way, it could mean extensive damage.*
6 **Screwdriver** – *Used to remove the seal from the hub (a long screwdriver would be preferred)*
7 **Socket/breaker bar** – *Needed to loosen the nut on the spindle if it's extremely tight*
8 **Brush** – *Together with some clean solvent, this will be used to remove old grease from the hub and spindle*

ing a torque wrench and special grease, are required for this procedure **(see illustration)**.

2   With the vehicle securely supported on jackstands, spin each wheel and check for noise, rolling resistance and free play.

3   Grasp the top of each tire with one hand and the bottom with the other. Move the wheel in-and-out on the spindle. If there's any noticeable movement, the bearings should be checked and then repacked with grease or replaced if necessary.

4   Remove the wheel(s).

5   Fabricate a wood block to slide between the brake pads to keep them separated. Remove the brake caliper (Chapter 9) and hang it out of the way on a piece of wire. Be careful not to kink or stretch the brake hose.

6   Pry the grease cap out of the hub using a screwdriver or hammer and chisel **(see illustration)**.

7   Straighten the bent ends of the cotter pin, then pull the cotter pin out. Discard the cotter pin and use a new one during reassembly.

8   Remove the nut lock, adjusting nut and thrust washer from the end of the spindle.

9   Pull the hub out slightly, then push it back into its original position. This should force the outer wheel bearing off the spindle enough so it can be removed.

10   Pull the hub/disc assembly off the spindle.

11   Use a screwdriver to pry the seal out of the rear of the hub **(see illustration)**. As this is done, note how the seal is installed.

12   Remove the inner wheel bearing from the hub.

13   Use solvent to remove all traces of the old grease from the bearings, hub and spindle. A small brush may prove helpful; however make sure no bristles from the brush embed themselves inside the bearing rollers. Allow the parts to air dry.

14   Carefully inspect the bearings for cracks, heat discoloration, worn rollers, etc. Check the bearing races inside the hub for wear and damage. If the bearing races are defective, the hubs should be taken to a machine shop with the facilities to remove the old races and press new ones in. Note that the bearings and races come as matched sets and old bearings should never be installed on new races.

15   Use high-temperature front wheel bearing grease to pack the bearings. Work the grease completely into the bearings, forcing it between the rollers, cone and cage from the back side **(see illustration)**.

16   Apply a thin coat of grease to the spindle at the outer bearing seat, inner bearing seat, shoulder and seal seat.

17   Put a small quantity of grease behind each bearing race inside the hub and cap. Using your finger, form a dam at these points to provide for extra grease and to keep thinned grease from flowing out of the bearing **(see illustration)**.

18   Place the grease-packed inner bearing into the rear of the hub and put a little more grease outside of the bearing.

19   Place a new seal over the inner bearing and tap the seal evenly into

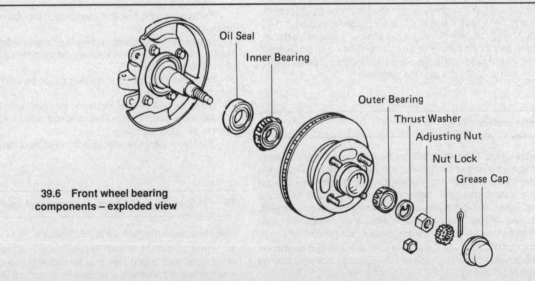

39.6   Front wheel bearing components – exploded view

Oil Seal
Inner Bearing
Outer Bearing
Thrust Washer
Adjusting Nut
Nut Lock
Grease Cap

39.11   Use a large screwdriver to pry the seal out of the rear of the hub

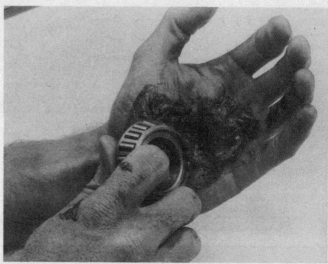

39.15   Work clean grease of the recommended type into each bearing until it's full

1

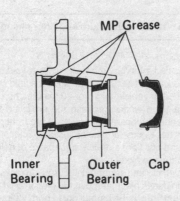

39.17   Hub lubrication details

MP Grease

Inner Bearing | Outer Bearing | Cap

39.19   Tap the seal into place with a block of wood and a hammer

place with a hammer and block of wood until it's flush with the hub **(see illustration)**.

20   Carefully place the hub assembly onto the spindle and push the grease-packed outer bearing into position.

21   Install the thrust washer and adjusting nut. Tighten the nut to the initial specified torque.

22   Spin the hub in a forward direction to seat the bearings and remove any grease or burrs which could cause excessive bearing play later.

23   On 1980 through 1983 models, unscrew the nut until it can be turned by hand. Using a socket only (do not use a ratchet or breaker bar), tighten the nut as much as possible by hand. Using a spring tension gauge, check for the specified preload **(see illustration)**. It should be 0.7 to 1.5 pounds. If the preload is incorrect, loosen or tighten the nut accordingly to obtain the specified preload. The nut should not be loosened at this point any more than one-half flat to install the new cotter pin.

24   On 1984 and later models, retighten the nut until to the specified torque. Loosen the adjusting nut until it can just be turned by hand. Attach a spring scale to one of the wheel studs and measure the force required to start the hub turning. This is the oil seal frictional drag. Record the measurement. Tighten the nut until the bearing preload is 0 to 2.3 pounds greater than the oil seal frictional drag (see illustration 39.23). The bearing preload is the force required to start the hub turning (as measured with the spring scale). The hub axial play should be less than 0.002-inch.

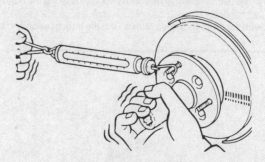

39.23   The wheel bearing preload is checked with a spring scale by pulling on the stud until the hub just starts to turn

25   Install the nut lock and a new cotter pin.

26   Bend the ends of the cotter pin until they're flat against the nut. Cut off any extra length which could interfere with the dust cap.

27   Install the grease cap. Tap it into place with a hammer.

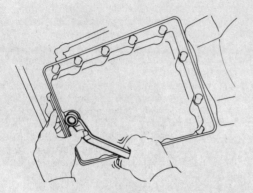

41.5   The automatic transmission fluid can be drained by removing the plug from the pan

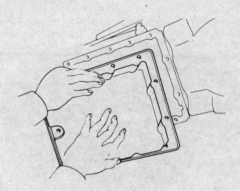

41.6   Lower the pan carefully – it'll still have some fluid in it

28   Place the brake caliper near the rotor and carefully remove the wood spacer. Install the caliper (Chapter 9).
29   Install the wheel and tighten the lug nuts.
30   Grasp the top and bottom of the tire and check the bearings in the manner described earlier in this Section.
31   Lower the vehicle.

40   Manual transmission lubricant change

1   Drive the vehicle for a few miles to thoroughly warm up the transmission oil.
2   Raise the vehicle and support it securely on jackstands.
3   Move a drain pan, rags, newspapers and a wrench under the vehicle. With the drain pan and newspapers in position under the transmission, use the wrench to remove the check/fill plug from the side of the transmission **(see illustration 24.3)**. Loosen the drain plug located in the bottom of the transmission case.
4   Carefully unscrew the plug with your fingers. Allow all of the lubricant to drain into the pan. If the plug is too hot to touch, use the wrench to remove it.
5   If the transmission is equipped with a magnetic drain plug, see if there are bits of metal clinging to it. If there are, it's a sign of excessive internal wear, indicating the transmission should be carefully inspected in the near future. If the transmission isn't equipped with a magnetic drain plug, allow the oil in the pan to cool, then feel with your hands along the bottom of the drain pan for debris.
6   Clean the drain plug, then reinstall it in the transmission and tighten it

securely.
7   Using a hand pump or syringe, fill the transmission with the correct amount and type of lubricant (see the Specifications), until the level is just at the bottom of the plug hole (see Section 24).
8   Reinstall the check/fill plug and tighten it securely.

41   Automatic transmission fluid and filter change

Refer to illustrations 41.5, 41.6, 41.7 and 41.8
1   At the specified intervals, the transmission fluid should be drained and replaced and a new filter installed. Since the fluid should be hot when it's drained, drive the vehicle for 15 or 20 minutes before proceeding.
2   Before beginning work, purchase the specified transmission fluid (see Recommended lubricants and fluids at the front of this Chapter).
3   Other tools necessary for this job include jackstands to support the vehicle in a raised position, a drain pan capable of holding at least eight pints, newspapers and clean rags.
4   Raise the vehicle and support it securely on jackstands.
5   With a drain pan in place, remove the plug and let the fluid drain into the pan **(see illustration)**. Be careful not to burn yourself on anything – it would be wise to wear gloves.
6   Remove the bolts and detach the transmission pan and filler tube **(see illustration)**. Discard the gasket. If the pan must be pried off, be very careful not to distort the pan or damage the transmission gasket surface!
7   Carefully pry the tubes loose with a screwdriver **(see illustration)**.
8   Remove the bolts and detach the filter/strainer from the transmission **(see illustration)**.

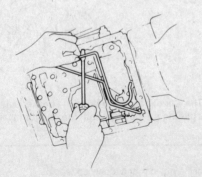

41.7   Use a screwdriver to carefully pry the tubes loose (later models)

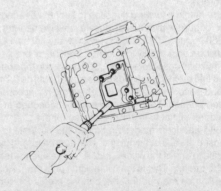

41.8   The filter is held in place with several bolts

9   Install the new filter/strainer and tighten the bolts securely, then press the tubes into place very carefully by hand only.

10   Carefully clean the gasket surface of the transmission to remove all traces of the old gasket and sealant.

11   Drain the fluid from the transmission pan, clean it with solvent and dry it with compressed air.

12   Apply a thin layer of RTV sealant to the transmission case side of the new gasket.

13   Make sure the gasket surface on the transmission pan is clean, then apply a thin layer of RTV sealant to it and position the new gasket on the pan. Put the pan in place against the transmission, install the bolts and, working around the pan, tighten each bolt a little at a time until the final torque is reached.

14   Lower the vehicle and add new automatic transmission fluid through the filler tube (Section 5). The amount should be equal to the amount of fluid that was drained (you don't want to overfill it).

15   With the transmission in Park and the parking brake set, run the engine at a fast idle, but don't race it.

16   Move the gear selector through each range and back to Park, then check the fluid level (Section 5). Add more fluid as required.

17   Check under the vehicle for leaks during the first few miles of driving.

42   Differential lubricant change

1   Drive the vehicle for several miles to warm up the differential oil, then raise the vehicle and support it securely on jackstands.

2   Move a drain pan, rags, newspapers and a wrench under the vehicle.

3   With the drain pan under the differential, use the wrench to loosen the drain plug. It's the lower of the two plugs **(see illustration 25.2)**.

4   Once loosened, carefully unscrew it with your fingers until you can remove it from the case.

5   Allow all of the lubricant to drain into the pan, then replace the drain plug and tighten it securely.

6   Feel with your hands along the bottom of the drain pan for any metal bits that may have come out with the lubricant. If there are any, it's a sign of excessive wear, indicating that the internal components should be carefully inspected in the near future.

7   Remove the differential check/fill plug (see Section 25). Using a hand pump, syringe or funnel, fill the differential with the correct amount and type of lubricant (see the Specifications) until the level is just at the bottom of the plug hole.

8   Reinstall the plug and tighten it securely.

9   Lower the vehicle. Check for leaks at the drain plug after the first few miles of driving.

43   Fuel tank cap gasket replacement

Refer to illustrations 43.2a and 43.2b

1   Obtain a new gasket.

2   Remove the tank cap, remove the screws (early model) and pry the gasket out of the recess **(see illustrations)**. Be careful not to damage the sealing surface inside the cap.

3   Install the new gasket.

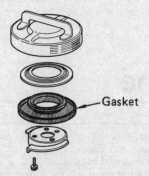

43.2a   **Early model fuel tank cap details**

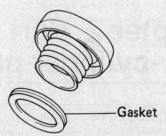

43.2b   **On later models the gasket can simply be pried out of the groove and a new one pressed in**

Chapter 2 Part A
Four-cylinder pushrod engine

Contents

Specifications

General

Displacement	1.8 liters
Cylinder numbers (front-to-rear)	1–2–3–4
Firing order	1-3-4-2
Compression	
Standard	164 psi
Minimum	128 psi

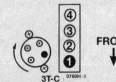

Cylinder location and distributor rotation

Camshaft

Lobe height	
USA	
Intake	1.5295 to 1.5335 in (38.85 to 38.95 mm)
Exhaust	1.5059 to 1.5098 in (38.25 to 38.35 mm)
Canada	
Intake	1.5102 to 1.5142 in (38.36 to 38.46 mm)
Exhaust	1.5059 to 1.5098 in (38.25 to 38.35 mm)
Thrust clearance (end play)	0.012 in (0.3 mm) maximum
Journal-to-bearing (oil) clearance	0.0010 to 0.0026 in (0.025 to 0.066 mm)
Journal out-of-round limit	0.0024 in (0.06 mm)
Journal diameter (journals numbered from front-to-rear of engine)	
No. 1	1.8291 to 1.8297 in (46.459 to 46.475 mm)
No. 2	1.8192 to 1.8199 in (46.209 to 45.975 mm)
No. 3	1.8094 to 1.8100 in (45.959 to 45.975 mm)
No. 4	1.7996 to 1.8002 in (45.709 to 45.725 mm)
No. 5	1.7897 to 1.7904 in (45.459 to 45.475 mm)

Torque specifications

	Ft-lbs (unless otherwise indicated)
Camshaft sprocket bolt	51 to 79
Camshaft thrust plate-to-block bolts	96 to 132 in-lbs
Crankshaft pulley bolt	55 to 75
Cylinder head/rocker arm assembly bolts	62 to 68
Exhaust manifold-to-cylinder head nuts	22 to 32
Flywheel bolts	42 to 47
Intake manifold-to-cylinder head bolts	14 to 18
Oil pan mounting bolts	44 to 69 in-lbs
Oil pump bolts	13 to 18

2A

1   General information

This Part of Chapter 2 is devoted to in-vehicle repair procedures for the 1.8 liter four-cylinder pushrod (3T-C) engine. Information concerning engine removal and installation, as well as engine block and cylinder head overhaul, is in Part C of this Chapter.

The following repair procedures are based on the assumption the engine is installed in the vehicle. If the engine has been removed from the vehicle and mounted on a stand, many of the steps included in this Part of Chapter 2 will not apply.

The Specifications included in this Part of Chapter 2 apply only to the engine and procedures in this Part. The Specifications necessary for rebuilding the block and cylinder head are found in Part C.

2   Repair operations possible with the engine in the vehicle

Many major repair operations can be accomplished without removing the engine from the vehicle.

Clean the engine compartment and the exterior of the engine with some type of pressure washer before any work is done. A clean engine will make the job easier and will help keep dirt out of the internal areas of the engine.

Depending on the components involved, remove the hood to improve access to the engine as repairs are performed (refer to Chapter 11 if necessary).

If vacuum, exhaust, oil or coolant leaks develop, indicating a need for gasket or seal replacement, the repairs can generally be made with the engine in the vehicle. The intake and exhaust manifold gaskets, oil pan gasket and cylinder head gasket are all accessible with the engine in place.

Exterior engine components such as the intake and exhaust manifolds, the oil pan (and the oil pump), the water pump, the starter motor, the alternator, the distributor and the carburetor or fuel injection components can be removed for repair with the engine in place.

Since the cylinder head can be removed without pulling the engine, valve component servicing can also be accomplished with the engine in the vehicle.

In extreme cases caused by a lack of necessary equipment, repair or replacement of piston rings, pistons, connecting rods and rod bearings is possible with the engine in the vehicle. However, this practice is not recommended because of the cleaning and preparation work that must be done to the components involved.

3   Top Dead Center (TDC) for number one piston – locating

Refer to illustration 3.8

Note: *The following procedure is based on the assumption the distributor is correctly installed. If you're trying to locate TDC to install the distributor correctly, piston position must be determined by feeling for compression at the number one spark plug hole, then aligning the ignition timing marks as described in Step 8.*

1   Top Dead Center (TDC) is the highest point in the cylinder that each piston reaches as it travels up-and-down when the crankshaft turns. Each piston reaches TDC on the compression stroke and again on the exhaust stroke, but TDC generally refers to piston position on the compression stroke.

2   Positioning the piston(s) at TDC is an essential part of many procedures such as rocker arm removal, camshaft and timing chain/sprocket removal and distributor removal.

3   Before beginning this procedure, be sure to place the transmission in Neutral and apply the parking brake or block the rear wheels. Also, remove the spark plugs (see Chapter 1) and disable the ignition system. On ignition systems with the ignition coil mounted separately from the distributor, detach the coil wire from the center terminal of the distributor cap and ground it on the block with a jumper wire.

4   To bring any piston to TDC, the crankshaft must be turned using one of the methods outlined below. When looking at the front of the engine, normal crankshaft rotation is clockwise.

   a) The preferred method is to turn the crankshaft with a socket and ratchet attached to the bolt threaded into the front of the crankshaft.
   b) A remote starter switch, which may save some time, can also be used. Follow the instructions included with the switch. Once the piston is close to TDC, use a socket and ratchet, as described in the previous Paragraph.

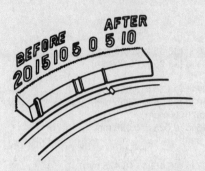

3.8   Turn the crankshaft clockwise until the notch aligns with the 0 mark

c)   If an assistant is available to turn the ignition switch to the Start position in short bursts, you can get the piston close to TDC without a remote starter switch. Make sure your assistant is out of the vehicle, away from the ignition switch, then use a socket and ratchet (as described in Paragraph a) to complete the procedure.

5   Note the position of the terminal for the number one spark plug wire on the distributor cap. If the terminal isn't marked, follow the plug wire from the number one cylinder spark plug to the cap.

6   Use a felt-tip pen or chalk to make a mark on the distributor body directly under the terminal.

7   Detach the cap from the distributor and set it aside (see Chapter 1 if necessary).

8   Turn the crankshaft (see Paragraph 3 above) until the notch in the crankshaft pulley is aligned with the 0 on the timing plate (located at the front of the engine) **(see illustration)**.

9   Look at the distributor rotor – it should be pointing directly at the mark you made on the distributor body. If it is, go to Step 12.

10   If the rotor is 180-degrees off, the number one piston is at TDC on the exhaust stroke. Go to Step 11.

11   To get the piston to TDC on the compression stroke, turn the crankshaft one complete turn (360-degrees) clockwise. The rotor should now be pointing at the mark on the distributor. When the rotor is pointing at the number one spark plug wire terminal in the distributor cap and the ignition timing marks are aligned, the number one piston is at TDC on the compression stroke.

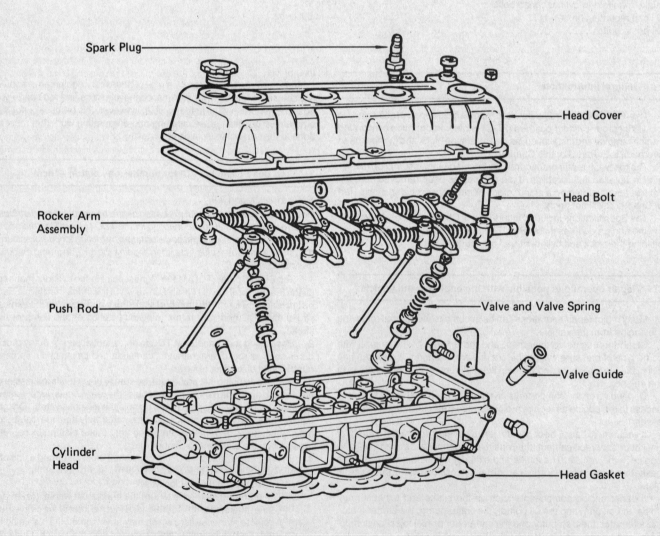

4.4a   Rocker arm cover, rocker arm assembly and related components – exploded view

4.4b   Lift the rocker arm cover off the cylinder head

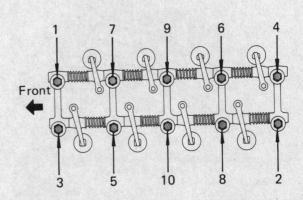

5.2   To prevent cylinder head distortion, loosen the cylinder head bolts in the order shown here

12   After the number one piston has been positioned at TDC on the compression stroke, TDC for any of the remaining pistons can be located by turning the crankshaft and following the firing order. Mark the remaining spark plug wire terminal locations on the distributor body just like you did for the number one terminal, then number the marks to correspond with the cylinder numbers. As you turn the crankshaft, the rotor will also turn. When it's pointing directly at one of the marks on the distributor, the piston for that particular cylinder is at TDC on the compression stroke.

4   Rocker arm cover – removal and installation

Refer to illustrations 4.4a and 4.4b
1   Disconnect the negative cable from the battery.
2   Remove the air cleaner (see Chapter 4).

5.3   Remove the retaining clips to disassemble the rocker arm shaft components

3   Label and remove all hoses and/or wires necessary to provide clearance for rocker arm cover removal.
4   Remove the rocker arm cover bolts **(see illustrations)** and lift off the cover. The cover may stick to the cylinder head – if it does, use a rubber hammer to jar it loose. Separate the rocker arm cover gasket with a putty knife or razor blade.
5   Prior to installation, remove all traces of dirt, oil and old gasket material from the cover and cylinder head with a scraper. Clean the mating surfaces with lacquer thinner or acetone and a clean rag.
6   Check the gasket mating surface on the cover for damage and distortion. If it's deformed, support it on a block of wood and flatten the flange with a hammer.
7   Place the rocker arm cover on the cylinder head while the sealant (if used) is still wet and install the mounting bolts. Tighten the bolts a little at a time until the specified torque is reached.
8   Complete the installation procedure by reversing the removal procedure.
9   Start the engine and check for oil leaks.

5   Rocker arm assembly and pushrods – removal, inspection and installation

Refer to illustrations 5.2, 5.3, 5.4, 5.5, 5.11, 5.12 and 5.13

Removal
Note: *The bolts that hold the rocker arm shaft assembly to the cylinder head also attach the head to the block; when the rocker arm shaft assembly is removed, the pressure on the head gasket is relieved. To avoid head gasket leaks, it's a good idea to remove the head and install a new gasket each time the rocker arm shaft assembly is removed for any reason (see Section 9).*

1   Detach the rocker arm cover (Section 4).
2   Beginning at the front of the cylinder head, loosen the head bolts in 1/4-turn increments until they can be removed by hand. Follow the recommended sequence **(see illustration)**. Remove the rocker arm assembly from the head.
3   Remove the retaining clips, supports, adjusters and rocker arms **(see illustration)**. Store them in marked containers (they must be reinstalled in their original locations).

5.4   Remove the pushrods and label them to ensure installation in their original locations

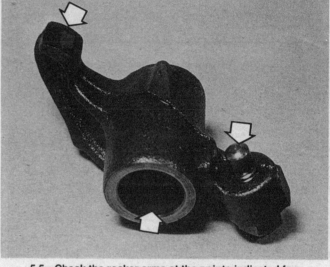

5.5   Check the rocker arms at the points indicated for excessive wear

4   Remove the pushrods and store them separately to make sure they don't get mixed up during installation **(see illustration)**.

Inspection

5   Check each rocker arm for wear, cracks and other damage, especially where the pushrods and valve stems contact the rocker arm faces **(see illustration)**.
6   Make sure the hole at the pushrod end of each rocker arm is open.
7   Check each rocker arm bushing for wear, cracks and galling. If the rocker arms are worn or damaged, replace them with new ones and check the shafts carefully as well.
8   Inspect the pushrods for cracks and excessive wear at the ends. Roll each pushrod across a piece of plate glass to see if it's bent (if it wobbles, it's bent).

Installation

9   Lubricate the lower ends of the pushrods with clean engine oil or moly-base grease and install them in their original locations. The short pushrods are for the intake valves, while the long pushrods are for the exhaust valves. Make sure each pushrod seats completely in the lifter socket.
10   Apply moly-base grease to the ends of the valve stems and the upper ends of the pushrods before installing the rocker arm assembly.

11   Assemble the rocker arm shafts so the oil circulating hole on the intake shaft (A) and the exhaust shaft (B) will be at the front of the engine **(see illustration)**. Apply moly-base grease to the rocker arm bushings.
12   Assemble the rocker shaft supports in the correct locations **(see illustration)**.
13   Set the rocker arm assembly in place and make sure the F mark faces the front of the engine **(see illustration)**. Tighten the cylinder head bolts (they hold the rocker arm shaft assembly in place) to the torque listed in this Chapter's Specifications.
14   Reinstall the rocker arm cover and run the engine. Check for oil leaks and unusual valve train noises.

6   Valve springs, retainers and seals – replacement

Since the cylinder head bolts must be removed to detach the rocker arm assembly to get at the valves for spring and seal replacement, it doesn't make sense to leave the head on the engine for these procedures. To do the job right, refer to Chapter 2, Part C, for the cylinder head disassembly and reassembly procedures if valve stem seals or springs must be replaced.

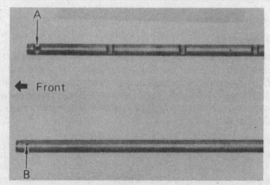

5.11   Make sure the oil hole in the shaft faces forward

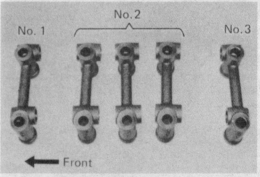

5.12   The rocker arm shaft supports must be assembled in the correct order

5.13 The rocker arm shaft support with the F mark (arrow) must face the front of the engine

7 Intake manifold – removal and installation

Refer to illustrations 7.7 and 7.8

1 Disconnect the negative cable from the battery.
2 Drain the cooling system (see Chapter 1).
3 Disconnect the throttle cable from the carburetor and remove the carburetor (see Chapter 4).
4 Label and then disconnect any wiring, hoses and control cables still connected to the intake manifold.
5 Unbolt the power steering pump (if equipped), and set it aside without disconnecting the hoses (see Chapter 10).
6 Disconnect the throttle valve (TV) cable, if equipped with an automatic transmission (see Chapter 7).
7 Remove the intake manifold bolts **(see illustration)**. Pull the manifold away from the engine slightly to disengage it from the dowel pins in the cylinder head, then lift the manifold off the engine. If the manifold sticks after all the bolts are removed, tap it with a soft-face hammer or a block of wood and a hammer to break the gasket seal (support it as this is done).

7.8 Remove the old intake manifold gasket with a scraper – don't leave any material on the mating surfaces

7.7 Remove the intake manifold bolts (cylinder head removed for clarity)

8 Remove all traces of old gasket material and sealant with a scraper **(see illustration)**, then clean the manifold and head mating surfaces with lacquer thinner or acetone.
9 If the manifold is being replaced, transfer all fittings to the new one.
10 Position the replacement gasket on the cylinder head and install the manifold.
11 Install the intake manifold bolts and tighten them in 1/4-turn increments to the torque listed in this Chapter's Specifications.
12 Reinstall the remaining parts in the reverse order of removal.
13 Run the engine and check for vacuum leaks and proper operation.

8 Exhaust manifold – removal and installation

Refer to illustration 8.5
Warning: *Allow the engine to cool completely before beginning this procedure.*

1 Raise the vehicle and support it on jackstands.
2 Remove the two nuts and bolts that secure the exhaust pipe to the exhaust manifold. You may have to apply penetrating oil to the threads.
3 Remove the hot air shroud from the exhaust manifold.
4 Remove the oxygen sensor (see Chapter 6).
5 Remove the mounting nuts and washers **(see illustration)** and detach the exhaust manifold from the engine.
6 Remove all traces of old gasket material with a scraper, then clean the manifold and head mating surfaces with lacquer thinner or acetone.
7 Reinstall the exhaust manifold.
8 Tighten the nuts in 1/4-turn increments to the torque listed in this Chapter's Specifications.
9 Reinstall the remaining components in the reverse order of removal.
10 Run the engine and check for exhaust leaks.

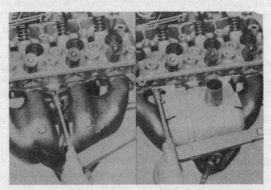

8.5 Remove the hot air shroud and the exhaust manifold mounting nuts

2A

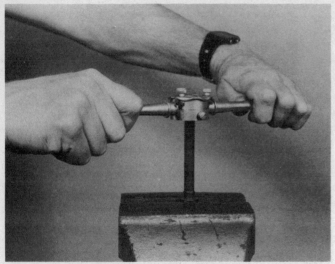

9.12   A die should be used to remove sealant and corrosion from the head bolt threads

9.15   Be sure the cylinder head gasket is properly installed so it doesn't block any coolant passages (circle)

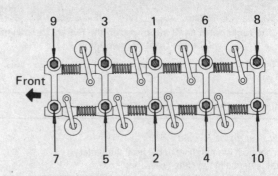

9.17   Cylinder head bolt/nut tightening sequence

---

9   Cylinder head – removal and installation

Refer to illustrations 9.12, 9.15 and 9.17

Warning: *Allow the engine to cool completely before beginning this procedure.*

Removal

1   Remove the rocker arm assembly and pushrods (see Section 5).
2   Remove the intake and exhaust manifolds (Sections 7 and 8).
3   Remove the drivebelt(s) and idler pulley bracket as described in Chapter 1.
4   Unbolt the power steering pump (if equipped) and tie it aside without disconnecting the hoses.
5   On air conditioned models, unbolt the compressor bracket from the engine. Set the compressor aside without disconnecting the hoses.
6   Label and disconnect the wire from the coolant temperature sending unit on the cylinder head.
7   Label the spark plug wires and remove the spark plugs.
8   Remove the bypass hose from the coolant outlet housing and the heater hose from the rear of the cylinder head.
9   Disconnect the hose from the air injection manifold.
10   Disconnect the solenoid valve connector, canister hose and any emission hoses that will hinder the removal of the cylinder head.
11   Lift the head off the engine (the bolts that hold the rocker arm assembly in place also attach the head to the block). If the head is stuck to the engine block, tap it with a soft-face hammer or a block of wood and a hammer to break the seal.
12   Stuff clean shop towels into the cylinders. Remove all traces of old gasket material and sealant from the head and block. Run an appropriate size tap into the bolt holes in the cylinder head and clean the head bolt threads with a die **(see illustration)**. Make sure all bolt holes are clean and dry.
13   Inspect the cylinder head for cracks and check it for warpage. Refer to Chapter 2, Part D, for cylinder head servicing procedures.

Installation

14   Clean the bolt holes in the engine block with compressed air to insure proper torque on the head bolts.
15   Install the new head gasket. Be sure the passages from the block to the cylinder head are clear **(see illustration)**.

16   Install the pushrods (see Section 5).
17   Install the cylinder head, the rocker arm assembly and the head bolts. Tighten the bolts in 1/4-turn increments to the torque listed in this Chapter's specifications **(see illustration)**.
18   Install the remaining components in the reverse order of removal.
19   Change the oil and filter (see Chapter 1).
20   Refill the cooling system and run the engine, then check for leaks and proper operation.

---

10   Lifters – removal, inspection and installation

---

1   A noisy valve lifter (which is actually just too much play in the valvetrain – lifter(s), pushrod(s), rocker arm(s), valve clearance(s), etc.) can be isolated when the engine is idling. Use a length of hose as a stethoscope on the rocker arm cover near the location of each valve. If excessive noise is heard, refer to Chapter 1 and check/adjust the valve clearances.
2   The most likely cause of a noisy valve lifter is a worn lifter or camshaft lobe.

Removal

Refer to illustration 10.6

3   Remove the rocker arm cover (see Section 4).
4   Remove the rocker arm assembly and pull out the pushrods for the cylinder with the noisy lifter (see Section 5).
5   Use a magnetic pick-up tool to remove the lifters through the pushrod openings in the cylinder head (if they won't fit through the openings, lift the head off the block first).
6   Store the lifters in an organized manner to ensure reinstallation in their original locations **(see illustration)**.

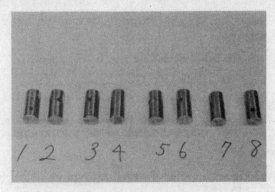

10.6   If you're removing more than one lifter, store them in an organized manner

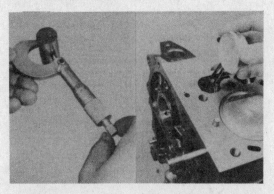

10.8   Use a micrometer to measure the diameter of each lifter (left) – measure the inside diameter of each lifter bore (right), then subtract the lifter diameter from the bore diameter to obtain the oil clearance

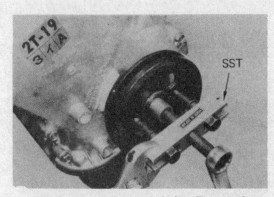

11.6   To remove the crankshaft pulley, use the special tool or an equivalent puller that attaches to the threaded holes in the hub – DO NOT use a gear puller that grips the outside of the pulley!

Inspection

Refer to illustration 10.8

7   Clean the lifters with solvent and dry them thoroughly. Do this one lifter at a time to avoid mixing them up.

8   Check each lifter wall, pushrod seat and foot for scuffing, score marks and uneven wear. Each lifter foot (the surface that rides on the cam lobe) must be slightly convex, although this can be difficult to determine by eye. If the base of the lifter is concave or rough, the lifters and camshaft must be replaced. If the lifter walls are damaged or worn (which isn't very likely), inspect the lifter bores in the engine block as well **(see illustration)**. If the pushrod seats are worn, check the pushrod ends.

9   If new lifters are being installed, a new camshaft must also be installed. If a new camshaft is installed, then use new lifters as well. Never install used lifters unless the original camshaft is used and the lifters can be installed in their original locations!

Installation

10   Used lifters must be installed in their original locations. Coat them with moly-base grease or engine assembly lube.

11   Install the lifter.

12   Install the pushrods and rocker arm assembly (see Section 5).

13   Install the rocker arm cover (see Section 4).

---

11   Crankshaft pulley – removal and installation

Refer to illustration 11.6

1   Remove the cable from the negative battery terminal.

2   Remove the drivebelts (see Chapter 1). Tag each belt as it's removed to simplify reinstallation. If the vehicle is equipped with a fan shroud, unscrew the mounting bolts and position the shroud out of the way.

3   Raise the vehicle and support it securely on jackstands.

4   If the vehicle is equipped with a manual transmission, apply the parking brake and put the transmission in gear to prevent the crankshaft from turning, then remove the drivebelt pulley bolts. If the vehicle is equipped with an automatic transmission, you may have to remove the starter motor (see Chapter 5) and immobilize the starter ring gear with a large screwdriver while an assistant loosens the bolts.

5   To loosen the large pulley-to-crankshaft bolt, install one of the drivebelt pulley bolts. Attach a breaker bar, extension and socket to the large bolt and immobilize the crankshaft by wedging a large screwdriver between the smaller bolt and the socket. Remove the large bolt.

6   Remove the crankshaft pulley. Use a puller if necessary **(see illustration)**.

7   Refer to Section 12 for the front oil seal replacement procedure.

8   Apply a thin layer of moly-base grease to the seal contact surface of the crankshaft pulley hub.

9   Slide the crankshaft pulley onto the crankshaft. The slot in the hub must be aligned with the Woodruff key in the end of the crankshaft. Once the key is aligned with the slot, tap the pulley onto the crankshaft with a soft-face hammer. The bolt can also be used to press the pulley into position.

10   Tighten the pulley-to-crankshaft bolt to the specified torque.

11   Install the drivebelt pulleys and tighten the bolts to the specified torque. Use thread locking compound on the bolt threads.

12   Install the drivebelt(s) (see Chapter 1) and replace the fan shroud (if equipped).

---

12   Crankshaft front oil seal – replacement

Note: *The crankshaft front oil seal can be replaced with the timing chain cover in place. However, due to the limited amount of room available, you may conclude the procedure would be easier if the cover were removed from the engine first. If so, refer to Section 13 for the removal and installation procedure.*

Timing chain cover in place

Refer to illustration 12.2

1   Disconnect the negative battery cable from the battery, then remove the crankshaft pulley (see Section 11).

2A

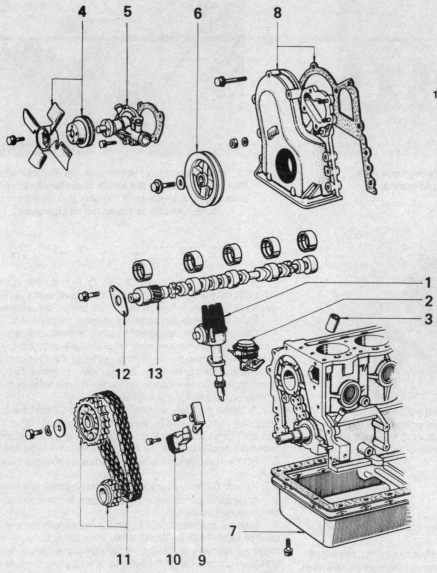

12.2   Timing chain cover and related components – exploded view

1	Distributor
2	Fuel pump and insulator
3	Lifter
4	Fan and fan pulley
5	Water pump
6	Crankshaft pulley
7	Oil pan
8	Timing chain cover and gasket
9	Chain damper
10	Chain tensioner
11	Timing chain and sprocket
12	Camshaft thrust plate
13	Camshaft

2   Note how the seal is installed – the new one must face the same direction! Carefully pry the oil seal out of the cover with a seal puller or screwdriver **(see illustration)**. Be very careful not to distort the cover or scratch the crankshaft!

3   Apply clean engine oil or multi-purpose grease to the outer edge of the new seal, then install it in the cover with the lip (open end) facing in. Drive the seal into place with a large socket and a hammer (if a large socket isn't available, a piece of pipe will also work). Make sure the seal enters the bore squarely and stop when the front face is flush with the cover.

4   Install the crankshaft pulley (see Section 11).

Timing chain cover removed

5   Remove the timing chain cover as described in Section 13.

6   If the engine has accumulated a lot of miles, apply penetrating oil to the seal-to-cover joint and allow it to soak in before attempting to remove the seal. Using a large screwdriver, pry the old seal out of the cover. Be careful not to distort the cover or scratch the wall of the seal bore.

7   Clean the bore to remove any old seal material and corrosion. Sup-

port the cover on a block of wood and position the new seal in the bore with the lip (open end) facing in. A small amount of oil applied to the outer edge of the new seal will make installation easier – don't overdo it!

8   Drive the seal into the bore with a large socket and hammer until it's completely seated. Select a socket that's the same outside diameter as the seal. A section of pipe or even a block of wood can be used if a socket isn't available).

9   Reinstall the timing chain cover.

13   Timing chain cover – removal and installation

Refer to illustration 13.6

1   Remove the crankshaft pulley (see Section 11).

2   Remove the cooling fan and hub assembly (see Chapter 3).

3   Remove the air conditioning compressor (if equipped) and the alternator bracket assembly from the cylinder head and set it aside.

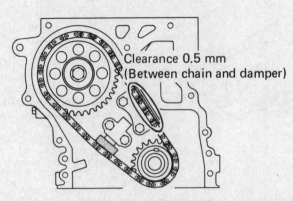

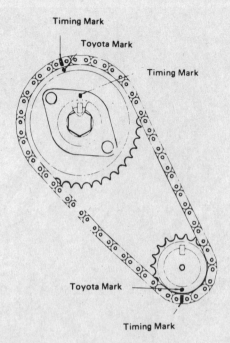

13.6 When the chain damper is installed, there should be 0.020-inch (0.5 mm) clearance between it and the chain

Clearance 0.5 mm (Between chain and damper)

Timing Mark
Toyota Mark
Timing Mark
Toyota Mark
Timing Mark

14.3 Timing mark alignment

2A

14.5 The timing chain and sprockets are removed and installed as an assembly

14.7a Align the bright chain links with the timing marks on the sprockets

4 Remove the oil pan-to-timing chain cover bolts and the timing chain cover-to-block bolts.

5 Separate the timing chain cover from the engine. To avoid damaging the sealing surfaces, do not force tools between the cover and block.

6 Use a scraper to remove all traces of old gasket material. Drive the old oil seal out from the rear of the timing chain cover and replace it with a new one (see Section 12). Also replace the timing chain damper if necessary **(see illustration)**.

7 Apply RTV sealant to both sides of the new cover gasket and position the gasket on the engine block.

8 Trim the tabs off the ends of the gasket to ensure a proper fit and apply sealant to the section of the oil pan gasket that will contact the bottom of the timing chain cover.

9 Lubricate the seal lip with moly-base grease.

10 Position the timing chain cover on the engine block.

11 Install the crankshaft pulley to center the timing chain cover.

12 Install the cover-to-block nuts and bolts and the oil pan-to-cover bolts and tighten them to the torque listed in this Chapter's Specifications.

13 Reinstall the remaining parts in the reverse order of removal.

14 Run the engine and check for oil leaks.

14 Timing chain and sprockets – removal, inspection and installation

Refer to illustrations 14.3, 14.5, 14.7a and 14.7b

1 Set the number one piston at Top Dead Center (see Section 3).

2 Remove the timing chain cover (see Section 13).

3 Reinstall the crankshaft pulley bolt and rotate the crankshaft until the zero timing mark on the crankshaft sprocket is lined up with the timing mark on the timing chain **(see illustration)**.

4 Remove the timing chain tensioner and damper.

5 Remove the camshaft sprocket bolt and slip both sprockets and the chain off as an assembly **(see illustration)**.

6 Clean the components and inspect them for wear and damage. Excessive chain slack and teeth that are deformed, chipped, pitted or discolored call for replacement. Always replace the sprockets and chain as a set. Inspect the tensioner and damper for excessive wear and replace them, if necessary.

7 Install the crankshaft/camshaft sprockets and timing chain. Make sure the marks on the sprockets are still properly aligned **(see illustrations)**.

**14.7b   Timing chain and sprockets assembled correctly
(number one piston at TDC)**

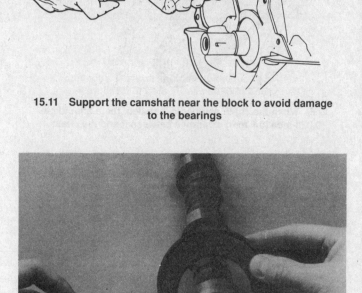

**15.11   Support the camshaft near the block to avoid damage
to the bearings**

8   Install the camshaft sprocket bolt and washer and tighten the bolt to the torque listed in this Chapter's Specifications. Install the chain tensioner and damper. Make sure there's a gap of 0.020-inch (0.5 mm) between the chain and damper **(see illustration 13.6).**

9   To verify correct installation of the timing chain, check to make sure the crankshaft keyway and the camshaft keyway are both aligned at the 12 o'clock position **(see illustration 14.7b).** This positions the crankshaft timing mark at TDC. Also see if the timing mark on the sprocket and the timing mark on the chain are properly aligned **(see illustration 14.3).**

10   Install the remaining parts in the reverse order of removal. Refer to the appropriate sections for instructions.

---

15   Camshaft and bearings – removal, inspection and installation

Removal

Refer to illustration 15.11

1   Set the number one piston at Top Dead Center (see Section 3).
2   Disconnect the negative cable from the battery.
3   Remove the radiator (see Chapter 3).
4   On models equipped with air conditioning, unbolt the air conditioning compressor and set it aside without disconnecting the refrigerant lines.
5   On carburetor-equipped models, remove the fuel pump (see Chapter 4).
6   Remove the distributor (see Chapter 5).
7   If not removed already, detach the rocker arm cover (see Section 4).
8   Remove the rocker arm assembly and pushrods (see Section 5).
9   Remove the lifters (see Section 10).
10   Remove the timing chain and sprockets. Remove the bolts and detach the camshaft thrust plate.
11   Install a bolt in the end of the camshaft to use as a handle. Carefully slide the camshaft out of the block **(see illustration). Caution:** *To avoid damage to the camshaft bearings as the lobes pass over them, support the camshaft near the block as it's withdrawn.*

**15.13   The camshaft bearing journal diameters are checked to
pinpoint excessive wear and out-of-round conditions**

Inspection

Refer to illustrations 15.13 and 15.14

12   After the camshaft has been removed from the engine, cleaned with solvent and dried, inspect the bearing journals for uneven wear, pitting and evidence of seizure. If the journals are damaged, the bearing inserts in the block are probably damaged also. Both the camshaft and bearings will have to be replaced.

13   If the bearing journals are in good condition, measure them with a micrometer **(see illustration).** Measure each journal at several locations around its circumference. If you get different measurements at different locations, the journal is out-of-round.

14   Measure the inside diameter of each camshaft bearing with an inside micrometer **(see illustration)** or a telescoping gauge and outside micrometer. Subtract each cam journal diameter from the corresponding camshaft bearing inside diameter to obtain the bearing oil clearance. Compare the clearance for each bearing to the specifications. If it's excessive, for any of the bearings, have new bearings installed by an automotive machine shop.

15   Measure each lobe to determine the height. If it isn't as specified, the lobe is worn.

16   Inspect the camshaft lobes (including the fuel pump lobe on carburetor-equipped models) for heat discoloration, score marks, chipped areas,

15.14 Use an inside micrometer (or telescoping gauge and outside micrometer) to measure the inside diameter of the camshaft bearings

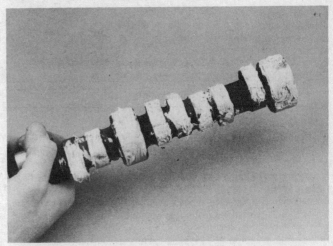

15.19 Be sure to apply moly-base grease or engine assembly lube to the cam lobes and bearing journals before installing the camshaft

15.21 The marks on the camshaft thrust plate must face out

pitting and uneven wear. If the lobes are in good condition and the lobe height measurements are as specified, the camshaft can be reused.

17 Check the distributor drive gear for wear. Replace the camshaft if the gear is worn.

Bearing replacement

18 Camshaft bearing replacement requires special tools and expertise that place it outside the scope of the home mechanic. Take the engine block (see Part C of this Chapter) to an automotive machine shop to ensure the job is done correctly.

Installation

Refer to illustrations 15.19 and 15.21

19 Lubricate the camshaft bearing journals and lobes with moly-base grease or engine assembly lube **(see illustration)**.

20 Slide the camshaft into the engine. Support the cam near the block and be careful not to scrape or nick the bearings.

21 Temporarily position the camshaft sprocket on the camshaft and turn the camshaft until the timing mark is aligned with the centerline of the crankshaft (see Section 14). Remove the sprocket. Install the thrust plate with the marked side out **(see illustration)** and tighten the bolts to the specified torque.

22 Install the timing chain and sprockets and the remaining components in the reverse order of removal. Refer to the appropriate Sections for installation instructions. **Note:** *If the original cam and lifters are being reinstalled, be sure to install the lifters in their original locations. If a new camshaft is used, be sure to install new lifters also.*

23 Add coolant and change the oil and filter (see Chapter 1).

24 Start the engine and check the ignition timing. Check for leaks and unusual noises.

2A

16 Oil pan – removal and installation

Refer to illustration 16.6

Note: *If the oil pan can't be maneuvered around enough to get it out with the engine in place, then the engine must be removed first or at least raised off the mounts with a hoist.*

1 Disconnect the cable from the negative battery terminal.

2 Raise the vehicle and support it securely on jackstands.

3 Drain the engine oil and remove the oil filter (Chapter 1).

4 Disconnect the exhaust pipe at the manifold (see Section 8) and hangers and tie it aside.

5 Remove the starter (see Chapter 5) and the bellhousing dust cover.

6 Remove the bolts and detach the oil pan **(see illustration)**. Don't pry between the block and pan or damage to the sealing surfaces may result and oil leaks could develop. If the pan is stuck, dislodge it with a soft-face hammer or a block of wood and a hammer.

7 Use a scraper to remove all traces of sealant from the pan and block, then clean the mating surfaces with lacquer thinner or acetone. If the oil pan flange is distorted, support it on a block of wood and flatten it with a hammer.

8 Using gasket sealant, position new oil pan seals and gaskets on the engine.

9 Install the oil pan and tighten the mounting bolts to the torque listed in this Chapter's specifications. Start at the center of the pan and work out toward the ends in a spiral pattern.

10 Install the bellhousing dust cover and the starter, then reconnect the exhaust pipe to the manifold and hanger brackets.

16.6 Oil pan removal (engine removed for clarity)

11   Lower the vehicle.
12   Install a new filter and add oil to the engine.
13   Reconnect the negative battery cable.
14   Start the engine and check for leaks.

17   Oil pump – removal and installation

Refer to illustrations 17.2 and 17.3

1   Remove the oil pan (see Section 16).
2   Remove the two oil pump mounting bolts from the engine block **(see illustration)**.
3   Detach the oil pump and strainer assembly from the block **(see illustration)**.
4   If the pump is defective, replace it with a new one. If the engine is being completely overhauled, install a new oil pump – don't reinstall the original or attempt to rebuild it.
5   To install the pump, turn the shaft so the gear tang mates with the slot on the lower end of the distributor drive. The oil pump should slide easily into place. If it doesn't, pull it off and turn the tang until it's aligned with the distributor drive.

17.2   Remove the oil pump mounting bolts

6   Install the pump mounting bolts. Tighten them to the torque listed in this Chapter's specifications.
7   Reinstall the oil pan (see Section 16).
8   Add oil, run the engine and check for leaks.

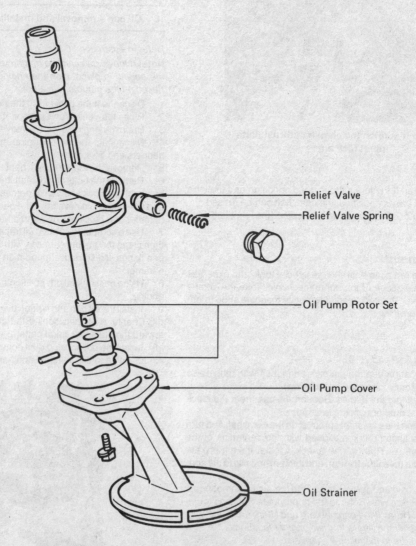

Relief Valve
Relief Valve Spring
Oil Pump Rotor Set
Oil Pump Cover
Oil Strainer

17.3   Oil pump and related components – exploded view

18.3   Before removing the flywheel, index it to the crankshaft (arrow)

18.4   To prevent the flywheel from turning, hold a pry bar against two bolts or wedge a large screwdriver into the flywheel ring gear

2A

18   Flywheel/driveplate – removal and installation

Refer to illustrations 18.3 and 18.4

1   Raise the vehicle and support it securely on jackstands, then refer to Chapter 7 and remove the transmission. If it's leaking, now would be a very good time to replace the front pump seal/O-ring (automatic transmission only).

2   Remove the pressure plate and clutch disc (see Chapter 8) (manual transmission equipped vehicles). Now is a good time to check/replace the clutch components and pilot bearing.

3   Use paint or a center punch to make alignment marks on the flywheel/driveplate and crankshaft to ensure correct alignment during reinstallation **(see illustration)**.

4   Remove the bolts that secure the flywheel/driveplate to the crankshaft. If the crankshaft turns, hold the flywheel with a pry bar or wedge a screwdriver into the ring gear teeth to jam the flywheel **(see illustration)**.

5   Remove the flywheel/driveplate from the crankshaft. Since the flywheel is heavy, be sure to support it while removing the last bolt.

6   Clean the flywheel to remove grease and oil. Inspect the clutch surface for cracks, rivet grooves, burned areas and score marks. Light score marks can be removed with emery cloth. Check for cracked and broken ring gear teeth or a loose ring gear. Lay the flywheel on a flat surface and use a straightedge to check for warpage.

7   Clean and inspect the mating surfaces of the flywheel/driveplate and crankshaft. If the crankshaft rear seal is leaking, replace it before reinstalling the flywheel/driveplate.

8   Position the flywheel/driveplate against the crankshaft. Be sure to align the marks made during removal. Note that some engines have an alignment dowel or staggered bolt holes to ensure correct installation. Before installing the bolts, apply thread locking compound to the threads.

9   Wedge a screwdriver into the ring gear teeth to keep the flywheel/driveplate from turning as you tighten the bolts to the torque listed in this Chapter's specifications

10   The remainder of installation is the reverse of the removal procedure.

19   Crankshaft rear oil seal – replacement

Refer to illustration 19.5

1   The crankshaft rear oil seal can be replaced without removing the oil pan or crankshaft.

2   Remove the transmission (see Chapter 7).

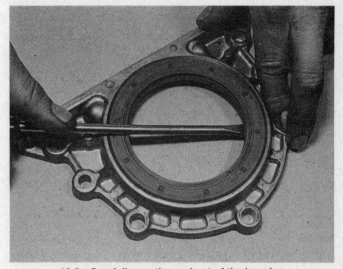

19.5   Carefully pry the seal out of the housing

3   If equipped with a manual transmission, remove the pressure plate and clutch disc (see Chapter 8).

4   Remove the flywheel or driveplate (see Section 18).

5   Remove the oil seal housing bolts and detach the housing and seal from the block. Carefully pry the seal out of the housing **(see illustration)**.

6   Clean the bore in the housing and the seal contact surface on the crankshaft. Check the crankshaft surface for scratches and nicks that could damage the new seal lip and cause oil leaks. If the crankshaft is damaged, the only alternative is a new or different crankshaft.

7   Apply a light coat of engine oil or multi-purpose grease to the outer edge of the new seal. Drive the seal squarely into the housing with a large section of pipe the same diameter as the seal and a hammer. If a piece of pipe isn't available, a large block of wood will also work.

8   Lubricate the seal lip with moly-base grease. Carefully work the seal lip over the end of the crankshaft until the housing is seated on the block. Install the bolts.

9   Install the flywheel or driveplate.

10   If equipped with a manual transmission, reinstall the clutch disc and pressure plate.

11   Reinstall the transmission as described in Chapter 7.

20   Engine mounts – check and replacement

Refer to illustration 20.8

1   Engine mounts seldom require attention, but broken or deteriorated mounts should be replaced immediately or the added strain placed on the driveline components may cause damage or wear.

Check

2   During the check, the engine must be raised slightly to remove the weight from the mounts.
3   Raise the vehicle and support it securely on jackstands, then position a jack under the engine oil pan. Place a large block of wood between the jack head and the oil pan, then carefully raise the engine just enough to take the weight off the mounts. **Warning:** *DO NOT place any part of your body under the engine when it's supported only by a jack!*
4   Check the mounts to see if the rubber is cracked, hardened or separated from the metal plates. Sometimes the rubber will split right down the center.
5   Check for relative movement between the mount plates and the engine or frame (use a large screwdriver or pry bar to attempt to move the mounts). If movement is noted, lower the engine and tighten the mount fasteners.
6   Rubber preservative should be applied to the mounts to slow deterioration.

Replacement

7   Disconnect the negative battery cable from the battery, then raise the vehicle and support it securely on jackstands (if not already done).

8   Remove the nuts from the studs that protrude from the mount (**see illustration**).
9   Raise the engine slightly with a jack or hoist (make sure the fan doesn't hit the radiator or shroud). Remove the mount.
10   Installation is the reverse of removal. Use thread locking compound on the mount nuts and be sure to tighten them securely.

20.8   Remove the nuts from the studs protruding from the mount (arrows), raise the engine and remove the mount

Chapter 2 Part B   Four-cylinder overhead camshaft (OHC) engines

Contents

Specifications

General

Engine type
  4A-C .... SOHC, two valves per cylinder
  4A-GE .... DOHC, four valves per cylinder
Cylinder numbers (front-to-rear) 1–2–3–4
Firing order 1-3-4-2

Timing belt

Idler pulley spring free length
  4A-C engine .... 1.512 in (38.4 mm)
  4A-GE engine .... 1.713 in (43.5 mm)
Timing belt deflection
  4A-C engine .... 0.24 to 0.28 in (6 to 7 mm) at 4.4 lbs
  4A-GE engine .... 0.16 in (4 mm) at 4.4 lbs

Cylinder location and distributor rotation

Camshaft

Endplay
  4A-C engine
    Standard .... 0.0031 to 0.0075 in (0.08 to 0.19 mm)
    Service limit .... 0.0118 in (0.30 mm)
  4A-GE engine
    Standard .... 0.0031 to 0.0075 in (0.08 to 0.19 mm)
    Service limit .... 0.0098 in (0.25 mm)
Bearing journal diameter
  4A-C engine .... 1.1015 to 1.1022 in (27.979 to 27.995 mm)
  4A-GE engine
    1985 .... 1.3768 to 1.3791 in (34.97 to 35.03 mm)
    1986 and 1987 .... 1.0610 to 1.0616 in (26.949 to 26.965 mm)
Bearing oil clearance
  4A-C engine
    Standard .... 0.0015 to 0.0029 in (0.037 to 0.073 mm)
    Service limit .... 0.0039 in (0.10 mm)
  4A-GE engine
    Standard .... 0.0014 to 0.0028 in (0.035 to 0.072 mm)
    Service limit .... 0.0039 in (0.10 mm)
Lobe height
  4A-C engine
    Standard (intake and exhaust) .... 1.5528 to 1.5531 in (39.44 to 39.55 mm)
    Service limit .... 1.5409 in (39.14 mm)
  4A-GE engine
    Standard (intake and exhaust) .... 1.3998 to 1.4002 in (35.555 to 35.565 mm)
    Service limit .... 1.3841 in (35.155 mm)

Valve lifters (4A-GE engine)

Diameter .... 1.1014 to 1.1018 in (27.975 to 27.985 mm)
Bore diameter .... 1.1020 to 1.1036 in (27.990 to 28.031 mm)
Oil clearance
  Standard .... 0.0006 to 0.0018 in (0.015 to 0.046 mm)
  Service limit .... 0.0039 in (0.10 mm)

Torque specifications

Ft-lbs (unless otherwise indicated)

Camshaft bearing cap bolts
  4A-C engine .... 108 in-lbs
  4A-GE engine .... 108 in-lbs
Camshaft idler pulley bolts (all) 27
Camshaft sprocket bolt
  4A-C engine 34
  4A-GE engine 34
Crankshaft pulley-to-crankshaft bolt
  4A-C engine 87
  4A-GE engine 105
Cylinder head bolts
  4A-C engine 43
  4A-GE engine 44
Exhaust manifold nuts/bolts (all) 18
Flywheel/driveplate bolts
  4A-C engine 58
  4A-GE engine 54
Intake manifold nuts/bolts
  4A-C engine 18
  4A-GE engine 20
Oil pan-to-block bolts
  4A-C engine .... 48 in-lbs
  4A-GE engine .... 43 in-lbs
Oil pump-to-block bolts (all) 18
Oil pick-up (strainer) nuts/bolts (all) .... 84 in-lbs
Rocker arm shaft (4A-C engine) 18

1 General information

This Part of Chapter 2 is devoted to in-vehicle repair procedures for the overhead cam engines. All information concerning engine removal and installation and engine block and cylinder head overhaul can be found in Part C of this Chapter.

The following repair procedures are based on the assumption the engine is installed in the vehicle. If the engine has been removed from the vehicle and mounted on a stand, many of the steps outlined in this Part of Chapter 2 will not apply.

The Specifications included in this Part of Chapter 2 apply only to the procedures contained in this Part. Part C of Chapter 2 contains the Specifications necessary for cylinder head and engine block rebuilding.

Two different overhead camshaft (OHC) engines are covered in this Chapter. One version is a dual overhead camshaft (DOHC) design and is designated 4A-GE. The other engine has a single overhead camshaft (SOHC) and is known as the 4A-C.

2 Repair operations possible with the engine in the vehicle

Many major repair operations can be accomplished without removing the engine from the vehicle.

Clean the engine compartment and the exterior of the engine with some type of degreaser before any work is done. It will make the job easier and help keep dirt out of the internal areas of the engine.

Depending on the components involved, it may be helpful to remove the hood to improve access to the engine as repairs are performed (refer to Chapter 11 if necessary). Cover the fenders to prevent damage to the paint. Special pads are available, but an old bedspread or blanket will also work.

If vacuum, exhaust, oil or coolant leaks develop, indicating a need for gasket or seal replacement, the repairs can generally be made with the engine in the vehicle. The intake and exhaust manifold gaskets, oil pan gasket, crankshaft oil seals and cylinder head gasket are all accessible with the engine in place.

Exterior engine components, such as the intake and exhaust manifolds, the oil pan, the oil pump, the water pump, the starter motor, the alternator, the distributor and the fuel system components can be removed for repair with the engine in place.

Since the cylinder head can be removed without pulling the engine, camshaft and valve component servicing can also be accomplished with the engine in the vehicle. Replacement of the timing belt and sprockets is also possible with the engine in the vehicle.

In extreme cases caused by a lack of necessary equipment, repair or replacement of piston rings, pistons, connecting rods and rod bearings is possible with the engine in the vehicle. However, this practice is not recommended because of the cleaning and preparation work that must be done to the components involved.

3 Top Dead Center (TDC) for number one piston – locating

Refer to illustrations 3.8 and 3.11

Note: *The following procedure is based on the assumption that the distributor is correctly installed. If you are trying to locate TDC to install the distributor correctly, piston position must be determined by feeling for compression at the number one spark plug hole, then aligning the ignition timing marks as described in step 8.*

1 Top Dead Center (TDC) is the highest point in the cylinder that each piston reaches as it travels up-and-down when the crankshaft turns. Each piston reaches TDC on the compression stroke and again on the exhaust stroke, but TDC generally refers to piston position on the compression stroke.

2 Positioning the piston(s) at TDC is an essential part of many procedures such as camshaft and timing belt/sprocket removal and distributor removal.

3 Before beginning this procedure, be sure to place the transmission in Neutral and apply the parking brake or block the rear wheels. Also, disable the ignition system by detaching the coil wire from the center terminal of the distributor cap and grounding it on the block with a jumper wire. Remove the spark plugs (see Chapter 1).

4 In order to bring any piston to TDC, the crankshaft must be turned using one of the methods outlined below. When looking at the drivebelt end of the engine, normal crankshaft rotation is clockwise.

   a) The preferred method is to turn the crankshaft with a socket and ratchet attached to the bolt threaded into the front of the crankshaft.

   b) A remote starter switch, which may save some time, can also be used. Follow the instructions included with the switch. Once the piston is close to TDC, use a socket and ratchet as described in the previous paragraph.

   c) If an assistant is available to turn the ignition switch to the Start position in short bursts, you can get the piston close to TDC without a remote starter switch. Make sure your assistant is out of the vehicle, away from the ignition switch, then use a socket and ratchet as described in Paragraph a) to complete the procedure.

5 Detach the cap from the distributor and set it aside (see Chapter 1 if necessary).

6 Note the position of the terminal for the number one spark plug wire on the distributor cap. If the terminal isn't marked, follow the plug wire from the number one cylinder spark plug to the cap.

7 Use a felt-tip pen or chalk to make a mark on the distributor body directly under the terminal. **Note:** *The location of the wires on the outside of the cap doesn't correspond with the inside terminals – use the position of the inside terminals for rotor alignment.*

8 Turn the crankshaft (see Paragraph 3 above) until the notch in the crankshaft pulley is aligned with the 0 on the timing scale (located at the front of the engine) **(see illustration)**.

9 Look at the distributor rotor – it should be pointing directly at the mark you made on the distributor body.

10 If the rotor is 180-degrees off, the number one piston is at TDC on the exhaust stroke.

11 If the number one piston is at TDC on the exhaust stroke, turn the crankshaft one complete turn (360-degrees) clockwise. The rotor should now be pointing at the mark on the distributor. When the rotor is pointing at the number one spark plug wire terminal in the distributor cap and the ignition timing marks are aligned, the number one piston is at TDC on the compression stroke. If it's impossible to align the ignition timing marks when the rotor is pointing at the mark on the distributor body, the distributor may be installed wrong, the timing belt may have jumped the teeth on the sprockets or may have been installed incorrectly. **Note:** *On 4A-GE engines, it is possible to verify TDC by removing the oil filler cap* **(see illustration)**.

3.8 The notch in the crankshaft pulley must be aligned with the zero on the timing scale (arrows)

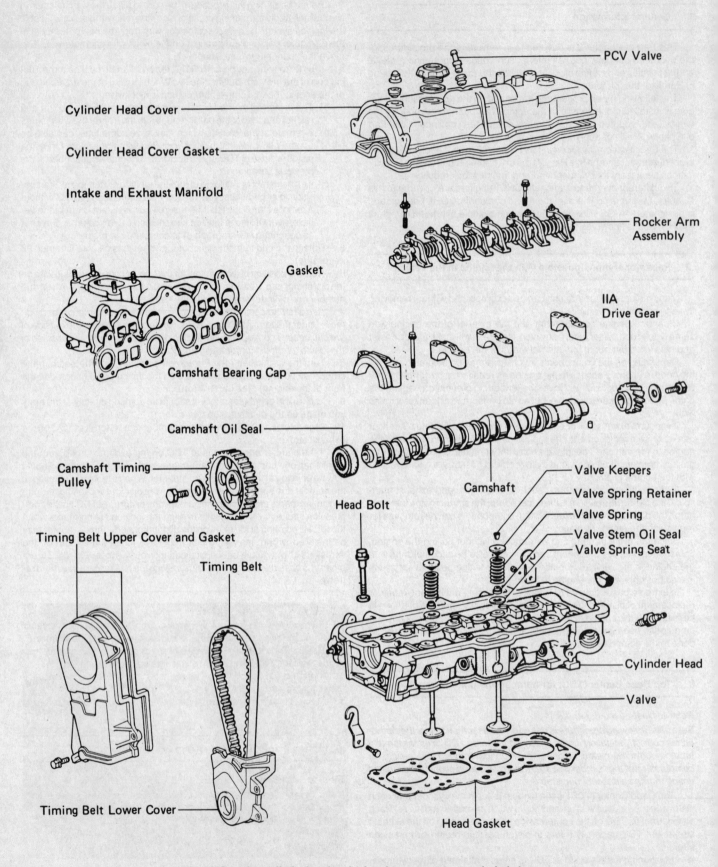

4.3 4A-C engine cylinder head and related components – exploded view

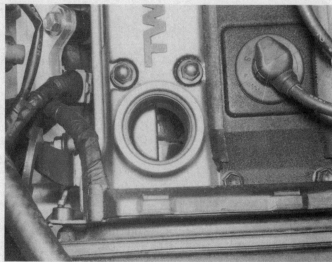

3.11 On the 4A-GE engine, to verify the number one piston is at TDC on the compression stroke, remove the oil filler cap and look for a little dimple in the camshaft – the dimple should be aligned with the straight edge of the filler neck opening

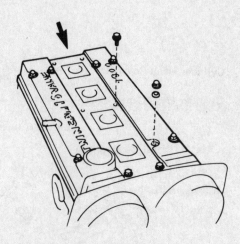

4.7 On the 4A-GE engine, remove the center cover (arrow) first

12   After the number one piston has been positioned at TDC on the compression stroke, TDC for any of the remaining pistons can be located by turning the crankshaft and following the firing order. Mark the remaining spark plug wire terminal locations on the distributor body just like you did for the number one terminal, then number the marks to correspond with the cylinder numbers. As you turn the crankshaft, the rotor will also turn. When it's pointing directly at one of the marks on the distributor, the piston for that particular cylinder is at TDC on the compression stroke.

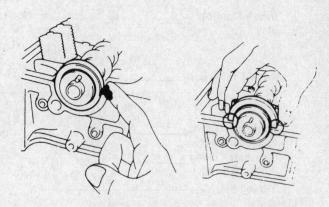

4.10 On the 4A-GE engine, apply sealant to the front bearing cap-to-seal joints

---

4   Camshaft cover(s) – removal and installation

Refer to illustrations 4.3, 4.7, 4.8, and 4.10

Removal

1   Disconnect the negative cable from the battery.
2   On 4A-C engines, remove the air cleaner assembly.
3   Detach the PCV valve and breather hose from the camshaft cover **(see illustration)**.
4   If you're working on a 4A-GE engine, remove the spark plug wires from the spark plugs.
5   Label, detach and move aside any wiring harness that is in the way.
6   On 4A-C engines, remove the upper timing belt cover and unclip the throttle cable from the cover and tie it aside.
7   On 4A-GE engines, remove the throttle cable (see Chapter 4) and the center cover and gasket **(see illustration)**.
8   Remove the mounting nuts/bolts and sealing washers, then detach the cover and gasket from the head **(see illustration on following page)**. If the cover is stuck to the head, bump the end with a block of wood and a hammer to jar it loose. If that doesn't work, try to slip a flexible putty knife between the head and cover to break the seal. **Caution:** *Don't pry at the cover-to-head joint or damage to the sealing surfaces may occur, leading to oil leaks after the cover is reinstalled.*

Installation

9   The mating surfaces of the cylinder head and cover must be clean when the cover is installed. Use a gasket scraper to remove all traces of sealant and old gasket material, then clean the mating surfaces with lacquer thinner or acetone. If there's residue or oil on the mating surfaces when the cover is installed, oil leaks may develop.

10   If you're working on a 4A-GE engine, apply a thin, uniform layer of sealant to the gasket mating surface and seal joints **(see illustration)**.
11   Position a new gasket and seals (if used) on the cylinder head, then install the camshaft cover, sealing washers and nuts.
12   Tighten the nuts/bolts to the torque listed in this Chapter's Specifications in three equal steps.
13   Reinstall the remaining parts, run the engine and check for oil leaks.

---

5   Intake manifold – removal and installation

Refer to illustrations 5.4, 5.6, 5.7a, 5.7b, 5.7c, 5.8 and 5.9

Note: *On 4A-C engines, the intake and exhaust manifolds share a common gasket. Therefore, it is necessary to remove the exhaust manifold (see Section 6) to change the gasket.*

Removal

1   Disconnect the negative cable from the battery.
2   Drain the cooling system (see Chapter 1).
3   Remove the air cleaner and carburetor or throttle body, fuel injectors

2B

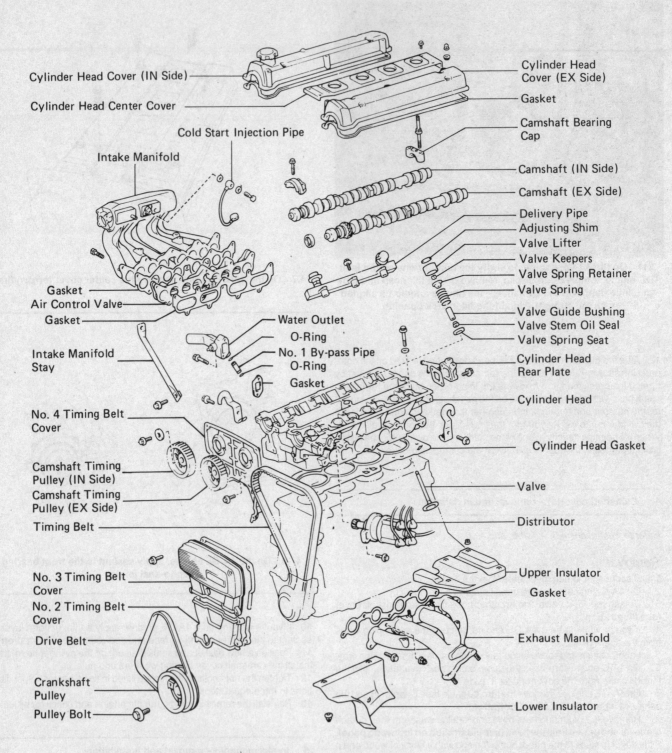

Cylinder Head Cover (IN Side)

Cylinder Head Center Cover

Cold Start Injection Pipe

Intake Manifold

Gasket
Air Control Valve
Gasket

Intake Manifold
Stay

No. 4 Timing Belt
Cover

Camshaft Timing
Pulley (IN Side)
Camshaft Timing
Pulley (EX Side)

Timing Belt

No. 3 Timing Belt
Cover
No. 2 Timing Belt
Cover

Drive Belt

Crankshaft
Pulley

Pulley Bolt

Cylinder Head
Cover (EX Side)

Gasket

Camshaft Bearing
Cap

Camshaft (IN Side)

Camshaft (EX Side)

Delivery Pipe
Adjusting Shim
Valve Lifter
Valve Keepers
Valve Spring Retainer
Valve Spring

Valve Guide Bushing
Valve Stem Oil Seal
Valve Spring Seat

Cylinder Head
Rear Plate

Cylinder Head

Cylinder Head Gasket

Valve

Distributor

Upper Insulator

Gasket

Exhaust Manifold

Lower Insulator

Water Outlet
O-Ring
No. 1 By-pass Pipe
O-Ring
Gasket

4.8   4A-GE engine cylinder head and related components – exploded view

and fuel rail (see Chapter 4).

4   Remove the heat shield (if equipped) from the manifold (**see illustration**).

5   Label and detach all wire harnesses, control cables, tubes, hoses and switches still connected to the intake manifold.

6   Unbolt any braces still in place (**see illustration**).

7   Remove the nuts/bolts, then detach the manifold from the engine

(**see illustrations**). On 4A-C engines, remove the exhaust manifold (see Section 6).

8   Use a scraper to remove all traces of old gasket material and sealant from the manifold and cylinder head (**see illustration**), then clean the mating surfaces with lacquer thinner or acetone. If the gasket was leaking, have the manifold checked for warpage at an automotive machine shop and resurfaced if necessary.

5.4 Remove the heat shield (arrow) – 4A-C engine shown

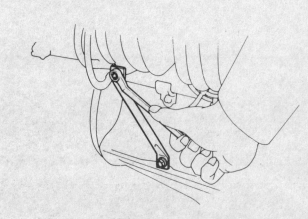

5.6 Remove all braces – note their locations for correct installation

2B

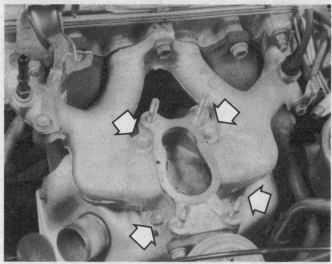

5.7a On the 4A-C engine, remove the intake-to-exhaust manifold bolts (arrows)

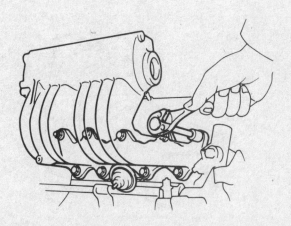

5.7b Intake manifold fastener locations (4A-GE engine)

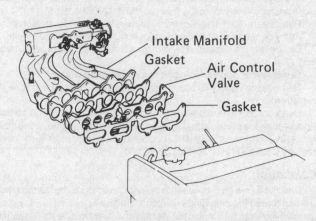

Intake Manifold
Gasket
Air Control Valve
Gasket

5.7c On the 4A-GE engine, remove the air control valve with the manifold

5.8 Be very careful when scraping off the gasket to avoid gouging the aluminum head

5.9   The 4A-C engine intake and exhaust manifolds share a
common gasket

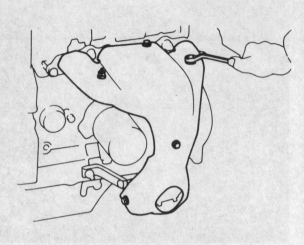

6.3a   Remove the outer heat shield (4A-GE
engine shown)

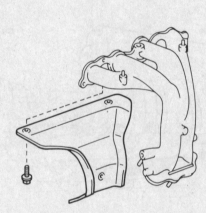

6.3b   Unbolt the inner heat shield, if equipped

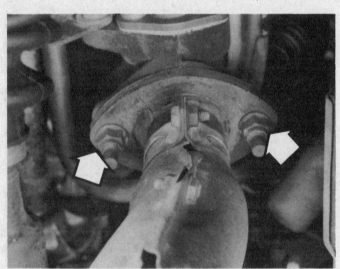

6.5   Remove the exhaust pipe-to-manifold mounting nuts

Installation

9   Install a new gasket **(see illustration)**, then position the manifold on the head and install the nuts/bolts.
10   Tighten the nuts/bolts in three equal steps to the torque listed in this Chapter's Specifications. Work from the center out towards the ends to avoid warping the manifold.
11   Install the remaining parts in the reverse order of removal.
12   Before starting the engine, check the throttle linkage for smooth operation.
13   Run the engine and check for coolant and vacuum leaks.
14   Road test the vehicle and check for proper operation of all accessories, including the cruise control system.

6   Exhaust manifold – removal and installation

Refer to illustrations 6.3a, 6.3b, 6.5, 6.6 and 6.7
Warning: *The engine must be completely cool before beginning this procedure.*
Note: *On 4A-C engines, the intake and exhaust manifolds share the same gasket. Refer to Section 5 for instructions on intake manifold removal.*

Removal

1   Disconnect the negative cable from the battery.
2   Unplug the oxygen sensor wire harness. If you're replacing the manifold, transfer the sensor to the new manifold (see Chapter 6).
3   Remove the heat shield(s) from the manifold **(see illustrations)**.
4   Apply penetrating oil to the exhaust manifold mounting nuts/bolts.
5   Disconnect the exhaust pipe from the exhaust manifold **(see illustration)**.
6   Remove any manifold-to-block braces **(see illustration)**.
7   Remove the nuts/bolts and detach the manifold and gasket **(see illustration)**.
8   Use a scraper to remove all traces of old gasket material and carbon deposits from the manifold and cylinder head mating surfaces. If the gasket was leaking, have the manifold checked for warpage at an automotive machine shop and resurfaced if necessary.

Installation

9   Position a new gasket over the cylinder head studs. Install the manifold and thread the mounting nuts/bolts into place.
10   Working from the center out, tighten the nuts/bolts to the specified torque in three equal steps.
11   Reinstall the remaining parts in the reverse order of removal.
12   Run the engine and check for exhaust leaks.

6.6   Remove the exhaust manifold braces (arrows) – 4A-GE engine shown

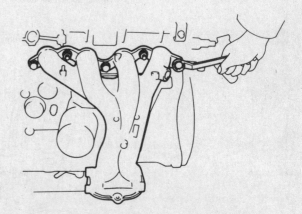

6.7   4A-GE engine exhaust manifold fastener locations

---

7   Timing belt – removal, inspection and installation

Removal

Refer to illustrations 7.1, 7.3, 7.10a, 7.10b, 7.10c, 7.10d, 7.11a, 7.11b, 7.12a, 7.12b, 7.13, 7.14a, 7.14b, 7.14c, 7.14d, 7.15a, 7.15b, 7.16a, 7.16b, 7.18a and 7.18b

1   The timing belt matchmarks may be checked without removing the covers **(see illustration)**.
2   Disconnect the negative cable from the battery.
3   Remove the air cleaner on 4A-C engines. Remove the air cleaner hose number 2 from the air cleaner on 4A-GE engines **(see illustration)**.
4   If equipped, remove the power steering pump and set it off to the side (see Chapter 10).
5   Remove the power steering pump pulley.
6   If equipped, remove the air conditioning compressor belt.
7   Unbolt the cruise control actuator (if equipped) and set it aside.
8   Remove the crankshaft pulley.
9   Remove the water pump pulley bolts and pulley.
10   Remove the upper (number one) timing belt cover and gaskets **(see illustrations)**.

7.1   The covers have removable plugs (arrows) that allow you to check the timing belt match marks without removing the covers (4A-C engine shown)

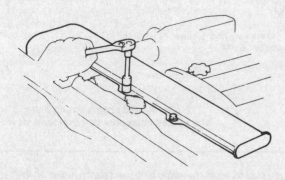

7.3   Remove the long inlet tube attached to the air cleaner (4A-GE engine)

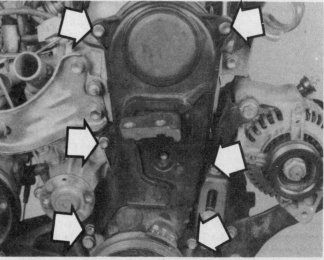

7.10a   4A-C engine timing belt cover bolt locations (arrows)

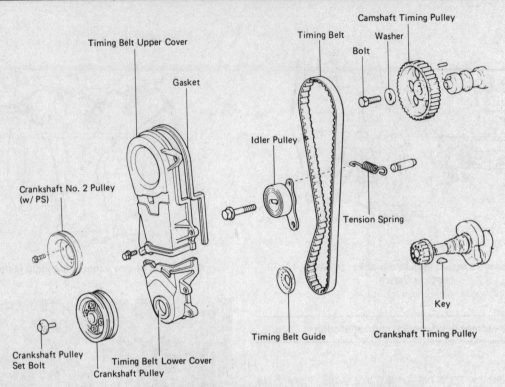

7.10b 4A-C engine timing belt and related components – exploded view

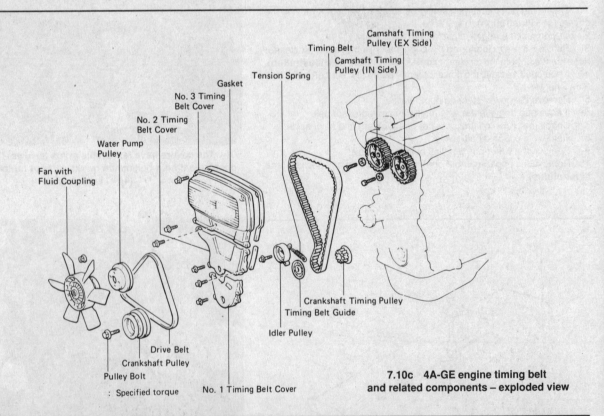

7.10c 4A-GE engine timing belt
and related components – exploded view

11   Position the number one piston at TDC on the compression stroke (see Section 3). On 4A-C, make sure the small hole in the camshaft sprocket is aligned with the TDC mark on the cam bearing cap. On 4A-GE engines, align the marks on the sprockets with the marks on the rear cover (see illustrations).

12   If you plan to reuse the timing belt, paint match marks on the pulley and belt and an arrow indicating direction of travel on the belt (see illustrations).

13   Loosen the timing belt idler pulley set bolt (see illustration) and push the pulley down (against spring tension) as far as it will go, then temporari-

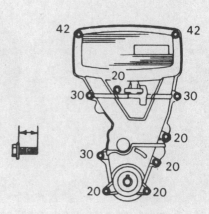

7.10d   4A-GE engine timing belt cover bolt locations – the bolt lengths are marked in millimeters

7.11a   On the 4A-C engine, align the camshaft sprocket timing hole (arrow) with the central mark on the cylinder head

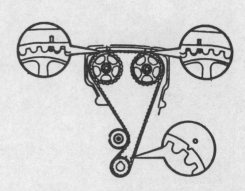

7.11b   On the 4A-GE engine, align the marks on the sprockets with the marks on the rear cover as shown

7.12a   Also index the belt to the camshaft sprockets (4A-GE engine shown)

7.12b   Before removing the timing belt, be sure to mark the direction of rotation, then index it to the crankshaft sprocket

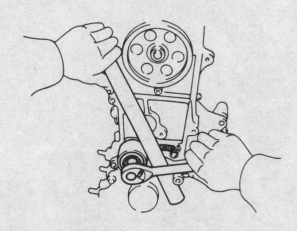

7.13   Temporarily move the pulley aside and retighten the bolt

2B

7.14a   To loosen the camshaft sprocket bolt, hold the camshaft with a large wrench on the hex as the bolt is turned – DO NOT use the timing belt tension to keep the camshaft from turning!

7.14b   On the 4A-GE engine, make sure the camshaft sprocket index marks are aligned with the stationary marks on the rear timing belt cover when removing/installing the sprockets

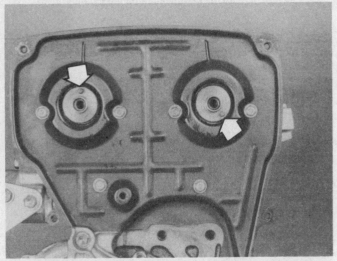

7.14c   On the 4A-GE engine, the knock pins (arrows) in the camshafts should be positioned as shown, with the pin in the intake camshaft at 12 o'clock and the pin in the exhaust cam at five o'clock

7.14d   On the 4A-C engine, the knock pin should be at approximately 11 o'clock (arrow)

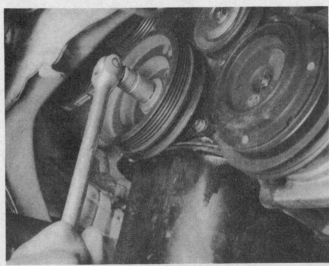

7.15a   Remove the crankshaft pulley bolt, . . .

7.15b   . . . then use a puller that bolts to the hub to remove the pulley – a jaw-type puller will damage it

7.16a   Remove the idler pulley retaining nut (arrow)

7.16b   The cupped edge (arrow) of the timing belt guide must face out when it's reinstalled

2B

7.18a   The match marks on the crankshaft sprocket and oil pump housing must be aligned (arrows)

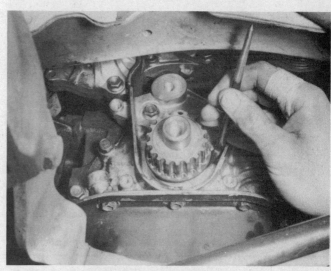

7.18b   The crankshaft sprocket can usually be pried off with a small pry bar – if it's stuck, use a puller

ly tighten it. Slip the timing belt off the pulley. If you're removing the belt for camshaft oil seal replacement or cylinder head removal, it isn't necessary to detach the belt from the crankshaft pulley.

14   If a camshaft sprocket is worn or damaged, remove the camshaft cover, hold the camshaft with a large wrench and remove the bolt, then detach the sprocket **(see illustration)**. Note the locations of the knock pins for correct sprocket reinstallation **(see illustrations)**. On 4A-GE engines, after the camshaft sprockets are removed, the rear cover bolts may be accessed.

15   To proceed with timing belt removal, keep the crankshaft from turning with a large screwdriver or a pry bar (see Section 16). Remove the bolt and detach the pulley **(see illustrations)**. Sometimes the pulley can be removed by hand. **Caution:** *Do not use a jaw-type puller!*

16   Remove the lower timing belt cover(s) and gaskets. It may be necessary to remove the air conditioner idler pulley **(see illustration)**. Slip the belt guide off the crankshaft **(see illustration)**.

17   If you plan to reuse the timing belt, paint match marks on the lower sprocket and belt, also.

18   The matchmarks on the crankshaft sprocket and oil pump housing must be aligned **(see illustration)**. Slip the timing belt off the crankshaft sprocket and remove it. If the sprocket is worn or damaged, or if you need to get at the oil pump or front crankshaft oil seal, remove the sprocket from the crankshaft **(see illustration)**.

Inspection

Refer to illustrations 7.19a, 7.19b, 7.21, 7.22 and 7.23

Caution: *Do not bend, twist or turn the timing belt inside out. Do not allow it to come in contact with oil, coolant or fuel. Do not utilize timing belt tension to keep the camshaft or crankshaft from turning when installing the pulley bolt(s). Do not turn the crankshaft or camshaft more than a few degrees (necessary for tooth alignment) while the timing belt is removed.*

7.19a   **To remove the timing belt idler pulley, remove the bolt and detach the spring (arrows)**

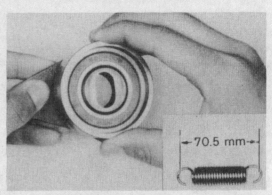

7.19b   **Check the idler pulley bearing for smooth operation and measure the free length of the tension spring**

7.22   **If the belt is cracked or worn, check the sprockets for nicks and burrs**

7.21   **Check the timing belt for cracked and missing teeth**

7.23   **Wear on one side of the belt indicates sprocket misalignment**

19   Remove the idler pulley and check the bearings for smooth operation and excessive play. Inspect the spring for damage and compare the free length to the Specifications **(see illustrations)**.

20   If the timing belt broke during engine operation, the valves and/or pistons may be damaged.

21   If the belt teeth are cracked or pulled off **(see illustration)**, the distributor, water pump, oil pump or camshaft(s) may have seized.

22   If there is noticeable wear or cracks in the belt, check to see if there are nicks or burrs on the sprockets **(see illustration)**.

23   If there is wear or damage on only one side of the belt, check the belt guide and the alignment of all sprockets and the idler pulley **(see illustration)**.

24   Replace the timing belt with a new one if obvious wear or damage is noted or if it is the least bit questionable. Correct any problems which contributed to belt failure prior to belt installation.

Installation

Refer to illustrations 7.35a and 7.35b

25   Remove all dirt and oil from the timing belt area.

26   If it was removed, install the idler pulley and tension spring. The idler should be pulled back against spring tension as far as possible and the bolt

temporarily tightened.

27   Recheck the camshaft and crankshaft timing marks to be sure they are properly aligned (see Steps 11, 12 and 18).

28   Install the timing belt on the crankshaft and camshaft sprockets and idler pulley. If the original belt is being reinstalled, align the marks made during removal.

29   Slip the belt guide onto the crankshaft with the cupped side facing out **(see illustration 7.16b)**.

30   Keep tension on the side nearest the front of the vehicle. If the original belt is being reinstalled, align the marks made during removal.

31   Loosen the idler pulley bolt 1/2-turn, allowing the spring to apply pressure to the idler pulley.

32   Tighten the idler pulley mounting bolt to the torque listed in this Chapter's Specifications.

33   Slowly turn the crankshaft clockwise by hand two complete revolutions (720-degrees). If anything hits, stop and recheck your work. Do not force the crankshaft to turn.

34   Recheck the timing matchmarks. If the marks are not aligned exactly, repeat the belt installation procedure. **Caution:** *DO NOT start the engine until you're absolutely certain that the timing belt is installed correctly. Serious and costly engine damage could occur if the belt is installed wrong.*

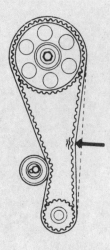

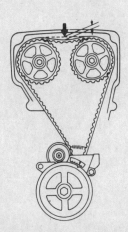

7.35a   On the 4A-C engine, check the timing belt deflection here (arrow)

7.35b   On the 4A-GE engine, check the timing belt deflection at the top (arrows)

35   Measure the timing belt deflection **(see illustrations)** and compare to this Chapter's Specifications. If the belt tension is too loose or tight, repeat the adjustment procedure and recheck.
36   Reinstall the remaining parts in the reverse order of removal.
37   Run the engine and check for proper operation.

8   Crankshaft front oil seal – replacement

Refer to illustrations 8.2 and 8.4

1   Remove the timing belt and crankshaft pulley (see Section 7).
2   Note how far the seal is seated in the bore, then carefully pry it out of the oil pump housing with a screwdriver or seal removal tool **(see illustration)**. Don't scratch the housing bore or damage the crankshaft in the process (if the crankshaft is damaged, the new seal will end up leaking).
3   Clean the bore in the housing and coat the outer edge of the new seal with engine oil or multi-purpose grease. Apply moly-base grease to the

seal lip.
4   Using a socket with an outside diameter slightly smaller than the outside diameter of the seal, carefully drive the new seal into place with a hammer **(see illustration)**. Make sure it's installed squarely and driven into the same depth as the original. If a socket isn't available, a short section of large diameter pipe will also work. Check the seal after installation to make sure the garter spring didn't pop out of place.
5   Reinstall the crankshaft sprocket and timing belt (see Section 7).
6   Run the engine and check for oil leaks at the front seal.

9   Camshaft oil seal – replacement

Refer to illustrations 9.2 and 9.4

1   Remove the timing belt, camshaft sprocket(s) and rear timing belt cover, if equipped (see Section 7).
2   Note how far the seal is seated in the bore, then carefully pry it out with

8.2   Carefully pry the old seal out of the oil pump housing

8.4   Gently tap the new seal into place with a hammer and deep socket

9.2   Pry the old seal out with a small screwdriver

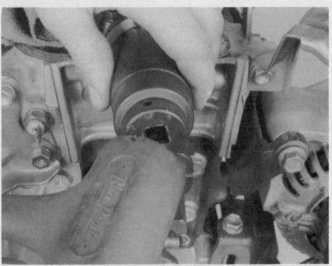

9.4   Carefully drive the new seal into place with a hammer and deep socket

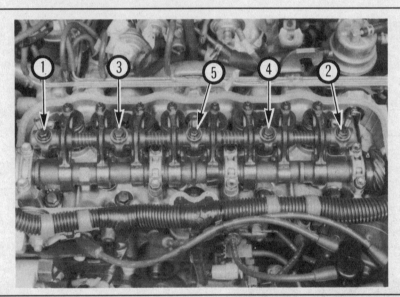

10.5   Rocker arm pedestal bolt loosening sequence (4A-C engine)

10.6   Leave the bolts in place to hold the rocker arm assembly together and lift it off

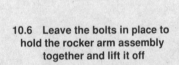

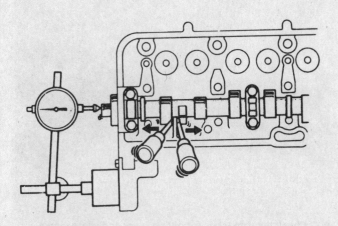

10.8   Pry the camshaft back-and-forth to check the endplay

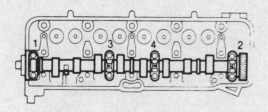

10.10a   Camshaft bearing cap bolt loosening sequence

a small screwdriver **(see illustration)**. Don't scratch the bore or damage the camshaft in the process (if the camshaft is damaged, the new seal will end up leaking).

3   Clean the bore and coat the outer edge of the new seal with engine oil or multi-purpose grease. Apply moly-base grease to the seal lip.

4   Using a socket with an outside diameter slightly smaller than the outside diameter of the seal, carefully drive the new seal into place with a hammer and deep socket **(see illustration)**. Make sure it's installed squarely and driven in to the same depth as the original. If a socket isn't available, a short section of pipe will also work.

5   Reinstall the camshaft sprocket and timing belt (see Section 7).

6   Run the engine and check for oil leaks at the camshaft seal.

10.10b   Slip the old oil seal off

and lift the bearing caps off. Remove the camshaft from the cylinder head and slip the oil seal off the end **(see illustration)**.

Rocker arm and shaft inspection

Refer to illustrations 10.11a and 10.11b

11   Check the clearance between the rocker arms and shaft by moving the rocker arms as shown **(see illustration)**. Little or no movement should be felt. If movement is felt, disassemble the rocker arm assembly and measure the oil clearance as follows:

---

10   Camshaft and rocker arms (4A-C engine) – removal, inspection and installation

Rocker arm removal

Refer to illustrations 10.5 and 10.6

1   Remove the negative cable from the battery.

2   Set the engine at Top Dead Center (see Section 3).

3   Remove the camshaft cover (see Section 4).

4   Loosen the lock nuts and back off the adjustment screws until they no longer open the valves.

5   Remove the rocker arm shaft by loosening each bolt a little at a time in the sequence shown **(see illustration)**.

6   Leave the bolts in place to hold the rocker arm assembly together and lift the rocker arm assembly up as a unit **(see illustration)**.

Camshaft removal

Refer to illustrations 10.8, 10.10a and 10.10b

7   Remove the timing belt and the camshaft pulley (see Section 7).

8   With the camshaft still in the cylinder head, use a dial indicator to check the endplay. Attach the gauge to the end of the head and move the camshaft all the way to the rear. Next, use a screwdriver to pry it all the way forward **(see illustration)**. If the endplay exceeds the specified limit, replace the camshaft and/or the cylinder head.

9   Remove the distributor and fuel pump (see Chapters 4 and 5).

10   Mark the bearing caps to ensure reinstallation in the same location. Loosen the bearing cap bolts in the sequence shown **(see illustration)**

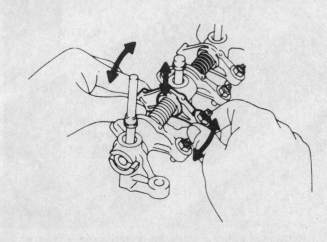

10.11a   Wiggle the rocker arms back-and-forth to check for play

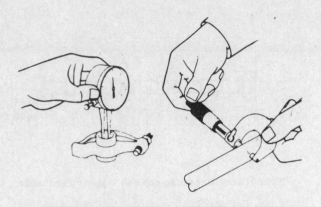

10.11b   Measure the inside diameter of each rocker arm bore and the outside diameter of the rocker arm shaft where each rocker arm rides

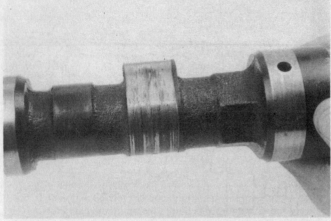

10.12 Check the cam lobes for pitting, wear and score marks – if scoring is excessive, as is the case here, replace the camshaft

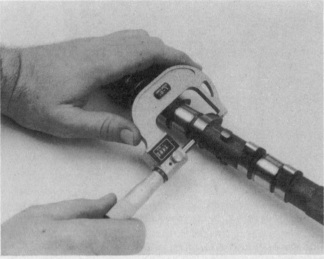

10.13   Measure the lobe heights on each camshaft – if any lobe height is less than the specified allowable minimum, replace that camshaft

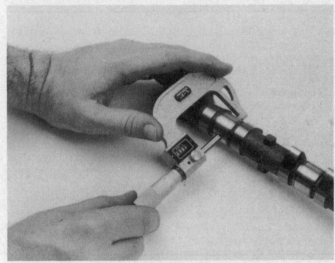

10.14   Measure each journal diameter with a micrometer (if any journal measures less than the specified limit, replace the camshaft)

10.15a   Lay a strip of Plastigage on each camshaft journal

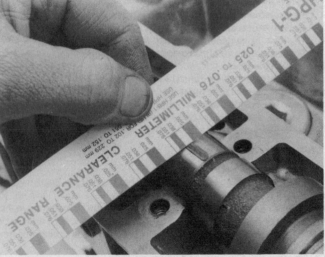

10.15b   Compare the width of the crushed Plastigage to the scale on the envelope to determine the oil clearance

10.17   Apply engine assembly lube or moly-base grease to the cam lobes and journals before installing the camshaft in the engine

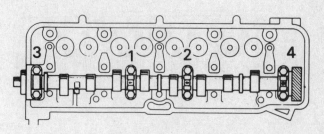

10.18a   Camshaft bearing cap bolt tightening sequence

a) Using an inside micrometer or dial indicator, measure the inside diameter of the rocker arm **(see illustration)**. Subtract the shaft diameter from the rocker arm diameter and compare the result to this Chapter's Specifications. Replace the rocker arms and/or shafts as necessary.

b) Visually inspect the rocker arm-to-camshaft contact surface. Replace any rockers that are worn excessively.

Camshaft inspection

Refer to illustrations 10.12, 10.13, 10.14, 10.15a and 10.15b

12   Visually inspect the camshaft journals, lobes and distributor gear. Check for score marks, pitting and evidence of wear or overheating (blue, discolored areas) **(see illustration)**. If wear is excessive or damage is evident, the component will have to be replaced.

13   Using a micrometer, measure the cam lobe height and compare it to this Chapter's Specifications. If the lobe height is less than the minimum allowable, the camshaft is worn and must be replaced **(see illustration)**.

14   Using a micrometer, measure the diameter of each journal and compare it to the Specifications **(see illustration)**. If the journals are worn or damaged, replace the camshaft.

15   Check the oil clearance for each camshaft journal as follows:

a) Clean the bearing caps and the camshaft journals with lacquer thinner or acetone.

b) Carefully lay the camshaft in place in the head. Don't use any lubrication.

c) Lay a strip of Plastigage on each journal **(see illustration)**.

d) Install the bearing caps with the arrows pointing toward the front (timing belt end) of the engine.

e) Tighten the bolts to the specified torque in 1/4 turn increments. **Note:** *Don't turn the camshaft while the Plastigage is in place.*

f) Remove the bolts and detach the caps.

g) Compare the width of the crushed Plastigage (at its widest point) to the scale on the Plastigage envelope **(see illustration)**.

h) If the clearance is greater than specified, replace the camshaft and/or the cylinder head.

i) Scrape off the Plastigage with your fingernail or the edge of a credit card – don't scratch or nick the journals or caps.

Camshaft installation

Refer to illustrations 10.17, 10.18a and 10.18b

16   Installation is basically the reverse of the removal procedure. However, keep the following points in mind.

17   Apply engine assembly lube or moly-base grease to the camshaft lobes and journals **(see illustration)**. Also apply the same lubricant to the rocker arms and oil seal lips. Slip a new oil seal over the end of the camshaft with the spring side facing in.

18   Place the camshaft in the cylinder head with the seal correctly positioned. Install the bearing caps in the original locations and apply a dab of RTV sealant at the number one cap-to-head joint **(see illustration 4.10)**.

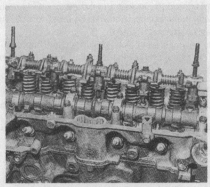

10.18b   Install the studs in these locations (arrows)

Tighten the bolts in three steps, in the sequence shown **(see illustration)** to the specified torque. Be sure the studs that fasten the camshaft cover are in the correct places **(see illustration)**.

Rocker arm installation

Refer to illustrations 10.19 and 10.20

19   If the rocker arms and shaft were disassembled, install the rocker arms on the shaft with the oil holes pointing left, right and down as shown **(see illustration)**. Be sure to apply engine assembly lube or moly-base grease to the moving surfaces.

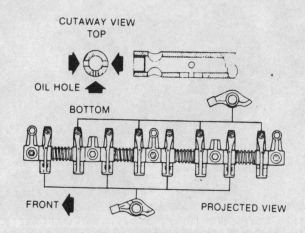

10.19   The oil holes must be positioned as shown

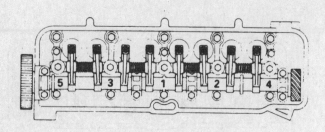

10.20   Rocker arm bolt tightening sequence

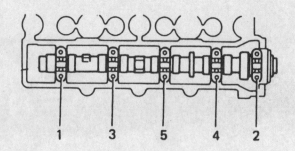

11.5   On the 4A-GE engine, loosen the cam bearing cap bolts in the sequence shown

20   Install and tighten the rocker arm mounting bolts gradually in three passes following the sequence shown **(see illustration)** until the torque specified in this Chapter is reached.
21   Adjust the valve clearances as described in Chapter 1.
22   Reinstall the remaining components in the reverse order of removal.

11   Camshafts and valve lifters (4A-GE engine) – removal, inspection and installation

Removal

Refer to illustration 11.5

1   Remove the camshaft covers (see Section 4).
2   Remove the timing belt, camshaft sprockets and rear timing belt cover (see Section 7).
3   Remove the distributor (see Chapter 5).
4   Measure the camshaft endplay with a dial indicator **(see illustration 10.8).** If the play is greater than the specified maximum, replace the camshaft and/or the cylinder head.
5   Check the bearing caps for numbers and mark them, if necessary, for proper reinstallation. Loosen the camshaft bearing cap bolts in the sequence shown **(see illustration)**. Now remove the bearing caps and lift each camshaft out of the engine.

Inspection

Camshaft

6   Refer to Section 10 for camshaft inspection and lobe height and oil clearance measurement procedures.

Lifters

Refer to illustrations 11.7, 11.8, 11.9a and 11.9b

7   Carefully label, then remove the valve lifters and shims **(see illustration)**.
8   Inspect each lifter for scuffing and score marks **(see illustration)**.
9   Measure the outside diameter of each lifter and the corresponding lifter bore inside diameter **(see illustrations)**. Subtract the lifter diameter from the lifter bore diameter to determine the oil clearance. Compare it to the Specifications. If the oil clearance is excessive, a new head and/or new lifters will be required.
10   Store the lifters in a clean box, separated from each other, so they won't be damaged. Make sure the shims stay with the lifters (don't mix them up).

Installation

Refer to illustrations 11.13a, 11.13b and 11.13c

11   Installation is basically the reverse of the removal procedure. However, keep the following points in mind.

11.7   Wipe the oil off the valve shims and mark the intakes I and the exhausts E – a magnetic tool works well for removing lifters

11.8   Wipe off the oil and inspect each lifter for wear and scuffing

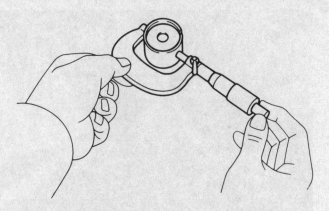

11.9a   Use a micrometer to measure each lifter diameter

11.9b   Use a telescoping gauge and micrometer to measure the lifter bores

12   Apply engine assembly lube or moly-base grease to the camshaft lobes and journals **(see illustration 10.17)**. Also apply the same lubricant to the sides of the lifters and the lifter shims. Install the lifters and shims in the same locations they were removed from.

13   Slip a new oil seal over the end of the camshaft with the spring side facing in. Place the camshaft in the cylinder head with the seal correctly positioned and the knock pin positioned as shown **(see illustration)**. Install the bearing caps in the original locations **(see illustration)**. Tighten the bolts in three steps, in the sequence shown **(see illustration)** to the specified torque.

12   Valve springs, retainers and seals (4A-C engine) – replacement

Refer to illustrations 12.4, 12.9a, 12.9b, 12.15 and 12.17

Note: *Broken valve springs and defective valve stem seals can be replaced without removing the cylinder head. Two special tools and a compressed air source are normally required to perform this operation, so read through this Section carefully and rent or buy the tools before beginning the job. If compressed air isn't available, a length of nylon rope can be used to keep the valves from falling into the cylinder during this procedure.*

1   Refer to Section 10 and remove the rocker arm assembly.

2   Remove the spark plug from the cylinder which has the defective component. If all of the valve stem seals are being replaced, all of the spark plugs should be removed.

3   Turn the crankshaft until the piston in the affected cylinder is at top dead center on the compression stroke (refer to Section 3 for instructions). If you're replacing all of the valve stem seals, begin with cylinder number one and work on the valves for one cylinder at a time. Move from cylinder-to-cylinder following the firing order sequence (1-3-4-2).

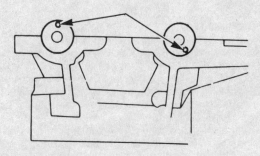

11.13a   When installing the camshafts, position the knock pins as shown (arrows)

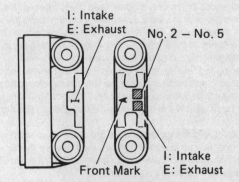

11.13b   The arrows point toward the front of the engine

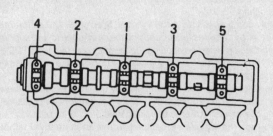

11.13c   On the 4A-GE engine, tighten the cam bearing cap bolts in the sequence shown here

2B

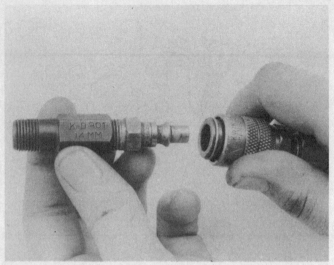

12.4   This is what the air hose adapter that threads into the spark plug hole looks like – they're commonly available from auto parts stores

12.9a   This type of spring compressor attaches to the camshaft – pull down on the handle until the keepers are free

12.9b   Use a small magnet or needle-nose pliers to remove the valve keepers (be careful not to drop them into the engine) – a different type of compressor is shown here

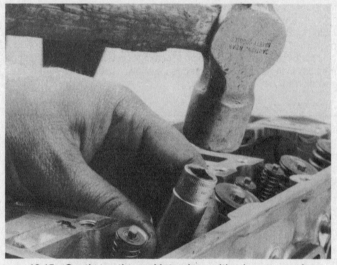

12.15   Gently tap the seal into place with a hammer and deep socket

4   Thread an adapter into the spark plug hole **(see illustration)** and connect an air hose from a compressed air source to it. Most auto parts stores can supply the air hose adapter. **Note:** *Many cylinder compression gauges utilize a screw-in fitting that may work with your air hose quick-disconnect fitting.*

5   Apply compressed air to the cylinder. **Warning:** *The piston may be forced down by compressed air, causing the crankshaft to turn suddenly. If the wrench used when positioning the number one piston at TDC is still attached to the bolt in the crankshaft nose, it could cause damage or injury when the crankshaft moves.*

6   The valves should be held in place by the air pressure. If the valve faces or seats are in poor condition, leaks may prevent air pressure from retaining the valves – refer to the alternative procedure below.

7   If you don't have access to compressed air, an alternative method can be used. Position the piston at a point just before TDC on the compression stroke, then feed a long piece of nylon rope through the spark plug hole until it fills the combustion chamber. Be sure to leave the end of the rope hanging out of the engine so it can be removed easily.

8   Use a large ratchet and socket to rotate the crankshaft in the normal direction of rotation (clockwise, viewed from the drivebelt end) until slight resistance is felt.

9   Stuff shop rags into the cylinder head holes above and below the valves to prevent parts and tools from falling into the engine, then use a valve spring compressor to compress the spring. Remove the keepers with small needle-nose pliers or a magnet **(see illustrations)**. **Note:** *A couple of different types of tools are available for compressing the valve springs with the head in place. One type grips the lower spring coils and presses on the retainer as the knob is turned, while the other type, utilizes a lever pulling against the camshaft. Both types work very well.*

10   Remove the spring retainer and valve spring, then remove the stem oil seal. **Note:** *If air pressure fails to hold the valve in the closed position during this operation, the valve face and/or seat is probably damaged. If so, the cylinder head will have to be removed for additional repair operations.*

11   Wrap a rubber band or tape around the top of the valve stem so the valve won't fall into the combustion chamber, then release the air pressure. **Note:** *If a rope was used instead of air pressure, turn the crankshaft slightly in the direction opposite normal rotation.*

12   Inspect the valve stem for damage. Rotate the valve in the guide and check the end for eccentric movement, which would indicate that the valve is bent.

13   Move the valve up-and-down in the guide and make sure it doesn't

12.17 Apply a small dab of grease to each keeper before installation to hold it in place on the valve stem until the spring is released

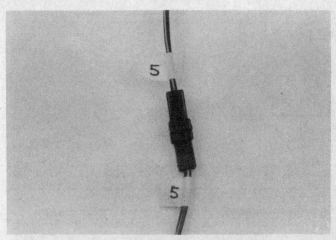

13.13 Clearly label each item before removal

bind. If the valve stem binds, either the valve is bent or the guide is damaged. In either case, the head will have to be removed for repair.

14 Reapply air pressure to the cylinder to retain the valve in the closed position, then remove the tape or rubber band from the valve stem. If a rope was used instead of air pressure, rotate the crankshaft in the normal direction of rotation until slight resistance is felt.

15 Lubricate the valve stem with engine oil and install a new oil seal **(see illustration)**.

16 Install the spring in position over the valve. Be sure the closely wound coils are next to the head.

17 Install the valve spring retainer. Compress the valve spring and carefully position the keepers in the groove. Apply a small dab of grease to the inside of each keeper to hold it in place if necessary **(see illustration)**.

18 Remove the pressure from the spring tool and make sure the keepers are seated.

19 Disconnect the air hose and remove the adapter from the spark plug hole. If a rope was used in place of air pressure, pull it out of the cylinder.

20 Refer to Section 10 and install the rocker arm assembly.

21 Install the spark plug(s) and connect the wire(s).

22 Start and run the engine, then check for oil leaks and unusual sounds coming from the camshaft cover area.

13 Cylinder head – removal and installation

Note: *The engine must be completely cool before beginning this procedure.*

Removal

Refer to illustrations 13.13, 13.14 and 13.15

1 Disconnect the negative cable from the battery.

2 Drain the coolant from the engine block and radiator. Drain the engine oil and remove the oil filter (see Chapter 1).

3 Remove the spark plugs.

4 Remove the carburetor or throttle body, fuel injectors and fuel rails (see Chapter 4).

5 Remove the intake and exhaust manifolds (see Sections 5 and 6).

Note: *On 4A-C engines, the manifolds may be left on the cylinder head until after the head is removed from the engine. However, this makes it more difficult to lift the head.*

6 Remove the camshaft cover(s) as described in Section 4.

7 Remove the timing belt and camshaft sprockets (see Section 7).

8 On 4A-C engines, remove the camshaft and rocker arms (see Section 10).

9 On 4A-GE engines, remove the camshafts and lifters (Section 11).

10 Remove the alternator and distributor (see Chapter 5).

11 Unbolt the power steering pump (if equipped) and set it aside without disconnecting the hoses (see Chapter 10).

12 Unbolt any brackets from the engine (below the camshaft sprocket).

13 Check the cylinder head. Label and remove any remaining items, such as coolant lines, tubes, cables, hoses or wires **(see illustration)**. At this point the head should be ready for removal.

14 Using a socket and a breaker bar, loosen the cylinder head bolts in 1/4-turn increments until they can be removed by hand. Follow the recommended sequence **(see illustration)** to avoid warping or cracking the head.

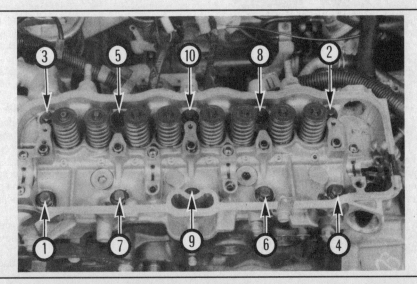

13.14 Cylinder head bolt loosening sequence (4A-C engine shown, 4A-GE uses same sequence)

2B

13.15   Pry on a protrusion (arrow) if the head is stuck – this way, the gasket mating surfaces won't be damaged

13.18   Scrape off all the old gasket material

13.23   Install the new gasket over the dowels (arrows)

15   Lift the cylinder head off the engine block. If it's stuck, very carefully pry up on a protrusion, beyond the gasket surface **(see illustration)**.

16   Remove all external components from the head to allow for thorough cleaning and inspection. See Chapter 2, Part C, for cylinder head servicing procedures.

Installation

Refer to illustrations 13.18, 13.23, 13.26a and 13.26b

17   The mating surfaces of the cylinder head and block must be perfectly clean when the head is installed.

18   Use a gasket scraper to remove all traces of carbon and old gasket material **(see illustration)**, then clean the mating surfaces with lacquer thinner or acetone. If there's oil on the mating surfaces when the head is installed, the gasket may not seal correctly and leaks could develop. When working on the block, stuff the cylinders with clean shop rags to keep out debris. Use a vacuum cleaner to remove material that falls into the cylinders.

13.26a   Cylinder head bolt tightening sequence (4A-C engine shown, 4A-GE uses same sequence)

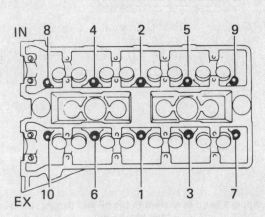

13.26b Cylinder head bolt tightening sequence – 4A-GE engine

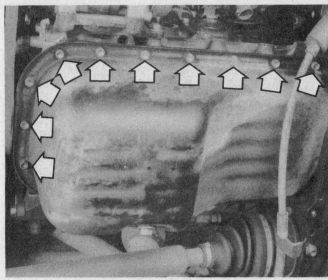

14.7a Remove the bolt/nuts (arrows) around the edge of the oil pan (4A-C engine shown)

2B

19 Check the block and head mating surfaces for nicks, deep scratches and other damage. If damage is slight, it can be removed with a file; if it's excessive, machining may be the only alternative.

20 Use a tap of the correct size to chase the threads in the head bolt holes, then clean the holes with compressed air – make sure that nothing remains in the holes. **Warning:** *Wear eye protection!*

21 Mount each bolt in a vise and run a die down the threads to remove corrosion and restore the threads. Dirt, corrosion, sealant and damaged threads will affect torque readings.

22 Install the components that were removed from the head.

23 Position the new gasket over the dowel pins in the block **(see illustration)**. Be sure to look for marks such as "Top" or "This side up".

24 Carefully set the head on the engine block without disturbing the gasket.

25 Before installing the head bolts, apply a small amount of clean engine oil to the threads.

26 Install the bolts in their original locations and tighten them finger tight. Following the recommended sequence **(see illustrations)**, tighten the bolts in several steps to the torque (and angle of rotation on 4A-GE engines) listed in this Chapter's Specifications. **Note:** *On 4A-GE engines, the exhaust side bolts are 4.25-inches long and the intake side bolts are 3.45-inches long.*

27 The remaining installation steps are the reverse of removal.

28 Check and adjust the valves as necessary (see Chapter 1).

29 Refill the cooling system, install a new oil filter and add oil to the engine (see Chapter 1).

30 Run the engine and check for leaks. Set the ignition timing and road test the vehicle.

14 Oil pan – removal and installation

Refer to illustrations 14.7a, 14.7b, 14.11 and 14.14

Removal

1 Disconnect the negative cable from the battery.

2 Set the parking brake and block the rear wheels.

3 Raise the front of the vehicle and support it securely on jackstands. Apply the parking brake and block the rear wheels.

14.7b Tap the oil pan with a soft-face hammer to break the gasket seal

4 Remove the splash shields from under the oil pan.

5 Drain the engine oil and remove the filter (see Chapter 1).

6 Remove the front exhaust pipe (and bracket) from the exhaust manifold and catalytic converter.

7 Remove the bolts **(see illustration)** and detach the oil pan (and baffle plate on 4A-GE engines). If it's stuck, pry it loose very carefully with a putty knife or tap it loose with a soft-face hammer **(see illustration)**. Don't damage the mating surfaces of the pan and block or oil leaks could develop.

8 Use a scraper to remove all traces of old gasket material and sealant from the block and oil pan. Clean the mating surfaces with lacquer thinner or acetone.

9 Make sure the threaded bolt holes in the block are clean.

10 Check the oil pan flange for distortion, particularly around the bolt holes. If necessary, place the pan on a block of wood and use a hammer to flatten and restore the gasket surface.

14.11   The oil pick-up tube assembly is secured by three bolts (arrows)

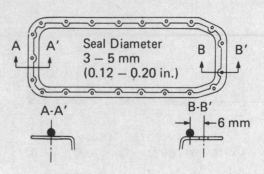

14.14   Apply a bead of sealant to the oil pan flange, to the inside of the bolt holes

11   Inspect the oil pump pick-up tube assembly for cracks or a blocked strainer **(see illustration)**.

Installation

12   If the pick-up was removed, install it now, using a new gasket. Tighten the bolts to the torque listed in this Chapter's Specifications.

13   If the oil pan was originally installed with a gasket, use a new gasket during installation. Hold it in place with sealant.

14   If the oil pan was originally installed with RTV sealant only (no gasket), apply a bead of RTV sealant to the oil pan flange **(see illustration)**. **Note:** *The oil pan must be installed within three minutes once the sealant has been applied.*

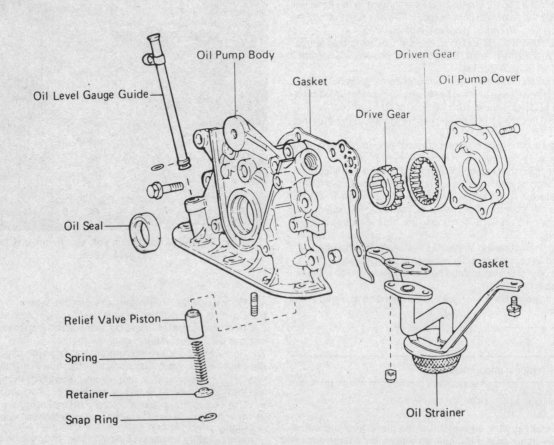

15.3   Oil pump components – exploded view

15.4a Remove the oil pump mounting bolts (arrows)

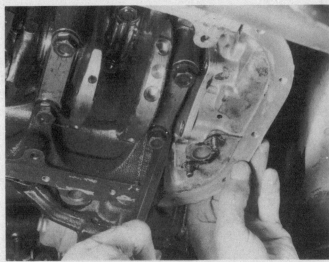

15.4b To break the gasket seal between the oil pump housing and block, insert a pry bar or large screwdriver between the number one main bearing cap and the pump cover – do not attempt to pry between the mating surfaces or you may damage them

2B

15   Carefully position the oil pan on the engine block and install the bolts. Working from the center out, tighten them to the torque listed in this Chapter's Specifications in three steps.
16   The remainder of installation is the reverse of removal. Be sure to add oil and install a new oil filter.
17   Run the engine and check for oil pressure and leaks.

15   Oil pump – removal and installation

Removal
Refer to illustrations 15.3, 15.4a, 15.4b, 15.6a, 15.6b and 15.6c
1   Remove the oil pan and oil pick-up tube assembly (and baffle plate on 4A-GE engines) as described in Section 14. **Note:** *Since the oil pan has*

been removed, the engine must be supported securely from above when removing the following components.
2   Remove the timing belt and crankshaft sprocket (see Section 7). On 4A-C engines, remove the timing belt idler pulley. On 4A-GE engines, temporarily pry it aside and retighten the adjustment bolt.
3   Remove the dipstick tube **(see illustration)**.
4   Remove the bolts and detach the oil pump from the engine **(see illustration)**. You may have to pry carefully between the front main bearing cap and the pump with a screwdriver **(see illustration)**.
5   Use a scraper to remove all traces of sealant and old gasket material from the pump and engine block, then clean the mating surfaces with lacquer thinner or acetone.
6   Pry the old oil seal out with a screwdriver. Using a deep socket and a hammer, carefully drive a new seal into place. Apply moly-base grease to the seal lip **(see illustrations)**.

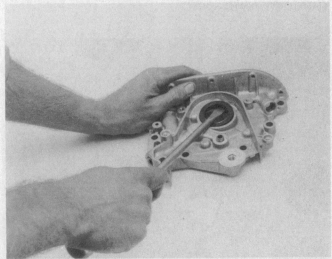

15.6a Carefully pry the oil seal out of the pump housing with a screwdriver – if the seal is difficult to remove, lay a large socket or ratchet extension between the screwdriver and housing to act as a fulcrum and protect the housing from damage

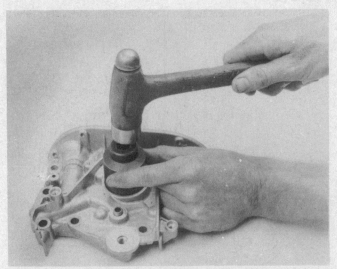

15.6b Drive the new seal into the bore with a hammer and a socket slightly smaller in diameter than the outside diameter of the new seal – make sure the seal doesn't get cocked in the bore or it'll leak

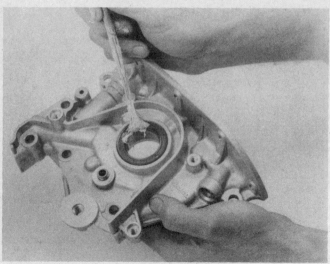

15.6c   Coat the lip of the new seal with multi-purpose grease so it won't be damaged by the nose of the crankshaft when the oil pump housing is reinstalled on the block

15.7   It's a good idea to apply gasket sealant to the mating surfaces of the oil pump housing

Installation

Refer to illustrations 15.7 and 15.8

7   Apply a light coat of RTV sealant to the gasket mating surfaces **(see illustration)**. Place a new gasket on the engine block (the dowel pins should hold it in place).
8   Position the pump against the block **(see illustration)** and install the mounting bolts.
9   Tighten the bolts to the specified torque in three steps. Follow a criss-cross pattern to avoid warping the pump.
10   Reinstall the remaining parts in the reverse order of removal.
11   Add oil, start the engine and check for oil pressure and leaks.
12   Recheck the engine oil level.

---

16   Flywheel/driveplate – removal and installation

Refer to illustrations 16.3, 16.4 and 16.9

Removal

1   Raise the vehicle and support it securely on jackstands, then refer to

Chapter 7 and remove the transmission. If it's leaking, now would be a very good time to replace the front pump seal (automatic transmission only).
2   Remove the pressure plate and clutch disc (see Chapter 8) (manual transmission equipped vehicles). Now is a good time to check/replace the clutch components.
3   Use a center punch or paint to make alignment marks on the flywheel/driveplate and crankshaft to ensure correct alignment during reinstallation **(see illustration)**.
4   Remove the bolts that secure the flywheel/driveplate to the crankshaft. If the crankshaft turns, wedge a screwdriver in the ring gear teeth **(see illustration)**.
5   Detach the flywheel/driveplate from the crankshaft. Since the flywheel is fairly heavy, be sure to support it while removing the last bolt.
6   Clean the flywheel to remove grease and oil. Inspect the clutch surface for cracks, rivet grooves, burned areas and score marks. Light scoring can be removed with emery cloth. Check for cracked and broken ring gear teeth. Lay the flywheel on a flat surface and use a straightedge to check for warpage.
7   Clean and inspect the mating surfaces of the flywheel/driveplate and the crankshaft. If the crankshaft rear seal is leaking, replace it before reinstalling the flywheel/driveplate.

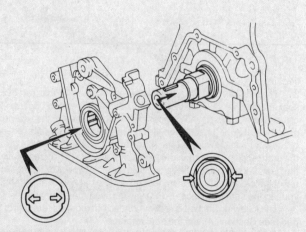

15.8   When installing the oil pump housing on the block, make sure the splines on the drive gear are engaged with the flats on the crankshaft

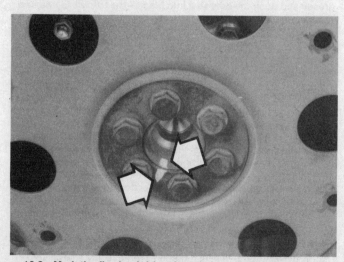

16.3   Mark the flywheel/driveplate and crankshaft (arrows) to ensure correct alignment during reassembly

16.4 Have an assistant engage a screwdriver in the ring gear to prevent the crankshaft from turning as the bolts are loosened

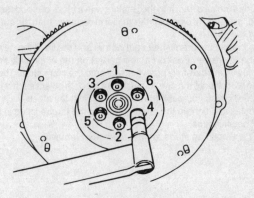

16.9 Tighten the flywheel/driveplate bolts following this sequence

2B

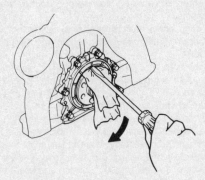

17.2 The quick way to replace the crankshaft rear oil seal is to simply pry the old one out with a screwdriver, lubricate the crankshaft journal and the lip of the new seal with moly-base grease and push the new seal into place – the trouble is, the seal lip is pretty stiff and can be easily damaged during installation if you're not careful

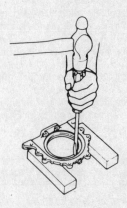

17.5 After removing the retainer from the block, support it on a couple of wood blocks and drive out the old seal with a screwdriver and hammer

Installation

8 Position the flywheel/driveplate against the crankshaft. Be sure to align the marks made during removal. Note that some engines have an alignment dowel or staggered bolt holes to ensure correct installation. Before installing the bolts, apply thread locking compound to the threads.

9 Wedge a screwdriver in the ring gear teeth to keep the flywheel/driveplate from turning as you tighten the bolts to the torque listed in this Chapter's Specifications. Follow a criss-cross pattern (see illustration) and work up to the final torque in three steps.

10 The remainder of installation is the reverse of the removal procedure.

17 Crankshaft rear oil seal – replacement

Refer to illustrations 17.2, 17.5 and 17.6

1 The flywheel/driveplate must be removed from the vehicle for this pro-cedure (see Section 16).

2 The seal can be replaced without dropping the oil pan or removing the seal retainer. However, this method is not recommended because the lip of the seal is quite stiff and it's possible to cock the seal in the retainer bore or damage it during installation. If you want to take the chance, pry out the old seal with a screwdriver (see illustration). Apply moly-base grease to the crankshaft seal journal and the lip of the new seal and carefully push the new seal into place. The lip is stiff so carefully work it onto the seal journal of the crankshaft with a smooth object like the end of an extension as you tap the seal into place. Don't rush it or you may damage the seal.

3 The following method is recommended but requires removal of the oil pan (see Section 14) and the seal retainer.

4 After the oil pan has been removed, remove the bolts, detach the seal retainer and peel off the old gasket.

5 Position the seal and retainer assembly on a couple of wood blocks on a workbench and drive the old seal out from the back side with a screwdriver (see illustration).

6   Drive the new seal into the retainer with a block of wood **(see illustration)** or a section of pipe slightly smaller in diameter than the outside diameter of the seal.

7   Lubricate the crankshaft seal journal and the lip of the new seal with moly-base grease. Position a new gasket on the engine block.

8   Slowly and carefully push the seal onto the crankshaft. The seal lip is stiff, so work it onto the crankshaft with a smooth object such as the end of an extension as you push the retainer against the block.

9   Install and tighten the retainer bolts to the torque listed in this Chapter's Specifications.

10   The remaining steps are the reverse of removal.

17.6   Drive the new seal into the retainer with a block of wood or a section of pipe, if you have one large enough – make sure you don't cock the seal in the retainer bore

Chapter 2 Part C
General engine overhaul procedures

Contents

Specifications

3T-C (pushrod) engine

General

Cylinder compression pressure at 250 rpm	
Standard	164 psi
Minimum	128 psi
Oil pressure (engine hot)	
At 3000 rpm	43 to 78 psi
At idle	4.3 psi minimum

Cylinder head warpage limits

Head-to-block surface	0.002 in (0.05 mm)
Manifold surface	0.004 in (0.1 mm)

3T-C (pushrod) engine (continued)

Valves and related components

Minimum valve margin width	0.020 in (0.5 mm)
Intake valve	
Stem diameter	0.3136 to 0.3142 in (7.965 to 7.980 mm)
Stem-to-guide clearance	
Standard	0.001 to 0.0024 in (0.025 to 0.060 mm)
Service limit	0.0031 in (0.08 mm)
Length	
Standard	4.291 in (109.0 mm)
Minimum	Not available
Exhaust valve	
Stem diameter	0.3136 to 0.3142 in (7.965 to 7.980 mm)
Stem-to-guide clearance	
Standard	0.0012 to 0.0026 in (0.030 to 0.065 mm)
Service limit	0.0039 in (0.10 mm)
Length	
Standard	4.291 in (109.0 mm)
Minimum	Not available
Valve spring	
Pressure	58.0 lbs at 1.48 in (26.3 kg at 37.7 mm)
Free length	1.657 in (42.1 mm)
Out-of-square limit	0.075 in (2.0 mm)
Valve lifter	
Diameter	0.8731 to 0.8740 in (22.178 to 22.199 mm)
Lifter-to-bore clearance	
Standard	0.0008 to 0.0012 in (0.02 to 0.03 mm)
Service limit	0.004 in (0.10 mm)

Crankshaft and connecting rods

Connecting rod journal	
Diameter	1.8888 to 1.8898 in (47.976 to 48.000 mm)
Taper and out-of-round limits	0.0004 in (0.01 mm)
Bearing oil clearance	
Standard	0.0009 to 0.0019 in (0.024 to 0.048 mm)
Service limit	0.0031 in (0.08 mm)
Connecting rod side clearance (endplay)	
Standard	0.0063 to 0.0102 in (0.16 to 0.26 mm)
Service limit	0.012 in (0.30 mm)
Main bearing journal	
Diameter	2.2825 to 2.2835 in (57.976 to 58.000 mm)
Taper and out-of-round limits	0.0004 in (0.01 mm)
Bearing oil clearance	
Standard	0.0009 to 0.0019 in (0.024 to 0.048 mm)
Service limit	0.0039 in (0.10 mm)
Crankshaft endplay	
Standard	0.0008 to 0.0087 in (0.02 to 0.22 mm)
Service limit	0.0118 in (0.30 mm)
Thrust bearing thickness	
Standard	0.0961 to 0.0980 in (2.440 to 2.490 mm)
O/S type 0.125	0.0985 to 0.1005 in (2.503 to 2.553 mm)
O/S type 0.250	0.1018 to 0.1030 in (2.585 to 2.615 mm)

Engine block

Deck warpage limit	0.002 in (0.05 mm)
Cylinder bore	
Diameter	
Standard	3.3465 to 3.3484 in (85.000 to 85.050 mm)
Service limit	0.008 in (0.20 mm)
Taper and out-of-round limits	0.0008 in (0.02 mm)

Pistons and rings

Piston diameter (standard)	3.3437 to 3.3457 in (84.93 to 84.98 mm)
Piston-to-bore clearance	0.0020 to 0.0028 in (0.05 to 0.07 mm)

Piston ring end gap
   No. 1 (top) compression ring .... 0.0039 to 0.0098 in (0.100 to 0.250 mm)
   No. 2 (middle) compression ring .... 0.0059 to 0.0118 in (0.150 to 0.300 mm)
   Oil control ring .... 0.0079 to 0.0276 in (0.200 to 0.700 mm)
Piston ring side clearance
   No. 1 (top) compression ring .... 0.0008 to 0.0024 in (0.020 to 0.060 mm)
   No. 2 (middle) compression ring .... 0.0006 to 0.0022 in (0.015 to 0.055 mm)

Torque specifications*   **Ft-lbs**
Main bearing cap bolts .... 53 to 63
Connecting rod cap nuts .... 29 to 36

* Note: *Refer to Part A for additional torque specifications.*

4A-C (SOHC) and 4A-GE (DOHC) engines

General
Cylinder compression pressure
  4A-C engine
    Standard .... 178 psi
    Minimum .... 128 psi
  4A-GE engine
    Standard .... 179 psi
    Minimum .... 128 psi
Oil pressure (engine warm)
  At 3000 rpm .... 36 to 71 psi
  At idle .... 4.3 psi minimum

Cylinder head warpage limits
4A-C engine
  Block surface .... 0.002 in (0.05 mm)
  Camshaft surface .... 0.002 in (0.05 mm)
  Manifold surface .... 0.0039 in (0.10 mm)
4A-GE engine
  Block surface .... 0.002 in (0.05 mm)
  Manifold surfaces
    Intake .... 0.0020 in (0.05 mm)
    Exhaust .... 0.0039 in (0.10 mm)
    Air control valve .... 0.0020 in (0.05 mm)

Valves and related components
Minimum valve margin width
  Intake .... 0.020 in (0.5 mm)
  Exhaust
    4A-C engine .... 0.039 in (1.0 mm)
    4A-GE engine .... 0.020 in (0.5 mm)
Intake valve
  Stem diameter
    4A-C engine .... 0.2744 to 0.2750 in (6.970 to 6.985 mm)
    4A-GE engine .... 0.2350 to 0.2356 in (5.970 to 5.985 mm)
  Stem-to-guide clearance
    Standard .... 0.0010 to 0.0024 in (0.025 to 0.060 mm)
    Service limit .... 0.0031 in (0.08 mm)
  Length
    4-AC engine
      Standard .... 4.208 in (106.9 mm)
      Minimum .... 4.188 in (106.4 mm)
    4A-GE engine
      Standard .... 3.921 in (99.60 mm)
      Minimum .... 3.902 in (99.10 mm)
Exhaust valve
  Stem diameter
    4A-C engine .... 0.2742 to 0.2748 in (6.965 to 6.980 mm)
    4A-GE engine .... 0.2348 to 0.2354 in (5.965 to 5.980 mm)

2C

Valves and related components (continued)

Stem-to-guide clearance
  Standard . . . . 0.0012 to 0.0026 in (0.030 to 0.065 mm)
  Service limit . . . . 0.0039 in (0.10 mm)
Length
  4A-C engine
    Standard . . . . 4.204 in (106.8 mm)
    Minimum . . . . 4.184 in (106.3 mm)
  4A-GE engine
    Standard . . . . 3.9272 in (99.75 mm)
    Minimum . . . . 3.9075 in (99.25 mm)
Valve spring
  Out-of-square limit
    4A-C engine . . . . 0.079 in (2.0 mm)
    4A-GE engine . . . . 0.098 in (2.5 mm)
  Free length
    4A-C engine . . . . 1.756 in (44.6 mm)
    4A-GE engine . . . . 1.645 in (41.8 mm)
  Pressure/length
    4A-C engine . . . . 52.0 lbs at 1.520 in (23.6 kg at 38.6 mm)
    4A-GE engine . . . . 34.8 lbs at 1.366 in (15.8 kg at 34.7 mm)
  Installed height
    4A-C engine . . . . 1.520 in (38.6 mm)
    4A-GE engine . . . . 1.366 in (34.7 mm)

Crankshaft and connecting rods

Connecting rod journal
  Diameter . . . . 1.5742 to 1.5748 in (39.985 to 40.000 mm)
  Taper and out-of-round limits . . . . 0.0008 in (0.02 mm)
  Bearing oil clearance
    Standard . . . . 0.0008 to 0.0020 in (0.020 to 0.051 mm)
    Service limit . . . . 0.0031 in (0.08 mm)
Connecting rod side clearance (endplay)
  Standard . . . . 0.0059 to 0.0098 in (0.15 to 0.25 mm)
  Service limit . . . . 0.012 in (0.30 mm)
Main bearing journal
  Diameter
    4A-C engine . . . . 1.8891 to 1.8898 in (47.982 to 48.000 mm)
    4A-GE engine (1985 and 1986) . . . . 1.8892 to 1.8898 in (47.985 to 48.000 mm)
    4A-Ge engine (1987)
      Marked "0" . . . . 1.8895 to 1.8898 in (47.994 to 48.000 mm)
      Marked "1" . . . . 1.8895 to 1.8893 in (47.994 to 47.988 mm)
      Marked "2" . . . . 1.8893 to 1.8891 in (47.988 to 47.982 mm)
  Taper and out-of-round limits . . . . 0.0008 in (0.02 mm)
  Runout limit . . . . 0.0024 in (0.06 mm)
  Bearing oil clearance
    4A-C engine (standard) . . . . 0.0012 to 0.0026 in (0.030 to 0.065 mm)
    4A-GE engine (standard)
      1985 . . . . 0.0005 to 0.0019 in (0.012 to 0.049 mm)
      1986 and 1987 . . . . 0.0005 to 0.0015 in (0.012 to 0.039 mm)
    Service limit (all) . . . . 0.0039 in (0.10 mm)
Crankshaft endplay
  Standard . . . . 0.0008 to 0.0087 in (0.020 to 0.220 mm)
  Service limit . . . . 0.012 in (0.30 mm)
Thrust bearing thickness . . . . 0.0961 to 0.0980 in (2.440 to 2.490 mm)

Engine block

Deck warpage limit . . . . 0.0020 in (0.05 mm)
Cylinder bore
  Diameter
    Standard . . . . 3.1890 to 3.1902 in (81.00 to 81.03 mm)
    Service limit . . . . 3.1980 in (81.23 mm)
  Taper and out-of-round limits . . . . 0.0008 in (0.020 mm)

Pistons and rings

Piston diameter	
4A-C engine	
1983 through 1985	
Size number 1	3.1846 to 3.1850 in (80.89 to 80.90 mm)
Size number 2	3.1850 to 3.1854 in (80.90 to 80.91 mm)
Size number 3	3.1854 to 3.1858 in (80.91 to 80.92 mm)
1986	3.1846 to 3.1858 in (80.89 to 80.92 mm)
1987	3.1850 to 3.1864 in (80.90 to 80.93 mm)
4A-GE engine	3.1846 to 3.1858 in (80.89 to 80.92 mm)
Piston-to-bore clearance	0.0039 to 0.0047 in (0.10 to 0.12 mm)
Piston ring end gap	
4A-C engine	
No. 1 (top) compression ring	0.0098 to 0.0185 in (0.250 to 0.470 mm)
No. 2 (middle) compression ring	0.0059 to 0.0165 in (0.150 to 0.420 mm)
Oil control ring	0.0118 to 0.0401 in (0.300 to 1.020 mm)
4A-GE engine	
No. 1 (top) compression ring	0.0098 to 0.0185 in (0.250 to 0.470 mm)
No. 2 (middle) compression ring	
1985	0.0059 to 0.0165 in (0.150 to 0.420 mm)
1986-on	0.0078 to 0.0165 in (0.20 to 0.42 mm)
Oil control ring	0.0118 to 0.0401 in (0.30 to 1.02 mm)
Piston ring side clearance	
No. 1 (top) compression ring	0.0016 to 0.0031 in (0.040 to 0.080 mm)
No. 2 (middle) compression ring	0.0012 to 0.0028 in (0.03 to 0.07 mm)

Torque specifications*

	Ft-lbs
Main bearing cap bolts	43
Connecting rod cap nuts	36

* Note: *Refer to Part B for additional torque specifications.*

1   General information

Included in this portion of Chapter 2 are the general overhaul procedures for the cylinder head and internal engine components.

The information ranges from advice concerning preparation for an overhaul and the purchase of replacement parts to detailed, step-by step procedures covering removal and installation of internal engine components and the inspection of parts.

The following Sections have been written based on the assumption the engine has been removed from the vehicle. For information concerning in-vehicle engine repair, as well as removal and installation of the external components necessary for the overhaul, see Part A or B of this Chapter and Section 7 of this Part.

The Specifications included in this Part are only those necessary for the inspection and overhaul procedures which follow. Refer to Parts A and B for additional Specifications.

2   Engine overhaul – general information

Refer to illustrations 2.4a and 2.4b

It's not always easy to determine when, or if, an engine should be completely overhauled, as a number of factors must be considered.

High mileage is not necessarily an indication that an overhaul is needed, while low mileage doesn't preclude the need for an overhaul. Frequency of servicing is probably the most important consideration. An engine that's had regular and frequent oil and filter changes, as well as other required maintenance, will most likely give many thousands of miles of reliable service. Conversely, a neglected engine may require an overhaul very early in its life.

Excessive oil consumption is an indication that piston rings, valve seals and/or valve guides are in need of attention. Make sure that oil leaks aren't responsible before deciding that the rings and/or guides are bad. Perform a cylinder compression check to determine the extent of the work required (see Section 3).

Check the oil pressure with a gauge installed in place of the oil pressure sending unit **(see illustrations)** and compare it to the Specifications. If it's extremely low, the bearings and/or oil pump are probably worn out.

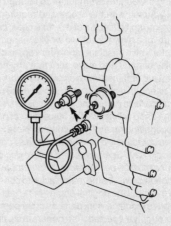

2.4a   On the 3T-C engine, the oil pressure sending unit is located near the distributor

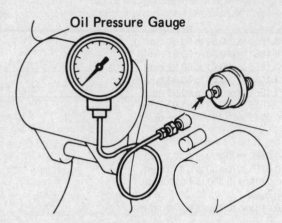

Oil Pressure Gauge

2.4b   On 4A-C and 4A-GE engines, the oil pressure sending unit is located above the oil filter

Loss of power, rough running, knocking or metallic engine noises, excessive valve train noise and high fuel consumption rates may also point to the need for an overhaul, especially if they're all present at the same time. If a complete tune-up doesn't remedy the situation, major mechanical work is the only solution.

An engine overhaul involves restoring the internal parts to the specifications of a new engine. During an overhaul, the piston rings are replaced and the cylinder walls are reconditioned (rebored and/or honed). If a rebore is done by an automotive machine shop, new oversize pistons will also be installed. The main bearings, connecting rod bearings and camshaft bearings are generally replaced with new ones and, if necessary, the crankshaft may be reground to restore the journals. Generally, the valves are serviced as well, since they're usually in less-than-perfect condition at this point. While the engine is being overhauled, other components, such as the distributor, starter and alternator, can be rebuilt as well. The end result should be a like new engine that will give many trouble free miles. **Note:** *Critical cooling system components such as the hoses, drivebelts, thermostat and water pump MUST be replaced with new parts when an engine is overhauled. The radiator should be checked carefully to ensure that it isn't clogged or leaking (see Chapter 3). Also, we don't recommend overhauling the oil pump – always install a new one when an engine is rebuilt.*

Before beginning the engine overhaul, read through the entire procedure to familiarize yourself with the scope and requirements of the job. Overhauling an engine isn't difficult, but it is time consuming. Plan on the vehicle being tied up for a minimum of two weeks, especially if parts must be taken to an automotive machine shop for repair or reconditioning. Check on availability of parts and make sure that any necessary special tools and equipment are obtained in advance. Most work can be done with typical hand tools, although a number of precision measuring tools are required for inspecting parts to determine if they must be replaced. Often an automotive machine shop will handle the inspection of parts and offer advice concerning reconditioning and replacement. **Note:** *Always wait until the engine has been completely disassembled and all components, especially the engine block, have been inspected before deciding what service and repair operations must be performed by an automotive machine shop.* Since the block's condition will be the major factor to consider when determining whether to overhaul the original engine or buy a rebuilt one, never purchase parts or have machine work done on other components until the block has been thoroughly inspected. As a general rule, time is the primary cost of an overhaul, so it doesn't pay to install worn or substandard parts.

As a final note, to ensure maximum life and minimum trouble from a rebuilt engine, everything must be assembled with care in a spotlessly clean environment.

3   Cylinder compression check

Refer to illustration 3.6

1   A compression check will tell you what mechanical condition the upper end (pistons, rings, valves, head gasket[s]) of your engine is in. Specifically, it can tell you if the compression is down due to leakage caused by worn piston rings, defective valves and seats or a blown head gasket. **Note:** *The engine must be at normal operating temperature and the battery must be fully charged for this check.*

2   Begin by cleaning the area around the spark plugs before you remove them (compressed air should be used, if available, otherwise a small brush or even a bicycle tire pump will work). The idea is to prevent dirt from getting into the cylinders as the compression check is being done.

3   Remove all of the spark plugs from the engine (Chapter 1).

4   Block the throttle wide open.

5   Detach the coil wire from the center of the distributor cap and ground it on the engine block. Use a jumper wire with alligator clips on each end to ensure a good ground. On EFI equipped vehicles, the fuel pump circuit should also be disabled (see Chapter 4).

6   Install the compression gauge in the spark plug hole **(see illustration)**.

7   Crank the engine over at least seven compression strokes and watch the gauge. The compression should build up quickly in a healthy engine. Low compression on the first stroke, followed by gradually increasing pressure on successive strokes, indicates worn piston rings. A low compression reading on the first stroke, which doesn't build up during successive strokes, indicates leaking valves or a blown head gasket (a cracked head could also be the cause). Deposits on the undersides of the valve heads can also cause low compression. Record the highest gauge reading obtained.

8   Repeat the procedure for the remaining cylinders and compare the results to the Specifications listed in this Chapter.

9   Add some engine oil (about three squirts from a plunger-type oil can) to each cylinder, through the spark plug hole, and repeat the test.

10   If the compression increases after the oil is added, the piston rings are definitely worn. If the compression doesn't increase significantly, the leakage is occurring at the valves or head gasket. Leakage past the valves may be caused by burned valve seats and/or faces or warped, cracked or bent valves.

11   If two adjacent cylinders have equally low compression, there's a strong possibility that the head gasket between them is blown. The appearance of coolant in the combustion chambers or the crankcase would verify this condition.

12   If one cylinder is 20 percent lower than the others, and the engine has a slightly rough idle, a worn exhaust lobe on the camshaft could be the cause.

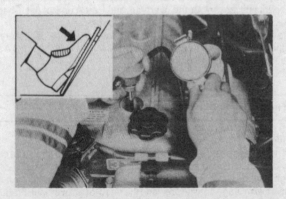

3.6   A compression gauge with a threaded fitting for the spark plug hole is preferred over the type that requires hand pressure to maintain the seal – be sure to open the throttle valve as far as possible during the compression check!

13   If the compression is unusually high, the combustion chambers are probably coated with carbon deposits. If that's the case, the cylinder head(s) should be removed and decarbonized.

14   If compression is way down or varies greatly between cylinders, it would be a good idea to have a leak-down test performed by an automotive repair shop. This test will pinpoint exactly where the leakage is occurring and how severe it is.

4   Engine removal – methods and precautions

If you've decided that an engine must be removed for overhaul or major repair work, several preliminary steps should be taken.

Locating a suitable place to work is extremely important. Adequate work space, along with storage space for the vehicle, will be needed. If a shop or garage isn't available, at the very least a flat, level, clean work surface made of concrete or asphalt is required.

Cleaning the engine compartment and engine before beginning the removal procedure will help keep tools clean and organized.

An engine hoist or A-frame will also be necessary. Make sure the equipment is rated in excess of the combined weight of the engine and transmission. Safety is of primary importance, considering the potential hazards involved in lifting the engine out of the vehicle.

If the engine is being removed by a novice, a helper should be available. Advice and aid from someone more experienced would also be helpful. There are many instances when one person cannot simultaneously perform all of the operations required when lifting the engine out of the vehicle.

Plan the operation ahead of time. Arrange for or obtain all of the tools and equipment you'll need prior to beginning the job. Some of the equipment necessary to perform engine removal and installation safely and with relative ease are (in addition to an engine hoist) a heavy duty floor jack, complete sets of wrenches and sockets as described in the front of this manual, wooden blocks and plenty of rags and cleaning solvent for mopping up spilled oil, coolant and gasoline. If the hoist must be rented, make sure that you arrange for it in advance and perform all of the operations possible without it beforehand. This will save you money and time.

Plan for the vehicle to be out of use for quite a while. A machine shop will be required to perform some of the work which the do-it-yourselfer can't accomplish without special equipment. These shops often have a busy schedule, so it would be a good idea to consult them before removing the engine in order to accurately estimate the amount of time required to rebuild or repair components that may need work.

Always be extremely careful when removing and installing the engine. Serious injury can result from careless actions. Plan ahead, take your time and a job of this nature, although major, can be accomplished successfully.

5   Engine – removal and installation

Refer to illustrations 5.6, 5.12, 5.15, 5.16, 5.17, 5.18 and 5.19

Note: *Read through the entire Section before beginning this procedure. The engine and transmission are removed as a unit and then separated outside the vehicle.*

Removal

1   On fuel injected vehicles, relieve the fuel system pressure (see Chapter 4).

2   Disconnect the negative cable from the battery.

3   Place protective covers on the fenders and cowl and remove the hood (see Chapter 11).

4   Remove the air cleaner assembly (see Chapter 4).

5   Raise the vehicle and support it securely on jackstands. Drain the cooling system and engine oil and remove the drivebelts (see Chapter 1).

6   Clearly label, then disconnect all vacuum lines, coolant and emissions hoses, wiring harness connectors, ground straps and fuel lines. Masking tape and/or a touch up paint applicator work well for marking items **(see illustration)**. Take instant photos or sketch the locations of components and brackets.

7   Remove the cooling fan(s), shroud(s) and radiator (Chapter 3).

8   Release the residual fuel pressure in the tank by removing the gas cap, then undo the fuel lines connecting the engine to the chassis (see Chapter 4). Plug or cap all open fittings.

9   Disconnect the throttle linkage (and TV linkage and speed control cable, if equipped) from the engine (see Chapter 4).

10   Disconnect the oxygen sensor wire.

11   On power steering equipped vehicles, unbolt the power steering pump. If clearance allows, tie the pump aside without disconnecting the hoses. If necessary, remove the pump (see Chapter 10).

12   On vehicles equipped with air conditioning, unbolt the compressor and set it aside **(see illustration)**. Do not disconnect the refrigerant hoses.

13   Detach the exhaust pipe(s) from the manifold(s) (Chapter 4).

14   Remove the driveshaft (see Chapter 8), wire harness, shift linkage and speedometer cable from the transmission (Chapter 7).

2C

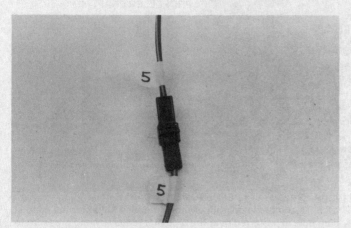

5.6   Label both ends of each wire before disconnecting them

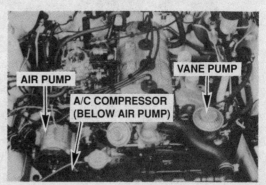

5.12   Unbolt the A/C compressor and use wire or rope to tie it out of the way

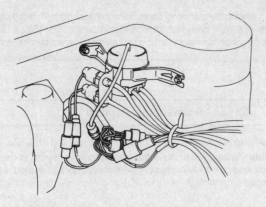

5.15　Remove the emission control valves from the fender well

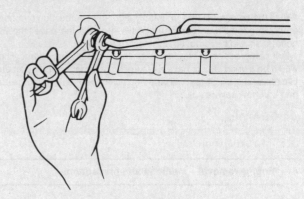

5.16　Use a flare-nut wrench and a back-up wrench to loosen the transmission lines

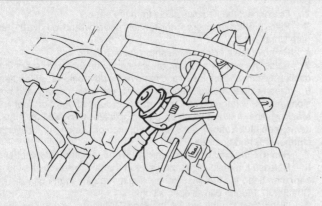

5.17　Detach the fuel hose and remove the pulsation damper from the delivery pipe

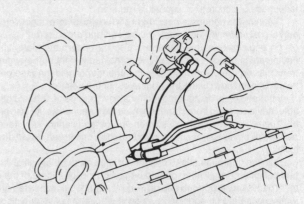

5.18　Remove the cold start injector pipe

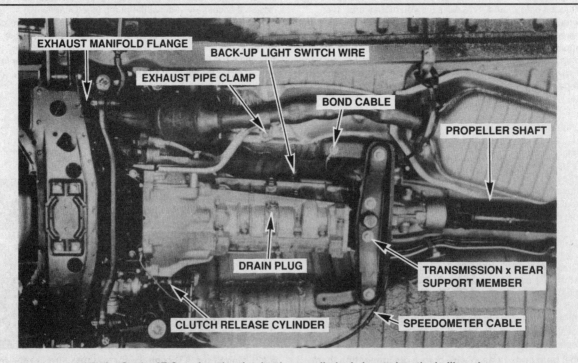

5.19　On the 3T-C engine, the clutch release cylinder is located on the bellhousing

4A-C engine

15   Remove the emission control valve set. Disconnect the two mounting bolts and six connectors from the emission control valve set and lay the valve set on the engine **(see illustration)**.
16   If equipped, disconnect the two oil cooler lines from the automatic transmission **(see illustration)**.

4A-GE engine

17   Remove the fuel hose from the pulsation damper and pressure regulator **(see illustration)**.
18   Remove the cold start injector pipe from the cold start injector and the fuel delivery pipe **(see illustration)**.

All engines

19   Disconnect the wires from the starter and remove the clutch release cylinder **(see illustration)**.
20   Attach a lifting sling to the brackets on the engine. Position a hoist and connect the sling to it. Take up the slack until there is slight tension on the hoist.
21   Recheck to be sure nothing except the mounts are still connecting the engine/transmission to the vehicle. Disconnect anything still remaining.
22   Support the transmission with a floor jack. Place a block of wood on the jack head to prevent damage to the transmission. Remove the bolts from the engine and transmission mounts. **Warning:** *Do Not place any part of your body under the engine/transmission when it's supported only by a hoist or other lifting device.*
23   Slowly lift the engine/transmission out of the vehicle. It may be necessary to pry the mounts away from the frame brackets.
24   Move the engine/transmission away from the vehicle and carefully lower the hoist until the transmission is supported in a level position. Support the engine/transmission assembly with jackstands or large wood blocks before proceeding to the next Step.
25   On automatic transmission equipped models, detach the torque converter dust shield from the lower bellhousing. Remove the torque converter-to-driveplate fasteners (see Chapter 7) and push the converter back slightly into the bellhousing.
26   Remove the engine-to-transmission bolts and separate the engine from the transmission. The torque converter should remain in the transmission.
27   Place the engine on the floor or remove the flywheel/driveplate and mount the engine on an engine stand.

Installation

28   Check the engine/transmission mounts. If they're worn or damaged, replace them.
29   On manual transmission equipped models, inspect the clutch components (see Chapter 8) and on automatic models inspect the converter seal and bushing.
30   On manual transmission equipped vehicles, apply a dab of high-temperature grease to the pilot bearing.
31   On automatic transmission equipped models, apply a dab of grease to the nose of the converter and to the seal lips.
32   Carefully guide the transmission into place, following the procedure outlined in Chapter 7. **Caution:** *Do Not use the bolts to force the engine and transmission into alignment. It may crack or damage major components.*
33   Install the engine-to-transmission bolts and tighten them securely.
34   Attach the hoist to the engine and carefully lower the engine/transmission assembly into the engine compartment.
35   Install the mount bolts and tighten them securely.
36   Reinstall the remaining components and fasteners in the reverse order of removal.
37   Add coolant, oil, power steering and transmission fluids as needed (see Chapter 1).
38   Run the engine and check for proper operation and leaks. Shut off the engine and recheck the fluid levels.

6   Engine rebuilding alternatives

The do-it-yourselfer is faced with a number of options when performing an engine overhaul. The decision to replace the engine block, piston/connecting rod assemblies and crankshaft depends on a number of factors, with the number one consideration being the condition of the block. Other considerations are cost, access to machine shop facilities, parts availability, time required to complete the project and the extent of prior mechanical experience on the part of the do-it-yourselfer.

Some of the rebuilding alternatives include:

Individual parts – If the inspection procedures reveal that the engine block and most engine components are in reusable condition, purchasing individual parts may be the most economical alternative. The block, crankshaft and piston/connecting rod assemblies should all be inspected carefully. Even if the block shows little wear, the cylinder bores should be surface honed.

Short block – A short block consists of an engine block with a crankshaft and piston/connecting rod assemblies already installed. All new bearings are incorporated and all clearances will be correct. The existing camshaft, valve train components, cylinder head(s) and external parts can be bolted to the short block with little or no machine shop work necessary.

Long block – A long block consists of a short block plus an oil pump, oil pan, cylinder head(s), rocker arm cover(s), camshaft and valve train components, timing sprockets and chain or gears and timing cover. All components are installed with new bearings, seals and gaskets incorporated throughout. The installation of manifolds and external parts is all that's necessary.

Give careful thought to which alternative is best for you and discuss the situation with local automotive machine shops, auto parts dealers and experienced rebuilders before ordering or purchasing replacement parts.

2C

7   Engine overhaul – disassembly sequence

Refer to illustration 7.5

1   It's much easier to disassemble and work on the engine if it's mounted on a portable engine stand. A stand can often be rented quite cheaply from an equipment rental yard. Before the engine is mounted on a stand, the flywheel/driveplate and rear oil seal retainer should be removed from the engine.
2   If a stand isn't available, it's possible to disassemble the engine with it blocked up on the floor. Be extra careful not to tip or drop the engine when working without a stand.
3   If you're going to obtain a rebuilt engine, all external components must come off first, to be transferred to the replacement engine, just as they will if you're doing a complete engine overhaul yourself. These include:

Alternator and brackets
Emissions control components
Distributor, spark plug wires and spark plugs
Thermostat and housing cover
Water pump
EFI components
Intake/exhaust manifolds
Oil filter
Engine mounts
Clutch and flywheel/driveplate
Engine rear end plate

Note: *When removing the external components from the engine, pay close attention to details that may be helpful or important during installation. Note the installed position of gaskets, seals, spacers, pins, brackets, washers, bolts and other small items.*

4   If you're obtaining a short block, which consists of the engine block, crankshaft, pistons and connecting rods all assembled, then the cylinder head(s), oil pan and oil pump will have to be removed as well. See Engine rebuilding alternatives for additional information regarding the different possibilities to be considered.

5   If you're planning a complete overhaul, the engine must be disassembled and the internal components removed in the following order **(see illustration)**.

Camshaft cover(s)
Intake and exhaust manifolds
Timing belt covers
Timing belt and sprockets
Cylinder head
Oil pan

Oil pump
Piston/connecting rod assemblies
Crankshaft rear oil seal retainer
Crankshaft and main bearings

6   Before beginning the disassembly and overhaul procedures, make sure the following items are available. Also, refer to Engine overhaul – reassembly sequence for a list of tools and materials needed for engine reassembly.

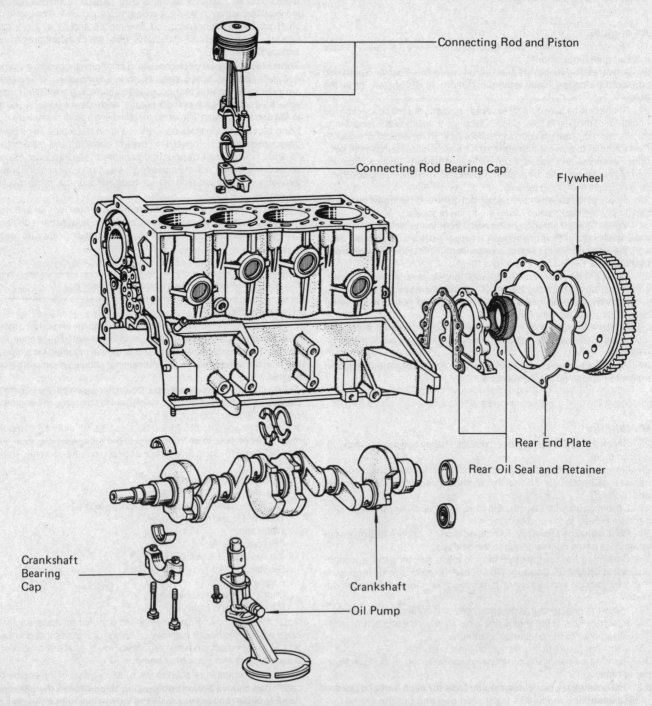

Connecting Rod and Piston

Connecting Rod Bearing Cap

Flywheel

Rear End Plate

Rear Oil Seal and Retainer

Crankshaft
Bearing
Cap

Crankshaft

Oil Pump

7.5   Typical engine lower end components – exploded view

Common hand tools
Small cardboard boxes or plastic bags for storing parts
Gasket scraper
Ridge reamer
Vibration damper puller
Micrometers
Telescoping gauges
Dial indicator set
Valve spring compressor
Cylinder surfacing hone
Piston ring groove cleaning tool
Electric drill motor
Tap and die set
Wire brushes
Oil gallery brushes
Cleaning solvent

8   Cylinder head – disassembly

Refer to illustrations 8.2 and 8.3

Note: *New and rebuilt cylinder heads are commonly available for most engines at dealerships and auto parts stores. Due to the fact that some specialized tools are necessary for the disassembly and inspection procedures, and replacement parts may not be readily available, it may be more practical and economical for the home mechanic to purchase a replacement head rather than taking the time to disassemble, inspect and recondition the original.*

1   Cylinder head disassembly involves removal of the intake and exhaust valves and related components. It's assumed that the lifters or rocker arms and camshaft(s) have already been removed (see Part A or B as needed).

2   Before the valves are removed, arrange to label and store them, along with their related components, so they can be kept separate and reinstalled in the same valve guides they are removed from **(see illustration)**.

3   Compress the springs on the first valve with a spring compressor and remove the keepers **(see illustration)**. Carefully release the valve spring compressor and remove the retainer, the spring and the spring seat (if used). **Caution:** Be very careful not to nick or otherwise damage the lifter bores when compressing the valve springs.

4   Pull the valve out of the head, then remove the oil seal from the guide. If the valve binds in the guide (won't pull through), push it back into the

head and deburr the area around the keeper groove with a fine file or whetstone.

5   Repeat the procedure for the remaining valves. Remember to keep all the parts for each valve together so they can be reinstalled in the same locations.

6   Once the valves and related components have been removed and stored in an organized manner, the head should be thoroughly cleaned and inspected. If a complete engine overhaul is being done, finish the engine disassembly procedures before beginning the cylinder head cleaning and inspection process.

9   Cylinder head – cleaning and inspection

Refer to illustrations 9.12, 9.14, 9.16, 9.17 and 9.18

1   Thorough cleaning of the cylinder head and related valve train components, followed by a detailed inspection, will enable you to decide how much valve service work must be done during the engine overhaul. **Note:** *If the engine was severely overheated, the cylinder head is probably warped (see Step 12).*

Cleaning

2   Scrape all traces of old gasket material and sealing compound off the head gasket, intake manifold and exhaust manifold sealing surfaces. Be very careful not to gouge the cylinder head. Special gasket removal solvents that soften gaskets and make removal much easier are available at auto parts stores.

3   Remove all built up scale from the coolant passages.

4   Run a stiff wire brush through the various holes to remove deposits that may have formed in them.

5   Run an appropriate size tap into each of the threaded holes to remove corrosion and thread sealant that may be present. If compressed air is available, use it to clear the holes of debris produced by this operation. **Warning:** *Wear eye protection when using compressed air!*

6   Clean the exhaust and intake manifold bolt/stud threads with a wire brush.

7   Clean the cylinder head with solvent and dry it thoroughly. Compressed air will speed the drying process and ensure that all holes and recessed areas are clean. **Note:** *Decarbonizing chemicals are available and may prove very useful when cleaning cylinder heads and valve train components. They are very caustic and should be used with caution. Be sure to follow the instructions on the container.*

2C

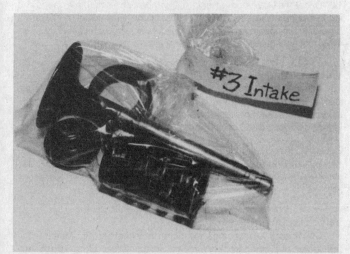

8.2   Have several plastic bags ready (one for each valve) before disassembling the head – label each bag and put the entire contents of each valve assembly in one bag as shown

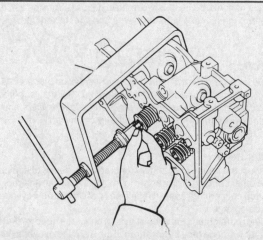

8.3   Use a valve spring compressor to compress the springs, then remove the keepers from the valve stem with a magnet or small needle-nose pliers

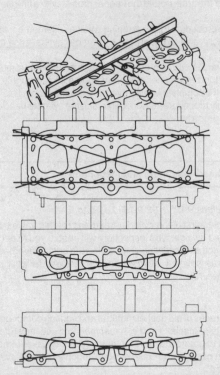

9.12   Check the cylinder head gasket surfaces for warpage by trying to slip a feeler gauge under the precision straightedge (see this Chapter's Specifications for the maximum warpage allowed and use a feeler gauge of that thickness)

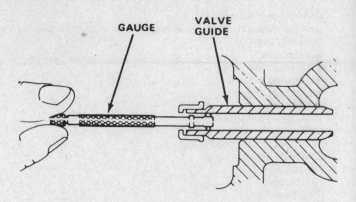

9.14   Use a small hole gauge to determine the inside diameter of each valve guide (the gauge is then measured with a micrometer)

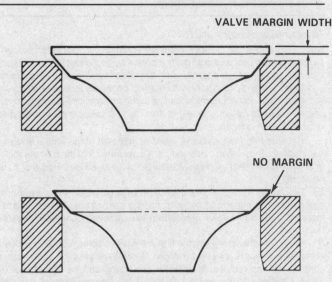

9.16   The margin width on each valve must be as specified (if no margin exists, the valve cannot be reused)

8   Clean the lifters and rocker arms (if used) with solvent and dry them thoroughly (don't mix them up during the cleaning process). Compressed air will speed the drying process and can be used to clean out the oil passages.
9   Clean all the valve springs, spring seats, keepers and retainers with solvent and dry them thoroughly. Do the components from one valve at a time to avoid mixing up the parts.
10   Scrape off any heavy deposits that may have formed on the valves, then use a motorized wire brush to remove deposits from the valve heads and stems. Again, make sure the valves don't get mixed up.

Inspection

Note: *Be sure to perform all of the following inspection procedures before concluding that machine shop work is required. Make a list of the items that need attention. The inspection procedures for the lifters and rocker arms, as well as the camshaft(s), can be found in Part A.*

Cylinder head

11   Inspect the head very carefully for cracks, evidence of coolant leakage and other damage. If cracks are found, check with an automotive machine shop concerning repair. If repair isn't possible, a new cylinder head should be obtained.
12   Using a straightedge and feeler gauge, check the head gasket mating surface for warpage **(see illustration)**. If the warpage exceeds the specified limit, it can be resurfaced at an automotive machine shop.
13   Examine the valve seats in each of the combustion chambers. If they're pitted, cracked or burned, the head will require valve service that's beyond the scope of the home mechanic.

14   Check the valve stem-to-guide clearance with a small hole gauge and micrometer **(see illustration)**. After this is done, if there's still some doubt regarding the condition of the valve guides they should be checked by an automotive machine shop (the cost should be minimal).

Valves

15   Carefully inspect each valve face for uneven wear, deformation, cracks, pits and burned areas. Check the valve stem for scuffing and galling and the neck for cracks. Rotate the valve and check for any obvious indication that it's bent. Look for pits and excessive wear on the end of the stem. The presence of any of these conditions indicates the need for valve service by an automotive machine shop.
16   Measure the margin width on each valve **(see illustration)**. Any valve with a margin narrower than specified will have to be replaced with a new one.

Valve components

17   Check each valve spring for wear (on the ends) and pits. Measure the free length and compare it to the Specifications **(see illustration)**. Any springs that are shorter than specified have sagged and should not be re-used. The tension of all springs should be checked with a special fixture before deciding that they're suitable for use in a rebuilt engine (take the springs to an automotive machine shop for this check).

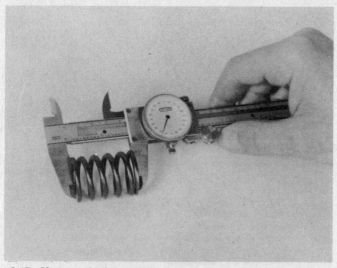

9.17   Measure the free length of each valve spring with a dial or vernier caliper

9.18   Check each valve spring for squareness

18   Stand each spring on a flat surface and check it for squareness **(see illustration)**. If any of the springs are distorted or sagged, replace all of them with new parts.
19   Check the spring retainers and keepers for obvious wear and cracks. Any questionable parts should be replaced with new ones, as extensive damage will occur if they fail during engine operation.
20   Any damaged or excessively worn parts must be replaced with new ones.
21   If the inspection process indicates that the valve components are in generally poor condition and worn beyond the limits specified, which is usually the case in an engine that's being overhauled, reassemble the valves in the cylinder head and refer to Section 10 for valve servicing recommendations.

2C

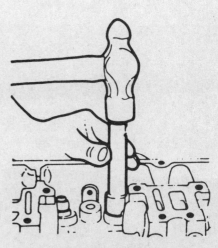

11.3   Gently tap the valve seals into place with a deep socket and hammer

10   Valves – servicing

1   Because of the complex nature of the job and the special tools and equipment needed, servicing of the valves, the valve seats and the valve guides, commonly known as a valve job, should be done by a professional.
2   The home mechanic can remove and disassemble the head, do the initial cleaning and inspection, then reassemble and deliver it to a dealer service department or an automotive machine shop for the actual service work. Doing the inspection will enable you to see what condition the head and valvetrain components are in and will ensure that you know what work and new parts are required when dealing with an automotive machine shop.
3   The dealer service department, or automotive machine shop, will remove the valves and springs, recondition or replace the valves and valve seats, recondition the valve guides, check and replace the valve springs, spring retainers and keepers (as necessary), replace the valve seals with new ones, reassemble the valve components and make sure the installed spring height is correct. The cylinder head gasket surface will also be resurfaced if it's warped.
4   After the valve job has been performed by a professional, the head will be in like new condition. When the head is returned, be sure to clean it again before installation on the engine to remove any metal particles and abrasive grit that may still be present from the valve service or head resurfacing operations. Use compressed air, if available, to blow out all the oil holes and passages.

11   Cylinder head – reassembly

Refer to illustration 11.3
1   Regardless of whether or not the head was sent to an automotive repair shop for valve servicing, make sure it's clean before beginning reassembly.
2   If the head was sent out for valve servicing, the valves and related components will already be in place. Begin the reassembly procedure with Step 8.
3   Install new seals on each of the valve guides. **Note:** *Intake and exhaust valves require different seals – DO NOT mix them up! Gently tap each intake valve seal into place until it's seated on the guide* **(see illustration)**. **Caution:** *Don't hammer on the valve seals once they're seated or you may damage them. Don't twist or cock the seals during installation or they won't seat properly on the valve stems.*
4   Beginning at one end of the head, lubricate and install the first valve. Apply moly-base grease or clean engine oil to the valve stem.
5   Drop the spring seat or shim(s) over the valve guide and set the valve spring and retainer in place.

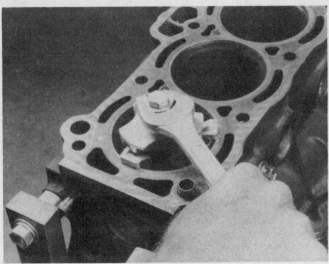

12.1   A ridge reamer is required to remove the ridge from the top of each cylinder – do this before removing the pistons!

12.3   Check the connecting rod side clearance with a feeler gauge as shown here

12.4   The connecting rods and caps should be marked to indicate which cylinder they're installed in – if they aren't, mark them with a center punch to avoid confusion during reassembly

12.6   To prevent damage to the crankshaft journals and cylinder walls, slip sections of rubber or plastic hose over the rod bolts before removing the pistons

6   Compress the springs with a valve spring compressor and carefully install the keepers in the upper groove, then slowly release the compressor and make sure the keepers seat properly. Apply a small dab of grease to each keeper to hold it in place if necessary **(see illustration 6.17 in Part A)**.

7   Repeat the procedure for the remaining valves. Be sure to return the components to their original locations – don't mix them up!

12   Pistons/connecting rods – removal

Refer to illustrations 12.1, 12.3, 12.4 and 12.6

Note: *Prior to removing the piston/connecting rod assemblies, remove the cylinder head, the oil pan and the oil pump pick-up tube by referring to the appropriate Sections in Chapter 2.*

1   Use your fingernail to feel if a ridge has formed at the upper limit of ring travel (about 1/4-inch down from the top of each cylinder). If carbon deposits or cylinder wear have produced ridges, they must be completely removed with a special tool **(see illustration)**. Follow the manufacturer's instructions provided with the tool. Failure to remove the ridges before at-tempting to remove the piston/connecting rod assemblies may result in piston breakage.

2   After the cylinder ridges have been removed, turn the engine upside-down so the crankshaft is facing up.

3   Before the connecting rods are removed, check the endplay with feeler gauges. Slide them between the first connecting rod and the crankshaft throw until the play is removed **(see illustration)**. The endplay is equal to the thickness of the feeler gauge(s). If the endplay exceeds the service limit, new connecting rods will be required. If new rods (or a new crankshaft) are installed, the endplay may fall under the specified minimum (if it does, the rods will have to be machined to restore it – consult an automotive machine shop for advice if necessary). Repeat the procedure for the remaining connecting rods.

4   Check the connecting rods and caps for identification marks. If they aren't plainly marked, use a small center punch to make the appropriate number of indentations on each rod and cap (1, 2, 3, etc., depending on the cylinder they're associated with) **(see illustration)**.

5   Loosen each of the connecting rod cap nuts 1/2-turn at a time until they can be removed by hand. Remove the number one connecting rod cap and bearing insert. Don't drop the bearing insert out of the cap.

6   Slip a short length of plastic or rubber hose over each connecting rod cap bolt to protect the crankshaft journal and cylinder wall as the piston is removed **(see illustration)**.

7   Remove the bearing insert and push the connecting rod/piston assembly out through the top of the engine. Use a wooden hammer handle to push on the upper bearing surface in the connecting rod. If resistance is felt, double-check to make sure that all of the ridge was removed from the cylinder.

8   Repeat the procedure for the remaining cylinders.

9   After removal, reassemble the connecting rod caps and bearing inserts in their respective connecting rods and install the cap nuts finger-tight. Leaving the old bearing inserts in place until reassembly will help prevent the connecting rod bearing surfaces from being accidentally nicked or gouged.

10   Don't separate the pistons from the connecting rods (see Section 17 for additional information).

13   Crankshaft – removal

Refer to illustrations 13.1, 13.3 and 13.4

Note: *The crankshaft can be removed only after the engine has been removed from the vehicle. It's assumed the flywheel or driveplate, crankshaft pulley (vibration damper), timing belt, oil pan, oil pick-up tube, oil pump and piston/connecting rod assemblies have already been removed. The rear main oil seal retainer must be unbolted and separated from the block before proceeding with crankshaft removal.*

1   Before the crankshaft is removed, check the endplay. Mount a dial indicator on the block with the stem in line with the crankshaft, and touching one of the crank throws or the end of the crankshaft **(see illustration)**.

2   Push the crankshaft all the way to the rear and zero the dial indicator. Next, pry the crankshaft to the front as far as possible and check the reading on the dial indicator. The distance that it moves is the endplay. If it's greater than specified, check the crankshaft thrust surfaces for wear. If no wear is evident, new thrust bearings should correct the endplay.

3   If a dial indicator isn't available, feeler gauges can be used. Gently pry or push the crankshaft all the way to the front of the engine. Slip feeler gauges between the crankshaft and the front face of the thrust bearing to determine the clearance **(see illustration)**.

4   Check the main bearing caps to see if they're marked to indicate their locations. They should be numbered consecutively from the front of the engine to the rear. If they aren't, mark them with number stamping dies or a center punch. Main bearing caps generally have a cast-in arrow, which points to the front of the engine. Loosen the main bearing cap bolts 1/4-turn at a time each, in the recommended sequence **(see illustration)**, until they can be removed by hand. Note if any stud bolts are used and make sure they're returned to their original locations when the crankshaft is reinstalled.

5   Gently tap the caps with a soft-face hammer, then separate them from the engine block. If necessary, use the bolts as levers to remove the caps. Try not to drop the bearing inserts if they come out with the caps.

6   Carefully lift the crankshaft out of the engine. It may be a good idea to have an assistant available, since the crankshaft is quite heavy. With the bearing inserts in place in the engine block and main bearing caps or cap assembly, return the caps to their respective locations on the engine block and tighten the bolts finger-tight.

2C

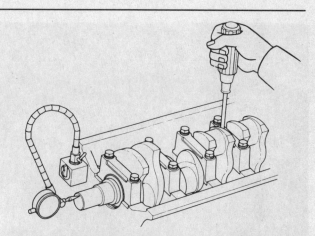

13.1   Check crankshaft endplay with a dial indicator . . .

13.3   . . . or slip feeler gauges between the crankshaft and thrust bearings – the endplay is equal to the feeler gauge thickness

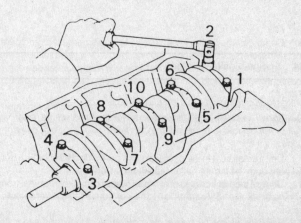

13.4   Loosen the main bearing cap bolts in this numerical order

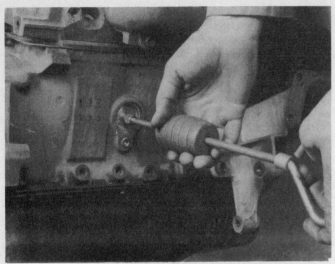

14.1   Remove the core plugs with a puller – if they're driven into the block they may be impossible to retrieve

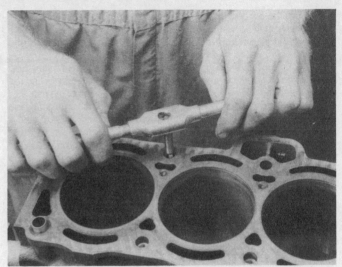

14.8   Clean and restore all threaded holes in the block – especially the main bearing cap and head bolt holes – with a tap (be sure to remove debris from the holes when you're done)

14.10   A large socket on an extension can be used to drive the new core plugs into the bores

14   Engine block – cleaning

Refer to illustrations 14.1, 14.8 and 14.10

Caution: *The core plugs (also known as freeze or soft plugs) may be difficult or impossible to retrieve if they're driven into the block coolant passages.*

1   Drill a small hole in the center of each core plug and pull them out with an auto body type dent puller **(see illustration)**.

2   Using a gasket scraper, remove all traces of gasket material from the engine block. Be very careful not to nick or gouge the gasket sealing surfaces.

3   Remove the main bearing caps or cap assembly and separate the bearing inserts from the caps and the engine block. Tag the bearings, indicating which cylinder they were removed from and whether they were in the cap or the block, then set them aside.

4   Remove all of the threaded oil gallery plugs from the block. The plugs are usually very tight – they may have to be drilled out and the holes re-tapped. Use new plugs when the engine is reassembled.

5   If the engine is extremely dirty it should be taken to an automotive machine shop to be steam cleaned or hot tanked.

6   After the block is returned, clean all oil holes and oil galleries one more time. Brushes specifically designed for this purpose are available at most auto parts stores. Flush the passages with warm water until the water runs clear, dry the block thoroughly and wipe all machined surfaces with a light, rust preventive oil. If you have access to compressed air, use it to speed the drying process and to blow out all the oil holes and galleries. **Warning:** *Wear eye protection when using compressed air!*

7   If the block isn't extremely dirty or sludged up, you can do an adequate cleaning job with hot soapy water and a stiff brush. Take plenty of time and do a thorough job. Regardless of the cleaning method used, be sure to clean all oil holes and galleries very thoroughly, dry the block completely and coat all machined surfaces with light oil.

8   The threaded holes in the block must be clean to ensure accurate torque readings during reassembly. Run the proper size tap into each of the holes to remove rust, corrosion, thread sealant or sludge and restore damaged threads **(see illustration)**. If possible, use compressed air to clear the holes of debris produced by this operation. Now is a good time to clean the threads on the head bolts and the main bearing cap bolts as well.

9   Reinstall the main bearing caps and tighten the bolts finger-tight.

10   After coating the sealing surfaces of the new core plugs with sealant, install them in the engine block **(see illustration)**. Make sure they're driven in straight and seated properly or leakage could result. Special tools are available for this purpose, but a large socket, with an outside diameter that will just slip into the core plug, a 1/2-inch drive extension and a hammer will work just as well.

11   Apply non-hardening sealant or Teflon tape to the new oil gallery plugs and thread them into the holes in the block. Make sure they're tightened securely.

12   If the engine isn't going to be reassembled right away, cover it with a large plastic trash bag to keep it clean.

15   Engine block – inspection

Refer to illustrations 15.4a, 15.4b, 15.4c and 15.12

1   Before the block is inspected, it should be cleaned as described in Section 14.

2   Visually check the block for cracks, rust and corrosion. Look for stripped threads in the threaded holes. It's also a good idea to have the

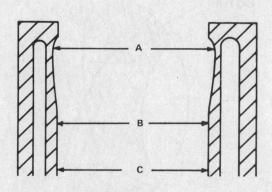

15.4a   Measure the diameter of each cylinder just under the wear ridge (A), at the center (B) and at the bottom (C)

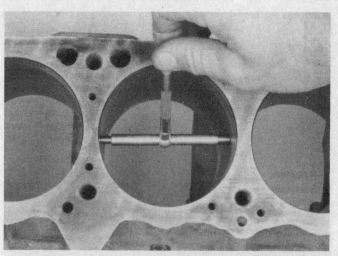

15.4b   The ability to "feel" when the telescoping gauge is at the correct point will be developed over time, so work slowly and repeat the check until you're satisfied the bore measurement is accurate

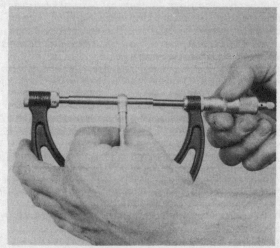

15.4c   The gauge is then measured with a micrometer to determine the bore size

15.12   Lay the straightedge across the block, diagonally and from end-to-end when making the check

2C

block checked for hidden cracks by an automotive machine shop that has the special equipment to do this type of work. If defects are found, have the block repaired, if possible, or replaced.

3   Check the cylinder bores for scuffing and scoring.

4   Measure the diameter of each cylinder at the top (just under the ridge area), center and bottom of the cylinder bore, parallel to the crankshaft axis **(see illustrations)**.

5   Next, measure each cylinder's diameter at the same three locations across the crankshaft axis. Compare the results to the Specifications listed in this Chapter.

6   If the required precision measuring tools aren't available, the piston-to-cylinder clearances can be obtained, though not quite as accurately, using feeler gauge stock. Feeler gauge stock comes in 12-inch lengths and various thicknesses and is generally available at auto parts stores.

7   To check the clearance, select a feeler gauge and slip it into the cylinder along with the matching piston. The piston must be positioned exactly as it normally would be. The feeler gauge must be between the piston and cylinder on one of the thrust faces (90-degrees to the piston pin bore).

8   The piston should slip through the cylinder (with the feeler gauge in place) with moderate pressure.

9   If it falls through or slides through easily, the clearance is excessive and a new piston will be required. If the piston binds at the lower end of the cylinder and is loose toward the top, the cylinder is tapered. If tight spots are encountered as the piston/feeler gauge is rotated in the cylinder, the cylinder is out-of-round.

10   Repeat the procedure for the remaining pistons and cylinders.

11   If the cylinder walls are badly scuffed or scored, or if they're out-of-round or tapered beyond the limits given in the Specifications, have the engine block rebored and honed at an automotive machine shop. If a rebore is done, oversize pistons and rings will be required.

12   Using a precision straightedge and feeler gauge, check the block deck (the surface that mates with the cylinder head) for distortion **(see illustration)**. If it's distorted beyond the specified limit, it can be resurfaced by an automotive machine shop.

13   If the cylinders are in reasonably good condition and not worn to the outside of the limits, and if the piston-to-cylinder clearances can be maintained properly, then they don't have to be rebored. Honing is all that's necessary (Section 16).

16.3a   If this is the first time you've ever honed cylinders, you'll get better results with a "bottle brush" hone than you will with a traditional spring-loaded hone

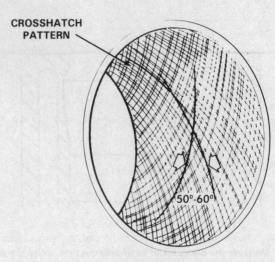

16.3b   The cylinder hone should leave a smooth, crosshatch pattern with the lines intersecting at approximately a 60-degree angle

16   Cylinder honing

Refer to illustrations 16.3a and 16.3b

1   Prior to engine reassembly, the cylinder bores must be honed so the new piston rings will seat correctly and provide the best possible combustion chamber seal. **Note:** *If you don't have the tools or don't want to tackle the honing operation, most automotive machine shops will do it for a reasonable fee.*

2   Before honing the cylinders, install the main bearing caps or cap assembly (without bearing inserts) and tighten the bolts to the torque listed in this Chapter's Specifications.

3   Two types of cylinder hones are commonly available – the flex hone or "bottle brush" type and the more traditional surfacing hone with spring-loaded stones. Both will do the job, but for the less experienced mechanic the "bottle brush" hone will probably be easier to use. You'll also need some kerosene or honing oil, rags and an electric drill motor. Proceed as follows:

   a) Mount the hone in the drill motor, compress the stones and slip it into the first cylinder **(see illustration)**. Be sure to wear safety goggles or a face shield!
   b) Lubricate the cylinder with plenty of honing oil, turn on the drill and move the hone up-and-down in the cylinder at a pace that will produce a fine crosshatch pattern on the cylinder walls. Ideally, the crosshatch lines should intersect at approximately a 60-degree angle **(see illustration)**. Be sure to use plenty of lubricant and don't take off any more material than is absolutely necessary to produce the desired finish. **Note:** *Piston ring manufacturers may specify a smaller crosshatch angle than the traditional 60-degrees – read and follow any instructions included with the new rings.*
   c) Don't withdraw the hone from the cylinder while it's running. Instead, shut off the drill and continue moving the hone up-and-down in the cylinder until it comes to a complete stop, then compress the stones and withdraw the hone. If you're using a "bottle brush" type hone, stop the drill motor, then turn the chuck in the normal direction of rotation while withdrawing the hone from the cylinder.
   d) Wipe the oil out of the cylinder and repeat the procedure for the remaining cylinders.

4   After the honing job is complete, chamfer the top edges of the cylinder bores with a small file so the rings won't catch when the pistons are installed. Be very careful not to nick the cylinder walls with the end of the file.

5   The entire engine block must be washed again very thoroughly with warm, soapy water to remove all traces of the abrasive grit produced during the honing operation. **Note:** *The bores can be considered clean when a lint-free white cloth – dampened with clean engine oil – used to wipe them out doesn't pick up any more honing residue, which will show up as gray areas on the cloth. Be sure to run a brush through all oil holes and galleries and flush them with running water.*

6   After rinsing, dry the block and apply a coat of light rust preventive oil to all machined surfaces. Wrap the block in a plastic trash bag to keep it clean and set it aside until reassembly.

17   Pistons/connecting rods – inspection

Refer to illustrations 17.4a, 17.4b, 17.10, 17.11a, and 17.11b

1   Before the inspection process can be carried out, the piston/connecting rod assemblies must be cleaned and the original piston rings removed from the pistons. **Note:** *Always use new piston rings when the engine is reassembled.*

2   Using a piston ring installation tool, carefully remove the rings from the pistons. Be careful not to nick or gouge the pistons in the process.

3   Scrape all traces of carbon from the top of the piston. A handheld wire brush or a piece of fine emery cloth can be used once the majority of the deposits have been scraped away. Do not, under any circumstances, use a wire brush mounted in a drill motor to remove deposits from the pistons. The piston material is soft and may be eroded away by the wire brush.

4   Use a piston ring groove cleaning tool to remove carbon deposits from the ring grooves. If a tool isn't available, a piece broken off the old ring will do the job. Be very careful to remove only the carbon deposits – don't remove any metal and do not nick or scratch the sides of the ring grooves **(see illustrations)**.

5   Once the deposits have been removed, clean the piston/rod assemblies with solvent and dry them with compressed air (if available). Make sure the oil return holes in the back sides of the ring grooves and the oil hole in the lower end of each rod are clear.

6   If the pistons and cylinder walls aren't damaged or worn excessively, and if the engine block is not rebored, new pistons won't be necessary. Normal piston wear appears as even vertical wear on the piston thrust surfaces and slight looseness of the top ring in its groove. New piston rings, however, should always be used when an engine is rebuilt.

7   Carefully inspect each piston for cracks around the skirt, at the pin bosses and at the ring lands.

8   Look for scoring and scuffing on the thrust faces of the skirt, holes in the piston crown and burned areas at the edge of the crown. If the skirt is scored or scuffed, the engine may have been suffering from overheating

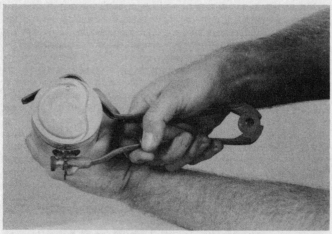

17.4a   The piston ring grooves can be cleaned with a special tool, as shown here, . . .

17.4b   . . . or a piece of broken piston ring

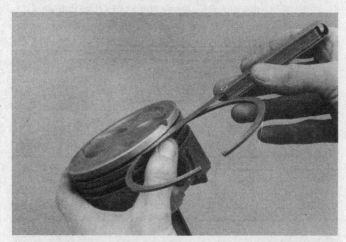

17.10   Check the ring side clearance with a feeler gauge at several points around the groove

17.11a   Measure the piston diameter at a 90-degree angle to the piston pin – depending on the model, the pistons must be measured at a precise point

2C

and/or abnormal combustion, which caused excessively high operating temperatures. The cooling and lubrication systems should be checked thoroughly. A hole in the piston crown is an indication that abnormal combustion (preignition) was occurring. Burned areas at the edge of the piston crown are usually evidence of spark knock (detonation). If any of the above problems exist, the causes must be corrected or the damage will occur again. The causes may include intake air leaks, incorrect fuel/air mixture, incorrect ignition timing and EGR system malfunctions.

9   Corrosion of the piston, in the form of small pits, indicates that coolant is leaking into the combustion chamber and/or the crankcase. Again, the cause must be corrected or the problem may persist in the rebuilt engine.

10   Measure the piston ring side clearance by laying a new piston ring in each ring groove and slipping a feeler gauge in beside it **(see illustration)**. Check the clearance at three or four locations around each groove. Be sure to use the correct ring for each groove – they are different. If the side clearance is greater than specified, new pistons will have to be used.

11   Check the piston-to-bore clearance by measuring the bore (see Section 15) and the piston diameter. Make sure the pistons and bores are correctly matched. Measure the piston across the skirt, at a 90-degree angle to the piston pin, the specified distance down from the top of the piston or the lower edge of the oil ring groove **(see illustration)**. Subtract the piston diameter from the bore diameter to obtain the clearance. If it's greater than specified, the block will have to be rebored and new pistons and rings installed. **Note:** *The piston grade designation (1, 2 or 3) is stamped on the piston crown* **(see illustration)**.

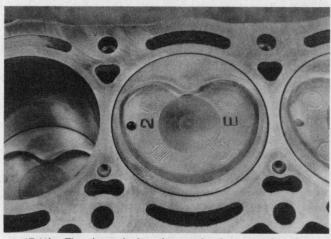

17.11b   The piston designation number is stamped on the piston crown

12   Check the piston-to-rod clearance by twisting the piston and rod in opposite directions. Any noticeable play indicates excessive wear, which must be corrected. The piston/connecting rod assemblies should be taken

18.1   Clean the crankshaft oil passages with a wire or stiff plastic bristle brush and flush them out with solvent (typical crankshaft shown)

18.3   Rubbing a penny lengthwise on each journal will give you a quick idea of its condition – if copper rubs off the penny and adheres to the crankshaft, the journals should be reground (typical crankshaft shown)

18.4   Chamfer the oil holes to remove sharp edges that might gouge or scratch the new bearings (typical crankshaft shown)

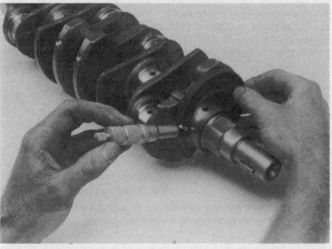

18.6   Measure the diameter of each crankshaft journal at several points to detect taper and out-of-round conditions

to an automotive machine shop to have the pistons and rods resized and new pins installed.

13   If the pistons must be removed from the connecting rods for any reason, they should be taken to an automotive machine shop. While they are there have the connecting rods checked for bend and twist, since automotive machine shops have special equipment for this purpose. **Note:** *Unless new pistons and/or connecting rods must be installed, do not disassemble the pistons and connecting rods.*

14   Check the connecting rods for cracks and other damage. Temporarily remove the rod caps, lift out the old bearing inserts, wipe the rod and cap bearing surfaces clean and inspect them for nicks, gouges and scratches. After checking the rods, replace the old bearings, slip the caps into place and tighten the nuts finger-tight. **Note:** *If the engine is being rebuilt because of a connecting rod knock, be sure to install new rods.*

---

18   Crankshaft – inspection

Refer to illustrations 18.1, 18.3, 18.4, 18.6 and 18.8

1   Clean the crankshaft with solvent and dry it with compressed air (if available). Be sure to clean the oil holes with a stiff brush and flush them with solvent **(see illustration)**.

2   Check the main and connecting rod bearing journals for uneven wear, scoring, pits and cracks.

3   Rub a penny across each journal several times **(see illustration)**. If a journal picks up copper from the penny, it's too rough and must be reground.

4   Remove all burrs from the crankshaft oil holes with a stone, file or scraper **(see illustration)**.

5   Check the rest of the crankshaft for cracks and other damage. It should be magnafluxed to reveal hidden cracks – an automotive machine shop will handle the procedure.

6   Using a micrometer, measure the diameter of the main and connecting rod journals and compare the results to the Specifications **(see illustration)**. By measuring the diameter at a number of points around each journal's circumference, you'll be able to determine whether or not the journal is out-of-round. Take the measurement at each end of the journal, near the crank throws, to determine if the journal is tapered. Crankshaft runout should be checked also, but large V-blocks and a dial indicator are needed to do it correctly. If you don't have the equipment, have a machine shop check the runout.

7   If the crankshaft journals are damaged, tapered, out-of-round or worn beyond the limits given in the Specifications, have the crankshaft reground by an automotive machine shop. Be sure to use the correct size bearing inserts if the crankshaft is reconditioned.

18.8   If the seals have worn grooves in the crankshaft journals, or if the seal journals are nicked or scratched, the new seal(s) will leak (typical crankshaft shown)

8   Check the oil seal journals at each end of the crankshaft for wear and damage **(see illustration)**. If the seal has worn a groove in the journal, or if it's nicked or scratched, the new seal may leak when the engine is reassembled. In some cases, an automotive machine shop may be able to repair the journal by pressing on a thin sleeve. If repair isn't feasible, a new or different crankshaft should be installed.
9   Refer to Section 19 and examine the main and rod bearing inserts.

---

19   Main and connecting rod bearings – inspection and bearing selection

Inspection
Refer to illustration 19.1

1   Even though the main and connecting rod bearings should be replaced with new ones during the engine overhaul, the old bearings should be retained for close examination, as they may reveal valuable information about the condition of the engine **(see illustration)**.
2   Bearing failure occurs because of lack of lubrication, the presence of dirt or other foreign particles, overloading the engine and corrosion. Regardless of the cause of bearing failure, it must be corrected before the engine is reassembled to prevent it from happening again.
3   When examining the bearings, remove them from the engine block, the main bearing caps, the connecting rods and the rod caps and lay them out on a clean surface in the same general position as their location in the engine. This will enable you to match any bearing problems with the corresponding crankshaft journal.
4   Dirt and other foreign particles get into the engine in a variety of ways. It may be left in the engine during assembly, or it may pass through filters or the PCV system. It may get into the oil, and from there into the bearings. Metal chips from machining operations and normal engine wear are often present. Abrasives are sometimes left in engine components after reconditioning, especially when parts are not thoroughly cleaned using the proper cleaning methods. Whatever the source, these foreign objects often end up embedded in the soft bearing material and are easily recognized. Large particles will not embed in the bearing and will score or gouge the bearing and journal. The best prevention for this cause of bearing failure is to clean all parts thoroughly and keep everything spotlessly clean during engine assembly. Frequent and regular engine oil and filter changes are also recommended.
5   Lack of lubrication (or lubrication breakdown) has a number of interrelated causes. Excessive heat (which thins the oil), overloading (which

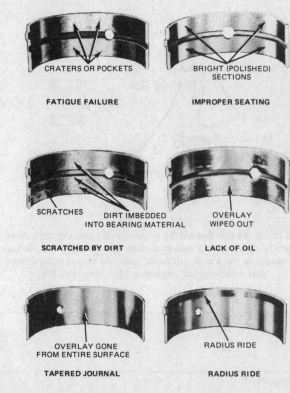

19.1   When inspecting the main and connecting rod bearings, look for these problems

squeezes the oil from the bearing face) and oil leakage or throw off (from excessive bearing clearances, worn oil pump or high engine speeds) all contribute to lubrication breakdown. Blocked oil passages, which usually are the result of misaligned oil holes in a bearing shell, will also oil starve a bearing and destroy it. When lack of lubrication is the cause of bearing failure, the bearing material is wiped or extruded from the steel backing of the bearing. Temperatures may increase to the point where the steel backing turns blue from overheating.
6   Driving habits can have a definite effect on bearing life. Full throttle, low speed operation (lugging the engine) puts very high loads on bearings, which tends to squeeze out the oil film. These loads cause the bearings to flex, which produces fine cracks in the bearing face (fatigue failure). Eventually the bearing material will loosen in pieces and tear away from the steel backing. Short trip driving leads to corrosion of bearings because insufficient engine heat is produced to drive off the condensed water and corrosive gases. These products collect in the engine oil, forming acid and sludge. As the oil is carried to the engine bearings, the acid attacks and corrodes the bearing material.
7   Incorrect bearing installation during engine assembly will lead to bearing failure as well. Tight fitting bearings leave insufficient bearing oil clearance and will result in oil starvation. Dirt or foreign particles trapped behind a bearing insert result in high spots on the bearing which lead to failure.

Bearing selection
Refer to illustrations 19.10, 19.11, 19.12 and 19.13

8   If the original bearings are worn or damaged, or if the oil clearances are incorrect (Section 22 or 24), the following procedures should be used to select the correct new bearings for engine reassembly. However, if the crankshaft has been reground, new undersize bearings must be installed – the following procedure should not be used if undersize bearings are required! The automotive machine shop that reconditions the crankshaft will provide or help you select the correct size bearings. Regardless of how the

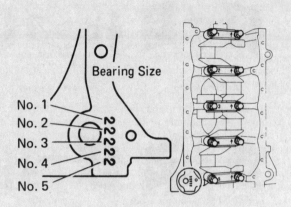

19.10   If the number on the original main bearing isn't clear, install a new bearing with a number that matches the number stamped into the block – different journals may require different size bearings (all engines – 1981 through 1986)

Cylinder Block No.	1	2	3	1	2	3	1	2	3
Crankshaft No.	0	0	0	1	1	1	2	2	2
Bearing No.	1	2	3	2	3	4	3	4	5

Example: Cylinder Block No. 2, Crankshaft No. 1 = Bearing No. 3

19.12   1987 4A-C and 4A-GE engine main bearing selection table

bearing sizes are determined, use the oil clearance, measured with Plastigage, as a guide to ensure the bearings are the right size.

Main bearings

9   If you need to use a STANDARD size main bearing, install one that has the same number as the original bearing (see illustrations 19.10 and 19.11 for the bearing number locations).

10   If you're working on a 1981 through 1986 engine and the number on the original main bearing has been obscured, install one that has the same number as the number stamped into the block for the corresponding cap location **(see illustration)**.

11   If you're working on a 1987 engine and the number on the original main bearing has been obscured, locate the main journal grade numbers stamped into the oil pan mating surface on the engine block **(see illustration)** and the main journal grade numbers on the crankshaft as well.

12   Use the accompanying chart to determine the correct bearings for each journal **(see illustration)**.

Connecting rod bearings

13   If you need to use a STANDARD size rod bearing, install one that has the same number as the number stamped into the connecting rod cap **(see illustration)**.

All bearings

14   Remember, the oil clearance is the final judge when selecting new bearing sizes. If you have any questions or are unsure which bearings to use, get help from a Toyota dealer parts or service department.

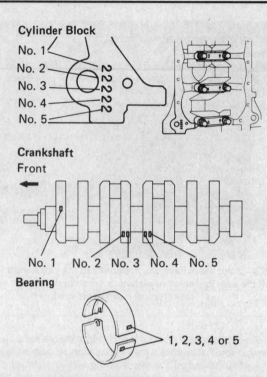

19.11   On 1987 4A-C and 4A-GE engines, the grade numbers are marked on the block as well as the crankshaft – use the accompanying table to select the correct main bearings

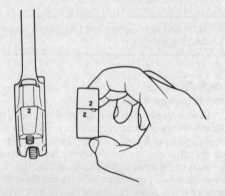

19.13   Connecting rod bearing size location

20   Engine overhaul – reassembly sequence

1   Before beginning engine reassembly, make sure you have all the necessary new parts, gaskets and seals as well as the following items on hand:

Common hand tools
A 1/2-inch drive torque wrench
Piston ring installation tool
Piston ring compressor
Short lengths of rubber or plastic hose to fit over connecting rod bolts
Plastigage
Feeler gauges
A fine-tooth file
New engine oil
Engine assembly lube or moly-base grease
Gasket sealer
Thread locking compound

2   In order to save time and avoid problems, engine reassembly must be done in the following general order:

Piston rings (Part C)
Crankshaft and main bearings (Part C)
Piston/connecting rod assemblies (Part C)
Rear crankshaft oil seal (Part C)
Cylinder head and rocker arms or lifters (Part A or B)
Camshaft (Part A or B)
Timing belt and sprockets (Part A or B)
Timing belt cover (Part B)
Oil pump (Part A or B)
Oil pick-up (Part A or B)
Oil pan (Part A or B)
Intake and exhaust manifolds (Part A or B)
Camshaft cover (Part A or B)
Flywheel/driveplate (Part A or B)

6   Excess end gap isn't critical unless it's greater than 0.040-inch. Again, double-check to make sure you have the correct rings for your engine.

7   Repeat the procedure for each ring that will be installed in the first cylinder and for each ring in the remaining cylinders. Remember to keep rings, pistons and cylinders matched up.

8   Once the ring end gaps have been checked/corrected, the rings can be installed on the pistons.

9   The oil control ring (lowest one on the piston) is usually installed first. It's composed of three separate components. Slip the spacer/expander into the groove (see illustration). If an anti-rotation tang is used, make sure it's inserted into the drilled hole in the ring groove. Next, install the lower side rail. Don't use a piston ring installation tool on the oil ring side rails, as they may be damaged. Instead, place one end of the side rail into the groove between the spacer/expander and the ring land, hold it firmly in place and slide a finger around the piston while pushing the rail into the

21   Piston rings – installation

Refer to illustrations 21.3, 21.4, 21.9a, 21.9b and 21.12

1   Before installing the new piston rings, the ring end gaps must be checked. It's assumed that the piston ring side clearance has been checked and verified correct (Section 17).

2   Lay out the piston/connecting rod assemblies and the new ring sets so the ring sets will be matched with the same piston and cylinder during the end gap measurement and engine assembly.

3   Insert the top (number one) ring into the first cylinder and square it up with the cylinder walls by pushing it in with the top of the piston (see illustration). The ring should be near the bottom of the cylinder, at the lower limit of ring travel.

4   To measure the end gap, slip feeler gauges between the ends of the ring until a gauge equal to the gap width is found (see illustration). The feeler gauge should slide between the ring ends with a slight amount of drag. Compare the measurement to the Specifications listed in this Chapter. If the gap is larger or smaller than specified, double-check to make sure you have the correct rings before proceeding.

5   If the gap is too small, replace the rings – DO NOT file the ends to increase the clearance.

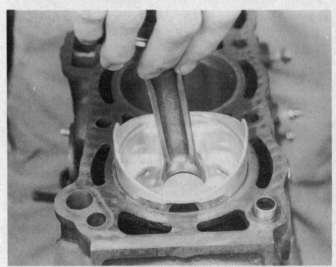

21.3   When checking piston ring end gap, the ring must be square in the cylinder bore – this is done by pushing it down with the top of a piston

21.4   Once the ring is at the lower limit of travel and square in the cylinder, measure the end gap with a feeler gauge

21.9a   Install the three-piece oil control ring first, one part at a time, beginning with the spacer/expander, . . .

2C

21.9b   . . . followed by the side rails – DO NOT use a piston ring installation tool to install the oil ring side rails

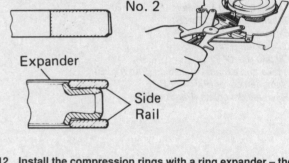

21.12   Install the compression rings with a ring expander – the beveled edge on the number two piston ring faces down

groove **(see illustration)**. Next, install the upper side rail in the same manner.

10   After the three oil ring components have been installed, check to make sure that both the upper and lower side rails can be turned smoothly in the ring groove.

11   The number two (middle) ring is installed next. It's usually stamped with a mark which must face up, toward the top of the piston. **Note:** *Always follow the instructions printed on the ring package or box – different manufacturers may require different approaches. Do not mix up the top and middle rings, as they have different cross sections.*

12   Use a piston ring installation tool and make sure the identification mark is facing the top of the piston, then slip the ring into the middle groove on the piston **(see illustration)**. Don't expand the ring any more than necessary to slide it over the piston.

13   Install the number one (top) ring in the same manner. Make sure the mark is facing up. Be careful not to confuse the number one and number two rings.

14   Repeat the procedure for the remaining pistons and rings.

22   Crankshaft – installation and main bearing oil clearance check

Refer to illustrations 22.10, 22.12, 22.14, 22.19a and 22.19b

1   Crankshaft installation is the first major step in engine reassembly. It's assumed at this point that the engine block and crankshaft have been cleaned, inspected and repaired or reconditioned.

2   Position the engine with the bottom facing up.

3   Remove the main bearing cap bolts and lift out the caps or cap assembly. Lay the caps out in the proper order to ensure correct installation.

4   If they're still in place, remove the old bearing inserts from the block and the main bearing caps. Wipe the main bearing surfaces of the block and caps with a clean, lint free cloth. They must be kept spotlessly clean!

Main bearing oil clearance check

5   Clean the back sides of the new main bearing inserts and lay the bearing half with the oil groove in each main bearing saddle in the block. Lay the other bearing half from each bearing set in the corresponding main bearing cap. Make sure the tab on each bearing insert fits into the recess in the block or cap. Also, the oil holes in the block must line up with the oil holes in

the bearing insert. **Caution:** *Do not hammer the bearings into place and don't nick or gouge the bearing faces. No lubrication should be used at this time.*

6   The thrust bearings must be installed in the number three (center) cap.

7   Clean the faces of the bearings in the block and the crankshaft main bearing journals with a clean, lint free cloth. Check or clean the oil holes in the crankshaft, as any dirt here can go only one way – straight through the new bearings.

8   Once you're certain the crankshaft is clean, carefully lay it in position in the main bearings.

9   Before the crankshaft can be permanently installed, the main bearing oil clearance must be checked.

10   Trim several pieces of the appropriate size Plastigage (they must be slightly shorter than the width of the main bearings) and place one piece on each crankshaft main bearing journal, parallel with the journal axis **(see illustration)**.

11   Clean the faces of the bearings in the caps and install the caps in their respective positions (don't mix them up) with the arrows pointing toward the front of the engine.

22.10   Lay the Plastigage strips (arrow) on the main bearing journals, parallel to the crankshaft centerline

22.12 Main bearing cap bolt tightening sequence

22.14 Compare the width of the crushed Plastigage to the scale on the envelope to determine the main bearing oil clearance (always take the measurement at the widest point of the Plastigage); be sure to use the correct scale – standard and metric ones are included

12 Following the recommended sequence **(see illustration)**, tighten the main bearing cap bolts, in three steps, to the specified torque. Don't rotate the crankshaft at any time during this operation!

13 Remove the bolts and carefully lift off the main bearing caps or cap assembly. Keep them in order. Don't disturb the Plastigage or rotate the crankshaft. If any of the main bearing caps are difficult to remove, tap them gently from side-to-side with a soft-face hammer to loosen them.

14 Compare the width of the crushed Plastigage on each journal to the scale printed on the Plastigage envelope to obtain the main bearing oil clearance **(see illustration)**. Check the Specifications to make sure it's correct.

15 If the clearance is not as specified, the bearing inserts may be the wrong size (which means different ones will be required – see Section 19). Before deciding that different inserts are needed, make sure that no dirt or oil was between the bearing inserts and the caps or block when the clearance was measured. If the Plastigage is noticeably wider at one end than the other, the journal may be tapered (see Section 18).

16 Carefully scrape all traces of the Plastigage material off the main bearing journals and/or the bearing faces. Don't nick or scratch the bearing faces.

Final crankshaft installation

17 Carefully lift the crankshaft out of the engine. Clean the bearing faces in the block, then apply a thin, uniform layer of clean moly-base grease or engine assembly lube to each of the bearing surfaces. Coat the thrust bearings as well.

18 Lubricate the crankshaft surfaces that contact the oil seals with moly-base grease, engine assembly lube or clean engine oil.

19 Make sure the crankshaft journals are clean, then lay the crankshaft back in place in the block. Clean the faces of the bearings in the caps or cap assembly, then apply lubricant to them. Install the caps in their respective positions with the arrows pointing toward the front of the engine. **Note:** *Be sure to install the thrust bearings* **(see illustrations)**.

20 Apply a light coat of oil to the bolt threads and the under sides of the bolt heads, then install them. Tighten all except the center (number three) cap bolts (the one with the thrust bearings) to the specified torque (work from the center out and approach the final torque in three steps). Tighten the center cap bolts to 10-to-12 ft-lbs. Tap the ends of the crankshaft forward and backward with a lead or brass hammer to line up the thrust washer and crankshaft surfaces. Retighten all main bearing cap bolts to the

2C

22.19a Rotate the thrust bearings into position on the number three crankshaft journal with the oil grooves facing OUT

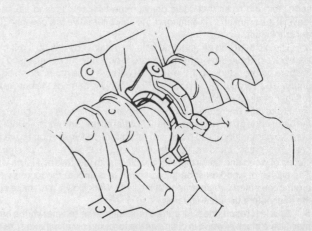

22.19b Install the thrust bearings in the number three cap with the oil grooves facing OUT

23.3 Support the retainer on a couple of wood blocks and drive out the old seal with a punch or screwdriver and hammer

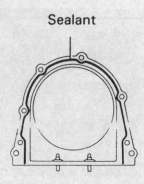

Sealant

23.6 Apply sealant to the retainer before bolting it to the block

specified torque, following the recommended sequence.

21   On manual transmission equipped models, install a new pilot bearing in the end of the crankshaft (see Chapter 8).

22   Rotate the crankshaft a number of times by hand to check for any obvious binding.

23   Check the crankshaft endplay with a feeler gauge or a dial indicator as described in Section 13. The endplay should be correct if the crankshaft thrust faces aren't worn or damaged and new thrust bearings have been installed.

24   Install a new rear oil seal, then bolt the retainer to the block (see Section 23).

23   Rear main oil seal installation

Refer to illustrations 23.3 and 23.6

1   The crankshaft must be installed first and the main bearing caps bolted in place, then the new seal should be installed in the retainer and the retainer bolted to the block.

2   Check the seal contact surface on the crankshaft very carefully for scratches and nicks that could damage the new seal lip and cause oil leaks. If the crankshaft is damaged, the only alternative is a new or different crankshaft.

3   The old seal can be removed from the retainer by driving it out from the back side **(see illustration)**. Be sure to note how far it's recessed into the bore before removing it; the new seal will have to be recessed an equal amount. Be very careful not to scratch or otherwise damage the bore in the retainer or oil leaks could develop.

4   Make sure the retainer is clean, then apply a thin coat of engine oil to the outer edge of the new seal. The seal must be pressed squarely into the bore, so hammering it into place isn't recommended. If you don't have access to a press, sandwich the housing and seal between two smooth pieces of wood and press the seal into place with the jaws of a large vise. The pieces of wood must be thick enough to distribute the force evenly around the entire circumference of the seal. Work slowly and make sure the seal enters the bore squarely.

5   As a last resort, the seal can be tapped into the retainer with a hammer. Use a block of wood to distribute the force evenly and make sure the seal is driven in squarely.

6   The seal lips must be lubricated with clean engine oil or moly-base grease before the seal/retainer is slipped over the crankshaft and bolted to

the block. Use a new gasket – and sealant – and make sure the dowel pins are in place before installing the retainer **(see illustration)**.

7   Tighten the bolts a little at a time until they're all at the torque listed in this Chapter's Specifications.

24   Pistons/connecting rods – installation and rod bearing oil clearance check

Refer to illustrations 24.3, 24.5, 24.9, 24.11, 24.13, 24.14 and 24.17

1   Before installing the piston/connecting rod assemblies, the cylinder walls must be perfectly clean, the top edge of each cylinder must be chamfered, and the crankshaft must be in place.

2   Remove the cap from the end of the number one connecting rod (refer to the marks made during removal). Remove the original bearing inserts and wipe the bearing surfaces of the connecting rod and cap with a clean, lint-free cloth. They must be kept spotlessly clean.

Connecting rod bearing oil clearance check

3   Clean the back side of the new upper bearing insert, then lay it in place in the connecting rod. Make sure the tab on the bearing fits into the recess in the rod so the oil holes line up **(see illustration)**. Don't hammer the bearing insert into place and be very careful not to nick or gouge the bearing face. Don't lubricate the bearing at this time.

4   Clean the back side of the other bearing insert and install it in the rod cap. Again, make sure the tab on the bearing fits into the recess in the cap, and don't apply any lubricant. It's critically important that the mating surfaces of the bearing and connecting rod are perfectly clean and oil free when they're assembled.

5   Position the piston ring gaps at staggered intervals around the piston **(see illustration)**.

6   Slip a section of plastic or rubber hose over each connecting rod cap bolt.

7   Lubricate the piston and rings with clean engine oil and attach a piston ring compressor to the piston. Leave the skirt protruding about 1/4-inch to guide the piston into the cylinder. The rings must be compressed until they're flush with the piston.

8   Rotate the crankshaft until the number one connecting rod journal is at BDC (bottom dead center) and apply a coat of engine oil to the cylinder walls.

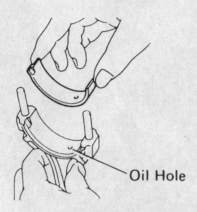

24.3   Align the oil hole in the bearing with the oil hole in the connecting rod

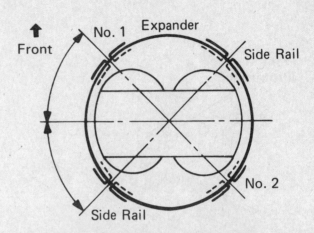

24.5   Stagger the ring end gaps before installing the pistons

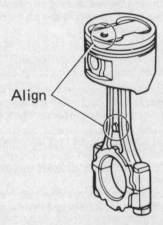

24.9   Check to be sure both the mark on the piston and the mark on the connecting rod are aligned as shown and facing the front of the engine

24.11   Drive the piston gently into the cylinder bore with the end of a wooden or plastic hammer handle

9   With the dimple on top of the piston (see illustration) facing the front of the engine, gently insert the piston/connecting rod assembly into the number one cylinder bore and rest the bottom edge of the ring compressor on the engine block.

10   Tap the top edge of the ring compressor to make sure it's contacting the block around its entire circumference.

11   Gently tap on the top of the piston with the end of a wood or plastic hammer handle (see illustration) while guiding the end of the connecting rod into place on the crankshaft journal. The piston rings may try to pop out of the ring compressor just before entering the cylinder bore, so keep some downward pressure on the ring compressor. Work slowly, and if any resistance is felt as the piston enters the cylinder, stop immediately. Find out what's hanging up and fix it before proceeding. Do not, for any reason, force the piston into the cylinder – you might break a ring and/or the piston.

12   Once the piston/connecting rod assembly is installed, the connecting rod bearing oil clearance must be checked before the rod cap is permanently bolted in place.

13   Cut a piece of the appropriate size Plastigage slightly shorter than the width of the connecting rod bearing and lay it in place on the number one connecting rod journal, parallel with the journal axis (see illustration).

24.13   Lay the Plastigage strips on each rod bearing journal, parallel to the crankshaft centerline

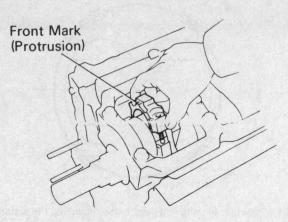

24.14   Install the connecting rod caps with the front mark facing the timing belt end of the engine

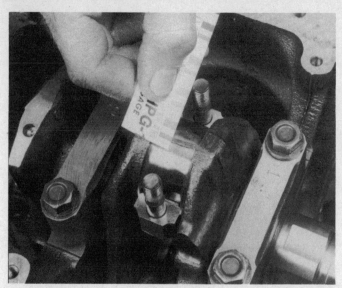

24.17   Measure the width of the crushed Plastigage with the scale on the envelope to determine the rod bearing oil clearance (be sure to use the correct scale – standard and metric ones are included)

14   Clean the connecting rod cap bearing face, remove the protective hoses from the connecting rod bolts and install the rod cap. Make sure the mating mark on the cap is on the same side as the mark on the connecting rod **(see illustration)**.

15   Apply a light coat of oil to the under sides of the nuts, then install and tighten them to the specified torque, working up to it in three steps. Use a thin-wall socket to avoid erroneous torque readings that can result if the socket is wedged between the rod cap and nut. If the socket tends to wedge itself between the nut and the cap, lift up on it slightly until it no longer contacts the cap. Do not rotate the crankshaft at any time during this operation.

16   Remove the nuts and detach the rod cap, being very careful not to disturb the Plastigage.

17   Compare the width of the crushed Plastigage to the scale printed on the Plastigage envelope to obtain the oil clearance **(see illustration)**. Compare it to the Specifications to make sure the clearance is correct.

18   If the clearance is not as specified, the bearing inserts may be the wrong size (which means different ones will be required). Before deciding that different inserts are needed, make sure that no dirt or oil was between the bearing inserts and the connecting rod or cap when the clearance was measured. Also, recheck the journal diameter. If the Plastigage was wider at one end than the other, the journal may be tapered (refer to Section 18).

Final connecting rod installation

19   Carefully scrape all traces of the Plastigage material off the rod journal and/or bearing face. Be very careful not to scratch the bearing – use your fingernail or the edge of a credit card.

20   Make sure the bearing faces are perfectly clean, then apply a uniform layer of clean moly-base grease or engine assembly lube to both of them. You'll have to push the piston into the cylinder to expose the face of the bearing insert in the connecting rod – be sure to slip the protective hoses over the rod bolts first.

21   Slide the connecting rod back into place on the journal, remove the protective hoses from the rod cap bolts, install the rod cap and tighten the nuts to the specified torque. Again, work up to the torque in three steps.

22   Repeat the entire procedure for the remaining pistons/connecting rods.

23   The important points to remember are . . .

a)   Keep the back sides of the bearing inserts and the insides of the connecting rods and caps perfectly clean when assembling them.

b)   Make sure you have the correct piston/rod assembly for each cylinder.

c)   The dimple on the piston must face the front of the engine.

d)   Lubricate the cylinder walls with clean oil.

e)   Lubricate the bearing faces when installing the rod caps after the oil clearance has been checked.

24   After all the piston/connecting rod assemblies have been properly installed, rotate the crankshaft a number of times by hand to check for any obvious binding.

25   As a final step, the connecting rod endplay must be checked. Refer to Section 12 for this procedure.

26   Compare the measured endplay to the Specifications to make sure it's correct. If it was correct before disassembly and the original crankshaft and rods were reinstalled, it should still be right. If new rods or a new crankshaft were installed, the endplay may be inadequate. If so, the rods will have to be removed and taken to an automotive machine shop for resizing.

25   Initial start-up and break-in after overhaul

Warning: *Have a fire extinguisher handy when starting the engine for the first time.*

1   Once the engine has been installed in the vehicle, double-check the engine oil and coolant levels.

2   With the spark plugs out of the engine and the ignition system disabled (see Section 3), crank the engine until oil pressure registers on the gauge or the light goes out.

3   Install the spark plugs, hook up the plug wires and restore the ignition system functions (Section 3).

4   Start the engine. It may take a few moments for the fuel system to build up pressure, but the engine should start without a great deal of effort.

5   After the engine starts, it should be allowed to warm up to normal operating temperature. While the engine is warming up, make a thorough check for fuel, oil and coolant leaks.

6   Shut the engine off and recheck the engine oil and coolant levels.

7   Drive the vehicle to an area with minimum traffic, accelerate at full throttle from 30 to 50 mph, then allow the vehicle to slow to 30 mph with the

throttle closed. Repeat the procedure 10 or 12 times. This will load the piston rings and cause them to seat properly against the cylinder walls. Check again for oil and coolant leaks.

8   Drive the vehicle gently for the first 500 miles (no sustained high speeds) and keep a constant check on the oil level. It is not unusual for an engine to use oil during the break-in period.

9   At approximately 500 to 600 miles, change the oil and filter.

10   For the next few hundred miles, drive the vehicle normally. Do not pamper it or abuse it.

11   After 2000 miles, change the oil and filter again and consider the engine broken in.

Chapter 3   Cooling, heating and air conditioning systems

Contents

Specifications

General

Radiator cap pressure rating .... 10.7 to 14.9 psi
Thermostat rating (opening temperature)
   3T-C engine .... 187 to 194-degrees F (86 to 90-degrees C)
   4A-C and 4A-GE engines .... 176 to 183-degrees F (80 to 84-degrees C)
Cooling system capacity .... See Chapter 1
Refrigerant capacity .... 1.4 to 1.7 lbs

Torque specifications   Ft-lbs

Water pump-to-engine bolts 11
Thermostat housing cover bolts 7

---

1   General information

Refer to illustration 1.1

Engine cooling system

All vehicles covered by this manual employ a pressurized engine cooling system with thermostatically controlled coolant circulation **(see illustration)**. An impeller type water pump mounted on the front (drivebelt end) of the block pumps coolant through the engine. The coolant flows around each cylinder and toward the rear of the engine. Cast-in coolant passages direct coolant around the intake and exhaust ports, near the spark plug areas and in close proximity to the exhaust valve guides.

A wax pellet type thermostat is located in a housing near the front of the engine. During warm up, the closed thermostat prevents coolant from circulating through the radiator. As the engine nears normal operating temperature, the thermostat opens and allows hot coolant to travel through the radiator, where it's cooled before returning to the engine.

The cooling system is sealed by a pressure type radiator cap, which raises the boiling point of the coolant and increases the cooling efficiency of the radiator. If the system pressure exceeds the cap pressure relief value, the excess pressure in the system forces the spring-loaded valve inside the cap off its seat and allows the coolant to escape through the overflow tube into a coolant reservoir. When the system cools, the excess coolant is automatically drawn from the reservoir back into the radiator.

The coolant reservoir does double duty as both the point at which fresh coolant is added to the cooling system to maintain the proper fluid level and as a holding tank for overheated coolant.

This type of cooling system is known as a closed design because coolant that escapes past the pressure cap is saved and reused.

Heating system

The heating system consists of a blower fan and heater core located in the heater box, the hoses connecting the heater core to the engine cooling system and the heater/air conditioning control head on the dashboard. Hot engine coolant is circulated through the heater core. When the heater mode is activated, a flap door opens to expose the heater box to the passenger compartment. A fan switch on the control head activates the blower motor, which forces air through the core, heating the air.

Air conditioning system

The air conditioning system consists of a condenser mounted in front of the radiator, an evaporator mounted adjacent to the heater core, a compressor mounted on the engine, a filter-drier which contains a high pressure relief valve and the plumbing connecting all of the above components.

A blower fan forces the warmer air of the passenger compartment through the evaporator core (sort of a radiator-in-reverse), transferring the heat from the air to the refrigerant. The liquid refrigerant boils off into low pressure vapor, taking the heat with it when it leaves the evaporator.

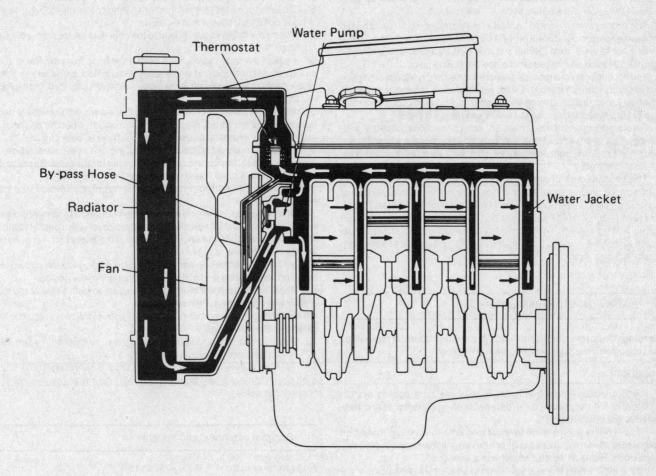

1.1   Cross-sectional view of a typical cooling system

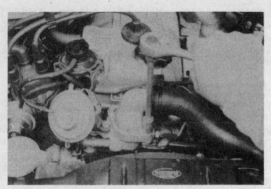

3.10 Remove the two thermostat housing cover bolts to gain access to the thermostat (3T-C engine shown, others similar)

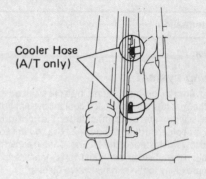

Cooler Hose
(A/T only)

4.5 On automatic transmission-equipped vehicles, disconnect the lines at the bottom of the radiator and cap the lines and fittings

2 Antifreeze – general information

Warning: *Do not allow antifreeze to come in contact with your skin or painted surfaces of the vehicle. Rinse off spills immediately with plenty of water. Antifreeze, if consumed, can be fatal, so wipe up garage floor and drip pan spills immediately. Keep antifreeze containers covered and repair leaks in the cooling system as soon as they're noticed.*

The cooling system should be filled with a water/ethylene glycol based antifreeze solution, which will prevent freezing down to at least – 20-degrees F, or lower if local climate requires it. It also provides protection against corrosion and increases the coolant boiling point.

The cooling system should be drained, flushed and refilled at the specified intervals (see Chapter 1). Old or contaminated antifreeze solutions are likely to cause damage and encourage the formation of corrosion and scale in the system. Use distilled water with the antifreeze.

Before adding antifreeze, check all hose connections, because antifreeze tends to search out and leak through very minute openings. Engines don't normally consume coolant, so if the level goes down, find the cause and correct it.

The exact mixture of antifreeze-to-water which you should use depends on the relative weather conditions. The mixture should contain at least 50-percent antifreeze, but should never contain more than 70-percent antifreeze. Consult the mixture ratio chart on the antifreeze container before adding coolant. Hydrometers are available at most auto parts stores to test the coolant. Use antifreeze which meets the vehicle manufacturer's specifications.

3 Thermostat – check and replacement

Warning: *Do not remove the radiator cap, drain the coolant or replace the thermostat until the engine has cooled completely.*

Check

1   Before assuming the thermostat is to blame for a cooling system problem, check the coolant level, drivebelt tension (Chapter 1) and temperature gauge operation.
2   If the engine seems to be taking a long time to warm up (based on heater output or temperature gauge operation), the thermostat is probably stuck open. Replace the thermostat with a new one.
3   If the engine runs hot, use your hand to check the temperature of the upper radiator hose. If the hose isn't hot, but the engine is, the thermostat is probably stuck closed, preventing the coolant inside the engine from escaping to the radiator. Replace the thermostat. **Caution:** *Don't drive the vehicle without a thermostat. The computer may stay in open loop and emissions and fuel economy will suffer.*

4   If the upper radiator hose is hot, it means the coolant is flowing and the thermostat is open. Consult the Troubleshooting Section at the front of this manual for cooling system diagnosis.

Replacement

Refer to illustration 3.10

5   Disconnect the negative battery cable from the battery.
6   Drain the cooling system (Chapter 1). If the coolant is relatively new or in good condition, save it and reuse it.
7   Follow the upper radiator hose to the engine to locate the thermostat housing.
8   Loosen the hose clamp, then detach the hose from the fitting. If it's stuck, grasp it near the end with a pair of Channelock pliers and twist it to break the seal, then pull it off. If the hose is old or deteriorated, cut it off and install a new one.
9   If the outer surface of the large fitting that mates with the hose is deteriorated (corroded, pitted, etc.) it may be damaged further by hose removal. If it is, the thermostat housing cover will have to be replaced.
10   Remove the bolts and detach the housing cover **(see illustration)**. If the cover is stuck, tap it with a soft-face hammer to jar it loose. Be prepared for some coolant to spill as the gasket seal is broken.
11   Note how it's installed (which end is facing up), then remove the thermostat.
12   Stuff a rag into the engine opening, then remove all traces of old gasket material and sealant from the housing and cover with a gasket scraper. Remove the rag from the opening and clean the gasket mating surfaces with lacquer thinner or acetone.
13   Install the new thermostat in the housing. Make sure the correct end faces up – the spring end is normally directed into the engine.
14   Apply a thin, uniform layer of RTV sealant to both sides of the new gasket and position it on the housing.
15   Install the cover and bolts. Tighten the bolts to the torque listed in this Chapter's Specifications.
16   Reattach the hose to the fitting and tighten the hose clamp securely.
17   Refill the cooling system (Chapter 1).
18   Start the engine and allow it to reach normal operating temperature, then check for leaks and proper thermostat operation (as described in Steps 2 through 4).

4 Radiator – removal and installation

Refer to illustrations 4.5, 4.8a, 4.8b and 4.9
Warning: *Wait until the engine is completely cool before beginning this procedure.*
1   Disconnect the negative battery cable from the battery.
2   Drain the cooling system (see Chapter 1). If the coolant is relatively new or in good condition, save it and reuse it.

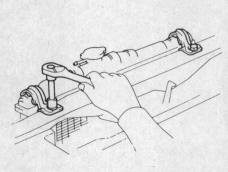

4.8a   On the 3T-C engine, the mounting bolts are located along the sides of the radiator

4.8b   On 4A-C and 4A-GE engines, two brackets at the top secure the radiator – remove the bolts to detach the brackets

4.9   Carefully lift the radiator out of the engine compartment (3T-C engine shown)

3   Loosen the hose clamps, then detach the radiator hoses from the fittings. If they're stuck, grasp each hose near the end with a pair of Channellock pliers and twist it to break the seal, then pull it off – be careful not to distort the radiator fittings! If the hoses are old or deteriorated, cut them off and install new ones.

4   Disconnect the reservoir hose from the radiator filler neck.

5   If the vehicle is equipped with an automatic transmission, disconnect the cooler lines **(see illustration)**.

6   Plug the lines and fittings to prevent leakage.

7   Remove the grille (see Chapter 11).

8   Remove the radiator mounting bolts **(see illustrations)**.

9   Carefully lift out the radiator **(see illustration)**. Don't spill coolant on the vehicle or scratch the paint.

10   With the radiator removed, it can be inspected for leaks and damage. If repair is required, have a radiator shop or dealer service department perform the work as special techniques are required.

11   Bugs and dirt can be removed from the radiator with compressed air and a soft brush. Don't bend the cooling fins as this is done.

12   Installation is the reverse of the removal procedure.

13   After installation, fill the cooling system with the proper mixture of antifreeze and water. Refer to Chapter 1 if necessary.

14   Start the engine and check for leaks. Allow the engine to reach normal operating temperature, indicated by the upper radiator hose becoming hot. Recheck the coolant level and add more if required.

15   If you're working on an automatic transmission equipped vehicle, check and add fluid as needed.

5   Engine cooling fan and clutch – check and replacement

Fan clutch check

1   The engine cooling fan is controlled by a fluid filled clutch. When the fluid reaches a predetermined temperature and the viscosity of the fluid changes, the clutch allows the fan to rotate faster.

2   Begin the clutch check with a warm engine (start it when cold and let it run for two minutes only).

3   Remove the key from the ignition switch for safety purposes.

4   Turn the fan blades and note the resistance. There should be moderate resistance, depending on temperature.

5   Drive the vehicle until the engine is warmed up. Shut it off and remove the key.

6   Turn the fan blades and again note the resistance. There should be a noticeable increase in resistance.

7   If the fan clutch fails this check or is locked up solid, replace it. If excessive fluid is leaking from the hub or lateral play over 1/4-inch is noted, replace the fan clutch.

8   If any fan blades are bent, don't straighten them! The plastic will be weakened and blades could fly off during engine operation. Replace the fan with a new one.

Replacement

9   Remove the fan shroud from the radiator.

10   Remove the four nuts that retain the fan assembly to the water pump.

11   Detach the fan assembly from the engine.

12   Remove the bolts that retain the fan to the fan clutch and separate the two components.

13   Installation is the reverse of removal.

6   Coolant temperature sending unit – check and replacement

Warning: *The engine must be completely cool before removing the sending unit.*

Check

1   If the coolant temperature gauge is inoperative, check the fuses first (Chapter 12).

2   If the temperature indicator shows excessive temperature after running a while, see the Troubleshooting Section in the front of the manual.

3   If the temperature gauge indicates Hot shortly after the engine is started cold, disconnect the wire(s) at the coolant temperature sending unit. If the gauge reading drops, replace the sending unit. If the reading remains high, the wire to the gauge or light may be shorted to ground or the gauge is faulty.

4   If the coolant temperature gauge fails to indicate after the engine has been warmed up (approximately 10 minutes) and the fuses checked out okay, shut off the engine. Disconnect the wire at the sending unit and, using a jumper wire, connect it to a clean ground on the engine. Turn on the ignition without starting the engine. If the gauge now indicates Hot, replace the sending unit.

5   If the gauge still doesn't work, the circuit may be open or the gauge may be faulty. See Chapter 12 for additional information.

Replacement

6   With the engine completely cool, remove the cap from the radiator to release any pressure, then replace the cap. This reduces coolant loss during sending unit replacement.

7   Disconnect the wire from the sending unit.

8   Prepare the new sending unit for installation by applying sealant to the threads.

9   Unscrew the sending unit from the engine and quickly install the new one to prevent coolant loss.

10   Tighten the sending unit securely and connect the wire.

11   Refill the cooling system and run the engine. Check for leaks and proper gauge operation.

3

7.1   Remove the cap and overflow hose from the coolant reservoir

9.4   Remove the idler pulley bracket and the drivebelt (3T-C engine)

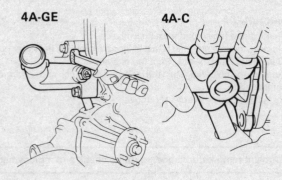

9.9   Unscrew the mounting bolts and remove the coolant outlet housing and by-pass pipe

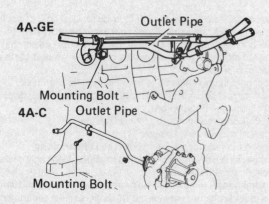

9.10   Remove the mounting bolt and outlet pipe (4A-C and 4A-GE engines)

---

7   Coolant reservoir – removal and installation

Refer to illustration 7.1

1   Lift the cap off the coolant reservoir and withdraw the overflow hose **(see illustration)**.
2   Remove the coolant reservoir-to-fender bolt and lift the coolant reservoir out. The windshield washer reservoir can remain in place.
3   Installation is the reverse of removal.

8   Water pump – check

1   Water pump failure can cause serious engine damage due to overheating.
2   There are three ways to check the operation of the water pump while it's installed on the engine. If the pump is defective, it should be replaced with a new or rebuilt unit.
3   With the engine running at normal operating temperature, squeeze the upper radiator hose. If the water pump is working properly, a pressure surge should be felt as the hose is released. **Warning:** *Keep your hands away from the fan blades!*
4   Water pumps are equipped with weep or vent holes. If a failure occurs in the pump seal, coolant will leak out of the hole. In most cases you'll need a flashlight to find the hole on the water pump from underneath to check for leaks.
5   If the water pump shaft bearings fail there may be a howling sound at the front of the engine while it's running. Shaft wear can be felt if the water

pump pulley is rocked up-and-down. Don't mistake drivebelt slippage, which causes a squealing sound, for water pump bearing failure.

9   Water pump – removal and installation

Warning: *Wait until the engine is completely cool before beginning this procedure.*
1   Disconnect the negative battery cable from the battery.
2   Drain the cooling system (Chapter 1). If the coolant is relatively new or in good condition, save it and reuse it.

3T-C engine
Refer to illustration 9.4
3   If the vehicle is equipped with power steering, remove the power steering pump drive pulley.
4   Remove the idler pulley bracket and drivebelt **(see illustration)**.
5   Loosen the alternator pivot and adjusting bolts and swing the alternator toward the engine (see Chapter 1).
6   Remove the fan assembly (see Section 5) and water pump pulley.
7   Remove the bolts and detach the water pump from the engine. Note the locations of the various lengths and different types of bolts as they're removed to ensure correct installation.

4A-C and 4A-GE engines
Refer to illustrations 9.9, 9.10 and 9.11
8   Remove the fan assembly and the water pump pulley from the water pump (see Section 5).

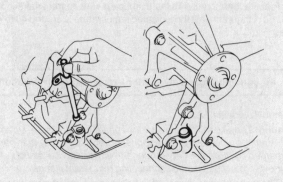

9.11 Remove the oil dipstick tube from the lower portion of the block (4A-C and 4A-GE engines)

9   Remove the coolant outlet housing and the by-pass pipe **(see illustration)**.

10   Remove the heater outlet pipe **(see illustration)**.

11   Remove the mounting bolt and pull out the oil dipstick tube **(see illustration)**. **Note:** *After pulling out the tube, be sure to plug the hole so oil doesn't leak out.*

12   Remove the timing belt cover and gasket (Chapter 2, Part A).

13   Remove the bolts and detach the water pump from the engine. Note the locations of the various lengths and different types of bolts as they're removed to ensure correct installation.

All engines

14   Clean the bolt threads and the threaded holes in the engine to remove corrosion and sealant.

15   Compare the new pump to the old one to make sure they're identical.

16   Remove all traces of old gasket material from the engine with a gasket scraper.

17   Clean the engine and new water pump mating surfaces with lacquer thinner or acetone.

18   On 4A-C and 4A-GE engines, install new O-rings in the grooves at the front end of the by-pass pipe and lubricate the O-rings with coolant. Install the by-pass pipe and heater outlet pipe.

19   Apply a thin coat of RTV sealant to the engine side of the new gasket and to the gasket mating surface of the new pump, then carefully mate the gasket and the pump. Slip a couple of bolts through the pump mounting holes to hold the gasket in place.

20   Carefully attach the pump and gasket to the engine and thread the bolts into the holes finger-tight.

21   Install the remaining bolts. Tighten them to the specified torque in 1/4-turn increments. Don't overtighten them or the pump may be distorted.

22   Reinstall all parts removed for access to the pump.

23   Refill the cooling system and check the drivebelt tension (Chapter 1). Run the engine and check for leaks.

10   Heater blower – removal and installation

Refer to illustration 10.3

1   Disconnect the negative cable from the battery.

2   Remove the glove compartment (see Chapter 11) and the blower duct on models without air conditioning.

3   Disconnect the wiring harnesses from the blower **(see illustration)**.

3

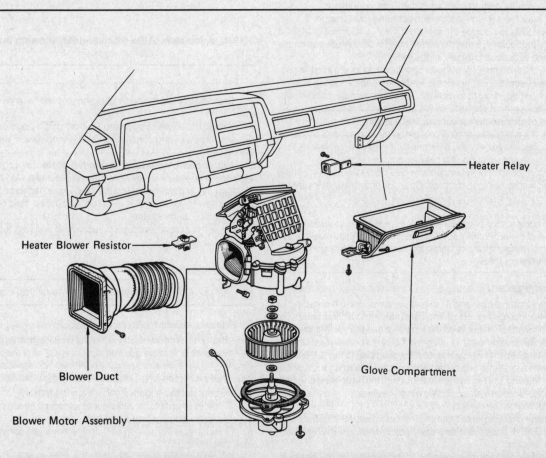

Heater Relay

Heater Blower Resistor

Blower Duct

Blower Motor Assembly

Glove Compartment

10.3 Typical blower motor assembly – exploded view

4   Remove the screws holding the blower motor to the heater housing and lift the unit out.
5   If you're replacing the motor, detach the fan and transfer it to the new motor.
6   Installation is the reverse of removal. Run the blower and check for proper operation.

11   Air conditioning system – check and maintenance

Refer to illustrations 11.1a and 11.1b
Warning: *The air conditioning system is under high pressure. Do not loosen any hose fittings or remove any components until after the system has been discharged by a dealer service department or service station. Always wear eye protection when disconnecting air conditioning system fittings.*

Check

1   The following maintenance checks should be performed on a regular basis to ensure the air conditioner continues to operate at peak efficiency **(see illustrations)**.
  a) Check the compressor drivebelt. If it's worn or deteriorated, replace it (see Chapter 1).
  b) Check the drivebelt tension and, if necessary, adjust it (see Chapter 1).
  c) Check the system hoses. Look for cracks, bubbles, hard spots and deterioration. Inspect the hoses and all fittings for oil bubbles and seepage. If there's any evidence of wear, damage or leaks, replace the hose(s).
  d) Inspect the condenser fins for leaves, bugs and other debris. Use a "fin comb" or compressed air to clean the condenser.
  e) Make sure the system has the correct refrigerant charge.
2   It's a good idea to operate the system for about 10 minutes at least once a month, particularly during the winter. Long term non-use can cause hardening, and subsequent failure, of the seals.
3   Because of the complexity of the air conditioning system and the special equipment necessary to service it, in-depth troubleshooting and repairs are not included in this manual. However, simple checks and component replacement procedures are provided in this Chapter.
4   The most common cause of poor cooling is simply a low system refrigerant charge. If a noticeable drop in cool air output occurs, one of the following quick checks will help you determine if the refrigerant level is low.
5   Warm the engine up to normal operating temperature.
6   Place the air conditioning temperature selector at the coldest setting and put the blower at the highest setting. Open the doors (to make sure the air conditioning system doesn't cycle off as soon as it cools the passenger compartment).
7   With the compressor engaged – the clutch will make an audible click and the center of the clutch will rotate – inspect the sight glass (see illustration 12.2). If the refrigerant looks foamy, it's low. Charge the system as described later in this Section.

Adding refrigerant

8   Buy an automotive charging kit at an auto parts store. A charging kit includes a 14-ounce can of refrigerant, a tap valve and a short section of hose that can be attached between the tap valve and the system low side service valve. Because one can of refrigerant may not be sufficient to bring the system charge up to the proper level, it's a good idea to buy a few additional cans. Make sure that one of the cans contains red refrigerant dye. If the system is leaking, the red dye will leak out with the refrigerant and help you pinpoint the location of the leak. **Warning:** *Never add more than three cans of refrigerant to the system.*
9   Hook up the charging kit by following the manufacturer's instructions. **Warning:** *DO NOT hook the charging kit hose to the system high side! Wear eye protection.*
10   Warm up the engine and turn on the air conditioner. Keep the charging kit hose away from the fan and other moving parts.

11   Place a thermometer in the dashboard vent nearest the evaporator and add refrigerant until the indicated temperature is around 40 to 45 degrees F.

12   Air conditioning receiver/drier – removal and installation

Refer to illustration 12.2
Warning: *The air conditioning system is under high pressure. Do not loosen any fittings or remove any components until after the system has been discharged by a dealer service department or service station. Always wear eye protection when disconnecting refrigerant fittings.*
1   The receiver/drier, which acts as a reservoir and filter for the refrigerant, is mounted adjacent to the condenser in the engine compartment.
2   Detach the two refrigerant lines from the receiver/drier **(see illustration)**.

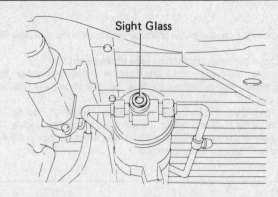

Sight Glass

12.2   A top view of the receiver-drier, showing the sight glass

3   Immediately cap the open fittings to prevent the entry of dirt and moisture.
4   Unbolt the receiver/drier and lift it out of the engine compartment.
5   Install new O-rings on the lines and lubricate them with clean refrigerant oil.
6   Installation is the reverse of removal. **Note:** *Do not remove the sealing caps until you're ready to reconnect the lines. Don't mix up the inlet (marked IN) and the outlet (marked OUT) connections.*
7   If a new receiver/drier is installed, add 0.7 US fluid ounces (20 cc) of refrigerant oil to the system.
8   Have the system evacuated, recharged and leak tested by the shop that discharged it.

13   Air conditioning compressor – removal and installation

Refer to illustrations 13.7a, 13.7b and 13.7c
Warning: *The air conditioning system is under high pressure. Do not loosen any fittings or remove any components until after the system has been discharged by a dealer service department or service station. Always wear eye protection when disconnecting refrigerant fittings.*
1   Disconnect the negative cable from the battery.
2   Raise the front of the vehicle and support it securely on jackstands.
3   Apply the parking brake and block the rear tires.
4   Unbolt the lower splash pan and remove the compressor drivebelt (see Chapter 1).
5   Disconnect the clutch wire from the compressor.
6   Detach the refrigerant lines from the back of the compressor and im-

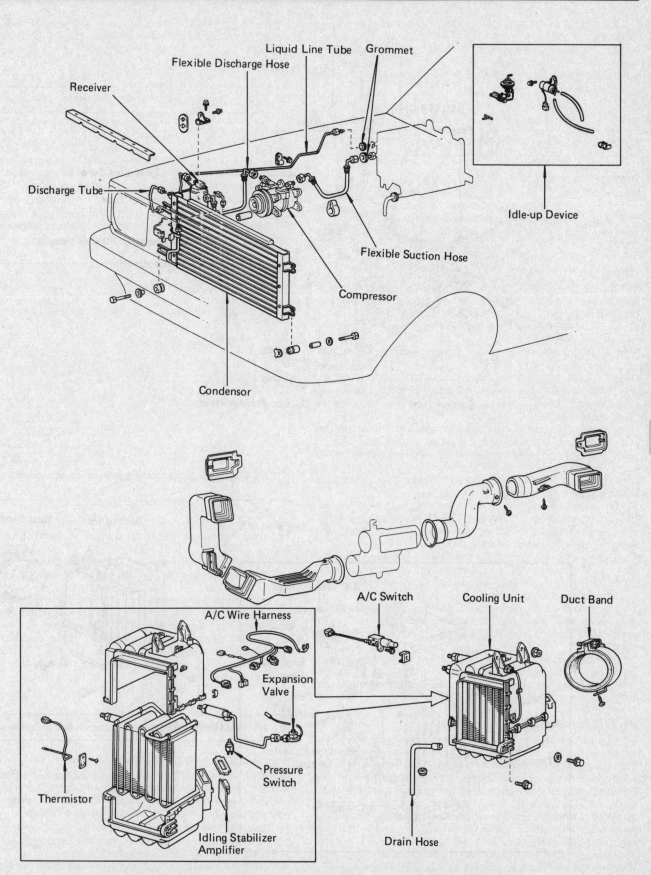

Receiver

Flexible Discharge Hose

Liquid Line Tube

Grommet

Discharge Tube

Idle-up Device

Flexible Suction Hose

Compressor

Condensor

A/C Switch

Cooling Unit

Duct Band

A/C Wire Harness

Expansion Valve

Pressure Switch

Thermistor

Idling Stabilizer Amplifier

Drain Hose

11.1a   Exploded view of the air conditioning system components – 3T-C engine

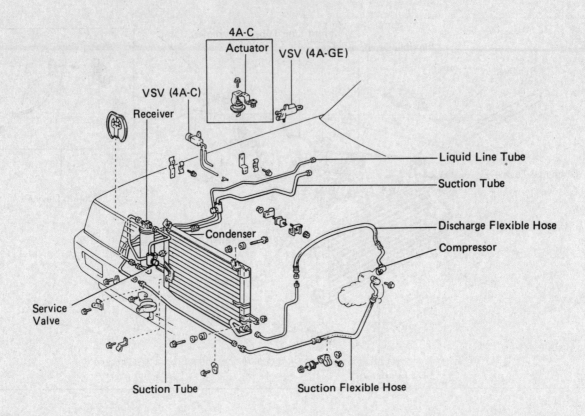

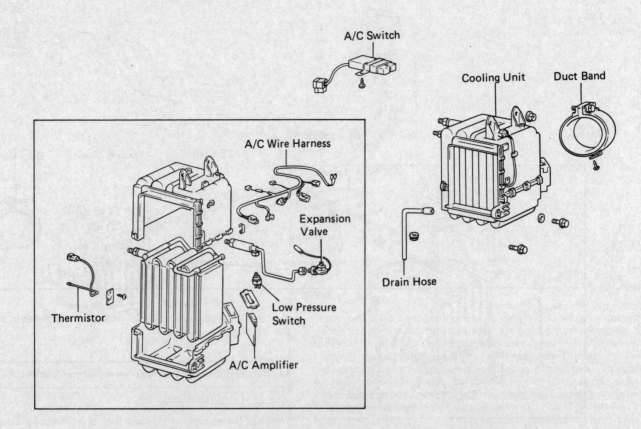

11.1b Exploded view of the air conditioning system components – 4A-C and 4A-GE engines

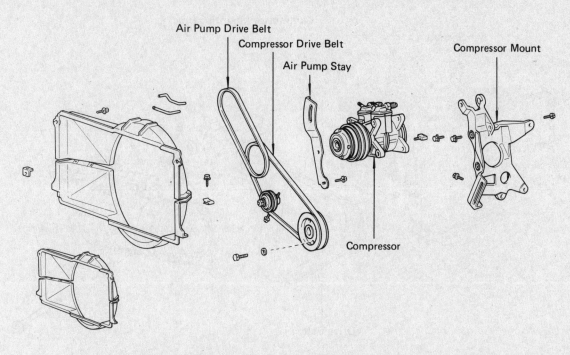

13.7a   An exploded view of the compressor and related components on a 3T-C engine

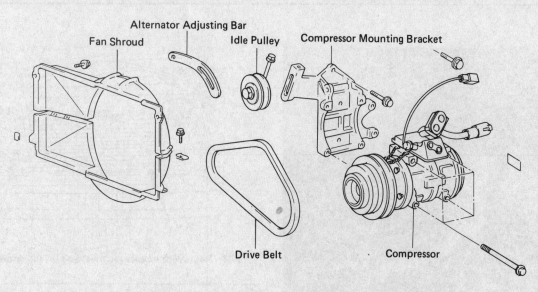

13.7b   An exploded view of the compressor and related components on a 4A-C engine

mediately cap the open fittings to prevent the entry of dirt and moisture.

7   Remove the mounting bolts **(see illustrations)** and lower the compressor from the engine compartment. Note the location and thickness of any shims and reinstall them in the same place. **Note:** *Keep the compressor level during handling and storage. If the compressor seized or you find metal particles in the refrigerant lines, the system must be flushed out by an air conditioning shop and the receiver/drier must be replaced.*

8   Prior to installation, turn the center of the clutch six times to disperse any oil that has collected in the head.

9   Install the compressor in the reverse order of removal.

10   If you're installing a new compressor, refer to the manufacturer's instructions for adding refrigerant oil to the system.

11   Have the system evacuated, recharged and leak tested by the shop that discharged it.

14   Air conditioning condenser – removal and installation

Refer to illustrations 14.2 and 14.4

Warning: *The air conditioning system is under high pressure. Do not loosen any fittings or remove any components until after the system has been discharged by a dealer service department or service station. Always wear eye protection when disconnecting refrigerant fittings.*

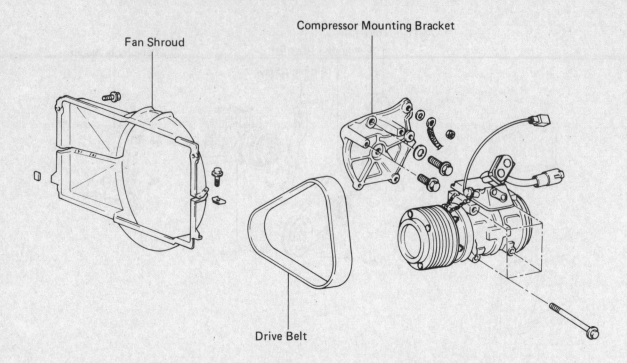

13.7c   An exploded view of the compressor and related components on a 4A-GE engine with power steering

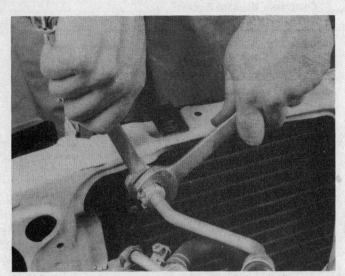

14.2   Use a back-up wrench to avoid twisting the lines

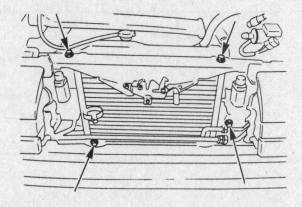

14.4   Remove the bolts (arrows) and lift the condenser out

7   Have the system evacuated, recharged and leak tested by the shop that discharged it.

1   Remove the hood, grille and vertical brace (see Chapter 11).
2   Disconnect the refrigerant lines from the condenser. Be sure to use a back-up wrench to avoid twisting the lines **(see illustration)**.
3   Immediately cap the open fittings to prevent the entry of dirt and moisture.
4   Unbolt the condenser **(see illustration)** and lift it out of the vehicle. Store it upright to prevent oil loss.
5   Installation is the reverse of removal.
6   If a new condenser was installed, add 1.4 to 1.7 ounces (40 to 50 cc) of refrigerant oil to the system.

15   Air conditioner and heater control assembly – removal, installation and cable adjustment

Removal and installation
Refer to illustrations 15.2a, 15.2b, 15.3, 15.4a, 15.4b, 15.4c, 15.4d and 15.6

1   Disconnect the negative cable from the battery.
2   Remove the finish panel **(see illustrations)** which surrounds the control assembly (see Chapter 11).

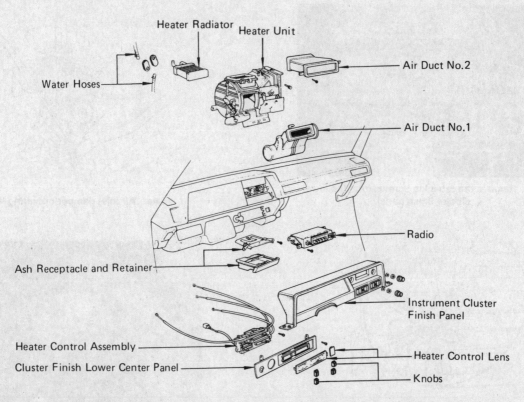

15.2a An Exploded view of the heater unit and controls used on typical sedan and station wagon models

3

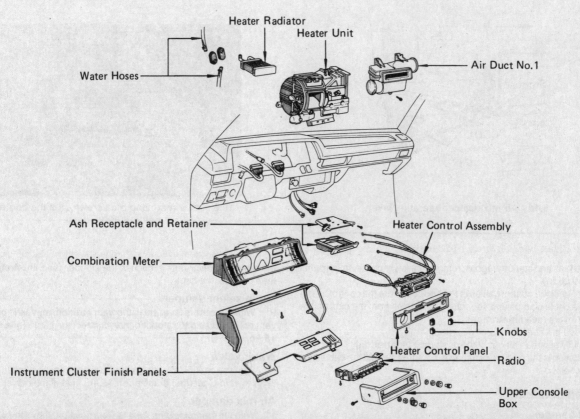

15.2b An exploded view of the heater unit and controls used on typical coupe and hatchback models

15.3   Remove the retaining screws from the lower cluster finish panel

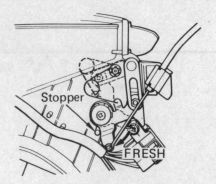

15.4a   Air inlet damper operating lever

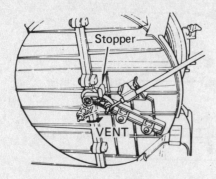

15.4b   Mode select damper operating lever

15.4c   Water valve operating lever

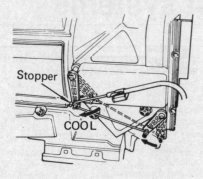

15.4d   Air mix damper operating lever

15.6   After removing the screws, pull the control unit out of the dash

3   On sedans and station wagons, remove the lower cluster finish panel **(see illustration)**.

4   Disconnect the control cables at the ends opposite the control by detaching the cable clamps and separating the cables from the pins on the operating levers **(see illustrations)**.

5   Remove the control mounting screws.

6   Carefully slip the unit out of the dash **(see illustration)**.

7   Installation is the reverse of removal. Be sure to adjust the cables, as explained below.

Cable adjustment

Air inlet damper

8   With the control lever all the way toward the fresh air position, move the operating lever until it touches the stopper **(see illustration 15.4a)**, then connect the cable.

Mode select damper

9   With the control lever set in the Vent position, move the operating lever until it contacts the stopper, then connect the cable **(see illustration 15.4b)**.

Water valve

10   With the control lever set in the Cool position, position the operating lever toward Cool **(see illustration 15.4c)**. Install the cable.

Air mix damper

11   With the control lever set in the Cool position, move the operating lever against the stopper **(see illustration 15.4d)**. Install the cable.

Chapter 4   Fuel and exhaust systems

Contents

Specifications

Fuel pressure

3T-C engine	Not available
4A-C engine	Not available
4A-GE engine	
At idle	27 to 31 psi
With vacuum sensing hose off	33 to 40 psi

Torque specifications

	Ft-lbs
Throttle body mounting bolts	14 to 16
Carburetor mounting bolts	18
Catalytic converter-to-exhaust pipe bolts	32
Fuel tank bolts	10
Fuel tank drain plug	9

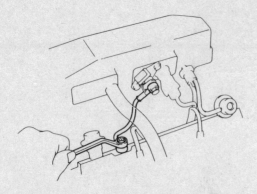

2.6   Slowly loosen the union bolt on the cold start injection pipe – fuel may spray out, so wear eye protection

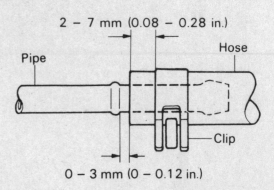

2 – 7 mm (0.08 – 0.28 in.)

Pipe

Hose

Clip

0 – 3 mm (0 – 0.12 in.)

3.6   When attaching a section of rubber hose to a metal fuel line, be sure to overlap the hose as shown and secure it to the line with a new worm-drive hose clamp

1   General information

The fuel system consists of a rear-mounted tank, fuel lines, an engine-mounted mechanical pump (carburetor-equipped vehicles) or an electric pump (fuel injected vehicles), and either a two-stage, two barrel carburetor or an electronic fuel injection system.

The exhaust system is composed of an exhaust manifold, a catalytic converter and a combination muffler and tailpipe assembly.

The emission control systems modify the functions of both the exhaust and fuel systems. There may be some cross-references throughout this Chapter to sections in Chapter 6 because the emissions control systems are integrated with the fuel and exhaust systems.

2   Fuel pressure relief procedure

Refer to illustration 2.6

Warning: *Gasoline is extremely flammable, so extra precautions must be taken when working on any part of the fuel system. Do not smoke or allow open flames or bare light bulbs in or near the work area. Also, don't work in a garage if a natural gas-type appliance with a pilot light is present. Always keep a dry chemical (Class B) fire extinguisher on hand.*

1   To minimize the risk of fire and personal injury, relieve the fuel pressure before disconnecting any fuel injection system components.
2   Unscrew the fuel filler cap to release the pressure caused by fuel vapor.
3   Disconnect the negative cable from the battery.
4   Disconnect the wiring connector from the cold start injector.
5   Place shop towels underneath the cold start injection pipe to absorb the fuel as the pressure is relieved.
6   Slowly loosen the union bolt on the cold start injection pipe **(see illustration)**. It's a good idea to wear safety goggles, since fuel may spray out.
7   After repairs are completed, reinstall the union bolt, using new crush washers. Tighten the union bolt securely, start the engine and check for fuel leaks.

3   Fuel lines and fittings – inspection and replacement

Warning: *Gasoline is extremely flammable, so extra precautions must be taken when working on any part of the fuel system. Do not smoke or allow open flames or bare light bulbs in or near the work area. Also, don't work in a garage if a natural gas-type appliance with a pilot light is present. Always keep a dry chemical (Class B) fire extinguisher on hand.*

Inspection

1   Once in a while, you'll have to raise the vehicle to service or replace some component (an exhaust pipe hanger, for example). Whenever you work under the vehicle, always inspect the fuel lines and all fittings and connections for damage and deterioration.
2   Check all hoses and lines for cracks, kinks and distortion.
3   Make sure all hoses and lines are securely attached to the under side of the vehicle.
4   Verify all hose clamps attaching rubber hoses to metal fuel lines are snug enough to ensure a tight fit between the hoses and lines.

Replacement

Refer to illustration 3.6

5   If you must replace any damaged sections, use original equipment replacement hoses or lines constructed from exactly the same material as the section being replaced. Do not install substitutes constructed from inferior or inappropriate materials.
6   Always, before detaching or disassembling any lines, note the routing of all hoses and lines and the orientation of all clamps and clips to ensure that replacement sections are installed in exactly the same manner. When attaching hoses to metal lines, overlap them as shown **(see illustration)**.
7   Before detaching any part of the fuel system, be sure to relieve the fuel line and tank pressure (Section 2).
8   While you're under the vehicle, it's a good idea to check the condition of the fuel filter – make sure it's not leaking or damaged (see Chapter 1).

4   Fuel pump – check

Warning: *Gasoline is extremely flammable, so extra precautions must be taken when working on any part of the fuel system. Do not smoke or allow open flames or bare light bulbs in or near the work area. Also, don't work in a garage if a natural gas-type appliance with a pilot light is present. Always keep a dry chemical (Class B) fire extinguisher on hand.*

Note: *The following checks assume the fuel filter is in good condition. If you doubt it's condition, install a new one (see Chapter 1).*

1   Make sure there's adequate fuel in the tank. If you doubt the reading on the gauge, insert a long wooden dowel into the filler opening; it will serve as a dipstick.

Mechanical pump (carburetor-equipped vehicles)

Refer to illustration 4.3

2   Raise the vehicle and support it securely on jackstands. With the engine running, examine all fuel lines between the fuel tank and fuel pump for leaks, loose connections, kinks or distortion of the rubber hoses. Do this quickly, before the engine gets hot. Air leaks upstream of the fuel pump can seriously affect the pump's output.

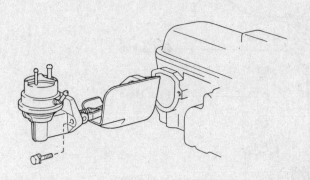

4.3   The fuel pump on carburetor-equipped engines is located at the front of the cylinder head

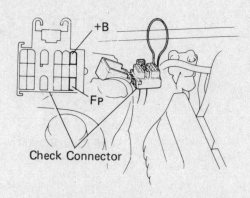

4.8a   On 1985 models, the check connector is located in the wiring harness near the windshield wiper motor and the windshield washer reservoir – connect a jumper wire as shown

3   Check the pump body for leaks **(see illustration)**. Shut off the engine.
4   Remove the fuel filler cap to relieve the fuel tank pressure. Disconnect the fuel line at the carburetor. Also disconnect the primary wiring connectors to the distributor so the engine can be cranked without starting. Place an approved gasoline container at the end of the detached fuel line and have an assistant crank the engine for several seconds. There should be a strong spurt of gasoline from the line on every second revolution.
5   If little or no gasoline emerges from the line, either the fuel line is clogged or the fuel pump isn't working properly. Disconnect the fuel feed line from the pump and blow air through it to be sure the line is clear. If the line isn't clogged, the pump should be replaced with a new one.

Electric pump (fuel injected vehicles)
Refer to illustrations 4.8a and 4.8b

6   Although the best way to check the operation of the fuel pump is with a fuel pressure gauge, to do so on these vehicles requires special adapters not normally available to the home mechanic. It is possible, however, to determine if the fuel pump is receiving power and rotating, which is usually a pretty good indication that it's pumping fuel.
7   Turn the ignition key to the Off position and remove the fuel filler cap. With the help of an assistant, put your ear next to the opening, crank the engine over and listen for fuel pump operation, which is characterized by a whirring sound. After listening, turn the ignition switch to Off.
8   If the fuel pump isn't working, check the ignition fuse, the EFI fuse, the stop fuse and the fusible links (see Chapter 12). If the fuse is okay, find the check connector **(see illustrations)**. Using a jumper wire, bridge the indicated terminals. Turn the ignition switch to On. If the fuel pump now works, replace the fuel pump relay.
9   If the fuel pump is still not working, a problem could exist with the wiring harness to the pump or the pump itself. Any further checks should be done by a dealer service department or an automotive repair shop.

---

5   Fuel pump – removal and installation

Warning: *Gasoline is extremely flammable, so extra precautions must be taken when working on any part of the fuel system. Do not smoke or allow open flames or bare light bulbs in or near the work area. Also, don't work in garage if a natural gas-type appliance with a pilot light is present. Always keep a dry chemical (Class B) fire extinguisher on hand.*

1   Disconnect the cable from the negative terminal of the battery.
2   Relieve the fuel system pressure (see Section 2).

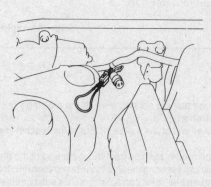

4.8b   On 1986 and 1987 models, jump terminals +B and Fp of the check connector to activate the fuel pump – the connector is located near the wiper motor

---

Mechanical pump (carburetor-equipped vehicles)

3   Relieve the fuel tank pressure by removing the fuel filler cap.
4   Locate the fuel pump mounted on the front of the cylinder head **(see illustration 4.3)**. Place rags underneath the pump to catch any spilled fuel.
5   Loosen the hose clamps and slide them down the hoses, past the fittings. Disconnect the hoses from the pump (use a twisting motion as you pull them off the fittings). Immediately plug the hoses to prevent leakage of fuel and the entry of dirt.
6   Unscrew the fasteners and detach the pump from the head. Inspect the fuel pump arm for wear. Coat it with clean engine oil before installing it.
7   Using a gasket scraper or putty knife, remove all traces of old gasket material from the mating surfaces on the cylinder head (and the fuel pump, if the same one will be reinstalled). While scraping, be careful not to gouge the soft aluminum surfaces.
8   Installation is the reverse of the removal procedure, but be sure to use a new gasket and tighten the mounting fasteners securely.

Electric pump (fuel injected vehicles)
Refer to illustration 5.10, 5.11, 5.13 and 5.14

9   Remove the fuel tank following the procedure described in Section 6.

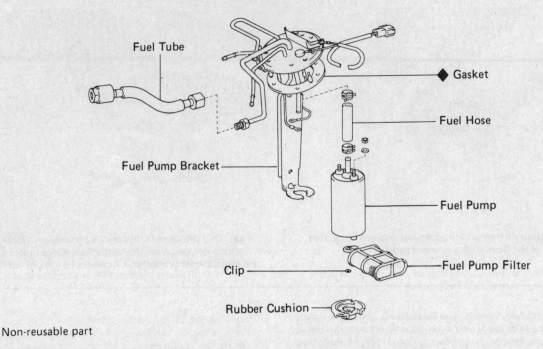

Fuel Tube

Gasket

Fuel Hose

Fuel Pump Bracket

Fuel Pump

Clip

Fuel Pump Filter

Rubber Cushion

◆   Non-reusable part

5.10   An exploded view of a typical fuel pump assembly

10   Remove the retaining screws, then lift the assembly out of the fuel tank **(see illustration)**.
11   Pull the lower end of the fuel pump out of the bracket **(see illustration)**.
12   Remove the rubber cushion from the lower end of the fuel pump.
13   Remove the clip securing the filter to the pump **(see illustration)**. Pull out the filter and inspect it for contamination. If it's dirty, replace it.
14   Loosen the hose clamp at the upper end of the pump, disconnect the pump from the hose, then disconnect the wires from the pump terminals **(see illustration)**.
15   Installation is the reverse of the removal procedure. Be sure to replace the pump gasket if it's deteriorated.

6   Fuel tank – removal and installation

Refer to illustrations 6.6, 6.8a, 6.8b, 6.8c and 6.10

Warning: Gasoline is extremely flammable, so extra precautions must be taken when working on any part of the fuel system. Do not smoke or allow open flames or bare light bulbs in or near the work area. Also, don't work in a garage if a natural gas-type appliance with a pilot light is present. While performing any work on the fuel tank, wear safety glasses and have a dry chemical (Class B) fire extinguisher on hand. If you spill any fuel on your skin, rinse it off immediately with soap and water.

5.11   Pull the lower end of the fuel pump off the bracket and remove the rubber cushion that insulates the bottom of the pump

5.13   Pry off the clip that holds the filter to the fuel pump and pull the filter off – replace the clip if it's a loose fit

5.14   Pull the fuel pump off the hose far enough to get at the wire near the bracket

6.6   Remove the fuel tank protectors (arrow)

Note: *The following procedure is much easier if the fuel tank is empty. Some tanks have a drain plug for this purpose. If the tank doesn't have a drain plug, simply run the engine until the tank is empty.*

1   Remove the fuel filler cap to relieve fuel tank pressure.
2   Relieve the fuel pressure (see Section 2).
3   Detach the cable from the negative terminal of the battery.
4   If the tank has a drain plug, remove it and allow the fuel to collect in an approved gasoline container.

5   Raise the vehicle and support it securely on jackstands.
6   Remove the fuel tank protectors **(see illustration)**.
7   Detach the parking brake cable from the fuel tank strap.
8   Disconnect the fuel lines, the vapor return lines and the fuel inlet tube **(see illustrations)**. **Note:** *The fuel lines are usually different diameters, so reattachment is simplified. If you have any doubts, however, clearly label the lines and the fittings. Be sure to plug the hoses to prevent leakage and contamination of the fuel system.*

4

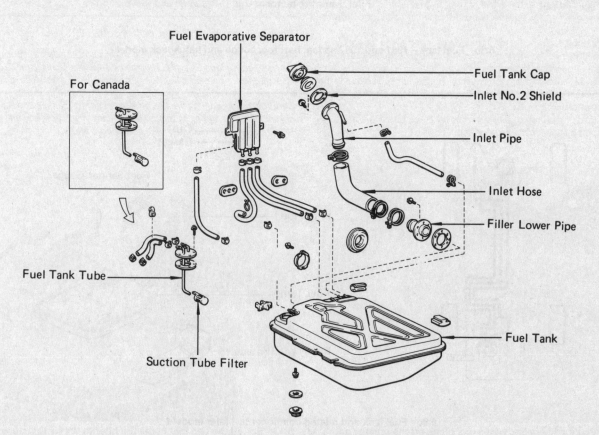

Fuel Evaporative Separator

For Canada

Fuel Tank Cap
Inlet No.2 Shield
Inlet Pipe
Inlet Hose
Filler Lower Pipe
Fuel Tank Tube
Fuel Tank
Suction Tube Filter

6.8a   Fuel tank – 1981 and 1982 station wagon models

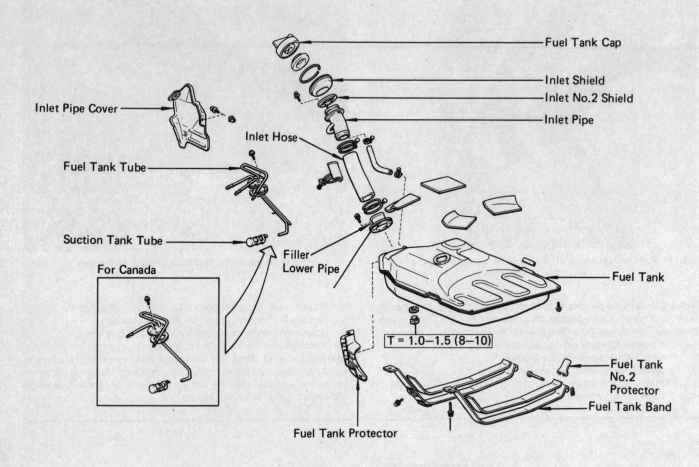

Fuel Tank Cap

Inlet Shield

Inlet No.2 Shield

Inlet Pipe

Inlet Pipe Cover

Inlet Hose

Fuel Tank Tube

Suction Tank Tube

Filler
Lower Pipe

For Canada

Fuel Tank

T = 1.0—1.5 (8—10)

Fuel Tank
No.2
Protector

Fuel Tank Band

Fuel Tank Protector

6.8b Fuel tank – 1981 and 1982 sedan, hardtop, coupe and hatchback models

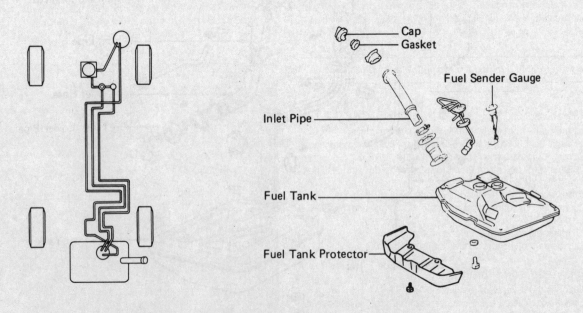

Cap

Gasket

Fuel Sender Gauge

Inlet Pipe

Fuel Tank

Fuel Tank Protector

6.8c Fuel tank and related components – later models

6.10   Remove the fuel tank strap bolts (arrows) and swing the
straps down out of the way

8.2   Accelerator cable on a typical 3T-C engine

9   Support the fuel tank with a floor jack. Position a piece of wood between the jack head and the fuel tank to protect the tank.
10   Disconnect both fuel tank straps and pivot them down until they're
hanging out of the way **(see illustration)**.
11   Lower the tank enough to disconnect the wires and ground strap from
the fuel pump/fuel gauge sending unit, if you have not already done so.
12   Remove the tank from the vehicle.
13   Installation is the reverse of removal.

7   Fuel tank cleaning and repair – general information

1   Any repairs to the fuel tank or filler neck should be done by a professional who has experience in this critical and potentially dangerous work.
Even after cleaning and flushing of the fuel system, explosive fumes can
remain and ignite during repair of the tank.
2   If the fuel tank is removed from the vehicle, it should not be placed in
an area where sparks or open flames could ignite the fumes coming out of
the tank. Be especially careful inside garages where a natural gas-type
appliance is located, because the pilot light could cause an explosion.

8.3   Grasp the throttle lever arm and rotate it to put some slack
in the cable, then slip the cable end out of the slot in the arm

8   Accelerator cable – removal, installation and adjustment

Removal
Refer to illustrations 8.2, 8.3 and 8.5
1   Detach the cable from the negative terminal of the battery.
2   Unscrew the locknut on the threaded portion of the accelerator cable
at the carburetor or throttle body **(see illustration)**.
3   Rotate the throttle lever arm **(see illustration)** to put some slack in
the cable, then slip the cable end out of the slot in the arm.
4   Trace the cable to the firewall, detaching it from all brackets.
5   On later models, the cable must be detached from inside the vehicle
(see illustration).
6   Detach the cable from the accelerator pedal.
7   Working inside the vehicle, pull the cable through the firewall.

Installation and adjustment
8   Installation is the reverse of removal.
9   To adjust the cable, depress the accelerator pedal as far as possible
and make sure the throttle is all the way open.
10   If it isn't, loosen the locknuts, depress the accelerator pedal and adjust the cable.
11   Tighten the locknuts and recheck the adjustment.

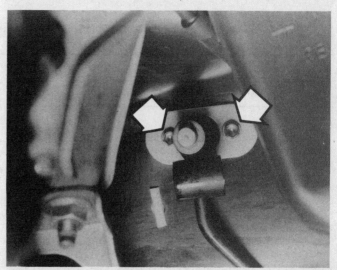

8.5   On some models, you'll have to detach the cable ferrule
from inside the vehicle – remove the bolts (arrows)

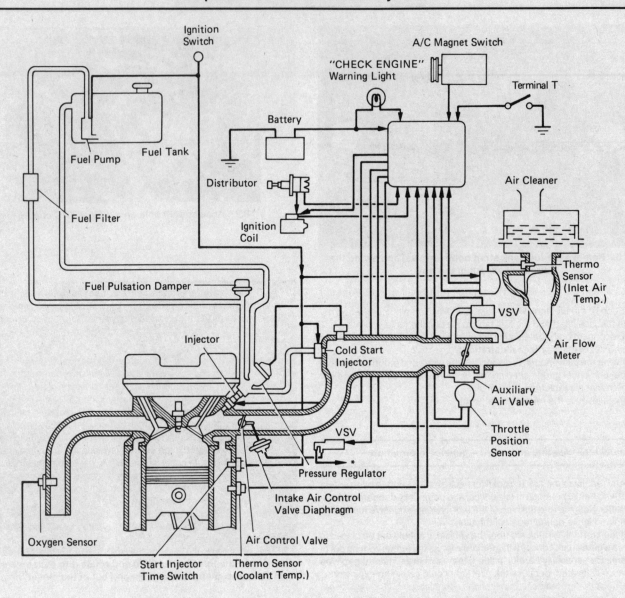

9.1   Electronic Fuel Injection (EFI) system installed on 4A-GE engines – 1985 through 1987

9   Fuel injection system – general information

Refer to illustration 9.1

The engine is equipped with an Electronic Fuel Injection (EFI) system. The EFI system is composed of three basic sub systems: fuel system, air system and electronic control system **(see illustration).**

Fuel system

An electric fuel pump located inside the fuel tank supplies fuel under constant pressure to the fuel rail, which distributes fuel evenly to all injectors. From the fuel rail, fuel is injected into the intake ports, just above the intake valves, by four fuel injectors. The amount of fuel supplied by the injectors is precisely controlled by an Electronic Control Unit (ECU). An additional injector, known as the cold start injector, supplies extra fuel into the intake manifold for starting. A pressure regulator controls system pressure in relation to intake manifold vacuum. A fuel filter between the fuel pump and the fuel rail filters fuel to protect the components of the system.

Air system

The air system consists of an air filter housing and an air flow meter. The air flow meter is an information gathering device for the ECU. A potentiometer measures intake air flow and a temperature sensor measures intake air temperature. This information helps the ECU determine the amount (duration) of fuel to be injected by the injectors. The throttle plate inside the throttle body is controlled by the driver. As the throttle plate opens, the amount of air that can pass through the system increases, so the potentiometer opens further and the ECU signals the injectors to increase the amount of fuel delivered to the intake ports.

Electronic control system

The Computer Control System controls the EFI and other systems by means of an Electronic Control Unit (ECU), which employs a microcomputer. The ECU receives signals from a number of information sensors which monitor such variables as intake air volume, intake air temperature, coolant temperature, engine rpm, acceleration/deceleration and exhaust

10.6   Clean the throttle body casting thoroughly with solvent or carburetor cleaner – the area right behind the throttle plate is particularly susceptible to sludge build-up because the PCV hose vents crankcase vapors to the plenum

10.7   Use a stethoscope or screwdriver to determine if the injectors are working properly – they should make a steady clicking sound that rises and falls with engine speed changes

oxygen content. These signals help the ECU determine the injection duration necessary for the optimum air/fuel ratio. Some of these sensors and their corresponding ECU-controlled relays are not contained within EFI components, but are located throughout the engine compartment. For further information regarding the ECU and its relationship to the engine electrical and ignition system, refer to Chapter 6.

10   Fuel injection system – check

Refer to illustrations 10.6 and 10.7

Warning: *Gasoline is extremely flammable, so extra precautions must be taken when working on any part of the fuel system. Don't smoke or allow open flames or bare light bulbs in or near the work area. Also, don't work in a garage where a natural gas-type appliance with a pilot light is present. Have a fire extinguisher rated for gasoline fires handy and know how to use it!*

1   Check the ground wire connections. Check all wiring harness connectors that are related to the system. Loose connectors and poor grounds can cause many problems that resemble more serious malfunctions.

2   Make sure the battery is fully charged, as the control unit and sensors depend on an accurate supply voltage in order to properly meter the fuel.
3   Check the air filter element – a dirty or partially blocked filter will severely impede performance and economy (Chapter 1).
4   If a blown fuse is found, replace it and see if it blows again. If it does, search for a grounded wire in the harness related to the system.
5   Check the air intake duct from the air flow meter to the intake manifold for leaks, which will result in an excessively lean mixture. Also check the condition of the vacuum hoses connected to the intake manifold.
6   Remove the air intake duct from the throttle body and check for dirt, carbon and other residue build-up. If it's dirty, clean it with carburetor cleaner and a toothbrush **(see illustration)**.
7   With the engine running, place a screwdriver or a stethoscope against each injector, one at a time, and listen for a clicking sound, indicating operation **(see illustration)**.
8   The remainder of the system checks should be left to a dealer service department or a repair shop, since there's a chance the ECU may be damaged if the system isn't checked properly.

11   Fuel injection system – component removal and installation

Warning: *Gasoline is extremely flammable, so extra precautions must be taken when working on any part of the fuel system. Don't smoke or allow open flames or bare light bulbs in or near the work area. Also, don't work in a garage where a natural gas-type appliance with a pilot light is present. Have a fire extinguisher rated for gasoline fires handy and know how to use it!*

Throttle body
Refer to illustrations 11.6, 11.7 and 11.8
1   Detach the cable from the negative terminal of the battery.
2   Drain about a gallon of coolant (see Chapter 1).
3   Loosen the hose clamps and remove the air intake duct.
4   Detach the accelerator cable from the throttle lever arm (see Section 8), then detach the throttle cable bracket and set it aside (it's not necessary to detach the throttle cable from the bracket).
5   If the vehicle is equipped with an automatic transmission, detach the throttle valve (TV) cable from the throttle linkage (see Chapter 7B), detach the TV cable brackets from the engine and set the cable and brackets aside.
6   Clearly label, then detach, all vacuum and coolant hoses from the throttle body **(see illustration)**.

11.6   Label and detach all vacuum hoses from the throttle body

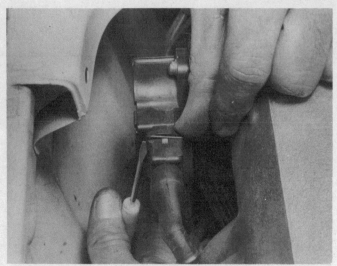

11.7   Pry the spring clip up far enough to release the electrical connector plug from the throttle position sensor (TPS) and unplug the connector

11.8   Remove the bolts (arrows) to detach the throttle body from the air intake chamber – DOHC engine shown, others similar

7   Unplug the electrical connector from the throttle position sensor **(see illustration)**.
8   Remove the throttle body mounting bolts **(see illustration)** and detach the throttle body and gasket from the air intake chamber.
9   Using a soft brush and carburetor cleaner, thoroughly clean the throttle body casting, then blow out all passages with compressed air. **Caution:** *Do not clean the throttle position sensor with anything. Just wipe it off carefully with a clean soft cloth.*
10   Installation of the throttle body is the reverse of removal. Be sure to tighten the throttle body mounting bolts to the torque listed in this Chapter's specifications.

Fuel pressure regulator

Refer to illustration 11.16
11   Relieve the fuel pressure (see Section 2).
12   Detach the cable from the negative terminal of the battery.
13   Detach the vacuum sensing hose.
14   Place a metal container or shop towel under the fuel return line at the regulator.
15   Disconnect the fuel return line.

16   Remove the pressure regulator mounting bolts **(see illustration)** and detach the pressure regulator from the fuel rail.
17   Installation is the reverse of removal.

Fuel rail and fuel injectors

Refer to illustrations 11.23, 11.24, 11.25, 11.27, 11.28, 11.30a and 11.30b
18   Remove the fuel filler cap to relieve the fuel tank pressure.
19   Relieve the system fuel pressure (see Section 2).
20   Detach the cable from the negative terminal of the battery.
21   Detach the accelerator cable from the throttle linkage and from its bracket on the air intake (see Section 8).
22   Detach the vacuum sensing hose from the fuel pressure regulator **(see illustration 11.16)**.
23   Unplug the cold start injector connector and remove the cold start injector pipe bolt **(see illustration)**.
24   Unplug the four fuel injector electrical connectors **(see illustration)** and set the injector wire harness aside.
25   Remove the pulsation damper and detach the fuel feed line **(see illustration)**.
26   Remove the two fuel rail mounting bolts and detach the fuel rail/injec-

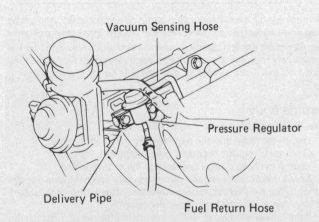

11.16   To detach the fuel pressure regulator from the fuel rail, disconnect the fuel return line, remove the two mounting bolts, then separate the regulator from the fuel rail

11.23   Unplug the electrical connector, remove the banjo bolt (arrow) and crush washers, then separate the line from the cold start injector

11.24   The injector connectors can be tricky to unplug – depress the tang (arrow) to unlock each connector

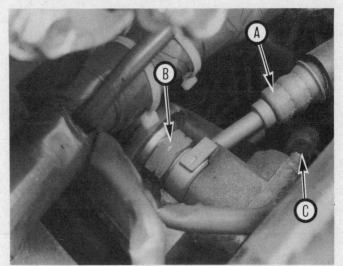

11.25   To detach the fuel feed line (A) from the fuel rail, remove the pulsation damper (B) – discard the crush washers – the fuel return line (C) is also visible in the lower right corner of this photo but you can't detach it until the fuel rail is removed from the head

tor assembly from the cylinder head by pulling on it while wiggling it back-and-forth.

27   Remove the fuel injectors from the fuel rail and set them aside in a clearly labelled storage container **(see illustration).**

11.27   Unless you're only removing one fuel injector at a time, it's a good idea to place the injectors in a clearly labelled container, like an egg carton, to prevent mixing them up

28   Remove the fuel rail **(see illustration).**

29   Remove the four fuel rail insulators from the cylinder head and set them aside.

30   If you are replacing the injector(s), discard the old injector, the grommet and the O-ring. If you are simply replacing leaking injector O-rings, and intend to re-use the same injectors, remove the old grommet and O-ring **(see illustrations)** and discard them.

31   Testing of the injector(s) is beyond the scope of the home mechanic. If you are in doubt as to the status of any injector(s), it can be bench tested for volume and leakage at a dealer service department.

32   Installation of the fuel injectors is the reverse of removal. Be sure to use new grommets and O-rings on the injector(s).

12   Carburetor – diagnosis and overhaul

Warning: *Gasoline is extremely flammable, so extra precautions must be taken when working on any part of the fuel system. Do not smoke or allow open flames or bare light bulbs in or near the work area. Also, don't work in a garage if a natural gas-type appliance with a pilot light is present. Have a fire extinguisher handy and know how to use it!*

11.28   Carefully remove the fuel rail assembly through the space between the camshaft covers and the air intake chamber (DOHC engine)

11.30a   Even if you plan to reinstall the same injector(s), be sure to remove and discard the old O-rings and replace them with new ones

11.30b   Also remove and discard the old grommets and replace them with new ones

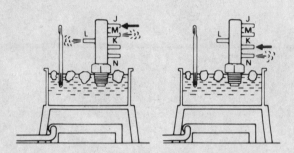

12.5a   With the temperature of the valve below 45-degrees F, blow through pipe J (air should exit through pipes M and L); next, blow through pipe K (air should exit pipe N)

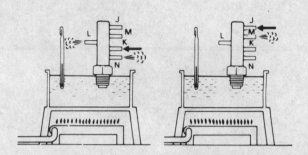

12.5b   With the temperature of the valve at about 100-degrees F, blow through pipe K (air should exit through pipes N and L); next, blow through pipe j (air should exit pipe M)

General diagnosis

1   A thorough road test and check of carburetor adjustments should be done before any major carburetor service work. Specifications for some adjustments are listed on the Vehicle Emissions Control Information (VECI) label found in the engine compartment.

2   Carburetor problems usually show up as flooding, hard starting, stalling, severe backfiring and poor acceleration. A carburetor that's leaking fuel and/or covered with wet looking deposits definitely needs attention.

3   Some performance complaints directed at the carburetor are actually a result of loose, out-of-adjustment or malfunctioning engine or electrical components. Others develop when vacuum hoses leak, are disconnected or are incorrectly routed. The proper approach to analyzing carburetor problems should include the following items:

a) Inspect all vacuum hoses and actuators for leaks and correct installation (see Chapters 1 and 6).
b) Tighten the intake manifold and carburetor mounting nuts/bolts evenly and securely.
c) Perform a cylinder compression test (see Chapter 2).
d) Clean or replace the spark plugs as necessary (Chapter1).
e) Check the spark plug wires (see Chapter 1).
f) Inspect the ignition primary wires.
g) Check the ignition timing (follow the instructions printed on the Emissions Control Information label).
h) Check the fuel pump (see Section 4).
i) Check the heat control valve in the air cleaner for proper operation (see Chapter 1).
j) Check/replace the air filter element (see Chapter 1).
k) Check the PCV system (see Chapters 1 and 6).
l) Check/replace the fuel filter (see Chapter 1). Also, the strainer in the tank could be restricted.
m) Check for a plugged exhaust system.
n) Check EGR valve operation (see Chapter 6).

o) Check the choke – it should be completely open at normal engine operating temperature (see Chapter 1).
p) Check for fuel leaks and kinked or dented fuel lines (see Chapters 1 and 4).
q) Check accelerator pump operation with the engine off (remove the air cleaner cover and operate the throttle as you look into the carburetor throat – you should see a stream of gasoline enter the carburetor).
r) Check for incorrect fuel or bad gasoline.
s) Check the valve clearances (if applicable) and camshaft lobe lift (see Chapters 1 and 2).
t) Have a dealer service department or repair shop check the electronic engine and carburetor controls.

4   Diagnosing carburetor problems may require the engine to be started and run with the air cleaner off. While running the engine without the air cleaner, backfires are possible. This situation is likely to occur if the carburetor is malfunctioning, but just the removal of the air cleaner can lean the fuel/air mixture enough to produce an engine backfire. **Warning:** *Don't position any part of your body, especially your face, directly over the carburetor during inspection and servicing procedures. Wear eye protection!*

Feedback carburetor inspection

Refer to illustrations 12.5a, 12.5b, 12.5c, 12.6a and 12.6b

5   Check the Thermostatic Vacuum Switching Valve (TVSV).
a) The coolant temperature should be below 45-degrees F. Drain the coolant (see Chapter 1).
b) Remove the TVSV.
c) Check that air flows from pipe J to pipe M and L, and from pipe K to pipe N **(see illustration)**.
d) Heat the TVSV to about 100-degrees F.
e) Check that air flows from pipe K to pipe N and L, and from pipe J to pipe M **(see illustration)**.

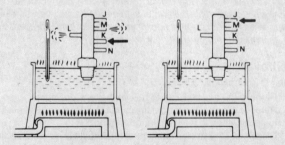

12.5c   With the temperature of the valve above 154-degrees F, blow through pipe K (air should exit through pipes M and L); next, try to blow through pipe J (air should not exit through any of the pipes)

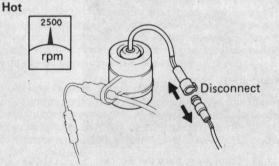

12.6a   With the EBCV disconnected, maintain the engine rpm at 2500 rpm

Below 7°C

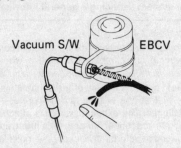

Vacuum S/W   EBCV

12.6b   With the vacuum line off the EBCV, the engine RPM should not change during testing

12.9   Before buying a carburetor rebuild kit, look for a tag like this and write the number down – it will ensure that you get the correct rebuild kit for the carburetor

f) Heat the TVSV above 154-degrees F.
g) Check that air flows from pipe K to pipe M and L, and does not flow from pipe J to other pipes **(see illustration)**.
6   Check the Electronic Air Bleed Control Valve (EBCV).
a) Warm up the engine to normal operating temperature.
b) Disconnect the EBCV connector **(see illustration)**.
c) Maintain engine speed at 2,500 rpm.
d) Reconnect the EBCV connector and the engine rpm should drop about 300 rpm momentarily.
e) With the engine idling, repeat steps b) and d).
f) Make sure the engine speed does not change.
g) Disconnect the vacuum hose from the vacuum switch **(see illustration)**.
h) Repeat steps b), c) and d). Check that the engine speed does not change.
7   If no problems are found during this inspection, the system is okay. Additional checks should be done by a dealer service department or an automotive repair shop.

Overhaul

Refer to illustration 12.9

8   Once it's determined the carburetor needs an overhaul, several options are available. If you're going to attempt to overhaul the carburetor yourself, first obtain a good quality carburetor rebuild kit (which will include all necessary gaskets, internal parts, instructions and a parts list). You'll also need some special solvent and a means of blowing out the internal passages of the carburetor with air.

9   An alternative is to obtain a new or rebuilt carburetor. They're readily available from dealers and auto parts stores. Make absolutely sure the exchange carburetor is identical to the original. A tag is usually attached to the top of the carburetor or a number is stamped on the float bowl **(see illustration)**. It'll help determine the exact type of carburetor you have. When obtaining a rebuilt carburetor or a rebuild kit, make sure the kit or carburetor matches your application exactly. Seemingly insignificant differences can make a large difference in engine performance.

10   Because carburetor designs are constantly modified by the manufacturer in order to meet increasingly more stringent emissions regulations, it isn't feasible to include a step-by-step overhaul of each type. You'll receive a detailed, well illustrated set of instructions with any carburetor overhaul kit; they'll apply in a more specific manner to the carburetor on your vehicle.

11   If you choose to overhaul the carburetor, allow enough time to disassemble it carefully, soak the necessary parts in the cleaning solvent (usually for at least one-half day or according to the instructions listed on the carburetor cleaner) and reassemble it, which will usually take much longer than disassembly. When disassembling the carburetor, match each part with the illustration in the carburetor kit and lay the parts out in order on a clean work surface. Overhauls by inexperienced mechanics can result in an engine which runs poorly or not at all. To avoid this, use care and patience when disassembling the carburetor so you can reassemble it correctly.

13.5   Clearly label all vacuum hoses before disconnecting them

13   Carburetor – removal and installation

Warning: *Gasoline is extremely flammable, so extra precautions must be taken when working on any part of the fuel system. Do not smoke or allow open flames or bare light bulbs in or near the work area. Also, don't work in a garage if a natural gas-type appliance with a pilot light is present. Have a fire extinguisher handy and know how to use it!*

Removal

Refer to illustrations 13.5 and 13.7

1   Remove the fuel tank cap to relieve the tank pressure.
2   Remove the air cleaner from the carburetor. Be sure to label all vacuum hoses attached to the air cleaner housing.
3   Disconnect the throttle cable from the throttle lever (see Section 8).
4   If the vehicle is equipped with an automatic transmission, disconnect the TV cable from the throttle lever.
5   Clearly label all vacuum hoses and fittings, then disconnect the hoses **(see illustration)**.
6   Disconnect the fuel line from the carburetor.

4

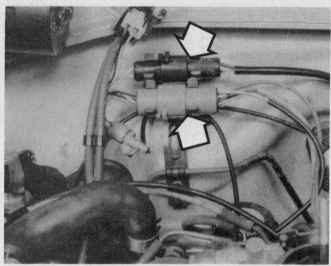

13.7   Label and unplug the carburetor electrical connectors (arrows)

7   Label the wires and terminals, then unplug all wire harness connectors **(see illustration)**.
8   Remove the mounting fasteners, move the EGR modulator bracket out of the way and lift the carburetor off the intake manifold. Remove the carburetor gasket. Do not remove the cold mixture heater. Stuff a shop rag into the intake manifold openings.

Installation

9   Use a gasket scraper to remove all traces of gasket material from the mating surfaces, being careful not to damage the delicate aluminum surfaces. Then remove the shop rag from the manifold openings. Clean the mating surfaces with lacquer thinner or acetone.
10   Place a new gasket on the cold mixture heater.
11   Position the carburetor on the gasket, attach the EGR modulator bracket, then install the mounting fasteners.
12   To prevent carburetor distortion or damage, tighten the fasteners, in a criss-cross pattern, 1/4-turn at a time.
13   The remaining installation steps are the reverse of removal.
14   Check and, if necessary, adjust the idle speed (Chapter 1).
15   If the vehicle is equipped with an automatic transmission, refer to Chapter 7, Part B, for the TV cable adjustment procedure.
16   Start the engine and check carefully for fuel leaks.

14   Exhaust system servicing – general information

Refer to illustrations 14.1 and 14.4
Warning: *Inspection and repair of exhaust system components should be done only when they are completely cool. Also, when working under the vehicle, make sure it's securely supported on jackstands.*
1   The exhaust system consists of the exhaust manifold, the catalytic converter, the muffler, the tailpipe and all connecting pipes, brackets, hangers and clamps. The exhaust system is attached to the body with mounting brackets and rubber hangers **(see illustration)**. If any of these parts are damaged or deteriorated, excessive noise and vibration will be transmitted to the body.
2   Regular inspections of the exhaust system will keep it safe and quiet. Look for damaged and bent parts, open seams, holes, loose connections, excessive corrosion and other defects which could allow exhaust fumes to enter the vehicle. Deteriorated exhaust system components should not be repaired – they should be replaced with new parts.
3   If the exhaust system components are extremely corroded or rusted together, they will probably have to be cut out of the exhaust system. The convenient way to accomplish this is to have a muffler repair shop remove the corroded sections with a cutting torch. If, however, you want to save money by doing it yourself (and you don't have an oxy-acetylene welding outfit with a cutting torch), simply cut off the old components with a hacksaw. If you have compressed air, special pneumatic cutting chisels can also be used. If you do decide to tackle the job at home, be sure to wear eye protection to protect your eyes from metal chips and work gloves to protect your hands.
4   Here are some simple guidelines to apply when repairing the exhaust system:
   a) Work from the back to the front when removing exhaust system components.
   b) Apply penetrating oil to the exhaust system component fasteners to make them easier to remove **(see illustration)**.
   c) Use new gaskets, hangers and clamps when installing exhaust system components.
   d) Apply anti-seize compound to the threads of all exhaust system fasteners during reassembly.
   e) Be sure to allow sufficient clearance between newly installed parts and all points on the underbody to avoid overheating the floor pan and possibly damaging the interior carpet and insulation. Pay particularly close attention to the catalytic converter and heat shield.
   Warning: *The catalytic converter operates at very high temperatures and takes about 30 minutes to cool. Wait half an hour before attempting to remove the converter. Failure to do so could result in serious burns.*

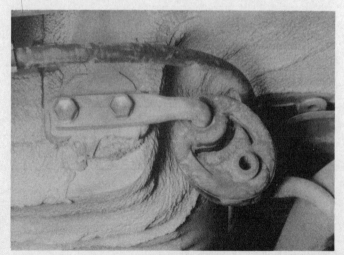

14.1   Here's a typical exhaust system hanger – they should be inspected for cracks and replaced if deteriorated

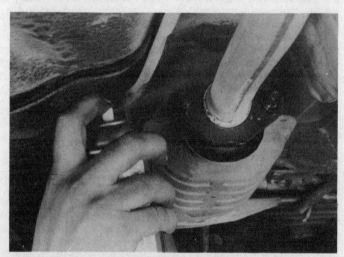

14.4   Exhaust system bolts and nuts, particularly those on the exhaust manifold and catalytic converter, can be very difficult to loosen – spraying them with penetrating oil will help

Chapter 5 Engine electrical systems

Contents

5

Specifications

Ignition coil

Primary resistance

3T-C engine	0.8 to 1.1 ohms
4A-GE engine	0.5 to 0.7 ohms
4A-C engine	
USA	0.3 to 0.5 ohms
Canada	1.2 to 1.5 ohms

Secondary resistance

3T-C engine	11,500 to 15,500 ohms
4A-GE engine	11,000 to 16,000 ohms
4A-C engine	
USA	7,700 to 10,400 ohms
Canada	10,200 to 13,800 ohms

Igniter transistor voltage

3T-C engine .... 5 volts
4A-GE engine .... 12 volts
4A-C engine
  USA .... 5 volts
  Canada .... 0 to 3 volts

Pick-up coil

Resistance .... 140 to 180 ohms
Air gap .... 0.008 to 0.016 in

Alternator brush minimum length .... 0.217 in

1   General information

The engine electrical systems include all ignition, charging and starting components. Because of their engine-related functions, these components are discussed separately from chassis electrical devices such as the lights, instruments, etc. (which are included in Chapter 12).

Always observe the following precautions when working on the electrical systems:

a) Be extremely careful when servicing engine electrical components. They are easily damaged if checked, connected or handled improperly.

b) Never leave the ignition switch on for long periods of time with the engine off.

c) Don't disconnect the battery cables while the engine is running.

d) Maintain correct polarity when connecting a battery cable from another vehicle during jump starting.

e) Always disconnect the negative cable first and hook it up last or the battery may be shorted by the tool being used to loosen the cable clamps.

It's also a good idea to review the safety-related information regarding the engine electrical systems located in the Safety first! Section near the front of this manual before beginning any operation included in this Chapter.

2   Battery – emergency jump starting

Refer to the *Booster battery (jump) starting* procedure at the front of this manual.

3   Battery – removal and installation

1   **Caution:** *Always disconnect the negative cable first and hook it up last or the battery may be shorted by the tool being used to loosen the cable clamps.* Disconnect both cables from the battery terminals.
2   Remove the battery hold-down clamp.
3   Lift out the battery. Be careful – it's heavy.
4   While the battery is out, inspect the carrier (tray) for corrosion (see Chapter 1).
5   If you're replacing the battery, make sure you buy one that's identical, with the same dimensions, amperage rating, cold cranking rating, etc.
6   Installation is the reverse of removal.

4   Battery cables – check and replacement

1   Periodically inspect the entire length of each battery cable for damage, cracked or burned insulation and corrosion. Poor battery cable connections can cause starting problems and decreased engine performance.
2   Check the cable-to-terminal connections at the ends of the cables for cracks, loose wire strands and corrosion. The presence of white, fluffy deposits under the insulation at the cable terminal connection is a sign that the cable is corroded and should be replaced. Check the terminals for distortion, missing mounting bolts and corrosion.
3   When removing the cables, always disconnect the negative cable first and hook it up last or the battery may be shorted by the tool used to loosen the cable clamps. Even if only the positive cable is being replaced, be sure to disconnect the negative cable from the battery first (see Chapter 1 for further information regarding battery cable removal).
4   Disconnect the old cables from the battery, then trace each of them to their opposite ends and detach them from the starter solenoid and ground terminals. Note the routing of each cable to ensure correct installation.
5   If you are replacing either or both of the old cables, take them with you when buying new cables. It is vitally important that you replace the cables with identical parts. Cables have characteristics that make them easy to identify: positive cables are usually red, larger in cross-section and have a larger diameter battery post clamp; ground cables are usually black, smaller in cross-section and have a slightly smaller diameter clamp for the negative post.
6   Clean the threads of the solenoid or ground connection with a wire brush to remove rust and corrosion. Apply a light coat of battery terminal corrosion inhibitor, or petroleum jelly, to the threads to prevent future corrosion.
7   Attach the cable to the solenoid or ground connection and tighten the mounting nut/bolt securely.
8   Before connecting a new cable to the battery, make sure that it reaches the battery post without having to be stretched.
9   Connect the positive cable first, followed by the negative cable.

5   Ignition system – general information and precautions

The ignition system includes the ignition switch, the battery, the igniter, the coil, the primary (low voltage) and secondary (high voltage) circuits, the distributor and the spark plugs. On later 1987 models, the ignition system is controlled by the Electronic Control Unit (ECU). Using data provided by information sensors which monitor various engine functions (such as rpm, intake air volume, engine temperature, etc.), the ECU ensures perfectly timed sparks under all conditions.

When working on the ignition system, take the following precautions:

a) Do not keep the ignition switch on for more than 10 seconds if the engine will not start.

b) Always connect a tachometer in accordance with the manufacturer's instructions. Some tachometers may be incompatible with this ignition system. Consult a dealer service department before buying a tachometer for use with this vehicle.

c) Never allow the ignition coil terminals to touch ground. Grounding the coil could result in damage to the igniter and/or the ignition coil.

d) Do not disconnect the battery when the engine is running.

e) Make sure the igniter is properly grounded.

6 Ignition system – check

1   If the engine won't start, the following quick checks should pinpoint the problem.

2   Attach an inductive timing light to each plug wire, close to the plug, one at a time, and crank the engine.

a) If the light flashes, voltage is reaching the plug, but the plug may still be faulty. Check it (see Chapter 1).

b) If the light does not flash, proceed to the next step.

3   Inspect the spark plug wire(s), distributor cap, rotor and spark plug(s) (see Chapter 1).

4   If the engine still won't start, check the ignition coil (see Section 7).

7 Ignition coil – check and replacement

Check
Refer to illustrations 7.3a, 7.3b, 7.3c and 7.3d

1   Detach the cable from the negative terminal of the battery.

2   Locate the coil in the engine compartment.

3   Using an ohmmeter, check the coil:

a) Measure the resistance between the positive and negative terminals **(see illustrations)**. Compare your reading with the specified primary coil resistance.

b) Detach the high tension lead from the coil. Measure the resistance between the positive terminal and high tension terminal **(see illustrations)**. Compare your reading with the specified secondary coil resistance.

4   If either of the above tests yield resistance values outside the specified resistance, replace the coil.

Replacement

3T-C and 4A-GE engines

5   Detach the wires from the coil primary terminals.

6   Remove the coil mounting bracket bolts and lift the coil and ignitor assembly up far enough to get at the ignitor mounting bolts.

7   Remove the ignitor from the ignition coil.

8   Installation is the reverse of removal.

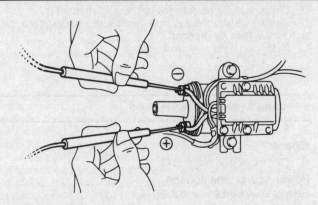

7.3a   Check the primary resistance of the coil between the positive and negative terminals – 3T-C and 4A-GE engines

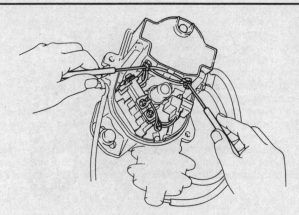

7.3b   Check the primary resistance of the coil between the positive and negative terminals – 4A-C engine

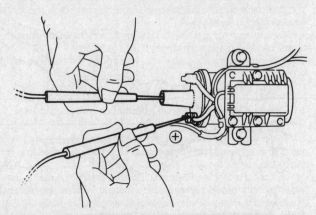

7.3c   Check the secondary coil resistance between the high tension terminal and primary positive terminal – 3T-C and 4A-GE engines

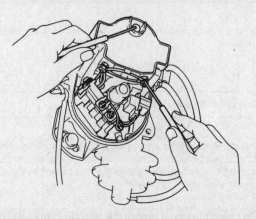

7.3d   Checking secondary coil resistance on a 4A-C engine

5

7.10   To remove the coil dust cover, spread the tangs (arrows) at each side and slide it off the coil

7.11   Label the coil primary wires, remove the nuts (arrows) and detach the wires

7.12   Remove the four coil mounting screws to separate the coil from the distributor – 4A-C engine

4A-C engine

Refer to illustrations 7.10, 7.11 and 7.12

9   Remove the distributor from the engine (see Section 10).

10   Remove the ignition coil dust cover **(see illustration)**.

11   Disconnect all wires from the coil **(see illustration)**.

12   Remove the bolts that secure the ignition coil to the distributor and detach the coil **(see illustration)**.

13   Installation is the reverse of removal.

---

8   Igniter – check and replacement

Check

1   Turn the ignition switch to On.

Power source line voltage

Refer to illustration 8.2a and 8.2b

2   Using a voltmeter, connect the positive probe to the ignition coil positive terminal and the negative probe to body ground **(see illustrations)**. It should be about 12-volts.

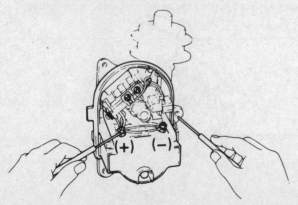

8.2a   To check the power source line voltage to the igniter on the 4A-C engine, connect the positive probe of a voltmeter to the coil positive terminal and the negative probe to a good ground – it should be about 12-volts

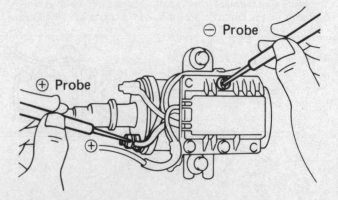

8.2b   To check the power source line voltage on 3T-C and 4A-GE engines, hook up a voltmeter as shown – the reading should be approximately 12-volts

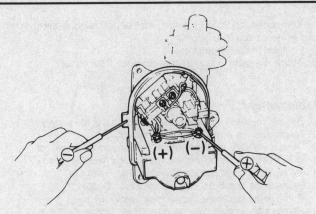

8.3a   On the 4A-C engine, connect the positive probe of a voltmeter to the ignition coil negative terminal and the negative probe to a good ground – the reading should be about 12-volts

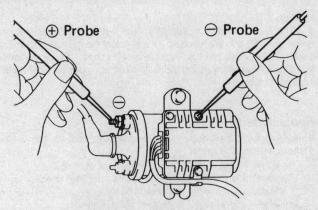

8.3b   On 3T-C and 4A-GE engines, hook up a voltmeter as shown – the reading should be about 12-volts

Power transistor in igniter

1980 through 1985

Refer to illustrations 8.3a, 8.3b, 8.4a, 8.4b, 8.5a and 8.5b

3   Using a voltmeter, connect the positive probe to the ignition coil negative terminal and the negative probe to the body ground **(see illustrations)**. It should be about 12-volts.

4   Using a dry cell battery (1.5V), connect the positive pole of the battery to the pink wire terminal and the negative pole to the white wire terminal

(see illustrations). Caution: *Do not apply voltage for more than five seconds or you could destroy the power transistor in the igniter.*

5   Using a voltmeter, connect the positive probe to the ignition coil negative terminal and the negative probe to body ground **(see illustrations)**. Check the voltage reading in this Chapter's specifications.

6   If the voltage reading from either of these tests is not within the specified voltage, replace the igniter.

7   Turn the ignition switch off.

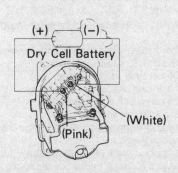

8.4a   On 4A-C engines, connect the positive side of a 1.5-volt dry cell battery to the pink wire terminal and the negative side to the white wire terminal (don't apply voltage for more than five seconds or you could destroy the power transistor in the igniter)

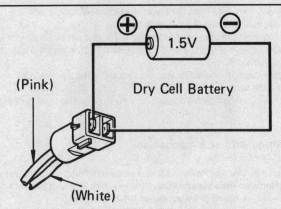

8.4b   On 3T-C and 4A-GE engines, hook up a 1.5-volt dry cell battery as shown (don't apply voltage for more than five seconds or you could destroy the power transistor in the igniter)

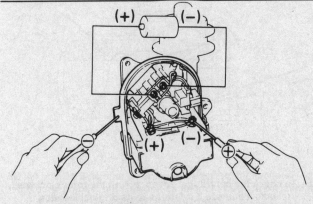

8.5a   On 4A-C engines, hook up a voltmeter as shown

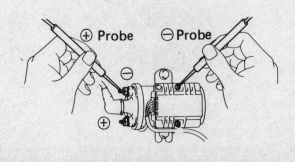

8.5b   On 3T-C and 4A-GE engines, hook up a voltmeter as shown

1986-on

8   There is no specific procedure for checking the power transistor in the igniter on 1986 and later models – if a check of the ignition system (see Section 6) rules out all other possible malfunctions, replace the igniter. Make sure, however, that you eliminate all other possibilities before buying a new igniter.

Replacement

Note: *Refer to the exploded views of the distributor assemblies in Section 9 when replacing the igniter.*

9   Detach the cable from the negative terminal of the battery.
10   Remove the distributor cap, packing and rotor (see Chapter 1).
11   If equipped, remove the igniter dust cover.
12   Remove the ignition coil dust cover (4A-C engine).
13   Remove the ignition coil (see Section 7).
14   Remove the igniter mounting screws and nuts, disconnect the wires from the igniter terminals and remove the two screws and the igniter.
15   Installation is the reverse of removal.

---

9   Vacuum and centrifugal advance units – check and replacement (3T-C and 4A-C engines only)

Check

Vacuum advance unit
Refer to illustration 9.4

1   Detach the cable from the negative terminal of the battery.
2   Remove the distributor cap (see Chapter 1).
3   Disconnect the vacuum hose(s) from the vacuum advance unit and connect a vacuum pump to the fitting(s). Use a T-fitting and two hoses on dual vacuum units.
4   Apply vacuum and verify that the vacuum advancer link rod moves **(see illustration)**.
5   If the vacuum advancer doesn't work, replace it as necessary (see below).

Centrifugal advance mechanism
Refer to illustration 9.6

6   Turn the rotor clockwise, release it and verify that it snaps back to its original location **(see illustration)**.
7   Make sure the rotor fits snugly on the shaft.

8   If the centrifugal advance doesn't work as described, repair or replace parts as necessary (see below).
9   Reinstall the distributor cap.
10   Attach the cable to the negative terminal of the battery.

Replacement

11   Detach the cable from the negative terminal of the battery.
12   Disconnect the wires from the distributor.
13   Detach the vacuum hose(s) from the vacuum advance unit.
14   Disconnect the wires from the spark plugs (see Chapter 1).
15   Remove the distributor (see Section 10).
16   Remove the distributor cap and rotor (see Chapter 1).
17   Remove the igniter dust cover (see Section 8).
18   Remove the ignition coil dust cover (see Section 7).
19   Remove the ignition coil (see Section 7).
20   Remove the igniter (see Section 8).
21   If you're replacing the vacuum advance unit, proceed to the next Step. Even if you're only replacing the centrifugal advance assembly, you must still remove the vacuum advance unit first, so follow the instructions in Steps 22 and 23, then proceed to Step 25.

Vacuum advance unit
Refer to illustrations 9.22a, 9.22b and 9.23

22   Remove the retaining screw from the vacuum advance unit **(see illustrations)**.
23   Disconnect the link rod from the breaker plate **(see illustration)** and remove the advance unit.
24   Installation is the reverse of removal.

Centrifugal advance mechanism
Refer to illustrations 9.31, 9.32, 9.33 and 9.38

25   Using a small screwdriver, pry out the set spring, then pull out the signal rotor.
26   Remove the breaker plate screws and washers, then detach the breaker plate and pick-up coil as an assembly.
27   Remove the advance weight springs.
28   Remove the grease stopper.
29   Remove the screw at the top of the shaft.
30   Pull off the signal rotor shaft.
31   Using a small screwdriver, pop off the E-clips **(see illustration)** and remove the advance weights.
32   Check the breaker plate **(see illustration)**. Turn it to make sure there's a slight drag. If strong resistance or binding is felt, replace the breaker plate and pick-up coil assembly.

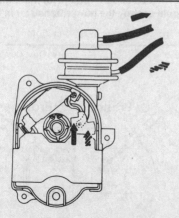

9.4   To check the vacuum advance unit, connect a vacuum pump to each fitting, apply vacuum and verify that the link rod moves (4A-C engine shown, 3T-C similar)

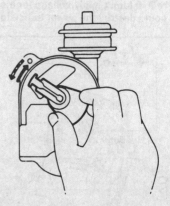

9.6   To check the centrifugal advance, turn the rotor clockwise, release it and see if it returns to its original location

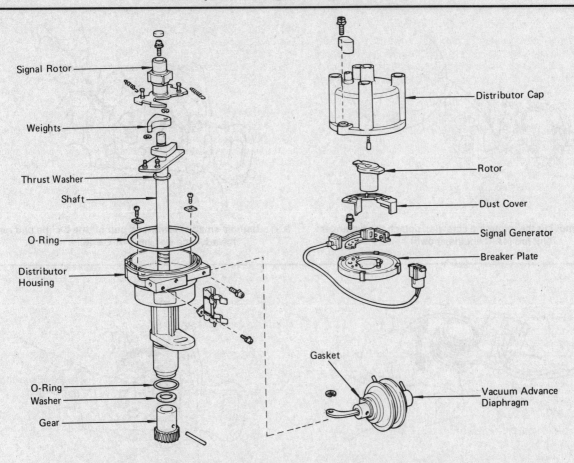

9.22a   An exploded view of the distributor used on 3T-C engines (1981 and 1982 shown, others similar)

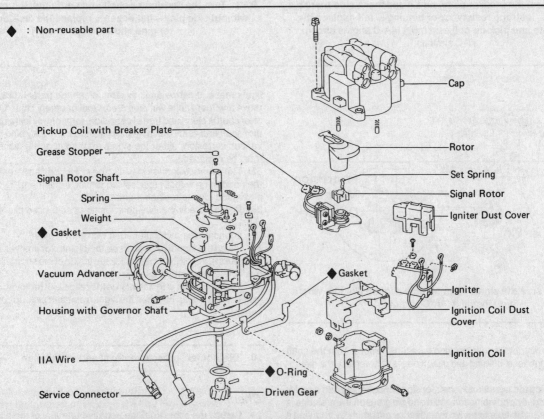

9.22b   An exploded view of the Integrated Ignition Assembly (IIA) distributor used on 4A-C engines

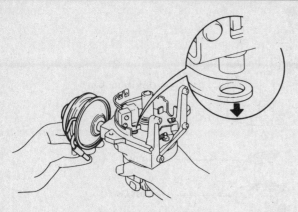

9.23   After removing the mounting screw(s), detach the advancer link rod (4A-C engine shown)

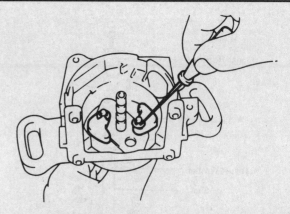

9.31   Using a small screwdriver, pop off the E-clips and remove the advance weights (4A-C engine shown)

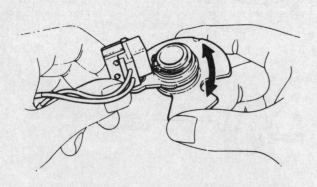

9.32   To inspect the breaker plate, turn it and make sure there's a slight drag – if strong resistance or binding is felt, replace the breaker plate and pick-up coil assembly (4A-C engine shown, 3T-C similar)

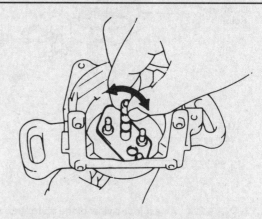

9.33   Turn the distributor shaft and verify that it turns smoothly without side play – if it doesn't, replace the distributor (4A-C engine shown, 3T-C similar)

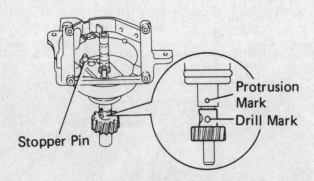

Protrusion Mark

Drill Mark

Stopper Pin

9.38   Make sure the signal rotor shaft is aligned like this when you install it (4A-C engine)

33   Check the distributor shaft bearing **(see illustration)**. Turn the shaft to check for roughness, binding and play. If necessary, replace the distributor.

34   Check inside the signal rotor shaft for signs of corrosion and a build-up of sludge (usually a combination of dirt and old grease). If any sludge is present, you might be able to revive the advance assembly by spraying it with carburetor cleaner or washing it with solvent, then lubricating it with

light grease. If corrosion is evident, clean the parts thoroughly, then remove any rust or pits with fine steel wool or emery cloth. Once the signal rotor shaft is clean and free of corrosion, temporarily install it on the distributor shaft and verify that both parts fit properly. If they bind because of advanced corrosion, either the signal rotor shaft or the distributor, or both, must be replaced.

35   The advance springs may also be stretched, but it's difficult to assess their operation without specialized testing equipment. If you're in doubt, it's a good idea to replace them.

36   Install the advance weights. Using needle-nose pliers, install the E-clips.

37   Lubricate the distributor shaft with light grease.

38   Install the signal rotor shaft on the distributor shaft as shown **(see illustration)**, install the screw, pack the inside of the shaft with grease, then push the grease stopper into place with your finger.

39   The remainder of installation is the reverse of removal. It's a good idea to check the air gap between the signal rotor and pick-up coil to be sure it's correct.

---

10   Distributor – check, removal and installation

Check

1   Detach the cable from the negative terminal of the battery.

2   Remove the distributor cap (see Chapter 1).

10.3   Measure the air gap between the signal rotor and the pick-up coil projection – if the gap is not within specification, replace the distributor (4A-C engine shown, others similar)

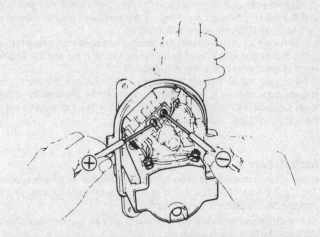

10.4a   To check the pick-up coil on 1980 through 1986 4A-C engines, measure the resistance between the two terminals on top and compare it to the Specifications

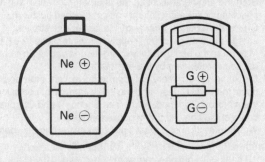

10.4b   To check the pick-up coil on 1987 4A-C engines, measure the resistance between terminals G+ and G- and between NE+ and NE- and compare it to the Specifications

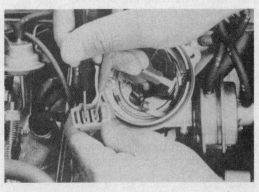

10.4c   Checking the pick-up coil resistance on a 3T-C engine

Air gap
Refer to illustration 10.3

3   Using a feeler gauge, measure the gap between the signal rotor and the pick-up coil projection **(see illustration)**. Compare your measurement to the specified air gap. If the air gap is not as specified, replace the distributor. **Note:** *On 1981 and 1982 3T-C engines, the air gap is adjustable. Loosen the two screws and move the signal generator until the gap is correct. Tighten the two screws.*

Signal generator (pick-up coil) resistance
Refer to illustrations 10.4a, 10.4b and 10.4c

4   Using an ohmmeter, measure the resistance between the terminals **(see illustrations)** and compare your measurement to the specified pick-up coil resistance. If the resistance is not as specified, replace the distributor.

Removal
Refer to illustration 10.6

5   Unplug the electrical connectors from the distributor.
6   Look for a raised "1" on the distributor cap **(see illustration)**. This marks the location for the number one cylinder spark plug wire terminal. If the cap doesn't have a mark for the number one spark plug, locate the number one spark plug and trace the wire back to the terminal on the cap.

10.6   Look for a raised "1" (arrow) on top of the distributor cap to find the number one spark plug terminal (if there is no raised "1" indicating the number one terminal, trace the wire from the number one spark plug back to the distributor cap)

7   Remove the distributor cap (see Chapter 1) and turn the engine over until the rotor is pointing toward the number one spark plug wire terminal (see locating TDC procedure in Chapter 2).

8   Make a mark on the edge of the distributor base directly below the rotor tip and in line with it. Also, mark the distributor base and the engine block to ensure the distributor is reinstalled correctly.

9   Remove the distributor hold-down bolt, then pull the distributor straight out to remove it. Be careful not to disturb the intermediate driveshaft. **Caution:** *DO NOT turn the crankshaft while the distributor is out or the alignment marks will be useless.*

Installation

Note: *If the crankshaft has been moved while the distributor is out, locate Top Dead Center (TDC) for the number one piston (see Chapter 2) and position the distributor and rotor accordingly.*

10   Insert the distributor into the engine in exactly the same relationship to the block it was in when removed.

11   If the distributor doesn't seat completely, recheck the alignment marks between the distributor base and the block to verify that the distributor is in the same position it was in before removal. Also check the rotor to see if it's aligned with the mark you made on the edge of the distributor base.

12   Loosely install the distributor hold-down bolt.

13   Install the distributor cap.

14   Plug in the electrical connectors.

15   Reattach the spark plug wires to the plugs (if removed).

16   Connect the cable to the negative terminal of the battery.

17   Check the ignition timing (see Chapter 1), then tighten the distributor hold-down bolt securely.

11   Charging system – general information and precautions

The charging system includes the alternator, an internal or external voltage regulator, a charge indicator, the battery, a fusible link and the wiring between all the components. The charging system supplies electrical power for the ignition system, the lights, the radio, etc. The alternator is driven by a drivebelt at the front of the engine.

The purpose of the voltage regulator is to limit the alternator's voltage to a preset value. This prevents power surges, circuit overloads, etc., during peak voltage output.

The fusible link is a short length of insulated wire integral with the engine compartment wiring harness. The link is four wire gauges smaller in diameter than the circuit it protects. Production fusible links and their identification flags are identified by the flag color. See Chapter 12 for additional information regarding fusible links.

The charging system doesn't ordinarily require periodic maintenance. However, the drivebelt, battery and wires and connections should be inspected at the intervals outlined in Chapter 1.

The dashboard warning light should come on when the ignition key is turned to Start, then should go off immediately. If it remains on, there's a malfunction in the charging system (see Section 12). Some vehicles are also equipped with a voltmeter. If the voltmeter indicates abnormally high or low voltage, check the charging system (see Section 12).

Be very careful when making electrical circuit connections to a vehicle equipped with an alternator and note the following:

a) When reconnecting wires to the alternator from the battery, be sure to note the polarity.

b) Before using arc welding equipment to repair any part of the vehicle, disconnect the wires from the alternator and the battery terminals.

c) Never start the engine with a battery charger connected.

d) Always disconnect both battery cables before using a battery charger.

e) The alternator is driven by an engine drivebelt which could cause serious injury if your hands, hair or clothes become entangled in it with the engine running.

f) Because the alternator is connected directly to the battery, it could arc or cause a fire if overloaded or shorted out.

g) Wrap a plastic bag over the alternator and secure it with rubber bands before steam cleaning the engine.

12   Charging system – check

Refer to illustrations 12.7, 12.8a and 12.8b

1   If a malfunction occurs in the charging system, don't automatically assume the alternator is causing the problem. First check the following items:

a) Check the drivebelt tension and condition. Replace it if worn or deteriorated.

b) Make sure the alternator mounting and adjustment bolts are tight.

c) Inspect the alternator wiring harness and the connectors at the alternator and voltage regulator. They must be in good condition and tight.

d) Check the fusible link (if equipped) located between the starter solenoid and alternator. If it's burned, determine the cause, repair the circuit and replace the link (the engine won't start and/or the accessories won't work if the fusible link blows).

e) Start the engine and check the alternator for abnormal noises (a shrieking or squealing sound indicates a bad bushing).

f) Check the specific gravity of the battery electrolyte. If it's low, charge the battery (doesn't apply to maintenance free batteries).

g) Make sure the battery is fully charged (one bad cell in a battery can cause overcharging by the alternator).

h) Disconnect the battery cables (negative first, then positive). Inspect the battery posts and the cable clamps for corrosion. Clean them thoroughly if necessary (see Section 4 and Chapter 1). Reconnect the cable to the negative terminal.

i) With the key off, insert a test light between the negative battery post and the disconnected negative cable clamp.

   1) If the test light does not come on, reattach the clamp and proceed to the next Step.

   2) If the test light comes on, there is a short in the electrical system of the vehicle. The short must be repaired before the charging system can be checked.

   3) Disconnect the alternator wiring harness.

      (a) If the light goes out, the alternator is bad.

      (b) If the light stays on, pull each fuse until the light goes out (this will tell you which component is shorted).

2   Using a voltmeter, check the battery voltage with the engine off. It should be approximately 12-volts.

3   Start the engine and check the battery voltage again. It should now be approximately 14-to-15 volts.

4   Turn on the headlights. The voltage should drop and then come back up, if the charging system is working properly.

5   If the voltage reading is greater than the specified charging voltage, replace the voltage regulator (see Section 14).

6   If the voltage reading is less than specified, check the regulator and alternator as follows.

7   Ground terminal F, start the engine, check the voltage at terminal B **(see illustration)** and compare your reading to the standard voltage.

a) If the voltmeter reading is greater than 14-to-15 volts, replace the regulator.

b) If the voltmeter reading is less than 14-to-15 volts, check the alternator (or have it checked by a dealer service department if you don't have an ammeter).

8   If you have an ammeter, hook it up to the charging system as shown **(see illustration)**. If you don't have a professional ammeter, you can also use an inductive-type current indicator **(see illustration)**. This device is inexpensive, readily available at auto parts stores and accurate enough to perform simple amperage checks like the following test.

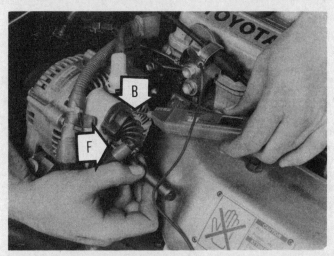

12.7   If the alternator is putting out low voltage, ground terminal F, start the engine and check the voltage at terminal B

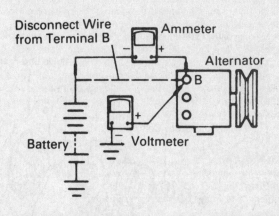

12.8a   Hook up an ammeter as shown

9   With the engine running at 2000 rpm, turn on the headlights (High beam), turn the heater blower switch to the HI position, check the reading on the ammeter and compare your reading to the standard amperage.
10   If the ammeter reading is less than standard amperage, have the alternator repaired or replace it.

13   Alternator – removal and installation

Refer to illustrations 13.3a and 13.3b

1   Detach the cable from the negative terminal of the battery.
2   Detach the wires from the alternator.
3   Loosen the alternator adjustment and pivot bolts (see illustrations) and detach the drivebelt.
4   Remove the adjustment and pivot bolts and separate the alternator from the engine.
5   If you're replacing the alternator, take the old alternator with you when purchasing a replacement. Make sure the new/rebuilt one is identical to the old alternator. Look at the terminals – they should be the same in number, size and location as the terminals on the old alternator. Finally, look at the identification marks – they'll be stamped on the housing or printed on a tag attached to the housing. Make sure the numbers are the same on both alternators.
6   Many new/rebuilt alternators don't have a pulley installed, so you may have to switch the pulley from the old one to the new/rebuilt one. When buying an alternator, find out the shop's policy regarding installation of pulleys – some shops will perform this service free of charge.

12.8b   An inductive type ammeter like this one, which is available at most auto parts stores, is much cheaper than a professional ammeter, but it's accurate enough for a quick check of the charging system and is quite easy to use: Simply place it on the alternator output lead, start the engine and check charging amperage

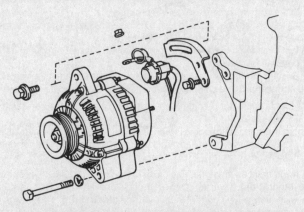

13.3a   Alternator mounting details – 4A-GE engine

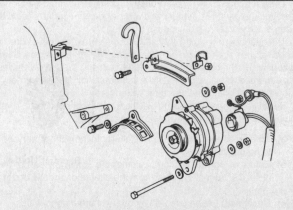

13.3b   Alternator mounting details – 4A-C engine

50A Type

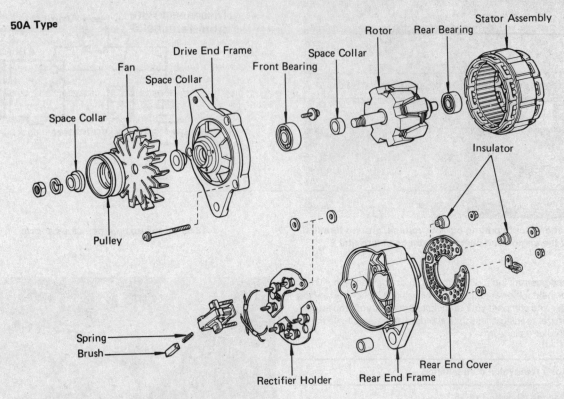

50A·55A Type (With IC Regulator)

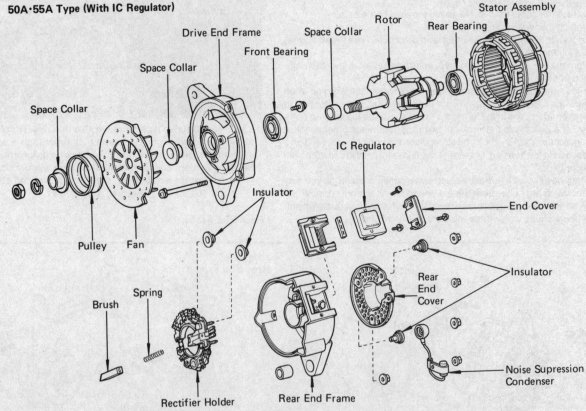

14.2a   An exploded view of the alternator used on early 3T-C engines

7   Installation is the reverse of removal.

8   After the alternator is installed, adjust the drivebelt tension (see Chapter 1).

9   Check the charging voltage to verify proper operation of the alternator (see Section 12).

14   Voltage regulator and alternator brushes – replacement

Refer to illustrations 14.2a, 14.2b, 14.2c and 14.5

Note: *Some models are equipped with an external voltage regulator mounted on the fender.*

1   Remove the alternator (Section 13) and place it on a clean workbench.

2   Remove the nuts and terminal insulator and detach the rear cover **(see illustrations)**.

3   Remove the voltage regulator (if equipped) and brush holder mounting screws.

4   Remove the brush holder and the regulator from the rear end frame. If you're only replacing the regulator, proceed to Step 8, install the new unit, reassemble the alternator and install it on the engine (see Section 13). If you're going to replace the brushes, proceed as follows.

5   Measure the exposed length of each brush **(see illustration)** and compare it to the specified minimum length. If the length of either brush is less than the specified minimum, replace the brushes.

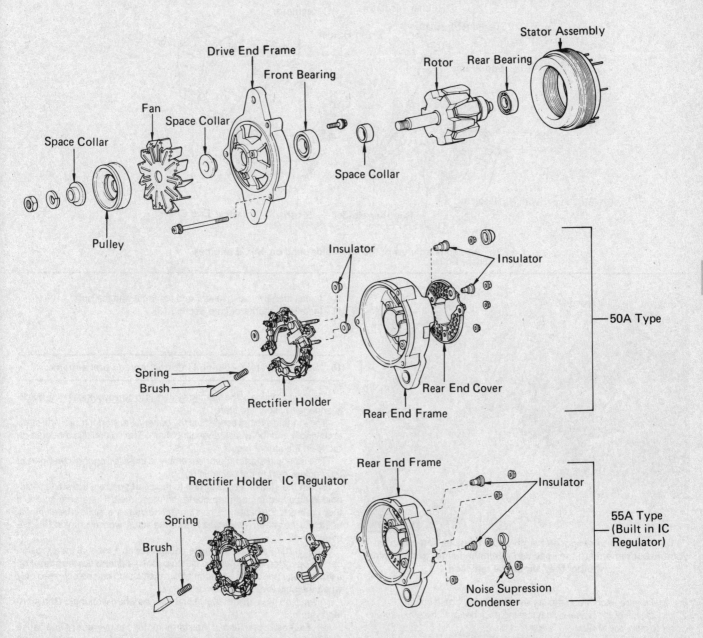

14.2b   An exploded view of the alternator used on 4A-C and later 3T-C engines

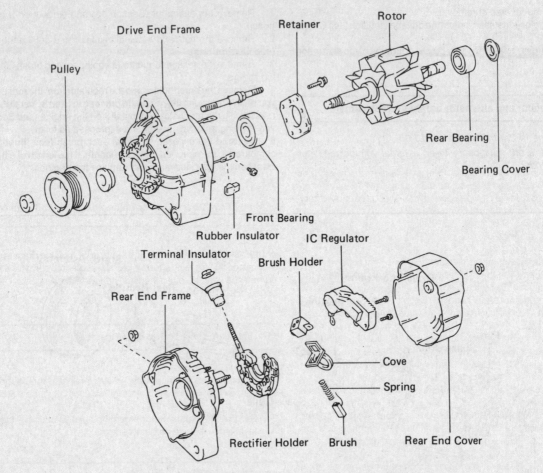

14.2c   An exploded view of the alternator used on 4A-GE engines

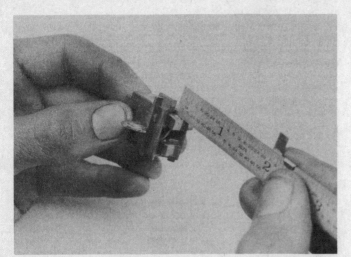

14.5   Measure the exposed length of the brushes and compare your measurements to the specified minimum length to determine whether they should be replaced

6   Make sure each brush moves smoothly in the brush holder.

7   Install the brush holder by depressing each brush with a small screw-driver to clear the shaft.

8   Install the voltage regulator and brush holder screws in the rear frame.

9   Install the rear cover and tighten the nuts securely.

10   Install the terminal insulator and tighten it with the nuts.

11   Install the alternator (see Section 13).

15   Starting system – general information and precautions

The sole function of the starting system is to turn over the engine quickly enough to allow it to start.

The starting system consists of the battery, the starter motor, the starter solenoid and the wires connecting them. The solenoid is mounted directly on the starter motor.

The solenoid/starter motor assembly is installed on the lower part of the engine, next to the bellhousing.

When the ignition key is turned to the Start position, the starter solenoid is actuated through the starter control circuit. The starter solenoid then connects the battery to the starter. The battery supplies the electrical energy to the starter motor, which does the actual work of cranking the engine.

The starter motor on a vehicle equipped with a manual transmission can be operated only when the clutch pedal is depressed; the starter on a vehicle equipped with an automatic transmission can be operated only when the shift lever is in Park or Neutral.

Always observe the following precautions when working on the starting system:

a) Excessive cranking of the starter motor can overheat it and cause serious damage. Never operate the starter motor for more than 30 seconds at a time without pausing to allow it to cool for at least two minutes.

b) The starter is connected directly to the battery and could arc or cause a fire if mishandled, overloaded or shorted out.

c) Always detach the cable from the negative terminal of the battery before working on the starting system.

16   Starter motor – in-vehicle check

Note: *Before diagnosing starter problems, make sure the battery is fully charged.*

1   If the starter motor doesn't turn at all when the switch is operated, make sure the shift lever is in Neutral or Park (automatic transmission) or the clutch pedal is depressed (manual transmission).

2   Make sure the battery is charged and all cables, both at the battery and starter solenoid terminals, are clean and secure.

3   If the starter motor spins but the engine isn't cranking, the overrunning clutch in the starter motor is slipping and the starter motor must be replaced.

4   If, when the switch is actuated, the starter motor doesn't operate at all but the solenoid clicks, then the problem lies with either the battery, the main solenoid contacts or the starter motor (or the engine is seized).

5   If the solenoid plunger cannot be heard when the switch is actuated, the battery is bad, the fusible link is burned (the circuit is open) or the solenoid is defective.

6   To check the solenoid, connect a jumper wire between the battery (+) and the ignition switch terminal (the small terminal) on the solenoid. If the starter motor now operates, the solenoid is okay and the problem is in the ignition switch, Neutral start switch or the wires.

7   If the starter motor still doesn't operate, remove the starter/solenoid for disassembly, testing and repair.

8   If the starter motor cranks the engine at an abnormally slow speed, first make sure the battery is charged and all terminal connections are tight. If the engine is partially seized, or has the wrong viscosity oil in it, it'll crank slowly.

9   Run the engine until normal operating temperature is reached, then disconnect the coil wire from the distributor cap and ground it on the engine.

10   Connect a voltmeter positive lead to the battery positive post and connect the negative lead to the negative post.

11   Crank the engine and take the voltmeter readings as soon as a steady figure is indicated. Do not allow the starter motor to turn for more than 30 seconds at a time. A reading of 9-volts or more, with the starter motor turning at normal cranking speed, is normal. If the reading is 9-volts or more

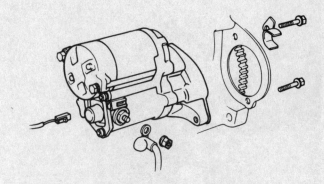

17.2   Starter motor/solenoid installation details

but the cranking speed is slow, the motor is faulty. If the reading is less than 9-volts and the cranking speed is slow, the solenoid contacts are probably burned, the starter motor is bad, the battery is discharged or there's a bad connection.

17   Starter motor – removal and installation

Refer to illustration 17.2

1   Detach the cable from the negative terminal of the battery.

2   Detach the wires from the starter/solenoid assembly **(see illustration)**.

3   Remove the starter motor mounting bolts. Detach the starter.

4   Installation is the reverse of removal.

18   Starter solenoid – removal and installation

Refer to illustrations 18.2, 18.3, 18.4, 18.5, 18.6a and 18.6b

1   Remove the starter motor (see Section 17).

2   Scribe a mark across the starter motor and gear reduction assembly **(see illustration)**.

3   Disconnect the strap from the solenoid to the starter motor terminal **(see illustration)**.

5

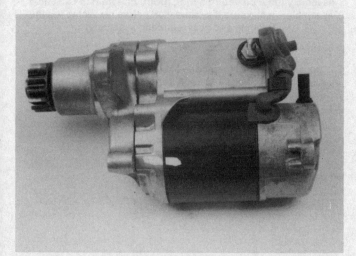

18.2   Before disassembling the starter motor, solenoid and gear reduction assembly, scribe or paint an alignment mark across them as shown here

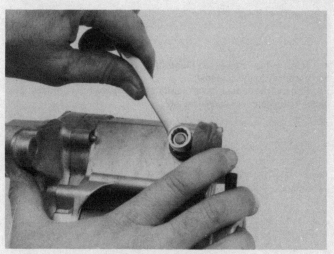

18.3   To disconnect the strap that connects the starter to the solenoid, remove this nut

18.4   To detach the solenoid from the starter motor, remove the screws (arrows) which secure the gear reduction assembly to the solenoid, . . .

18.5   . . . then remove the through-bolts (arrows) which secure the starter motor to the gear reduction assembly

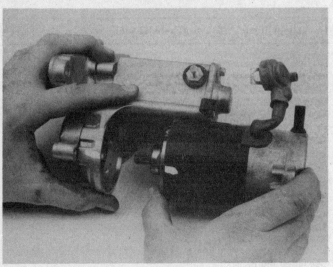

18.6a   Separate the starter from the gear reduction assembly, . . .

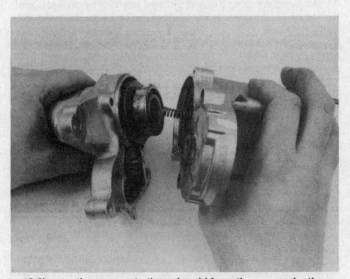

18.6b   . . . then separate the solenoid from the gear reduction assembly (note the return spring protruding from the solenoid assembly – make sure it's reinstalled before reassembling the solenoid and gear reduction assembly)

4   Remove the screws **(see illustration)** which secure the gear reduction assembly to the solenoid.

5   Remove the through-bolts **(see illustration)** which secure the starter motor to the gear reduction assembly.

6   Separate the starter from the gear reduction assembly, then separate the solenoid from the gear reduction assembly **(see illustrations)**.

7   Installation is the reverse of removal. Be sure to align the scribed mark.

Chapter 6 Emissions control systems

Contents

6

---

1 General information

Refer to illustrations 1.1a, 1.1b, 1.1c, 1.1d, 1.1e and 1.1f

To minimize pollution of the atmosphere from incompletely burned and evaporating gases and to maintain good driveability and fuel economy, a number of emission control systems are used on these vehicles **(see illustrations)**. They include the:

Positive Crankcase Ventilation (PCV) system, which reduces hydrocarbons from crankcase blowby
Evaporative Emission Control (EVAP) system, which reduces evaporative hydrocarbons
Feedback carburetor system (some models), which reduces hydro dro carbons and carbon monoxide by regulating the operating conditions of the engine
Exhaust Gas Recirculation (EGR) system, which reduces oxides of nitrogen emissions
Catalytic converter, which reduces hydrocarbons, carbon monoxide and oxides of nitrogen
Electronic Fuel Injection (EFI) system (some models), which reduces all exhaust emissions by regulating the operating conditions of the engine

The Sections in this chapter include general descriptions, checking procedures within the scope of the home mechanic and component replacement procedures (when possible) for each of the systems listed above.

Before assuming an emissions control system is malfunctioning, check the fuel and ignition systems carefully. The diagnosis of some emission control devices requires specialized tools, equipment and training. If checking and servicing become too difficult or if a procedure is beyond your ability, consult a dealer service department.

This doesn't mean, however, that emission control systems are particularly difficult to maintain and repair. You can quickly and easily perform many checks and do most of the regular maintenance at home with common tune-up and hand tools. **Note:** *The most frequent cause of emissions problems is simply a loose or broken wire or vacuum hose, so always check the electrical connectors and vacuum hoses first.*

Pay close attention to any special precautions outlined in this Chapter. It should be noted that the illustrations of the various systems may not exactly match the system installed on your vehicle because of changes made by the manufacturer during production or from year-to-year.

The Vehicle Emissions Control Information (VECI) label is located in the engine compartment. This label contains important emissions specifications and adjustment procedures, as well as a vacuum hose schematic with emissions components identified. When servicing the engine or emissions systems, the VECI label in your particular vehicle should always be checked for up-to-date information.

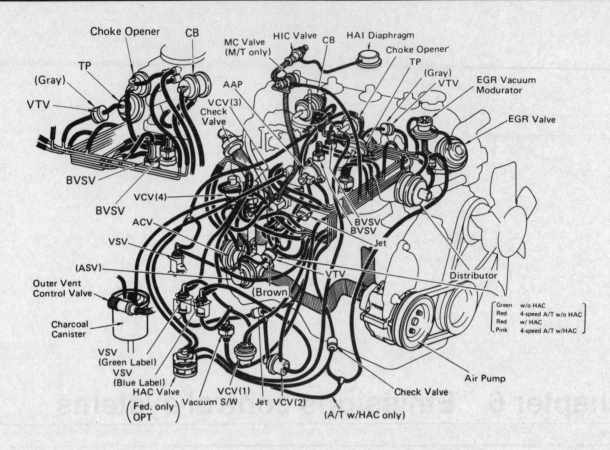

1.1a   Emission control system component locations – 1981 and 1982 US models

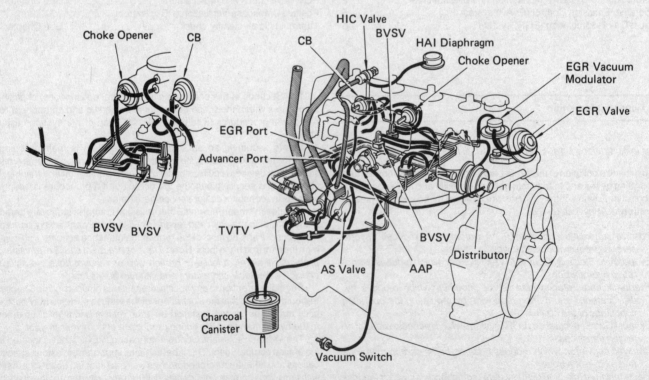

1.1b   Emission control system component locations – 1981 and 1982 Canadian models

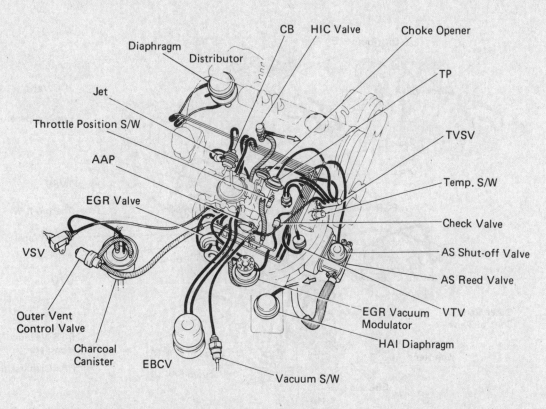

1.1c   Emission control system component locations – carburetor-equipped 1983 and later Federal models (early models have two vacuum S/W's)

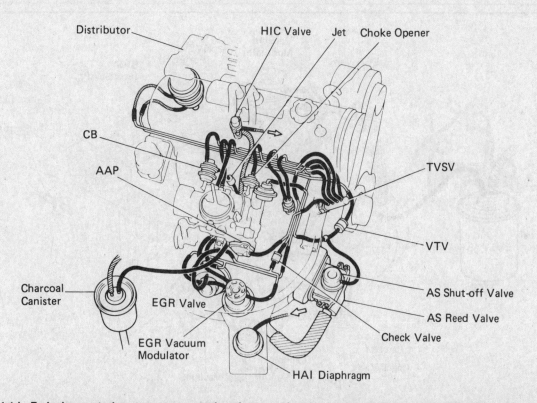

1.1d   Emission control system component locations – carburetor-equipped 1983 and later Canadian models

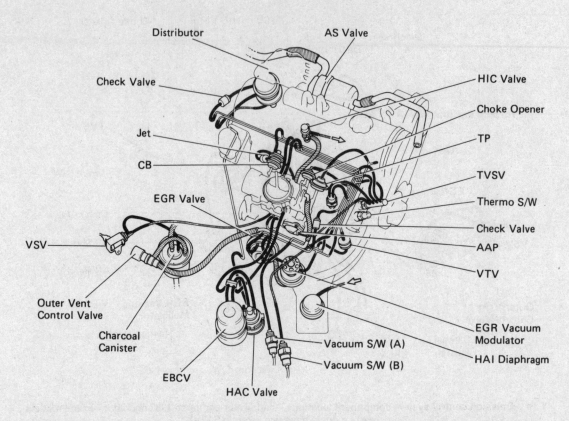

Distributor
AS Valve
Check Valve
HIC Valve
Choke Opener
Jet
TP
CB
TVSV
EGR Valve
Thermo S/W
Check Valve
VSV
AAP
VTV
Outer Vent
Control Valve
EGR Vacuum
Modulator
Charcoal
Canister
HAI Diaphragm
Vacuum S/W (A)
Vacuum S/W (B)
EBCV
HAC Valve

**1.1e   Emission control system component locations – carburetor-equipped 1983 and later California models
(later models have only one vacuum S/W)**

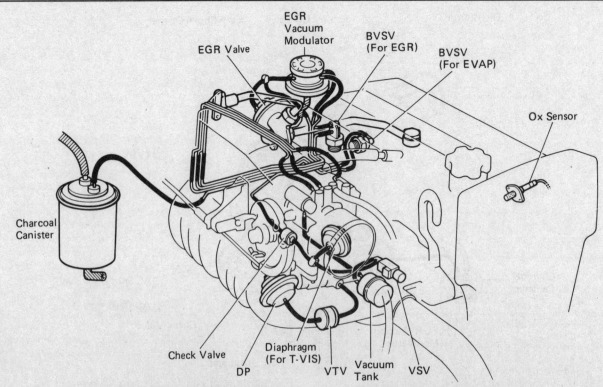

EGR
Vacuum
Modulator
EGR Valve
BVSV
(For EGR)
BVSV
(For EVAP)
Ox Sensor
Charcoal
Canister
Check Valve
Diaphragm
(For T-VIS)
DP
VTV
Vacuum
Tank
VSV

1.1f   Emission control system component locations – 1985 and later fuel injected models

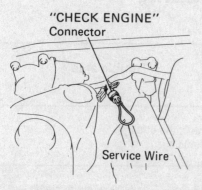

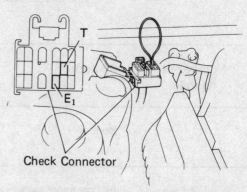

3.3a   To display the diagnostic code output on 1985 models, use a jumper wire to bridge the terminals of the CHECK ENGINE connector (located next to the wiper motor)

3.3b   To display the diagnostic code output on 1986 and later models, use a jumper wire to bridge terminals T and E1 of the check connector (located in the engine compartment)

2   Electronic control system – description and precautions

Description

The electronic control system controls the fuel injection system or feedback carburetor system through a microcomputer known as the Electronic Control Unit (ECU).

The ECU receives signals from various sensors which monitor changing engine operating conditions such as intake air volume, intake air temperature, coolant temperature, engine rpm, acceleration/deceleration, exhaust oxygen content, etc. These signals are utilized by the ECU to determine the correct injection duration or the fuel/air mixture in the carburetor.

The system is analogous to the central nervous system in the human body: The sensors (nerve endings) constantly relay signals to the ECU (brain), which processes the data and, if necessary, sends out a command to change the operating parameters of the engine (body).

Here's a specific example of how one portion of this system operates: An oxygen sensor, located in the exhaust manifold, constantly monitors the oxygen content of the exhaust gas. If the percentage of oxygen in the exhaust gas is incorrect, an electrical signal is sent to the ECU. The ECU takes this information, processes it and then sends a command to the fuel injection system or feedback carburetor telling it to change the fuel/air mixture. This happens in a fraction of a second and it goes on continuously when the engine is running. The end result is an fuel/air mixture ratio which is constantly maintained at a predetermined ratio, regardless of driving conditions.

In the event of a sensor malfunction, a backup circuit will take over to provide driveability until the problem is identified and fixed.

Precautions

a) Always disconnect the power by either turning off the ignition switch or disconnecting the battery terminals before removing ECU wiring connectors.

b) When installing a battery, do not reverse the positive and negative battery cables.

c) Do not subject EFI, emissions related components, feedback carburetor components or the ECU to severe impact during removal or installation.

d) Do not be careless during troubleshooting. Even slight terminal contact can invalidate a testing procedure and even damage one of the numerous transistor circuits.

e) Never attempt to work on the ECU or open the ECU cover. It's protected by a government mandated extended warranty that will be nullified if you tamper with or damage the ECU.

f) If you're inspecting electronic control system components during rainy weather, make sure water doesn't enter any part. When washing the engine compartment, do not spray these parts or their connectors with water.

3   Diagnosis system – general information and obtaining code output

Note: *Only fuel injected models are equipped with a diagnosis system.*

General information

The ECU contains a built-in self-diagnosis system which detects and identifies malfunctions occurring in the network. When the ECU detects a problem, three things happen: the Check Engine light comes on, the trouble is identified and a diagnostic code is recorded and stored. The ECU stores the failure code assigned to the specific problem area until the diagnosis system is cancelled by removing the stop fuse with the ignition switch off.

The Check Engine warning light, which is located on the instrument panel, comes on when the ignition switch is turned to On and the engine is not running. When the engine is started, the warning light should go out. If the light remains on, the diagnosis system has detected a malfunction in the system.

Obtaining code output

Refer to illustrations 3.3a and 3.3b

1   To obtain diagnostic code output, verify first that the battery voltage is above 11-volts, the throttle is fully closed, the transmission is in Neutral, the accessory switches are off and the engine is at normal operating temperature.

2   Turn the ignition switch to On. Do not start the engine.

3   On 1986 and later models, use a jumper wire to bridge terminals T and E1 of the check connector (**see illustration**). On 1985 models, use a jumper wire to bridge both terminals of the check connector located near the windshield wiper motor (**see illustration**).

Trouble code chart (applies to fuel injected models only)

Code No.	Number of flashes	System	Diagnosis	Trouble area
1	1	Normal	This appears when none of the other codes (2 thru 11) are identified.	
2	2	Air flow meter signal	Vc circuit open or Vs-E2 short circuited. Vc-Vs short circuited.	1. Air flow meter circuit 2. Air flow meter 3. ECU
3	3	Ignition signal	No signal from igniter four times in succession.	1. Ignition circuit (+B, IGf) 2. Igniter 3. ECU
4	4	Coolant temp. sensor	Open or short circuit in coolant temp. sensor or circuit.	1. Coolant temp. sensor circuit 2. Coolant temp sensor 3. ECU
5	5	Oxygen sensor	Open circuit in oxygen sensor or circuit (only lean indication).	1. Oxygen sensor circuit 2. Oxygen sensor 3. ECU
6	6	RPM signal	No neg. signal to ECU while cranking.	1. Distributor circuit 2. Distributor 3. Igniter 4. Starter signal circuit 5. ECU
7	7	Throttle position sensor	Open or short circuit in throttle position sensor or circuit.	1. Throttle position sensor circuit 2. Throttle position sensor 3. ECU
8	8	Intake air temp. sensor	Open or short circuit in intake air temp. sensor or circuit.	1. Air temp. sensor circuit 2. ECU
10	10	Starter motor	No STA signal to ECU (vehicle stopped and engine running over 800 rpm).	1. Starter relay circuit 2. IG switch circuit 3. IG switch circuit (starter) 4. ECU
11	11	A/C switch	Air conditioner switch On, idle switch Off during diagnosis check.	1. Air conditioner S/W 2. Idle S/W 3. ECU

4   Read the diagnosis code as indicated by the number of flashes of the "Check Engine" light on the dash. Normal system operation is indicated by code one (no malfunctions) for all models. The "Check Engine" light displays a code one by blinking once every few seconds.

5   If there are any malfunctions in the system, their corresponding trouble codes are stored in computer memory and the light will blink the requisite number of times for the indicated trouble codes. If there's more than one trouble code in the memory, they'll be displayed in numerical order (from lowest to highest) with a pause between each one. After the code with the largest number of flashes has been displayed, there will be another pause and then the sequence will begin all over again.

6   To ensure correct interpretation of the blinking "Check Engine" light, watch carefully for the interval between the end of one code and the beginning of the next (otherwise, you'll become confused by the apparent number of blinks and misinterpret the display). The length of this interval varies with the model year.

Cancelling a diagnostic code

7   After the malfunctioning component has been repaired/replaced, the trouble code(s) stored in computer memory must be cancelled. To accomplish this, simply remove the 15 amp stop fuse for at least ten seconds with the ignition switch off (the lower the temperature, the longer the fuse must be left out). The location of the fuse varies with the model year.

8   Cancellation can also be affected by removing the cable from the negative battery terminal, but other memory systems (such as the clock) will also be cancelled.

9   If the diagnosis code isn't cancelled, it'll be stored by the ECU and appear with any new codes in the event of future trouble.

10   If you have to disconnect the battery cables for any reason, first check to see if a diagnostic code has been recorded.

---

4   Information sensors

Note: *Most of the components described in this Section are protected by a Federally-mandated extended warranty. See your dealer for the details regarding your vehicle. It therefore makes little sense to either check or replace any of these parts yourself as long as they are still under warranty. However, once the warranty has expired, you may wish to perform some* of the component checks and\or replacement procedures in this Chapter to save money.

Oxygen sensor (all models)

1   The oxygen sensor is located in the exhaust manifold. It's purpose is to detect the concentration of oxygen in the exhaust gases. On some models, a second oxygen sensor is located in the catalytic converter. This sensor rechecks the emission level after the exhaust gases pass through the converter and feeds the results back to the main oxygen sensor so the air\fuel ratio is maintained as precisely as possible.

2   A fault in the oxygen sensor circuit will set a code five.

3   To replace the oxygen sensor, disconnect the wire and unscrew the sensor. Screw in the new sensor, tighten it securely and reconnect the wire.

Carburetor-equipped models

4   See Section 8 for information on the feedback carburetor system.

Fuel injected models

Coolant Temperature sensor

Refer to illustrations 4.6a and 4.6b

5   The coolant sensor is a thermistor (a resistor which varies the value of its voltage output in accordance with temperature changes). A failure in the coolant sensor or circuit will set a code four. The coolant temperature sensor is located in the thermostat housing or behind the distributor housing.

6   To check the coolant temperature sensor, unplug the electrical connector and use an ohmmeter to measure the resistance between the two terminals **(see illustrations)**.

7   If the indicated resistance is not as specified, replace the water temperature sensor. Be sure to use Teflon tape or thread sealant on the threads of the new switch to prevent leaks.

Air temperature sensor

8   The air temperature sensor, located in the side of the air cleaner housing, is a thermistor which constantly measures the temperature of the air entering the intake manifold. As air temperature varies, the ECU monitors the air temperature sensor and adjusts the amount of fuel according to the air temperature. A failure in the air temperature sensor or circuit will set a code eight. Diagnosis of the air temperature sensor should be left to a dealer service department.

6

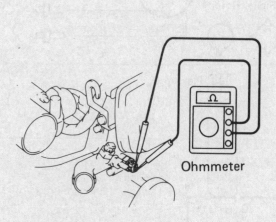

4.6a   To check the coolant temperature sensor, use an ohmmeter to measure the resistance between the two terminals

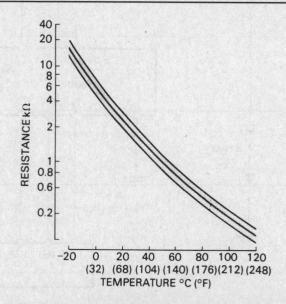

4.6b   Compare the indicated resistance to the resistance values specified on this graph – note that as the temperature increases (as the engine warms up), resistance decreases

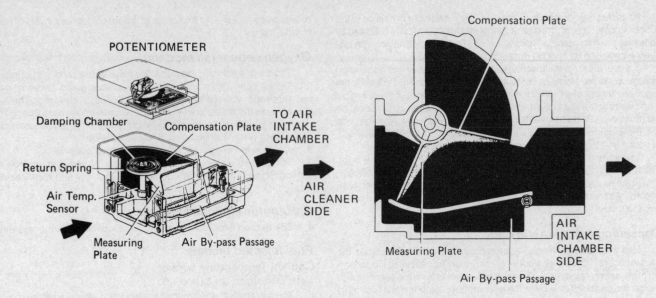

4.9   A typical air flow meter and related components

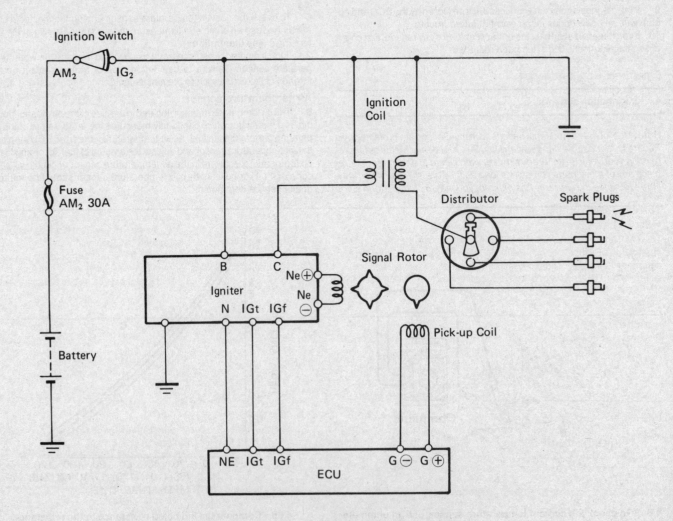

4.10   Schematic of the electronic spark advance system

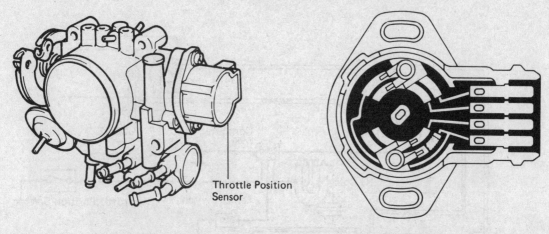

4.12   A Typical Throttle Position Sensor (TPS) mounted on the throttle body

Air flow meter

Refer to illustration 4.9

9   The air flow meter, which is located near the battery, measures the amount of air which passes through it in a given time. The ECU uses this information to control fuel delivery. A large quantity of air indicates acceleration, while a small quantity indicates deceleration or idle **(see illustration)**. A failure in the meter or its circuit will set a code two. The diagnosis of the air flow meter should be left to a dealership service department.

Electronic Spark Advance

Refer to illustration 4.10

10   Using data provided by the sensors which monitor various engine functions (rpm, air intake volume, engine temperature etc.), the ECU triggers the spark at precisely the right moment. The electronic spark advance system utilizes an igniter, pick-up coil, distributor, ignition coil and a signal rotor **(see illustration)**.

11   The codes for this system (3 or 6) could indicate several possibilities of component failure. Have the system tested by a dealership service department.

Throttle Position Sensor (TPS)

Refer to illustration 4.12

12   The Throttle Position sensor (TPS) is located on the throttle body **(see illustration)**. By monitoring the output voltage from the TPS, the ECU can determine fuel delivery based on throttle valve angle (driver demand). A failure in the TPS sensor or circuit will set a code seven. Should the TPS

need replacement or diagnosis, it should be left to a dealer service department because of the need for special tools and test equipment.

Air Conditioner (A/C) amplifier

13   The A/C amplifier supplies a signal to the ECU when the A/C is selected. This signal allows the ECU to adjust engine speed to compensate for the additional load on the engine. A code 11 will set if this signal is not present. Any diagnosis should be left to a dealer service department.

Engine Start Signal

14   This signal is sent from the engine starter circuit. Receiving it, the ECU detects that the engine is cranking and uses it as one of the signals to control the fuel injectors.

---

5   Evaporative Emission Control (EVAP) system

General description

Refer to illustrations 5.2a, 5.2b and 5.2c

1   This system is designed to trap and store fuel that evaporates from the fuel tank, carburetor and intake manifold that would normally enter the atmosphere in the form of hydrocarbon (HC) emissions.

2   The Evaporative Emission Control (EVAP) system consists of a charcoal-filled canister, the lines connecting the canister to the fuel tank and a thermo switch or an ECU-controlled solenoid valve **(see illustrations)**.

6

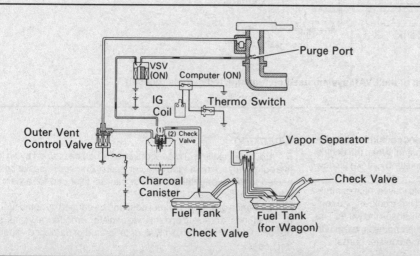

5.2a   Diagram of the EVAP system used on 1981 and 1982 models (typical)

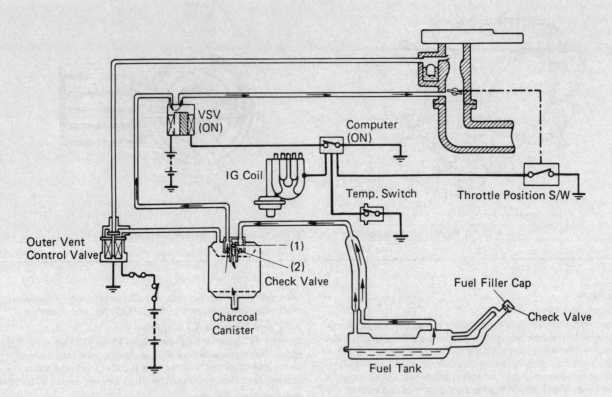

5.2b   Diagram of the EVAP system used on 1983 and later carburetor-equipped models (typical)

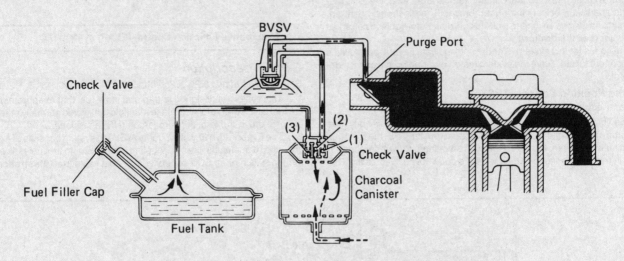

5.2c   Diagram of the EVAP system used on fuel injected models (typical)

3   Fuel vapors are transferred from the fuel tank and carburetor to a canister where they're stored when the engine isn't running. When the engine is running, the fuel vapors are purged from the canister by intake air flow and consumed in the normal combustion process.

4   On some models, the ECU operates a solenoid valve which controls vacuum to the purge valve in the charcoal canister. Under cold engine conditions, the solenoid is turned on by the ECU, which closes the valve. The ECU turns off the valve and allows purge when the engine is warm. On some models, a bi-metal thermo switch controls the canister purge.

Checking

5   Poor idle, stalling and poor driveability can be caused by an inoperative purge valve, a damaged canister, split or cracked hoses or hoses connected to the wrong fittings. Check the fuel filler cap for a damaged or deformed gasket (see Chapter 1).

6   Evidence of fuel loss or fuel odor can be caused by liquid fuel leaking from fuel lines, a cracked or damaged canister, an inoperative purge valve, disconnected, misrouted, kinked, deteriorated or damaged vapor or control hoses.

7   Inspect each hose attached to the canister for kinks, leaks and cracks along its entire length. Repair or replace as necessary.

8   Inspect the canister. If it's cracked or damaged, replace it.

9   Look for fuel leaking from the bottom of the canister. If fuel is leaking, replace the canister and check the hoses and hose routing.

10   Any further testing should be left to a dealer service department.

Charcoal canister replacement

Refer to illustration 5.13

11   Detach the negative cable from the battery.

12   Unplug the solenoid electrical connectors, if equipped.

13   Clearly label, then detach the vacuum hoses from the canister (see illustration).

14   Remove the canister mounting bolts and lift it out of the vehicle.

15   Installation is the reverse of removal.

---

6   Exhaust Gas Recirculation (EGR) system

General description

Refer to illustrations 6.2 and 6.3

1   To reduce oxides of nitrogen emissions, some of the exhaust gases are recirculated through the EGR valve to the intake manifold to lower combustion temperatures.

2   On carburetor-equipped vehicles, the EGR system (see illustration) consists of the EGR valve, EGR vacuum modulator, a check valve and a TVSV (thermo) valve. The EGR valve, which is operated by ported vacuum recirculates gases in accordance with engine load (intake air volume). To eliminate recirculation at idle, the vacuum signal is ported above the idle throttle position. During cold engine operation, the TVSV opens, bleeding off ported vacuum and keeping the EGR valve closed. When the engine coolant temperature exceeds the set temperature of the TVSV, it closes and ported vacuum is applied to the EGR valve. The EGR vacuum modulator controls the EGR valve by controlling the vacuum signal to the EGR valve with an atmospheric bleed. This bleed is controlled by the amount of exhaust pressure which acts on the bottom of the EGR vacuum modulator.

3   On fuel-injected vehicles, the EGR system (see illustration) consists of an EGR valve, EGR vacuum modulator, vacuum switching (BVSV) valve, the Electronic Control Unit (ECU) and various sensors. The ECU memory is programmed to produce the ideal EGR valve lift for each operating condition.

5.13   To remove the charcoal canister, label and detach the hoses (arrows) from the top and bottom, loosen the mounting bracket pinch bolt (arrow) and lift the canister straight up

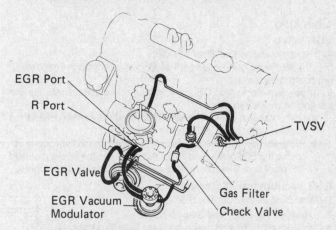

6.2   Typical EGR system used on carburetor-equipped models

6

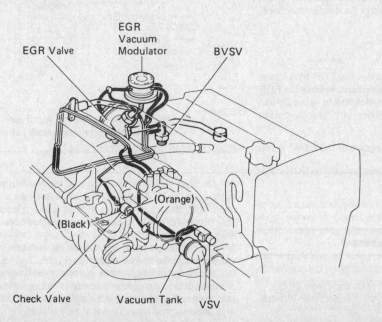

6.3   Typical EGR system used on fuel injected models

6.8a   To remove the EGR vacuum modulator filters for cleaning, remove this cap, . . .

6.8b   . . . then pull out the two filters and clean them with compressed air – be sure the coarse side of the outer filter faces out when reinstalling them

Checking

EGR valve

4   Start the engine and allow it to idle.

5   Detach the vacuum hose from the EGR valve and attach a hand vacuum pump in its place.

6   Apply vacuum to the EGR valve. Vacuum should remain steady and the engine should run poorly.

   a) If the vacuum doesn't remain steady and the engine doesn't run poorly, replace the EGR valve and recheck it.

   b) If the vacuum remains steady but the engine doesn't run poorly, remove the EGR valve and check the valve and the intake manifold for blockage. Clean or replace parts as necessary and recheck.

EGR vacuum modulator valve

Refer to illustrations 6.8a and 6.8b

7   Remove the valve (see Step 13 below).

8   Pull the cover off and check the filters **(see illustrations)**.

9   Clean them with compressed air, reinstall the cover and the modulator.

EGR system

10   Any further checking of the EGR system requires special tools and test equipment. Take the vehicle to a dealer service department for checking.

Component replacement

EGR valve

11   Disconnect the threaded fitting that attaches the EGR pipe to the EGR valve, remove the two EGR valve mounting bolts, remove the EGR valve from the intake manifold and check it for sticking and heavy carbon deposits. If the valve is sticking or clogged with deposits, clean or replace it.

12   Installation is the reverse of removal.

EGR vacuum modulator valve

13   Label and disconnect the vacuum hoses and remove the EGR vacuum modulator from its bracket.

14   Installation is the reverse of removal.

---

7   Positive Crankcase Ventilation (PCV) system

Refer to illustration 7.1

1   To reduce hydrocarbon (HC) emissions, crankcase blow-by gas is routed to the intake manifold for combustion in the cylinders **(see illustration)**.

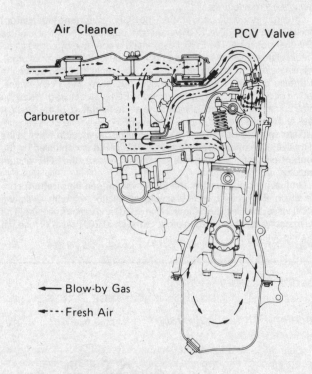

7.1   Typical Positive Crankcase Ventilation (PCV) system (carburetor-equipped model shown)

---

2   On carburetor-equipped models, the main components of the PCV system are the PCV valve, a fresh air filtered inlet and the vacuum hoses connecting these components with the engine. On fuel injected models, it only consists of a PCV hose between the valve cover and the intake manifold.

3   On carburetor-equipped models, to maintain idle quality, the PCV valve restricts the flow when the intake manifold vacuum is high. If abnormal operating conditions arise, the system is designed to allow excessive amounts of blow-by gases to flow back through the crankcase vent tube into the air cleaner to be consumed by normal combustion.

4   Checking and replacement of the PCV valve is covered in Chapter 1.

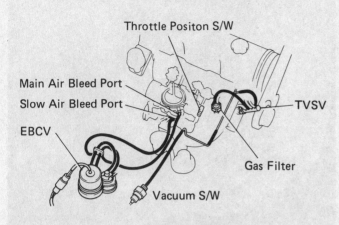

8.1 **Typical feedback carburetor system**

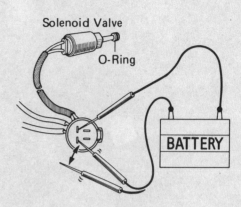

8.7 **Apply battery voltage to the fuel cut solenoid valve**

8   Feedback carburetor system

Note: *The Feedback Carburetor system and all components related to the system is covered by a Federally mandated warranty. Check with a dealer service department before replacing or repairing the system at your own expense.*

General description
Refer to illustration 8.1

1   The feedback carburetor (FBC) system's purpose is to maintain the optimum fuel/air ratio for all driving conditions. By means of signals from information sensors (see Section 4), the carburetor main and slow air bleeds are controlled, thereby reducing HC, CO and NOx emissions **(see illustration)**.

2   The various sub-systems and components of the feedback system are discussed below. Checking and component replacement information is provided, where possible.

Evaporative Emission Control (EVAP) system

3   See Section 5 for information on this system.

Feedback control system

4   See Chapter 4 for information on this system.

Deceleration fuel cut system
Refer to illustration 8.7

5   During deceleration, this system cuts off part of the fuel flow in the idle circuit of the carburetor to prevent overheating and afterburning in the exhaust system. The fuel cut solenoid is kept energized by the ECU whenever the engine is running, except when the throttle is closed with the rpm's above 2290.

6   To check the system, locate and remove the fuel cut solenoid valve.

7   Connect the battery to the valve's connector **(see illustration)**.

8   Listen for a "click" when the battery is connected and disconnected. If you don't hear one, replace the valve.

9   If no problems are found, the system is okay. Any further checks or repairs should be left to a dealer service department.

Cold Mixture Heater (CMH) system
Refer to illustration 8.13

10   The Cold Mixture Heater (CMH) system reduces cold engine emissions and improves driveability during engine warm up. The intake manifold is heated during cold engine operation to accelerate vaporization of the liquid fuel. The relay turns the CMH on and off according to engine coolant temperature.

11   To check the cold mixture heater, locate the connector, unplug it and, using an ohmmeter, measure the resistance between the terminals. It should be between 0.5 and 2.0 ohms. If the readings are not within specification, replace the heater. Any further checks should be done by a dealer service department.

12   To replace the cold mixture heater, first remove the carburetor (see Chapter 4).

13   Unplug the cold mixture heater connector, remove the PCV hose and lift the heater off the intake manifold **(see illustration)**.

14   Installation is the reverse of removal.

Positive Crankcase Ventilation (PCV) system

15   See Section 7 for information on this system.

Throttle Positioner (TP)

16   To reduce HC and CO emissions, the throttle positioner opens the throttle valve slightly when decelerating. This keeps the fuel/air ratio from becoming excessively rich when the throttle valve is quickly closed. The TP is also used to increase idle speed when power steering fluid pressure exceeds a pre-set value and when a large electrical load is placed on the electrical system. Any checks or repairs should be left to a dealer service department.

6

8.13 **Carefully lift the cold mixture heater (arrow) off the intake manifold**

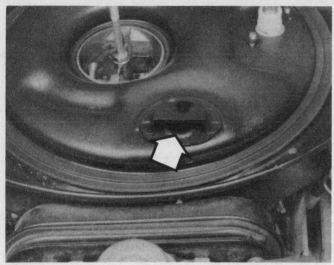

8.21   With the engine running, listen for a burbling noise from the air suction inlet (arrow)

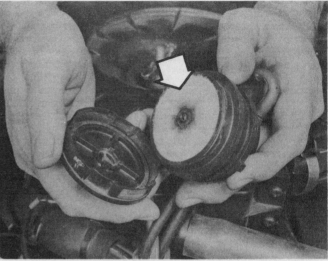

8.24   Remove the HAC cover, peel the filter out, clean it with compressed air, inspect it and, if necessary, replace it

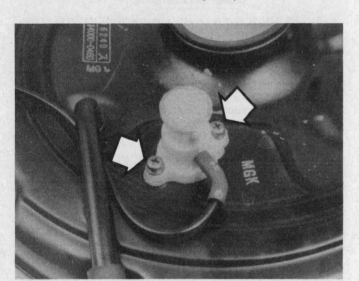

8.28   To remove the HIC valve, label and detach the vacuum hoses, then remove the mounting screws (arrows)

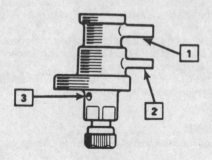

8.29   Typical HIC valve

1   Carburetor port
2   Hot air intake diaphragm port
3   Atmospheric port

Exhaust Gas Recirculation (EGR) system

17   See Section 6 for information on this system.

Catalytic Converter

18   See Section 9 for further information on the catalytic converter.

Air Suction (AS) system

Refer to illustration 8.21

19   Additional air is needed to aid the oxidation of HC and CO in the catalytic converter. The air suction valve is a simple reed-type valve that opens when vacuum is present in the exhaust system. When open, air is drawn into the exhaust to aid the converter with the oxidation process.

20   To check the system, first check the hoses and fittings for cracks, kinks, damage and loose connections.

21   Remove the air cleaner top cover and, with the engine idling, see if a burbling noise is heard from the air suction valve inlet **(see illustration)**. Any further checks or repairs should be left to a dealer service department.

High Altitude Compensation (HAC) system (Federal models only)

Refer to illustration 8.24

22   As altitude increases, air density decreases so the fuel/air mixture becomes richer. The High Altitude Compensation (HAC) system insures proper fuel/air mixture by supplying additional air to the primary and high-speed circuit of the carburetor. The system also advances the ignition timing to improve driveability at high altitudes.

23   To check the system, first inspect all hoses for cracks, kinks, damage and loose connections.

24   Check and clean the air filter in the HAC valve **(see illustration)**. Any further checks or repairs should be left to a dealer service department.

Thermostatic Air Cleaner (TAC) system

25   This system directs hot air to the carburetor in cold weather to improve driveability and to prevent carburetor icing in extremely cold weather.

26   See Chapter 1 for the TAC system check.

Hot Idle Compensation (HIC) system

Refer to illustrations 8.28 and 8.29

27   The Hot Idle Compensation (HIC) system allows additional air to enter the intake manifold to maintain proper fuel/air mixture during high temperatures at idle.

28   To check the system, remove the HIC valve from the air cleaner housing **(see illustration)**.

8.34   When the engine is cold, make sure the valve is in the upper position – when the engine is hot, make sure the valve is in the lower position

29   With the temperature above 72-degrees F, check the operation of the valve by placing a finger over the atmospheric port and blowing into the port for the HIC diaphragm **(see illustration)**. Air should flow from the port normally connected to the carburetor.

30   At temperatures below 72-degrees F, carry out a similar air flow test. Place a finger over the port normally connected to the carburetor. Blow through the port for the HIC diaphragm and make sure that air does not pass out of the atmospheric port.

Automatic Choke

31   The automatic choke temporarily supplies a rich fuel/air mixture to the engine by closing the choke valve when the engine is cold. It automatically opens the choke as the engine warms up. See Chapter 1 for the choke check procedure. Any further checks or repairs should be left to a dealer service department.

Auxiliary Acceleration Pump (APP)

32   When accelerating with a cold engine, the main acceleration pump's capacity is insufficient. The auxiliary acceleration pump system compensates for this by forcing more fuel into the acceleration nozzle to obtain better cold engine performance. A thermostatic control valve controls the APP system. After the engine is warmed up, the valve lets the main acceleration pump take over. Any checks or repairs should be left to a dealer service department.

Heat Control Valve

Refer to illustration 8.34

33   When the engine is cold, the heat control valve improves fuel vaporization for better driveability by quickly heating the intake manifold. Once the engine has warmed up, the valve helps to keep the intake manifold at the proper temperature. The valve is located in the exhaust manifold and can be seen best from under the vehicle.

34   Check the heat control valve when the engine is cold. The counterweight of the heat control valve should be in it's upper position **(see illustration)**. After warm-up, check that the counterweight is in it's lower position.

35   If the valve is stuck, apply some penetrating oil to the shaft – this will normally free it up.

9.3   If the catalytic converter is mounted under the vehicle, periodically inspect the protector for dents and other damage – if a dent is deep enough to touch the surface of the converter, replace the protector

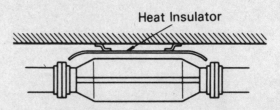

Heat Insulator

9.4   If the catalytic converter is mounted under the vehicle, periodically inspect the heat insulator to make sure there's adequate clearance between it and the converter

9   Catalytic converter

Note: *Because of a federally mandated extended warranty which covers emissions-related components such as the catalytic converter, check with a dealer service department before replacing the converter at your own expense.*

General description

1   To reduce hydrocarbon, carbon monoxide and oxides of nitrogen emissions, all vehicles are equipped with a three-way catalyst system which oxidizes and reduces these chemicals, converting them into harmless nitrogen, carbon dioxide and water.

Checking

Refer to illustrations 9.3 and 9.4

2   Periodically inspect the catalytic converter-to-exhaust pipe mating flanges and bolts. Make sure there are no loose bolts and no leaks between the flanges.

3   Look for dents in or damage to the catalytic converter protector **(see illustration)**. If any part of the protector is damaged or dented enough to touch the converter, repair or replace it.

4   Inspect the heat insulator for damage. Make sure there's adequate clearance between the heat insulator and the catalytic converter **(see illustration)**.

Replacement

5   To replace the catalytic converter, refer to Chapter 4.

6

Chapter 7 Part A   Manual transmission

Contents

Specifications

Output shaft (service limits)

Gear journal diameter
  2nd . . . .   1.4488 in (36.80 mm)
  3rd . . . .   1.4482 in (37.80 mm)
  5th . . . .   1.0748 in (27.30 mm)
Flange thickness . . . .   0.157 in (4.0 mm)
Runout limit . . . .   0.0024 in (0.06 mm)

Gear thrust clearances

1st gear
  Standard . . . .   0.0059 to 0.0108 in (0.150 to 0.275 mm)
  Service limit . . . .   0.020 in (0.5 mm)
2nd gear
  Standard . . . .   0.0059 to 0.0098 in (0.150 to 0.250 mm)
  Service limit . . . .   0.020 in (0.5mm)
3rd gear
  Standard . . . .   0.0059 to 0.0118 in (0.1520 to 0.19 mm)
  Service limit . . . .   0.024 in (0.6 mm)
5th gear
  Standard . . . .   0.0039 to 0.0366 in (0.100 to 0.930 mm)
  Service limit . . . .   0.039 in (1.0 mm)
Reverse
  Standard . . . .   0.0079 to 0.0128 in (0.200 to 0.325 mm)
  Service limit . . . .   0.024 in (0.6 mm)
Reverse idler gear
  Standard . . . .   0.0020 to 0.0197 in (0.05 to 0.50 mm)
  Service limit . . . .   0.039 in (1.0 mm)

Gear journal oil clearances *(service limits)*

1st, 2nd, 5th and Reverse .... 0.0059 in (0.150 mm)
3rd and Reverse Idler .... 0.0079 in (0.200 mm)

Shift fork-to-hub sleeve clearance *(service limit)* ..   0.031 in (0.8 mm)

Synchronizer ring-to-gear clearance

Standard .... 0.030 to 0.079 in (1.0 to 2.0 mm)
Service limit .... 0.031 in (0.8 mm)

Inner race

Flange thickness (service limit) .... 0.150 in (3.8 mm)
Outer diameter (service limit) .... 1.4508 in (36.85 mm)

Input shaft snap-ring thickness

A .... 0.0925 to 0.0945 in (2.35 to 2.40 mm)
B .... 0.0945 to 0.0965 in (2.40 to 2.45 mm)
C .... 0.0965 to 0.0984 in (2.45 to 2.50 mm)
D .... 0.0984 to 0.1004 in (2.50 to 2.55 mm)
E .... 0.1004 to 0.1024 in (2.55 to 2.60 mm)

Input bearing spacer thickness

1 .... 0.0719 to 0.0738 in (1.825 to 1.875 mm)
2 .... 0.0762 to 0.0781 in (1.935 to 1.985 mm)
3 .... 0.0805 to 0.0825 in (2.045 to 2.095 mm)
4 .... 0.0845 to 0.0868 in (2.155 to 2.205 mm)
5 .... 0.0892 to 0.0911 in (2.265 to 2.315 mm)
6 .... 0.0935 to 0.0955 in (2.375 to 2.425 mm)

Output shaft snap-ring thickness

No. 2 clutch hub

0 .... 0.0768 to 0.0787 in (1.95 to 2.00 mm)
1 .... 0.0787 to 0.0807 in (2.00 to 2.05 mm)
2 .... 0.0807 to 0.0827 in (2.05 to 2.10 mm)
3 .... 0.0827 to 0.0846 in (2.10 to 2.15 mm)
4 .... 0.0846 to 0.0866 in (2.15 to 2.20 mm)

No. 3 clutch hub

A .... 0.1024 to 0.1043 in (2.60 to 2.65 mm)
B .... 0.1043 to 0.1063 in (2.65 to 2.70 mm)
C .... 0.1063 to 0.1083 in (2.70 to 2.75 mm)
D .... 0.1083 to 0.1102 in (2.75 to 2.80 mm)
E .... 0.1102 to 0.1122 in (2.80 to 2.85 mm)
F .... 0.1122 to 0.1142 in (2.85 to 2.90 mm)
G .... 0.1142 to 0.1161 in (2.90 to 2.95 mm)
H .... 0.1161 to 0.1181 in (2.95 to 3.00 mm)
I .... 0.1181 to 0.1201 in (3.00 to 3.05 mm)
J .... 0.1201 to 0.1220 in (3.05 to 3.10 mm)
K .... 0.1220 to 0.1240 in (3.10 to 3.15 mm)
L .... 0.1240 to 0.1260 in (3.15 to 3.20 mm)
M .... 0.1260 to 0.1280 in (3.20 to 3.25 mm)
N .... 0.1280 to 0.1299 in (3.25 to 3.30 mm)
O .... 0.1299 to 0.1319 in (3.30 to 3.35 mm)

Center bearing

A .... 0.1063 to 0.1083 in (2.70 to 2.75 mm)
D .... 0.1083 to 0.1102 in (2.75 to 2.80 mm)
V .... 0.1102 to 0.1122 in (2.80 to 2.85 mm)
E .... 0.1122 to 0.1142 in (2.85 to 2.90 mm)
F .... 0.1142 to 0.1161 in (2.90 to 2.95 mm)
G .... 0.1161 to 0.2281 in (2.95 to 3.00 mm)
H .... 0.1181 to 0.1201 in (3.00 to 3.05 mm)
J .... 0.1201 to 0.1220 in (3.05 to 3.10 mm)
K .... 0.1220 to 0.1240 in (3.10 to 3.15 mm
L .... 0.1240 to 0.1260 in (3.15 to 3.20 mm)

7A

Output shaft snap-ring thickness (continued)
Rear bearing

1	0.0925 to 0.0945 in (2.35 to 2.40 mm)
2	0.0945 to 0.0965 in (2.40 to 2.45 mm)
3	0.0965 to 0.0984 in (2.45 to 2.50 mm)
4	0.0984 to 0.1004 in (2.50 to 2.55 mm)
5	0.1004 to 0.1024 in (2.55 to 2.60 mm)
6	0.1024 to 0.1043 in (2.60 to 2.65 mm)
7	0.1043 to 0.1063 in (2.65 to 2.70 mm)

Counter gear snap-ring thickness

1	0.0787 to 0.0807 in (2.00 to 2.05 mm)
2	0.0709 to 0.0728 in (1.80 to 1.85 mm)
3	0.0630 to 0.0650 in (1.60 to 1.65 mm)

Torque specifications

	Ft-lbs
Clutch bellhousing-to-engine bolts	47
Clutch bellhousing-to-transmission bolts	27
Transmission case right-to-left half bolts	14
Extension housing-to-transmission bolts	27
Front bearing retainer-to-clutch housing bolts	13
Counter gear front bearing lockplate bolts	27
Shift lever screws	9
Stiffener plate bolts	27

1   General information

All vehicles covered in this manual come equipped with either a four or five-speed manual transmission or an automatic transmission. All information on the manual transmission is included in this Part of Chapter 7. Information on the automatic transmission can be found in Part B of this Chapter.

Overhauling a manual transmission can be expensive and time consuming, since the unit is complex and parts are not always readily available. As an alternative to overhauling the transmission yourself (see Section 6), it may be a good idea to replace the unit with either a new or rebuilt one. Your local dealer or transmission shop should be able to supply you with information concerning cost, availability and exchange policy. Regardless of how you decide to remedy a transmission problem, you can still save a lot of money by removing and installing the unit yourself.

2   Oil seal replacement

1   Oil leaks frequently occur due to wear of the extension housing oil seal and bushing, and/or the speedometer drive gear oil seal and O-ring. Replacement of these seals is relatively easy, since the repairs can usually be performed without removing the transmission from the vehicle.

Extension housing
Refer to illustration 2.4

2   The extension housing oil seal is located at the extreme rear of the transmission, where the driveshaft is attached. If leakage at the seal is suspected, raise the rear of the vehicle and support it securely on jackstands. Be sure to block the front wheels to keep the vehicle from rolling. If the seal is leaking, transmission lubricant will be built up on the front of the driveshaft and may be dripping from the dust shield at the rear of the transmission.

3   Refer to Chapter 8 and remove the driveshaft.

4   Using a hooked tool, carefully pry the oil seal and bushing out of the rear of the transmission (see illustration). Do not damage the splines on the transmission output shaft.

5   If the oil seal cannot be removed with a hooked tool, it may be necessary to obtain a special seal removal tool, available at your dealer or an auto parts store.

6   Using a large section of pipe or a very large deep socket as a drift, install the new oil seal. Drive it into the bore squarely and make sure that it is completely seated.

7   Lubricate the splines of the transmission output shaft and the outside of the driveshaft sleeve yoke with lightweight grease, then install the driveshaft. Be careful not to damage the lip of the new seal.

Speedometer driven gear
Refer to illustrations 2.9, 2.10, 2.12 and 2.13

8   The speedometer cable and driven gear housing is located on the side of the extension housing. Look for transmission oil around the cable housing to determine if the seal and O-ring are leaking.

2.4   With the driveshaft out, the rear oil seal can be removed with a hooked tool – be careful not to damage the output shaft splines

2.9 Unscrew the collar with pliers and disconnect the speedometer cable from the driven gear housing

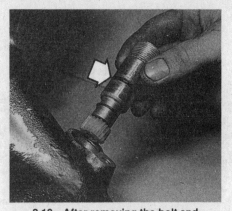

2.10 After removing the bolt and retainer, pull the driven gear housing out of the transmission and replace the O-ring (arrow)

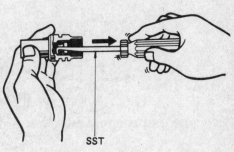

2.12 Use a hooked tool to remove the seal from the housing

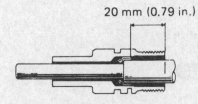

2.13 Be sure to drive the new seal in to the proper depth in the housing

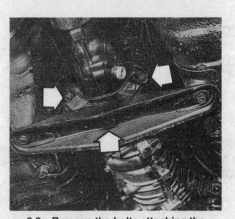

3.3 Remove the bolts attaching the insulator to the transmission and crossmember (arrows)

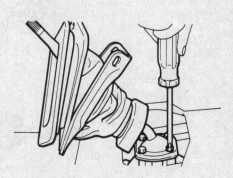

4.3a On some models, the shift lever is retained by screws, . . .

9 Disconnect the cable housing with pliers (**see illustration**).
10 Remove the retaining bolt, then pull the driven gear housing out of the transmission (**see illustration**). Replace the O-ring on the housing.
11 Remove the driven gear from the housing.
12 Using a hooked tool, remove the seal (**see illustration**).
13 Using a small socket of the appropriate diameter or other similar tool as a drift, install the new seal (**see illustration**).
14 Reinstall the driven gear housing and cable assembly on the extension housing.

3 Transmission mount – check and replacement

Refer to illustration 3.3

1 Insert a large screwdriver or pry bar into the space between the transmission extension housing and the crossmember and try to pry the transmission up slightly.
2 The transmission should not move away from the insulator much at all.
3 To replace the mount, remove the bolt(s) attaching the insulator to the crossmember and the bolts attaching the insulator to the transmission (**see illustration**).
4 Raise the transmission slightly with a jack and remove the insulator, noting which holes are used in the crossmember for proper alignment during installation.
5 Installation is the reverse of the removal procedure. Be sure to tighten the nuts/bolts securely.

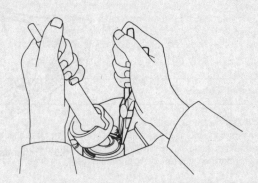

4.3b . . . while on others a snap-ring is used to retain the lever

4 Shift lever – removal and installation

Refer to illustrations 4.3a and 4.3b

1 Remove the console (if equipped) and shift boot screws.
2 Place the shift lever in Neutral.
3 Remove the shift lever retainer-to-transmission screws or circlip (**see illustrations**).

7A

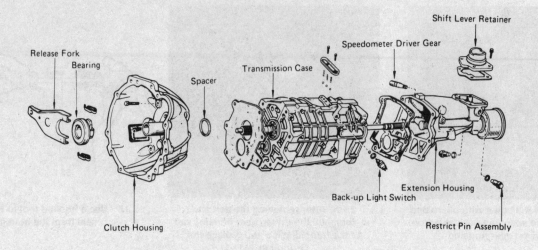

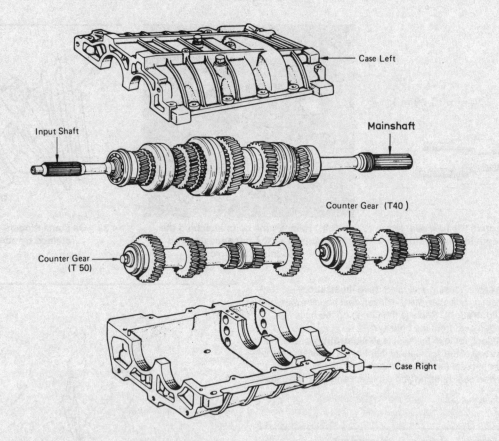

6.5   Transmission components – exploded view

4   Disconnect the shift lever from the transmission.
5   Lift the shift lever assembly from the transmission.
6   Installation is the reverse of removal.

5   Manual transmission – removal and installation

Removal

1   Disconnect the negative cable at the battery.

2   From inside the vehicle, remove the shift lever (Section 4).
3   Raise the vehicle and support it securely on jackstands.
4   Disconnect the speedometer cable and electrical connections from the transmission.
5   Remove the driveshaft (Chapter 8). Use a plastic bag to cover the end of the transmission to prevent fluid loss and contamination.
6   Drain the transmission lubricant (see Chapter 1).
7   Remove the starter motor.
8   Unbolt the clutch release cylinder and fasten it out of the way.
9   Remove the exhaust system components as necessary for clearance (Chapter 4).

6.6   When the bellhousing is removed, note the locations of the washers and don't lose them!

6.10   Unscrew the restrict pins

6.11   Support the extension housing when pulling it off the main housing

10   Support the engine. This can be done from above by using an engine hoist, or by placing a jack (with a block of wood as an insulator) under the engine oil pan. The engine should remain supported at all times while the transmission is out of the vehicle.
11   Support the transmission with a jack – preferably a special jack made for this purpose. Safety chains will help steady the transmission on the jack.
12   Remove the rear transmission mount-to-crossmember nuts and bolts.
13   Remove the nuts from the crossmember bolts. Raise the transmission slightly and remove the crossmember.
14   Remove the bolts securing the transmission clutch housing to the engine.
15   Make a final check that all wires and hoses have been disconnected from the transmission and then move the transmission and jack toward the rear of the vehicle until the clutch housing is clear of the engine dowel pins. Keep the transmission level as this is done. Be careful not to damage the extension housing dust deflector.
16   Lower the transmission and remove it from under the vehicle. **Caution:** *Do not depress the clutch pedal while the transmission is removed from the vehicle.*
17   The clutch components now can be inspected (Chapter 8). In most cases, new clutch components should be installed as a matter of course if the transmission is removed.

Installation

18   If removed, install the clutch components (Chapter 8)
19   With the transmission clutch housing secured to the jack as on removal, raise it into position behind the engine and then carefully slide it forward, engaging the clutch housing over the dowel pins. Do not use excessive force to install the transmission – if it does not slide into place, readjust the angle of the transmission so it is level.
20   Install the transmission/clutch housing-to-engine bolts. Tighten the bolts to the specified torque.
21   Install the crossmember and transmission support. Tighten all nuts and bolts securely.
22   Remove the jacks supporting the transmission and the engine.
23   Install the various items removed previously, referring to Chapter 8 for the installation of the driveshaft and Chapter 4 for information regarding the exhaust system components.
24   Make a final check that all wires, hoses and the speedometer cable have been connected and that the transmission has been filled with lubricant to the proper level (Chapter 1). Lower the vehicle.
25   From inside the vehicle connect the shift lever (see Section 4).
26   Connect the negative battery cable. Road test the vehicle for proper operation and check for leakage.

6   Manual transmission – overhaul

Note: *This procedure covers overhaul of the four-speed (T40) and five-speed (T50) transmissions. Since the two transmissions are nearly identical, the various repair procedures are combined. Where differences between the two exist, they are noted in the text. Tools required for overhaul include internal and external snap-ring pliers, a bearing puller, pin punches, a dial indicator and a hydraulic press.*

Disassembly

Refer to illustrations 6.5, 6.6, 6.10, 6.11, 6.13, 6.14, 6.19, 6.21a and 6.21b

1   Drain the lubricant and clean the outside of the transmission with a stiff brush and water-soluble solvent.
2   Refer to Chapter 8 and remove the clutch release lever and bearing assembly.
3   Remove the four bolts and lock washers securing the input shaft bearing retainer.
4   Remove the gasket from the retainer or bellhousing face.
5   Remove the bolts and lock washers that secure the clutch bellhousing to the front face of the main housing. Detach the clutch housing **(see illustration)**.
6   Note the locations of the cone washers which will be exposed when the clutch housing is removed **(see illustration)**.
7   Remove the four bolts and lock washers securing the shift lever to the upper face of the extension housing. Lift off the retainer and remove the gasket.
8   Remove the bolt, lock washer and clip retaining the speedometer driven gear housing to the extension housing.
9   Using a screwdriver, carefully ease the assembly from its location in the extension housing (see Section 2).
10   Remove the restrict pins from the extension housing. Unless they are color coded, mark each pin to ensure correct installation **(see illustration)**.
11   Remove the bolts and lock washers securing the extension housing to the main housing. Pull the extension housing away from the main housing, moving the selector rod to the left and right to disengage it from the shift selectors **(see illustration)**. Remove the housing-to-transmission gasket.
12   On T50 transmissions, the reverse restrict pin can now be removed by removing the plug and driving out the roll pin.
13   Unbolt and remove the lock ball and spring cover and extract the balls and springs. Remove the bolts and lock washers securing the two halves of the transmission main housing. Note their lengths and locations. Lift off

7A

6.13 Carefully separate the housing halves – if they're stuck together, gently tap on them with a soft-face hammer

6.14 Use a magnet to remove the lock ball from the housing web

6.19 Remove the lockbolt (arrow) which retains the reverse idler gear and shaft assembly

6.21a Use a pin punch to drive out the shift fork roll pins

6.21b Sometimes you'll need to remove the plug (arrow) in the housing to allow enough clearance to drive out the roll pin

the upper main housing half. No gasket is used between the two mating faces **(see illustration)**.

14 Carefully remove the lock ball located in the central web **(see illustration)**.

15 Gently tap the countershaft assembly with a soft-face hammer and lift it slightly.

16 Carefully remove the lock ball from the countershaft bearing outer race.

17 Lift off the countershaft assembly.

18 Lift the mainshaft and input shaft off the main housing half.

19 If necessary, unscrew and remove the bolt and lock washer securing the reverse idler gear shaft **(see illustration)**.

20 Carefully tap the idler gear shaft and remove the gear and thrust washers.

21 Normally, it isn't necessary to remove the selector forks and rods. If you have to remove them, mark the relative positions of the selector forks and rods and tap out the fork retaining roll pins with a pin punch **(see illustration)**. Where necessary, remove the plug from the housing to allow the roll pin to be driven through the hole in the housing **(see illustration)**.

22 Pull out the selector shafts and remove the interlock pins, detent balls, spring and spring seat.

Inspection

Note: *You cannot inspect many of the components until you have further disassembled the transmission (see the appropriate procedure below).*

23 Inspect the disassembled parts after cleaning them with solvent and drying them thoroughly. Repair and replace and parts that are defective.

24 Check the transmission case and extension housing for cracks and damage, especially at the bearing outer race bosses. Small nicks and

burrs can be removed with a fine file.

25 Check the shafts for worn or damaged gear mounting areas and worn or damaged splines. Check the spacers and bushings for damage and wear.

26 Inspect the gears for worn or damaged teeth. Check the inner diameter and both ends of each gear for wear and damage. Also check the contact surface of the synchronizer cone for wear and damage.

27 With the synchronizer rings assembled to their mating gears, check the synchronizer ring-to-gear clearance. If the clearance is greater than specified, replace the synchronizer ring.

28 Assemble the hub and sleeve and see if the sleeve slides smoothly. Also, check for excessive play in the direction of rotation. If either part is defective, both the hub and sleeve must be replaced as an assembly.

29 Check the clearance between the shift fork and groove in the synchronizer and compare it to this Chapter's Specifications.

30 Check the needle bearings for roller surface damage such as pitting, cracks and scoring. Assemble the needle bearings and gears in their respective shafts and check to see if they rotate smoothly and quietly. Inspect all ball-bearings for wear and damage. See if they rotate smoothly and quietly. If there's any doubt as to the condition of the bearing, replace it.

31 Inspect the interlock pins, springs and snap-rings for damage and wear, replacing them as necessary.

Input shaft overhaul

Refer to illustrations 6.34a, 6.34b and 6.36

32 If the synchromesh hub assemblies are disassembled, be sure to mark the component relationships with a dab of paint.

33 Pull the input shaft off the front of the mainshaft.

6.34a Slide the synchro ring off the input shaft

6.34b Remove the roller bearings from the input shaft

6.36 Remove the snap-ring from the input shaft bearing

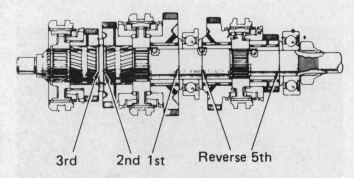

3rd   2nd 1st   Reverse 5th

6.42 Check the thrust clearances at the indicated points before disassembling the mainshaft

34 Remove the synchro ring and extract the needle roller bearings from the input shaft **(see illustrations)**.

35 The shaft and bearing are held on the front of the main housing by a large snap-ring in the outer race of the bearing.

36 To replace the bearing, first remove the snap-ring from the front of the bearing **(see illustration)**.

37 Place the outer edge of the bearing on a workbench and drive the input shaft through the bearing. Note that the bearing is installed with the snap-ring groove towards the forward end of the input shaft. Lift off the bearing.

38 If the bearing is worn or damaged, it must be replaced. Drive the new bearing onto the shaft using a section of pipe. Make sure the bearing outer snap-ring groove is offset to the front. Install a new outer snap-ring.

39 A new bearing retaining snap-ring must also be installed. This is a selective snap-ring which is available in a range of different thicknesses as listed in the Specifications. Select a snap-ring to provide the minimum amount of axial play in the groove. When installed, make sure the snap-ring is engaged in the groove.

40 It's always a good idea to replace the needle roller bearings as a matter of course. When placing them in position, coat them with grease to retain them against the walls of the housing. The grease on the rollers will hold them in position when the input shaft is reinstalled on the mainshaft.

41 If the synchro ring shows any sign of wear, replace it.

Mainshaft overhaul

Refer to illustrations 6.42, 6.43, 6.44a, 6.44b, 6.46, 6.47, 6.48a, 6.48b, 6.49a, 6.49b, 6.49c, 6.49d, 6.50, 6.57, 6.60, 6.61, 6.62, 6.64, 6.67, 6.68a, 6.68b, 6.69a, 6.69b, 6.69c, 6.69d, 6.69e, 6.70a, 6.70b, 6.71a, 6.71b, 6.71c, 6.71d, 6.72, 6.73a, 6.73b, 6.74a and 6.74b

42 Before disassembling the mainshaft, check each gear thrust clearance with feeler gauges **(see illustration)**. Make a note of the clearances so they can be compared with the recommended thrust clearances in the Specifications.

43 Remove the snap-ring from the front end of the mainshaft **(see illustration)**.

44 Pull the 3rd gear synchronizer unit **(see illustration)**, then the gear **(see illustration)** off the front end of the mainshaft.

45 Remove the snap-ring retaining the speedometer drive gear in position on the rear end of the mainshaft.

7A

6.43 Remove the snap-ring from the front end of the mainshaft

6.44a Slide 2nd gear . . .

6.44b . . . and 3rd gear off the shaft

6.46   Slide the speedometer gear off

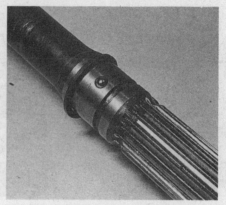

6.47   Remove the lock ball and snap-ring from the shaft

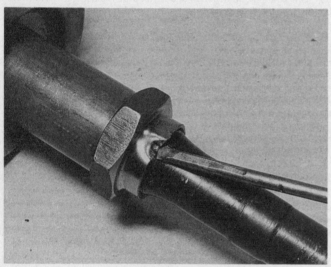

6.48a   On some early models, you'll have to unstake the locknut . . .

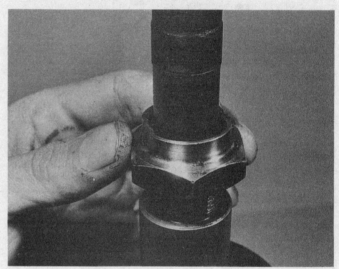

6.48b   . . . before it can be removed

6.49a   Lift off the spacer collar, . . .

6.49b   . . . followed by the shift stop plate (four-speed shown)

46 Pull the speedometer drive gear off the mainshaft, tapping it lightly with a soft-face hammer **(see illustration)**.

47 Remove the speedometer gear lock ball from the shaft and then remove the second snap-ring from the shaft groove **(see illustration)**.

48 Place the mainshaft securely in a vise and, on some early models, unstake the locking nut as shown and unscrew and remove the nut **(see illustrations)**. On later models, remove the snap-ring used to retain the gears.

a) T40 transmission – pull the spacer collar and the shift stop plate off the rear end of the mainshaft **(see illustrations)**.

b) T50 transmission – pull off the rear bearing, the bushing or spacer (if equipped), needle roller bearing, 5th gear, synchronizer ring and locking ball.

49 After removing the nut or snap-ring, proceed as follows according to transmission type **(see illustrations)**:

50 Remove the snap-ring, then support the mainshaft and tap the end

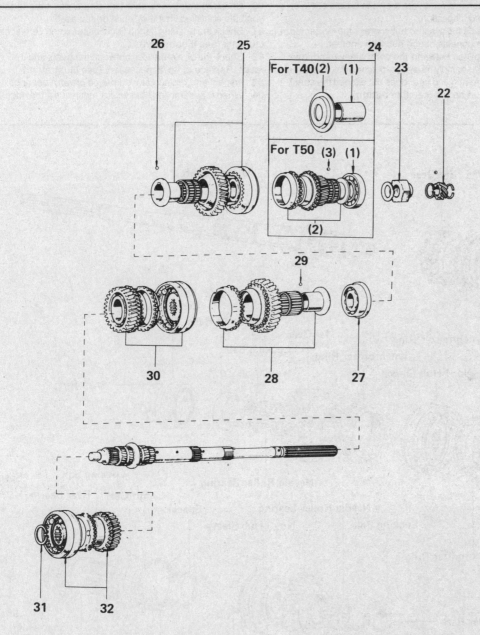

6.49c Mainshaft assembly components – exploded view (four-speed and early five-speed models)

22	Speedometer drive gear	25	No. 3 clutch hub and sleeve assembly	29	Lock ball
23	Rear bearing locknut	26	Lock ball	30	No. 1 clutch hub, sleeve, synchronizer ring and 2nd gear
24	T40 – spacer (1) and shift stop plate (2) T50 – Rear bearing (1), 5th gear and synchronizer assembly (2) and lock ball (3)	27	Center bearing	31	Snap-ring
		28	Bushing, needle roller bearing and 1st gear assembly	32	No. 2 clutch hub, sleeve, synchronizer ring and 3rd gear

7A

with a soft-face hammer to release the reverse gear assembly from the mainshaft **(see illustration)**.

51   Lift off the reverse gear assembly, needle bearing race, bushing and locking ball.

52   Remove the rear bearing retaining ball and slide off the rear bearing assembly, 1st gear assembly, needle roller race and bushing.

53   Slide off the thrust washer.

54   The 2nd gear assembly can now be removed from the mainshaft.

55   With the mainshaft components removed, they can be laid out in order for further disassembly and inspection.

56   If it's necessary to dismantle the synchro hubs, press the center out, taking care not to mix the components of one hub with another.

57   Check backlash in the splines between the outer sleeve and inner hub. If any is noted, the whole assembly must be replaced. Make sure the clearance between the synchro ring and gear does not exceed the specified limit using feeler gauges as shown **(see illustration)**.

58   Mark the hub and sleeve so they can be reassembled on the same splines. With the hub and sleeve separated, the teeth at the end of the splines (which engage with the corresponding teeth of the gears) must be checked for damage and wear.

59   If the synchronizing cones are being replaced, replace the sliding keys and springs which hold them in position. The hub assemblies are not interchangeable so they must be reassembled with their original or identical new parts.

60   Check the sleeve-to-shift fork clearances **(see illustration)**. If beyond the specified limit they must be replaced.

61   Check the bushing flange thicknesses using vernier calipers or a micrometer **(see illustration)**.

62   Check the oil clearances between the gears and their corresponding races. Replace parts as necessary **(see illustration)**.

63   Inspect and replace any damaged or worn bearings.

64   When reassembling the synchromesh hubs, the ridges on the sliding

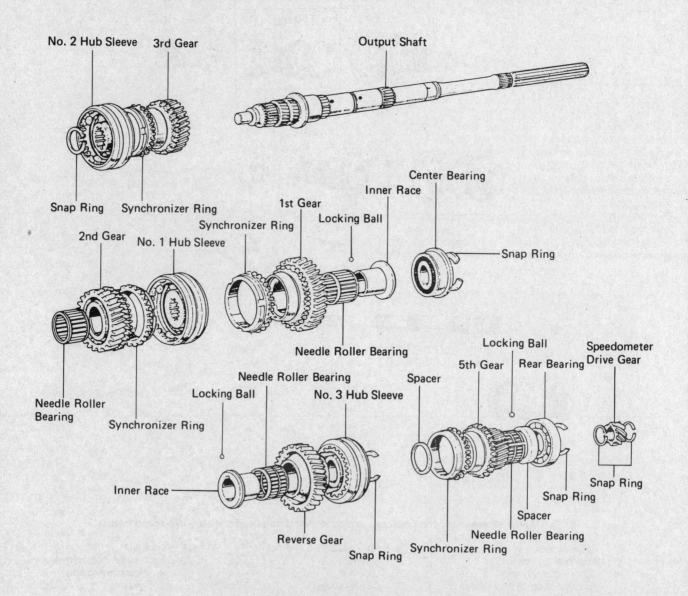

6.49d   Followed by the shift stop plate (four-speed shown)

6.50   Reverse gear removal details

6.57   Check the synchro ring-to-gear clearances

keys are symmetrical and can therefore be reinstalled either way in the hub during reassembly. Assemble the keys and springs in a staggered manner. Identification profiles and orientation for installing the hubs are as shown (see illustration). It should be noted that the keys for each synchromesh unit are different lengths. The turned out end of each spring must locate in the slotted key and be assembled in the hub in a counterclockwise direction as viewed from either side of the hub.

65   Slide the 3rd gear assembly and synchromesh assembly onto the front end of the mainshaft.

66   Reinstall the snap-ring and check the endplay. If the reading obtained is outside the limit, a new snap-ring will be required (see illustration 6.43).

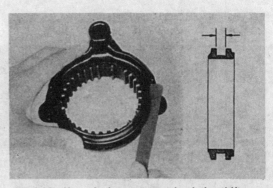

6.60   Use a feeler gauge to check the shift fork clearances

6.61   Check the bushing flange thickness

6.62   Use a dial indicator to check for bearing wear

7A

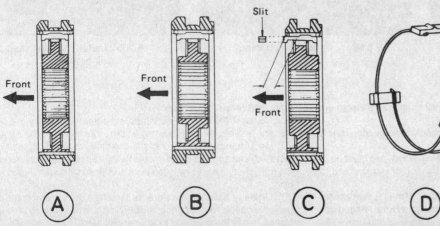

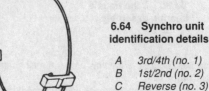

6.64   Synchro unit identification details

A   3rd/4th (no. 1)
B   1st/2nd (no. 2)
C   Reverse (no. 3)
D   Key assembly

A   B   C   D

6.67   Installing 2nd gear

6.68a   Place the synchro ring in
the hub, . . .

6.68b   . . . then slide the hub into
position on the shaft

6.69a   Place the opposing synchro ring
in the hub, . . .

6.69b   . . . followed by the lock ball

6.69c   Install 1st gear, . . .

6.69d . . . the needle
bearing assembly . . .

6.69e   . . . and the bushing

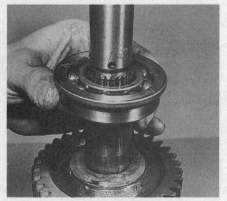

6.70a   Install the mainshaft
ball bearing, . . .

67   Slide the 2nd gear assembly onto the mainshaft from the rear end
(see illustration).
68   Follow it with the synchromesh unit and needle roller bearing **(see illustrations)**.
69   Slide on the 1st gear assembly and bushing. A lock ball must be installed in the hole in the mainshaft between the synchromesh unit and 1st
gear assembly **(see illustrations)**.
70   Slide on the ball race and push it up to the back of the 1st gear assembly **(see illustration)**. The bearing must be installed with the flanged face
to the rear. Lock the race with a ball bearing in the exposed hole in the

mainshaft **(see illustration)**.
71   Reinstall the reverse gear and synchromesh unit, along with the
bushing and needle roller bearing, in the order shown in the illustrations.
72   On T40 transmissions, reinstall the shift stop plate, spacer, shim (if
installed) and nut. Tighten the nut to the specified torque while supporting
the mainshaft in a vise with soft jaws and stake the locknut **(see illustration)**.
73   On early T50 transmissions, reassemble the synchronizer ring, 5th
gear, the needle roller bearing, the bushing and ball bearing **(see illustrations)**. Install the shim and locknut and tighten it to the specified torque.

6.70b ... then insert the lock ball into the shaft

6.71a Slide the bushing onto the shaft, ...

6.71b ... install the bearings, ...

6.71c ... install reverse gear and ...

6.71d ... the synchro hub

6.72 Stake the retaining nut collar (four-speed models)

6.73a Install 5th gear and the synchro ring, aligning the key slots with the shift keys (early five-speed models)

6.73b Install the ball bearing with the shielded face toward the rear (early five-speed models)

74   On later T50 transmissions (from August 1981-on), install the snap-ring (see illustration). Select a snap-ring allowing an axial play of up to 0.004-inch (0.1 mm). Having installed the selected snap-ring in position in the groove in the mainshaft, locate the needle roller bearing spacer ring. Then reinstall 5th gear with the synchronizer and needle bearing assembly. Make sure the synchronizer ring slots align with the shift keys when reassembling them. Now install the rear bearing spacer and lock ball, engaging the spacer groove over the ball (see illustration). Support the front end of the mainshaft and press the rear bearing into position while simultaneously retaining the 5th gear and spacer. With the bearing in position, select a snap-ring to provide an axial play of up to 0.004-inch (0.1 mm), then install the snap-ring to secure the bearing.

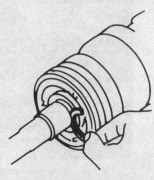

6.74a Select the correct snap-ring (early five-speed models)

7A

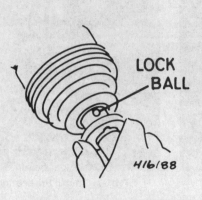

6.74b   Install the bearing spacer ring with the slot over the lock ball in the mainshaft (later five-speed models)

6.78   Secure the countershaft ball bearing with the bolt and washer

6.80   Remove the reverse gear snap-ring

6.81   Use a press to remove the countershaft

75   Install the first snap-ring on the end of the mainshaft, insert the lock ball and slide on the speedometer drive gear.

76   Retain the speedometer drive gear with the second snap-ring.

77   With the mainshaft now reassembled, use feeler gauges and measure each gear's thrust clearance to ensure that it's within the specified limits. If there's a significant difference, the cause must be found and rectified (see illustration 6.42).

Countershaft overhaul

Refer to illustrations 6.78, 6.80, 6.81, 6.82a and 6.82b

78   Remove the bolt, lock washer and plain washer holding the ball race on the end of the countershaft (see illustration).

79   Using a puller and thrust block, pull the bearing off the end of the countershaft. Note which way the bearing faces.

6.82a   Slide reverse gear off the countershaft, . . .

6.82b   . . . followed by the bearing

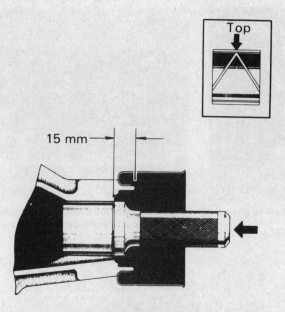

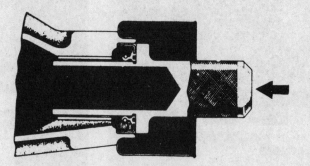

6.92 The hole in the top of the extension housing bushing must be facing up – use the special tool (shown) or a piece of pipe to drive the bushing in to the depth indicated

6.93 Use a seal driver (shown) or a piece of pipe to install the seal

80 On T40 transmissions, use a pair of snap-ring pliers to remove the snap-ring holding the reverse gear on the end of the countershaft (see illustration).

81 On T50 transmissions, support the front face of 5th gear and press or drive out the countershaft (see illustration).

82 Remove the reverse gear and center bearing from the countershaft. Note that the bearing roller cage is installed with the larger diameter facing forward (see illustrations).

83 Examine the various components and replace parts as necessary.

84 Reassembly of the countershaft is the reverse of disassembly. Be sure to install the bearings in the proper direction.

Reverse idler gear and shaft overhaul

85 If the reverse idler gear is still in position in the transmission, use a feeler gauge to check the thrust clearance. It should not exceed the limit listed in this Chapter's Specifications.

86 The gear can be removed by unscrewing the shaft retaining bolt, pulling out the gear and lifting out the thrust washers. Note which way the gear is installed (see illustration 6.19).

87 Check the shaft for wear. The outer diameter should not be less than 0.626-inch (15.9 mm). replace the shaft if necessary.

88 Measure the inside diameter of the gear bushing. Replace it if it's worn beyond 0.634-inch (16.1 mm). The bushing must be pressed out of the gear for replacement. When pressing the new bushing into position, make sure the oil holes in the gear and bushing align.

89 When reinstalling the gear in the transmission, engage the projecting part of the thrust washer in the slot in the housing. Tighten the bolt to the specified torque.

Extension housing overhaul

Refer to illustrations 6.92 and 6.93

90 If you have to disassemble the extension housing, remove the shift lever retainer, then drive out the roll pin to release the selector control rod from the shift lever housing.

91 The oil seal in the end of the housing can be replaced by prying out the old one (see Section 2).

92 To remove the extension housing bushing, heat the housing to 200-degrees F, then drive the bushing out with a punch. When driving the new bushing into position, make sure the oil hole is at the top (see illustration).

93 Tap the new oil seal into position using a piece of pipe with a diameter slightly smaller than the diameter of the seal (see illustration). Lubricate the seal lip with grease.

94 When reinstalling the selector control rod, use a new roll pin to retain it.

95 The speedometer driven gear housing oil seal can be pulled out with a hooked tool (see Section 2).

Reassembly

Refer to illustrations 6.96, 6.97a, 6.97b, 6.98, 6.100, 6.101, 6.102a, 6.102b, 6.102c, 6.104, 6.108, 6.109a, 6.109b, 6.110 and 6.111

96 If the selector forks and rods have been removed, they should be reinstalled. Reverse the removal procedure (see illustration).

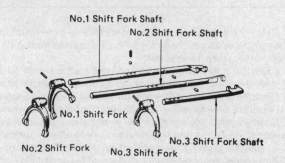

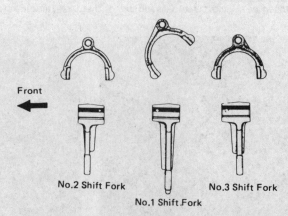

6.96 Shift fork assembly components – exploded view

7A

6.97a   Lower the countershaft into position and . . .

6.97b   . . . insert the lock ball as shown

6.98   Lower the mainshaft and input shaft assemblies into the housing

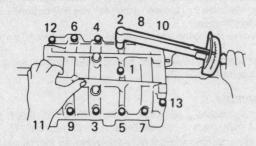

6.100   Tighten the housing bolts, in the sequence shown, to the torque listed in this Chapter's Specifications

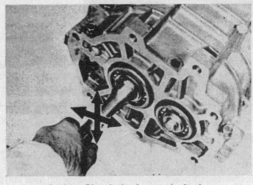

6.101   Check the input shaft play

97   Check that the main housing halves are clean and then carefully lower the assembled countershaft into position. Place the lock ball in the bearing central web (see illustrations).
98   Lower the combined mainshaft and input shaft assembly into position, engaging it with the selector forks as it's installed (see illustration).
99   Place the detent ball into the hole in the central web, then apply a coat of RTV sealant to the mounting face of the housing (see illustration 6.14).
100 Carefully reassemble the two halves of the housing. Coat the bolt threads with RTV sealant and insert the bolts. Tighten them in three steps, in the sequence shown, to the specified torque (see illustration).
101 Now check the input shaft endplay. It should be about 0.012-inch (0.3 mm) play (see illustration).
102 Insert the selector detent balls and springs, then install the gasket and

plate cover and secure it with the two bolts (see illustrations).
103 Operate the selector shafts to check for smooth operation.
104 Coat the rear face of the transmission housing with RTV sealant, then position the gasket on the housing (see illustration). Coat the mating surface of the extension housing with RTV sealant and reinstall the extension housing on the end of the transmission, engaging the lug of the selector lever rod in the slot in the no. 2 selector fork shaft. Install and tighten the bolts to the specified torque. Take care when installing the extension housing so you don't damage the oil seal on the splines of the mainshaft.
105 Before inserting the speedometer driven gear housing, make sure the oil seal is in good condition and correctly installed.
106 Reinstall the speedometer driven gear housing (see Section 2). Tighten the bolt securely.

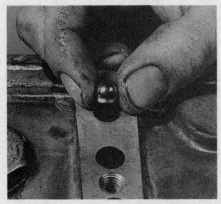

6.102a   Insert the selector balls, . . .

6.102b   . . . followed by the springs, then . . .

6.102c   . . . install the gasket and cover

6.104   Place the new gasket in position on the housing

6.108   Use a new gasket when installing the shift lever retainer

6.109a   Install the coned washer in the countershaft recess

6.109b   The large coned washer fits into the input shaft opening

6.110   Install the clutch bellhousing on the transmission housing

6.111   Tighten the clutch bellhousing bolts to the torque listed in this Chapter's Specifications

107 Reinstall the restrict pins in the extension housing using a new washer for each pin. Make sure the pins are correctly installed as marked during removal or with the white pin on the left side and black pin on the right if color coded. Tighten the pins securely.

108 Install the shift lever retainer, using a new gasket (see illustration).

109 Install the flat washer, followed by the small coned washer in the recess in the countershaft opening in the clutch housing. Install the large cone washer in the recess in the input shaft opening (see illustrations). The coned washers are installed with the concave section facing the transmission. Grease the washers to retain them when installing the clutch housing.

110 Coat the clutch housing-to-transmission mating surface with sealant, then install it on the front end of the transmission, taking care not to damage the front oil seal in the input shaft bearing retainer, if installed at this stage (see illustration).

111 Tighten the clutch housing retaining bolts to the specified torque (see illustration).

112 If the input shaft bearing retainer hasn't been installed, make sure the oil seal (use a new one) is correctly positioned. Lubricate the lips of the seal with multi-purpose grease and coat the retainer and clutch housing mating surfaces with RTV sealant. Position the gasket on one surface, then install the bearing retainer. Secure it with the four bolts and lock washers and tighten the bolts securely.

113 Reinstall the clutch release arm and bearing carrier (Chapter 8).

114 The transmission is now ready for installation.

7A

Chapter 7 Part B Automatic transmission

Contents

Specifications

Torque converter-to-bellhousing face clearance
1980 and 1981 .... 7/16 in (11.5 mm)
1982-on .... 1-1/64 in (26 mm)

Torque specifications   Ft-lbs
Transmission-to-engine bolts 47
Torque converter-to-driveplate bolts
   1980 through 1985 13
   1986-on 20
Transmission crossmember-to-body bolts 38

Torque specifications (continued)

Ft-lbs

Transmission mount-to-crossmember bolts
    1980 through 1983 .... 18 to 20
    1984-on 10

---

1   General information

All vehicles covered in this manual are equipped with either a four or five-speed manual transmission or an automatic transmission. All information on the automatic transmission is included in this Part of Chapter 7. Information on the manual transmission can be found in Part A.

Due to the complexity of the automatic transmission and the need for specialized equipment to perform most service operations, this Chapter contains only general diagnosis, routine maintenance, adjustment and removal and installation procedures.

If the transmission requires major repair work, it should be left to a dealer service department or an automotive transmission repair shop. You can, however, remove and install the transmission yourself and save the expense, even if the repair work is done by a transmission specialist.

2   Diagnosis – general

Note: *Automatic transmission malfunctions may be caused by five general conditions: poor engine performance, improper adjustments, hydraulic malfunctions, mechanical malfunctions or malfunctions in the computer or its signal network. Diagnosis of these problems should always begin with a check of the easily repaired items: fluid level and condition (Chapter 1), shift linkage adjustment and throttle linkage adjustment. Next, perform a road test to determine if the problem has been corrected or if more diagnosis is necessary. If the problem persists after the preliminary tests and corrections are completed, additional diagnosis should be done by a dealer service department or transmission repair shop.*

Preliminary checks

1   Drive the vehicle to warm the transmission to normal operating temperature.

2   Check the fluid level as described in Chapter 1:
    a) If the fluid level is unusually low, add enough fluid to bring the level within the designated area of the dipstick, then check for external leaks (see below).
    b) If the fluid level is abnormally high, drain off the excess, then check the drained fluid for contamination by coolant. The presence of engine coolant in the automatic transmission fluid indicates that a failure has occurred in the internal radiator walls that separate the coolant from the transmission fluid (see Chapter 8).
    c) If the fluid is foaming, drain it and refill the transmission, then check for coolant in the fluid or a high fluid level.

3   Check the engine idle speed. **Note:** *If the engine is malfunctioning, do not proceed with the preliminary checks until it has been repaired and runs normally.*

4   Check the throttle valve cable for freedom of movement. Adjust it if necessary (Section 3). **Note:** *The throttle cable may function properly when the engine is shut off and cold, but it may malfunction once the engine is hot. Check it cold and at normal engine operating temperature.*

5   Inspect the shift control linkage (Section 4). Make sure that it's properly adjusted and that the linkage operates smoothly.

Fluid leak diagnosis

6   Most fluid leaks are easy to locate visually. Repair usually consists of replacing a seal or gasket. If a leak is difficult to find, the following procedure may help.

7   Identify the fluid. Make sure it's transmission fluid and not engine oil or brake fluid.

8   Try to pinpoint the source of the leak. Drive the vehicle several miles, then park it over a large sheet of cardboard. After a minute or two, you should be able to locate the leak by determining the source of the fluid dripping onto the cardboard.

9   Make a careful visual inspection of the suspected component and the area immediately around it. Pay particular attention to gasket mating surfaces. A mirror is often helpful for finding leaks in areas that are hard to see.

10   If the leak still cannot be found, clean the suspected area thoroughly with a degreaser or solvent, then dry it.

11   Drive the vehicle for several miles at normal operating temperature and varying speeds. After driving the vehicle, visually inspect the suspected component again.

12   Once the leak has been located, the cause must be determined before it can be properly repaired. If a gasket is replaced but the sealing flange is bent, the new gasket will not stop the leak. The bent flange must be straightened.

13   Before attempting to repair a leak, check to make sure that the following conditions are corrected or they may cause another leak. **Note:** *Some of the following conditions (a leaking torque converter, for instance) cannot be fixed without highly specialized tools and expertise. Such problems must be referred to a transmission shop or a dealer service department.*

Gasket leaks

14   Check the pan periodically. Make sure the bolts are tight, no bolts are missing, the gasket is in good condition and the pan is flat (dents in the pan may indicate damage to the valve body inside).

15   If the pan gasket is leaking, the fluid level or the fluid pressure may be too high, the vent may be plugged, the pan bolts may be too tight, the pan sealing flange may be warped, the sealing surface of the transmission housing may be damaged, the gasket may be damaged or the transmission casting may be cracked or porous. If sealant instead of gasket material has been used to form a seal between the pan and the transmission housing, it may be the wrong sealant.

Seal leaks

16   If a transmission seal is leaking, the fluid level or pressure may be too high, the vent may be plugged, the seal bore may be damaged, the seal itself may be damaged or improperly installed, the surface of the shaft protruding through the seal may be damaged or a loose bearing may be causing excessive shaft movement.

17   Make sure the dipstick tube seal is in good condition and the tube is properly seated. Periodically check the area around the speedometer gear or sensor for leakage. If transmission fluid is evident, check the O-ring for damage.

Case leaks

18   If the case itself appears to be leaking, the casting is porous and will have to be repaired or replaced.

19   Make sure the oil cooler hose fittings are tight and in good condition.

Fluid comes out vent pipe or fill tube

20   If this condition occurs, the transmission is overfilled, there is coolant in the fluid, the case is porous, the dipstick is incorrect, the vent is plugged or the drain back holes are plugged.

3   Throttle valve (TV) linkage – adjustment

Refer to illustration 3.3

1   Make sure the throttle cable bracket is not bent or loose before attempting to make this adjustment. Also, the rubber boot must be seated properly on the adjuster.

2   Have an assistant press the accelerator pedal all the way to the floor and hold it there. **Note:** *The throttle valve in the carburetor must be fully open; check and adjust if necessary (see Chapter 4).*

7B

WHEN THROTTLE VALVE IS FULLY OPENED

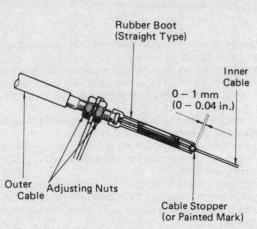

3.3   Throttle Valve (TV) linkage adjustment details

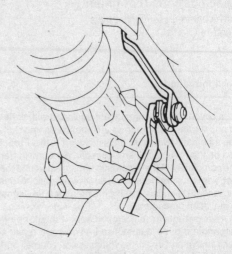

4.4   Use a wrench to loosen the nut on the shift linkage control rod

3   Check the distance between the end of the rubber boot and the stopper (or painted mark) on the cable. It must be as specified **(see illustration)**.

4   If the boot-to-stopper clearance is not as specified, loosen and back off the outer adjusting nut. Turn the inner adjusting nut to move the cable housing as required to produce the specified clearance. Be sure to tighten the outer nut to lock the housing in position.

4   Shift linkage – adjustment

Refer to illustration 4.4

1   This adjustment should not be considered routine and is not required unless wear in the linkage or misalignment of the shift position indicator occurs.

2   Position the shift lever in Drive, Second, Low and Reverse and make sure the transmission responds accordingly. Place the lever in Neutral, then verify that the transmission lever shifts to Neutral. Check to see if the shift position indicator registers correctly with the lever in each detent position.

3   If adjustment is required, the vehicle must be raised and supported securely on jackstands.

4   Working from under the vehicle, loosen the nut on the swivel connection that joins the shift lever to the transmission control rod **(see illustration)**.

1980 through 1983

5   Have an assistant position the shift lever in the Neutral position detent and hold it so it cannot move. Push the transmission control rod all the way forward; then pull it back exactly three notches. Tighten the nut on the swivel connection, then check the shift lever operation and position indicator alignment.

1984-on

6   Push the lever on the transmission all the way to the rear, then return it two notches to the Neutral position.

7   In the passenger compartment, place the shift lever in the Neutral position.

8   With an assistant holding the shift lever with light pressure toward the Reverse gear stop, tighten the linkage nut securely.

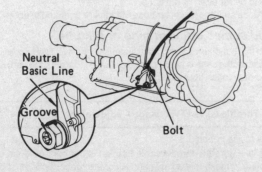

5.2a   Neutral start switch adjustment details (1980 through 1983 models)

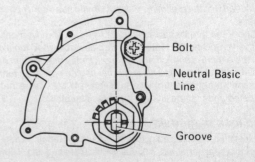

5.2b   Neutral start switch adjustment details (1984 and later models)

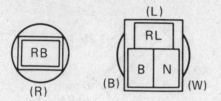

	B	N	RB	RL
P	○—	—○		
R			○—	—○
N	○—	—○		

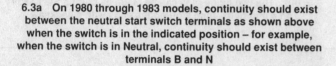

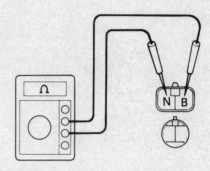

6.3a   On 1980 through 1983 models, continuity should exist between the neutral start switch terminals as shown above when the switch is in the indicated position – for example, when the switch is in Neutral, continuity should exist between terminals B and N

6.3b   On 1984 and later models, continuity should exist between terminals B and N when the transmission is in Neutral

5   Neutral start switch – check and adjustment

Refer to illustration 5.2a and 5.2b

1   If the engine can be started with the shift lever in any position other than Park or Neutral, the Neutral safety switch should be checked and adjusted. The vehicle must be raised and supported on jackstands for this procedure.

2   Position the shift lever in Neutral, then refer to the accompanying illustrations and loosen the switch bolt.

3   The groove in the end of the control shaft should be positioned vertically and directly in line with the neutral basic line on the switch. If it isn't, pivot the switch to align them, then tighten the bolt.

6   Neutral start switch – continuity check and replacement

Refer to illustrations 6.3a, 6.3b and 6.5

1   The neutral start switch is located on the right side of the automatic transmission housing. Its purpose is to allow the starter to operate only when the selector lever is in Neutral or Park. The switch also operates the back-up lights (lever in Reverse).

2   Before proceeding with the neutral start switch electrical continuity check, refer to Section 5 and make sure the it is properly adjusted.

3   If the switch is properly adjusted, check for continuity between the switch wiring terminals as shown in the accompanying illustrations.

4   If the switch is defective, disconnect the negative cable from the battery.

5   Unscrew the control shaft nut and disconnect the lever (see illustration).

6   Unscrew the switch retaining nut (you will have to bend back the washer lock lugs to unscrew the nut) and note the washer and grommet under the nut. Remove the switch mounting bolt as well.

7   Withdraw the switch. Unscrew the switch wire retaining clip bolt and then disconnect the wires at the block connectors.

8   Installation of the switch is the reverse of removal. Be sure to locate the grooved side of the grommet washer towards the transmission. Adjust the switch as discussed in Section 5 and then bend over the lugs of the lockwasher to secure the nut in position. Don't forget to relocate the wire retaining clip and take care not to pinch the hose.

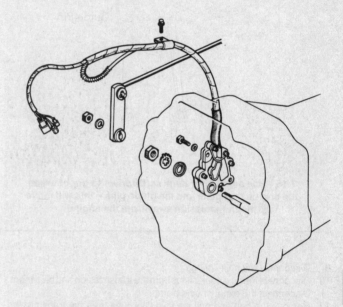

6.5   Typical neutral start switch installation details

7   Automatic transmission – removal and installation

Removal

Refer to illustrations 7.14a, 7.14b, 7.16 and 7.17

1   Disconnect the cable from the negative battery terminal.

2   Remove the air cleaner assembly and disconnect the throttle linkage cable at the carburetor or throttle body.

3   Raise the vehicle and support it securely on jackstands.

4   Drain the fluid from the transmission (Chapter 1).

5   Disconnect any wiring connectors which would interfere with removal.

6   Remove the starter motor (see Chapter 5).

7   Remove the driveshaft (Chapter 8).

8   Disconnect the speedometer drive cable.

7B

7.14a   Use a socket and ratchet to remove each of the six torque converter bolts – rotate the crankshaft to expose the bolts

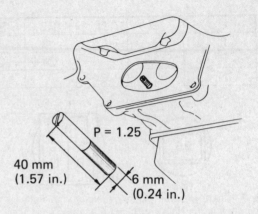

7.14b   The two guide pins can be made by cutting the heads off 6 mm bolts, then slotting the ends with a hacksaw

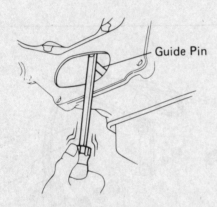

7.16   Use a prybar or large screwdriver to pry between the engine rear plate and the guide pins – this will move the transmission away from the engine

7.17   Grasp the torque converter securely and pull it away from the transmission; be careful, it's heavy

9   Disconnect the shift linkage.
10   Disconnect the fluid cooler lines from the transmission and plug them.
11   Disconnect the exhaust pipe clamp.
12   Remove the bolt and pull the fluid filler tube from the transmission tube, taking care not to lose any O-rings.
13   Remove the driveplate cover.
14   Support the transmission with a jack, then remove the rear support crossmember and mount. Through the open lower half of the torque converter housing, remove the six bolts which join the driveplate and converter **(see illustration)**. Remove them one at a time by rotating the driveplate. To do this, turn the crankshaft with a wrench attached to the front pulley securing bolt. Now screw two guide pins (made from two old bolts) into opposite bolt holes in the front of the driveplate, then rotate the engine until they are horizontal **(see illustration)**. These pins will act as pivot points during removal of the transmission.
15   Place a jack under the engine oil pan (use a block of wood to protect it), and remove the bolts which attach the torque converter housing to the engine.
16   Lower both jacks progressively until the transmission will clear the lower edge of the firewall. Insert two levers, or large screwdrivers, between the engine rear plate and the guide pins and pry the transmission away from the engine **(see illustration)**. Catch the fluid which will run from the torque converter during this operation. Never position the levers between the driveplate and the torque converter as damage or distortion will

result.
17   The torque converter can now be pulled forward to remove it from the housing **(see illustration)**.

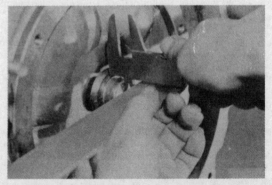

7.18a   On 1980 and 1981 models, measure the distance between the torque converter hub and the bellhousing face – if it's as listed in this Chapter's Specifications, the torque converter is properly seated

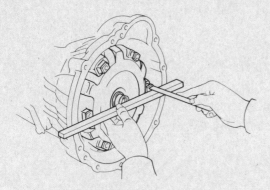

7.18b   On 1982 and later models, measure the distance from the converter mounting surface to the bellhousing face to make sure it's as listed in this Chapter's Specifications

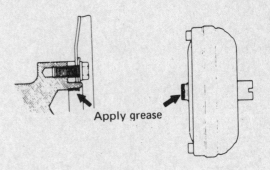

7.19   Apply multi-purpose grease to the areas indicated before rejoining the engine and transmission

Installation

Refer to illustrations 7.18a, 7.18b, 7.19 and 7.20

18   Prior to installation, make sure the torque converter is securely seated in the converter housing. On 1980 through 1982 models, measure the distance from the center of the hub to the housing face **(see illustration)**. On 1983 and later models, the driveplate mounting bosses should be the specified distance from the housing-to-block mating surface **(see illustration)**.

19   Apply a layer of multi-purpose grease to the recess in the end of the crankshaft **(see illustration)**.

20   Install one of the guide bolts in one of the lower torque converter-to-driveplate bolt holes **(see illustration)**.

21   Support the transmission and carefully guide it into position on the engine. The guide bolt should pass through the lower driveplate hole and the torque converter should enter the crankshaft recess.

22   Align the engine block dowel pins with the holes in the housing, then install the mounting bolts and tighten them securely.

23   Install the torque converter-to-driveplate mounting bolts and tighten them, using a criss-cross pattern, to the specified torque. Turn the crankshaft as required to expose the bolts. Install the cover.

24   The remainder of installation is the reverse of removal. Tighten all bolts and nuts securely. Be sure to refill the transmission with the specified fluid (see Chapter 1). Adjust the shift and throttle valve linkages as described in this Chapter before road testing the vehicle.

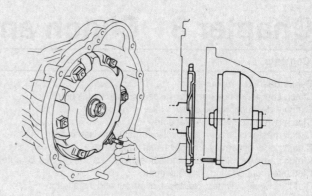

7.20   When installing the transmission, use the guide bolts to help align it with the engine

7B

Chapter 8   Clutch and drivetrain

Contents

Specifications

Clutch

Fluid type	See Chapter 1
Disc rivet head depth limit	1/16 in (0.3 mm)
Diaphragm spring tip out-of-alignment limit	0.020 in (0.5 mm)

Driveshaft

Runout limit	0.031 in (0.8 mm)
U-joint snap-rings	
Color code	**Thickness**
None	0.0935 to 0.0955 in (2.375 to 2.425 mm)
Brown	0.0955 to 0.0774 in (2.425 to 2.475 mm)
Blue	0.0974 to 0.0994 in (2.475 to 2.525 mm)
None	0.0974 to 0.1014 in (2.525 to 2.575 mm)
U-joint spider bearing axial play	
Solid-type	0.0 in (0.0 mm)
Shell-type	Less than 0.0020 in (0.05 mm)

Rear axle shaft

Maximum shaft runout	0.079 in (2.0 mm)
Maximum flange runout	0.008 in (0.2 mm)

Differential drive pinion preload

New bearing	8.7 to 13.9 in-lbs (10 to 16 kg-cm)
Used bearing	4.3 to 6.9 in-lbs (5 to 8 kg-cm)

Torque specifications

	Ft-lbs
Clutch pressure plate-to-flywheel	11 to 15
Bellhousing-to-engine	37 to 57
Clutch master cylinder reservoir mounting nut	9 to 15
Driveshaft center bearing-to-front shaft	
Step one	123 to 144
Step two	Loosen
Step three	
1980 through 1984	19 to 25
1985-on	51
Front-to-rear driveshaft flange bolts	22 to 28
Driveshaft-to-companion flange on differential	22 to 36
Center bearing bracket bolt	22 to 32
Differential carrier bolts	23
Rear axle shaft-to-rear axle housing nuts	44 to 53
Drive pinion nut	
Before preload test	80
Maximum	173
Wheel lug nuts	See Chapter 1

1   General information

The information in this Chapter deals with the components from the rear of the engine to the rear wheels, except for the transmission, which is dealt with in the previous Chapter. For the purposes of this Chapter, these components are grouped into three categories; clutch, driveshaft and rear axle. Separate Sections within this Chapter offer general descriptions and checking procedures for each of these three groups.

Since nearly all the procedures covered in this Chapter involve working under the vehicle, make sure it's securely supported on sturdy jackstands or on a hoist where the vehicle can be easily raised and lowered.

2   Clutch – description and check

Refer to illustration 2.1

1   All models equipped with a manual transmission feature a single dry plate, diaphragm spring-type clutch **(see illustration)**. The actuation is through a hydraulic system.

2   When the clutch pedal is depressed, hydraulic fluid (under pressure from the clutch master cylinder) flows into the slave cylinder. Because the slave cylinder is connected to the clutch fork, the fork moves the release bearing into contact with the pressure plate release fingers, disengaging the clutch plate.

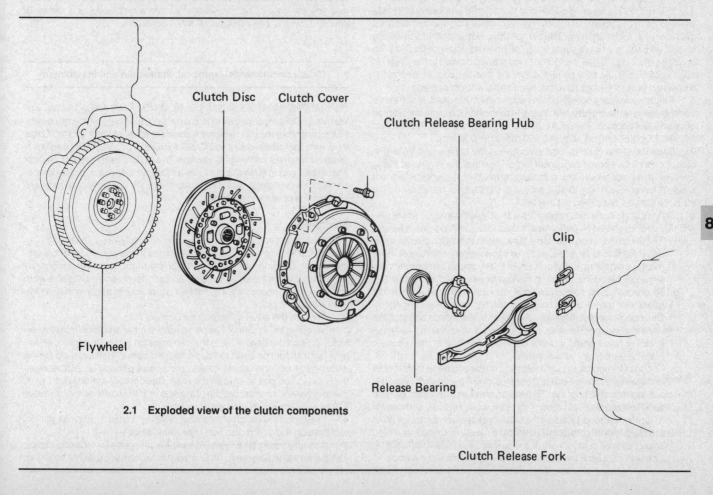

2.1   **Exploded view of the clutch components**

Clutch Disc

Clutch Cover

Clutch Release Bearing Hub

Clip

Flywheel

Release Bearing

Clutch Release Fork

8

3.4 A clutch alignment tool can be used to prevent the disc from falling out as the pressure plate is removed

3.5 Be sure to mark the pressure plate and flywheel to ensure proper alignment during installation

3   The hydraulic system locates the clutch pedal and provides clutch adjustment automatically, so no adjustment of the linkage is required.

4   Terminology can be a problem regarding the clutch components because common names have in some cases changed from that used by the manufacturer. For example, the driven plate is also called the clutch plate or disc, the clutch release bearing is sometimes called a throwout bearing, the release fork is sometimes called the clutch fork or shift fork, and the slave cylinder is sometimes called the operating or release cylinder.

5   Due to the slow wearing qualities of the clutch, it is not easy to decide when to go to the trouble of removing the transmission in order to check the wear on the friction lining. The only positive indication that something should be done is when it starts to slip or when squealing noises during engagement indicate that the friction lining has worn down to the rivets. In such instances it can only be hoped that the friction surfaces on the flywheel and pressure plate have not been badly worn or scored.

6   A clutch will wear according to the way in which it is used. Much intentional slipping of the clutch while driving – rather than the correct selection of gears – will accelerate wear. It is best to assume, however, that the disc will need replacement at about 40,000 miles (64,000 km).

7   Because of the clutch's location between the engine and transmission, it cannot be worked on without removing either the engine or transmission. If repairs which would require removal of the engine are not needed, the quickest way to gain access to the clutch is by removing the transmission, as described in Chapter 7.

8   Other than to replace components with obvious damage, some preliminary checks should be performed to diagnose a clutch system failure.

   a) The first check should be of the fluid level in the clutch master cylinder. If the fluid level is low, add fluid as necessary and re-test. If the master cylinder runs dry, or if any of the hydraulic components are serviced, bleed the hydraulic system as described in Section 8.

   b) To check "clutch spin down time", run the engine at normal idle speed with the transmission in Neutral (clutch pedal up – engaged). Disengage the clutch (pedal down), wait nine seconds and shift the transmission into Reverse. No grinding noise should be heard. A grinding noise would indicate component failure in the pressure plate assembly or the clutch disc.

   c) To check for complete clutch release, run the engine (with the brake on to prevent movement) and hold the clutch pedal approximately 1/2-inch from the floor mat. Shift the transmission between 1st gear and Reverse several times. If the shift is not smooth, component failure is indicated. Measure the slave cylinder pushrod travel. With the clutch pedal completely depressed the slave cylinder pushrod should extend substantially. If the pushrod will not extend very far or not at all, check the fluid level in the clutch master cylinder.

   d) Visually inspect the clutch pedal bushing at the top of the clutch pedal to make sure there is no sticking or excessive wear.

   e) Under the vehicle, check that the clutch fork is solidly mounted on the ball stud.

Note: *Because access to the clutch components is an involved process, any time either the engine or transmission is removed, the clutch disc, pressure plate assembly and release bearing should be carefully inspected and, if necessary, replaced with new parts. Since the clutch disc is normally the item of highest wear, it should be replaced as a matter of course if there is any question about its condition.*

---

3   Clutch components – removal, inspection and installation

Refer to illustrations 3.4, 3.5, 3.8, 3.10, 3.12a, 3.12b and 3.14

Warning: *Dust produced by clutch wear and deposited on clutch components contains asbestos, which is hazardous to your health. DO NOT blow it out with compressed air and DO NOT inhale it. DO NOT use gasoline or petroleum-based solvents to remove the dust. Brake system cleaner should be used to flush the dust into a drain pan. After the clutch components are wiped clean with a rag, dispose of the contaminated rags and cleaner in a covered container.*

Removal

1   Access to the clutch components is normally accomplished by removing the transmission, leaving the engine in the vehicle. If, of course, the engine is being removed for major overhaul, then the opportunity should always be taken to check the clutch for wear and replace worn components as necessary. The following procedures assume that the engine will stay in place.

2   Remove the slave cylinder (see Section 7).

3   Referring to Chapter 7 Part A, remove the transmission from the vehicle. Support the engine while the transmission is out. Preferably, an engine hoist should be used to support it from above. However, if a jack is used underneath the engine, make sure a piece of wood is used between the jack and oil pan to spread the load. **Caution:** *The pickup for the oil pump is very close to the bottom of the oil pan. If the pan is bent or distorted in any way, engine oil starvation could occur.*

4   To support the clutch disc during removal, install a clutch alignment tool through the clutch disc hub **(see illustration)**.

5   Carefully inspect the flywheel and pressure plate for indexing marks. The marks are usually an X, an O or a white letter. If they cannot be found,

3.8   Check the flywheel for cracks, hot spots (as seen in this photo) and other obvious defects (slight imperfections can be removed by a machine shop)

3.10   Once the clutch disc is removed, the rivet depth can be measured and compared to the Specifications

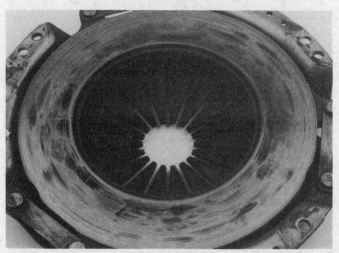

3.12a   Examine the pressure plate friction surface for score marks, cracks and evidence of overheating

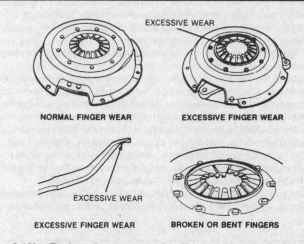

EXCESSIVE WEAR

NORMAL FINGER WEAR   EXCESSIVE FINGER WEAR

EXCESSIVE WEAR

EXCESSIVE FINGER WEAR   BROKEN OR BENT FINGERS

3.12b   Replace the pressure plate if excessive wear is noted

apply marks yourself so the pressure plate and the flywheel will be in the same alignment during installation **(see illustration)**.

6   Turning each bolt only 1/2-turn at a time, slowly loosen the pressure plate-to-flywheel bolts. Work in a diagonal pattern and loosen each bolt a little at a time until all spring pressure is relieved. Then hold the pressure plate securely and completely remove the bolts, followed by the pressure plate and clutch disc.

Inspection

7   Ordinarily, when a problem occurs in the clutch, it can be attributed to wear of the clutch driven disc assembly. However, all components should be inspected at this time.

8   Inspect the flywheel for cracks, heat checking, grooves or other signs of obvious defects **(see illustration)**. If the imperfections are slight, a machine shop can machine the surface flat and smooth, which is highly recommended regardless of the surface appearance. Refer to Chapter 2 for the flywheel removal and installation procedure.

9   Inspect the pilot bearing (Section 5).

10   Inspect the lining on the clutch disc. There should be at least 1/16-inch of lining above the rivet heads. Check for loose rivets, warpage, cracks, distorted springs or damper bushings and other obvious damage **(see illustration)**. As mentioned above, ordinarily the clutch disc is replaced as a matter of course, so if in doubt about the condition, replace it with a new one.

11   Ordinarily, the release bearing is also replaced along with the clutch disc (see Section 4).

12   Check the machined surfaces and the diaphragm spring fingers of the pressure plate **(see illustrations)**. If the surface is grooved or otherwise damaged, replace the pressure plate. Also check for obvious damage, distortion, cracking, etc. Light glazing can be removed with medium grit emery cloth. If a new pressure plate is indicated, new or factory-rebuilt units are available.

Installation

13   Before installation, carefully wipe the flywheel and pressure plate machined surfaces clean with a rubbing-alcohol dampened rag. It's important that no oil or grease is on these surfaces or the lining of the clutch disc. Handle these parts only with clean hands.

8

3.14   Insert a clutch alignment tool or metal bar through the middle of the clutch and move the disc until it's centered

4.5   Removing the retaining clips from the clutch release bearing

14   Position the clutch disc and pressure plate with the clutch held in place with an alignment tool **(see illustration)**. Make sure it's installed properly (most replacement clutch discs will be marked "flywheel side" or something similar – if not marked, install the clutch with the damper springs or bushings toward the transmission).

15   Tighten the pressure plate-to-flywheel bolts only finger-tight, working around the pressure plate.

16   Center the clutch disc by ensuring the alignment tool is through the splined hub and into the pilot bearing in the crankshaft. Wiggle the tool up, down or side-to-side as needed to bottom the tool in the pilot bearing. Tighten the pressure plate-to-flywheel bolts a little at a time, working in a criss-cross pattern to prevent distorting the cover. After all of the bolts are snug, tighten them to the specified torque. Remove the alignment tool.

17   Using high-temperature grease, lubricate the inner groove of the release bearing (refer to Section 4). Also place grease on the fork fingers.

18   Install the clutch release bearing as described in Section 4.

19   Install the transmission, slave cylinder and all components removed previously, tightening all fasteners to the proper torque specifications.

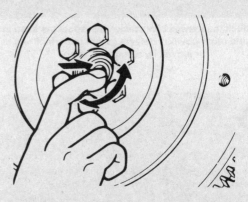

5.5   Turn the pilot bearing by hand while applying pressure – if it's rough or noisy, a new one should be installed

---

4   Clutch release bearing – replacement

Refer to illustration 4.5

1   The sealed release bearing, although designed for long life, is worth replacing at the same time that the other clutch components are being replaced or serviced.

2   Deterioration of the release bearing should be suspected when there are signs of grease leakage or if the unit is noisy when spun with the fingers.

3   Remove the rubber dust boot which surrounds the release lever at the bellhousing opening.

4   Using a screwdriver, unhook and detach the retaining spring from the pivot stud in the bellhousing.

5   Remove the retaining clips **(see illustration)**.

6   The clutch release bearing and hub assembly can now be removed. **Note:** *Make sure that the release fork has not been cracked or bent. Slowly turn the front face of the release bearing, making sure it turns freely and without any noise. The release bearing is prelubricated and should not be washed in solvent.*

7   If necessary, remove the release bearing from its hub using a two or three-jaw puller.

8   Press on the new bearing, but apply pressure only to the center race. If necessary, take the bearing and hub to a local repair shop, as considerable force may be needed to press the bearing on.

9   Reassembly is the reverse of disassembly, but apply multi-purpose grease to the internal recess of the release bearing hub.

10   Also apply similar grease to the pivot points of the clutch release lever, the sliding surface of the bearing sleeve and the splines on the transmission input shaft. **Note:** *Apply only a thin coat of grease to these points, as too much grease will run onto the friction lining when hot, causing damage to the clutch disc surfaces.*

---

5   Pilot bearing – inspection, removal and installation

Refer to illustrations 5.5, 5.9, 5.10 and 5.11

1   The clutch pilot bearing is a needle roller type bearing which is pressed into the rear of the crankshaft. Its primary purpose is to support the front of the transmission input shaft. The pilot bearing should be inspected whenever the clutch components are removed from the engine. Due to its inaccessibility, if you are in doubt as to its condition, replace it with a new one. **Note:** *If the engine has been removed from the vehicle, disregard the following steps which do not apply.*

2   Remove the transmission (refer to Chapter 7 Part A).

3   Remove the clutch components (Section 3).

Inspection

4   Using a clean rag, wipe the bearing clean and inspect for any excessive wear, scoring or obvious damage. A flashlight will be helpful to direct light into the recess.

5.9 Fill the opening behind the bearing with grease, . . .

5.10 . . . then force the bearing out hydraulically with a metal bar slightly smaller than the bore in the bearing – when the hammer strikes the bar, the grease will transmit force to the back side of the bearing and push it out

5   Check to make sure the pilot bearing turns smoothly and quietly **(see illustration)**. If the transmission input shaft contact surface is worn or damaged, replace the bearing with a new one.

Removal

6   Removal can be accomplished with a special puller but an alternative method also works very well.
7   Find a solid steel bar which is slightly smaller in diameter than the bearing. Alternatives to a solid bar would be a wood dowel or a socket with a bolt fixed in place to make it solid.
8   Check the bar for fit – it should just slip into the bearing with very little clearance.
9   Pack the bearing and the area behind it (in the crankshaft recess) with heavy grease **(see illustration)**. Pack it tightly to eliminate as much air as possible.
10   Insert the bar into the bearing bore and lightly hammer on the bar, which will force the grease to the backside of the bearing and push it out **(see illustration)**. Remove the bearing and clean all grease from the crankshaft recess.

Installation

11   To install the new bearing, lubricate the outside surface with oil, then drive it into the recess with a hammer and a socket with an outside diameter that matches the bearing outer race **(see illustration)**.
12   Install the clutch components, transmission and all other components removed to gain access to the pilot bearing.

---

6   Clutch master cylinder – removal, overhaul and installation

Refer to illustrations 6.2, 6.4 and 6.5
Caution: *Do not allow brake fluid to contact any painted surfaces of the vehicle, as damage to the finish may result.*

Removal

1   Disconnect the master cylinder pushrod from the clutch pedal.
2   Disconnect the hydraulic line from the master cylinder and drain the fluid into a suitable container **(see illustration)**.
3   Remove the master cylinder flange mounting nuts and withdraw the unit from the engine compartment.

5.11   Using a hammer and socket, carefully drive the new bearing into place

8

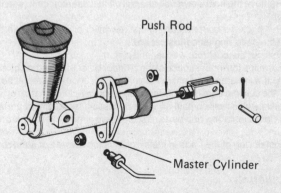

Push Rod

Master Cylinder

6.2 Clutch master cylinder mounting details

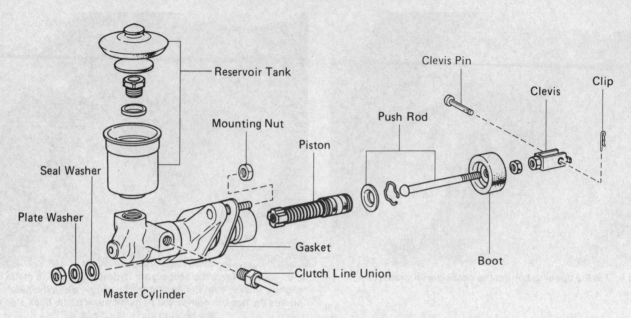

6.4   Exploded view of the clutch master cylinder components

6.5   Pry the snap-ring out of the clutch master cylinder with a small screwdriver

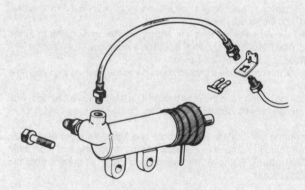

7.2   Clutch release cylinder mounting details

Overhaul

4   Remove the hold-down bolt and pull off the reservoir tank **(see illustration)**.

5   Pull back the boot and, using a screwdriver or snap-ring pliers, remove the snap-ring **(see illustration)**.

6   Pull out the pushrod, washer and piston.

7   Examine the inner surface of the cylinder bore. If it is scored or exhibits bright wear areas, the entire master cylinder should be replaced.

8   If the cylinder bore is in good condition, obtain a clutch master cylinder rebuild kit, which will contain all of the necessary replacement parts.

9   Prior to installing any parts, first dip them in brake fluid to lubricate them.

10   Installation of the parts in the cylinder is the reverse of removal.

Installation

11   Installation is the reverse of removal, but check the pedal height and freeplay as described in Chapter 1 and bleed the hydraulic system (see Section 8).

7   Clutch release cylinder – removal, overhaul and installation

Refer to illustrations 7.2 and 7.4

Removal

1   The clutch release cylinder is located at the left side of the transmission bellhousing.

2   Place a container under the release cylinder. Using a flare-nut wrench, disconnect the release cylinder hydraulic hose from the rigid hydraulic line at the bracket, then unscrew the hose from the cylinder **(see illustration)**.

3   Remove the two bolts and pull off the release cylinder.

Overhaul

4   Pull off the dust boot and pushrod, then tap the cylinder gently on a block of wood to extract the piston and spring **(see illustration)**.

5   Unscrew and remove the bleeder screw.

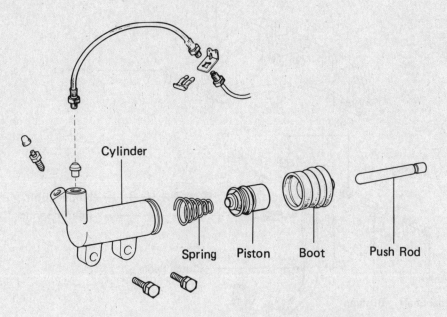

Cylinder

Spring   Piston   Boot   Push Rod

7.4   Exploded view of the clutch release cylinder components

6   Examine the surfaces of the piston and cylinder bore for scoring or bright wear areas. If any are found, discard the cylinder and purchase a new one.

7   If the components are in good condition, wash them in clean brake fluid. Remove the seal and discard it, noting carefully which way the seal lips face.

8   Obtain a repair kit which will contain all the necessary new items.

9   Install the new seal using your fingers only to manipulate it into position. Be sure the lips face in the proper direction.

10   Dip the piston assembly in clean brake fluid before installing it and the spring into the cylinder.

11   Reinstall the bleeder.

12   Complete the reassembly by installing the pushrod and the dust cover. Be sure the dust cover is secure on the cylinder housing.

Installation

13   Installation is the reverse of the removal procedure. After the cylinder has been installed, bleed the clutch hydraulic system as described in Section 8.

---

8   **Clutch hydraulic system – bleeding**

Refer to illustration 8.3

Caution: *Do not allow the brake fluid to contact any painted surface of the vehicle, as damage to the finish will result.*

1   Bleeding will be required whenever the hydraulic system has been dismantled and reassembled and air has entered the system.

2   First fill the fluid reservoir with clean brake fluid which has been stored in an airtight container. Never use fluid which has drained from the system or has bled out previously, as it may contain moisture or other contaminants.

3   Attach a rubber or plastic bleed tube to the bleeder screw on the release cylinder and immerse the open end of the tube in a glass jar containing an inch or two of fluid **(see illustration)**.

4   Open the bleeder screw about half a turn and have an assistant quickly depress the clutch pedal completely. Tighten the screw and then have

clutch pedal slowly released with the foot completely removed. Repeat this sequence of operations until air bubbles are no longer ejected from the open end of the tube beneath the fluid in the jar.

5   After two or three strokes of the pedal, make sure the fluid level in the reservoir has not fallen too low. Keep it full of fresh fluid, otherwise air will be drawn into the system.

6   Tighten the bleeder screw on a pedal down stroke (do not overtighten it), remove the bleed tube and jar, top-up the reservoir and install the cap.

7   If an assistant is not available, alternative 'one-man' bleeding operations can be carried out using a bleed tube equipped with a one-way valve or a pressure bleed kit, both of which should be used in accordance with the manufacturer's instructions.

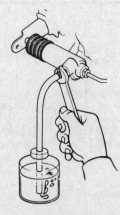

8.3   When bleeding the clutch hydraulic system, a hose is connected to the bleeder valve at the release cylinder and then submerged in brake fluid – air will be seen as bubbles in the container and the tube

8

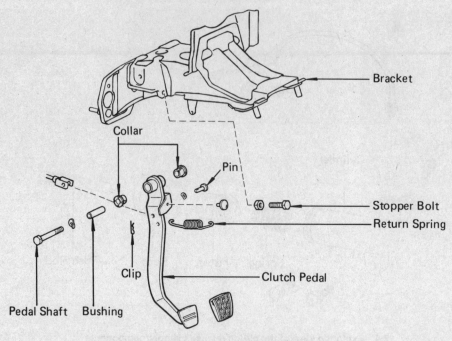

9.1   Clutch pedal mounting details

---

9   Clutch pedal assembly – removal and installation

Refer to illustration 9.1

1   Remove the pedal return spring **(see illustration)**.
2   Disconnect the master cylinder pushrod from the pedal by removing the spring clip and pulling out the pushrod pin.
3   Remove the pedal shaft.
4   Remove the clutch pedal with its bushings and collar.
5   Clean the parts in solvent and replace any that are damaged or excessively worn.
6   Installation is the reverse of the removal procedure. During installation, apply multi-purpose grease to the pedal boss, return spring, pedal shaft and pushrod pin.

10   Driveshafts, differentials and rear axles – general information

Refer to illustration 10.1

These models use a two-piece driveshaft which incorporates a center bearing at the rear of the front shaft. This driveshaft uses three universal joints; one at the transmission end, one behind the center bearing and one at the differential flange **(see illustration)**.

All universal joints are of the solid type and can be replaced separate from the driveshaft.

The driveshafts are finely balanced during production and whenever they are removed or disassembled, they must be reassembled and reinstalled in the exact manner and positions they were originally in, to avoid excessive vibration.

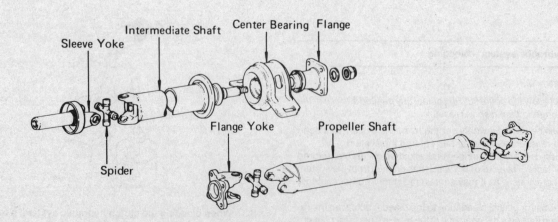

10.1   Typical early model driveshaft components – exploded view

12.2 Mark the relationship of the driveshaft flange and the differential companion flange to facilitate realignment

12.4 Remove the center bearing mounting bolts

12.6 Support the driveshaft as it's withdrawn from the transmission

The rear axle is of the semi-floating type, having a 'banjo' design axle housing, which is held in proper alignment with the body by the rear suspension.

Mounted in the center of the rear axle is the differential, which transfers the turning force of the driveshaft to the rear axleshafts, on which the rear wheels are mounted.

The axleshafts are splined at their inner ends to fit into the splines in the differential gears; outer support for the shaft is provided by the rear wheel bearing.

Because of the complexity and critical nature of the differential adjustments, as well as the special equipment needed to perform the operations, we recommend any disassembly of the differential be done by a Toyota dealer service department or other qualified repair facility.

11 Driveline inspection

1 Raise the rear of the vehicle and support it securely on jackstands.
2 Slide under the vehicle and visually inspect the condition of the driveshaft. Look for any dents or cracks in the tubing. If any are found, the driveshaft must be replaced.

3 Check for any oil leakage at the front and rear of the driveshaft. Leakage where the driveshaft enters the transmission indicates a defective rear transmission seal. Leakage where the driveshaft enters the differential indicates a defective pinion seal. For these repair operations refer to Chapters 7 and 8 respectively.
4 While still under the vehicle, have an assistant turn the rear wheel so the driveshaft will rotate. As it does, make sure that the universal joints are operating properly without binding, noise or looseness. On long bed models, listen for any noise from the center bearing, indicating it is worn or damaged. Also check the rubber portion of the center bearing for cracking or separation, which will necessitate replacement.
5 The universal joint can also be checked with the driveshaft motionless, by gripping your hands on either side of the joint and attempting to twist the joint. Any movement at all in the joint is a sign of considerable wear. Lifting up on the shaft will also indicate movement in the universal joints.
6 Finally, check the driveshaft mounting bolts at the ends to make sure they are tight.

12 Driveshafts – removal and installation

Refer to illustrations 12.2, 12.4, 12.6 and 12.8

Removal

1 Raise the rear of the vehicle and place it on jackstands.
2 Mark the edges of the driveshaft rear flange and the differential pinion flange so they can be realigned upon installation (**see illustration**).
3 Remove the four nuts and bolts.
4 Remove the two bolts holding the center support bearing to the chassis (**see illustration**).
5 Push the shaft forward slightly to disconnect the rear flange.
6 Pull the yoke from the transmission while supporting the driveshaft with your hand (**see illustration**).
7 While the driveshafts are removed, insert a plug in the transmission to prevent lubricant leakage.

Installation

8 Installation is the reverse of the removal procedures. During installation, make sure all flange marks line up. When connecting the center bearing support to the frame, first finger-tighten the two mounting bolts, then make sure that the bearing bracket is at right angles to the driveshaft and that the bearing center line is in the center of the bracket hole (**see illustration**). Tighten all nuts and bolts to the specified torque.

8

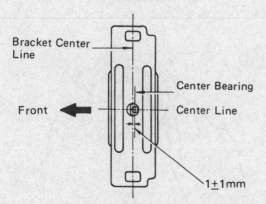

12.8 Correct alignment of the center bearing and bracket hole

**13.1   Make marks on the flanges before
separating the center universal joint**

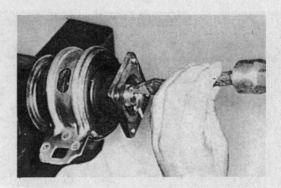

**13.3a   Use a punch or chisel to unstake the nut
retainer collar**

13   Center bearing – replacement

Refer to illustrations 13.1, 13.3a, 13.3b, 13.4, 13.5 and 13.8

1   Remove the driveshaft (Section 12). Mark the relationship of the center flange to the front section of the driveshaft **(see illustration)**.
2   Remove the four bolts that attach the center flange to the companion flange **(see illustration 13.1)**.
3   The center joint nut is staked to prevent it from working loose. To remove it, first use a punch to knock the staking back out, then unscrew it from the shaft **(see illustration)**. To keep the flange from turning, either obtain a special tool designed for this purpose, or one can be made using a flat steel bar and old bolts inserted through the flange holes **(see illustration)**. The bar should be drilled to match at least two of the flange holes.
4   Mark the companion flange in relation to the slot in the threaded shaft **(see illustration)**.
5   Clamp the flange in a vise and use a hammer and punch to tap the shaft out of the flange **(see illustration)**.
6   Using a dial indicator, inspect all driveshafts for damage and runout. If the shaft runout is greater than the specified maximum, replace the shaft with a new one.

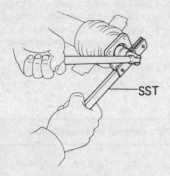

**13.3b   A special tool is required to unscrew the center
bearing nut**

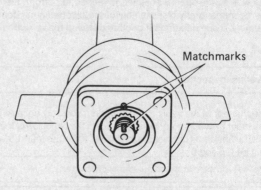

**13.4   Mark the relationship of the companion flange and
the threaded shaft**

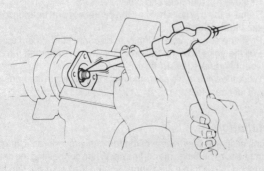

**13.5   Use a hammer and punch to tap the shaft out of
the center bearing flange**

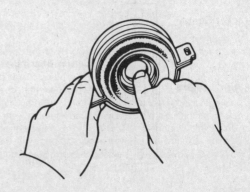

13.8   Make sure the center bearing turns freely

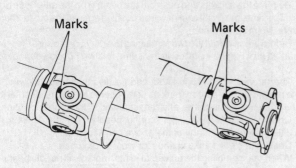

14.4   Mark the relationship of the driveshaft yoke and the flange yoke before disassembling the joint

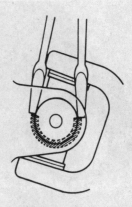

14.6   Push the snap-rings from the U-joint bearings with two small screwdrivers

7   Inspect the yokes and flanges for damage and wear. If damage or wear is found, replace the appropriate parts with new ones.

8   Inspect the center support bearing for wear or damage and make sure that the bearing turns freely **(see illustration)**. If any faults are found, replace the center bearing with a new one.

9   For inspection procedures for the universal joints, see Section 14.

10   Begin reassembly of the driveshaft by coating the splines of the intermediate shaft with multi-purpose grease and placing the bearing on the shaft.

11   Place the flange on the shaft and align the marks.

12   Using the special tool or the one you have fabricated (see Step 3) to hold the flange, tighten a new center joint nut to press the bearing into position.

13   Tighten the nut to 123 to 144 ft-lbs.

14   Loosen the nut, then tighten it to the torque listed in this Chapter's Specifications.

15   Using a hammer and punch, stake the center joint nut.

16   Attach the rear shaft to the center support bearing flange by aligning the marks on the flanges and connecting the four bolts and nuts.

14   Universal joints – inspection and replacement

Refer to illustrations 14.4, 14.6, 14.8a and 14.8b

Inspection

1   Wear in the needle roller bearings is characterized by vibration in the transmission, noise during acceleration, and in extreme cases of lack of lubrication, metallic squeaking and ultimately grating and shrieking sounds as the bearings disintegrate.

2   It is easy to check if the needle bearings are worn with the driveshaft in position by trying to turn the shaft with one hand, the other hand holding the rear axle flange when the rear universal joint is being checked or the front half coupling when the front universal joint is being checked. Any movement between the driveshaft and the front half couplings, and around the rear half couplings, is indicative of considerable wear.

3   With the driveshafts removed, the universal joints may be checked by holding the shaft in one hand and turning the yoke or flange with the other. If the axial movement is more than specified, replace the bearings with new ones.

Replacement

Note: *The universal joints can be replaced only on some 1980 through 1983 four-door models. On all other models, the driveshaft and/or inter-*

mediate shaft must be replaced as a unit if the universal joints are worn or damaged.

4   To replace the universal joints, with the driveshaft removed, place alignment marks on each shaft yoke and flange yoke **(see illustration)**.

5   Using a ratchet extension or similar tool and hammer, tap lightly on the bearing outer races of the universal joint to relieve pressure on the snap-rings.

6   Using two screwdrivers, remove the snap-rings from their grooves **(see illustration)**.

7   To remove the bearings from the yokes, you will need two sockets. One should be large enough to fit into the yoke where the snap-rings were installed and the other should have an inside diameter just large enough for the bearings to fit into when they are forced out of the yoke.

8   Mount the universal joint in a vise with the large socket on one side of the yoke and the small socket on the other side, pushing against the bearing. Carefully tighten the vise until the bearing is pushed out of the yoke and into the large socket **(see illustration)**. If it cannot be pushed all the

14.8a   Use a vise, a large socket (left) and a small socket (right) to press the bearing out of the universal joint

8

14.8b   Pliers may be needed to finish removing the bearing

way out, remove the universal joint from the vise and use pliers to finish removing the bearing **(see illustration)**.

9   Reverse the sockets and push out the bearing on the other side of the yoke. This time, the small socket will be pushing against the cross-shaped universal joint spider end.

10   Before pressing out the two remaining bearings, make sure the spider is marked so it can be installed in the same relative position during reassembly.

11   The remaining universal joints can be disassembled following the same procedure. Be sure to mark all components for each universal joint so they can be kept together and reassembled in the proper position.

12   Check the spider journals for scoring, needle roller impressions, rust and pitting. Replace it if any of the above conditions exist.

13   Check the sleeve yoke splines for wear and damage.

14   When reassembling the universal joints, replace all needle bearings, dust seals and snap-rings with new ones.

15   Before reassembly, pack each grease cavity in the spiders with a small amount of grease. Also, apply a thin coat of grease to the new needle bearing rollers and the roller contact areas on the spiders.

16   Apply a thin coat of grease to the dust seal lips and install the bearings and spider into the yoke using the vise and sockets that were used to remove the old bearings. Work slowly and be very careful not to damage the bearings as they are being pressed into the yokes.

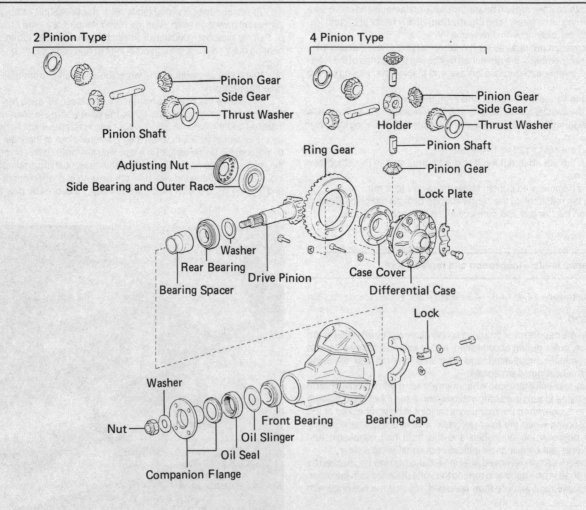

15.1   Differential components – exploded view

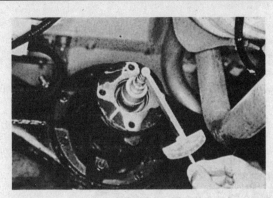

15.5   A torque wrench is used to measure drive pinion preload

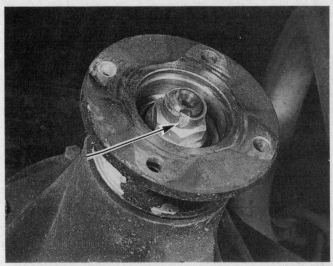

15.14   Use a hammer and small punch to stake the nut collar into the slot in the shaft

17   Press the bearings in until the width of the snap-ring grooves is approximately 0.0020-inch (0.05 mm). Install snap-rings of the same thickness on each side (four sizes are available) and make sure there is no clearance between the bearing cups and the snap-rings. Tap the yoke with a hammer to move the cups slightly.

18   Make sure that the spider moves freely in the bearings, then check the axial play. If it is excessive, thicker snap-rings must be used to reduce the play.

19   Assemble the remaining universal joint(s) and rejoin the two driveshafts.

15   Pinion oil seal – replacement

Refer to illustrations 15.1, 15.5 and 15.14

1   A pinion shaft oil seal failure results in the leakage of differential gear lubricant past the seal and onto the driveshaft yoke or flange. The seal is replaceable without removing or disassembling the differential **(see illustration)**.

2   Raise the vehicle and place it on jackstands.

3   Remove the drain and fill plugs from the differential housing and allow the differential lubricant to drain into a suitable container. When the draining is complete, loosely install the drain plug.

4   Disconnect the driveshaft from the companion flange (Section 12).

5   Using an inch-pound torque wrench, slowly turn the pinion shaft nut and measure the preload **(see illustration)** within the backlash of the drive pinion gear and the ring gear (if the axles and wheels turn, the backlash has been exceeded and the torque figure is incorrect). The preload should be within the Specifications. If it is not, the bearing spacer must be replace prior to installation of the new oil seal. This procedure should be performed by a dealer service department or a reputable repair shop, as special tools are required.

6   Using a hammer and chisel, loosen the staked part of the companion flange nut.

7   Using a holder (as described in Section 14, Step 4) to hold the flange, remove the nut.

8   Using a hammer, tap the companion flange off the shaft.

9   After noting what the visible side of the oil seal looks like, carefully pry it out of the differential with a screwdriver or pry bar. Be careful not to damage the splines on the pinion shaft.

10   Lubricate the new seal lip with molybdenum disulphide grease and carefully install it in position in the differential. Using a short section of pipe of the proper circumference and a hammer, carefully drive the seal into a depth of 0.157-inch (4.0 mm) for axles with a 6.7-inch ring gear and to a depth of 0.020-inch (0.5 mm) for axles with a 6.38-inch ring gear.

11   Clean the sealing lip contact surface of the differential companion flange. Apply a thin coat of molybdenum disulfide grease to the seal contact surface and the shaft spines and, using a plastic hammer, tap the companion flange onto the shaft.

12   Coat the threads of a new companion flange nut with multi-purpose grease and, using the holder to hold the flange, tighten the nut to the torque specified before the preload test.

13   Turn the companion flange several times to snug down the bearing.

14   Using a torque wrench, see how much torque is required to turn the pinion shaft within the range of gear backlash (if the axles and wheel turn, the backlash has been exceeded and the torque figure is incorrect). This torque is the drive pinion bearing preload. If the preload is greater then that specified, the bearing spacer will have to be replaced by an authorized dealer service department or reputable repair shop. If the preload is less than that specified, retighten the nut 5 to 10 degrees at a time until the specified preload is reached. If the maximum torque specified is reached before the preload figure is obtained, the bearing spacer must be replaced by a qualified repair facility. **Note:** *Do not back off the pinion nut to reduce the preload.* Once the proper preload is reached, stake the nut with a punch and hammer **(see illustration)**.

15   Connect the driveshaft to the companion flange (Section 12).

16   Tighten the drain plug in the rear axle housing and fill the housing to the proper level with the recommended gear lubricant (see the Recommended lubricants and fluids Section at the front of Chapter 1). Install the filler plug and tighten it fully.

17   Lower the vehicle to the ground, test drive it and check around the differential end yoke for evidence of leakage.

16   Rear axleshafts and oil seals – removal and installation

Refer to illustrations 16.1, 16.6, 16.7, 16.11, 16.12 and 16.16

Removal

1   The axleshafts can be removed without disturbing the differential assembly. They must be removed in order to replace the bearings and oil seals and when removing the differential carrier from the rear axle housing

8

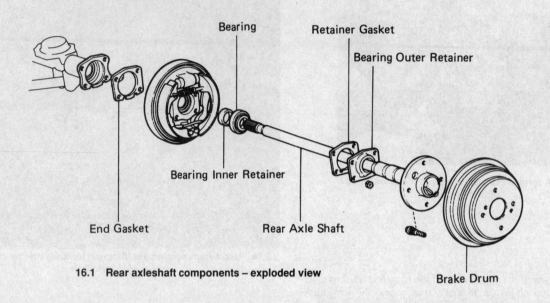

16.1   Rear axleshaft components – exploded view

16.6   Working through the hole in the axleshaft flange, remove
the backing plate nuts

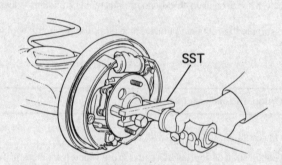

16.7   A rear axle adapter plate and slide hammer may be needed
to remove the rear axleshaft

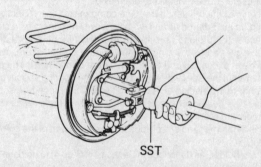

16.11   Pull the oil seal out of the axle housing with a
slide hammer

(see illustration). **Note:** *Read the entire Section before starting work.*
2   Raise the rear of the vehicle and support it securely on jackstands. Block the front wheels to keep the vehicle from rolling.
3   Remove the rear wheels and release the parking brake, then remove the brake drums or calipers and discs (see Chapter 9 for details).
4   Remove the drain plug and drain the differential oil into a suitable container. When the draining is complete, finger-tighten the drain plug in place.
5   Disconnect the brake line (see Chapter 9 for details).
6   Remove the brake backing plate mounting nuts **(see illustration)**.
7   The axleshaft, complete with the brake assembly, can now be pulled out from the rear axle. If the axleshaft will not pull out by hand, a slide hammer can be attached to the wheel studs using an adapter plate **(see illustration)**.
8   Since the wheel bearing is press fitted onto the axleshaft, its removal and installation will require the use of special tools and either a special puller or a hydraulic press. This operation should be left to a dealer or other suitably equipped shop.

9   Inspect the axleshaft for wear or damage.
10   Inspect the seal for wear or damage.
11   To replace the seal, remove it with a puller **(see illustration)**.

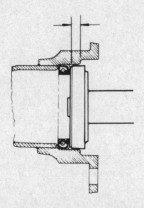

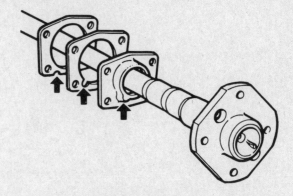

16.12 Press the new seal into the housing the specified distance

16.16 The notches in the gaskets must line up with the bulge in the bearing retainer (arrows)

Installation

12 Place the new seal in position, then use a seal driver or section of appropriately sized pipe and a hammer to drive in the new seal to a depth of 0.232-inch (5.9 mm) on drum brake models or 0.079-inch (2.0 mm) on disc brake models **(see illustration)**.

13 To install the axleshaft, first apply multi-purpose grease to the inner lip of the oil seal.

14 Clean the contact surfaces of the axle housing and brake backing plate. Apply gasket sealant to both sides of the end gasket and retainer gasket.

15 Place the end gasket in position on the axle housing with the notch facing down.

16 Place the backing plate and bearing retainer on the axleshaft. Install the axleshaft, aligning the gasket notches with the hole in the bearing retainer **(see illustration)**.

17 Attach the axle and backing plate assembly to the axle housing and tighten the four retaining nuts to the specified torque.

18 Following installation, tighten the drain plug and fill the differential with the proper grade and amount of lubricant as specified in Chapter 1.

19 Install the drum or caliper and disc and bleed the brakes (Chapter 9) and install the wheel.

17 Differential – removal and installation

Removal

1 Raise the rear of the vehicle and support it securely on jackstands. Block the front wheels to keep the vehicle from rolling.

2 Remove the drain plug and drain the differential oil into a suitable container, then reinstall the drain plug finger-tight.

3 Remove the rear axleshafts (see Section 16).

4 Disconnect the driveshaft flange from the companion flange (see Section 12).

5 Remove the nuts from the differential carrier assembly and pull out the differential assembly. The mounting nuts should be loosened in steps, following a criss-cross pattern.

6 The overhaul of the rear axle differential unit is not within the scope of the home mechanic, due to the specialized gauges and tools which are required. Where the unit requires servicing or repair, due to wear or excessive noise, it is most economical to exchange it for a factory reconditioned assembly.

7 Before reinstalling the rear differential, scrape all traces of old gasket from the mating surfaces of the axle housing. Position a new gasket on the housing (use a silicone-type gasket sealant).

Installation

8 Installation is the reverse of the removal procedure.

9 Following installation, fill the differential with the proper grade and quantity of lubricant (see Chapter 1).

18 Rear axle assembly – removal and installation

Removal

1 Loosen the rear wheel lug nuts, raise the vehicle and support it securely on jackstands placed underneath the frame. Remove the wheels.

2 Support the rear axle assembly with a floor jack placed underneath the differential.

3 Remove the shock absorber lower mounting nuts and compress the shocks to get them out of the way (Chapter 10).

4 Disconnect the driveshaft from the differential companion flange and hang it with a piece of wire from the underbody (Section 12).

5 Unbolt the stabilizer bar from the stabilizer bar link, if so equipped (Chapter 10).

6 Disconnect the parking brake cables.

7 Disconnect the flexible brake hose from the junction block on the rear axle housing. Plug the end of the hose or wrap a plastic bag tightly around it to prevent excessive fluid loss and contamination.

Leaf spring models

8 Remove the U-bolt nuts from under the leaf spring seats (Chapter 10).

9 Raise the rear axle assembly off of the leaf spring and carefully maneuver it out from between the leaf spring and the frame. It would be a good idea to have an assistant on hand, as the assembly is very heavy.

Coil spring models

10 Disconnect the lateral control rod and the upper and lower control arms (Chapter 10).

11 Slowly lower the axle to the floor with the jack while an assistant steadies it. Remove the axle from under the vehicle.

Installation

12 Installation is the reverse of the removal procedure. Be sure to tighten all suspension bolts and nuts (see Chapter 10) and the driveshaft companion flange bolts to the Specified torque.

8

Chapter 9   Brakes

Contents

Specifications

General

Brake fluid type . . . . See Chapter 1
Power brake booster pushrod-to-master cylinder piston clearance
   1980 through 1982 . . . . 0.004 to 0.020 in (0.01 to 0.05 mm)
   1983-on . . . . 0.0 in (0.0 mm)

Disc brakes

Minimum brake pad thickness . . . . See Chapter 1
Disc runout . . . . 0.0059 in (0.15 mm)
Minimum front disc thickness*
   1980 through 1983 . . . . 0.453 in (11.5 mm)
   1984-on . . . . 0.669 in (17.0 mm)
Minimum rear disc thickness* . . . . 0.354 in (9.0 mm)

Drum brakes

Minimum brake shoe lining thickness	See Chapter 1
Maximum drum diameter*	9.079 in (230.6 mm)
Parking brake adjusting lever-to-brake shoe clearance	0.138 in (0.35 mm)

Refer to the marks stamped on the disc or drum (they supersede information printed here)

Parking brake

Clicks until full engagement	
1980 through 1983	4 to 7
1984-on	
Drum	5 to 8
Disc	6 to 9

Torque specifications   Ft-lbs (unless otherwise indicated)

Brake booster mounting nuts	96 to 132 in-lbs
Master cylinder-to-brake booster nuts	96 to 132 in-lbs
Front brake caliper-to-torque plate	
1980 through 1983	40 to 54
1984-on	14
Torque plate-to-steering knuckle	
1980 through 1983	29 to 39
1984-on	47
Caliper bridge bolt	58 to 68
Brake disc-to-front hub	47
Rear brake caliper-to-torque plate	14
Rear disc brake torque plate bolts	34
Drum brake backing plate-to-rear axle housing	44 to 53
Wheel cylinder-to-backing plate	84 to 120 in-lbs
Wheel lug nuts	See Chapter 1

1   General information

General information

The brake system in the vehicles covered by this manual is a split system design. It incorporates two separate circuits, one for the front brakes and one for the rear brakes. With this system if one circuit fails, the other circuit will still function.

The master cylinder is designed for the split system and incorporates a primary piston for one circuit and a secondary piston for the other.

A vacuum booster unit is used which draws vacuum from the intake manifold to add power assistance to the normal brake pressure.

The front (and on some later models, the rear) wheels are equipped with disc brakes. These consist of a flat, disc-like rotor which is attached to the axle and wheel. Around one section of the rotor is mounted a stationary caliper assembly which houses two hydraulically-operated disc brake pads. On some models the inner pad is mounted to a piston facing the inner surface of the rotor, while the outer pad is mounted to a yoke and faces the outer surface of the rotor. When the brake pedal is applied, brake fluid pressure forces both pads against the rotor. The pressure and resultant friction on the rotor is what slows the wheel.

The rear drum brakes are of the leading-trailing shoe type. Fluid pressure from the master cylinder forces the rear wheel cylinder pistons outward, which in turn forces the brake shoes against the spinning brake drum attached to the rear wheel. The force of the brake shoes against the drum is what slows the wheel. The wheel cylinders contain two operating pistons which contact both brake shoes. Adjustment is automatic, occurring when the parking brake is applied.

Precautions

There are some general notes and cautions involving the brake system on this vehicle:

a) Use only DOT 3 brake fluid in this system.
b) The brake pads and linings may contain asbestos fibers which are hazardous to your health if inhaled. Whenever you work on brake system components, carefully clean all parts with brake cleaner. Do not allow the fine asbestos dust to become airborne.
c) Safety should be paramount whenever any servicing of the brake components is performed. Do not use parts or fasteners which are not in perfect condition, and be sure that all clearances and torque specifications are adhered to. If you are at all unsure about a certain procedure, seek professional advice. Upon completion of any brake system work, test the brakes carefully in a controlled area before putting the vehicle into normal service. If a problem is suspected in the brake system, do not drive the vehicle until the fault is corrected.
d) Tires, load and front end alignment are factors which also affect braking performance.

2   Brake pads – replacement

Warning: *Disc brake pads must be replaced on both wheels at the same time – never replace the pads on only one wheel. Also, the dust created by the brake system may contain asbestos, which is harmful to your health. NEVER blow it out with compressed air and don't inhale any of it. An approved filtering mask should be worn when working on the brakes. Do not, under any circumstances, use petroleum-based solvents to clean brake parts. Use brake cleaner or denatured alcohol only!*

Note: *It is a good idea to work on only one side at a time so that the other brake can be used as a guide if difficulties are encountered during reassembly. Also, use only high quality, nationally recognized brand name brake parts.*

Front brakes

1980 through 1983

Refer to illustrations 2.3, 2.4, 2.5 and 2.7

1   Remove the cover from the brake fluid reservoir, siphon off about two-thirds of the brake fluid into a container and discard it.

2   Loosen the wheel lug nuts, raise the front of the vehicle and support it securely on jackstands. Remove the front wheels.

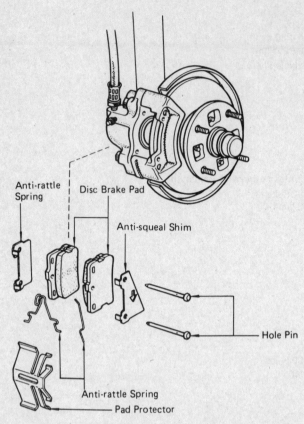

2.3   Brake pad arrangement – 1980 through 1983 models

8   Apply a thin coat of disc brake grease to the upper and lower openings of the caliper and to the anti-squeal shims. Insert the brake pads and anti-squeal shims into the caliper, making sure the arrows on the shims point in the direction of forward wheel rotation.
9   Install the anti-rattle spring, the pad retaining pins, springs and pad protector. Mount the front wheel and tighten the lug nuts to the specified torque.
10   Perform the same steps to the other side. **Warning:** *Pump the brake pedal several times before driving the vehicle to bring the pads in contact with the brake disc. Check the brake fluid level, topping it off if necessary. Make sure the brakes are working smoothly and make several low speed stops before taking the vehicle into a traffic situation.*

1984-on
Refer to illustrations 2.12, 2.13a, 2.13b and 2.14

11   Perform Steps 1 and 2 of this Section.
12   Using a large C-clamp, push the piston back into its bore **(see illustration)**.
13   Remove the slide pin and pivot the caliper up on the main pin **(see illustration)**. Insert a bolt into the torque plate to hold the caliper up out of the way **(see illustration)**.
14   Remove the two pads and anti-squeal shim, anti-rattle springs, pad guide plate and support plate from the torque plate **(see illustration)**.
15   Refer to Section 4 and inspect the brake disc.
16   Apply disc brake grease to the anti-squeal shim and install it to the inner pad.
17   Install new anti-rattle springs, pad guide plate and support plate in the torque plate.
18   Place the new pads (and anti-rattle springs, if equipped) in the torque plate.
19   Rotate the caliper down into position, tightening the slide pin to the specified torque. Install the front wheel and tighten the lug nuts to the specified torque.
20   Repeat the procedure on the other front brake. **Warning:** *Pump the brake pedal several times before driving the vehicle to bring the pads into contact with the brake disc. Check the brake fluid level, topping it off if necessary. Make sure the brakes are working smoothly and make several low speed stops before taking the vehicle into a traffic situation.*

Rear brakes
Refer to illustrations 2.22, 2.23, 2.27 and 2.28

21   Perform Steps 1 and 2 of this Section.
22   Remove the lower bolt and pivot the caliper up on the main pin **(see illustration)**.
23   Remove the two pads and anti-squeal shims, anti-rattle springs, pad guide plate and support plate from the torque plate **(see illustration)**.
24   Refer to Section 4 and inspect the brake disc.
25   Apply disc brake grease to the anti-squeal shims and install them.
26   Install new anti-rattle springs, pad guide plate and support plate in the torque plate.

3   Detach the pad protector from the caliper **(see illustration)**.
4   Use needle-nose pliers to detach the lower ends of the anti-rattle springs from the pad, then rotate the springs out **(see illustration)**.
5   Pull the pins out with a pair of pliers **(see illustration)**.
6   Using a pair of large pliers, squeeze each pad against the caliper housing to push the pistons into their bores, making room for the new brake pads. Do this slowly, alternating between each end of the pad, to ensure the pistons are compressed evenly and don't become cocked in the bores.
7   Slide the anti-squeal shims out, followed by the two pads, out of the caliper **(see illustration)**. Inspect the brake disc as described in Section 4.

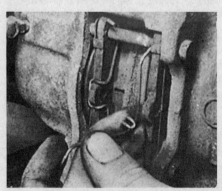

2.4   Detach the anti-rattle springs from the pads

2.5   Use pliers to pull the pad retaining pins out

2.7   Pull out the anti-squeal shims, followed by the pads

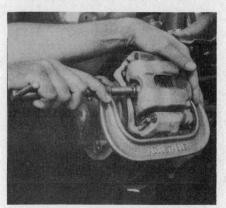

2.12   Using a large C-clamp, push the piston back into the caliper bore – note that one end of the clamp is on the flat area near the brake hose fitting and the other end (screw end) is pressing against the outer brake pad

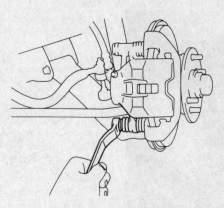

2.13a   Remove the slide pin and pivot the caliper up

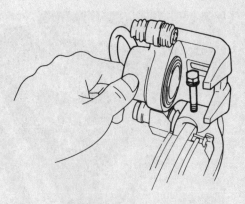

2.13b   Insert a bolt into the torque plate to hold the caliper up

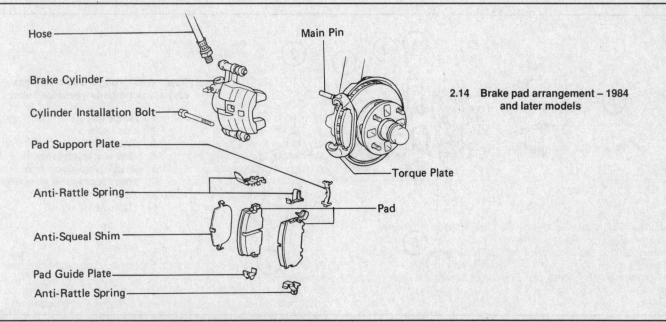

Hose

Brake Cylinder

Cylinder Installation Bolt

Pad Support Plate

Anti-Rattle Spring

Anti-Squeal Shim

Pad Guide Plate

Anti-Rattle Spring

Main Pin

Torque Plate

Pad

2.14   Brake pad arrangement – 1984 and later models

2.22 On rear calipers, after removing the lower mounting bolt, pivot the caliper up on the upper guide pin and separate the pads from the disc (note the locations of the wear indicator and the other pad components to help during installation)

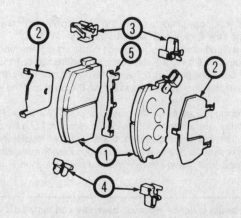

2.23   Along with the rear pads, remove the . . .

1   Brake pads
2   Anti-squeal shim
3   Anti-rattle springs
4   Pad support plate
5   Pad guide plate

9

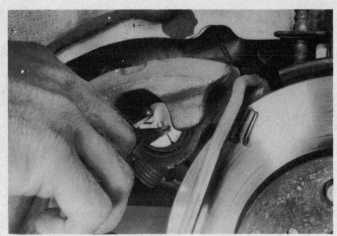

2.27   When installing the rear pads, you may have to push back the caliper piston – using needle-nose pliers, turn the piston clockwise while pushing in until it locks

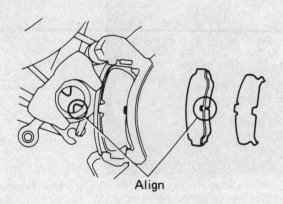

2.28   The protrusion on the rear pad fits into the cutout in the piston

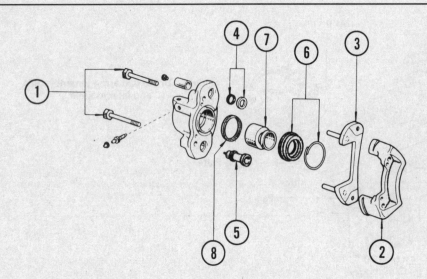

3.6a   1980 through 1983 disc brake caliper components – exploded view

1   Bridge bolt
2   Outer body
3   Torque plate
4   Dust seal and retainer
5   Torque plate pin bushing
6   Piston boot and retaining ring
7   Piston
8   Piston seal

27   Use needle-nose pliers to retract the caliper piston to make enough room for the new, thicker pad **(see illustration)**.

28   Place the pads and anti-rattle springs in the torque plate, making sure the pad protrusion fits into the piston notch **(see illustration)**, then rotate the caliper down into position, tightening the installation bolt to the specified torque. Install the rear wheel and tighten the lug nuts to the specified torque.

29   Repeat the procedure on the other rear brake. **Warning:** *Pump the brake pedal several times before driving the vehicle to bring the pads into contact with the brake disc. Check the brake fluid level, topping it off if necessary. Make sure the brakes are working smoothly and make several low speed stops before taking the vehicle into a traffic situation.*

3   Disc brake caliper – removal, overhaul and installation

Refer to illustrations 3.6a, 3.6b, 3.7, 3.9, 3.10 and 3.15

Note: *The following procedure applies to all caliper designs used on the vehicles covered by this manual. If an overhaul is indicated (usually because of fluid leakage or stuck pistons) explore all options before begin-*

ning the job. New and factory rebuilt calipers are available on an exchange basis, which makes this job quite easy. If it is decided to rebuild the calipers, make sure a rebuild kit is available before proceeding.

Removal

1   Disconnect the brake line from the caliper and plug it to keep contaminants out of the brake system and to prevent losing any more brake fluid than is necessary. Unbolt the brake line bracket from the caliper (on models so equipped).

Front brake

2   On 1980 thru 1983 models, remove the two caliper mounting bolts and lift the caliper off the brake disc.

3   On 1984 and later models, remove the lower slide pin, rotate the caliper up and slide it off the main pin.

Rear brake

Note: *Since disassembly and overhaul of the rear disc brake caliper requires special tools not usually available to the home mechanic, this job should be left to your Toyota dealer service department or a properly equipped brake shop. You can, however, remove the caliper yourself and reinstall it after it is overhauled (or replace it with a rebuilt unit).*

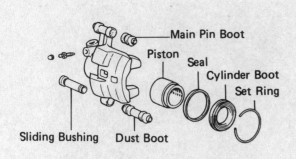

3.6b 1984 and later front brake caliper components – exploded view

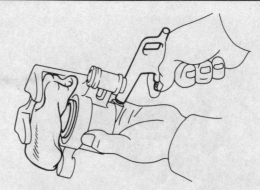

3.7 With the caliper padded to catch the piston, use compressed air to force the piston out of the bore – make sure your hands and fingers are not between the piston and caliper

3.9 Use a non-metallic tool to remove the piston seal from the groove in the cylinder – a pencil works well (metal tools can scratch the bore surface)

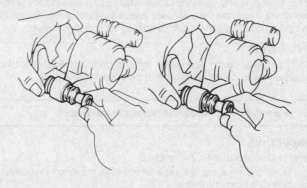

3.10 On each side of the caliper, push the sliding bushing up through the boot and pull it out, then remove the dust boots (1984 and later calipers only)

4   Remove the lower bolt, rotate the caliper up and slide it off the main pin.

Overhaul

Warning: *Do not, under any circumstances, use petroleum-based solvents to clean brake parts. Use only clean brake fluid, brake system cleaner or denatured alcohol. Allow all parts to dry, preferably using compressed air to blow out all passages. Make sure the compressed air is filtered, as a harmful lubricant residue will be present in unfiltered systems.*

5   On 1980 through 1983 models, place the caliper securely in a vise, remove the two bridge bolts and detach the caliper body from the bridge plate and outer body **(see illustration 3.6a)**. Set the bridge plate and outer body aside.

6   To overhaul the caliper, remove the rubber boot retaining ring and the rubber boot **(see illustrations)**. Before you remove the piston, place a wood block in the center of the caliper to prevent damage to the piston upon removal.

7   To remove the piston from the caliper, apply compressed air to the brake fluid hose connection on the caliper body **(see illustration)**. Place

rags or a wood block between the piston and caliper frame to prevent damage to the piston when it comes out. Use only enough air pressure to ease the piston out of the bore. **Warning:** *Be careful not to place your fingers between the piston and the caliper as the piston may come out with some force.*

8   Inspect the mating surfaces of the piston and caliper bore wall. If there is any scoring, rust, pitting or bright areas, replace the complete caliper unit with a new one.

9   If these components are in good condition, remove the rubber seal from the caliper bore using a wooden or plastic tool (metal tools may cause bore damage). Be careful not to damage the cylinder bore **(see illustration)**.

10   On 1984 and later models, push the sliding bushing out of the caliper housing and remove the two rubber boots from both ends **(see illustration)**. On 1980 through 1983 models the sliding bushings and boots are located in the torque plate.

11   Wash all the components in clean brake fluid, brake cleaner or alcohol.

12   To reassemble the caliper, you should already have the correct rebuild kit for your vehicle. **Note:** *During reassembly apply silicone based grease (supplied with the rebuild kit) between the sliding bushing and the bushing sleeve.*

13   Submerge the new piston seal and the piston in brake fluid and install them into the caliper bore. Do not force the piston into the bore, but make sure that it is squarely in place, then apply firm (but not excessive) pressure to install it.

14   Install the new rubber boot and retaining ring.

9

3.15   Press the torque plate pins evenly into the caliper body

4.4a   Check disc runout with a dial indicator – if the reading exceeds the maximum allowable runout, the disc must be resurfaced or replaced

15   On 1980 through 1983 models, apply brake assembly lube to the torque plate pins and insert the torque plate into the caliper body **(see illustration)**. Assemble the outer body, torque plate and caliper, then install the bridge bolts. Tighten the bridge bolts to the specified torque.

Installation

16   To install the caliper, reverse the removal procedure. Be sure to bleed the system by following the procedure described in Section 9.

---

4   Brake disc – inspection, removal and installation

Inspection

Refer to illustrations 4.4a, 4.4b and 4.9

1   Loosen the wheel lug nuts, raise the vehicle and support it securely on jackstands. Remove the wheel.

2   Remove the brake caliper as outlined in Section 3. It's not necessary to disconnect the brake hose. After removing the caliper bolts, suspend the caliper out of the way with a piece of wire. Don't let the caliper hang by the hose and don't stretch or twist the hose. On rear disc brakes, install two lug nuts so the disc will remain flat against the hub flange during inspection.

3   Visually check the disc surface for score marks and other damage. Light scratches and shallow grooves are normal after use and may not always be detrimental to brake operation, but deep score marks – over 0.015-inch (0.38 mm) – require disc removal and refinishing by an automotive machine shop. Be sure to check both sides of the disc. If pulsating

has been noticed during application of the brakes, suspect disc runout.

4   To check disc runout, place a dial indicator at a point about 1/2-inch from the outer edge of the disc **(see illustration)**. Set the indicator to zero and turn the disc. The indicator reading should not exceed the specified allowable runout limit. If it does, the disc should be refinished by an automotive machine shop. **Note:** *Professionals recommend resurfacing of brake discs regardless of the dial indicator reading (to produce a smooth, flat surface that will eliminate brake pedal pulsations and other undesirable symptoms related to questionable discs). At the very least, if you elect not to have the discs resurfaced, deglaze the brake pad surface with medium-grit emery cloth (use a swirling motion to ensure a non-directional finish)* **(see illustration)**.

5   The disc must not be machined to a thickness less than the specified minimum refinish thickness. The minimum wear (or discard) thickness is cast into the disc (either near the hub or on the outer edge). The disc thickness can be checked with a micrometer **(see illustration)**.

Removal and installation

Refer to illustration 4.9

6   If it has been determined while performing the inspection procedures in this Section that the brake disc must be removed and/or replaced, perform the following procedure. **Note:** *If the front disc is to be taken to a machine shop to be refinished, do not remove the disc from the axle hub. Take the entire disc/hub assembly.*

Front disc brake

7   On 1984 and later calipers, remove the two torque plate-to-steering knuckle bolts and the torque plate.

4.4b   Using a swirling motion, remove the glaze from the disc with emery cloth or sandpaper

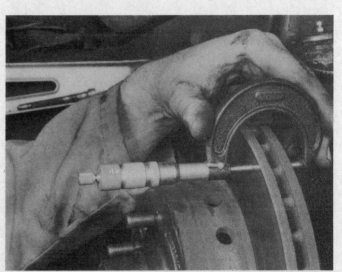

4.5   Measure the disc thickness at several points with a micrometer

4.9   The disc is retained to the hub by four bolts

8   Remove the axle hub (see Chapter 1).
9   Remove the disc from the axle hub by removing the four retaining bolts **(see illustration)**.
10   Install a new disc and tighten the four bolts, following a criss-cross pattern, to the specified torque.
11   Install the axle hub and adjust the front bearing preload (Chapter 1).

Rear disc brake

12   Remove the torque plate-to-rear hub bolts and lift the torque plate off.
13   Installation is the reverse of removal.

5   Rear brake shoes – replacement

Refer to illustrations 5.2a, 5.2b, 5.3, 5.6, 5.7, 5.10, 5.11, 5.20 and 5.23
Warning: *Drum brake shoes must be replaced on both wheels at the same time – never replace the shoes on only one wheel. Also, the dust created by the brake system may contain asbestos, which is harmful to your health. Never blow it out with compressed air and do not inhale any of it. An approved filtering mask should be worn whenever servicing the brake system. Do not, under any circumstances, use petroleum-based solvents to clean brake parts. Use brake cleaner or denatured alcohol only.*

Caution: *Whenever the brake shoes are replaced, the retractor and hold-down springs should also be replaced. Due to the continuous heating/cooling cycle that the springs are subjected to, they lose their tension over a period of time and may allow the shoes to drag on the drum and wear at a much faster rate than normal. When replacing the rear brake shoes, use only high quality nationally recognized brand name parts.*

1   Remove the rear wheels and drums according to the brake check instructions in Chapter 1. Perform all drum brake checks as described in Chapter 1. It is a good idea to disassemble only one brake at a time so the other brake can be used as a guide if difficulties are encountered during reassembly.
2   Using a brake spring tool, remove the adjuster return spring and adjuster **(see illustrations)**. Note the locations of the adjuster assembly components to facilitate installation. Also note that the right-hand adjuster screw has right-hand threads and that the left-hand adjuster has left-hand threads.

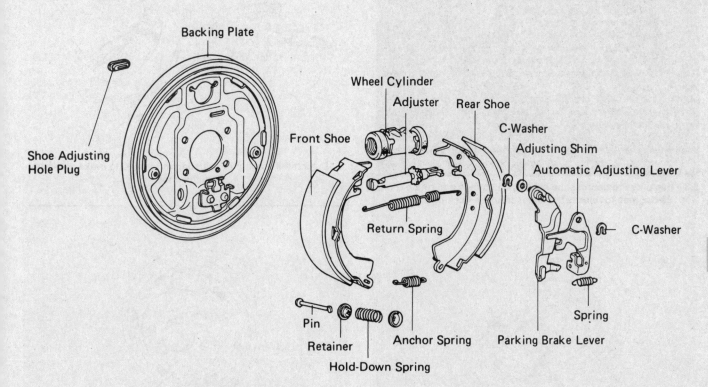

Backing Plate

Shoe Adjusting Hole Plug

Wheel Cylinder

Adjuster

Rear Shoe

Front Shoe

C-Washer

Adjusting Shim

Automatic Adjusting Lever

C-Washer

Return Spring

Spring

Pin

Retainer

Hold-Down Spring

Anchor Spring

Parking Brake Lever

5.2a   Exploded view of the drum brake components

9

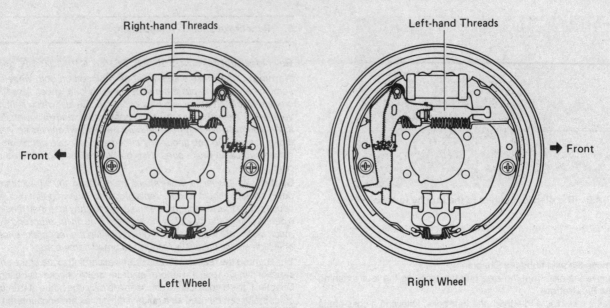

Right-hand Threads

Left-hand Threads

Front ◀

➡ Front

Left Wheel

Right Wheel

5.2b   Assembled view of the drum brake

5.3   Use pliers to depress the hold-down springs and rotate them 90-degrees to release the shoes from the backing plate

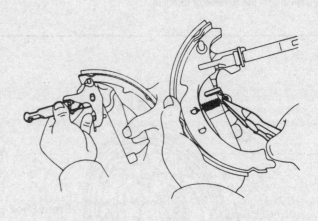

5.6   Detach the automatic adjusting strut/parking brake assembly from the shoe

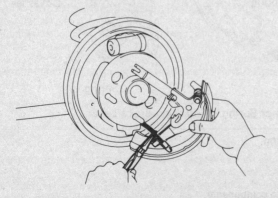

5.7   Compress the parking brake cable spring with a pair of pliers, then unhook the cable from the lever

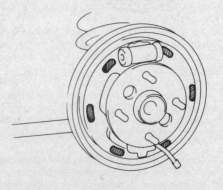

5.10   Lubricate the shoe contact points on the backing plate with high-temperature brake grease

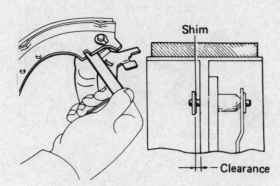

5.11   Replace the shim (available at a dealer) if the shoe-to-adjusting lever clearance is out of specification

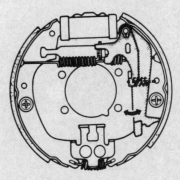

5.20   Check to see if the adjuster bolt turns by moving the bottom of the adjuster lever (arrow)

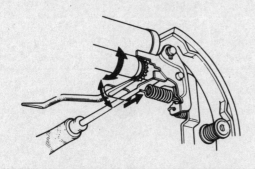

5.23   A screwdriver and brake adjuster tool (or two screwdrivers) are used to adjust the rear brake shoes – to retract the shoes, push the adjuster lever off the star wheel and turn the wheel as required

3   Using a pair of pliers or a hold-down tool, remove the front shoe hold-down spring and pin **(see illustration)**.

4   Remove the front brake shoe and tension spring that goes between the front and rear shoes.

5   Remove the rear shoe hold-down spring and pin, then remove the rear shoe.

6   Remove the automatic adjusting strut and tension spring from the automatic adjusting lever **(see illustration)**.

7   Disconnect the parking brake cable from the parking brake lever **(see illustration)**.

8   Using a screwdriver, remove the C-clips, parking brake lever and automatic adjusting lever from the rear shoe.

9   Be sure to check the wheel cylinders. Even if no leakage is found coming from the cylinders, it is advisable to rebuild or replace them when new linings are installed, as the new linings will put added strain on the cylinder components (see Section 6).

10   Installation is basically the reverse of removal. Lubricate the brake shoe contact points with a brake lube designed specifically for this purpose **(see illustration)**. Use grease sparingly and take care not to get it on the brake shoe lining material. Make sure the brake lining material is clean. Use a special cleaner for this purpose if any oil or grease has contacted the friction surface.

11   Using pliers, attach the parking brake lever and automatic adjusting lever to the new rear shoe with new C-clips. Check the clearance between the brake shoe and adjuster lever to make sure it is no more than 0.0138-inch (0.35 mm). If it is not within specification, replace the shim **(see illustration)**.

12   Connect the parking brake cable to the parking brake lever.

13   Connect the strut and shorter tension spring to the automatic adjusting lever.

14   Set the rear brake shoe in place with the end of the shoe inserted in the wheel cylinder.

15   Using a hold-down spring tool, install the rear shoe hold-down spring and pin.

16   Install the return spring between the front and rear shoes.

17   Position the adjuster, then set the front brake shoe in place with the end of the shoe inserted in the wheel cylinder. Make sure that the adjuster is properly seated in both brake shoes.

18   Install the front hold-down spring and pin with a hold-down spring tool.

19   Using a brake spring tool, install the adjuster return spring.

20   Move the bottom of the adjuster lever back and forth, checking to see that the adjusting bolt turns **(see illustration)**. If the adjuster bolt does not turn, recheck all components you have just installed for binding or improper fit and make adjustments as necessary.

21   Before reinstalling the drum it should be checked for cracks, score marks, deep scratches and hard spots, which will appear as small discolored areas. If the hard spots cannot be removed with fine emery cloth or if any of the other conditions listed above exist, the drum must be taken to an automotive machine shop to have it turned. **Note:** *Professionals recommend resurfacing the drums whenever a brake job is done. Resurfacing will eliminate the possibility of out-of-round drums. If the drums are worn so much that they can't be resurfaced without exceeding the maximum allowable diameter (stamped into the drum), then new ones will be required. At the very least, if you elect not to have the drums resurfaced, remove the glazing from the surface with medium-grit emery cloth using a swirling motion.*

22   Adjust the brake shoes so the drum just slips over them with very little clearance. Install the wheel and tighten the lug nuts to the specified torque.

23   Rotate the wheel slowly, listening for the brake shoes dragging on the drum. If they don't, turn the adjuster screw star wheel with a screwdriver inserted through the backing plate until a slight dragging sound is heard. Then, using another small screwdriver, hold the adjuster lever off the star wheel while turning the star wheel in the opposite direction, until no brake shoe drag can be detected when the drum is rotated **(see illustration)**.

6   Wheel cylinder – removal, overhaul and installation

Refer to illustrations 6.4 and 6.7

Note: *If an overhaul is indicated (usually because of fluid leakage or sticky operation) explore all options before beginning the job. New wheel cylinders are available, which makes this job quite easy. If it's decided to rebuild the wheel cylinder, make sure that a rebuild kit is available before proceeding. Never overhaul only one wheel cylinder- always rebuild both of them at the same time.*

9

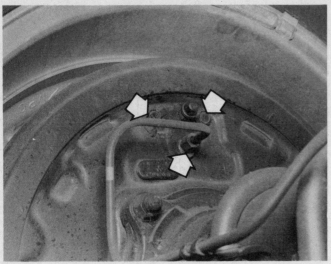

6.4   Completely loosen the brake line fitting then remove the two wheel cylinder mounting bolts (arrows)

Removal

1   Raise the rear of the vehicle and support it securely on jackstands. Block the front wheels to keep the vehicle from rolling.
2   Remove the brake shoe assembly (Section 5).
3   Remove all dirt and foreign material from around the wheel cylinder.
4   Disconnect the brake line **(see illustration)**. Don't pull the brake line away from the wheel cylinder.
5   Remove the wheel cylinder mounting bolts.
6   Detach the wheel cylinder from the brake backing plate and place it on a clean workbench. Immediately plug the brake line to prevent fluid loss and contamination.

Overhaul

7   Remove the bleeder valve, seals, pistons, boots and spring assembly from the wheel cylinder body **(see illustration)**.
8   Clean the wheel cylinder with brake fluid, denatured alcohol or brake system cleaner. **Warning:** *Do not, under any circumstances, use petroleum based solvents to clean brake parts!*
9   Use compressed air to remove excess fluid from the wheel cylinder and to blow out the passages.
10   Check the cylinder bore for corrosion and score marks. Crocus cloth can be used to remove light corrosion and stains, but the cylinder must be replaced with a new one if the defects cannot be removed easily, or if the bore is scored.
11   Lubricate the new seals with brake fluid.
12   Assemble the brake cylinder components. Make sure the seal lips face in.

Installation

13   Place the wheel cylinder in position and install the bolts.
14   Connect the brake line and install the brake shoe assembly.
15   Bleed the brakes following the procedure described in Section 10.

---

7   Master cylinder – removal, overhaul and installation

Refer to illustrations 7.6, 7.8a, 7.8b, 7.9, 7.10, 7.11a, 7.11b, 7.11c and 7.26
Note: *Before deciding to overhaul the master cylinder, check on the availability and cost of a new or factory rebuilt unit and also the availability of a rebuild kit.*

Removal

1   The master cylinder is located in the engine compartment, mounted to the power brake booster.
2   Remove as much fluid as you can from the reservoir with a syringe.

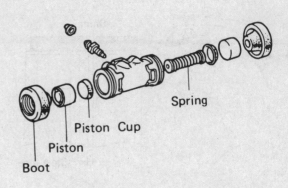

6.7   Exploded view of the wheel cylinder components

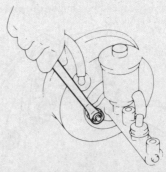

7.6   Unscrew the brake line fittings at the master cylinder, then remove the two mounting nuts

---

3   Place rags under the fittings and prepare caps or plastic bags to cover the ends of the lines once they are disconnected. **Caution:** *Brake fluid will damage paint. Cover all body parts and be careful not to spill fluid during this procedure.*
4   Loosen the tube nuts at the ends of the brake lines where they enter the master cylinder. To prevent rounding off the flats on these nuts, the use of a flare-nut wrench, which wraps around the nut, is preferred.
5   Pull the brake lines slightly away from the master cylinder and plug the ends to prevent contamination.
6   Disconnect the electrical connector at the master cylinder, then remove the two nuts attaching the master cylinder to the power booster **(see illustration)**. Pull the master cylinder off the studs and out of the engine compartment. Again, be careful not to spill the fluid as this is done.

Overhaul

7   Before attempting the overhaul of the master cylinder, obtain the proper rebuild kit, which will contain the necessary replacement parts and also any instructions which may be specific to your model.
8   Inspect the reservoir grommet for indications of leakage near the base of the reservoir. Remove the reservoir **(see illustrations)**.
9   Place the cylinder in a vise and use a punch or Phillips screwdriver to fully depress the pistons until they bottom against the other end of the master cylinder **(see illustration)**. Hold the pistons in this position and remove the stop bolt on the side of the master cylinder. Remove the two outlet plugs and the copper gaskets.
10   Carefully remove the snap-ring at the end of the master cylinder **(see illustration)**.
11   The internal components can now be removed from the cylinder bore **(see illustrations)**. Make a note of the proper order of the components so they can be returned to their original locations. **Note:** *The two springs are of different tension, so pay particular attention to their order.*

7.8a   Remove the set bolt inside the reservoir

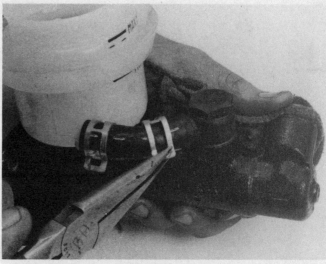

7.8b   Use pliers to release the hose clamp, then separate the hose from the master cylinder and remove the reservoir

7.9   Push the pistons in all the way and remove the piston stop bolt and copper gasket (also remove the two outlet plugs [arrows] and gaskets)

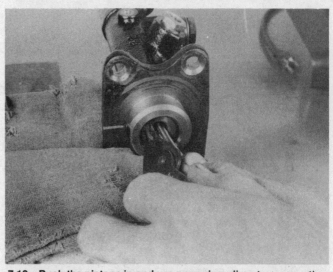

7.10   Push the pistons in and use snap-ring pliers to remove the snap-ring

7.11a   Tilt the cylinder and remove the no. 1 piston and spring

7.11b   To free the no. 2 piston and spring, tap the cylinder on a block of wood

9

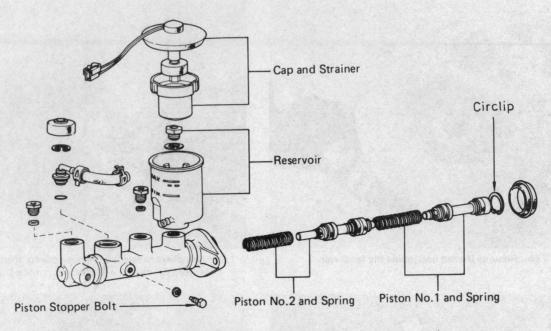

7.11c   Exploded view of the master cylinder components

7.26   Have an assistant pump the brake pedal several times, then hold it down – loosen the fitting nut, allowing the air and fluid to escape (repeat this procedure on both fittings until the fluid is clear – no air bubbles)

12   Carefully inspect the inside bore of the master cylinder. Any deep scoring or other damage will mean a new master cylinder is required.

13   Replace all parts included in the rebuild kit, following any instructions in the kit. Clean all reused parts with clean brake fluid, brake cleaner or denatured alcohol. Do not use any petroleum-based cleaners. During assembly, lubricate all parts liberally with clean brake fluid. Be sure to tighten all fittings and connections to the specified torque.

14   Push the assembled components into the bore, bottoming them against the end of the master cylinder, then install the stop bolt.

15   Install the new snap-ring, making sure it is seated properly in the groove.

16   Before installing the new master cylinder it should be bench bled. Because it will be necessary to apply pressure to the master cylinder piston and, at the same time, control flow from the brake line outlets, it is recommended that the master cylinder be mounted in a vise, with the jaws of the vise clamping on the mounting flange.

17   Insert threaded plugs into the brake line outlet holes and snug them down so that there will be no air leakage past them, but not so tight that they cannot be easily loosened.

18   Fill the reservoir with brake fluid of the recommended type (see Chapter 1).

19   Remove one plug and push the piston assembly into the master cylinder bore to expel the air from the master cylinder. A large Phillips screwdriver can be used to push on the piston assembly.

20   To prevent air from being drawn back into the master cylinder the plug must be replaced and snugged down before releasing the pressure on the piston assembly.

21   Repeat the procedure until only brake fluid is expelled from the brake line outlet hole. When only brake fluid is expelled, repeat the procedure with the other outlet hole and plug. Be sure to keep the master cylinder reservoir filled with brake fluid to prevent the introduction of air into the system.

22   Since high pressure is not involved in the bench bleeding procedure, an alternative to the removal and replacement of the plugs with each stroke of the piston assembly is available. Before pushing in on the piston assembly, remove the plug as described in Step 19. Before releasing the piston, however, instead of replacing the plug, simply put your finger tightly over the hole to keep air from being drawn back into the master cylinder. Wait several seconds for brake fluid to be drawn from the reservoir into the piston bore, then depress the piston again, removing your finger as brake fluid is expelled. Be sure to put your finger back over the hole each time before releasing the piston, and when the bleeding procedure is complete for that outlet, replace the plug and snug it before going on to the other port.

Installation

23   Install the master cylinder over the studs on the power brake booster and tighten the attaching nuts only finger-tight at this time.

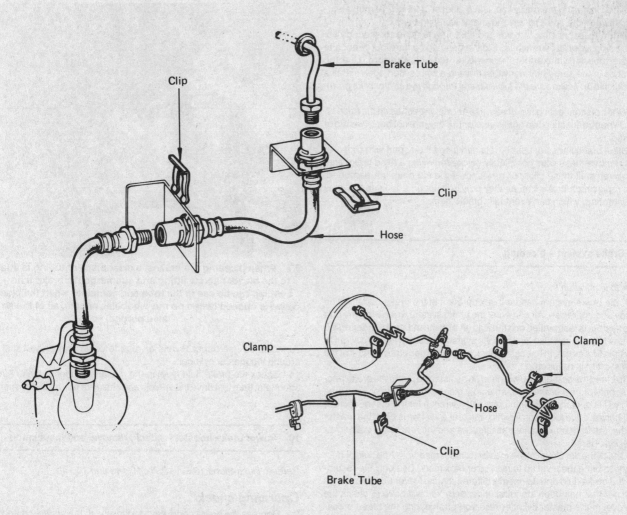

8.1 Rubber brake hoses should be inspected about every six months

24 Thread the brake line fittings into the master cylinder. Since the master cylinder is still a bit loose, it can be moved slightly in order for the fittings to thread in easily. Do not strip the threads as the fittings are tightened.

25 Tighten the mounting nuts and the brake fittings.

26 Fill the master cylinder reservoir with fluid, then bleed the master cylinder (only if it hasn't been bench bled) and the brake system as described in Section 10. To bleed the cylinder on the vehicle, have an assistant pump the brake pedal several times and then hold the pedal to the floor. Loosen the fitting nut to allow air and fluid to escape. Repeat this procedure on both fittings until the fluid is clear of air bubbles **(see illustration)**. Test the operation of the brake system carefully before placing the vehicle in normal service.

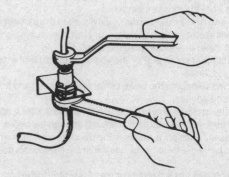

8.4 A back-up wrench must be used to keep the hose from turning, otherwise the steel brake line will twist

---

8   Brake lines and hoses – inspection and replacement

Refer to illustrations 8.1 and 8.4

1   About every six months the flexible hoses which connect the steel brake lines with the rear brakes and front calipers **(see illustration)** should be inspected for cracks, chafing of the outer cover, leaks, blisters, and other damage (see Chapter 1).

2   Replacement steel and flexible brake lines are commonly available from dealer parts departments and auto parts stores. Do not, under any circumstances, use anything other than genuine steel lines or approved flexible brake hoses as replacement items.

3   When installing the brake line, leave at least 3/4-inch (19 mm) clearance between the line and any moving or vibrating parts.

4   When disconnecting a hose and line, first remove the spring clip. Then, using a normal wrench to hold the hose and a flare-nut wrench to turn the tube nut, make the disconnection **(see illustration)**. Use the wrenches in the same manner when making a connection, then install a new clip. **Note:** *Make sure the tube passes through the center of its grommet.*

5   When disconnecting two hoses, use normal wrenches on the hose fittings. When connecting two hoses, make sure they are not bent, twisted or strained.

6   Steel brake lines are usually retained along their span with clips. Always remove these clips completely before removing a fixed brake line. Always reinstall these clips, or new ones if the old ones are damaged, when replacing a brake line, as they provide support and keep the lines from vibrating, which can eventually break them.

9   Brake system – bleeding

Refer to illustration 9.7

1   If the brake system has air in it, operation of the brake pedal will be spongy and imprecise. Air can enter the brake system whenever any part of the system is dismantled or if the fluid level in the master cylinder reservoir runs low. Air can also leak into the system through a leak too slight to allow fluid to leak out. In this case, it indicates that a general overhaul of the brake system is required.

2   To bleed the brakes, you will need an assistant to pump the brake pedal, a supply of new brake fluid, an empty glass jar, a plastic or vinyl tube which will fit over the bleeder nipple, and a wrench for the bleeder screw.

3   There are five locations at which the brake system is bled; the master cylinder, the front brake caliper assemblies and the rear brake calipers or wheel cylinders.

4   Check the fluid level at the master cylinder reservoir. Add fluid, if necessary, to bring the level up to the Full or Max mark. Use only the recommended brake fluid and do not mix different types. Never use fluid from a container that has been standing uncapped. You will have to check the fluid level in the master cylinder reservoir often during the bleed procedure. If the level drops too far, air will enter the system through the master cylinder.

5   Raise the vehicle and set it securely on jackstands, as instructed in the front of the book.

6   Remove the bleeder screw cap from the wheel cylinder or caliper assembly that is being bled. If more than one wheel must be bled, start with the one farthest from the master cylinder.

7   Attach one end of the clear plastic or vinyl tube to the bleeder screw fitting and place the other end in the glass or plastic jar submerged in a small amount of clean brake fluid **(see illustration)**.

8   Loosen the bleeder screw slightly, then tighten it to the point where it is snug yet easily loosened.

9   Have the assistant pump the brake pedal several times and hold it in the fully depressed position.

10   With pressure on the brake pedal, open the bleeder screw approximately one-half turn. As the brake fluid is flowing through the pedal, hold it in the fully depressed position, and loosen the bleeder screw momentarily. Do not allow the brake pedal to be released with the bleeder screw in the open position.

11   Repeat the procedure until no air bubbles are visible in the brake fluid flowing through the tube. Be sure to check the brake fluid level in the master cylinder reservoir while performing the bleeding operation.

12   Fully tighten the bleeder screw, remove the plastic or vinyl tube and install the bleeder screw cap.

13   Follow the same procedure to bleed the other wheel cylinder or caliper assemblies.

14   To bleed the master cylinder, have the assistant pump and hold the brake pedal. Momentarily loosen the brake line fittings, one at a time, where they attach to the master cylinder. Any air in the master cylinder will escape when the fittings are loosened. Brake fluid will damage painted

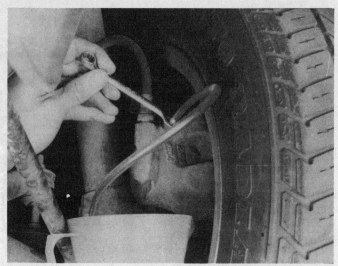

9.7   When bleeding the brakes, a clear piece of tubing is attached to the bleeder screw fitting and submerged in brake fluid – air bubbles can be see in the tube and container when the bleeder valve is opened (when no more bubbles appear, all of the air has been purged)

surfaces, so use paper towels or rags to cover and protect the areas around the master cylinder.

15   Check the brake fluid level in the master cylinder to make sure it is adequate, then test drive the vehicle and check for proper brake operation.

10   Power brake booster – check, removal and installation

Refer to illustrations 10.7a, 10.7b, 10.14a and 10.14b

Operating check

1   Depress the brake pedal several times with the engine off and make sure that there is no change in the pedal reserve distance.

2   Depress the pedal and start the engine. If the pedal goes down slightly, operation is normal.

Air tightness check

3   Start the engine and turn it off after one or two minutes. Depress the brake pedal several times slowly. If the pedal goes down farther the first time but gradually rises after the second or third depression, the booster is air tight.

4   Depress the brake pedal while the engine is running, then stop the engine with the pedal depressed. If there is no change in the pedal reserve travel after holding the pedal for 30 seconds, the booster is air tight.

Removal

5   Power brake booster units should not be disassembled. They require special tools not normally found in most automotive repair stations or shops. They are fairly complex and because of their critical relationship to brake performance it is best to replace a defective booster unit with a new or rebuilt one.

6   To remove the booster, first remove the brake master cylinder as described in Section 7.

7   Locate the pushrod clevis connecting the booster to the brake pedal **(see illustrations)**. This is accessible from the interior in front of the driver's seat.

8   Remove the clevis pin retaining clip with pliers and pull out the pin.

9   Holding the clevis with pliers, disconnect the clevis locknut with a wrench. The clevis is now loose.

10   Disconnect the hose leading from the engine to the booster. Be careful not to damage the hose when removing it from the booster fitting.

Hose

Clevis Pin   Clip   Gasket

Master Cylinder   Gasket   Brake Booster   Bracket

10.7a   Power brake booster installation details

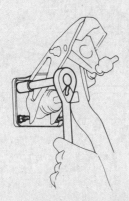

10.7b   Remove the nuts holding the brake booster and bracket to the firewall

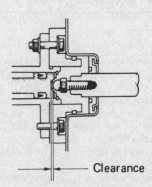

Clearance

10.14a   The booster pushrod-to-master cylinder piston clearance must be as specified

11   Remove the four nuts and washers holding the brake booster to the firewall. You may need a light to see these, as they are up under the dash area **(see illustration 10.7b).**

12   Slide the booster straight out from the firewall until the studs clear the holes and pull the booster, brackets and gaskets from the engine compartment area.

Installation

13   Installation procedures are basically the reverse of those for removal. Tighten the clevis locknut and booster mounting nuts to the specified torque figures.

14   If the power booster unit is being replaced, the clearance between the master cylinder piston and the pushrod in the vacuum booster must be measured. Using a depth micrometer or vernier calipers, measure the distance from the seat (recessed area) in the master cylinder to the master cylinder mounting flange. Next, measure the distance from the end of the vacuum booster pushrod to the mounting face of the booster (including gasket) where the master cylinder mounting flange seats. Subtract the two measurements to get the clearance **(see illustration).** If the clearance is more or less than specified, turn the adjusting screw on the end of the power booster pushrod until the clearance is within the specified limit **(see illustration).**

10.14b   To adjust the length of the booster pushrod, hold the serrated portion of the rod with a pair of pliers and turn the adjusting screw in-or-out, as necessary, to achieve the desired setting

9

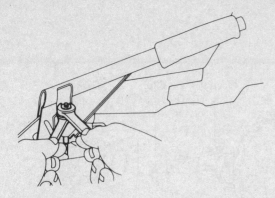

11.3   Turn the adjusting nut at the brake handle to take up slack in the parking brake cables (which will affect full engagement)

15   After the final installation of the master cylinder and brake hoses and lines, the brake pedal height and freeplay must be adjusted (see Chapter 1) and the system must be bled (see Section 9).

11   Parking brake – check and adjustment

Refer to illustration 11.3

Check

1   The parking brake system is activated by a handle assembly in the middle of the vehicle's interior which is attached to the cable system which activates are cables that run to each rear brake drum and hold the vehicle stationary by expanding the rear shoes in the brake drums or calipers. Adjustment for cable stretch is accomplished by a threaded nut at the handle. The parking brake system also is used to activate the automatic brake adjusters on the rear brake shoes. Each time the parking brake is activated, it adjusts the rear adjuster one notch until all of the slack is taken up in the brake system.
2   If the parking brake will not hold the vehicle while the check as described in Chapter 1 is performed, or if the parking brake lever does not respond within the lever click travel limit as designated in the Specifications while pulling the lever all the way up, check to confirm that the rear brake shoe clearance is correct (see Section 5). If the clearance is incorrect, adjust the clearance and recheck the parking brake operation.

Adjustment

3   Remove the center console, loosen the locknut and turn the lever adjusting screw until the travel is correct **(see illustration)**. This may require several trial-and-error adjustments to get the correct lever travel.
4   After adjusting the parking brake, confirm that the rear brakes are not dragging.
5   Tighten the locknut and install the center console.

12   Brake pedal – removal and installation

Refer to illustration 12.3

1   Remove the floor mat.
2   Disconnect the stoplight switch at the plastic connector. Pull it apart at the junction rather than pulling on the wires.
3   Remove the clip from the end of the clevis pin **(see illustration)**.
4   Pull out the clevis pin.
5   Remove the pedal spring.
6   Remove the nut from the left end of the pedal shaft while holding the right end of the shaft with a wrench.
7   Remove the pedal shaft. The brake pedal will pull down and out of the mounting bracket.
8   Disassemble the bushings and collar from the brake pedal.
9   Inspect all parts for wear or damage and replace them with new parts as needed.
10   Installation procedures are the reverse of those for removal. Coat all the bushings, the collar, the spring and the pedal pin with multipurpose light grease before installation. Before connecting the stoplight switch, adjust the pedal height (see Chapter 1).

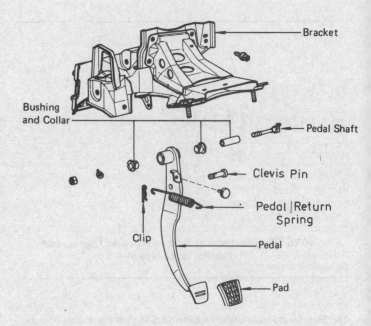

12.3   Brake pedal mounting details

Chapter 10
Suspension and steering systems

Contents

Specifications

Torque specifications

Front suspension   Ft-lbs (unless otherwise indicated)

Front strut/shock absorber upper mounting nuts	13
Strut bar-to-control arm nuts	34
Strut bar-to-bracket nut	67
Strut bar bracket-to-body bolt	48
Steering knuckle arm-to-strut assembly bolt	58
Control arm through-bolt	58

10

Torque specifications

Rear suspension

Ft-lbs (unless otherwise indicated)

Leaf spring-type
U-bolt nut	22 to 32
Shackle pin nut	37 to 50
Hanger pin nut	29 to 39
Hanger pin bolts	96 to 132 in-lbs
Shock absorber-to-body nut	14 to 22
Shock absorber-to-axle bolt	22 to 32

Coil spring-type
Lateral control rod-to-body bolt	87
Lateral control rod-to-axle bolt	47
Upper and lower control arm bolts	87
Shock absorber-to-body nut	14 to 22
Shock absorber-to-axle bolt	22 to 32

Steering system

Recirculating ball-type
Steering gear-to-frame bolt	26 to 36
Steering wheel nut	25
Pitman arm nut	101
Relay rod-to-Pitman arm nut	37 to 50
Steering shaft coupling bolt	15 to 21
Tie-rod end nut	37 to 50

Rack-and-pinion type
Tie-rod end-to-steering knuckle nut	43
Steering wheel nut	25
Steering gear-to-crossmember bolts	22 to 32
Intermediate shaft pinch bolts	26

Wheel lug nuts
Wheel lug nuts	See Chapter 1

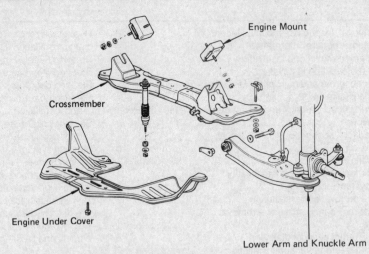

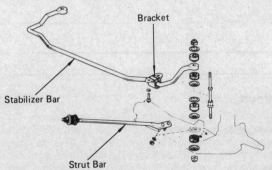

1.1   Front suspension components

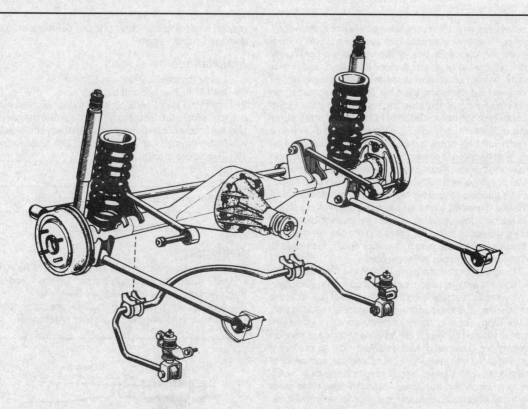

1.2a   Leaf spring rear suspension components

1.2b   Coil spring rear suspension components

10

1   General information

Refer to illustrations 1.1, 1.2a and 1.2b

The front suspension is a MacPherson strut design. The strut is attached to the chassis by studs at the top and bolts to the steering knuckle arm at the bottom. The steering knuckle is located by a control arm, which, in turn, is triangulated by a strut bar. A stabilizer bar, mounted to the front crossmember and connecting the control arms, minimizes body lean **(see illustration)**.

The rear suspension on early model consists of a solid rear axle fastened by U-bolts and plates to leaf springs with telescopic shock absorbers **(see illustration)**. On later models the axle is located by control arms, a lateral control arm and suspension is by coil springs and telescopic shock absorbers with a stabilizer bar **(see illustration)**.

Two types of steering are used on these models: a conventional recirculating ball-type steering box and rack-and-pinion. The recirculating ball steering box is bolted to the chassis and actuates the steering arms through a system of rods. The rack-and-pinion steering gear is clamped to the firewall and actuates the steering arms, which are integral with the steering knuckles. The steering column is designed to collapse in the event of an accident.

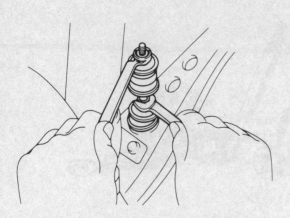

**2.3   Use two wrenches to remove the stabilizer
bar-to-control arm nut**

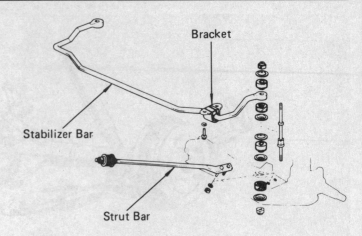

2.4   Stabilizer bar/strut bar details

Frequently, when working on the suspension or steering system components, you may come across fasteners which seem impossible to loosen. These fasteners on the under side of the vehicle are continually subjected to water, road grime, mud, etc., and can become rusted or "frozen," making them extremely difficult to remove. In order to unscrew these stubborn fasteners without damaging them (or other components), be sure to use lots of penetrating oil and allow it to soak in for awhile. Using a wire brush to clean exposed threads will also help removal of the nut or bolt and prevent damage to the threads. Sometimes a sharp blow with a hammer and punch will help break the bond between a nut and bolt threads, but care must be taken to prevent the punch from slipping off the fastener and ruining the threads. Heating the stuck fastener and surrounding area with a torch sometimes helps too, but isn't recommended because of the obvious dangers associated with fire. Long breaker bars and extension, or "cheater," pipes will increase leverage, but never use an extension pipe on a ratchet – the ratcheting mechanism could be damaged. Sometimes, turning the nut or bolt in the tightening (clockwise) direction first will help to break it loose. Fasteners that require drastic measures to unscrew should always be replaced with new ones.

Since most of the procedures that are dealt with in this Chapter involve jacking up the vehicle and working underneath it, a good pair of jackstands will be needed. A hydraulic floor jack is the preferred type of jack to lift the vehicle, and it can also be used to support certain components during various operations. **Warning:** *Never, under any circumstances, rely on a jack to support the vehicle while working on it. Whenever any of the suspension or steering fasteners are loosened or removed they must be inspected and, if necessary, replaced with new ones of the same part number or of original equipment quality and design. Torque specifications must be followed for proper reassembly and component retention. Never attempt to heat or straighten any suspension or steering components. Instead, replace bent or damaged parts with new ones.*

2   Front stabilizer bar – removal and installation

Refer to illustrations 2.3 and 2.4

Removal

1   Raise the front of the vehicle and support it securely on jackstands. Apply the parking brake and position blocks behind the rear wheels.
2   Remove one of the strut bars and its bracket (see Section 3).
3   Remove the stabilizer bar-to-control arm nut and bushings, noting how the bushings and washers are positioned **(see illustration)**.
4   Remove the stabilizer bar bracket bolts and detach the bar from the vehicle **(see illustration)**.
5   Pull the brackets off the stabilizer bar and inspect the bushings for

cracks, hardening and other signs of deterioration. If the bushings are damaged, replace them.

Installation

6   Guide the stabilizer bar into position.
7   Install the strut bar and bracket.
8   Insert the lower ends of the stabilizer bar brackets into their slots, push the brackets over the bushings and raise the bar up to the frame. Install the bracket bolts but don't tighten them completely at this time.
9   Install the stabilizer bar-to-control arm rubber bushings and nuts.
10   Tighten the bracket bolts.

3   Front strut bar – removal and installation

Refer to illustrations 3.2, 3.3a and 3.3b

Removal

1   Loosen the wheel lug nuts, raise the front of the vehicle and support it securely on jackstands. Apply the parking brake and position blocks behind the rear wheels. Remove the wheel.
2   If the bar is to be replaced, measure the distance from the staked nut to the forward mounting bolt hole **(see illustration)**.

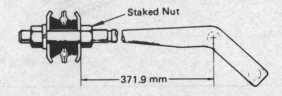

**3.2   Measure the distance from the staked nut to the first hole in
the strut bar – if it's not maintained, the caster adjustment will
be affected**

3   Remove the strut bar-to-bracket nut and the two bolts and nuts that secure the other end of the bar to the control arm **(see illustrations)**.
4   Remove the large washer and rubber bushing from the front of the bar then pull the bar straight back out of the bracket.
5   Check the bar for cracks and distortion. If the rod is distorted, it must be replaced – don't try to straighten it. Inspect the bushings for wear, cracks, hardness and general deterioration, replacing them if necessary.

3.3a To remove the strut bar, first unscrew the large nut at the front of the crossmember and remove the washer and bushing

Installation

6 Measure the distance between the staked nut and the first hole in the bar to make sure it's 14.6-inches (371.9 mm). If it is not, adjust the position of the staked nut. When installing a new strut bar, thread the staked nut onto the bar to the specified distance and stake in place.

7 Assemble the inner washer, rubber bushing and sleeve on the bar and insert it into the hole in the crossmember. Install the two bolts and nuts that secure the bar to the control arm and tighten them to the specified torque.

8 Install the outer rubber bushing, washer and nut on the front of the bar and tighten the nut to the specified torque.

9 Install the wheel and lug nuts, lower the vehicle and tighten the lug nuts to the specified torque.

10 It would be a good idea to drive the vehicle to an alignment shop to have the front wheel alignment checked and, if necessary, adjusted.

4 Front strut/shock absorber and coil spring assembly – removal, inspection and installation

Refer to illustrations 4.3, 4.4a, 4.4b and 4.5

Removal

1 Loosen the wheel lug nuts, raise the front of the vehicle and support it securely on jackstands. Apply the parking brake and position blocks behind the rear wheels. Remove the front wheel.

2 Disconnect and plug the brake hose at the bracket on the strut.

3 Remove the strut-to-body nuts **(see illustration)**.

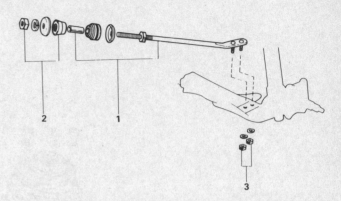

3.3b Strut bar and related components – exploded view

1	Strut bar retainer, bushing and collar	2	Bushing assembly
		3	Nuts and washers

4.3 Be sure to support the strut while removing the three strut-to-body nuts – the strut will fall if you don't (Note: Don't unscrew the nut in the center, under the plastic cover!)

4 Remove the strut-to-steering knuckle arm nuts and pry the control arm downward with a pry bar to detach the steering knuckle arm from the strut **(see illustrations)**.

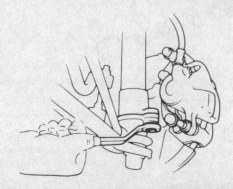

4.4a Remove the two bolts securing the steering arm to the strut, . . .

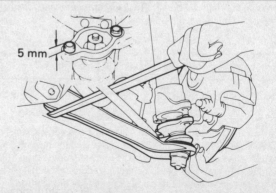

5 mm

4.4b . . . then separate the components with a pry bar (the steering arm bolt collars extend into the strut)

10

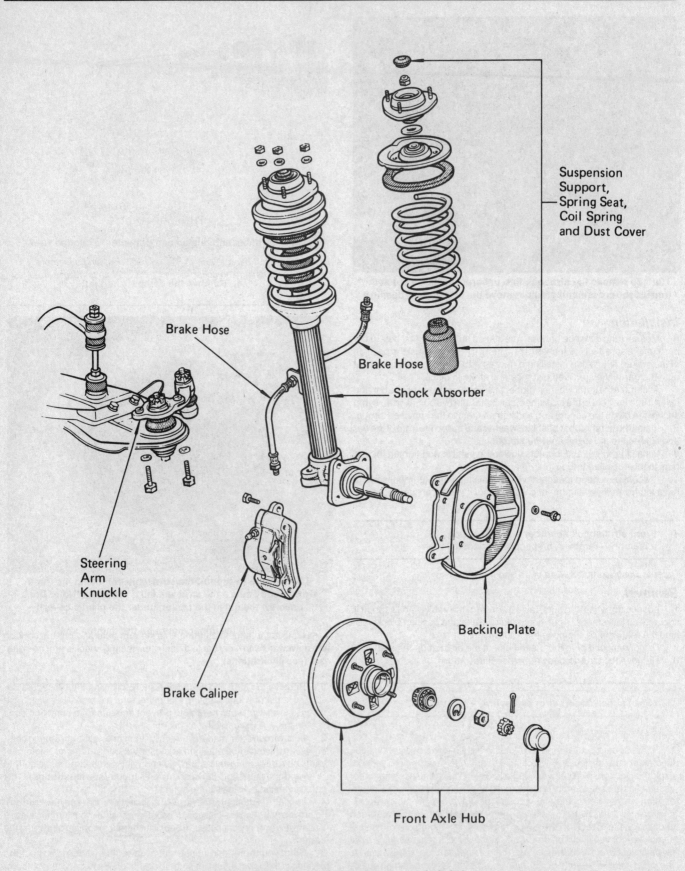

Suspension
Support,
Spring Seat,
Coil Spring
and Dust Cover

Brake Hose

Brake Hose

Shock Absorber

Steering
Arm
Knuckle

Backing Plate

Brake Caliper

Front Axle Hub

4.5   Front strut and related components – exploded view

5.3   Install the spring compressor according to the tool manufacturer's instructions and compress the spring until all pressure is relieved from the upper seat

5.4   Remove the damper shaft nut

5   Support the strut and spring assembly and remove the assembly out through the fender well **(see illustration)**.

Inspection

6   Check the strut body for leaking fluid, dents, cracks and other obvious damage which would warrant repair or replacement.
7   Check the coil spring for chips or cracks in the spring coating (this will cause premature spring failure due to corrosion).
8   If any undesirable conditions exist, proceed to Section 5 for the strut disassembly procedure.

Installation

9   Slide the steering knuckle arm into the strut flange and install the two bolts. Tighten the bolts to the specified torque.
10   Guide the strut assembly up into the fender well and insert the upper mounting studs through the holes in the body. This may require an assistant, as the strut is quite heavy and awkward. Once the studs protrude through the body, install the nuts. Tighten the nuts to the specified torque.
11   Connect the brake hose to the bracket on the strut, tightening securely. Bleed the brakes (Chapter 9).
12   Install the wheel, lower the vehicle and tighten the lug nuts to the specified torque.

5.5   Lift the upper mount off the damper shaft

5   Strut/shock absorber or coil spring – replacement

Refer to illustrations 5.3, 5.4, 5.5, 5.6, 5.12 and 5.14

1   If the struts or coil springs exhibit the telltale signs of wear (leaking fluid, loss of damping capability, chipped, sagging or cracked coil springs) explore all options before beginning any work. The strut/shock absorber assemblies are serviceable (the damper and oil can be replaced). However, strut assemblies complete with springs may be available on an exchange basis, which eliminates much time and work. Whichever route you choose to take, check on the cost and availability of parts before disassembling your vehicle. **Warning:** *Disassembling a strut assembly is a potentially dangerous undertaking and utmost attention must be directed to the job at hand, or serious bodily injury may result. Use only a high quality spring compressor and carefully follow the manufacturer's instructions furnished with the tool. After removing the coil spring from the strut assembly, set it aside in a safe, isolated area (a steel cabinet is preferred).*

2   Remove the strut and spring assembly following the procedure described in the previous Section. Mount the strut assembly in a vise. Line the vise jaws with wood or rags to prevent damage to the unit and don't tighten the vise excessively.
3   Following the tool manufacturer's instructions, install the spring compressor (which can be obtained at most auto parts stores or equipment yards on a daily rental basis) on the spring and compress it sufficiently to relieve all pressure from the suspension support **(see illustration)**. This can be verified by wiggling the spring.
4   Loosen the damper shaft nut with a socket wrench **(see illustration)**. To prevent the suspension support and damper shaft from turning, wedge a screwdriver or pry bar between one of the upper mounting studs and the socket.
5   Remove the nut and upper mount **(see illustration)**. Inspect the bearing in the upper mount for smooth operation. If it doesn't turn smoothly, replace the upper mount. Check the rubber portion of the mount for cracking and general deterioration. If there is any separation of the rubber, replace it.

10

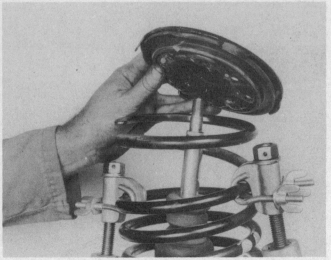

5.6   Remove the spring seat from the damper shaft

5.12   When installing the spring, make sure the lower end of the coil fits into the recessed portion of the lower seat (arrow)

5.14   The flats on the damper shaft (arrow) must match up with the flats in the spring seat

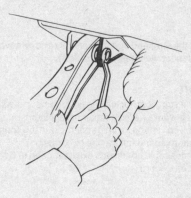

6.4   Remove the control arm through-bolt

6   Lift the spring seat and upper insulator from the damper shaft **(see illustration)**. Check the rubber spring seat for cracking and hardness, replacing it if necessary.

7   Slide the rubber bumper and dust boot off the damper shaft.

8   Carefully lift the compressed spring from the assembly and set it in a safe place, such as a steel cabinet. **Warning:** *Never place your head near the end of the spring!*

9   Check for fluid leaks around the damper shaft packing nut. Check for cracks in the strut body around this area also.

10   Check the operation of the damper by pulling the damper shaft out, making sure the resistance is constant throughout its travel. Move the shaft up-and-down, in short strokes – the resistance should be equal in both directions.

11   If the damper doesn't operate as described above, obtain a new or rebuilt strut unit and install the coil spring to it, or rebuild the strut by installing a new damper shaft/piston assembly and new shock oil.

12   Begin reassembly by carefully placing the coil spring onto the lower seat, with the end of the spring resting in the recessed portion of the seat **(see illustration)**.

13   Install the rubber bumper and dust boot to the damper shaft.

14   Install the upper insulator and spring seat, making sure that the flats in the hole in the seat match up with the flats on the damper shaft **(see illustration)**.

15   Install the dust seal and suspension support to the damper shaft.

16   Install the nut and tighten it to the specified torque.

17   Install the strut/shock absorber and coil spring assembly following the procedure outlined in the previous Section.

6   Control arm – removal, inspection and installation

Refer to illustration 6.4, 6.5a and 6.5b

Removal

1   Loosen the wheel lug nuts on the side to be dismantled, raise the front of the vehicle, support it securely on jackstands, apply the parking brake and place blocks behind the rear wheels. Remove the wheel.

2   Remove the bolts and detach the steering arm from the strut **(see illustrations 4.4a and 4.4b)**.

3   Remove the strut bar-to-control arm bolts and nuts and disconnect the stabilizer bar **(see illustration 2.4)**.

4   Remove the bolt and nut from the control arm pivot **(see illustration)**. Pry the arm from the crossmember if it is stuck.

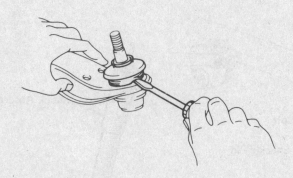

6.5a   Use a screwdriver to pry the boot from the balljoint

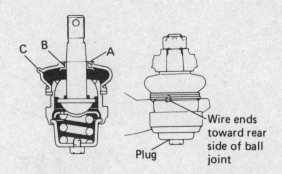

6.5b   Lubricate the contact surfaces (A and B) then install the boot with the vent (C) facing the rear of the vehicle

Inspection

5   Check the control arm for distortion and the bushings for wear, damage and deterioration. Replace a damaged or bent control arm with a new one. If the inner pivot bushing is worn, take the control arm to a dealer service department or a repair shop, as special tools are required to replace it. If the balljoint boot is torn or leaking, remove the steering knuckle arm from the balljoint by unscrewing the nut and using a puller to separate the arm from the balljoint. Cut the retaining wire and remove the boot **(see illustration)**. Install a new boot and secure it with mechanic's wire, then remove the plug and lubricate the balljoint (Chapter 1) **(see illustration)**. If the balljoint itself is damaged or worn, the control arm will have to be replaced with a new one.

Installation

6   Place the control arm into the crossmember. Install the bolt and nut, but don't tighten them completely yet.
7   Connect the outer end of the arm to the stabilizer bar and strut bar, tightening the nuts and bolts to the specified torque.
8   Place a jack under the balljoint, with a block of wood on the jack head as a cushion. Raise the control arm into position, connect the steering arm and strut and install the two bolts. Tighten the steering arm-to-strut and pivot bolts to the specified torque.
9   Install the wheel and lug nuts, lower the vehicle and tighten the lug nuts to the specified torque.

---

7   Rear shock absorber – removal and installation

Refer to illustrations 7.2 and 7.3

1   Loosen the wheel lug nuts, raise the rear of the vehicle, support it securely on jackstands. Place blocks in front of the front wheels. Remove the wheel.
2   Position a floor jack under the rear axle and raise it just enough to take some of the spring pressure off the shock absorber. Remove the shock absorber lower mounting bolt **(see illustration.)**
3   Remove the upper mounting nuts and detach the shock absorber **(see illustration)**.
4   Installation is the reverse of removal. Be sure to tighten the fasteners securely.

7.2   Rear shock absorber lower mounting details

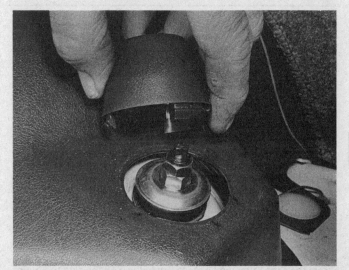

7.3   On some models a cover must be removed for access to the upper mounting nuts

10

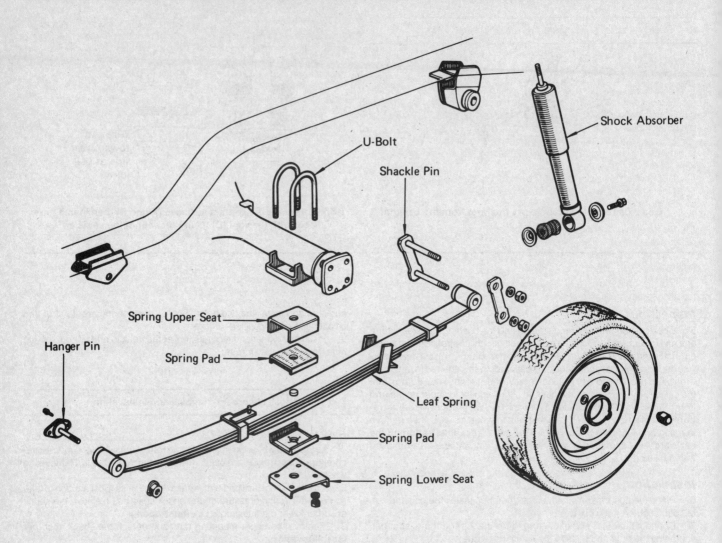

U-Bolt

Shackle Pin

Shock Absorber

Spring Upper Seat

Hanger Pin

Spring Pad

Leaf Spring

Spring Pad

Spring Lower Seat

8.5   Leaf spring rear suspension components – exploded view

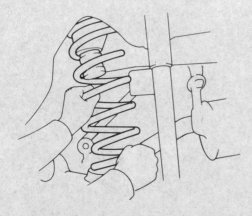

9.4   Once the coil spring is fully extended, it can be removed
from the seat – you may have to push down on the axle to obtain
adequate clearance for removal

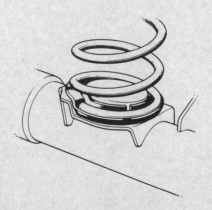

9.8   The lower end of the coil spring must be positioned
in the seat as shown

8   Rear leaf spring – removal and installation

Refer to illustration 8.5

Removal

1   Loosen the wheel lug nuts, raise the rear of the vehicle, support it securely on jackstands placed under the frame and place blocks in front of the front wheels. Remove the wheel.
2   Place a jack under the rear differential housing.
3   Lower the axle housing until the leaf spring tension is relieved, and lock the jack in this position.
4   Disconnect the shock absorber from its lower mount.
5   Remove the U-bolt mounting nuts **(see illustration)**.
6   Remove the spring seat and U-bolts.
7   Unbolt and remove the shackle pin and hanger pin assemblies.
8   Remove the rubber bushings from the spring ends and frame, then remove the spring.

Installation

9   Installation is the reverse of the removal procedure. When installing the hanger pin and shackle pin nuts, finger-tighten them until all other components are installed, then raise the jack under the differential until the vehicle is just free of the stands and tighten the hanger pin and shackle pin nuts to the specified torque. The U-bolts should be tightened to the specified torque as well.

9   Rear coil spring – removal and installation

Refer to illustrations 9.4 and 9.8

Removal

1   Raise the vehicle and support it securely on jackstands. The jackstands must be placed under the vehicle lifting points, not under the rear axle assembly. Remove the wheel(s).
2   Place a jack under the rear axle differential housing and raise it just enough to feel resistance from the spring.
3   Disconnect the shock absorber, stabilizer bar and lateral control rod from the axle housing.
4   Slowly lower the jack until the coil spring is fully extended, then guide the spring out of the mounts **(see illustration)**.

Installation

5   Before installing the coil spring, check the upper seat for cracks, hardening and general deterioration. Replace if necessary.
6   Check the bump stop on the frame for cracks and wear and replace it if necessary.
7   Check the coil spring for cracks, chips and excessive rust and deformation. Replace the spring if any of these conditions exist.
8   Place the coil spring in the seat on the axle, making sure it is positioned properly **(see illustration)**.
9   Raise the floor jack high enough enable the shock absorber and lateral control arm to be reconnected. Tighten the bolts securely.
10   Install the wheels and lower the vehicle.

10   Lateral control rod (coil spring models) – removal and installation

Refer to illustration 10.2

1   Raise the vehicle and support it securely on jackstands. Support the rear axle assembly with a jack or jackstands.
2   Remove the nut and disconnect the lateral control rod from the axle housing **(see illustration)**.
3   Remove the lateral control rod-to-frame bolt and lower the rod from the vehicle.
4   Use a jack to raise the axle housing slightly off the jackstands and install the lateral control rod, nuts and bolt.
5   Remove the jackstands and lower vehicle. Bounce the vehicle up-and-down on the rear suspension.
6   Raise the axle housing with a jack and tighten the control rod nuts/bolt to the specified torque.

11   Rear control arms (coil spring models) – removal and installation

Refer to illustration 11.3

Removal

1   Raise the rear of the vehicle and support it securely on jackstands. Place blocks in front of the front wheels.
2   Place a jack under the rear axle differential housing and raise it just enough to feel resistance from the spring.

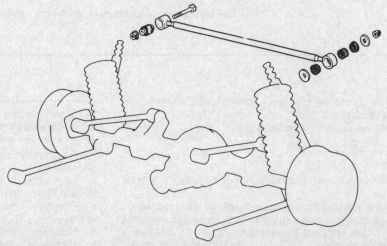

10.2   Lateral control rod mounting details

10

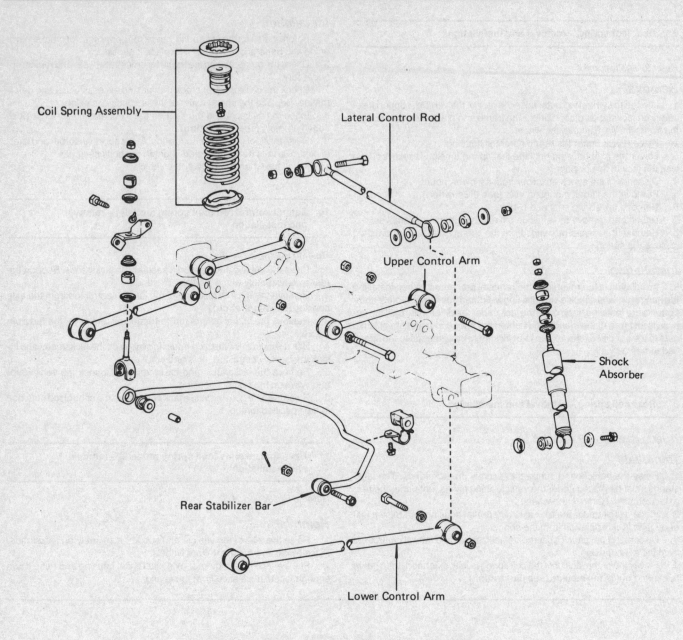

Coil Spring Assembly

Lateral Control Rod

Upper Control Arm

Shock Absorber

Rear Stabilizer Bar

Lower Control Arm

11.3   Coil spring rear suspension components – exploded view

3   Remove the control arm-to-body bolt, followed by the control arm-to-axle bolt **(see illustration)**.
4   Detach the control arm(s) from the vehicle.

Installation

5   Installation is the reverse of removal. Tighten the bolts and nuts finger-tight.
6   Lower the vehicle and bounce it up-and-down on the suspension.
7   Raise the vehicle and support it on jackstands. Raise the axle with the jack until the chassis just lifts off the jackstands. Tighten the control arm-to-body nuts/bolts and control arm-to-axle bolts to the specified torque.
8   Lower the vehicle.

12   Rear stabilizer bar (coil spring models) – removal and installation

1   Raise the vehicle, support it securely on jackstands and remove the rear wheels.
2   Remove the stabilizer bar-to-axle bracket bolts and detach the brackets **(see illustration 11.3)**.
3   Remove the stabilizer bar-to-body bolts and detach the bar from the vehicle.
4   Replace any worn or damaged bushings.
5   Installation is the reverse of removal. Tighten the nuts/bolts to the specified torque.

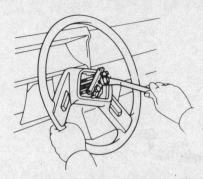

14.4   Use a puller to separate the steering wheel from the shaft – DO NOT hammer on the shaft in an attempt to remove the wheel!

13   Steering system – general information

Early models are equipped with conventional recirculating ball-type steering while later models use rack-and-pinion steering. The recirculating ball-type steering box is bolted to the frame and actuates the steering arms through a system of rods. The rack-and-pinion steering gear is bolted to the crossmember at the firewall and operates the steering arms via tie-rods. The inner ends of the tie-rods are protected by rubber boots which should be inspected periodically for secure attachment, tears and leaking lubricant.

Power assist was available on all later models.

14   Steering wheel – removal and installation

Refer to illustration 14.4

Removal

1   Disconnect the cable from the negative terminal of the battery.

2   Detach the horn pad from the steering wheel.

3   Remove the steering wheel retaining nut, then mark the relationship of the steering shaft to the hub to simplify installation and ensure steering wheel alignment.

4   Use a steering wheel puller to disconnect the steering wheel from the shaft **(see illustration)**.

Installation

5   To install the wheel, align the mark on the steering wheel hub with the mark on the shaft and slip the wheel onto the shaft. Install the hub nut and tighten it to the specified torque.

6   Install the horn pad.

7   Connect the negative battery cable.

15   Steering gear (recirculating ball-type) – removal and installation

Refer to illustration 15.6

Note: *The removal and installation procedures for manual and power steering gear housings are identical except that the inlet and outlet lines must be removed from the housing on power steering-equipped models before the housing can be removed. The steering system should be filled and power steering systems should be bled after the gear is reinstalled (see Section 21).*

Removal

1   Raise the front of the vehicle and support it securely on jackstands. Apply the parking brake and block the rear wheels.

2   Place an alignment mark on the steering coupling and the gear housing shaft to ensure correct reassembly.

3   Loosen the Pitman arm nut at the bottom of the steering gear housing.

4   Remove the cotter pin and castle nut securing the relay rod to the Pitman arm.

5   Using a puller, disconnect the relay rod end from the Pitman arm.

6   Remove the bolts securing the gear housing to the chassis and pull the gear housing off the coupling **(see illustration)**.

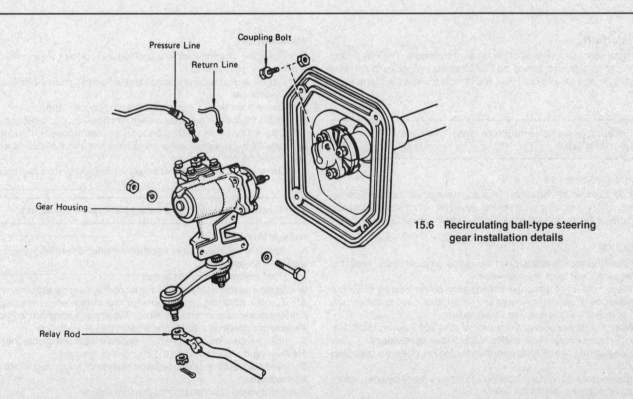

15.6   Recirculating ball-type steering gear installation details

10

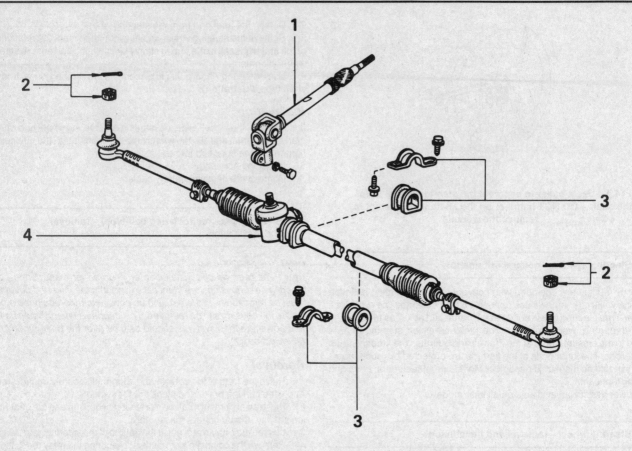

16.3   Rack-and-pinion steering gear mounting details

1	Intermediate shaft	3	Bracket and grommet
2	Cotter pin and nut	4	Steering gear

Installation

7   Installation is the reverse of the removal procedure. The Pitman arm nut should be tightened before the Pitman arm is connected to the relay rod end. Be sure to tighten all nuts and bolts to the specified torque.

16   Steering gear (rack-and-pinion type) – removal and installation

Refer to illustration 16.3

Note: *This procedure applies to both manual and power steering gear assemblies. When working on a vehicle equipped with a manual steering gear, simply ignore any references to the power steering system.*

Removal

1   Raise the vehicle and support it securely on jackstands. Apply the parking brake and block the rear wheels.
2   Place a drain pan under the steering gear (power steering only). Remove the power steering pressure and return lines and cap the ends to prevent excessive fluid loss and contamination.
3   Mark the relationship of the universal joint and steering shaft. Remove the lower intermediate shaft pinch bolt **(see illustration)**.
4   Separate the tie-rod ends from the steering knuckle arms (see Section 19).
5   Support the steering gear housing and remove the clamp bolts. Lower the unit and remove it from the vehicle.

Installation

6   Raise the steering gear into position and connect the intermediate shaft, aligning the marks.
7   Install the gear housing clamps and bolts and tighten the bolts to the specified torque.
8   Connect the tie-rod ends to the steering knuckle arms.
9   Install the lower intermediate shaft pinch bolt and tighten it securely.
10   Connect the power steering pressure and return hoses to the steering gear and fill the power steering pump reservoir with the recommended fluid (see Chapter 1).
11   Lower the vehicle and bleed the power steering system (Section 21).

17   Steering freeplay (recirculating ball-type) – adjustment

Refer to illustration 17.6

1   Raise the vehicle with a jack so the front wheels are off the ground and support it on jackstands.
2   Point the wheels straight ahead.
3   Using a wrench, loosen the locknut on the steering gear.
4   Turn the adjusting screw clockwise to decrease wheel freeplay and counterclockwise to increase it. **Note:** *Turn the adjusting screw in small increments, checking the steering wheel freeplay each time.*
5   Turn the steering wheel halfway around in both directions, checking the steering freeplay between the changes of direction.
6   Hold the adjusting screw so it won't turn and tighten the locknut **(see illustration)**.
7   Remove the jackstands and lower the vehicle.

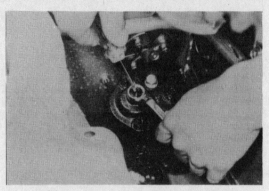

17.6   The adjusting screw must be held stationary while tightening the locknut

18   Steering linkage (recirculating ball-type) – removal and installation

Refer to illustrations 18.4, 18.12 and 18.13

1   All steering linkage removal and installation procedures should be done with the front end of the vehicle raised and supported securely on jackstands. Apply the parking brake and block the rear wheels.
2   Before removing any steering linkage components, obtain a balljoint separator. It may be a screw-type puller or a wedge-type tool, although the wedge-type tool tends to damage the balljoint seals. It is possible to jar a balljoint taper pin free by striking opposite sides of the eye simultaneously with two large hammers, but the space available to do so is usually very limited.
3   After installing any of the steering linkage components, the front wheel alignment should be checked by a front end alignment shop.

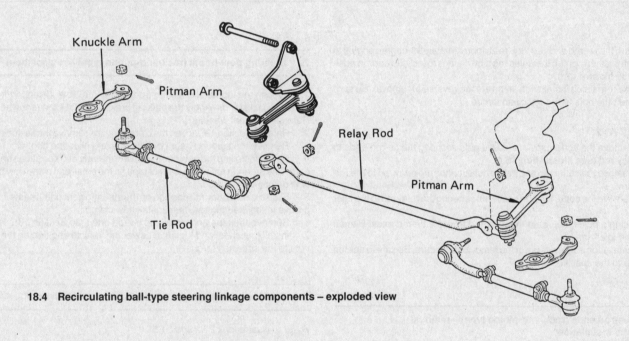

18.4   Recirculating ball-type steering linkage components – exploded view

Knuckle Arm
Pitman Arm
Relay Rod
Pitman Arm
Tie Rod

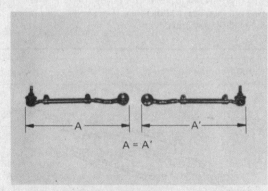

18.12   The exposed thread area and adjusting clamp position should be equal on both sides of the sleeve – the overall length of the tie-rods should be as specified (recirculating ball-type steering)

A = A'

Pitman arm

4   Remove the nut securing the Pitman arm to the steering gear sector shaft **(see illustration)**.
5   Scribe or paint match marks on the arm and shaft.
6   Using a puller, disconnect the Pitman arm from the shaft splines.
7   Remove the cotter pin and castle nut securing the Pitman arm to the relay rod.
8   Using a puller, disconnect the Pitman arm from the relay rod.
9   Installation is the reverse of the removal procedure. Be sure to tighten the nuts to the specified torque.

Tie-rod

10   Remove the cotter pins and castle nuts securing the tie-rod to the relay rod and knuckle arm **(see illustration 18.4)**.
11   Separate the tie-rod from the relay rod and knuckle arm with a puller.
12   Before installation, if both tie-rods have been removed and disassembled, adjust the tie-rod ends in the adjusting clamps until the measurements are equal. The tie-rods should be approximately 12.36-inches (314 mm) long **(see illustration)**.

10

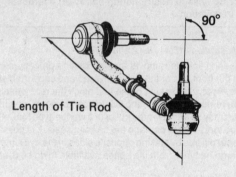

18.13   The tie-rod balljoint studs should be situated 90-degrees to each other (recirculating ball-type steering)

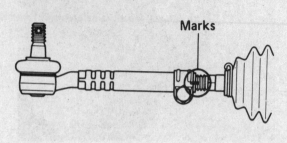

19.2   The relationship of the tie-rod end to the tie-rod can be marked with white paint

13   Turn the tie-rod ends so they're at approximately 90-degree angles to each other, then tighten the adjusting tube clamps to lock the ends in position **(see illustration)**.

14   The remaining installation steps are the reverse of removal. Be sure to tighten the nuts to the specified torque.

Relay rod

15   Remove the cotter pins and castle nuts securing the tie-rod ends to the relay rod **(see illustration 18.4).**

16   Remove the cotter pin and castle nut securing the relay rod to the Pitman arm.

17   Remove the cotter pin and castle nut securing the relay rod to the idler arm.

18   Using a puller, separate the relay rod from the tie-rod ends, Pitman arm and idler arm.

19   Installation is the reverse of the removal procedure. Be sure to tighten all nuts to the specified torque.

19   Tie-rod ends (rack-and-pinion type) – removal and installation

Refer to illustration 19.2

Removal

1   Loosen the wheel lug nuts. Raise the front of the vehicle, support it securely, block the rear wheels and apply the parking brake. Remove the front wheel(s).

2   Mark the position of the tie-rod end in relation to the threads **(see illustration)**.

3   Remove the cotter pin and loosen the nut on the tie-rod end stud.

4   Disconnect the tie-rod from the steering knuckle arm with a puller. Remove the nut and separate the tie-rod.

5   Unscrew the tie-rod end from the tie-rod.

Installation

6   Thread the tie-rod end on to the marked position and insert the tie-rod stud into the steering knuckle arm. Tighten the clamp nut securely.

7   Install the castellated nut on the stud and tighten it to the specified torque. Install a new cotter pin.

8   Install the wheel and lug nuts. Lower the vehicle and tighten the lug nuts to the specified torque.

9   Have the alignment checked by a dealer service department or an alignment shop.

20   Steering gear boots (rack-and-pinion type) – replacement

1   Loosen the lug nuts, raise the front of the vehicle and support it securely on jackstands. Apply the parking brake and block the rear wheels. Remove the front wheel(s).

2   Refer to Section 19, loosen the clamp nut and remove the tie-rod end.

3   Remove the steering gear boot clamps and slide the boot off.

4   Before installing the new boot, wrap the threads and serrations on the end of the steering rod with a layer of tape so the small end of the new boot isn't damaged.

5   Slide the new boot into position on the steering gear until it seats in the groove in the steering rod, then install new clamps.

6   Remove the tape and install the tie-rod end (see Section 18).

7   Install the wheel and lug nuts. Lower the vehicle and tighten the lug nuts to the specified torque.

21   Power steering pump – removal and installation

Refer to illustrations 21.2 and 21.5

Removal

1   Disconnect the cable from the negative battery terminal.

2   Push on the drivebelt to prevent the pulley from turning and loosen the drive pulley nut **(see illustration)**

3   Remove the pulley and drivebelt.

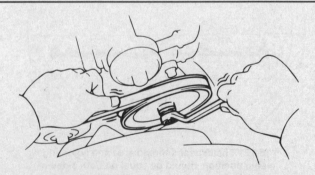

21.2   Push down on the drivebelt to prevent the pump pulley from turning when the pulley nut is loosened

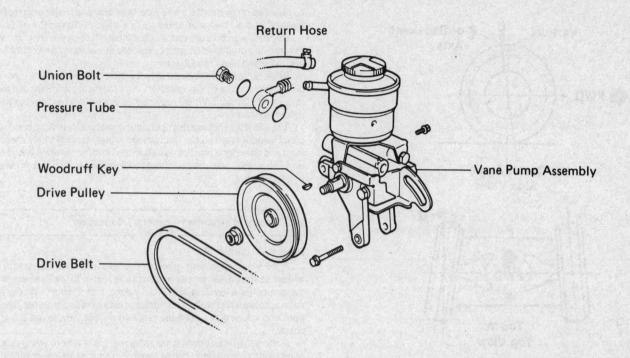

Return Hose

Union Bolt

Pressure Tube

Woodruff Key

Drive Pulley

Drive Belt

Vane Pump Assembly

21.5 Power steering pump installation details (1985 models shown, others similar)

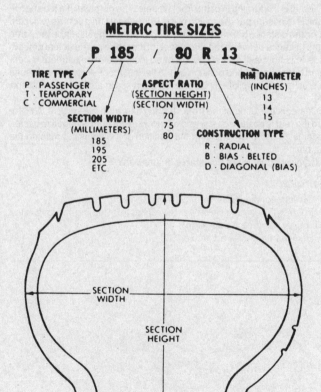

METRIC TIRE SIZES

P 185 / 80 R 13

TIRE TYPE
P - PASSENGER
T - TEMPORARY
C - COMMERCIAL

SECTION WIDTH
(MILLIMETERS)
185
195
205
ETC

ASPECT RATIO
(SECTION HEIGHT)
(SECTION WIDTH)
70
75
80

CONSTRUCTION TYPE
R - RADIAL
B - BIAS - BELTED
D - DIAGONAL (BIAS)

RIM DIAMETER
(INCHES)
13
14
15

SECTION WIDTH

SECTION HEIGHT

23.1 Metric tire size code

4   Using a suction gun, remove as much fluid from the reservoir as possible. Place a drain pan under the vehicle to catch any fluid that may spill out when the hoses are disconnected.
5   Disconnect the pressure and return lines from the pump **(see illustration)**. Unbolt the high pressure line bracket from the pump.
6   Remove the adjuster and pivot bolts from the pump **(see illustration 21.5)** and detach the pump from the vehicle.

Installation

7   Installation is the reverse of the removal procedure. Be sure to adjust the power steering pump drivebelt tension and top up the power steering fluid reservoir (Chapter 1).
8   Bleed the power steering system as described in Section 22.

---

22   Power steering system – bleeding

---

1   Following any operation in which the power steering lines have been disconnected, the power steering system must be bled to remove all air and obtain proper steering performance.
2   With the front wheels in the straight ahead position, check the power steering fluid level and, if low, add fluid (see Chapter 1).
3   Start the engine and allow it to run at fast idle (approximately 1000 rpm). Recheck the fluid level and add more if necessary.
4   Bleed the system by turning the steering wheel from side-to-side, without hitting the stops. This will work the air out of the system. Keep the reservoir full of fluid as this is done.
5   When the air is out of the system, return the wheels to the straight ahead position and leave the vehicle running for several more minutes before shutting it off.
6   Road test the vehicle to be sure the steering system is functioning normally and noise free.
7   Recheck the fluid level to be sure it's correct. Add fluid if necessary (see Chapter 1).

10

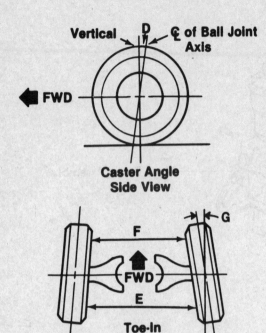

24.1   Front end alignment details

D = caster (measured in degrees)
E minus F = toe-in (measured in inches)
G = toe-in (expressed in degrees)

23   Wheels and tires – general information

Refer to illustration 23.1

All vehicles covered by this manual are equipped with metric-sized fiberglass or steel belted radial tires **(see illustration)**. Use of other size or type of tires may affect the ride and handling of the vehicle. Don't mix different types of tires, such as radials and bias belted, on the same vehicle as handling may be seriously affected. It's recommended that tires be replaced in pairs on the same axle, but if only one tire is being replaced, be sure it's the same size, structure and tread design as the other.

Because tire pressure has a substantial effect on handling and wear, the pressure on all tires should be checked at least once a month or before any extended trips (see Chapter 1).

Wheels must be replaced if they are bent, dented, leak air, have elongated bolt holes, are heavily rusted, out of vertical symmetry or if the lug nuts won't stay tight. Wheel repairs that use welding or peening are not recommended.

Tire and wheel balance is important in the overall handling, braking and performance of the vehicle. Unbalanced wheels can adversely affect handling and ride characteristics as well as tire life. Whenever a tire is installed on a wheel, the tire and wheel should be balanced by a shop with the proper equipment.

24   Front end alignment – general information

Refer to illustration 24.1

A front end alignment refers to the adjustments made to the front wheels so they are in proper angular relationship to the suspension and the ground **(see illustration)**. Front wheels that are out of proper alignment not only affect steering control, but also increase tire wear. The only front end adjustments normally required on this vehicle are toe-in and caster.

Getting the proper front wheel alignment is a very exacting process, one in which complicated and expensive machines are necessary to perform the job properly. Because of this, you should have a technician with the proper equipment perform these tasks. We will, however, use this space to give you a basic idea of what is involved with front end alignment so you can better understand the process and deal intelligently with the shop that does the work.

Toe-in is the turning in of the front wheels. The purpose of a toe specification is to ensure parallel rolling of the front wheels. In a vehicle with zero toe-in, the distance between the front edges of the wheels will be the same as the distance between the rear edges of the wheels. The actual amount of toe-in is normally only a fraction of an inch. Toe-in adjustment is controlled by the tie-rod end position on the tie-rod. Incorrect toe-in will cause the tires to wear improperly by making them scrub against the road surface.

Caster is the tilting of the front steering axis from the vertical. A tilt toward the rear is positive caster and a tilt toward the front is negative caster. Caster is adjusted by changing the position of the adjusting nuts on the strut bar.

Camber angle is not adjustable on this vehicle.

Chapter 11   Body

Contents

---

1   General information

These models feature a "unibody" layout, using a floor pan with front and rear frame side rails which support the body components, front and rear suspension systems and other mechanical components.

Certain components are particularly vulnerable to accident damage and can be unbolted and repaired or replaced. Among these parts are the body moldings, bumpers, the hood and trunk lids and all glass.

Only general body maintenance practices and body panel repair procedures within the scope of the do-it-yourselfer are included in this Chapter.

2   Body – maintenance

1   The condition of your vehicle's body is very important, because the resale value depends a great deal on it. It's much more difficult to repair a neglected or damaged body than it is to repair mechanical components. The hidden areas of the body, such as the wheel wells, the frame and the engine compartment, are equally important, although they don't require as frequent attention as the rest of the body.

2   Once a year, or every 12,000 miles, it's a good idea to have the underside of the body steam cleaned. All traces of dirt and oil will be removed and the area can then be inspected carefully for rust, damaged brake

lines, frayed electrical wires, damaged cables and other problems. The front suspension components should be greased after completion of this job.

3   At the same time, clean the engine and the engine compartment with a steam cleaner or water soluble degreaser.

4   The wheel wells should be given close attention, since undercoating can peel away and stones and dirt thrown up by the tires can cause the paint to chip and flake, allowing rust to set in. If rust is found, clean down to the bare metal and apply an anti-rust paint.

5   The body should be washed about once a week. Wet the vehicle thoroughly to soften the dirt, then wash it down with a soft sponge and plenty of clean soapy water. If the surplus dirt is not washed off very carefully, it can wear down the paint.

6   Spots of tar or asphalt thrown up from the road should be removed with a cloth soaked in solvent.

7   Once every six months, wax the body and chrome trim. If a chrome cleaner is used to remove rust from any of the vehicle's plated parts, remember that the cleaner also removes part of the chrome, so use it sparingly.

3   Vinyl trim – maintenance

Don't clean vinyl trim with detergents, caustic soap or petroleum-based cleaners. Plain soap and water works just fine, with a soft brush to clean dirt that may be ingrained. Wash the vinyl as frequently as the rest of the vehicle.

After cleaning, application of a high quality rubber and vinyl protectant will help prevent oxidation and cracks. The protectant can also be applied to weatherstripping, vacuum lines and rubber hoses, which often fail as a result of chemical degradation, and to the tires.

4   Upholstery and carpets – maintenance

1   Every three months remove the carpets or mats and clean the interior of the vehicle (more frequently if necessary). Vacuum the upholstery and carpets to remove loose dirt and dust.

2   Leather upholstery requires special care. Stains should be removed with warm water and a very mild soap solution. Use a clean, damp cloth to remove the soap, then wipe again with a dry cloth. Never use alcohol, gasoline, nail polish remover or thinner to clean leather upholstery.

3   After cleaning, regularly treat leather upholstery with a leather wax. Never use car wax on leather upholstery.

4   In areas where the interior of the vehicle is subject to bright sunlight, cover leather seats with a sheet if the vehicle is to be left out for any length of time.

5   Body repair – minor damage

See photo sequence

Repair of scratches

1   If the scratch is superficial and does not penetrate to the metal of the body, repair is very simple. Lightly rub the scratched area with a fine rubbing compound to remove loose paint and built up wax. Rinse the area with clean water.

2   Apply touch-up paint to the scratch, using a small brush. Continue to apply thin layers of paint until the surface of the paint in the scratch is level with the surrounding paint. Allow the new paint at least two weeks to harden, then blend it into the surrounding paint by rubbing with a very fine rubbing compound. Finally, apply a coat of wax to the scratch area.

3   If the scratch has penetrated the paint and exposed the metal of the body, causing the metal to rust, a different repair technique is required. Remove all loose rust from the bottom of the scratch with a pocket knife, then apply rust inhibiting paint to prevent the formation of rust in the future. Us-

ing a rubber or nylon applicator, coat the scratched area with glaze-type filler. If required, the filler can be mixed with thinner to provide a very thin paste, which is ideal for filling narrow scratches. Before the glaze filler in the scratch hardens, wrap a piece of smooth cotton cloth around the tip of a finger. Dip the cloth in thinner and then quickly wipe it along the surface of the scratch. This will ensure that the surface of the filler is slightly hollow. The scratch can now be painted over as described earlier in this section.

Repair of dents

4   When repairing dents, the first job is to pull the dent out until the affected area is as close as possible to its original shape. There is no point in trying to restore the original shape completely as the metal in the damaged area will have stretched on impact and cannot be restored to its original contours. It is better to bring the level of the dent up to a point which is about 1/8-inch below the level of the surrounding metal. In cases where the dent is very shallow, it is not worth trying to pull it out at all.

5   If the back side of the dent is accessible, it can be hammered out gently from behind using a soft-face hammer. While doing this, hold a block of wood firmly against the opposite side of the metal to absorb the hammer blows and prevent the metal from being stretched.

6   If the dent is in a section of the body which has double layers, or some other factor makes it inaccessible from behind, a different technique is required. Drill several small holes through the metal inside the damaged area, particularly in the deeper sections. Screw long, self tapping screws into the holes just enough for them to get a good grip in the metal. Now the dent can be pulled out by pulling on the protruding heads of the screws with locking pliers.

7   The next stage of repair is the removal of paint from the damaged area and from an inch or so of the surrounding metal. This is easily done with a wire brush or sanding disk in a drill motor, although it can be done just as effectively by hand with sandpaper. To complete the preparation for filling, score the surface of the bare metal with a screwdriver or the tang of a file or drill small holes in the affected area. This will provide a good grip for the filler material. To complete the repair, see the Section on filling and painting.

Repair of rust holes or gashes

8   Remove all paint from the affected area and from an inch or so of the surrounding metal using a sanding disk or wire brush mounted in a drill motor. If these are not available, a few sheets of sandpaper will do the job just as effectively.

9   With the paint removed, you will be able to determine the severity of the corrosion and decide whether to replace the whole panel, if possible, or repair the affected area. New body panels are not as expensive as most people think and it is often quicker to install a new panel than to repair large areas of rust.

10   Remove all trim pieces from the affected area except those which will act as a guide to the original shape of the damaged body, such as headlight shells, etc. Using metal snips or a hacksaw blade, remove all loose metal and any other metal that is badly affected by rust. Hammer the edges of the hole inward to create a slight depression for the filler material.

11   Wire brush the affected area to remove the powdery rust from the surface of the metal. If the back of the rusted area is accessible, treat it with rust inhibiting paint.

12   Before filling is done, block the hole in some way. This can be done with sheet metal riveted or screwed into place, or by stuffing the hole with wire mesh.

13   Once the hole is blocked off, the affected area can be filled and painted. See the following subsection on filling and painting.

Filling and painting

14   Many types of body fillers are available, but generally speaking, body repair kits which contain filler paste and a tube of resin hardener are best for this type of repair work. A wide, flexible plastic or nylon applicator will be necessary for imparting a smooth and contoured finish to the surface of the filler material. Mix up a small amount of filler on a clean piece of wood or cardboard (use the hardener sparingly). Follow the manufacturer's in-

structions on the package, otherwise the filler will set incorrectly.

15   Using the applicator, apply the filler paste to the prepared area. Draw the applicator across the surface of the filler to achieve the desired contour and to level the filler surface. As soon as a contour that approximates the original one is achieved, stop working the paste. If you continue, the paste will begin to stick to the applicator. Continue to add thin layers of paste at 20-minute intervals until the level of the filler is just above the surrounding metal.

16   Once the filler has hardened, the excess can be removed with a body file. From then on, progressively finer grades of sandpaper should be used, starting with a 180-grit paper and finishing with 600-grit wet-or-dry paper. Always wrap the sandpaper around a flat rubber or wooden block, otherwise the surface of the filler will not be completely flat. During the sanding of the filler surface, the wet-or-dry paper should be periodically rinsed in water. This will ensure that a very smooth finish is produced in the final stage.

17   At this point, the repair area should be surrounded by a ring of bare metal, which in turn should be encircled by the finely feathered edge of good paint. Rinse the repair area with clean water until all of the dust produced by the sanding operation is gone.

18   Spray the entire area with a light coat of primer. This will reveal any imperfections in the surface of the filler. Repair the imperfections with fresh filler paste or glaze filler and once more smooth the surface with sandpaper. Repeat this spray-and-repair procedure until you are satisfied that the surface of the filler and the feathered edge of the paint are perfect. Rinse the area with clean water and allow it to dry completely.

19   The repair area is now ready for painting. Spray painting must be carried out in a warm, dry, windless and dust free atmosphere. These conditions can be created if you have access to a large indoor work area, but if you are forced to work in the open, you will have to pick the day very carefully. If you are working indoors, dousing the floor in the work area with water will help settle the dust which would otherwise be in the air. If the repair area is confined to one body panel, mask off the surrounding panels. This will help minimize the effects of a slight mismatch in paint color. Trim pieces such as chrome strips, door handles, etc., will also need to be masked off or removed. Use masking tape and several thicknesses of newspaper for the masking operations.

20   Before spraying, shake the paint can thoroughly, then spray a test area until the spray painting technique is mastered. Cover the repair area with a thick coat of primer. The thickness should be built up using several thin layers of primer rather than one thick one. Using 600-grit wet-or-dry sandpaper, rub down the surface of the primer until it is very smooth. While doing this, the work area should be thoroughly rinsed with water and the wet-or-dry sandpaper periodically rinsed as well. Allow the primer to dry before spraying additional coats.

21   Spray on the top coat, again building up the thickness by using several thin layers of paint. Begin spraying in the center of the repair area and then, using a circular motion, work out until the whole repair area and about two inches of the surrounding original paint is covered. Remove all masking material 10 to 15 minutes after spraying on the final coat of paint. Allow the new paint at least two weeks to harden, then use a very fine rubbing compound to blend the edges of the new paint into the existing paint. Finally, apply a coat of wax.

6   Body repair – major damage

1   Major damage must be repaired by an auto body shop specifically equipped to perform unibody repairs. These shops have the specialized equipment required to do the job properly.

2   If the damage is extensive, the body must be checked for proper alignment or the vehicle's handling characteristics may be adversely affected and other components may wear at an accelerated rate.

3   Due to the fact that all of the major body components (hood, fenders, etc.) are separate and replaceable units, any seriously damaged components should be replaced rather than repaired. Sometimes the components can be found in a wrecking yard that specializes in used vehicle components, often at considerable savings over the cost of new parts.

7   Hinges and locks – maintenance

Once every 3000 miles, or every three months, the hinges and latch assemblies on the doors, hood and trunk should be given a few drops of light oil or lock lubricant. The door latch strikers should also be lubricated with a thin coat of grease to reduce wear and ensure free movement. Lubricate the door and trunk locks with spray-on graphite lubricant.

8   Fixed glass – replacement

Replacement of the windshield and fixed glass requires the use of special fast-setting adhesive/caulk materials and some specialized tools and techniques. These operations should be left to a dealer service department or a shop specializing in glass work.

9   Hood – removal, installation and adjustment

Refer to illustrations 9.2, 9.10 and 9.11
Note: *The hood is heavy and somewhat awkward to remove and install – at least two people should perform this procedure.*

Removal and installation

1   Use blankets or pads to cover the cowl area of the body and the fenders. This will protect the body and paint as the hood is lifted off.

2   Scribe or paint alignment marks around the bolt heads to insure proper alignment during installation **(see illustration)**.

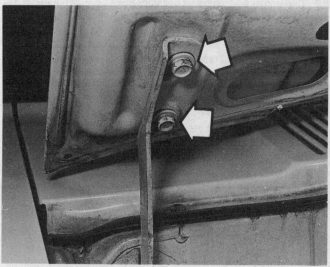

9.2   Scribe or mark around the bolt heads (arrows) on the hinge plate – mark around the entire hinge plate before adjusting the hood

3   Disconnect any cables or wire harnesses which will interfere with removal.

4   Have an assistant support the weight of the hood. Remove the hinge-to-hood nuts or bolts.

5   Lift off the hood.

6   Installation is the reverse of removal.

Adjustment

7   Fore-and-aft and side-to-side adjustment of the hood is done by moving the hood in relation to the hinge plate after loosening the bolts or nuts.

11

9.10 To adjust the hood in relation to the fenders, loosen the hood latch bolts and move the latch as necessary

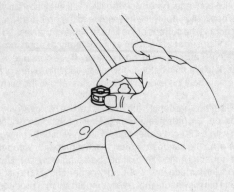

9.11 Screw the hood bumpers in-or-out to adjust the front edge of the hood in relation to the fenders

8   Scribe a line around the entire hinge plate so you can judge the amount of movement.

9   Loosen the bolts or nuts and move the hood into correct alignment. Move it only a little at a time. Tighten the hinge bolts or nuts and carefully lower the hood to check the alignment.

10   If necessary after installation, the entire hood latch assembly can be adjusted up-and-down as well as from side-to-side on the radiator support so the hood closes securely and is flush with the fenders. To do this, scribe a line around the hood latch mounting bolts to provide a reference point. Then loosen the bolts and reposition the latch assembly as necessary. Following adjustment, retighten the mounting bolts **(see illustration)**.

11   Finally, adjust the hood bumpers on the radiator support so the hood, when closed, is flush with the fenders **(see illustration)**.

12   The hood latch assembly, as well as the hinges, should be periodically lubricated with white lithium-base grease to prevent sticking and wear.

10   Headlight cover (1984 and later models) – adjustment

Refer to illustrations 10.1, 10.2 and 10.3
Caution: *When raising or lowering the headlights, always use the light control switch. Disconnect the negative battery cable before working on the headlight or it's mechanism.*

1   The headlight cover can be adjusted in relation to the surrounding bodywork by loosening the cover screws and repositioning it **(see illustration)**.

2   Headlight slant angle is adjusted by loosening the stopper locknut, then lowering the headlight. Check the crank arm and link to make sure they are aligned **(see illustration)**. If necessary, adjust the length of the link rod until it lines up the crank arm.

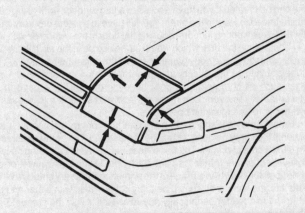

10.1 You can adjust the headlight cover in relation to the body after loosening the cover screws

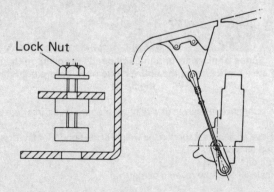

Lock Nut

10.2 Loosen the stopper locknut to adjust the link rod and crank arm

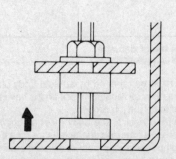

10.3 The stopper should just contact the headlight bracket

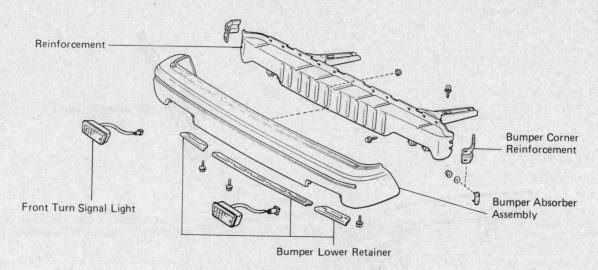

Reinforcement

Front Turn Signal Light

Bumper Corner Reinforcement

Bumper Absorber Assembly

Bumper Lower Retainer

11.3a Typical front bumper installation details

3   The stopper should just touch the headlight bracket **(see illustration)**. Raise the headlight, loosen the locknut and turn the stopper counterclockwise until it touches the bracket, then turn it an additional 1/2-turn. Tighten the locknut.

11   Bumpers – removal and installation

Refer to illustrations 11.3a and 11.3b

1   Detach the bumper cover (if equipped).
2   Disconnect any wiring or other components that would interfere with bumper removal.
3   Support the bumper with a jack or jackstand. Alternatively, have an assistant support the bumper as the bolts are removed **(see illustrations)**.

4   Remove the retaining bolts and detach the bumper.
5   Installation is the reverse of removal.
6   Tighten the retaining bolts securely.
7   Install the bumper cover and any other components that were removed.

12   Front fender – removal and installation

Refer to illustration 12.3

1   Raise the vehicle, support it securely on jackstands and remove the front wheel.
2   Disconnect the antenna and all light bulb wiring harness connectors and other components that would interfere with fender removal.
3   Remove the clips and/or bolts, detach the fender liner, then remove

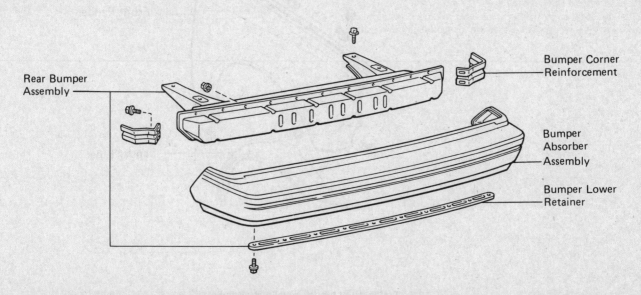

Rear Bumper Assembly

Bumper Corner Reinforcement

Bumper Absorber Assembly

Bumper Lower Retainer

11.3b Typical rear bumper installation details

11

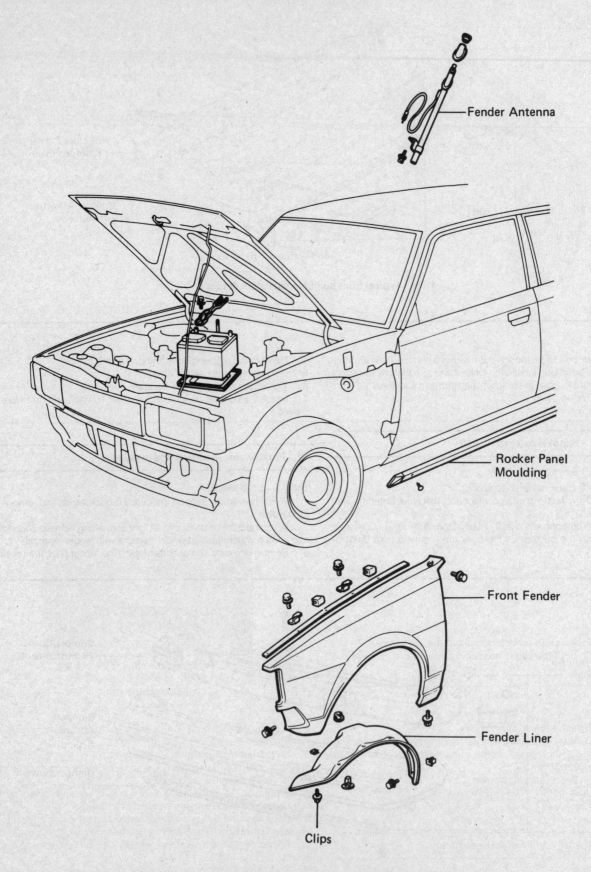

Fender Antenna

Rocker Panel
Moulding

Front Fender

Fender Liner

Clips

12.3 Typical front fender installation details

Door Inside Handle

Service Hole Cover

Door Trim Panel

Window Regulator Handle

Armrest

Door Inside Handle Bezel

13.2   Typical door panel installation details

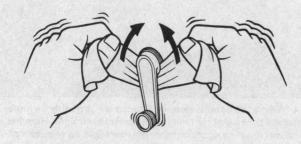

13.3   Work a cloth up behind the handle and move it back-and-forth until the clip is pushed up so you can remove it

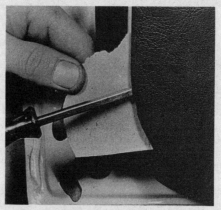

13.4   Pry under the clips to detach the trim panel – a piece of cardboard will protect the paint

the fender mounting bolts **(see illustration)**.

4   Detach the fender. It is a good idea to have an assistant support the fender while it's being moved away from the vehicle to prevent damage to the surrounding body panels.

5   Installation is the reverse of removal.

6   Tighten all nuts, bolts and screws securely.

13   Door trim panel – removal and installation

Refer to illustrations 13.2, 13.3, 13.4, 13.8a and 13.8b

1   Disconnect the negative cable from the battery.

2   Remove all door trim panel retaining screws and door pull/armrest assemblies **(see illustration)**.

3   On manual window regulator equipped models, remove the window regulator crank **(see illustration)**. On power regulator models, pry off the control switch assembly and unplug it.

4   Disengage the trim panel-to-door retaining clips. Work around the outer edge until the panel is free **(see illustration)**.

5   Once all of the clips are disengaged, detach the trim panel, unplug any wire harness connectors and remove the trim panel from the vehicle.

6   For access to the inner door, carefully peel back the plastic watershield.

7   Prior to installation of the door panel, be sure to reinstall any clips in the panel which may have come out during the removal procedure and remain in the door itself.

11

These photos illustrate a method of repairing simple dents. They are intended to supplement *Body repair - minor damage* in this Chapter and should not be used as the sole instructions for body repair on these vehicles.

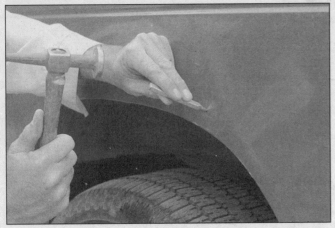

1 If you can't access the backside of the body panel to hammer out the dent, pull it out with a slide-hammer-type dent puller. In the deepest portion of the dent or along the crease line, drill or punch hole(s) at least one inch apart . . .

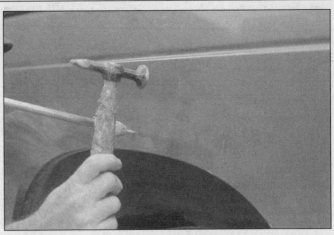

2 . . . then screw the slide-hammer into the hole and operate it. Tap with a hammer near the edge of the dent to help 'pop' the metal back to its original shape. When you're finished, the dent area should be close to its original contour and about 1/8-inch below the surface of the surrounding metal

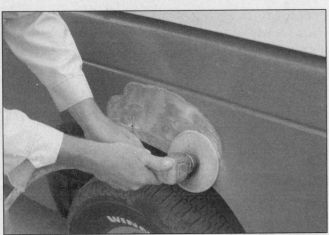

3 Using coarse-grit sandpaper, remove the paint down to the bare metal. Hand sanding works fine, but the disc sander shown here makes the job faster. Use finer (about 320-grit) sandpaper to feather-edge the paint at least one inch around the dent area

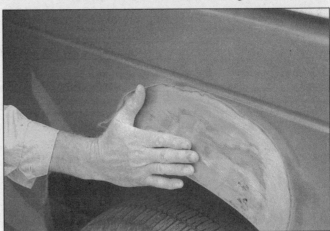

4 When the paint is removed, touch will probably be more helpful than sight for telling if the metal is straight. Hammer down the high spots or raise the low spots as necessary. Clean the repair area with wax/silicone remover

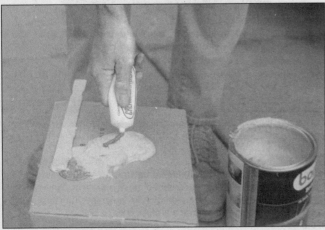

5 Following label instructions, mix up a batch of plastic filler and hardener. The ratio of filler to hardener is critical, and, if you mix it incorrectly, it will either not cure properly or cure too quickly (you won't have time to file and sand it into shape)

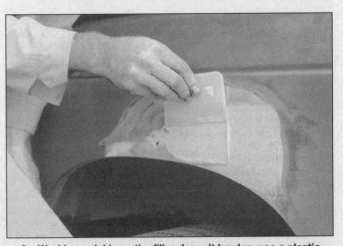

6 Working quickly so the filler doesn't harden, use a plastic applicator to press the body filler firmly into the metal, assuring it bonds completely. Work the filler until it matches the original contour and is slightly above the surrounding metal

7   Let the filler harden until you can just dent it with your fingernail. Use a body file or Surform tool (shown here) to rough-shape the filler

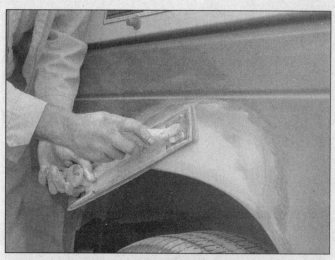

8   Use coarse-grit sandpaper and a sanding board or block to work the filler down until it's smooth and even. Work down to finer grits of sandpaper - always using a board or block - ending up with 360 or 400 grit

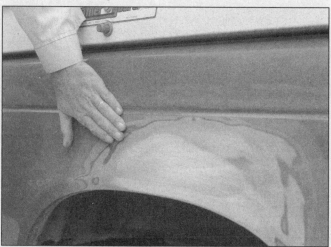

9   You shouldn't be able to feel any ridge at the transition from the filler to the bare metal or from the bare metal to the old paint. As soon as the repair is flat and uniform, remove the dust and mask off the adjacent panels or trim pieces

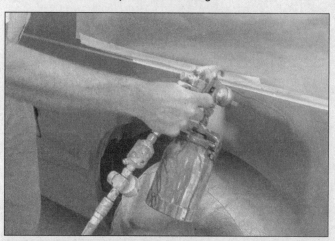

10   Apply several layers of primer to the area. Don't spray the primer on too heavy, so it sags or runs, and make sure each coat is dry before you spray on the next one. A professional-type spray gun is being used here, but aerosol spray primer is available inexpensively from auto parts stores

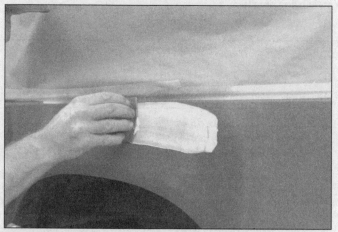

11   The primer will help reveal imperfections or scratches. Fill these with glazing compound. Follow the label instructions and sand it with 360 or 400-grit sandpaper until it's smooth. Repeat the glazing, sanding and respraying until the primer reveals a perfectly smooth surface

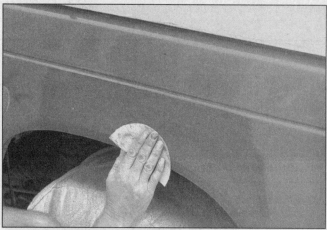

12   Finish sand the primer with very fine sandpaper (400 or 600-grit) to remove the primer overspray. Clean the area with water and allow it to dry. Use a tack rag to remove any dust, then apply the finish coat. Don't attempt to rub out or wax the repair area until the paint has dried completely (at least two weeks)

13.8a   Install the clip as shown so you can snap it into place after pressing the handle onto the shaft

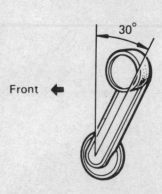

13.8b   With the window all the way up, install the handle 30-degrees from the vertical position

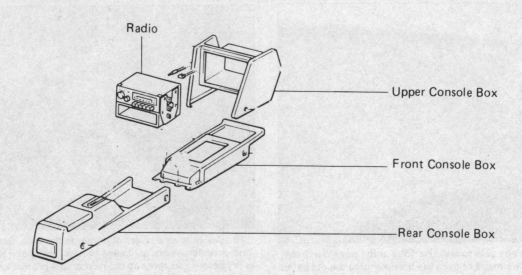

14.3   Center console installation details

8   Plug in the wire harness connectors and place the panel in position in the door. Press the door panel into place until the clips are seated and install the armrest/door pulls. Install the manual regulator window crank **(see illustrations)**.

14   Center console – removal and installation

Refer to illustration 14.3

1   Disconnect the negative battery cable.
2   Remove the shift knob or handle.
3   Remove the retaining screws **(see illustration)**. If necessary, move the seats forward for access to the rear console screws.
4   Detach the console from the vehicle.
5   Installation is the reverse of removal.

15   Door – removal and installation

Refer to illustrations 15.4a, 15.4b, 15.6a, 15.6b and 15.6c

1   Remove the door trim panel. Disconnect any wire harness connectors and push them through the door opening so they won't interfere with door removal.
2   Place a jack or jackstand under the door or have an assistant on hand to support it when the hinge bolts are removed. **Note:** *If a jack or jackstand is used, place a rag between it and the door to protect the door's painted surfaces.*
3   Scribe around the door hinges.
4   Remove the check pin and detach the door check strap **(see illustration)**. Remove the hinge-to-door mounting bolts and carefully lift off the door **(see illustration)**.
5   Installation is the reverse of removal.

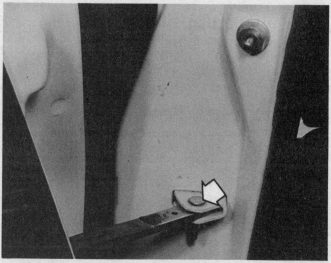

15.4a   Drive the pin out and detach the check strap

6   Following installation of the door, check the alignment and adjust it if necessary as follows:
   a) Up-and-down and forward-and-backward adjustments are made by loosening the hinge-to-body bolts and moving the door as necessary **(see illustration)**. To adjust the door in or out, loosen the hinge-to-door bolts **(see illustration)**.
   b) The door lock striker can also be adjusted both up-and-down and sideways to provide positive engagement with the lock mechanism. This is done by loosening the mounting bolts and moving the striker as necessary **(see illustration)**.

16   Trunk lid – removal, installation and adjustment

Refer to illustration 16.4
1   Open the trunk lid and cover the edges of the trunk compartment with pads or cloths to protect the painted surfaces when the lid is removed.
2   Disconnect any cables or wire harness connectors attached to the trunk lid that would interfere with removal.
3   Scribe or paint alignment marks around the hinge bolt mounting flanges.

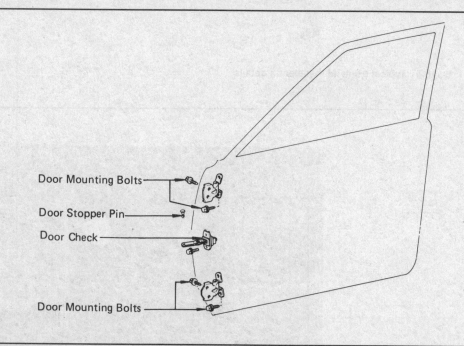

Door Mounting Bolts

Door Stopper Pin

Door Check

Door Mounting Bolts

15.4b   Typical door installation details

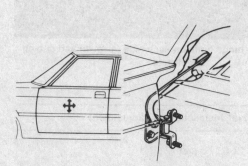

15.6a   Loosen the hinge-to-body bolts to adjust the door – a special offset wrench will make the job easier

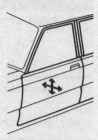

15.6b   To adjust the door, loosen the hinge-to-door bolts

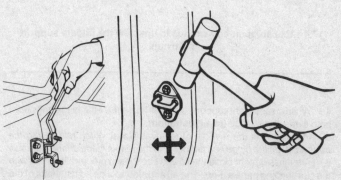

15.6c   Adjust the door lock striker by loosening the retaining screws and tapping the striker in the desired direction with a soft-face hammer

11

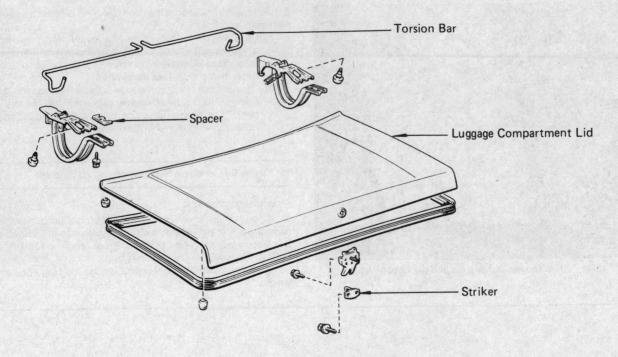

16.4   Typical trunk lid installation details

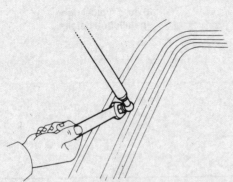

17.4   Use an open-end wrench to unscrew the liftgate support strut nuts

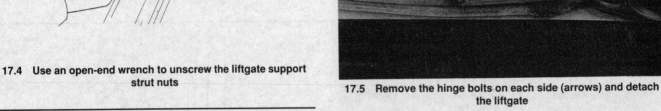

17.5   Remove the hinge bolts on each side (arrows) and detach the liftgate

4   While an assistant supports the trunk lid, remove the hinge bolts from both sides and lift it off **(see illustration)**.

5   Installation is the reverse of removal. **Note:** *When reinstalling the trunk lid, align the hinge bolt flanges with the marks made during removal.*

6   After installation, close the lid and see if it's in proper alignment with the surrounding panels. Fore-and-aft and side-to-side adjustments of the lid are controlled by the position of the hinge bolts in the slots. To adjust it, loosen the hinge bolts, reposition the lid and retighten the bolts.

7   The height of the lid in relation to the surrounding body panels when closed can be adjusted by loosening the lock striker bolts, repositioning the striker and retightening the bolts.

17   Liftgate – removal, installation and adjustment

Refer to illustrations 17.4, 17.5 and 17.8

1   Open the liftgate and cover the upper body area around the opening with pads or cloths to protect the painted surfaces when the liftgate is removed.

2   Disconnect all cables and wire harness connectors that would interfere with removal of the liftgate.

3   Paint or scribe around the hinge flanges.

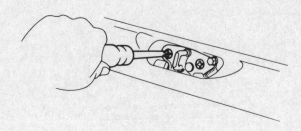

17.8   Typical liftgate striker adjustment details

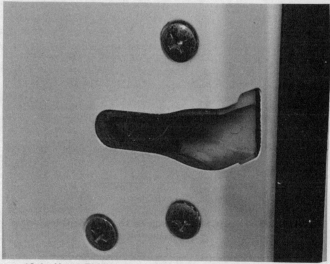

18.4   Use a Phillips screwdriver to remove the door latch retaining screws from the end of the door

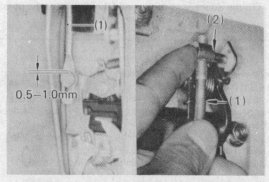

18.5   On 1980 through 1983 models, the outside handle link rod (1) can be adjusted by turning the nut (2)

0.5 – 1.0mm

4   While an assistant supports the liftgate, detach the support struts **(see illustration)**.
5   Remove the hinge bolts **(see illustration)** and detach the liftgate from the vehicle.
6   Installation is the reverse of removal.
7   After installation, close the liftgate and make sure it's in proper alignment with the surrounding body panels. Adjustments are made by moving the position of the hinge bolts in the slots. To adjust it, loosen the hinge bolts and reposition the hinges either side-to-side or fore-and-aft the desired amount and retighten the bolts.
8   The engagement of the liftgate can be adjusted by loosening the lock striker bolts, repositioning the striker and retightening the bolts **(see illustration)**.

18   Door latch, lock cylinder and handles – removal and installation

1   Remove the door trim panel and watershield (Section 13).
2   Remove the door window glass (Section 19).

Door latch

Refer to illustrations 18.4 and 18.5

3   Reach in through the door service hole and disconnect the control link from the latch.
4   Remove the three door latch retaining screws from the end of the door **(see illustration)**.
5   Installation is the reverse of removal **(see illustration)**.

Lock cylinder

Refer to illustration 18.7

6   Disconnect the control link from the lock cylinder.

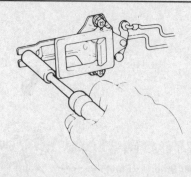

18.7   Use pliers to pull off the lock cylinder retaining clip

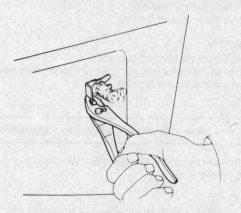

18.9   Use a nut driver or Phillips screwdriver to remove the inside door handle retaining screws

7   Use pliers to slide the retaining clip off and remove the lock cylinder from the door **(see illustration)**.
8   Installation is the reverse of removal.

Inside handle

Refer to illustration 18.9

9   Remove the retaining screws **(see illustration)**.

11

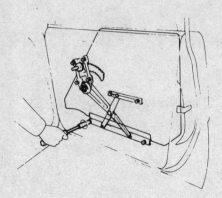

19.3   After marking their positions, remove the two window glass retaining nuts

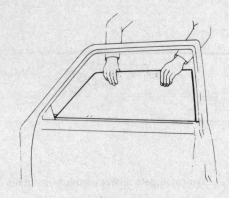

19.4   Lift the door glass up and pull it out, toward the outside of the door

10   Rotate the handle assembly away, disconnect the control rods from the handle and detach it from the door.
11   Installation is the reverse of removal.

Outside handle

12   Disconnect the control link from the handle.
13   Remove the nuts inside the door and detach the handle from the door.
14   Installation is the reverse of removal.

19   Door window glass – removal, installation and adjustment

1   Remove the door trim panel and watershield (Section 13).
2   Lower the window glass.

Front door

Refer to illustrations 19.3, 19.4, 19.6a, 19.6b and 19.6c

3   Scribe or paint marks on the two window-to-glass channel nuts and remove them **(see illustration)**.
4   Remove the window glass by tilting it to detach the glass from the glass channel studs and then sliding the glass up and out of the door **(see illustration)**.
5   If necessary, remove the regulator retaining bolts and slide the assembly up and out of the access hole in the door.
6   Installation is the reverse of removal **(see illustrations)**.

Rear door

Refer to illustrations 19.7, 19.8 and 19.9

7   Remove the retaining screws and pull the glass run and division bar out of the door **(see illustration)**.
8   Detach the glass from the regulator and pull the glass up and out of the door **(see illustration)**.
9   If you are replacing the glass, apply soapy water to the channel and tap the glass into place with a plastic mallet **(see illustration)**.
10   Lower the glass into the door and attach it to the regulator roller.

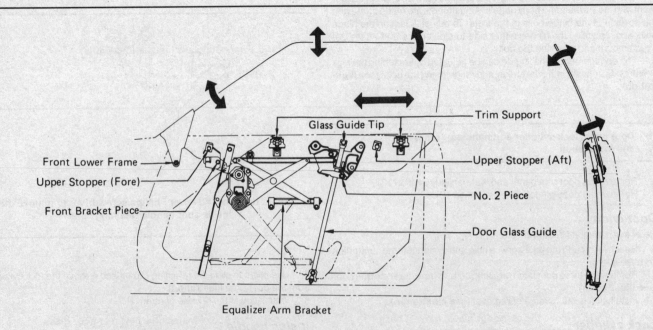

19.6a   Front door window glass adjustment details (1980 through 1983 models shown)

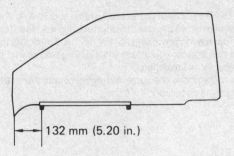

19.6b   On 1984 and later models, if you're installing a new front door glass, position the sash the specified distance from the front of the glass

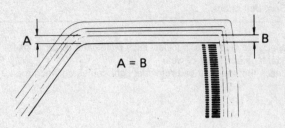

19.6c   On 1984 and later models, adjust the glass so the top edge is level

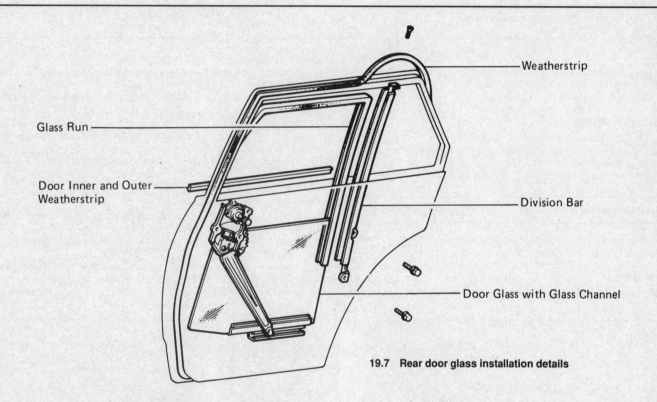

19.7   Rear door glass installation details

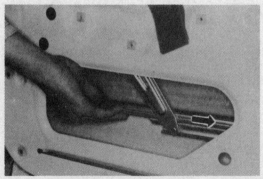

19.8   To remove the rear door glass, move it back and detach it from the regulator roller

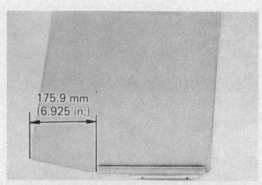

19.9   If you're installing a new rear door glass, position the sash the specified distance from the front of the glass

11

20   Seat belt check

1   Check the seat belts, buckles, latch plates and guide loops for obvious damage and signs of wear.
2   Check that the seat belt reminder light comes on when the key is turned to the Run or Start positions. A chime should also sound.
3   The seat belts are designed to lock up during a sudden stop or impact, yet allow free movement during normal driving. Check that the retractors return the belt against your chest while driving and rewind the belt fully when the buckle is unlatched.
4   If any of the above checks reveal problems with the seat belt system, replace parts as necessary.

Chapter 12   Chassis electrical system

Contents

12

1   General information

The electrical system is a 12-volt, negative ground type. Power for the lights and all electrical accessories is supplied by a lead/acid-type battery which is charged by the alternator.

This Chapter covers repair and service procedures for the various electrical components not associated with the engine. Information on the battery, alternator, distributor and starter motor can be found in Chapter 5.

It should be noted that when portions of the electrical system are serviced, the cable should be disconnected from the negative battery terminal to prevent electrical shorts and/or fires.

2   Electrical troubleshooting – general information

A typical electrical circuit consists of an electrical component, any switches, relays, motors, fuses, fusible links or circuit breakers related to that component and the wiring and connectors that link the component to both the battery and the chassis. To help you pinpoint an electrical circuit problem, wiring diagrams are included at the end of this book.

Before tackling any troublesome electrical circuit, first study the appropriate wiring diagrams to get a complete understanding of what makes up that individual circuit. Trouble spots, for instance, can often be narrowed down by noting if other components related to the circuit are operating properly. If several components or circuits fail at one time, chances are the problem is in a fuse or ground connection, because several circuits are often routed through the same fuse and ground connections.

Electrical problems usually stem from simple causes, such as loose or corroded connections, a blown fuse, a melted fusible link or a bad relay. Visually inspect the condition of all fuses, wires and connections in a problem circuit before troubleshooting it.

If testing instruments are going to be utilized, use the diagrams to plan ahead of time where you will make the necessary connections in order to accurately pinpoint the trouble spot.

The basic tools needed for electrical troubleshooting include a circuit tester or voltmeter (a 12-volt bulb with a set of test leads can also be used), a continuity tester, which includes a bulb, battery and set of test leads, and a jumper wire, preferably with a circuit breaker incorporated, which can be used to bypass electrical components. Before attempting to locate a problem with test instruments, use the wiring diagram(s) to decide where to make the connections.

Voltage checks

Voltage checks should be performed if a circuit is not functioning properly. Connect one lead of a circuit tester to either the negative battery terminal or a known good ground. Connect the other lead to a connector in the circuit being tested, preferably nearest to the battery or fuse. If the bulb of the tester lights, voltage is present, which means that the part of the circuit between the connector and the battery is problem free. Continue checking the rest of the circuit in the same fashion. When you reach a point at which no voltage is present, the problem lies between that point and the last test point with voltage. Most of the time the problem can be traced to a loose connection. **Note:** *Keep in mind that some circuits receive voltage only when the ignition key is in the Accessory or Run position.*

Finding a short

One method of finding shorts in a circuit is to remove the fuse and connect a test light or voltmeter in its place to the fuse terminals. There should be no voltage present in the circuit. Move the wiring harness from side to side while watching the test light. If the bulb goes on, there is a short to ground somewhere in that area, probably where the insulation has rubbed through. The same test can be performed on each component in the circuit, even a switch.

Ground check

Perform a ground test to check whether a component is properly grounded. Disconnect the battery and connect one lead of a selfpowered test light, known as a continuity tester, to a known good ground. Connect the other lead to the wire or ground connection being tested. If the bulb goes on, the ground is good. If the bulb does not go on, the ground is not good.

Continuity check

A continuity check is done to determine if there are any breaks in a circuit – if it is passing electricity properly. With the circuit off (no power in the circuit), a self-powered continuity tester can be used to check the circuit. Connect the test leads to both ends of the circuit (or to the "power" end and a good ground), and if the test light comes on the circuit is passing current properly. If the light doesn't come on, there is a break somewhere in the circuit. The same procedure can be used to test a switch, by con-

necting the continuity tester to the power in and power out sides of the switch. With the switch turned On, the test light should come on.

Finding an open circuit

When diagnosing for possible open circuits, it is often difficult to locate them by sight because oxidation or terminal misalignment are hidden by the connectors. Merely wiggling a connector on a sensor or in the wiring harness may correct the open circuit condition. Remember this when an open circuit is indicated when troubleshooting a circuit. Intermittent problems may also be caused by oxidized or loose connections.

Electrical troubleshooting is simple if you keep in mind that all electrical circuits are basically electricity running from the battery, through the wires, switches, relays, fuses and fusible links to each electrical component (light bulb, motor, etc.) and to ground, from which it is passed back to the battery. Any electrical problem is an interruption in the flow of electricity to and from the battery.

3   Fuses – general information

Refer to illustrations 3.1 and 3.3

The electrical circuits of the vehicle are protected by a combination of fuses, circuit breakers and fusible links. The fuse blocks are located on the driver's side kick panel, on the passenger's side kick panel (1984 and later models) and next to the battery in the engine compartment **(see illustration)**.

Each of the fuses is designed to protect a specific circuit, and the various circuits are identified on the fuse panel itself.

Miniaturized fuses are employed in the fuse block. These compact fuses, with blade terminal design, allow fingertip removal and replacement. If an electrical component fails, always check the fuse first. A blown fuse is easily identified through the clear plastic body. Visually inspect the element for evidence of damage **(see illustration)**. If a continuity check is called for, the blade terminal tips are exposed in the fuse body.

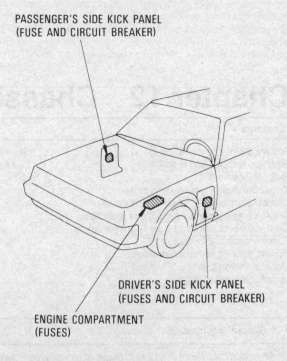

PASSENGER'S SIDE KICK PANEL
(FUSE AND CIRCUIT BREAKER)

DRIVER'S SIDE KICK PANEL
(FUSES AND CIRCUIT BREAKER)

ENGINE COMPARTMENT
(FUSES)

3.1   Typical fuse block locations

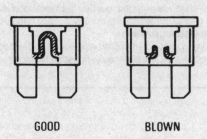

3.3   The fuses used on these models can be checked visually to determine if they're blown

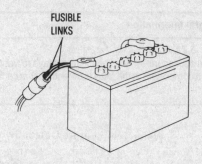

4.2a   On 1980 through 1983 models the fusible links are connected to the positive battery cable

Be sure to replace blown fuses with the correct type. Fuses of different ratings are physically interchangeable, but only fuses of the proper rating should be used. Replacing a fuse with one of a higher or lower value than pecified is not recommended. Each electrical circuit needs a specific amount of protection. The amperage value of each fuse is molded into the fuse body.

If the replacement fuse immediately fails, don't replace it again until the cause of the problem is isolated and corrected. In most cases, this will be a short circuit in the wiring caused by a broken or deteriorated wire.

4   Fusible links – general information

Refer to illustrations 4.2a and 4.2b

Some circuits are protected by fusible links. The links are used in circuits which are not ordinarily fused, such as the ignition circuit.

The fusible links on 1980 through 1983 models are located in the main wiring harness next to the battery or in the positive battery cable **(see illustration)**. The fusible links cannot be repaired, but a new link of the same size (available from your dealer) can be put in its place. On 1984 and later models the fusible links are similar to fuses in that they can be visually checked to determine if they are melted **(see illustration)**.

To replace a fusible link, first disconnect the negative cable from the battery. Unplug the burned out link and replace it with a new one (available from your dealer). Always determine the cause for the overload which melted the fusible link before installing a new one.

5   Circuit breakers – general information

Refer to illustration 5.3

Circuit breakers protect components such as power windows, power door locks and headlights. Some circuit breakers are located in the fuse box.

Because on some models the circuit breaker resets itself automatically, an electrical overload in a circuit breaker protected system will cause the circuit to fail momentarily, then come back on. If the circuit does not come back on, check it immediately. Note, however, that on 1984 and later models, some circuit breakers must be reset manually. Once the condition is corrected, the circuit breaker will resume its normal function.

To reset a manual circuit breaker, first turn off the ignition switch. Insert a toothpick into the reset hole and push in until your hear a click **(see illustration)**.

4.2b   On 1984 and later models, the fusible links can be checked visually to determine if they're melted

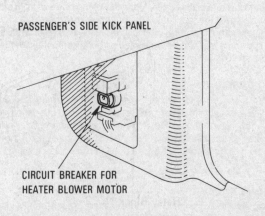

5.3   Some circuit breakers used on 1984 and later models can be reset without removing them from the vehicle – insert a toothpick or paper clip into the circuit breaker reset hole and push in to reset it

12

6   Relays – general information

Refer to illustrations 6.2a, 6.2b, 6.2c and 6.2d

Several electrical accessories in the vehicle use relays to transmit the electrical signal to the component. If the relay is defective, that component will not operate properly.

The various relays are grouped together in several locations under the dash and in the engine compartment for convenience in the event of needed replacement **(see illustrations)**.

If a faulty relay is suspected, it can be removed and tested by a dealer or other qualified shop. Defective relays must be replaced as a unit.

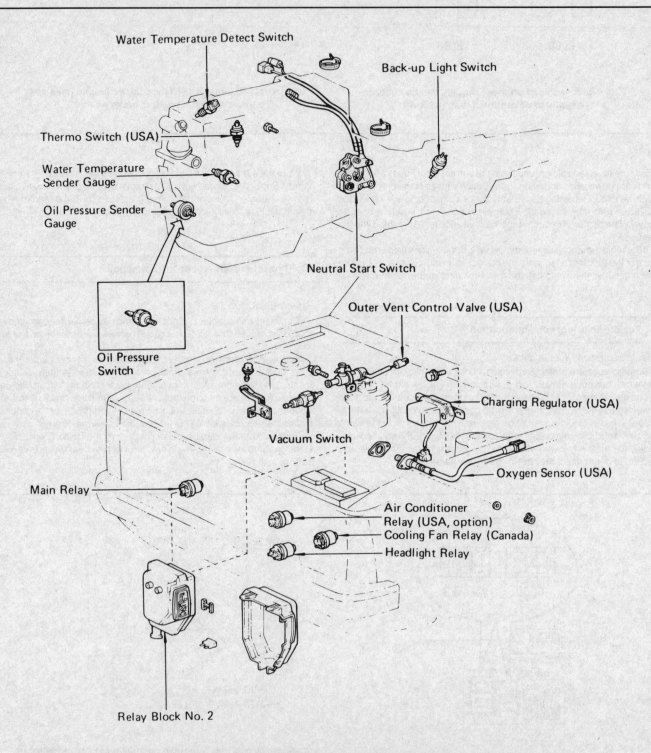

6.2a   Typical engine compartment electrical components (1980 through 1983 models)

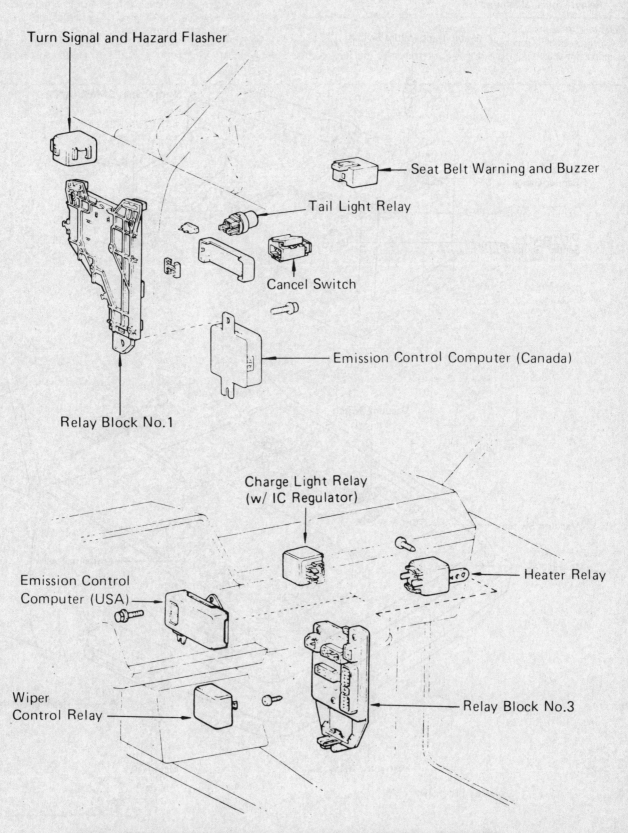

6.2b   Typical passenger compartment electrical components (1980 through 1983 models)

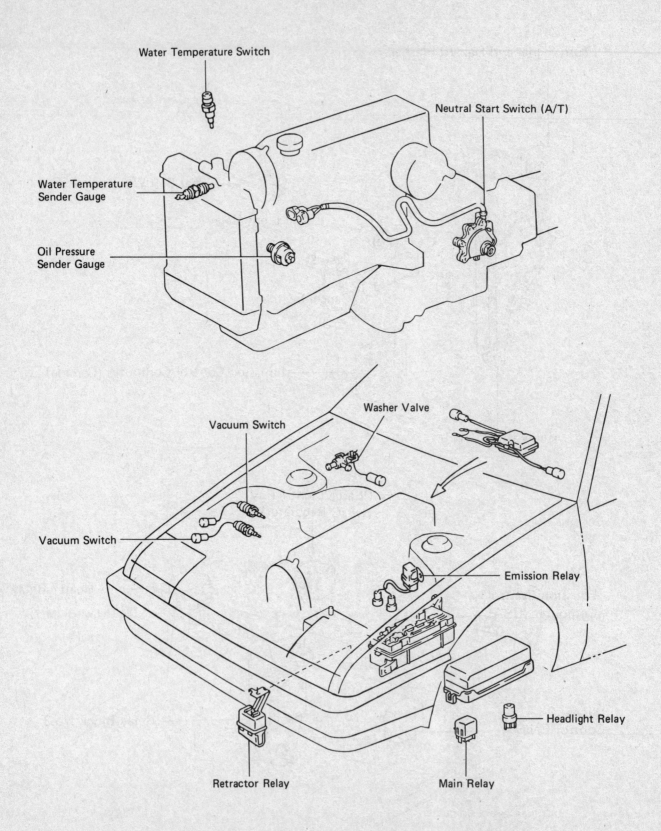

6.2c   Typical engine compartment electrical components (1984 and later models)

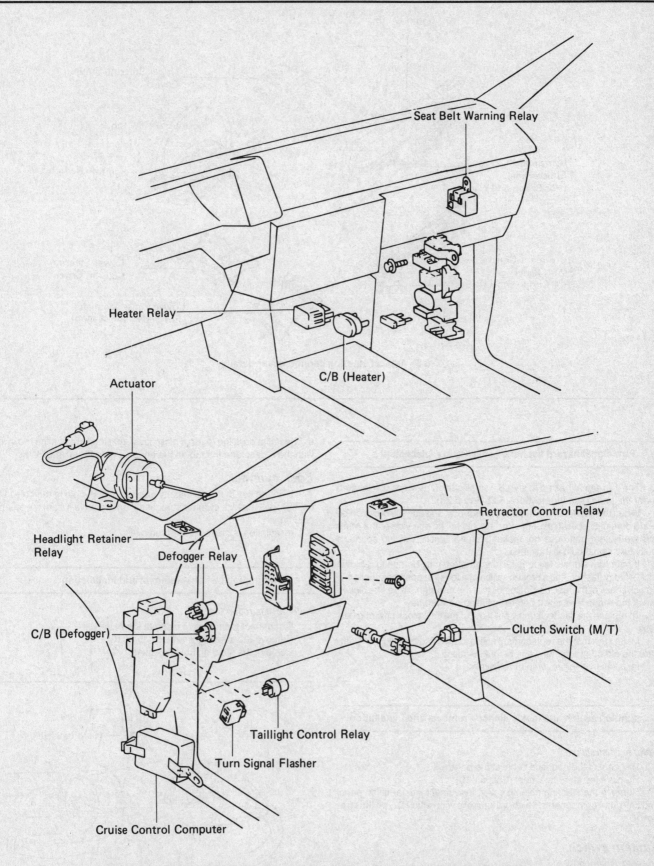

6.2d Typical passenger compartment electrical components (1984 and later models)

Seat Belt Warning Relay

Heater Relay

Actuator

C/B (Heater)

Retractor Control Relay

Headlight Retainer Relay

Defogger Relay

C/B (Defogger)

Clutch Switch (M/T)

Taillight Control Relay

Turn Signal Flasher

Cruise Control Computer

12

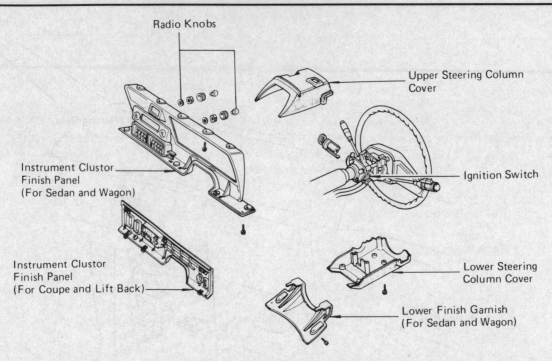

Radio Knobs

Upper Steering Column Cover

Instrument Clustor Finish Panel (For Sedan and Wagon)

Ignition Switch

Instrument Clustor Finish Panel (For Coupe and Lift Back)

Lower Steering Column Cover

Lower Finish Garnish (For Sedan and Wagon)

8.3   Typical steering column cover details

7   Turn signal/hazard flashers – check and replacement

1   The turn signal/hazard flasher is a small canister shaped unit located under the dash **(see illustrations 6.2b and 6.2d)**.

2   When the flasher unit is functioning properly, and audible click can be heard during its operation. If the turn signals fail on one side or the other and the flasher unit does not make its characteristic clicking sound, a faulty turn signal bulb is indicated.

3   If both turn signals fail to blink, the problem may be due to a blown fuse, a faulty flasher unit, a broken switch or a loose or open connection. If a quick check of the fuse box indicates that the turn signal fuse has blown, check the wiring for a short before installing a new fuse.

4   To replace the flasher, simply pull it out of the fuse block or wiring harness.

5   Make sure that the replacement unit is identical to the original. Compare the old one to the new one before installing it.

6   Installation is the reverse of removal.

8   Ignition switch and lock cylinder – removal and installation

Refer to illustration 8.3

1   Disconnect the negative cable at the battery.

2   Remove the steering wheel (Chapter 10).

3   Remove the steering column cover, instrument cluster finish panel and any other components which will interfere with removal **(see illustration)**.

Ignition switch

Refer to illustration 8.6

4   Remove the retaining screws and bend back the wiring retainer.

5   Unplug the electrical connector and detach the switch from the steering column.

6   Installation is the reverse of removal, making sure to align the switch with the recess and the tab on the housing **(see illustration)**.

Lock cylinder

7   With the key in the Accessory position, insert a pin in the hole in the casting, pull the lock cylinder straight out and remove it from the steering column.

8   Installation is the reverse of removal.

9   Combination switch – removal and installation

Refer to illustration 9.4

1   Disconnect the negative cable at the battery.

2   Remove the steering wheel (Chapter 10).

3   Remove the steering column covers.

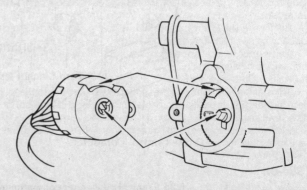

8.6   Line up the slot and recess in the switch with the housing (some models)

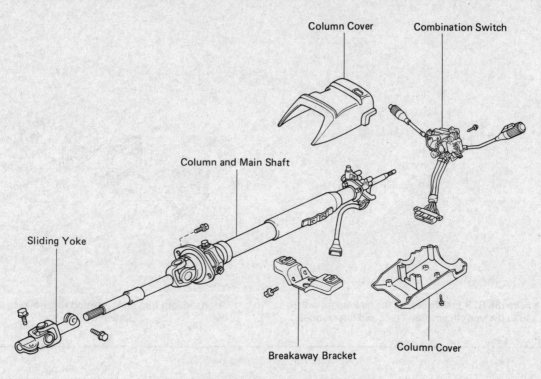

Column Cover

Combination Switch

Column and Main Shaft

Sliding Yoke

Breakaway Bracket

Column Cover

9.4   Combination switch installation details

4   Remove the switch retaining screws **(see illustration)**.
5   Trace the switch wiring harness down the steering column to the connector and unplug it. Remove the switch.
6   Installation is the reverse of removal.

10   Headlights – removal and installation

1   Disconnect the negative cable from the battery.

1980 through 1983

Refer to illustrations 10.2 and 10.3

2   Open the hood. Remove the parking light lens, insert a screwdriver blade into the clips, release them and detach the headlight bezel **(see illustration)**.
3   Remove the headlight retainer screws, taking care not to disturb the adjusting screws **(see illustration)**.
4   Remove the retainer and pull the headlight out sufficiently to allow the connector to be unplugged.
5   Remove the headlight.
6   To install the headlight, plug the connector securely into the headlight, place the headlight in position and install the retainer and screws. Tighten the screws securely.
7   Place the headlight bezel in position, press it into place and reinstall the parking light lens.

1984-on

Refer to illustrations 10.8 and 10.9

8   Open the hood. Push the headlight switch in and rotate it to the third stop to raise the headlight. In the engine compartment, pull out the RTR

10.2   After removing the parking light, insert a flat screwdriver blade into the clips and turn it to unlock the bezel (1980 through 1983 models)

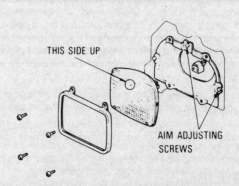

THIS SIDE UP

AIM ADJUSTING SCREWS

12

10.3   Remove the screws and detach the retainer – DO NOT disturb the headlight aim adjusting screws unless you're adjusting the headlights

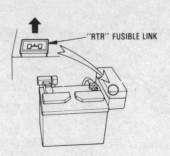

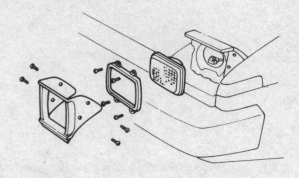

10.8   Remove the RTR fusible link so the headlights will remain locked in the upright position (1984 and later models)

10.9   Headlight trim and retaining ring details (1984 and later models)

fusible link located in the fusebox adjacent to the battery **(see illustration)**.

9   Remove the screws and detach the headlight trim and retaining rings, taking care not to disturb the adjusting screws **(see illustration)**.

10   Pull the headlight out sufficiently to allow the connector to be unplugged.

11   Remove the headlight.

12   To install the headlight, plug the connector securely into the headlight, place the headlight in position and install the retainer and screws. Tighten the screws securely.

13   Place the headlight trim ring in position, press it into place and tighten the retaining screws. Install the RTR fusible link.

11   Headlights – adjustment

Note: *The headlights must be aimed correctly. If adjusted incorrectly, they could blind the driver of an oncoming vehicle and cause an accident or seriously reduce your ability to see the road. The headlights should be checked for proper aim every 12 months and any time a new headlight is installed or front end body work is performed. It should be emphasized that the following procedure is only an interim step which will provide temporary adjustment until the headlights can be adjusted by a properly equipped shop.*

1   Headlights have two adjusting screws, one on the top controlling up and down movement and one on the side controlling left and right movement.

2   There are several methods of adjusting the headlights. The simplest method requires a blank wall 25 feet in front of the vehicle and a level floor.

3   Position masking tape vertically on the wall in reference to the vehicle centerline and the centerlines of both headlights.

4   Position a horizontal tape line in reference to the centerline of all the headlights. **Note:** *It may be easier to position the tape on the wall with the vehicle parked only a few inches away.*

5   Adjustment should be made with the vehicle sitting level, the gas tank half-full and no unusually heavy load in the vehicle.

6   Starting with the low beam adjustment, position the high intensity zone so it is two inches below the horizontal line and two inches to the right of the headlight vertical line. Adjustment is made by turning the top adjusting screw clockwise to raise the beam and counterclockwise to lower the beam **(see illustration 10.3)**. The adjusting screw on the side should be used in the same manner to move the beam left or right.

7   With the high beams on, the high intensity zone should be vertically centered with the exact center just below the horizontal line. **Note:** *It may not be possible to position the headlight aim exactly for both high and low beams. If a compromise must be made, keep in mind that the low beams are the most used and have the greatest effect on driver safety.*

8   Have the headlights adjusted by a dealer service department at the earliest opportunity.

12   Bulb replacement

Refer to illustrations 12.1, 12.2, 12.3a, 12.3b, 12.3c and 12.4

1   The lenses of many lights are held in place by screws, which makes it a simple procedure to gain access to the bulbs **(see illustration)**.

2   On some lights the lenses are held in place by clips. On these, the lenses can either be removed by unsnapping them or by using a small screwdriver to pry them off **(see illustration)**.

3   Several types of bulbs are used. Some are removed by pushing in and turning counterclockwise **(see illustrations)**. Others can simply be unclipped from the terminals or pulled straight out of the socket.

4   To gain access to the instrument panel illumination lights **(see illustration)**, the instrument cluster will have to be removed as described in Section 14.

13   Wiper motors – removal and installation

1   Disconnect the negative cable at the battery.

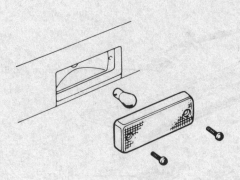

12.1   The front turn signal lens is held in place by two screws

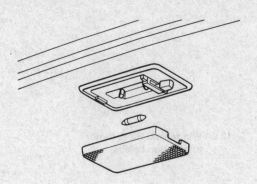

12.2   The dome light and lens are held in place by clips

12.3a   Parking light details (1980 through 1983 models)

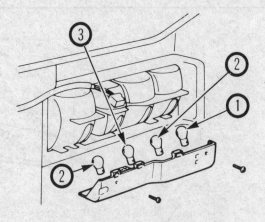

12.3b   The rear light bulbs on sedan and coupe models are located under a cover

1   Turn signal light
2   Brake and turn signal light
3   Back-up light

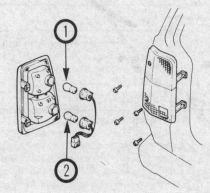

12.3c   The rear lights on station wagon models are accessible after removing the lens

1   Turn signal light
2   brake and turn signal light

12.4   After removing the instrument cluster, turn the bulb holders, lift them out and pull out the bulbs

12

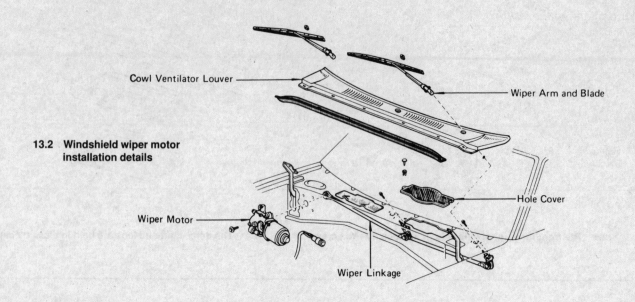

Cowl Ventilator Louver

Wiper Arm and Blade

13.2   Windshield wiper motor installation details

Hole Cover

Wiper Motor

Wiper Linkage

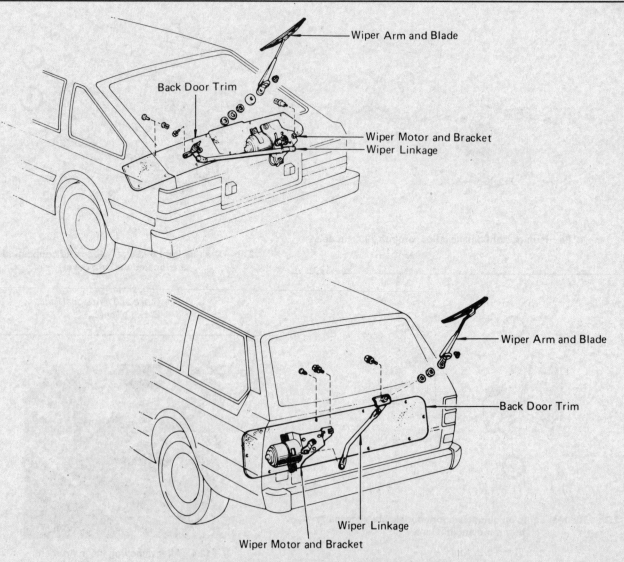

Wiper Arm and Blade

Back Door Trim

Wiper Motor and Bracket

Wiper Linkage

Wiper Arm and Blade

Back Door Trim

Wiper Linkage

Wiper Motor and Bracket

13.6   Typical rear wiper motor mounting details

Windshield wiper motor

Refer to illustration 13.2

2   Locate the wiper motor under the hood **(see illustration)**.
3   Unplug the electrical connector, remove the retaining bolts and lift the wiper motor from the engine compartment.
4   Installation is the reverse of removal.

Rear wiper motor

Refer to illustration 13.6

5   Remove the back door trim.
6   Disconnect the wiper linkage arm from the motor **(see illustration)**.

7   Unplug the electrical connector, remove the retaining screws and lower the motor from the vehicle.
8   Installation is the reverse of removal.

14   Instrument cluster – removal and installation

Refer to illustrations 14.3a, 14.3b, 14.3c, 14.5a and 14.5b

1   Disconnect the negative cable at the battery.
2   Remove the steering column covers.
3   Remove the retaining screws, then remove the cluster finish panels **(see illustrations)**.

Sedan and Wagon

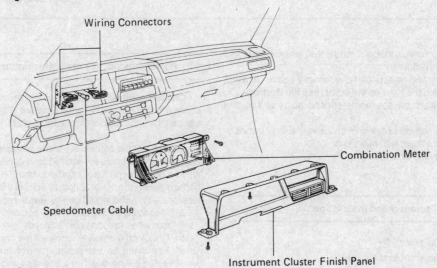

Hardtop, Coupe and Liftback

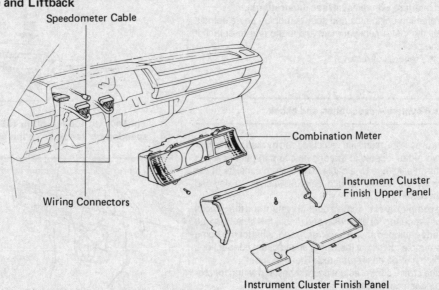

14.3a   Instrument cluster (combination meter) installation details (1980 through 1983 models)

12

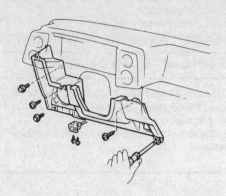

14.3b   Remove the left side finish panel (1984 and later models)

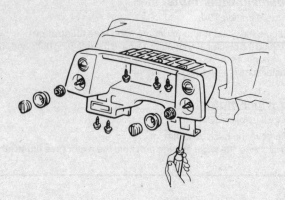

14.3c   Instrument cluster finish panel details (1984 and later models)

4   Remove the retaining screws, then pull out the instrument cluster and disconnect the wiring connectors.
5   Reach behind cluster and detach the speedometer cable. On 1980 through 1983 models, push the lever on the collar **(see illustration)**. On 1984 and later models, grasp the speedometer cable guide and push it back **(see illustration)**.
6   To replace any faulty components within the cluster, simply unbolt or unscrew them and replace them with new units.
7   Installation is the reverse of removal.

15   Instrument panel – removal and installation

Refer to illustrations 15.3a and 15.3b
1   Disconnect the negative cable at the battery.
2   Remove the steering wheel (Chapter 10).
3   Remove the steering column covers, finish panels, instrument cluster, ducts, nozzles, registers, radio, heater controls and any other components which would interfere with removal **(see illustrations)**.
4   Remove the retaining bolts, nuts and screws, unplug any electrical connectors and pull the instrument panel up and to the rear to detach it from the clips on the back.
5   Installation is the reverse of removal.

16   Cruise control system – description and check

The cruise control system maintains vehicle speed by means of a vacuum actuated servo motor located in the engine compartment which is connected to the throttle linkage by a cable. The system consists of the servo motor, clutch switch, stoplight switch, control switches, a relay and associated vacuum hoses.
Because of the complexity of the cruise control system and the special tools and techniques required for diagnosis and repair, this should be left to a dealer or properly equipped shop. However, it is possible for the home mechanic to make simple checks of the wiring and vacuum connections for minor faults which can be easily repaired. These include:
a) Inspecting the cruise control actuating switches and wiring for broken wires or loose connections.
b) Checking the cruise control fuse.
c) Checking the hoses in the engine compartment for tight connections, cracked hoses and obvious vacuum leaks. The cruise control system is operated by a vacuum so it is critical that all vacuum switches, hoses and connections be secure.

17   Power window system – description and check

The power window system operates the electric motors mounted in the doors which lower and raise the windows. The system consists of the control switches, the motors (regulators), glass mechanisms and associated wiring.
Because of the complexity of the power window system and the special tools and techniques required for diagnosis and repair, this should be left to a dealer or properly equipped shop. However, it is possible for the home mechanic to make simple checks of the wiring connections and motors for minor faults which can be easily repaired. These include:
a) Inspecting the power window actuating switches and wiring for broken wires or loose connections.
b) Checking the power window fuse and/or circuit breaker.
c) Removing the door panel(s) and checking the power window motor wiring connections for looseness and damage, and inspecting the glass mechanisms for damage which could cause binding.

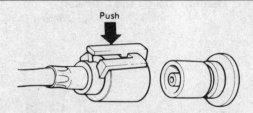

14.5a   On 1980 through 1983 models, disconnect the speedometer cable from the cluster by pushing the lever

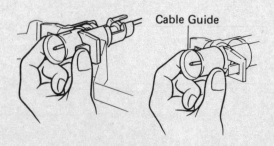

14.5b   On 1984 and later models, push the cable guide back to disconnect the speedometer cable

Sedan and Wagon

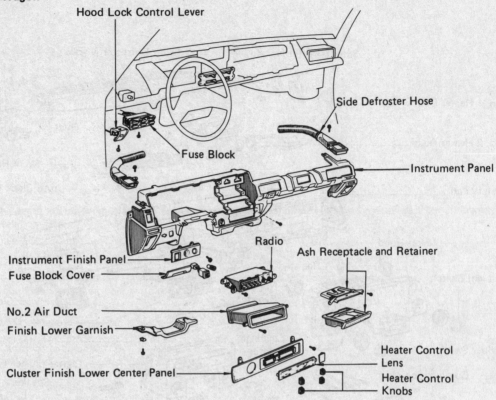

Hood Lock Control Lever

Side Defroster Hose

Fuse Block

Instrument Panel

Instrument Finish Panel

Fuse Block Cover

Radio

Ash Receptacle and Retainer

No.2 Air Duct

Finish Lower Garnish

Cluster Finish Lower Center Panel

Heater Control Lens

Heater Control Knobs

Hardtop, Coupe and Liftback

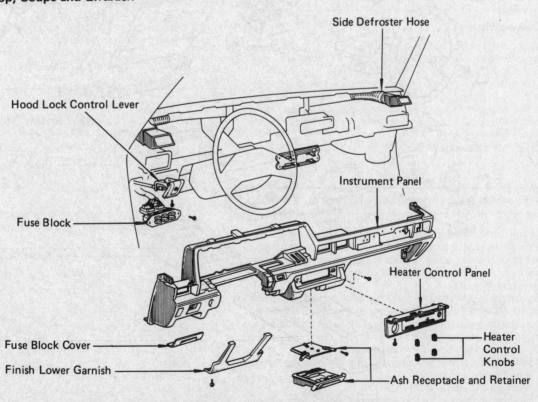

Side Defroster Hose

Hood Lock Control Lever

Instrument Panel

Fuse Block

Heater Control Panel

Fuse Block Cover

Finish Lower Garnish

Heater Control Knobs

Ash Receptacle and Retainer

15.3a   Instrument panel details (1980 through 1983 models)

12

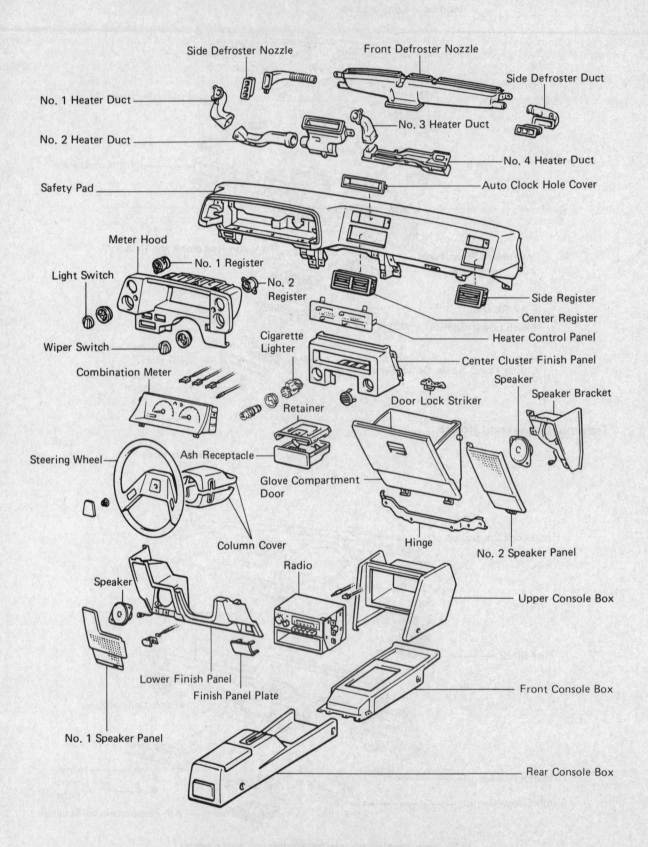

15.3b   Instrument panel details (1984 and later models)

18 Wiring diagrams – general information

Since it isn't possible to include all wiring diagrams for every year covered by this manual, the following diagrams are those that are typical and most commonly needed.

Prior to troubleshooting any circuits, check the fuse and circuit breakers (if equipped) to make sure they are in good condition. Make sure the battery is properly charged and has clean, tight cable connections (Chapter 1).

When checking the wiring system, make sure that all connectors are clean, with no broken or loose pins. When unplugging a connector, do not pull on the wires, only on the connector housings themselves.

Refer to the accompanying illustration for the wire color codes applicable to your vehicle.

Wire colors are indicated by an alphabetical code.

B	= Black	L	= Light Blue	R	= Red
BR	= Brown	LG	= Light Green	V	= Violet
G	= Green	O	= Orange	W	= White
GR	= Gray	P	= Pink	Y	= Yellow

The first letter indicates the basic wire color and the second letter indicates the color of the stripe.

Wiring diagram color code chart

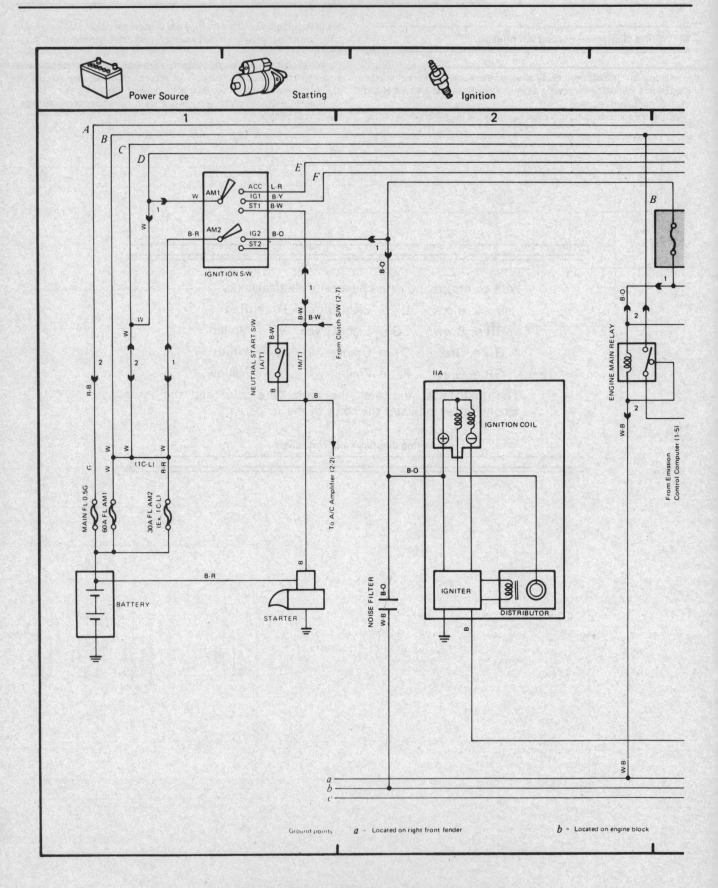

Typical wiring diagram – 1980 through 1984 models (1 of 12)

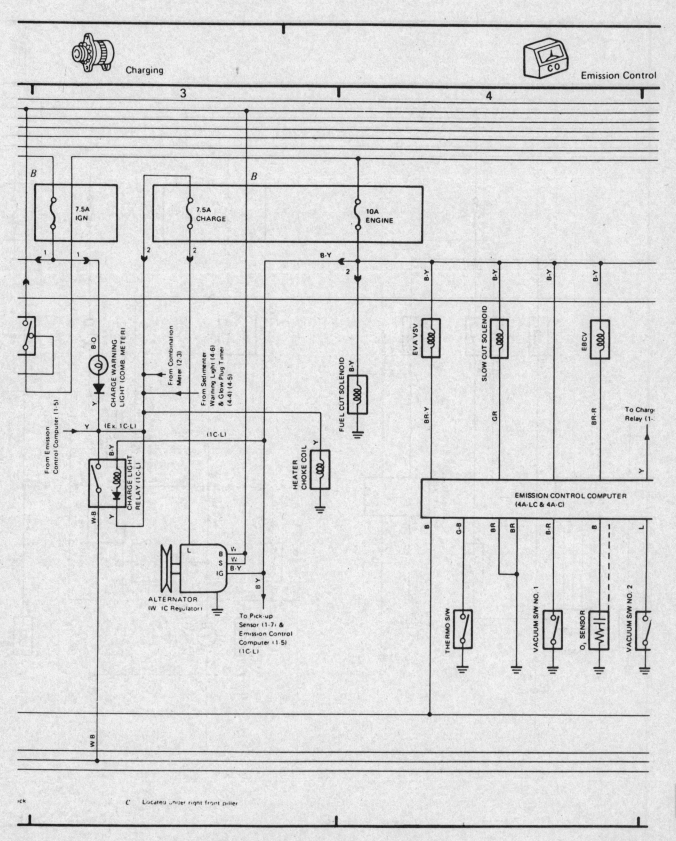

Typical wiring diagram – 1980 through 1984 models (2 of 12)

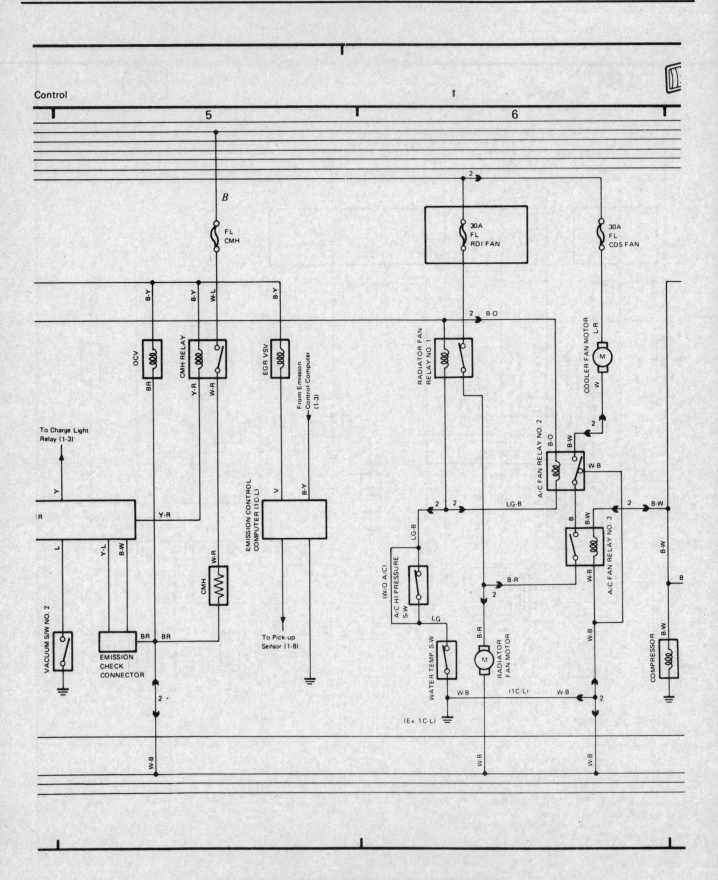

Typical wiring diagram – 1980 through 1984 models (3 of 12)

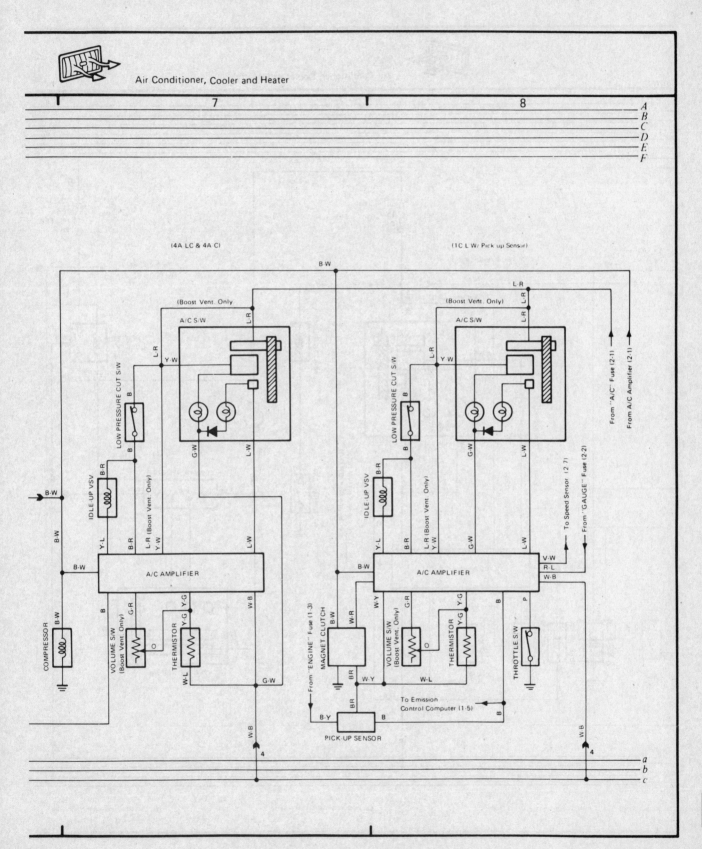

Air Conditioner, Cooler and Heater

Typical wiring diagram – 1980 through 1984 models (4 of 12)

12

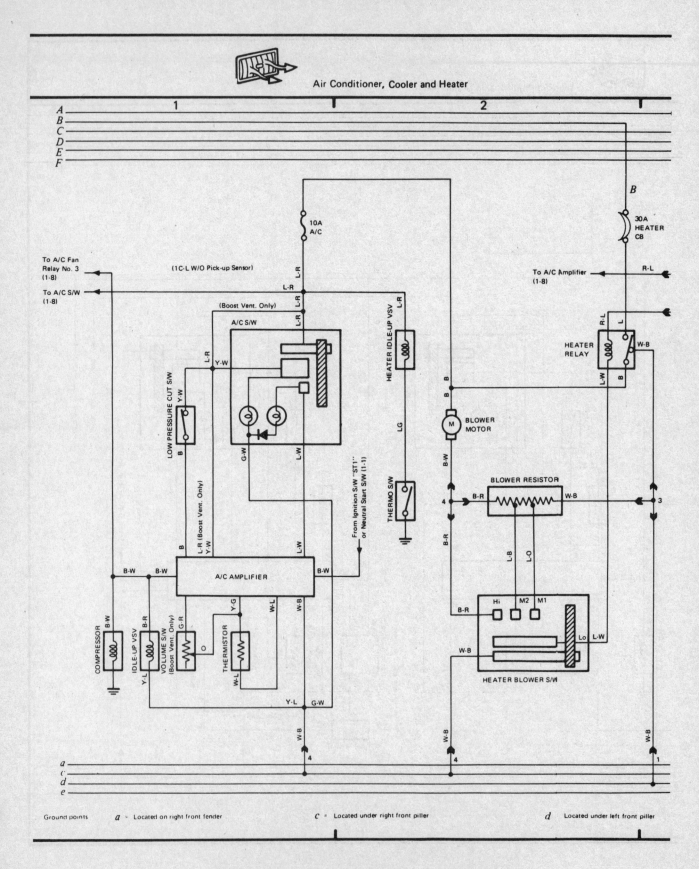

Typical wiring diagram – 1980 through 1984 models (5 of 12)

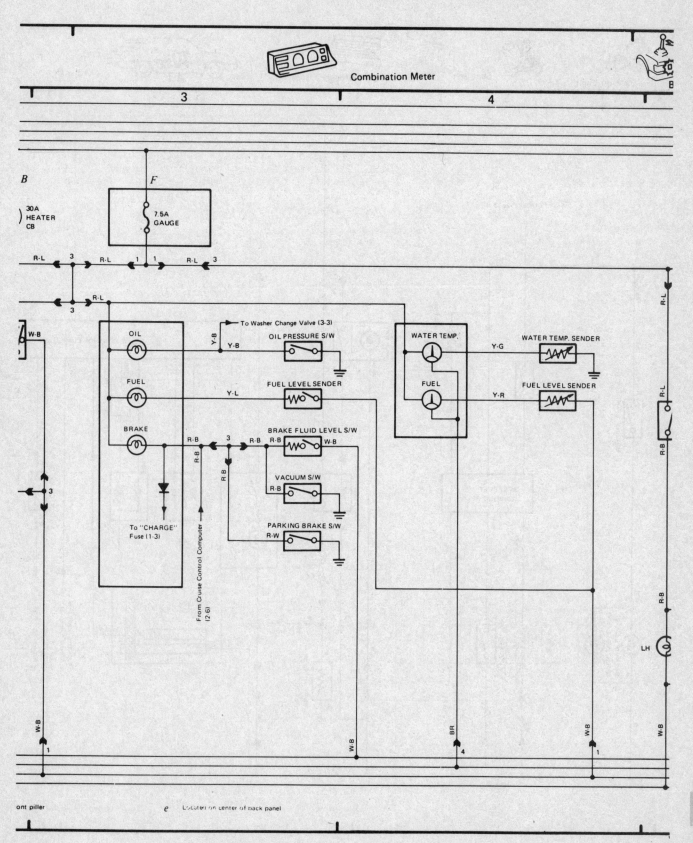

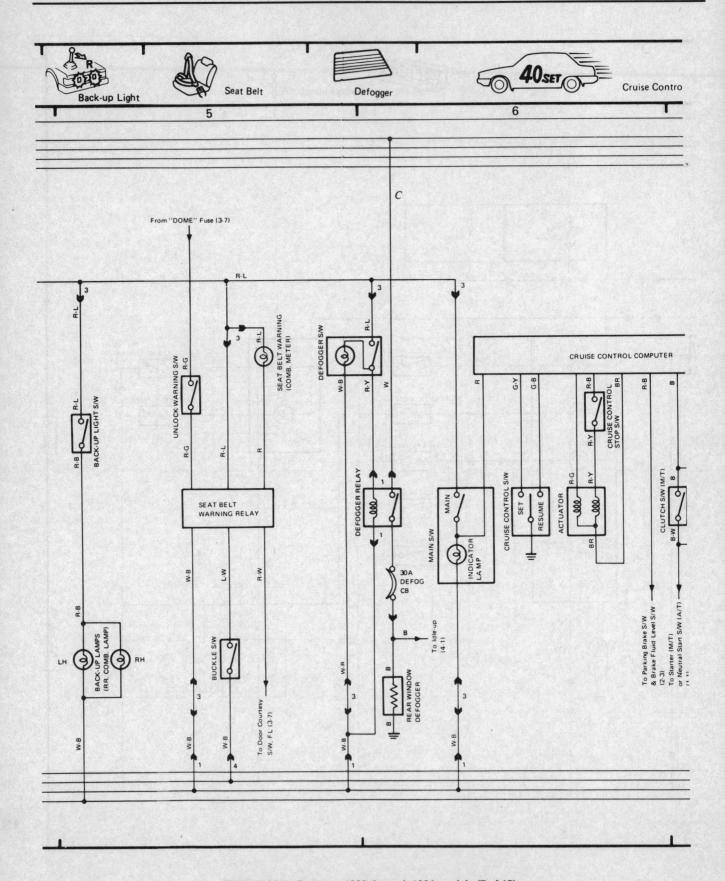

Typical wiring diagram – 1980 through 1984 models (7 of 12)

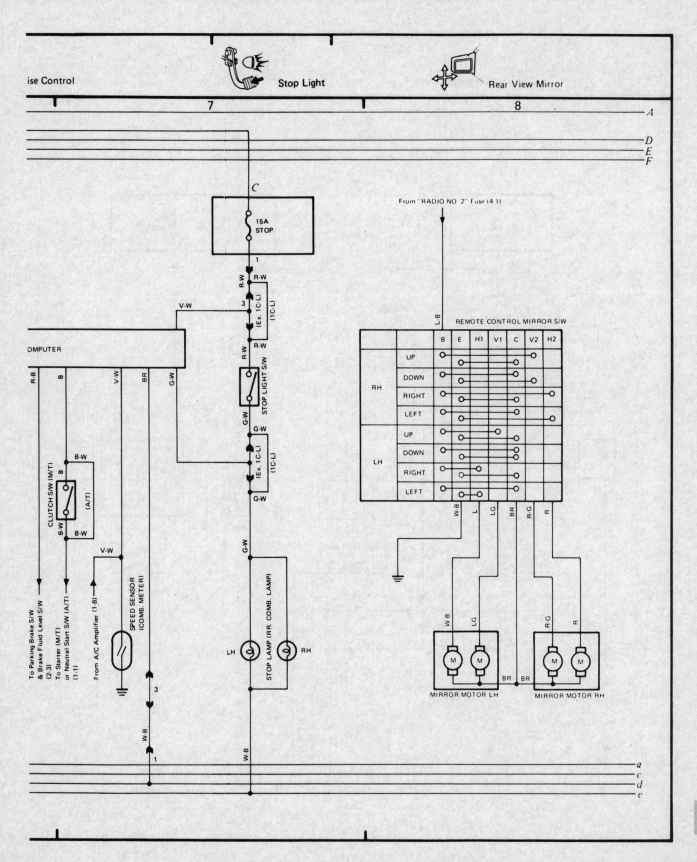

Typical wiring diagram – 1980 through 1984 models (8 of 12)

12

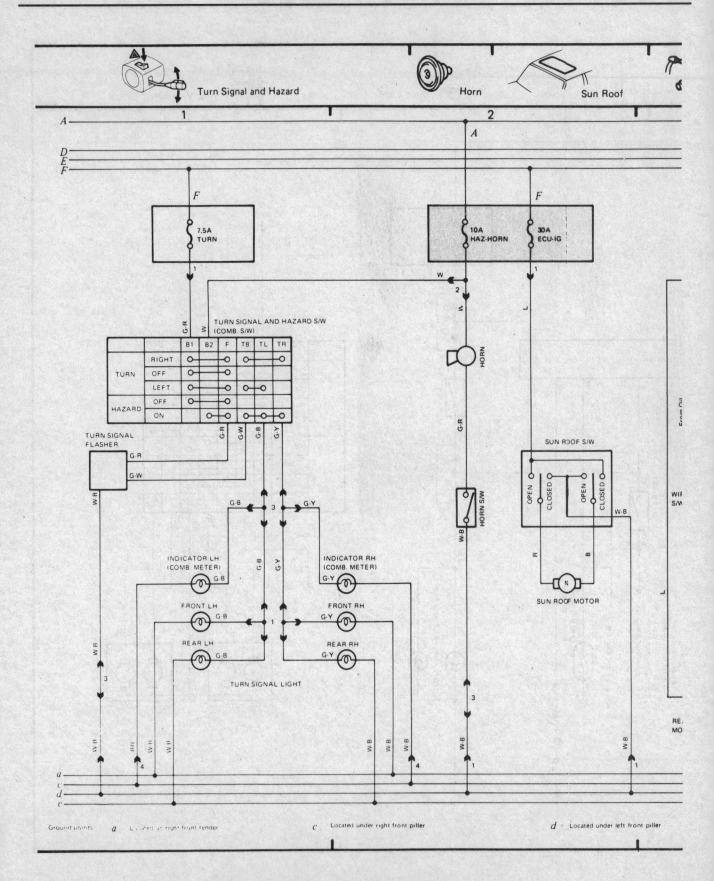

Typical wiring diagram – 1980 through 1984 models (9 of 12)

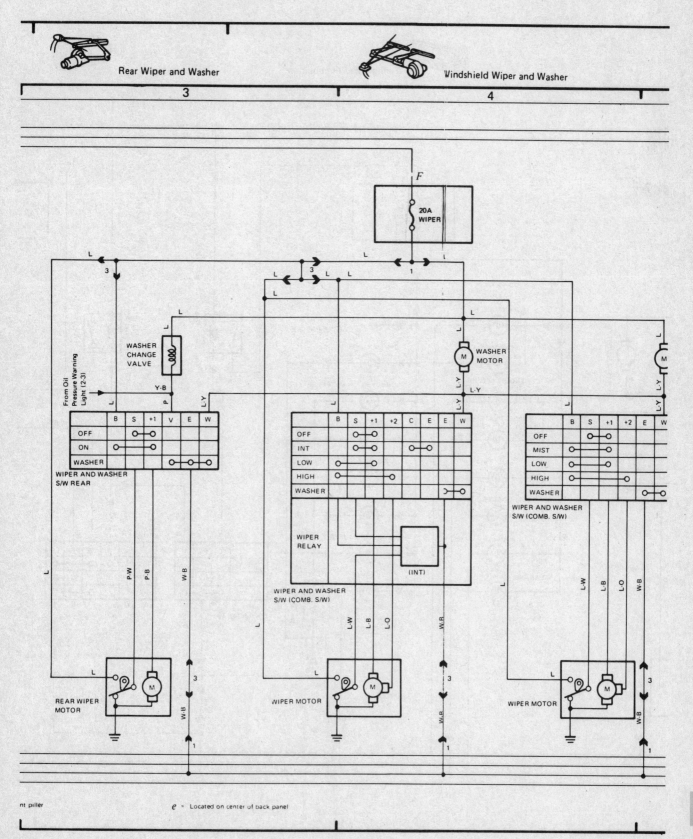

Rear Wiper and Washer

Windshield Wiper and Washer

3

4

F

20A
WIPER

WASHER
CHANGE
VALVE

WASHER
MOTOR

From Oil
Pressure Warning
Light (2-3)

Y-B

WIPER AND WASHER S/W REAR	B	S	+1	V	E	W
OFF						
ON						
WASHER						

WIPER AND WASHER S/W (COMB. S/W)	B	S	+1	+2	C	E	E	W
OFF								
INT								
LOW								
HIGH								
WASHER								

WIPER
RELAY

(INT)

WIPER AND WASHER S/W (COMB. S/W)	B	S	+1	+2	E	W
OFF						
MIST						
LOW						
HIGH						
WASHER						

REAR WIPER
MOTOR

WIPER MOTOR

WIPER MOTOR

nt piller

e = Located on center of back panel

Typical wiring diagram – 1980 through 1984 models (10 of 12)

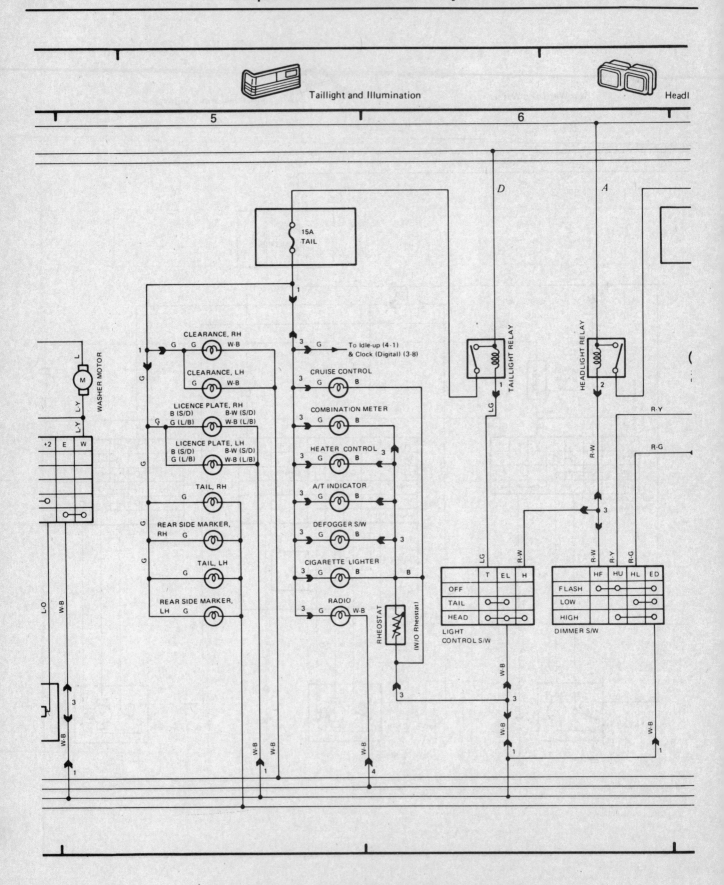

Typical wiring diagram – 1980 through 1984 models (11 of 12)

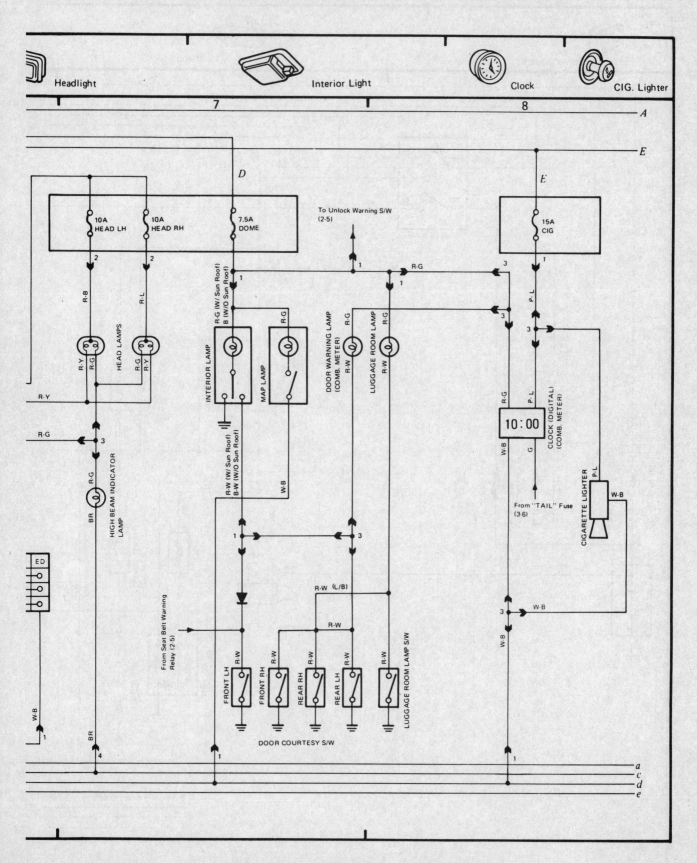

Typical wiring diagram – 1980 through 1984 models (12 of 12)

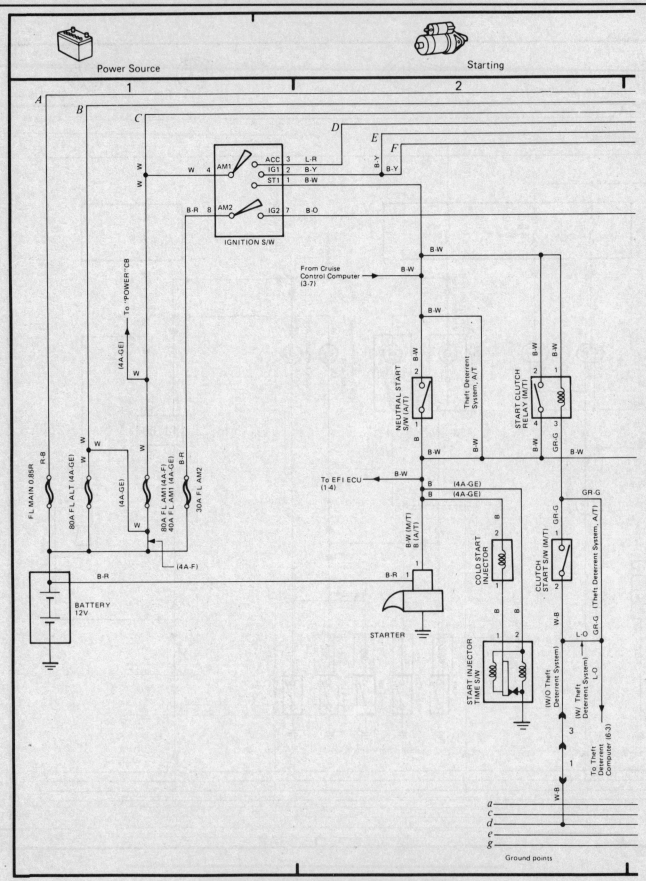

Typical wirng diagram – 1985 and later models (1 of 7)

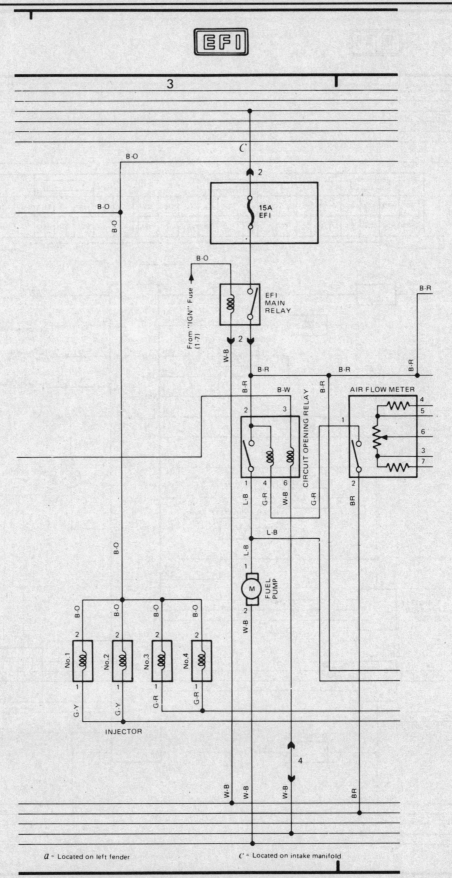

Typical wirng diagram – 1985 and later models (2 of 7)

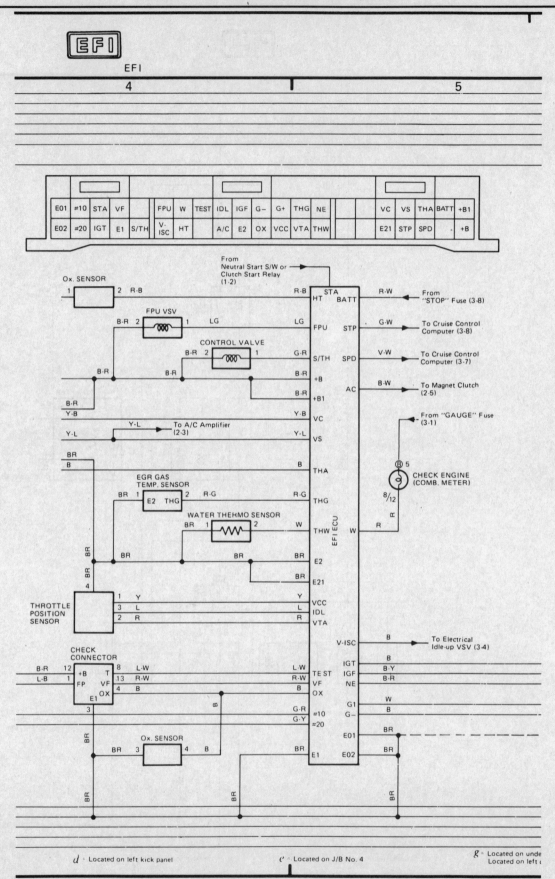

Typical wirng diagram – 1985 and later models (3 of 7)

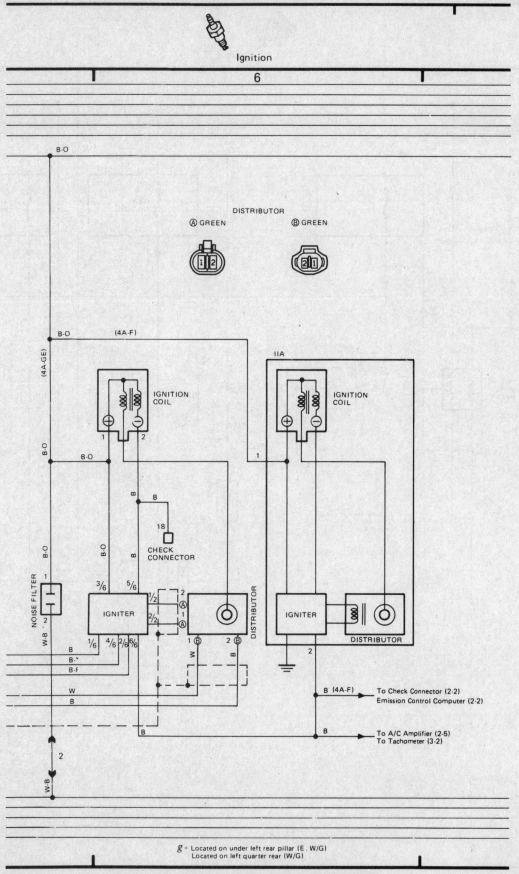

12

g = Located on under left rear pillar (E . W/G)
Located on left quarter rear (W/G)

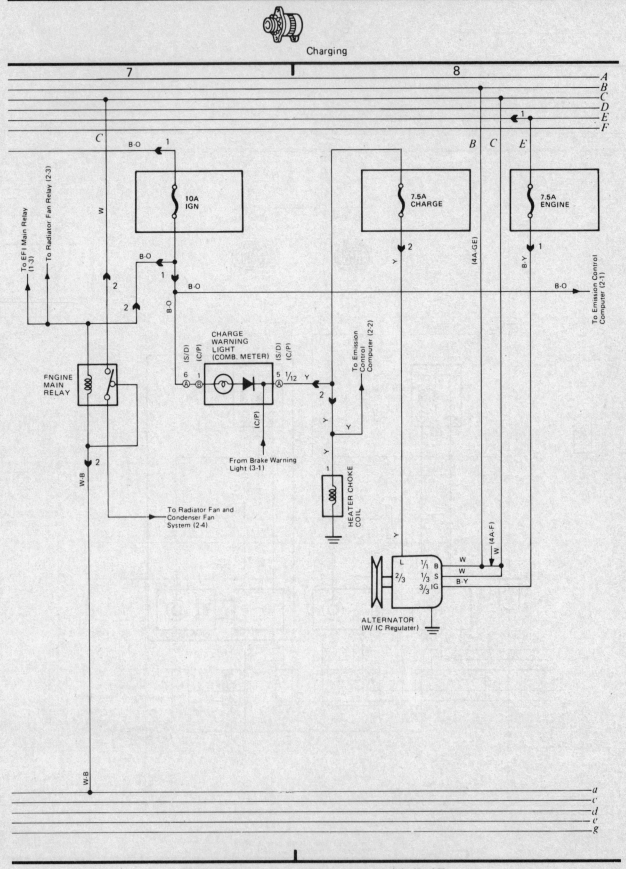

Charging

ALTERNATOR
(W/ IC Regulater)

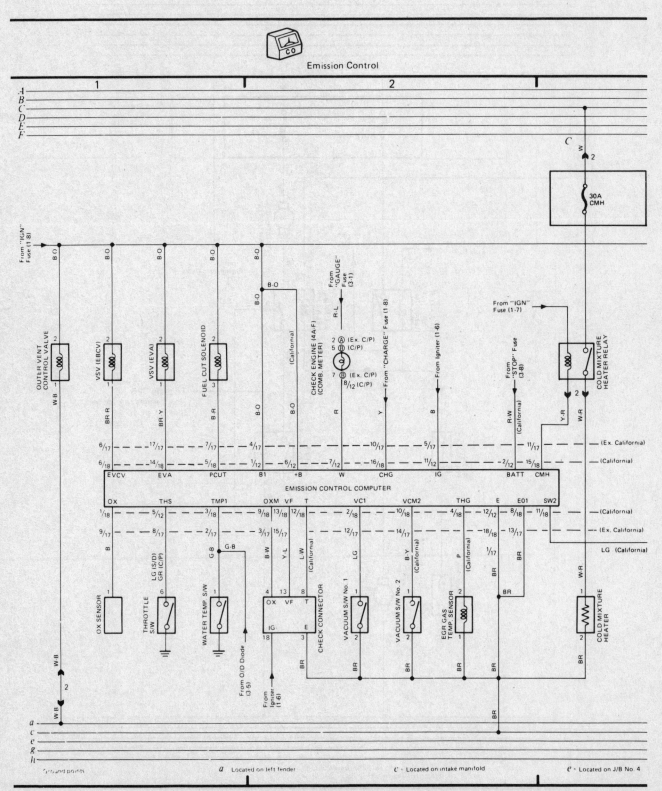

Typical wirng diagram – 1985 and later models (6 of 7)

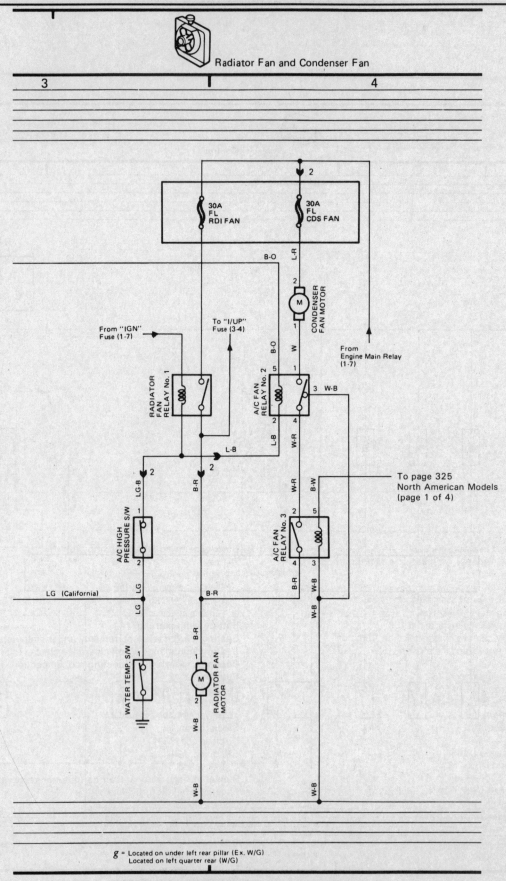

Radiator Fan and Condenser Fan

Index